Microsoft 365 Security, Compliance, and Identity Administration

Plan and implement security and compliance strategies for Microsoft 365 and hybrid environments

Peter Rising

BIRMINGHAM—MUMBAI

Microsoft 365 Security, Compliance, and Identity Administration

Group Product Manager: Pavan Ramchandani

Publishing Product Manager: Neha Sharma

Senior Editor: Shruti Menon

Technical Editor: Arjun Varma

Copy Editor: Safis Editing

Project Manager: Neil Dmello

Proofreader: Safis Editing

Indexer: Pratik Shirodkar

Production Designer: Alishon Mendonca

Marketing Coordinator: Marylou De Mello

First published: July 2023

Production reference: 180723

Published by Packt Publishing Ltd.

Grosvenor House

11 St Paul's Square

Birmingham

B3 1RB.

ISBN 978-1-80461-192-0

www.packtpub.com

To George, my oldest son. The world is tough and challenging, but it is also full of amazing opportunities, good surprises, and happy accidents. Go find yours and turn them into happiness above all else!

– Peter Rising

Contributors

About the author

Peter Rising has over 25 years of experience in IT. He has worked for several IT solutions providers and private organizations in a variety of technical and leadership roles, with a focus on Microsoft technologies. Since 2014, Peter has specialized in the Microsoft 365 platform, focusing most recently on security and compliance in his role as a consulting services manager for Insight. Peter is heavily involved in the wider Microsoft community and has been recognized by Microsoft as an MVP. He holds several Microsoft certifications, including MCSE: Productivity; Microsoft 365 Certified: Enterprise Administrator Expert; and Microsoft 365: Cybersecurity Architect Expert.

About the reviewers

Rahul Singh is a seasoned IT professional and Chief Teaching Officer at SV9 Academy, which is a Microsoft Learning Partner. Rahul has 17+ years of experience in the IT field as of 2023, and holds numerous certifications in the Microsoft technological stack. In addition, Rahul has also been a Microsoft Certified Trainer since 2020. He is deeply passionate about technology and demystifying complex technical architectures using various pedagogies and a systems-based learning mechanism, making learning an enjoyable and enriching experience.

With the ever-changing technical world, testing and reviewing technical content can be a very daunting task requiring perseverance and patience. I would like to take this opportunity to thank my lovely parents, who I have been blessed with by the Divine, as without their support I would not have been able to be a part of this amazing project from Packt.

Rogier Dijkman is a Principal Cloud Security Consultant at Nedscaper and a Microsoft Security MVP. With a background in architecture and software development, he is currently focusing on event-driven security in Microsoft Azure. Rogier specializes in cloud security testing and contributes to the development of tools for penetration and security teams. In his spare time, Rogier enjoys improving his coding skills and contributing to the Microsoft Security Community, but also has a passion for running and loves to train for marathons.

I would like to thank my wife, Liesbeth, for giving me the opportunity to be the best version of myself. Without her, I wouldn't have the time and space necessary to pursue my professional and personal interests.

Table of Contents

3

Implementing Conditional Access Policies   67

4

Managing Roles and Identity Governance   95

5

Azure AD Identity Protection   123

Part 2: Implementing and Managing Threat Protection

6

Configuring a Microsoft Defender for Identity Solution   151

7

Configuring Device Threat Protection with Microsoft Defender for Endpoint and Intune   175

8

Configuring Microsoft Defender for Office 365   203

9

Using Microsoft Sentinel to Monitor Microsoft 365 Security   241

10

Configuring Microsoft Defender for Cloud Apps   277

Part 3: Implementing and Managing Information Protection

11

Managing Sensitive Information   309

12

Managing Microsoft Purview Data Loss Prevention   351

13

Managing Microsoft Purview Data Lifecycle Management   387

Part 4: Managing Compliance Features in Microsoft 365

14

Monitoring and Analyzing Audit Logs and Reports in Microsoft Purview   429

15

Planning For, Conducting, and Managing eDiscovery Cases   451

16

Managing Regulatory and Privacy Requirements   483

17

Managing Insider Risk Solutions in Microsoft 365   539

Preface

In this book, you will learn how to manage the principles of security, compliance, identity, management, and privacy within a Microsoft 365 environment.

By the end of this guide, you will understand how to securely implement and manage hybrid identity and advanced security features to protect your users and devices. You will also have learned how to deploy compliance features for information protection and governance, to ensure that business and regulatory requirements for your organization are being fulfilled.

Azure Active Directory (Azure AD) was renamed by Microsoft in July 2023 as **Microsoft Entra ID**. This book references the Microsoft Entra portal frequently, but still refers to Azure AD in many places. Please note that only the name has changed; so, wherever you see Azure AD mentioned, this is in fact referring to Microsoft Entra ID. For more information, please refer to `https://learn.microsoft.com/en-gb/azure/active-directory/fundamentals/new-name`.

Who this book is for

This book is designed to help IT professionals, administrators, or anyone looking to pursue a career in security administration to enhance their skills in utilizing the Microsoft 365 security features. Readers of this book will ideally already be well versed in the basic implementation and administration principles of Microsoft 365 and Azure Active Directory. This book will help them learn how to apply modern security, compliance, and identity principles to Microsoft 365 hybrid environments in line with best practices, while providing a user environment that is accessible and easy to use.

What this book covers

Chapter 1, Planning for Hybrid Identity, teaches you how to plan your hybrid environment with Azure AD Connect and introduces you to additional authentication security methods.

Chapter 2, Authentication and Security, covers the implementation of Azure AD dynamic groups, Azure AD **self-service password reset (SSPR)**, **multi-factor authentication (MFA)**, and managing external identities.

Chapter 3, Implementing Conditional Access Policies, explains the principles of Azure AD Conditional Access, how it integrates with Microsoft Intune, and how Conditional Access may be used with device- and app-based policies.

Chapter 4, Managing Roles and Identity Governance, shows you how, with the help of **Privileged Identity Management (PIM)**, you can reduce your permanently assigned admin roles and implement eligibility with just-in-time access. You will also learn about **entitlement management** and **access reviews**.

Chapter 5, Azure AD Identity Protection, introduces the principles of identity protection, how to configure user- and sign-in-based risk policies, and how to manage and respond to alerts.

Chapter 6, Configuring a Microsoft Defender for Identity Solution, explains how to set up and manage a Defender for Identity instance and install sensors on servers.

Chapter 7, Configuring Device Threat Protection with Microsoft Defender for Endpoint and Intune, helps you to understand how to reduce your attack surface by configuring policies for Microsoft Defender Application Guard, Application Control, Exploit Guard, and Secure Boot. In addition, you will learn how BitLocker device encryption can protect Windows devices.

Chapter 8, Configuring Microsoft Defender for Office 365, covers how to protect users and domains with anti-phishing and anti-spam protection, and the application of safe attachments and safe links policies. It also covers running simulated attacks and running reports.

Chapter 9, Using Microsoft Sentinel to Monitor Microsoft 365 Security, shows you how to configure and use Microsoft Sentinel to respond to threats with playbooks.

Chapter 10, Configuring Microsoft Defender for Cloud Apps, demonstrates how to track your SaaS application usage, configure file and activity policies, integrate with Conditional Access, and navigate dashboards and logs.

Chapter 11, Managing Sensitive Information, explains how to create sensitive information types; how to plan, set up, and implement sensitivity labels and policies; and how to use content explorer and Activity explorer.

Chapter 12, Managing Microsoft Purview Data Loss Prevention, covers the planning and creation of DLP policies and how to review DLP alerts.

Chapter 13, Managing Microsoft Purview Data Lifecycle Management, teaches you how to understand retention requirements for your organization, how to configure retention labels and retention policies, how to find and recover deleted data, and how to use adaptive scopes.

Chapter 14, Managing and Analyzing Audit Logs and Reports in Microsoft Purview, teaches you how to plan for auditing and reporting, as well as understanding how to use the audit logs and alert policies and configure audit log retention.

Chapter 15, Planning For, Conducting, and Managing eDiscovery Cases, shows you how to identify and understand the different versions of eDiscovery, the roles needed to run cases, and how to manage cases.

Chapter 16, Managing Regulatory and Privacy Requirements, explains how to manage regulatory compliance in Microsoft Purview, as well as implementing privacy risk management and subject rights requests.

Chapter 17, Managing Insider Risk Solutions in Microsoft 365, teaches you the principles of privileged access management, Customer Lockbox, Insider risk management policies, and Communication Compliance policies. It also goes over Information Barriers segments and policies.

To get the most out of this book

To get the most out of this book, it is highly recommended to create a test or practice Microsoft 365 environment, where you can follow along and recreate the steps that are covered in each chapter. Unfortunately, trial licenses for Microsoft 365 E5 are not available. The best option for working along with this book is to sign up for an Office 365 E5 trial at `https://www.microsoft.com/en-gb/microsoft-365/business/office-365-enterprise-e5-business-software?activetab=pivot:overviewtab` and an EM+S E5 trial at `https://www.microsoft.com/en-us/microsoft-365/enterprise-mobility-security/compare-plans-and-pricing`. These trial subscriptions will allow you to recreate most of the steps covered in the chapters contained in this book. Should you wish to test the process of establishing a hybrid identity, it is recommended that you acquire a trial Azure subscription, which will allow you to create a Windows virtual server that you may use to install Azure AD Connect and synchronize to your test Microsoft 365 tenant.

This book also has some sample PowerShell commands that can be used instead of the Microsoft 365 admin centers. Therefore, it is recommended to have a Windows 10/11 device available to you where you can run PowerShell and practice some of the commands included in the chapters.

A **Windows 10/11** device will also be useful for the purposes of testing how to set up Microsoft 365 test profiles to fully test and deploy features such as Microsoft Intune, Azure AD Conditional Access, MFA, Information Protection, and many more of the features described in the book. A **mobile device**, such as an iOS or Android device, will also be useful for testing Microsoft Intune in particular.

Software/hardware covered in the book	Operating system requirements
Microsoft 365	Windows, macOS, or Linux

If you are using the digital version of this book, we advise you to type the code yourself or access the code from the book's GitHub repository (a link is available in the next section). Doing so will help you avoid any potential errors related to the copying and pasting of code.

Conventions used

There are a number of text conventions used throughout this book.

`Code in text`: Indicates code words in text, database table names, folder names, filenames, file extensions, pathnames, dummy URLs, user input, and Twitter handles. Here is an example: "The `Start-ADSyncSyncCycle -PolicyType Initial` command will initiate a full synchronization."

Any command-line input or output is written as follows:

```
New-RetentionPolicyTag -Name "Personal-2-year-move-to-archive" -Type
All -AgeLimitForRetention 730 -RetentionActionMoveToArchive
```

Bold: Indicates a new term, an important word, or words that you see on screen. For example, words in menus or dialog boxes appear in bold. Here is an example: "Click **Save** to complete the setup of your retention tag."

> **Tips or important notes**
> Appear like this.

Get in touch

Feedback from our readers is always welcome.

General feedback: If you have questions about any aspect of this book, email us at customercare@packtpub.com and mention the book title in the subject of your message.

Errata: Although we have taken every care to ensure the accuracy of our content, mistakes do happen. If you have found a mistake in this book, we would be grateful if you would report this to us. Please visit www.packtpub.com/support/errata and fill in the form.

Piracy: If you come across any illegal copies of our works in any form on the internet, we would be grateful if you would provide us with the location address or website name. Please contact us at copyright@packt.com with a link to the material.

If you are interested in becoming an author: If there is a topic that you have expertise in and you are interested in either writing or contributing to a book, please visit authors.packtpub.com.

Share Your Thoughts

Once you've read *Microsoft 365 Security, Compliance, and Identity Administration*, we'd love to hear your thoughts! Scan the QR code below to go straight to the Amazon review page for this book and share your feedback.

https://packt.link/r/1804611921

Your review is important to us and the tech community and will help us make sure we're delivering excellent quality content.

Download a free PDF copy of this book

Thanks for purchasing this book!

Do you like to read on the go but are unable to carry your print books everywhere?

Is your eBook purchase not compatible with the device of your choice?

Don't worry, now with every Packt book you get a DRM-free PDF version of that book at no cost.

Read anywhere, any place, on any device. Search, copy, and paste code from your favorite technical books directly into your application.

The perks don't stop there, you can get exclusive access to discounts, newsletters, and great free content in your inbox daily

Follow these simple steps to get the benefits:

1. Scan the QR code or visit the link below

https://packt.link/free-ebook/978-1-80461-192-0

2. Submit your proof of purchase
3. That's it! We'll send your free PDF and other benefits to your email directly

Part 1:
Implementing and Managing Identity and Access

In this part, you will learn how to configure and manage Microsoft 365 identity and access components. On completion, you will be able to describe authentication and synchronization methods, user security, Conditional Access, Privileged Identity Management, and Identity Protection.

This part has the following chapters:

- *Chapter 1, Planning for Hybrid Identity*
- *Chapter 2, Authentication and Security*
- *Chapter 3, Implementing Conditional Access Policies*
- *Chapter 4, Managing Roles and Identity Governance*
- *Chapter 5, Azure AD Identity Protection*

1

Planning for Hybrid Identity

This book aims to act as a general administration guide for security, compliance, identity, management, and privacy administrators of Microsoft 365 environments, whether they are cloud-only or hybrid. You will learn about umbrella terms for technology principles, such as **Microsoft Defender**, **Microsoft Purview**, and **Microsoft Entra**, and understand their purpose and how they relate to each other. You will see how to access, plan, and configure these technologies via administrative portals, as well as by using PowerShell. In this first chapter, we begin by focusing on identity.

Configuring a Microsoft 365 hybrid environment requires an understanding of your organization's identity needs. This will enable you to plan and deploy the correct Azure **Active Directory** (**AD**) authentication and synchronization method within your environment. This chapter discusses how you can plan your identity methodology and describes the process of monitoring and understanding the events recorded by **Azure AD Connect**.

By the end of this chapter, you will be able to determine your business needs, analyze on-premises identity infrastructure, and develop a plan for hybrid identity. You will understand how to design and implement authentication and application management solutions, how to enhance data security through strong identity, and how to analyze events and configure alerts in Azure AD Connect.

This chapter covers the following topics:

- Planning your hybrid environment
- Authentication methods in Azure AD
- Synchronization methods with Azure AD Connect
- Azure AD Connect cloud sync
- Event monitoring and troubleshooting in Azure AD Connect

Planning your hybrid environment

Identity is key when planning and implementing a Microsoft 365 environment. While the default identity method within Microsoft 365 is cloud-only, many organizations with reliance on legacy on-premises infrastructure and applications need to plan the deployment of hybrid identities when introducing Microsoft 365 to their organization.

So, what is a **hybrid identity**? In simple terms, it is the process of providing your users with an identity in the cloud that is based on their on-premises identity. There are several ways in which this can be achieved and they will be explained in detail throughout this chapter.

The basic principles of hybrid identity in Microsoft 365 are shown in the following diagram:

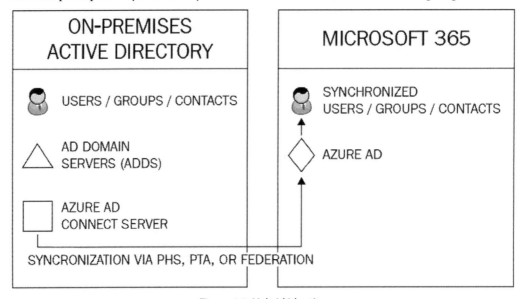

Figure 1.1: Hybrid identity

We will now explain how you can start planning for hybrid identities in Microsoft 365.

You should start by establishing the correct identity type for the business needs of your organization. It is important, at this stage, to recognize who your **stakeholders** will be in this process, understand their current working tools and practices, and assess how Microsoft 365 could be used best enabling them to work more efficiently and securely.

The following are some examples of your possible stakeholders:

- Users
- Power users
- IT team

- Security team

- Compliance team

- Business owners

Each stakeholder will have their challenges that need to be considered. However, your users account for the highest percentage of your stakeholders. Therefore, your primary focus should be to ensure that the transition to new ways of working is seamless. This is because many users will be nervous about change. How you introduce them to new technologies and working practices is directly related to the success or failure of your project. If your users buy into the changes you are introducing and can realize the benefits, then the rest of your stakeholders are also more likely to follow suit.

While your main users will be focused on doing their job, the remaining stakeholders will have a deeper interest in how a Microsoft 365 hybrid environment meets **business requirements**. Some of the common business requirements are as follows:

- The modernization of existing IT services and tools

- Providing and securing cloud **Software as a Service (SaaS)** applications

- Reducing risk by establishing a modern identity-based security perimeter

For addressing these requirements, a logical starting point is to examine how on-premises identities are currently configured. This will give you a better understanding of what you need to plan and implement for identity authentication in the cloud. You need to be aware of any current on-premises synchronization solutions that may be in place, including any third-party solutions. You will also need to consider any existing use of cloud applications in the organization. These will need to be identified and plans made for their continued use, integration, or possible replacement.

> **Note**
> Cloud App Discovery using Microsoft Defender for Cloud Apps can be used to analyze existing SaaS app usage within your organization. This will be covered in a later chapter of this book.

Understanding your on-premises identity infrastructure will help you to plan for modernization or digital transformation. So, what is **modernization** considered to be in the world of information technology? Essentially, it is based on the principle that IT users now wish and expect to be more mobile. They want quick and easy access to their emails, chats, and documents anywhere, anytime, and on any device.

This requirement creates the challenge of how to effectively secure and protect the services within the Microsoft 365 platform while simultaneously ensuring that they are easily available and accessible to users. How is this achieved? It is not possible to wrap a firewall around Microsoft 365 in the traditional sense. Instead, you need to look at the various modern authentication security methods that are available within Azure AD. Let's discuss these methods in detail in the next section.

Authentication methods in Azure AD

Several approaches can be leveraged to authenticate your users to Azure AD. In this section, you will explore these methods and understand their use cases.

The authentication security methods available in Microsoft 365 are as follows:

- **Multi-factor authentication (MFA)**
- **Self-service password reset (SSPR)**
- Conditional Access
- Passwordless

The following sections will briefly introduce the principles of these methods; however, each of these will be explored in greater detail in *Chapter 2, Authentication and Security*, and *Chapter 3, Implementing Conditional Access Policies*.

Multi-factor authentication

MFA in Azure AD provides two-step verification for Microsoft services via a combination of approved authentication methods determined by Microsoft 365 administrators. The available methods can be based on the following:

- Something you *know*, such as your password
- Something you *own*, such as your mobile phone or an OAuth hardware token
- Something you *are*, such as biometric identification (fingerprint or facial recognition)

When setting up MFA for users in your Microsoft 365 environment, users must first complete a registration process to provide information about themselves to Azure AD and set their authentication method preferences.

Once set, users will be challenged with an MFA prompt when accessing Microsoft 365 services and applications using their Azure AD credentials, as shown in the following diagram:

Figure 1.2: Azure MFA

MFA can also be configured to work in conjunction with **Conditional Access**, with trusted locations that you define by entering the IP ranges of your business operating units so that users will not be issued an MFA challenge when working in these locations. Conditional Access with MFA also enables you to apply another layer of security by ensuring that any access requests to specific apps and resources can be secured and protected, by requiring the requesting user to complete an MFA challenge before being granted the access they require.

> **Note**
>
> It is recommended that you configure MFA for *all* privileged user accounts within your Microsoft 365 environment, except for your permanent break-glass accounts, which should be cloud-only accounts with the domain suffix of the `.onmicrosoft.com` domain name. Alternative authentication protection should be applied to these break-glass accounts. Break-glass accounts will be covered in more detail in *Chapter 3, Implementing Conditional Access Policies*.

Self-service password reset

Whilst not strictly an authentication method in itself, SSPR is a user feature designed to remove the requirement of IT staff to respond to user requests to reset their passwords in Azure AD. An initial registration process is required at `https://aka.ms/SSPRSetup` for each user to set up SSPR, during which time they must provide authentication methods to verify their identity.

> **Note**
>
> To reset the password, the user visits `https://passwordreset.microsoftonline.com`.

SSPR can be used for both cloud-only and hybrid identity users. If the user is cloud-only, then their password is always stored encrypted in Azure AD, whereas hybrid users have their password written back to on-premises AD. This is achieved using a feature that can be enabled in Azure AD Connect called **password writeback**.

The basic principles of SSPR are illustrated in the following diagram:

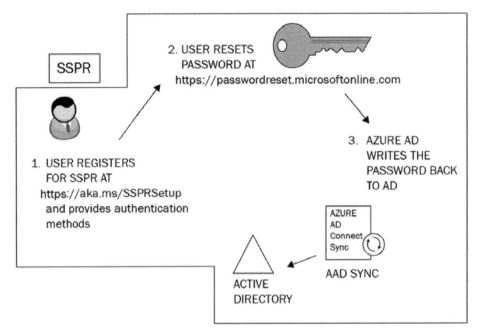

Figure 1.3: Self-service password reset

The process of registering your users for SSPR is now combined with that of the MFA registration process. Previously, there were two separate registration processes for these technologies.

When SSPR is enabled on your Azure AD environment, you can assist your users by configuring notifications that make them aware when their passwords have been reset. You can also increase security by setting administrator notifications to monitor and alert whenever an administrator changes a password. It is also possible to customize a helpdesk email or URL to provide immediate guidance to users who experience problems when attempting to reset their passwords.

> **Note**
> When using SSPR with password writeback for your hybrid identities, you will require Azure AD Premium P1 licenses.

Conditional Access

Conditional Access is a powerful feature of Azure AD Premium P1 that allows Microsoft 365 administrators to control access to applications and resources within your organization. With Conditional Access, you can automate the process of controlling the level of access that users will have to these applications and resources by setting Conditional Access policies. Azure AD will then make decisions on whether to grant or deny access based on the conditions that you set in these policies. The basic principles are shown in the following diagram:

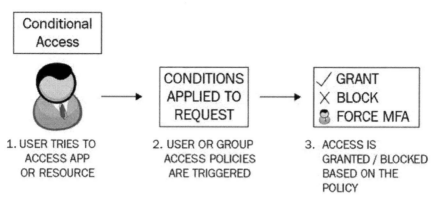

Figure 1.4: Conditional Access

While it is possible to apply some default security settings to your Microsoft 365 environment with security defaults (auto-applied on newer tenants), you will undoubtedly need to plan and define custom policies with specific conditions and exceptions. For example, you would not wish to force MFA on your permanent break-glass global administrator account. We will examine Conditional Access in greater detail in *Chapter 3, Implementing Conditional Access Policies*.

> **Note**
>
> Conditional Access settings frequently require some additional features of Azure AD to be configured, for example, **Azure AD Identity Protection**. This will have an impact on your decision-making process as it relates to licensing. While Conditional Access is a feature of Azure AD Premium P1, the use of Azure AD Identity Protection features would necessitate Azure AD Premium P2 licenses.

Passwordless authentication

Passwords are more vulnerable than ever before and can be exploited and compromised by malicious actors using techniques such as phishing, spray attacks, and social engineering attacks. Switching to a passwordless authentication method helps mitigate such risks.

Microsoft provides three types of passwordless authentication for Azure AD. These are as follows:

- **Microsoft Authenticator**: Can enable iOS or Android phones to be used as passwordless credentials by providing numerical challenges.

- **FIDO2-compliant security keys**: Hardware keys provided by a number of third-party manufacturers; ideal for highly privileged identities or shared machines in kiosks.

- **Windows Hello for Business**: Available on Windows computers and ideal for users with their own designated Windows device. Biometric and PIN credentials are directly configured on the device to prevent access from anyone but the authorized user.

> **Note**
>
> Links to further resources on Microsoft Authenticator, FIDO2-compliant security keys, and Windows Hello for Business can be found in the *Further reading* section at the end of this chapter.

Now that you understand the available authentication methods, let's explore the directory synchronization methods supported by Azure AD Connect.

Synchronization methods with Azure AD Connect

Having covered the concept of hybrid identity and authentication, you will now go through the process that makes hybrid identity possible—**directory synchronization**. The tool used to configure directory synchronization is called Azure AD Connect (previously known as **Azure AD Sync Service** and **DirSync**). Azure AD Connect consists of, or can leverage, the following components:

- Synchronization services

- **Active Directory Federation Services** (**AD FS**)—an optional component

- Health monitoring

Azure AD Connect supports multiple AD forests and multiple Exchange organizations to a single Microsoft 365 tenant. It leverages a one-way process, where it synchronizes users, groups, and contact objects from your on-premises AD to Microsoft 365.

Although this is almost exclusively a one-way process, there are some writeback capabilities that can be leveraged if chosen or required, which will allow attributes from passwords and groups set in Microsoft 365 to be written back to an on-premises AD.

The principles of Azure AD Connect are shown in the following diagram:

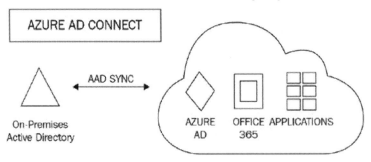

Figure 1.5: Azure AD Connect

Once Azure AD Connect is configured and in place, the source of authority for these newly synchronized objects remains with the on-premises AD. Therefore, these objects must be managed by on-premises tools, such as **AD Users and Computers** or **PowerShell**. Microsoft 365 administrators will, therefore, not be able to make changes to cloud objects in the Microsoft 365 portal that are synchronized from the on-premises AD.

When setting up Azure AD Connect for the first time, the installation wizard will guide you to select either an **Express Settings** installation or a customized settings installation. The **Express Settings** installation is the default setting for Azure AD Connect and is designed for use with password hash synchronization from a single AD forest. The installation dialog is shown in the following screenshot:

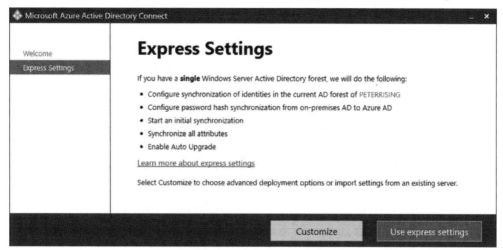

Figure 1.6: Express settings

The custom settings installation provides a richer selection of optional features that can be configured to provide enhanced functionality if required. You can start a custom settings installation by clicking on **Customize**:

Figure 1.7: Custom settings

With the custom settings installation, you are provided with the following options to extend your on-premises identities in the cloud using Azure AD Connect:

- **Password hash synchronization**
- **Pass-through authentication**
- **Federation with AD FS**
- **Federation with PingFederate**
- **Enable single sign-on**
- **Do not configure**

The following sections will explain how to configure the first five of these options in detail.

Password hash synchronization

Password hash synchronization is the simplest method to establish a hybrid identity with Azure AD. Also commonly known as **same sign-on**, password hash synchronization can be set up using Azure AD Connect. This will synchronize a hash of the user passwords to Azure AD from your on-premises AD.

With password hash synchronization, users logging onto their cloud accounts via the Microsoft 365 portal will authenticate directly to Microsoft 365 cloud services as opposed to leveraging on-premises authentication and security:

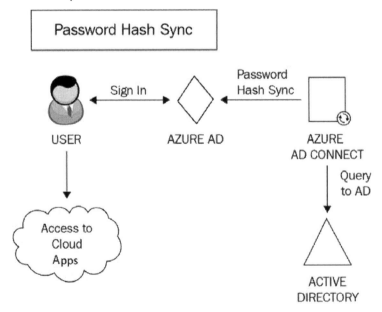

Figure 1.8: Password hash synchronization

How does this work? Here is the process in a few simple steps:

1. The password synchronization agent within Azure AD Connect will request the stored password hashes at 2-minute intervals from a domain controller. In response to this, the domain controller will encrypt the hash. This encryption is executed with a key that is acquired from the **Remote Procedure Call (RPC)** session key and then salted. **Salting** is a process pertaining to password hashing. Essentially it involves adding a unique value to the end of the password to create a different hash value. This provides an additional layer of security and helps protect against brute-force attacks.

2. The domain controller will then send the result, along with the salt, to the sync agent using RPC. The agent can now decrypt the envelope. It is important to point out that the sync agent never has any access to the password in cleartext.

3. Once decrypted, the sync agent performs a re-hash on the original password hash, changing it to a SHA256 hash by imputing this into the PKDF2 function.

4. The agent will then sync the resulting SHA256-hashed password hash from Azure AD Connect to Azure AD using SSL.

5. When Azure AD receives the hash, it will be encrypted with an AES algorithm and then stored in the Azure AD database.

Therefore, when a user signs into Azure AD with their on-premises AD username and password, the password is taken through this process. If the hash result is a match for the hash stored in Azure AD, the user will be successfully authenticated.

Pass-through authentication

Pass-through authentication is an alternative to password hash synchronization. This method is commonly used when Microsoft 365 administrators require users to authenticate their Microsoft 365 logins on-premises as opposed to directly to Azure AD:

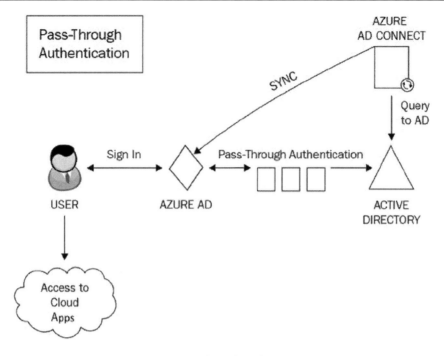

Figure 1.9: Pass-through authentication

Unlike password hash synchronization, pass-through authentication does not synchronize passwords from on-premises AD to Microsoft 365. Instead, it allows users to log on to both on-premises and cloud applications and services using the same password. This provides a far more cohesive experience for users, with the added benefit that on-premises passwords are never stored in the cloud in any form.

A lightweight agent is all that is needed to set this up with Azure AD Connect and this agent is automatically installed on the Azure AD Connect server when you run the initial setup for pass-through authentication. To provide resiliency to your pass-through authentication solution, the agent can be installed onto additional servers in your on-premises AD sites. The agents should ideally be installed on servers close to your domain controllers to improve sign-in latency. Servers on which the agent is installed should also be security hardened to the same extent that you would protect domain controllers.

> **Note**
>
> It is recommended to configure a minimum of three authentication agents in your environment. The maximum number of agents that can be installed is 40. It is generally good practice to have at least one agent deployed to each of your AD sites to make pass-through authentication resilient and highly available.

The authentication agents must be able to make outbound requests to Azure AD over the following ports in order to function:

Port	Requirement
80	SSL certificate validation and certificate revocation list download
443	Provides outbound communication for the service
8080	While this port is optional and not required for user sign-ins, it is useful to configure this as authentication agents will report status through port 8080 at 10-minute intervals.

Table 1.1: Azure AD ports

Federation

Federation, in simple terms, can be described as domains that trust each other. They share access to resources across organizations, with authentication and authorization settings configured to control the trust.

It is possible to federate your on-premises AD environment with Azure AD to provide authentication and authorization. As is the case with pass-through authentication, a federated sign-in method enforces all user authentication via on-premises methods as opposed to the cloud.

The main benefits of federation are that it provides enhanced access controls to administrators. However, the drawback of this method is that additional infrastructure will inevitably need to be provisioned and maintained.

In Azure AD Connect, there are two methods available to configure federation with Azure AD. These are AD FS and the more recently added PingFederate.

To explain the infrastructure requirements in more detail, AD FS can be used as an example. In order to configure AD FS in line with Microsoft's best practices, you will need to install and configure a minimum of two on-premises AD FS servers on your AD environment and two web application proxy servers on your perimeter network.

This configuration provides the necessary security principles to ensure that both internal and (especially) remote users authenticate to the services within your hybrid environment in a manner that provides appropriate authentication and authorization. The process of federation is shown in the following diagram:

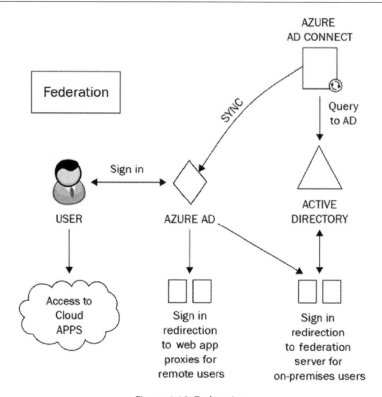

Figure 1.10: Federation

So, how does federation actually work? Well, there are two main principles that you need to understand. These are **claims-based authentication** and **federated trusts**. The following sections will explain each of these in detail.

Claims-based authentication

Claims-based authentication works on the principle of users making statements about themselves in order to authenticate and gain access to applications by using industry-standard security protocols. User claims rely on the claims issuer, which is the **Security Token Service (STS)**. The STS can be configured on your AD FS server. The statements provided by users can relate to name, identity, key, group, privilege, or capability.

A claim is issued by the user to the claims issuer. It is then assigned values and packaged into a security token by the claims issuer (the STS). This security token is essentially an envelope that contains the claims relating to the user. The token is sent back to the user and then passed to the application that the user wishes to access.

The claim relies on the explicit trust that is established with the issuer. The application that the user wishes to access will only trust the user's claim if it subsequently trusts the claims issuer (the STS).

With claims-based authentication, you can configure a number of authentication methods. The most commonly used ones are as follows:

- Kerberos authentication
- Forms authentication
- X.509 certificates
- Smart cards

Although many older applications do not support claims-based authentication, the main use-case argument for applications that do support it is that it simplifies the process of trust for those target applications. Instead of having to place their trust directly in the user making the claim, they can be secure in the knowledge that they can absolutely trust the claims issuer instead.

Federated trust

Federated trusts expand on the capabilities of claims-based authentication by enabling your issuer to accept security tokens from other issuers as opposed to a user having to directly authenticate. In this scenario, the issuer can both issue and accept security tokens from other trusted issuers utilizing the federation trust. This process essentially establishes a business relationship or partnership between two organizations.

Federated trusts enable trusted issuers to represent the users on their side of the trust. The benefit of this configuration is that should you need to revoke the trust, you can do so through a single action. Rather than revoking a trust with many individual external users, you can simply terminate the trust with the issuer.

A good example of how this works in practice would be that if you need to authenticate remote users to your environment, a federated trust will remove the requirement to provide direct authentication for those users. Instead, you will have a trust relationship with the remote user from their organization. This enables these remote users to continue using their own single sign-on methodology and provides an efficient, decentralized way for them to authenticate to your organization.

> **Note**
> An alternative method of providing many of the features that federation offers is to use pass-through authentication in conjunction with the rich features of Azure AD Premium, such as Conditional Access and Identity Protection.

Although additional licensing may be required within Azure AD to deploy these features, this method offers simplified setup and administration and also removes the requirement for any additional infrastructure.

Azure AD Seamless Single Sign-On

Azure AD Seamless Single Sign-On (Azure AD Seamless SSO) is a free-to-use feature of Azure AD that provides a single set of credentials for your users to authenticate to applications within Azure AD, when connecting to your organization's network using a business desktop device. This means that once connected to your organization's network on their Windows 10/11 domain-joined devices, they will not be asked to provide further credentials when opening any Azure AD applications. The principles of Seamless SSO are shown in the following diagram:

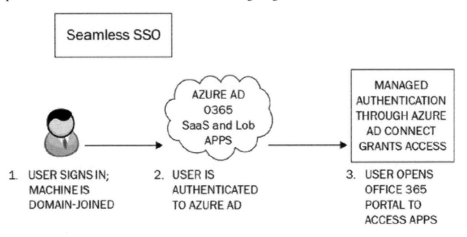

Figure 1.11: Seamless SSO

Seamless SSO is configured via the Azure AD Connect wizard or PowerShell and can be used in conjunction with password hash synchronization and pass-through authentication. It is not compatible with federations such as AD FS or PingFederate.

There are some prerequisites to be aware of when planning to implement Seamless SSO. These include the following:

- If you are using Azure AD Connect with password hash sync, ensure that you are using Azure AD Connect Version 1.1.644.0 or later. Further, if possible, ensure that your firewall or proxy is set to allow connections to the `*.msappproxy.net` URLs over port 443. Alternatively, allow access to the Azure data center IP ranges.

- Be aware of the supported topologies that are shown at `https://docs.microsoft.com/en-us/azure/active-directory/hybrid/plan-connect-topologies`.

- Ensure that modern authentication is enabled on your tenant.

- Ensure that the version of your users' Office desktop clients is a minimum of 16.0.8730.xxxx or above.

> **Note**
>
> Although at the time of writing this book, version 1.1.644.0 is still listed as the minimum required version of Azure AD Connect when using Seamless SSO with password hash synchronization, it is important to be aware that version 1 of AD Connect was retired by Microsoft at the end of August 2022. Further details of this can be found in the *Further reading* section at the end of the chapter.

Once you have verified these prerequisites, you can go ahead and enable the feature. This is most commonly done when setting up Azure AD Connect for the first time by performing a custom installation using the Azure AD Connect wizard and, from the **User sign-in** page, ensuring that the **Enable single sign-on** option is selected:

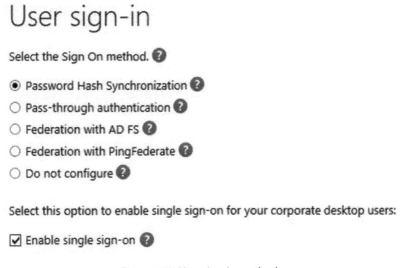

Figure 1.12: User sign-in methods

It is also possible to use PowerShell to set up Seamless SSO. This is a particularly useful method if you need to specify a particular domain(s) in your AD forest to use the feature.

If you need to enable the feature when you already have Azure AD Connect deployed, then you can rerun the setup wizard and choose the **Change user sign-in** option under the **Additional tasks** section:

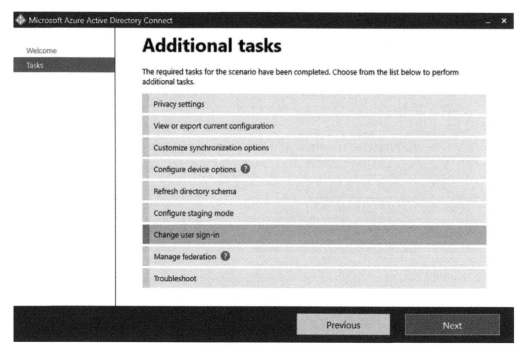

Figure 1.13: Additional tasks

> **Note**
>
> You will need domain administrator credentials to complete setting up Seamless SSO. However, these credentials are only required to enable the feature and will not be required after the setup is complete.

To verify that the setup of Seamless SSO has been completed successfully, log on as a global administrator to `https://portal.azure.com` and navigate to **Azure Active Directory | Azure AD Connect**.

From this page, you will be able to verify that Seamless SSO has the status **Enabled**:

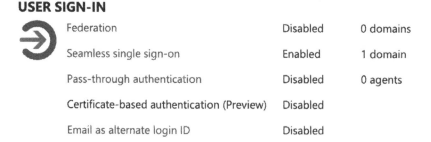

Figure 1.14: User sign-in settings

Finally, when completing your custom settings installation of Azure AD Connect, you are presented with several additional **Optional features**, as shown in the following screenshot:

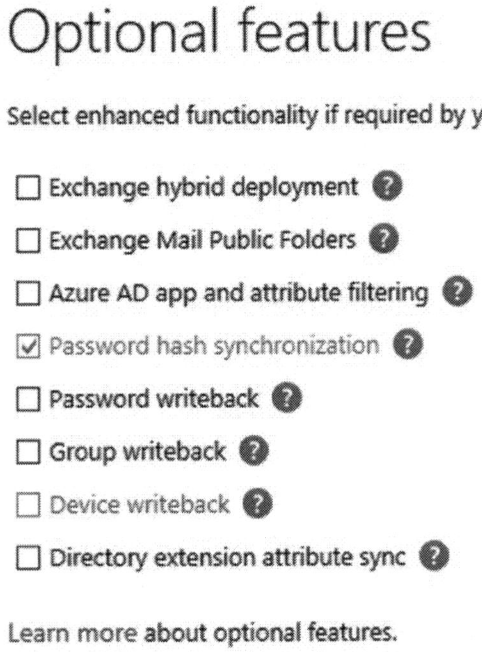

Optional features

Select enhanced functionality if required by your organization.

☐ Exchange hybrid deployment ❓

☐ Exchange Mail Public Folders ❓

☐ Azure AD app and attribute filtering ❓

☑ Password hash synchronization ❓

☐ Password writeback ❓

☐ Group writeback ❓

☐ Device writeback ❓

☐ Directory extension attribute sync ❓

Learn more about optional features.

Figure 1.15: Optional features

The most commonly used features are **Exchange hybrid deployment** and **Password writeback**. Further information on all of the available optional features can be viewed at https://docs. microsoft.com/en-us/azure/active-directory/hybrid/how-to-connect-install-custom#optional-features.

To deploy the Azure AD Seamless single sign-on feature for your users, you need to ensure that the following URL is added to the required user's Intranet Zone settings by using Group Policy: https://autologon.microsoftazuread-sso.com.

One of the advantages of deploying this setting with Group Policy is that you can roll out Seamless SSO to groups of users at your own pace.

A more recent alternative to Azure AD Connect to accomplish hybrid identity goals is Azure AD Connect cloud sync, which we will discuss in the next section.

Azure AD Connect cloud sync

Instead of the Azure AD Connect application, a cloud provisioning agent can be used. However, Azure AD Connect cloud sync can also be leveraged along with Azure AD Connect sync to enable the synchronization of data to a tenant from a multi-forest disconnected AD forest environment, which is a functionality that is often used in merger and acquisition scenarios. It also facilitates simplified installation using lightweight provisioning agents, with the management of all sync configuration taking place in the cloud. In addition, it offers multiple provisioning agents to simplify high-availability deployments. Azure AD Connect cloud sync is controlled by Microsoft Online services. Locally, only a lightweight agent needs to be deployed, which acts as a bridge between the on-premises AD and Azure AD.

A detailed comparison of features between Azure AD Connect and Azure AD Connect cloud sync can be viewed at `https://learn.microsoft.com/en-us/azure/active-directory/ cloudsync/what-is-cloud-sync#comparison-between-azure-ad-connect- and-cloud-sync`.

While Azure AD Connect cloud sync does include some powerful features, it also has some limitations. The most notable one is no support for Exchange hybrid writeback, which prevents many organizations still relying on Exchange on-premises from leveraging this technology.

> **Note**
> Federation is becoming less used in favor of pass-through authentication, but it is still important to understand AD FS scenarios.

Next, we will look at the monitoring and troubleshooting methods for Azure AD Connect.

Event monitoring and troubleshooting in Azure AD Connect

Now that you have your hybrid identity method configured, it should all run smoothly. However, occasionally, you may still encounter some problems. This is where the ability to assess and troubleshoot Azure AD Connect with tools from the Microsoft 365 portal can assist administrators in quickly identifying and resolving issues. Administrators will be able to perform the following tasks as part of troubleshooting in Azure AD Connect:

1. Review and interpret synchronization errors by accessing the Microsoft 365 admin center via `https://admin.microsoft.com` and examining the Azure AD Connect directory sync status. Here, you will see an overview of all directory synchronization errors. A common example may be a duplicate proxy address or UPNs causing conflicts and preventing an object from syncing. The following screenshot shows the Azure AD Connect tile in the admin center. Any issues with synchronization will be shown here by using red circles for critical warnings or yellow triangles for lesser warnings. A green circle means all is OK and healthy:

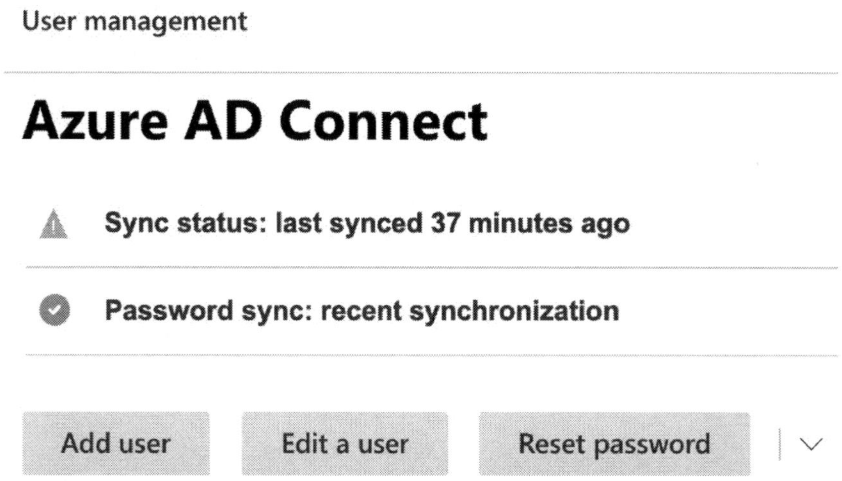

User management

Azure AD Connect

⚠ **Sync status: last synced 37 minutes ago**

✓ **Password sync: recent synchronization**

| Add user | Edit a user | Reset password | ⌄ |

Figure 1.16: Azure AD Connect sync status

The preceding figure shows a sync status of only **37 minutes ago**, which results in a yellow warning. *Figure 1.17* shows more serious red warnings when sync has not completed for 3 days:

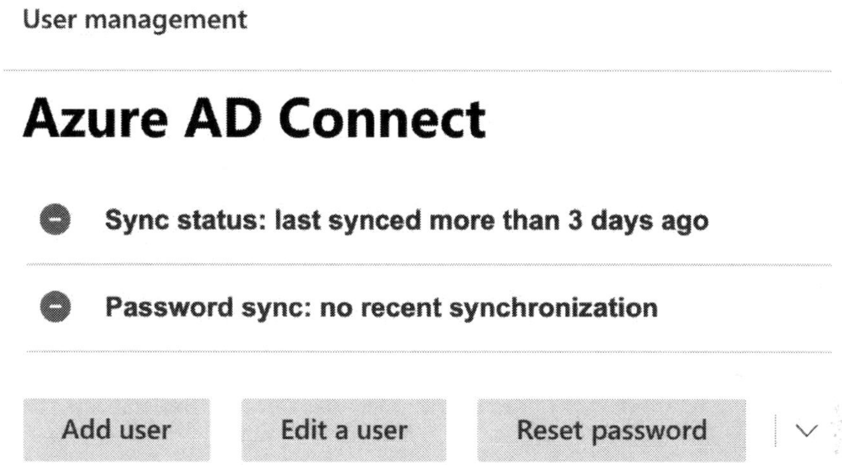

User management

Azure AD Connect

⊖ **Sync status: last synced more than 3 days ago**

⊖ **Password sync: no recent synchronization**

| Add user | Edit a user | Reset password | ⌄ |

Figure 1.17: Azure AD Connect status

2. If you scroll down further, you will see additional details about your **Directory sync status**, as shown in the following screenshot. One of the tools you can download from here is **IdFix**. You can run this tool from any domain-joined workstation in your environment. It provides detailed information on synchronization issues and guidelines on how to resolve them:

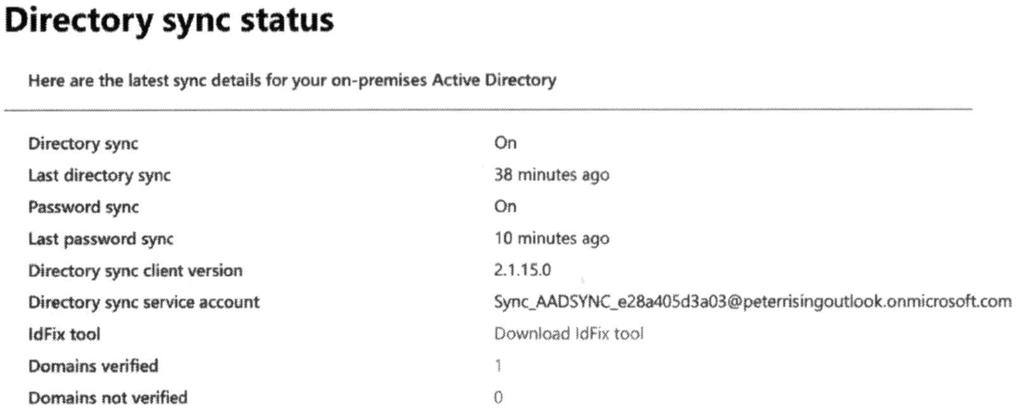

Directory sync status

Here are the latest sync details for your on-premises Active Directory

Directory sync	On
Last directory sync	38 minutes ago
Password sync	On
Last password sync	10 minutes ago
Directory sync client version	2.1.15.0
Directory sync service account	Sync_AADSYNC_e28a405d3a03@peterrisingoutlook.onmicrosoft.com
IdFix tool	Download IdFix tool
Domains verified	1
Domains not verified	0

Figure 1.18: Directory sync status

3. Receive and act on email notifications relating to an unhealthy identity synchronization. These email alerts are configured by default to alert only the technical contact defined in your Microsoft 365 tenant under the organization profile. The technical contact will continue receiving these emails until the issue is resolved.

4. Check **Synchronization Service Manager** on the **Azure AD Connect** server to confirm that the operations required for successful synchronization have been completed. If any errors occur, they will be displayed here with explanations for why the operation failed:

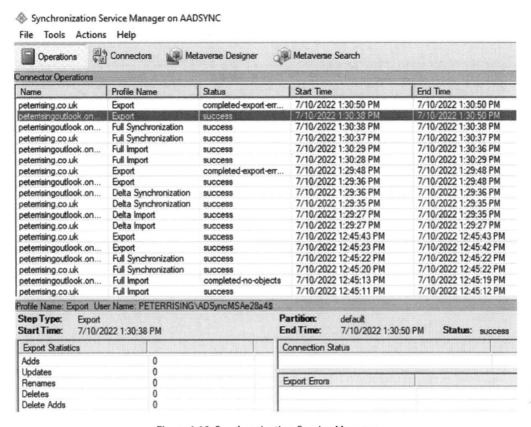

Figure 1.19: Synchronization Service Manager

5. Directory synchronization occurs every 30 minutes by default. However, you can generate a synchronization on demand by opening the **Connectors** tab and manually starting the process, as shown in the following screenshot:

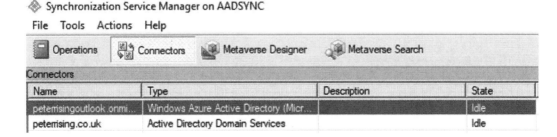

Figure 1.20: Synchronization Service Manager

6. Click on **Actions** and select **Run**:

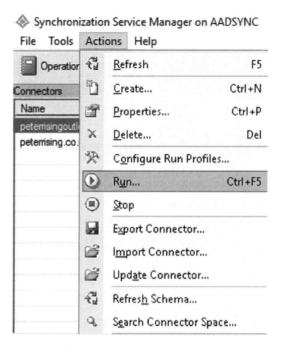

Figure 1.21: Connector actions

7.   You will be able to run the desired connectors from here, as shown:

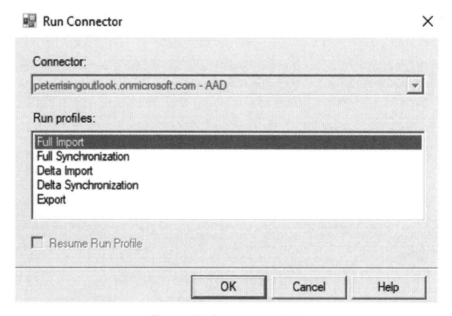

Figure 1.22: Connector options

8. It is also possible, and far simpler, to run a manual synchronization process using PowerShell from your AD Connect server with the following commands:

- To initiate a full synchronization:

```
Start-ADSyncSyncCycle -PolicyType Initial
```

- To initiate a delta synchronization

```
Start-ADSyncSyncCycle -PolicyType Delta
```

In this section, we examined event monitoring and troubleshooting techniques in Azure AD Connect. We learned how to review, interpret, and respond to synchronization errors in the Office 365 portal and by checking the Synchronization Service Manager tool. We also explored how you can manually trigger the synchronization process from the Synchronization Service Manager tool and by using PowerShell.

Summary

This chapter presented the steps and considerations for planning and implementing hybrid identity in Microsoft 365. You should now have an understanding of the synchronization methods available and how to choose the correct one for your environment, along with the principles of additional security authentication. You also learned how to troubleshoot events and alerts when required.

The next chapter will dive deeper into security and authentication features within Microsoft 365, including MFA and SSPR. You will also take a look at Azure AD dynamic groups and managing B2B and Office 365 external sharing.

Questions

1. Which of the following is not one of the identity methods available with Azure AD?

    A. Pass-through authentication

    B. Federation

    C. MFA

    D. Password hash sync

2. Your organization needs to synchronize an on-premises Active Directory with Azure AD. Users must authenticate to the on-premises infrastructure while connecting to services with their Microsoft 365 credentials. You need to recommend an identity methodology that accomplishes the goal but minimizes costs and complexity. What should you recommend?

    A. Cloud-only identity

    B. Pass-through authentication

C. Active Directory Federation Services

D. Password hash synchronization

3. True or false? Azure AD Connect Cloud sync includes support for Exchange hybrid writeback.

A. True

B. False

4. Which of the following Microsoft 365 licenses allows users to use SSPR (choose two)?

A. Azure AD Premium P2

B. Intune

C. Azure Information Protection P1

D. Azure AD Premium P1

5. Which of the following PowerShell commands could you use to run a full Azure AD Connect sync manually?

A. Start-ADSyncSyncCycle -PolicyType Initial

B. Start-ADSyncSyncCycle -PolicyType Delta

C. Start-ADSyncSyncCycle -PolicyType Full

D. Start-ADSyncSyncCycle -PolicyType Immediate

6. True or false? Self-service password reset is automatically enabled for Global Administrator accounts in Microsoft 365.

A. True

B. False

7. What is the maximum number of authentication agents that can be configured in Azure AD for pass-through authentication?

A. 5

B. 10

C. 30

D. 40

8. How frequently (by default) does Azure AD Connect automatically synchronize on-premises AD changes to Azure AD?

   A. Every 20 minutes

   B. Once an hour

   C. Every 30 minutes

   D. Every 15 minutes

9. Which of the following could be a possible cause for Azure AD Connect synchronization issues or errors?

   A. A duplicate proxy address is detected.

   B. SSPR has been incorrectly configured.

   C. You are using password hash sync rather than pass-through authentication.

   D. The AD Connect wizard was run with express installation settings rather than a customized installation.

10. When deploying federation with AD FS, what is the minimum number of web application proxy servers you should configure on your perimeter network?

    A. 5

    B. 2

    C. 3

    D. 7

Further reading

Please refer to the following links for more information:

- Refer to `https://learn.microsoft.com/en-us/azure/active-directory/hybrid/plan-hybrid-identity-design-considerations-business-needs?wt.mc_id=4039827` to help you to plan for hybrid identity.

- Information on how to select the most appropriate synchronization method for Azure AD Connect can be found at `https://learn.microsoft.com/en-us/azure/active-directory/hybrid/choose-ad-authn`.

- For help with additional authentication security, please refer to `https://learn.microsoft.com/en-us/azure/active-directory/authentication/concept-sspr-howitworks` and `https://learn.microsoft.com/en-us/azure/active-directory/conditional-access/overview`.

- Further guidance on troubleshooting synchronization with Azure AD Connect can be found at `https://learn.microsoft.com/en-us/azure/active-directory/hybrid/tshoot-connect-objectsync`.

- Read more about Windows Hello for Business at `https://learn.microsoft.com/en-us/azure/active-directory/authentication/concept-authentication-passwordless#windows-hello-for-business`

- To learn about FIDO2 security keys, refer to `https://learn.microsoft.com/en-us/azure/active-directory/authentication/concept-authentication-passwordless#fido2-security-keys`

- Details about Microsoft Authenticator can be found at `https://learn.microsoft.com/en-us/azure/active-directory/authentication/concept-authentication-passwordless#microsoft-authenticator`

- Learn more about Azure AD cloud sync at `https://learn.microsoft.com/en-us/azure/active-directory/cloud-sync/what-is-cloud-sync`

- For information regarding the retiring Azure AD Connect 1x versions, refer to `https://learn.microsoft.com/en-us/azure/active-directory/hybrid/reference-connect-version-history#retiring-azure-ad-connect-1x-versions`

2
Authentication and Security

Now that you have implemented your hybrid identity model, it is equally important to be able to assign access to applications and resources within your Microsoft 365 environment in a manner that is safe and secure but also user friendly. **Azure AD Premium** allows you to do this.

By the end of this chapter, you will be able to create Azure AD groups with dynamic membership rules and configure user authentication and registration, as well as **Self-Service Password Reset** (**SSPR**) capabilities for users. In addition, you will cover the setup of **Multi-Factor Authentication** (**MFA**) and understand how to implement device authentication methods such as Windows Hello.

This chapter covers the following topics:

- Implementing Azure AD dynamic group membership
- Implementing password management
- Implementing and managing external identities
- Implementing and managing MFA
- Planning and implementing device authentication methods

> **Note**
>
> Many of the features you will cover in this chapter are traditionally accessed from the Microsoft Azure portal. However, Microsoft has also recently introduced **Microsoft Entra** as the umbrella platform for all things related to identity in Azure AD. Therefore, many of the features described here are now also accessible from the new Microsoft Entra admin center.

Implementing Azure AD dynamic group membership

Before diving into the principles of Azure AD dynamic groups, it is important to take a step back and ensure you have an overall appreciation of the methods available for assigning access rights to your users in Azure AD. These methods are as follows:

- **Direct assignment**: Permissions to Azure AD resources are granted by manually assigning access for the resource to an Azure AD object that has a credential.

- **Group assignment**: Permissions to Azure AD resources are granted by manually assigning access for the resource to an Azure AD group containing a set of Azure AD user objects. These objects are added or removed from the group manually.

- **Rule-based assignment**: Permissions to resources are granted by dynamically assigning users to a group. The rules for membership are defined based on specific user object attributes (such as the `department` field).

- **External authority assignment**: Permissions to resources are granted by creating groups to provide access to resources for sources external to Azure AD. In this situation, the external source is given permission to manage group membership.

This essentially means that the basic way to provide access rights to resources in Azure AD is to grant access directly to individual users. However, this has obvious disadvantages compared to the use of group assignment. In group assignment, permissions to resources are assigned directly to all members of a group in a single action, instead of providing access to individual users. This can be a laborious and ongoing task for administrators, who constantly need to add and remove users from groups. Rule-based assignment using Azure AD dynamic groups simplifies this process and provides a secure method for maintaining appropriate access to resources. The following sections dive into how this works.

Creating a dynamic group in Azure AD using the Azure portal

To create a dynamic group, you need to log in to the Azure portal at `https://aad.portal.azure.com` or the Microsoft Entra admin center at `https://entra.micrososoft.com` as a Global Administrator, Intune Administrator, or User Administrator, and navigate to **Azure Active Directory | Groups | All groups**:

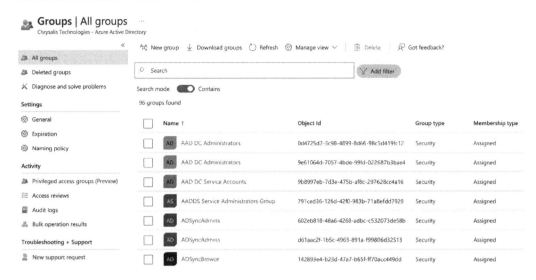

Figure 2.1: Azure AD groups

The following steps will enable you to set up the group:

1. Start by clicking on **New Group**:

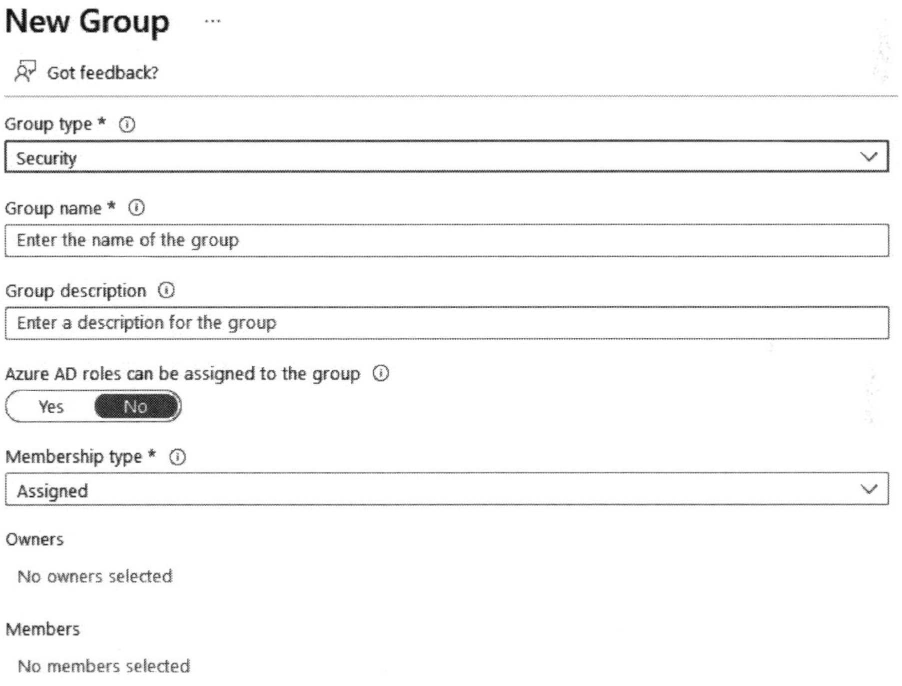

New Group   ...

🦜 Got feedback?

Group type * ⓘ

Security ⌄

Group name * ⓘ

Enter the name of the group

Group description ⓘ

Enter a description for the group

Azure AD roles can be assigned to the group ⓘ

Yes   No

Membership type * ⓘ

Assigned ⌄

Owners

No owners selected

Members

No members selected

Figure 2.2: New group settings

2. Choose between the available group types, that is, **Security**, which is used to grant access to users and devices, or **Microsoft 365**, which is used to grant access only to users and can be assigned to a group email address:

Figure 2.3: Group type

3. Enter a name and description for the group. This example uses the group name `Marketing Users` and provides a group description that states `For access to the Marketing Dept SharePoint Team Site`. You can choose your own name and description or copy this one, whichever makes it easier for you to follow along. It is advisable to always try and give logical names and descriptions that will be easy for your users to understand.

4. Choose the desired membership type: **Assigned**, **Dynamic User**, or **Dynamic Device** (only with security groups). This example has a **Security Group** for the **Marketing** department and the **Membership type** is set to **Dynamic User** with a single owner selected for the group:

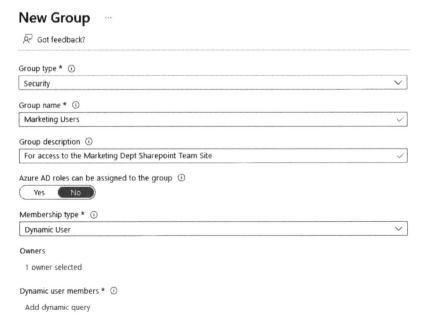

Figure 2.4: New group settings

5. You can now go ahead and select **Add dynamic query** to begin creating dynamic membership rules. The rule builder allows you to add up to five expressions by clicking on the **Add expression** button. The following example shows a simple rule configured for adding members to this group, where the user's department field equals **Marketing** and **accountEnabled** equals **All**:

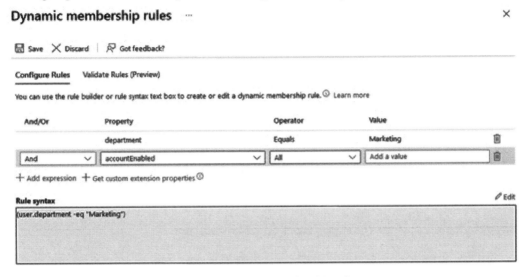

Figure 2.5: Dynamic membership rules

6. Once you've added up to five expressions, you can't add any more. Instead, you must use the **Rule syntax** text box to add more expressions and create more advanced rules. In addition, you can use the **Get custom extension properties** option to add an application ID (if applicable). This can be synced from either your on-premises AD or a connected SaaS application:

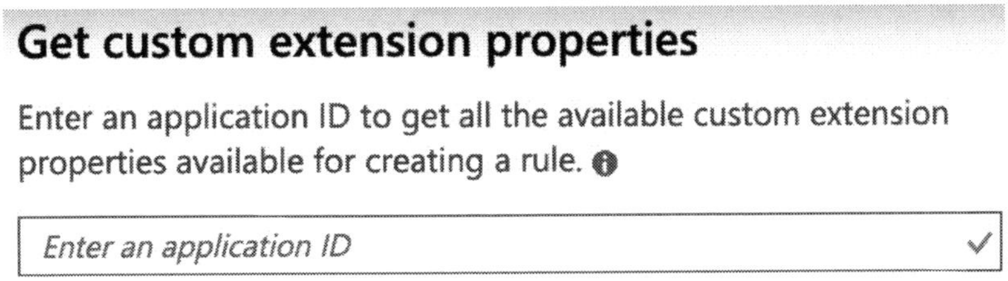

Get custom extension properties

Enter an application ID to get all the available custom extension properties available for creating a rule. ❶

| Enter an application ID | ✓ |

Figure 2.6: Get custom extension properties

7. When you are happy with your selections, click **Save** and then **Create**.

Next, we will look at how you can use PowerShell to create dynamic groups.

Creating dynamic groups with Azure AD PowerShell

It is also possible to create and manage Azure AD groups with PowerShell. Take a look at the **Marketing Users** group you created in the Azure portal using PowerShell.

1. First, you need to launch PowerShell. Running PowerShell as an administrator is often good practice. Once you have PowerShell open and ready, you need to perform the following steps:

   - Run `install-module azuread`.

   - Run `import-module azuread`.

   - Run `get-module azuread`.

   - Run `connect-azuread`.

2. You will be prompted for your credentials, and will need to connect as a **Global Administrator**, **Intune Administrator**, or **User Administrator**. This will connect you to Azure AD in the PowerShell session. Then, you can retrieve a full list of all Azure AD groups by running `Get-AzureADGroup`.

3. However, you need to view the **Marketing Users** group. To do this, filter the command as follows:

```
Get-AzureADGroup -Filter "DisplayName eq 'Marketing Users'"
```

The executed command is shown in the following screenshot:

```
Administrator: Administrator: Windows PowerShell                                    —

PS C:\WINDOWS\system32> Get-AzureADGroup -Filter "DisplayName eq 'Marketing Users'"

ObjectId                              DisplayName       Description
--------                              -----------       -----------
27d45089-6880-4d54-b8a8-c91ab84243ed  Marketing Users   For access to the Marketing Dept SharePoint Team Site

PS C:\WINDOWS\system32>
```

Figure 2.7: Viewing groups with PowerShell

The output of this command will show you the `ObjectID`, `DisplayName`, and `Description` values of your group.

4. Creating a group in PowerShell is just as simple. Suppose you need to create another dynamic security group with the same settings for the *Sales Department* users, but this time, you want to do this in PowerShell. To do this, run the following code:

```
New-AzureADMSGroup -Description "For access to the Sales Dept
SharePoint Team Site" -DisplayName "Sales Users"
-MailEnabled $false -SecurityEnabled $true -MailNickname
"SalesDynamic" -GroupTypes "DynamicMembership"
-MembershipRule "(user.department -eq ""Sales"")"
```

The executed command is shown in the following screenshot:

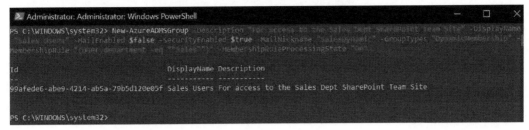

Figure 2.8: Creating a group with PowerShell

With this, the group is created for you. You can search for and view it in the Azure portal, as follows:

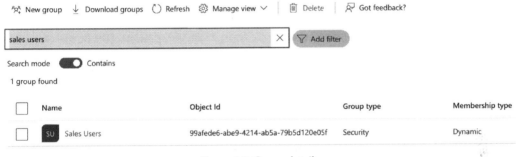

Figure 2.9: Group details

5. You can click on the group name (in this case, **Sales Users**) to open and inspect the group settings. This will show you the group **Overview**:

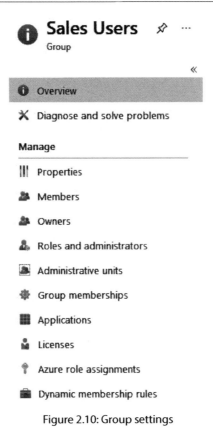

Figure 2.10: Group settings

6.   Select **Dynamic membership rules**. Here, you will see the **Rule syntax** that you defined in the PowerShell command in *step 4*:

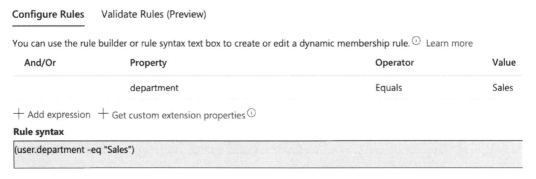

Figure 2.11: Dynamic membership rules

The `New-AzureADMSGroup` command allows you to create not only security groups but also Office 365 groups.

> **Note**
>
> When creating an Office 365 group, a welcome email is sent to all members of the group. It is possible to change this behavior, if desired, by using Exchange Online PowerShell with the `Set-UnifiedGroup` command and the **UnifiedGroupWelcomeMessage** switch set to enabled.

Links to all the relevant PowerShell commands related to Azure AD groups can be found in the *Further reading* section at the end of this chapter.

Using group-based licensing in Azure AD

It is also possible to use Azure AD groups to assign licenses to users within Microsoft 365. You can configure this from the Azure portal by navigating to Azure AD and then selecting **Licenses** followed by **All products**. Alternatively, you can also use the Microsoft Entra admin center at `https://entra.micrososoft.com` under **Azure Active Directory | Billing | Licenses | All products**:

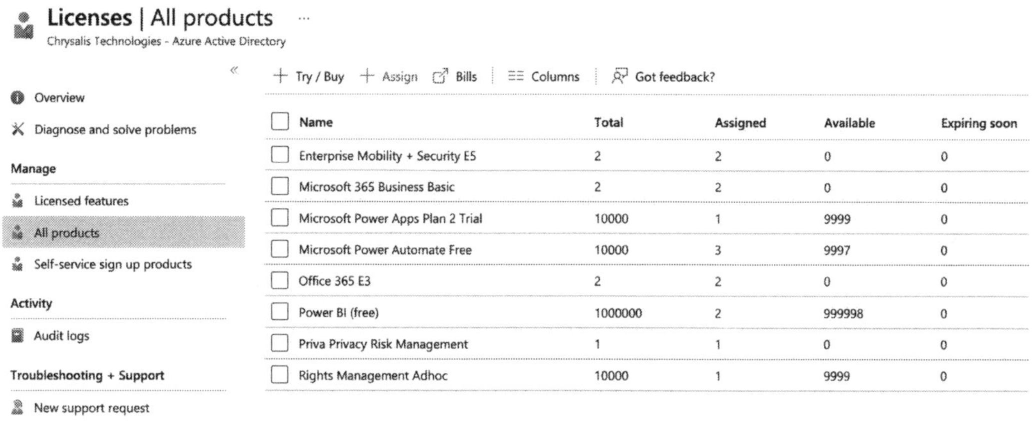

Licenses | All products ...
Chrysalis Technologies – Azure Active Directory

＋ Try / Buy   ＋ Assign   ☐ Bills   ☲☲ Columns   ☒ Got feedback?

Name	Total	Assigned	Available	Expiring soon
Enterprise Mobility + Security E5	2	2	0	0
Microsoft 365 Business Basic	2	2	0	0
Microsoft Power Apps Plan 2 Trial	10000	1	9999	0
Microsoft Power Automate Free	10000	3	9997	0
Office 365 E3	2	2	0	0
Power BI (free)	1000000	2	999998	0
Priva Privacy Risk Management	1	1	0	0
Rights Management Adhoc	10000	1	9999	0

Manage
- Overview
- Diagnose and solve problems
- Licensed features
- All products
- Self-service sign up products

Activity
- Audit logs

Troubleshooting + Support
- New support request

Figure 2.12: Licenses – All products

Suppose you wish to assign an Office 365 E3 license to everyone in the **Marketing Users** group created earlier in this chapter. To do this, you need to follow these steps:

1. Select the **Office 365 E3** license.

2. Select **Licensed groups** and click **Assign**.

3. Click on **Users and groups | + Add users and groups**, search for **Marketing Users**, select the group, and click on **Select**:

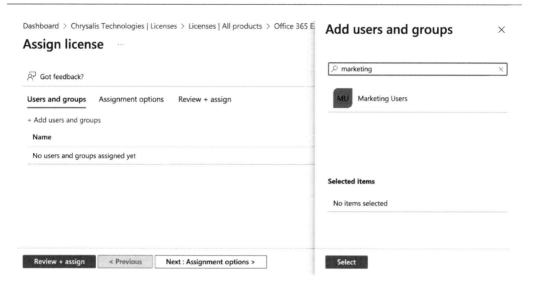

Figure 2.13: Assign license

4.   Now, click **Assignment options**. When assigning a license, you may not be ready to deploy and support all the features of the E3 license to users just yet. Therefore, you can turn off any unrequired features, as shown in the following screenshot:

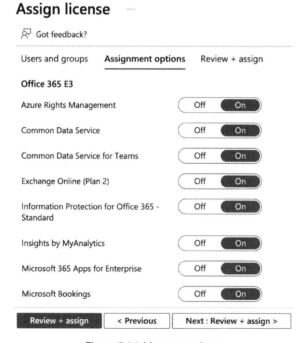

Figure 2.14: License options

5. Once you are happy with your selections, click **Review + Assign**. This will automatically assign all members of the **Marketing Users** group an E3 license with only the features you wish to release at the time. The assignment options can be modified at any time when you are ready to add or remove more features.

Here, you can see how these features can enable you, as an administrator, to empower your users to perform some easy administration. The following section deals with another feature of Azure AD Premium that promotes user convenience – Azure AD SSPR.

Implementing password management

One of the common challenges faced by IT administrators is responding to user requests to reset forgotten passwords. This issue is addressed in Azure AD by SSPR.

SSPR allows Azure AD users to reset their passwords without having to contact the IT department. In order to use this feature, users must complete a registration process during which they need to choose one or more authentication methods set up by the administrators in Azure AD.

When planning for SSPR, you need to consider the different types of user identities within your Microsoft 365 tenant and how SSPR will behave when users wish to reset their own passwords. These are as follows:

- In-cloud users only
- Hybrid identity users

Both user types can register for and use SSPR, but the experience and license requirements will differ. For **in-cloud users** only, passwords are stored within Azure AD. On the other hand, **hybrid identity users** need to have password writeback enabled, which is a feature of Azure AD Premium P1 licensing. With password writeback, users can use SSPR to reset their password; it is then written back to the on-premises AD.

Next, we will look at how you can set up self-service password reset or SSPR.

Setting up SSPR

The first step, as an administrator, is to enable this feature in Azure AD and set up the available user authentication methods. To do this, follow these steps:

1. From the Azure portal, select **Azure Active Directory | Users | Password reset**. Alternatively, go to the Entra admin center and select **Azure Active Directory | Users | User settings | Password reset**.

2. Here, you have the option to activate SSPR for selected users or groups, or for all users within the tenant:

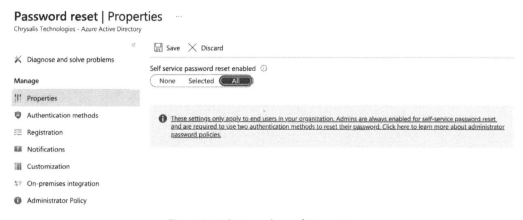

Figure 2.15: Password reset | Properties

3. Next, set up the **Authentication methods**. Requiring two methods to perform the password reset is recommended. There are six methods available in total, as shown in the following screenshot:

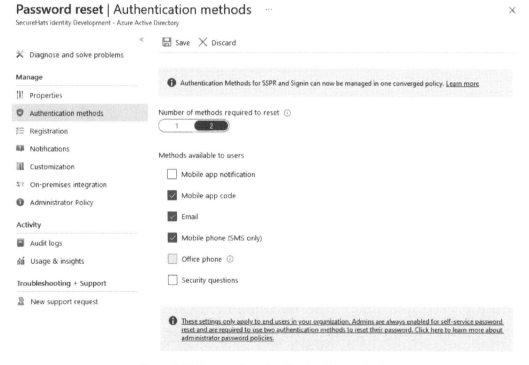

Figure 2.16: Password reset authentication methods

4. Next, configure the user registration options. This setting will determine whether users must register for SSPR the next time they sign in, as well as the number of days before the user must reconfirm their authentication information:

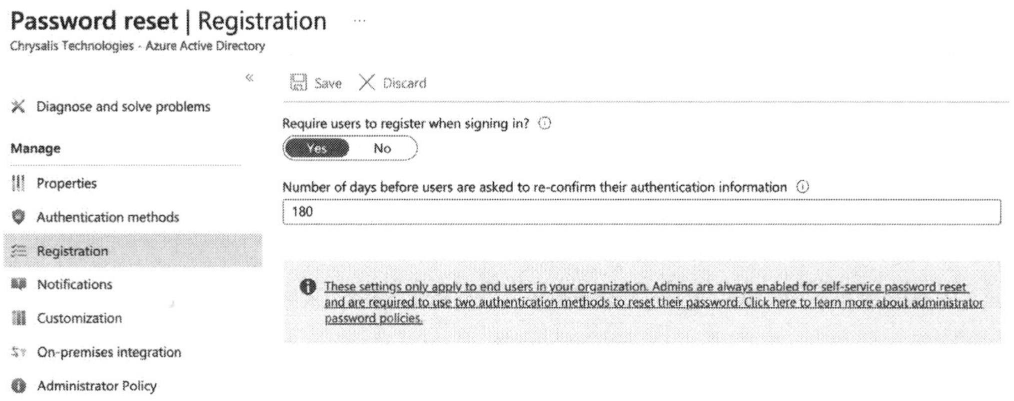

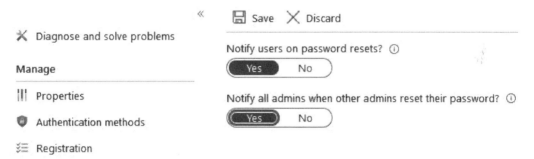

Figure 2.17: Password reset registration

5. It is also possible to set notifications to alert users when their password is reset and also to alert admins when another admin resets their password:

Password reset | Notifications ...

SecureHats Identity Development - Azure Active Directory

🗗 Save   ✕ Discard

Notify users on password resets? ⓘ

Yes   No

Notify all admins when other admins reset their password? ⓘ

Yes   No

Diagnose and solve problems

Manage

Properties

Authentication methods

Registration

Figure 2.18: Password reset: Notifications

6. There is also the option to enable a custom helpdesk link or email address for users who may be struggling with this feature:

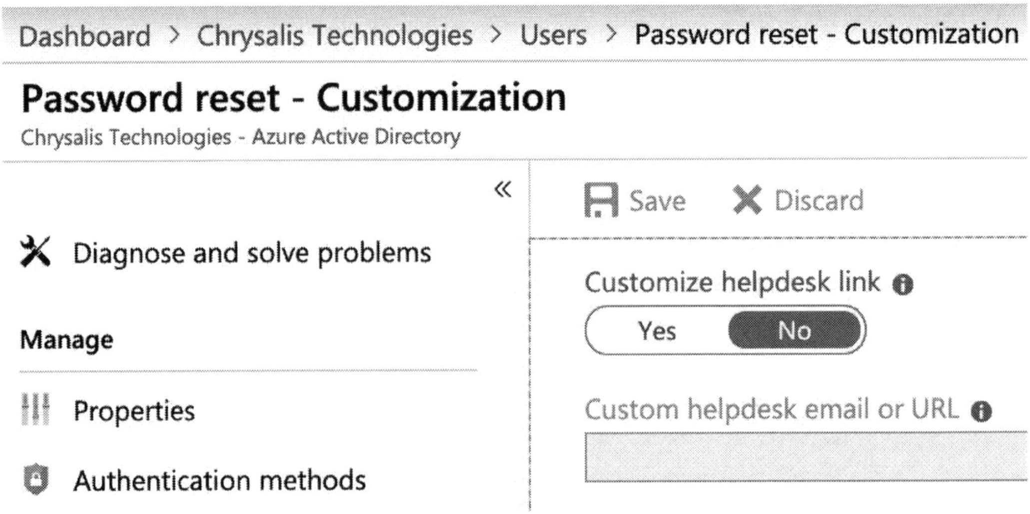
Dashboard > Chrysalis Technologies > Users > Password reset - Customization
Password reset - Customization
Chrysalis Technologies - Azure Active Directory
Save
Discard
Diagnose and solve problems
Customize helpdesk link
Yes
No
Manage
Properties
Custom helpdesk email or URL
Authentication methods

Figure 2.19: Password reset - Customization

7. Finally, configure the **On-premises integration**. If the **password writeback** feature is not enabled in your Azure AD Connect configuration, you will need to rerun the Azure AD Connect setup wizard with a custom installation and ensure that the setting is selected, as shown in the following screenshot:

Password reset | On-premises integration
Chrysalis Technologies - Azure Active Directory
No agents that are capable of performing password writeback have been detected. Install a sync agent and set up your sync engine before enabling password writeback
Learn more
Diagnose and solve problems
Manage
Properties
Authentication methods
Registration
Notifications
Customization
On-premises integration
Administrator Policy

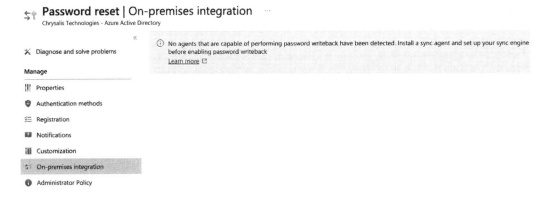

Figure 2.20: Password reset | On-premises integration

The **Password writeback** option can be enabled in the **Optional features** section of the Azure AD Connect setup wizard:

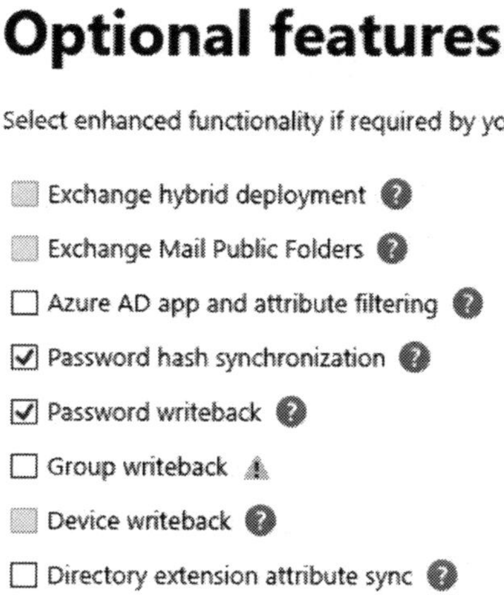

Optional features

Select enhanced functionality if required by your organization.

- ☐ Exchange hybrid deployment ❓
- ☐ Exchange Mail Public Folders ❓
- ☐ Azure AD app and attribute filtering ❓
- ☑ Password hash synchronization ❓
- ☑ Password writeback ❓
- ☐ Group writeback ⚠
- ☐ Device writeback ❓
- ☐ Directory extension attribute sync ❓

Figure 2.21: Optional features

Now that you have finished setting up SSPR, let's take a look at how users can register for the feature.

Registering for SSPR

Users can complete the registration process for SSPR by accessing `https://aka.ms/ssprsetup` and following these steps:.

1. The user will be prompted to provide more information, then click **Next**.

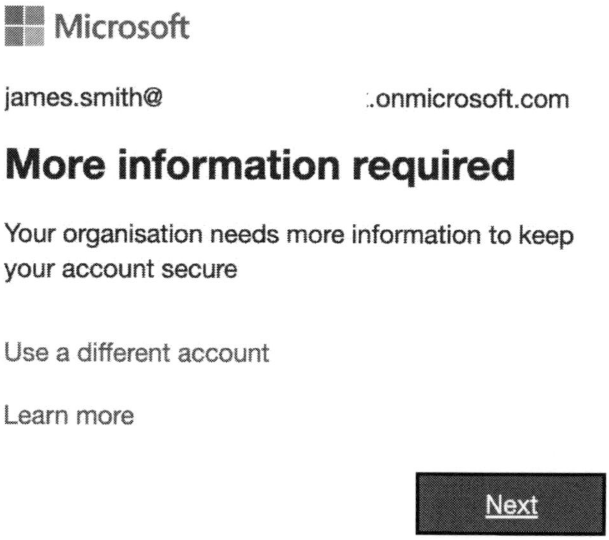

james.smith@   .onmicrosoft.com

More information required

Your organisation needs more information to keep your account secure

Use a different account

Learn more

Next

Figure 2.22: More information is required

2. Next, they will be prompted to enter authentication responses based on how their Microsoft 365 administrator has set up the SSPR. As shown in *Figure 2.17* earlier in the chapter, the user must register an authentication phone number along with an authentication email address. Once this is done, the process will be completed, and they will see the security information, as shown in the following screenshot:

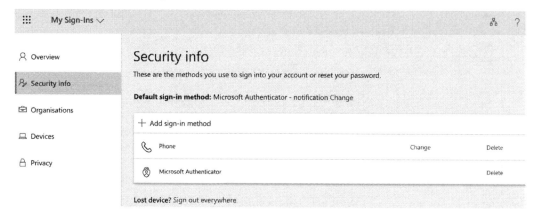

Figure 2.23: Security info shown with the two authentication types required

3. Finally, the user will click **Finish** to complete the registration process.

Now that the user has registered for SSPR, it is ready to be used when needed. Next, let's look at how passwords can be reset.

Using SSPR to reset passwords

If a user needs to reset their password, they can do so by going to `https://aka.ms/sspr/` and completing the following steps:

1. Enter your **User ID** and complete the CAPTCHA; then, click **Next**:

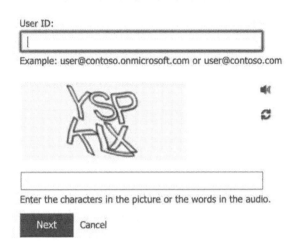

Microsoft

Get back into your account

Who are you?

To recover your account, begin by entering your user ID and the characters in the picture or audio below.

User ID:

Example: user@contoso.onmicrosoft.com or user@contoso.com

Enter the characters in the picture or the words in the audio.

Next   Cancel

Figure 2.24: Get back into your account

2. Based on the authentication challenges defined in the registration process earlier, the user now needs to enter their authentication email address and mobile phone details:

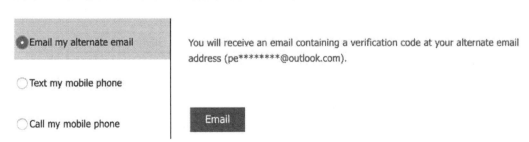

Get back into your account

verification step 1 > verification step 2 > choose a new password

Please choose the first contact method we should use for verification:

Email my alternate email

Text my mobile phone

Call my mobile phone

You will receive an email containing a verification code at your alternate email address (pe********@outlook.com).

Email

Figure 2.25: Get back into your account

3. Once they have completed the two-step authentication, they can enter a new password for their account:

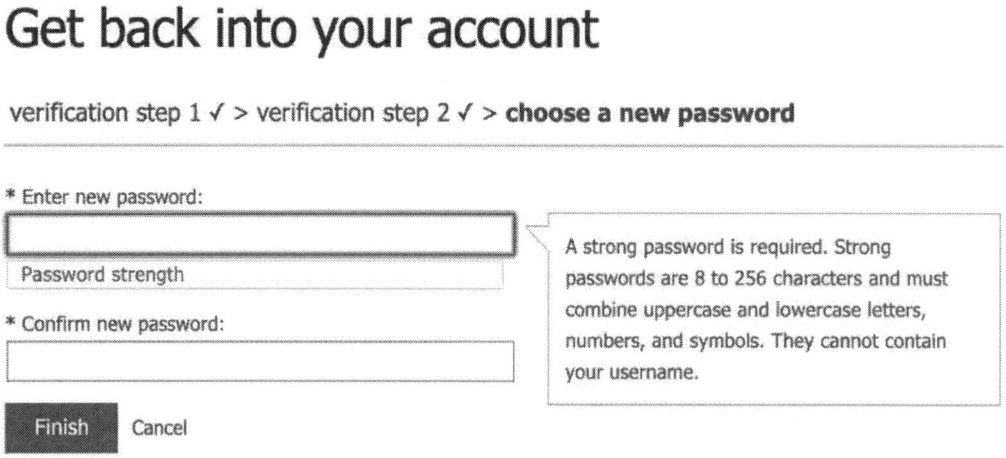

Get back into your account

verification step 1 ✓ > verification step 2 ✓ > **choose a new password**

---

* Enter new password:

Password strength

* Confirm new password:

> A strong password is required. Strong passwords are 8 to 256 characters and must combine uppercase and lowercase letters, numbers, and symbols. They cannot contain your username.

Finish   Cancel

Figure 2.26: Get back into your account

4. Once this is complete, they will see the following message.

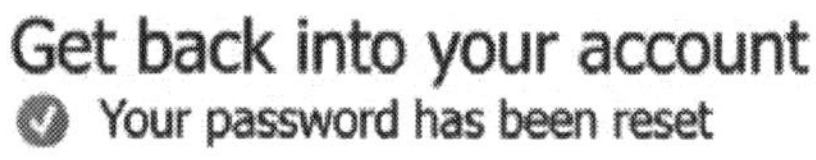

Get back into your account
✅ Your password has been reset

Figure 2.27: Password reset message

The registration process is now complete.

Combined registration for SSPR and MFA

If you are planning to deploy both SSPR and MFA within your Microsoft 365 environment, it is worth considering configuring **User settings** to enable the combined registration experience. This can be found in the Azure portal under **Azure Active Directory | Users | User settings**, or from the Entra admin center under **Azure Active Directory | Users**:

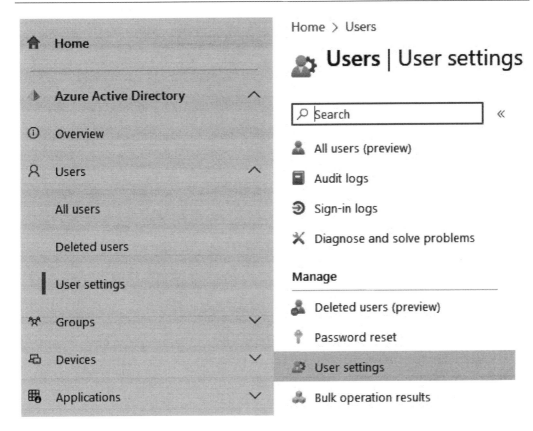

Figure 2.28: Accessing user settings from the Entra Admin center

Navigate to **User settings**, as shown in the following screenshot:

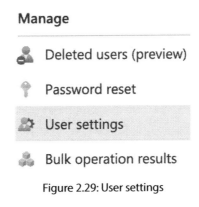

Figure 2.29: User settings

Once you click on **User settings**, you will see the option for **User features | Manage user feature settings**.

User features

Manage user feature settings

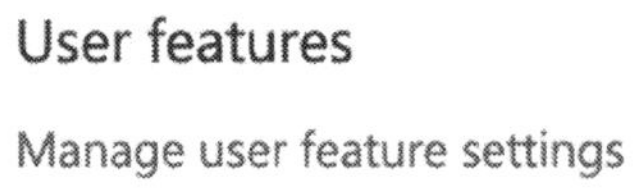

Figure 2.30: Manage user feature settings

In this section, you may set the option for **Users can use the combined security information registration experience**, as shown in the following screenshot:

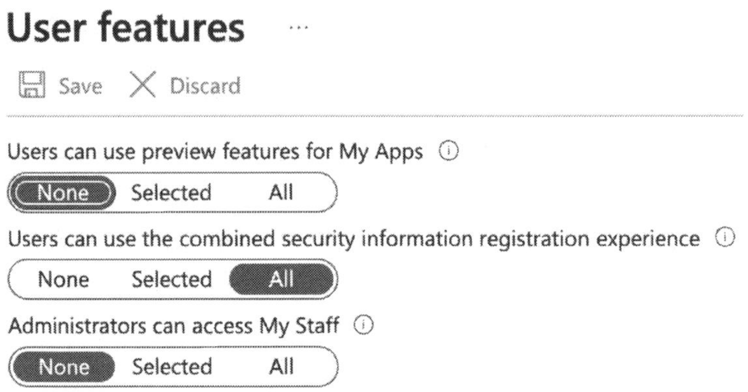

User features   ⋯

💾 Save   ✕ Discard

Users can use preview features for My Apps ⓘ

(**None**   Selected   All)

Users can use the combined security information registration experience ⓘ

(None   Selected   **All**)

Administrators can access My Staff ⓘ

(**None**   Selected   All)

Figure 2.31: Configuring the combined security information registration experience

When this feature is enabled, there is a single registration process for both SSPR and MFA for all users. This provides ease of administration and helps minimize user confusion.

> **Note**
>
> When planning your SSPR rollout, ensure that you test it with a pilot group first. You can do this by activating SSPR for specific users, or, preferably, groups.

Test thoroughly and diligently, and when you are ready to deploy SSPR to all your users, ensure that you communicate with them effectively and inform them that the feature will soon be available to them.

Next, we will examine how to implement and manage external identities.

Implementing and managing external identities

There will often be situations where you need to invite guest users to collaborate within your organization's Microsoft 365 environment. This can be achieved with Azure AD B2B collaboration. The **external identities** feature allows you to securely share your organization's apps and services with external users and maintain complete control.

This is achieved with an invitation process that allows external users to access your Microsoft 365 environment with their own credentials. When the invitee accepts the invitation, they are set up in Azure AD as a B2B user object as a **Guest**.

While B2B collaboration is enabled by default, admins have significant control over the settings. The following steps deal with how a guest user is created:

1. Go to the Azure portal at `https://aad.portal.azure.com` or the Entra admin center at `https://entra.microsoft.com` and log in with admin privileges. Navigate to **Azure Active Directory** | **Users**, and select **+ New user** | **Invite external user**:

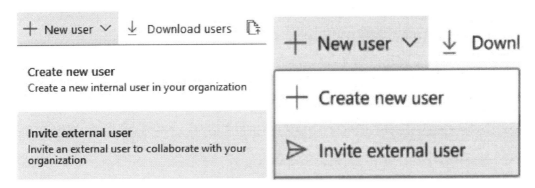

Figure 2.32: Invite external user

2. Fill in the required fields, as shown in the following screenshot, and click **Invite**:

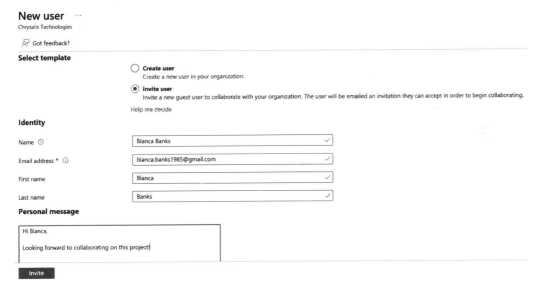

Figure 2.33: Invite settings

3. The invitee will then receive an email with a link that they can click on to accept the invitation. They must then review the permissions requested by the invitation and click **Accept**:

bianca.banks1985@gmail.com

Permission requested by:

C **Chrysalis Technologies**
peterrising.co.uk

By accepting, you allow this organisation to:

∨   Receive your profile data

Your profile data means your name, email address, and photo

∨   Collect and log your activity

Your activity data means your access, usage, and content associated with their apps and resources

∨   Use your profile data and activity data

This data may be used with your access and use of their apps and resources, as well as to create, control, and administer an account according to their policies

You should only accept if you trust Chrysalis Technologies. **Chrysalis Technologies has not provided a link to their privacy statement for you to review.** You can update these permissions at https://myaccount.microsoft.com/organizations Learn More

This resource is not shared by Microsoft.

Figure 2.34: Reviewing invitation permissions

4. Once accepted, the new guest user object will appear in the list of users within Azure AD:

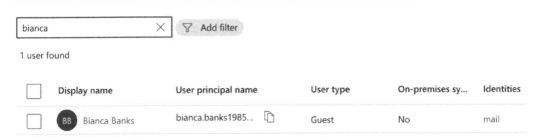

Figure 2.35: New guest user object shown in Azure AD

5. To control the central external collaboration settings for users, select **User settings** from within the **Azure AD Users** section:

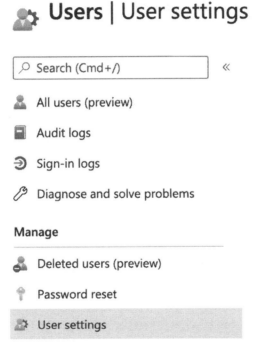

Figure 2.36: User settings in Azure AD

6. Select **External users | Manage external collaboration settings**:

External users

Manage external collaboration settings

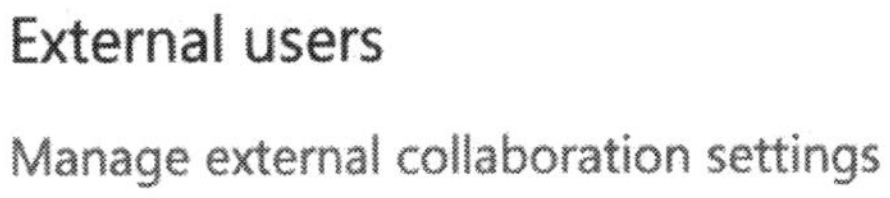

Figure 2.37: Manage external collaboration settings

7. The **External Collaboration settings** you can configure from here include **Guest user access**, **Guest invite settings**, **Enable guest self-service sign up via user flows**, **External user leave settings,** and **Collaboration restrictions**. These options may be set as follows:

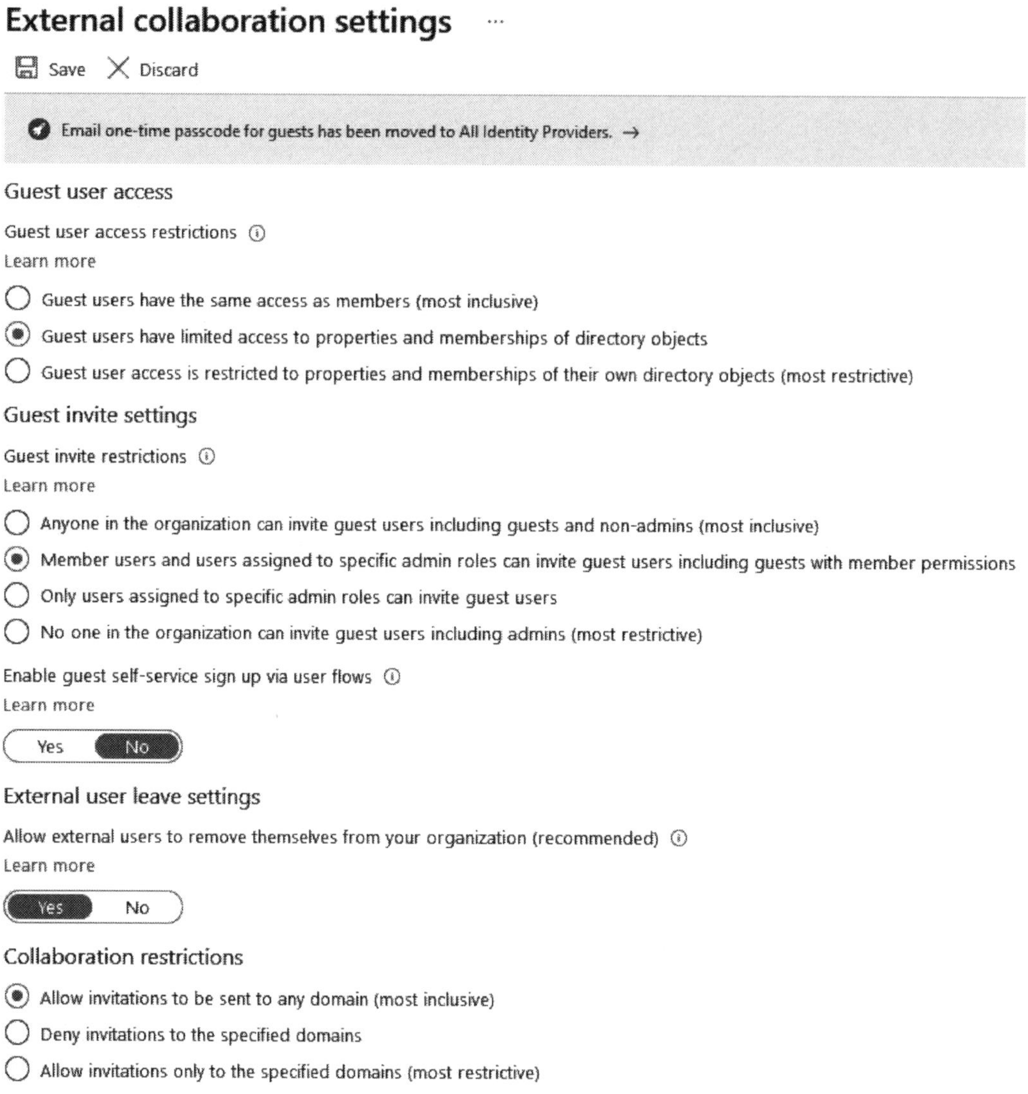

External collaboration settings   ···

🖫 Save   ✕ Discard

> 🛈 Email one-time passcode for guests has been moved to All Identity Providers. →

Guest user access

Guest user access restrictions ⓘ
Learn more

○ Guest users have the same access as members (most inclusive)

◉ Guest users have limited access to properties and memberships of directory objects

○ Guest user access is restricted to properties and memberships of their own directory objects (most restrictive)

Guest invite settings

Guest invite restrictions ⓘ
Learn more

○ Anyone in the organization can invite guest users including guests and non-admins (most inclusive)

◉ Member users and users assigned to specific admin roles can invite guest users including guests with member permissions

○ Only users assigned to specific admin roles can invite guest users

○ No one in the organization can invite guest users including admins (most restrictive)

Enable guest self-service sign up via user flows ⓘ
Learn more

(Yes **No**)

External user leave settings

Allow external users to remove themselves from your organization (recommended) ⓘ
Learn more

(**Yes** No)

Collaboration restrictions

◉ Allow invitations to be sent to any domain (most inclusive)

○ Deny invitations to the specified domains

○ Allow invitations only to the specified domains (most restrictive)

Figure 2.38: External collaboration settings

Once you have made your selections, these will be the defaults for all new guest invitations in Azure AD.

This section explained the principles of Azure AD B2B guest access. We learned how to invite an external guest user to collaborate in your Microsoft 365 organization, how the invited user views and accepts the invitation, and how the guest user object appears in Azure AD. We also learned how to control tenant-wide settings for external user collaboration.

The next section talks about the principles and importance of MFA.

Implementing and managing MFA

In the modern workplace, users are increasingly accessing their data from almost anywhere in the world and from multiple devices. This increases the burden on Microsoft 365 administrators, who not only need to support this modern and more agile way of working but also need to ensure that users, resources, and data are secure and protected. By default, Microsoft 365 user accounts authenticate to Azure AD with only a user ID and password. In the modern security landscape, this simply does not provide enough protection from threats such as phishing attacks.

As was briefly highlighted in *Chapter 1, Planning for Hybrid Identity*, MFA within Microsoft 365 can help protect your organization by providing two-step verification to Microsoft services via approved authentication methods. As a quick reminder, these authentication methods can be based upon the following aspects:

- Something you *know*, such as your password

- Something you *own*, such as your mobile phone or an OAuth token

- Something you *are*, such as biometric identification (fingerprint or facial recognition)

For instance, when a user logs on with their user ID and password, before they can gain access to Microsoft 365, they may also need to enter a six-digit code that has been sent to their smartphone through text message or, alternatively, a code provided by the Microsoft Authenticator app. If all the required authentication challenges are met, then the user is granted access.

Enabling MFA

There are some different methods of enabling MFA in Microsoft 365. Azure AD **Conditional Access** is the preferred method of configuration, and we will cover this in *Chapter 3, Implementing Conditional Access Policies*. However, it remains possible to configure MFA on a per-user basis – but this is not generally recommended anymore.

Per-user MFA can be enabled from the Microsoft 365 admin center at `https://admin.microsoft.com`, as follows:

1. Open **Org settings** from the **Settings** menu:

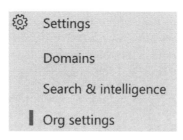

Figure 2.39: Org settings

2. From the **Services** tab, select **Multi-factor authentication**:

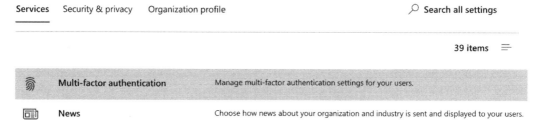

Figure 2.40: Multi-factor authentication

3. Now, select **Configure multi-factor authentication**:

Multi-factor authentication

Multi-factor authentication provides a second layer of security by requiring users to sign in with more than just their username and password.

Configure multi-factor authentication

Learn more about Azure multi-factor authentication

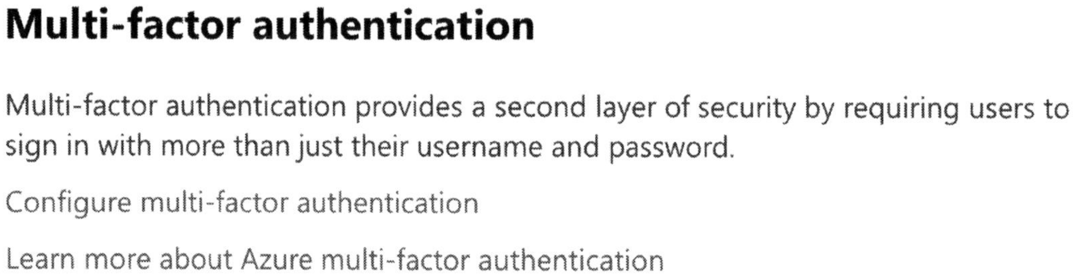

Figure 2.41: Configure multi-factor authentication

4. On the **multi-factor authentication** page, select the users you wish to use MFA and click **Enable**:

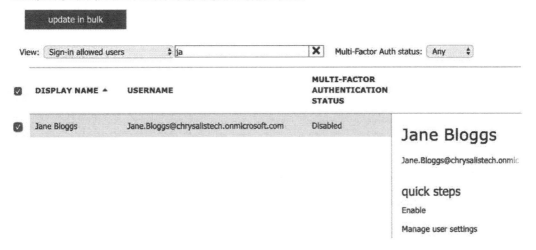

Figure 2.42: Managing MFA

5. You can also choose the **update in bulk** option if you wish to enable MFA for several users. You can download a sample CSV file from here, which you can then upload to enable multiple users.

You can also enable MFA for your users via PowerShell. The following example shows the process of enabling a single user via PowerShell:

1. First, connect to `MsolService` via PowerShell:

    ```
    $UserCredential = Get-Credential
    Import-Module MSOnline
    Connect-MsolService -Credential $UserCredential
    ```

2. Next, create a variable, as follows:

    ```
    $mfa = New-Object -TypeName Microsoft.Online. Administration.
    StrongAuthenticationRequirement
    $mfa.RelyingParty = "*"
    ```

3. Choose between `Enabled` or `Enforced` for your desired MFA state, as follows:

    ```
    $mfa.State = "Enabled"
    Then, to enable MFA for a single user, enter the following
    command:
    Set-MsolUser -UserPrincipalName <UserPrincipalName>
    -StrongAuthenticationRequirements $mfa
    ```

4. If you wish to enable MFA for all your users via PowerShell, you can use the following command:

```
comm Get-MsolUser -All | Foreach{ Set-MsolUser
-UserPrincipalName $_.UserPrincipalName
-StrongAuthenticationRequirements $mfa}and:
```

Next, we will go through the service settings.

Service settings

Administrators can also configure some additional service settings, which include the following:

- Allow/disallow users to create app passwords.

- Set a list of trusted IP addresses or IP ranges that may skip the MFA process.

- Choose from the available verification options, which include the following:

  - Call to phone

  - Text message to phone

  - Notification through mobile app

  - Verification code from mobile app

  - OAuth hardware token

Next, let's cover some secondary authentication methods.

Configuring secondary authentication methods

Once a user has been enabled for MFA, they will be prompted to configure their secondary authentication method the next time they log in with their Microsoft 365 user ID and password.

The user will see a screen with instructions when they log in with their credentials once MFA is enabled.

They will first see a prompt saying **More information required**:

jane.bloggs@chrysalistech.onmicrosoft.com

More information required

Your organization needs more information to keep your account secure

Use a different account

Learn more

Figure 2.43: More information required

The next stage of the process will prompt the user to get the **Microsoft Authenticator** app:

Figure 2.44: Keep your account secure

The user should follow this process until completion. When it's finished, they will be shown a **Success!** prompt, as follows:

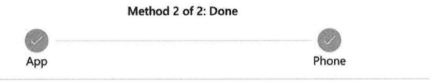

Figure 2.45: Success!

MFA is now set up for their account, and they will be prompted for it when logging into apps on their Windows, Mac, and mobile devices.

> **Note**
>
> If you have Microsoft 365 Business Premium or Azure AD Premium P1, you can configure MFA for Microsoft 365 via Conditional Access policies. This will be covered in the next chapter. In addition, with Azure AD Premium P2, you can configure Azure AD Identity Protection to trigger MFA verification based on user sign-in risk detections.

Please remember that if you are enabling both SSPR and MFA in your Microsoft 365 environment, you can also use the combined registration portal, as described earlier in this chapter.

This section showed you how to set up MFA in Azure AD. In the final section of this chapter, we will examine how to plan and implement the available device authentication methods.

Planning and implementing device authentication methods

With Azure AD MFA deployed in your environment, you need to consider the available authentication methods. There are many options available and they are all listed briefly in this section. Links to more detailed information and instructions on each of these methods are included in the *Further reading* section at the end of this chapter.

In Azure AD, a password is still typically the primary means of authentication. However, passwordless authentication methods are available and include Windows Hello, FIDO security keys, and the Microsoft Authenticator app (all of which are described briefly in *Chapter 1, Planning for Hybrid Identity*). These methods provide the most secure sign-in experience for users in Microsoft 365, and Microsoft recommends replacing passwords with a passwordless method where practical and possible.

The following table presents the different authentication methods available in Azure AD and the level of security they provide:

Method	Security
Windows Hello for Business	High
Microsoft Authenticator app	High
FIDO2 security key	High
OAuth hardware tokens	Medium
Oauth software tokens	Medium
SMS message	Medium
Voice message	Medium
Password	Low

Table 2.1: Authentication methods and their security level

These authentication methods may be configured via the Azure portal and via the Microsoft Graph REST API.

This section introduced the available device authentication methods in Azure AD. Wherever possible and practical, passwordless is recommended by Microsoft, but regardless of the method you choose, secure authentication is crucial to protecting your users and their devices as they access Microsoft 365 apps and services.

> **Note**
>
> The authentication methods listed in this section are not all configured from the same portal areas within Azure AD. Some are in Endpoint Manager, while others are in the Security section of Azure AD. Please refer to the references included for each method at the end of this chapter.

Summary

This chapter dived into the process of assigning access rights to users and groups by using Azure AD dynamic groups. You will now be able to configure dynamic groups, membership rules, and rules syntax for more advanced rules. You also learned how SSPR and MFA can provide authentication security within a Microsoft 365 environment, as well as how these services can be enabled via the combined registration portal.

Additionally, the principles of external user access to Azure AD with B2B users were covered, and finally, you learned how to plan for the available device authentication methods within Azure AD.

The next chapter focuses on Azure AD Conditional Access policies and how they can be used in conjunction with features such as MFA to promote compliance.

Questions

1. True or False: The `New-UnifiedGroup` PowerShell command is used by admins to create dynamic membership groups within Azure AD.

    A. True

    B. False

2. Where would you go to configure the combined MFA/SSPR registration experience in the Azure portal?

    A. **Azure Active Directory | Password reset | Registration**

    B. **Azure Active Directory | Password reset | Properties**

    C. **Azure Active Directory | Users | User settings**

    D. **Azure Active Directory | Users | Password reset**

3. Which of the following is not a method of passwordless authentication?

    A. Windows Hello for Business

    B. FIDO2 security key

    C. Microsoft Authenticator

    D. Enabling MFA

4. With Azure AD dynamic groups, how many expressions can be set in a dynamic query before you will need to use the textbox?

    A. Three

    B. Ten

C. Five

D. Fifteen

5. True or False: Microsoft B2B guest access is enabled by default in Microsoft 365 tenants.

A. True

B. False

6. Which of the following PowerShell commands could you use to create an Azure AD Dynamic Security group?

A. `New-AzureADMSGroup`

B. `New-AzureADGroup`

C. `New-UnifiedGroup`

D. `Set-UnifiedGroup`

7. True or False: Azure MFA may be enabled from the **Services & add-ins** section of the Microsoft 365 admin center?

A. True

B. False

8. Once a user has had MFA enabled for their Microsoft 365 account, when will they be forced to set up their authentication methods?

A. Immediately

B. The next time they log in with their Microsoft 365 account

C. After 14 days

D. At a time of their choosing

9. Where would you go in the Azure portal to configure group-based licensing settings?

A. **Licenses | License Features**

B. **Licenses | All products**

C. **Licenses | Self-Service sign up products**

D. **Licenses | Audit logs**

10. True or False: Azure AD dynamic group membership can be assigned to users based on the attributes of their Microsoft 365 account, such as the department field.

A. True

B. False

Further reading

Please refer to the following links for more information regarding the topics covered in this chapter:

- Creating a basic group and adding members via Azure AD: `https://docs.microsoft.com/en-us/azure/active-directory/fundamentals/active-directory-groups-create-azure-portal?context=azure/active-directory/users-groups-roles/context/ugr-context`

- Creating or updating a dynamic group in Azure AD: `https://docs.microsoft.com/en-us/azure/active-directory/users-groups-roles/groups-create-rule`

- Dynamic membership rules for groups in Azure AD: `https://docs.microsoft.com/en-us/azure/active-directory/users-groups-roles/groups-dynamic-membership`

- Azure AD version 2 cmdlets for group management: `https://docs.microsoft.com/en-us/azure/active-directory/users-groups-roles/groups-settings-v2-cmdlets`

- Using the `Set-UnifiedGroup` command in PowerShell: `https://docs.microsoft.com/en-gb/powershell/module/exchange/users-and-groups/Set-UnifiedGroup?view=exchange-ps`

- Planning for SSPR: `https://docs.microsoft.com/en-us/azure/active-directory/authentication/howto-sspr-deployment`

- Deploying SSPR without requiring user registration: `https://docs.microsoft.com/en-us/azure/active-directory/authentication/howto-sspr-authenticationdata`

- Tutorial for enabling SSPR: `https://docs.microsoft.com/en-us/azure/active-directory/authentication/howto-sspr-writeback`

- How to enable SSPR from the Windows login screen: `https://docs.microsoft.com/en-us/azure/active-directory/authentication/howto-sspr-windows`

- Combined security information registration overview: `https://docs.microsoft.com/en-us/azure/active-directory/authentication/concept-registration-mfa-sspr-combined`

- Setting up your security information from a sign-in prompt: `https://docs.microsoft.com/en-us/azure/active-directory/user-help/user-help-security-info-overview`

- How Azure MFA works: `https://docs.microsoft.com/en-us/azure/active-directory/authentication/concept-mfa-howitworks`

- Features and licenses for Azure MFA: `https://docs.microsoft.com/en-us/azure/active-directory/authentication/concept-mfa-licensing`

- When to use an Azure MFA provider: `https://docs.microsoft.com/en-us/azure/active-directory/authentication/concept-mfa-authprovider`

- Planning an Azure MFA deployment: `https://docs.microsoft.com/en-us/azure/active-directory/authentication/multi-factor-authentication-security-best-practices`

- B2B collaboration overview: `https://docs.microsoft.com/en-us/azure/active-directory/external-identities/what-is-b2b`

- Authentication methods in Azure AD: `https://docs.microsoft.com/en-us/azure/active-directory/authentication/concept-authentication-methods?WT.mc_id=EM-MVP-4039827`

- Windows Hello for Business: `https://docs.microsoft.com/en-us/windows/security/identity-protection/hello-for-business/hello-overview`

- Microsoft Authenticator app: `https://docs.microsoft.com/en-us/azure/active-directory/authentication/concept-authentication-authenticator-app`

- FIDO2 security keys: `https://docs.microsoft.com/en-us/azure/active-directory/authentication/concept-authentication-passwordless#fido2-security-keys`

- OAuth hardware tokens: `https://docs.microsoft.com/en-us/azure/active-directory/authentication/concept-authentication-oath-tokens#oath-hardware-tokens-preview`

- OAuth software tokens: `https://docs.microsoft.com/en-us/azure/active-directory/authentication/concept-authentication-oath-tokens#oath-software-tokens`

- SMS sign in and verification: `https://docs.microsoft.com/en-us/azure/active-directory/authentication/howto-authentication-sms-signin`

- Voice call verification: `https://docs.microsoft.com/en-us/azure/active-directory/authentication/concept-authentication-phone-options`

3

Implementing Conditional Access Policies

One of the common challenges faced by security administrators is finding a balance between usability and security. This is especially relevant in a Microsoft 365 environment where users access cloud-based resources. It is not possible to wrap a firewall around Microsoft 365 in the traditional sense. **Conditional Access** is an Azure **Active Directory** (**AD**) feature that helps you address this challenge.

This chapter will show you how you can configure compliance policies for Conditional Access within your Microsoft 365 environment. You will learn how to allow or block access to the features in your tenant and how device compliance can be enforced with system security settings, such as a minimum password length and data encryption.

These topics will be covered in the following order:

- Explaining Conditional Access

- Conditional Access and Microsoft Intune

- Device-based Conditional Access

- App-based Conditional Access

- Monitoring Conditional Access events

Explaining Conditional Access

Azure AD Conditional Access is a feature within Azure AD Premium P1 and P2 and Microsoft 365 Business Premium. It is designed to provide a balance between security and productivity in modern workplace environments amidst employees' increasing need to work from anywhere and on any device. Conditional Access enables Microsoft 365 administrators to control requests from devices and apps to access company resources.

This is achieved with granular access control policies that are used to define and apply conditions that determine whether access is granted or denied. The following are some examples of categories based on which conditions can be triggered:

- Location

- Device type

- Device state

- User state

- Application sensitivity

So, how does this work? The most basic description of a Conditional Access policy is *when this happens > do this*.

This combination of the condition with the access control makes up the Conditional Access policy. The access control result is either a step that must be completed by the requesting party to gain access, or it can be a restriction applied after sign-in that determines what the requesting party can or cannot do.

Conditional Access policies can be configured by Microsoft 365 administrators from the Azure portal at `https://portal.azure.com` by selecting **Azure Active Directory** | **Security** and then navigating to the **Protect** section and **Conditional Access**. Alternatively, you could go to the Microsoft Entra Admin center at `https://entra.micrososoft.com` and select **Azure Active Directory** | **Protect & secure**. All examples in this chapter use the Azure portal.

The following image shows **Conditional Access** in the **Protect** section.

Figure 3.1: Conditional Access

This takes you to the following page where you will see any existing Conditional Access policies and can create new ones:

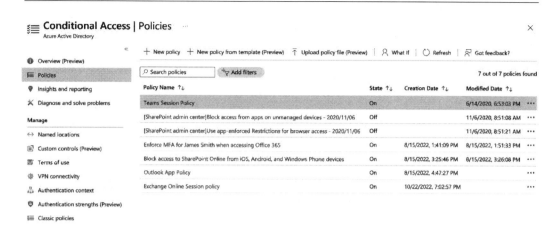

Figure 3.2: Conditional Access policies

Policies may be created from here either manually or via the use of templates that Microsoft provides. In the following section, we discuss how to configure a simple Conditional Access policy and apply it to a single user.

Creating a Simple Conditional Access policy

In the following example, you will create a Conditional Access policy to trigger these conditions and results:

Policy item	Policy setting
Policy Name	`Enforce MFA for James Smith when accessing Office 365`
Applied to	Specific users (in this case James Smith)
Cloud Apps or Actions	Office 365
Conditions	**Location** is set to **Any Location**
Access Controls	Require **multi-factor authentication** (**MFA**)

Table 3.1: Triggering conditions and their results

To create the policy, you need to navigate to **Conditional Access | Policies | New Policy**:

1. You will see the following screen. Enter a name for your policy. This example uses `Enforce MFA for James Smith when accessing Office 365`:

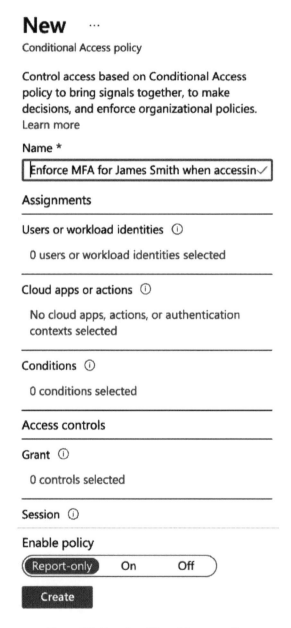

Figure 3.3: New Conditional Access policy

2. Under **Users or workload identities**, choose **Select users and groups** and you can select the targeted users or groups (in this case, **James Smith**):

Enforce MFA for James Smith when accessing Office 365

Conditional Access policy

🗑 Delete

Control access based on Conditional Access policy to bring signals together, to make decisions, and enforce organizational policies. Learn more

Name *

Enforce MFA for James Smith when accessi...

Assignments

Users or workload identities ⓘ
Specific users included

Cloud apps or actions ⓘ
1 app included

Conditions ⓘ
1 condition selected

Access controls

Grant ⓘ
1 control selected

Session ⓘ

Control access based on who the policy will apply to, such as users and groups, workload identities, directory roles, or external guests. Learn more

What does this policy apply to?

Users and groups ⌄

Include   Exclude

◯ None

◯ All users

⦿ Select users and groups

☐ All guest and external users ⓘ

☐ Directory roles ⓘ

☑ Users and groups

Select

1 user

(JS) James Smith   •••
      james.smith@peterrising.co.uk

Figure 3.4: Selecting users and groups

3.   Next, under **Cloud apps or actions**, click on the **Select apps** radio button and choose **Office 365**:

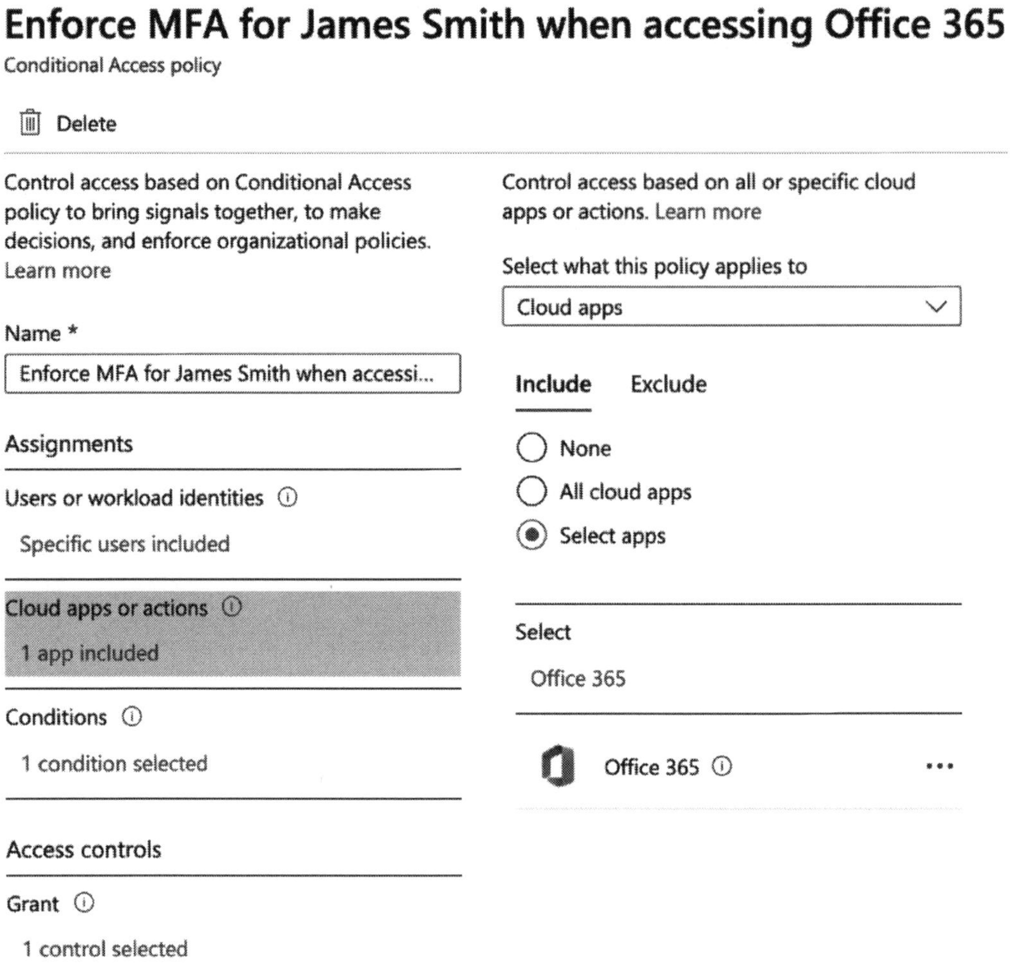

Enforce MFA for James Smith when accessing Office 365
Conditional Access policy

🗑 Delete

Control access based on Conditional Access policy to bring signals together, to make decisions, and enforce organizational policies. Learn more

Name *

Enforce MFA for James Smith when accessi...

Assignments

Users or workload identities ⓘ

Specific users included

Cloud apps or actions ⓘ

1 app included

Conditions ⓘ

1 condition selected

Access controls

Grant ⓘ

1 control selected

Control access based on all or specific cloud apps or actions. Learn more

Select what this policy applies to

Cloud apps ⌄

Include   Exclude

○ None

○ All cloud apps

◉ Select apps

Select

Office 365

▯ Office 365 ⓘ   •••

Figure 3.5: Choosing cloud apps or actions

4. Under **Conditions**, select **Locations**, and choose **Any location**:

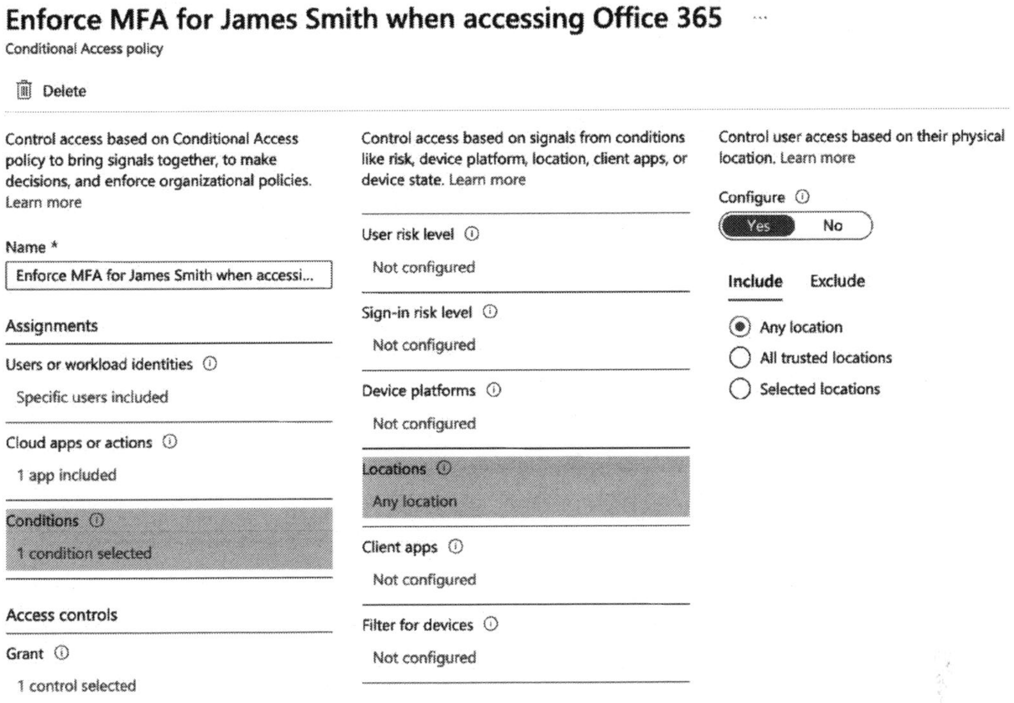

Enforce MFA for James Smith when accessing Office 365 ...

Conditional Access policy

🗑 Delete

Control access based on Conditional Access policy to bring signals together, to make decisions, and enforce organizational policies. Learn more

Name *

Enforce MFA for James Smith when accessi...

Assignments

Users or workload identities ⓘ

Specific users included

Cloud apps or actions ⓘ

1 app included

Conditions ⓘ

1 condition selected

Access controls

Grant ⓘ

1 control selected

Control access based on signals from conditions like risk, device platform, location, client apps, or device state. Learn more

User risk level ⓘ

Not configured

Sign-in risk level ⓘ

Not configured

Device platforms ⓘ

Not configured

Locations ⓘ

Any location

Client apps ⓘ

Not configured

Filter for devices ⓘ

Not configured

Control user access based on their physical location. Learn more

Configure ⓘ

(Yes   No)

Include   Exclude

◉ Any location

○ All trusted locations

○ Selected locations

Figure 3.6: Selecting conditions for the policy

5. Next, under **Access Controls**, select **Grant | Grant Access | Require multifactor authentication**.

6.   Click **Select**:

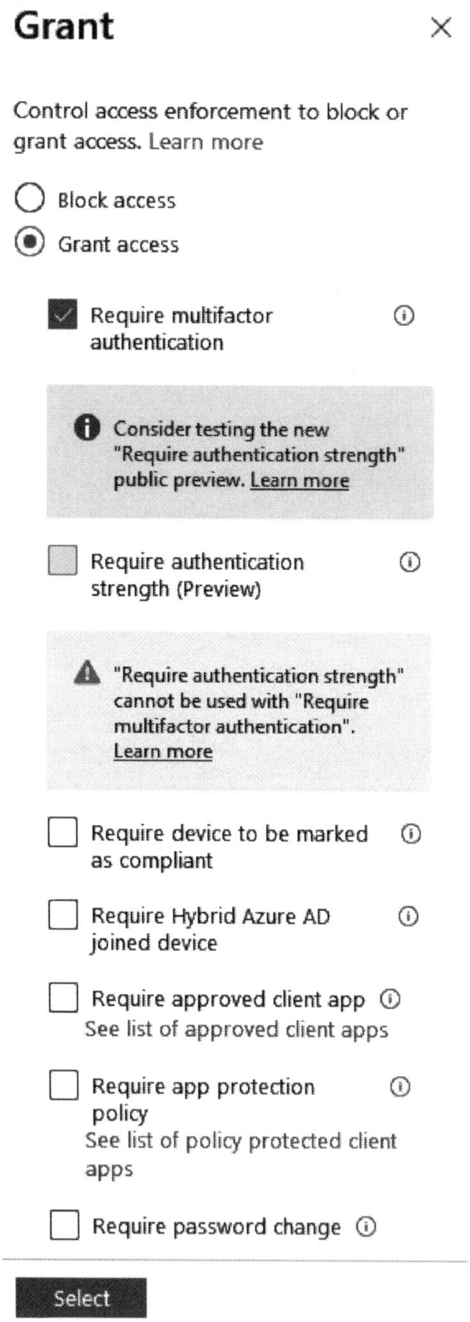

Grant   ✕

Control access enforcement to block or
grant access. Learn more

○ Block access

◉ Grant access

    ☑ Require multifactor   ⓘ
       authentication

    ┌──────────────────────────────────┐
    │ ❶ Consider testing the new   │
    │   "Require authentication strength" │
    │   public preview. Learn more   │
    └──────────────────────────────────┘

    ☐ Require authentication   ⓘ
       strength (Preview)

    ┌──────────────────────────────────┐
    │ ⚠ "Require authentication strength" │
    │   cannot be used with "Require │
    │   multifactor authentication". │
    │   Learn more   │
    └──────────────────────────────────┘

    ☐ Require device to be marked ⓘ
       as compliant

    ☐ Require Hybrid Azure AD   ⓘ
       joined device

    ☐ Require approved client app ⓘ
       See list of approved client apps

    ☐ Require app protection   ⓘ
       policy
       See list of policy protected client
       apps

    ☐ Require password change ⓘ

    ┌──────────┐
    │ Select │
    └──────────┘

Figure 3.7: Creating the policy

7.   Then set **Enable policy** to **On** and click **Create**. The default selection when creating a Conditional Access policy is to save it in **Report-only** mode:

Figure 3.8: Creating the policy

This enables administrators to test whether the policy is working correctly before turning it on fully. It also helps to prevent accidental lockout from Microsoft 365 due to misconfigured Conditional Access policies.

8.   The policy is now created and you will see the following screen:

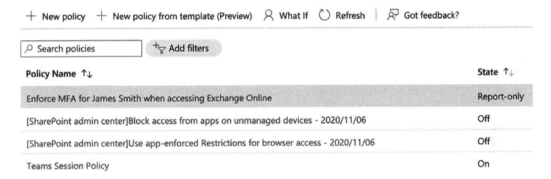

Figure 3.9: Conditional access policies

The result is that James Smith will be required to complete MFA whenever he logs in to Office 365 (regardless of his location).

Now that you understand the basic principles of Conditional Access in Azure AD, we'll examine how Conditional Access integrates with Microsoft Intune to support device-based and app-based policies.

Note

Should you wish to explore the complete range of assignments and access controls, please refer to the *Further reading* section at the end of this chapter.

Conditional Access and Microsoft Intune

While conditional access is a feature of Azure AD Premium, it integrates closely with **Microsoft Intune** to add mobile device compliance and mobile app management capabilities.

This is why Conditional Access may also be accessed by users with the appropriate roles and permissions from within Microsoft Intune (also commonly referred to as Microsoft Intune). The Microsoft Intune admin center is accessed via `https://intune.microsoft.com` and **Conditional access** may be found in the **Devices** section as shown in the following screenshot:

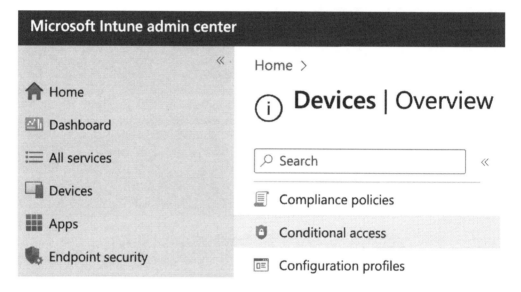

Figure 3.10: Conditional access from the Microsoft Intune admin center

Now that you understand the relationship between Conditional Access and Intune, let's examine two more types of conditional access—device-based conditional access and app-based conditional access.

Introducing the types of Conditional Access

There are different applications of Conditional Access, which we will discuss in this section, starting with device-based policies.

Device-based Conditional Access

With **device-based Conditional Access**, you can ensure that only devices that are managed and compliant can access the services provided by Microsoft 365, such as Exchange Online, **Software as a Service (SaaS)** apps, and even on-premises apps. It is also possible to set specific requirements; for instance, that computers must be hybrid Azure AD-joined or require an approved client app for enrolment in Intune to access services.

Device policies can be configured to ensure device compliance and give administrators visibility on the compliance status of devices that have been enrolled in Microsoft Intune. This compliance status is passed to Azure AD, which then triggers a Conditional Access policy when users attempt to access resources. The Conditional Access policy either allows or blocks access to resources based on the compliance status of the requesting device.

In the modern workplace, you will increasingly need to consider and plan for the following device types and Conditional Access scenarios:

- Corporate-owned devices, which can include the following:

  - On-premises domain-joined Azure AD

  - Domain-joined Azure AD

  - Domain-joined Azure AD registered with System Center Configuration Manager

- **Bring Your Own Device (BYOD)** devices, which can include the following:

  - Workplace

  - Joined

  - Managed by Intune

The following section explains how you can use Conditional Access to create a device-based policy.

Creating a device-based Conditional Access policy

In the following example, you will create a device-based Conditional Access policy that will be triggered on the following conditions and implement the results listed here:

Field name	Field purpose
Policy Name	Block access to SharePoint Online from iOS, Android, and Windows Phone devices
Cloud Apps or Actions	Office 365 SharePoint Online
Conditions	Include the following device platforms: Android, iOS, Windows Phone
Client Apps	To include the following: browser and mobile apps and desktop clients
Access Control	Block access

Table 3.2: Conditional Access policy conditions and results

To create the policy, you need to go to **Conditional Access | Policies | New Policy** and follow the given steps:

1. You will see the following screen, where you will be asked to enter a name for your policy:

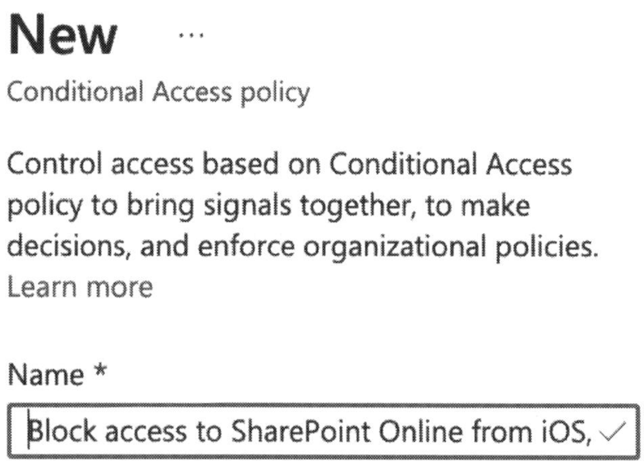

New   ···

Conditional Access policy

Control access based on Conditional Access policy to bring signals together, to make decisions, and enforce organizational policies. Learn more

Name *

Block access to SharePoint Online from iOS, ✓

Figure 3.11: New policy creation

This example uses `Block access to SharePoint Online from iOS, Android, and Windows Phone devices`.

2. Next, you need to target the users and groups to which you wish to apply the policy. This case targets two specific users—**Jane Bloggs** and **James Smith**. Go to **Assignments | Users or workload identities** in the new policy wizard, as shown here:

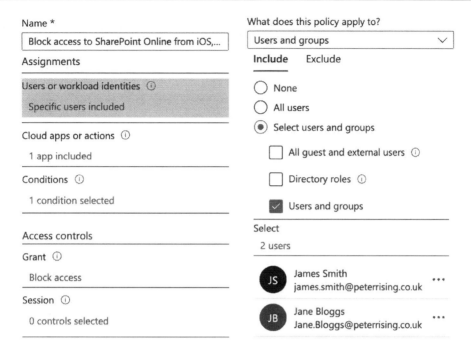

Figure 3.12: New policy user and group settings

3. Once you are happy with your selections, click **Select**.

4. Next, you need to select **Cloud apps or actions**. Choose **Office 365 SharePoint Online** as the targeted cloud app:

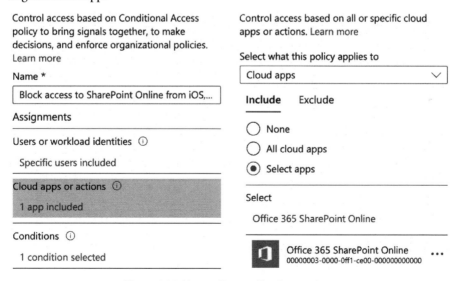

Figure 3.13: New policy application settings

5. You are not going to select any user actions or authentication context settings (at the time of writing, this is a preview feature), so go ahead and click on **Select** once again.

6. Now, you need to choose the conditions that will trigger the policy. Under **Conditions**, first select **Device platforms**:

Figure 3.14: New policy device platforms

7. Choose **Android**, **iOS**, and **Windows Phone**. Click on **Done**.

8. Next, under **Access Controls**, select **Grant**. For this example, choose **Block access**:

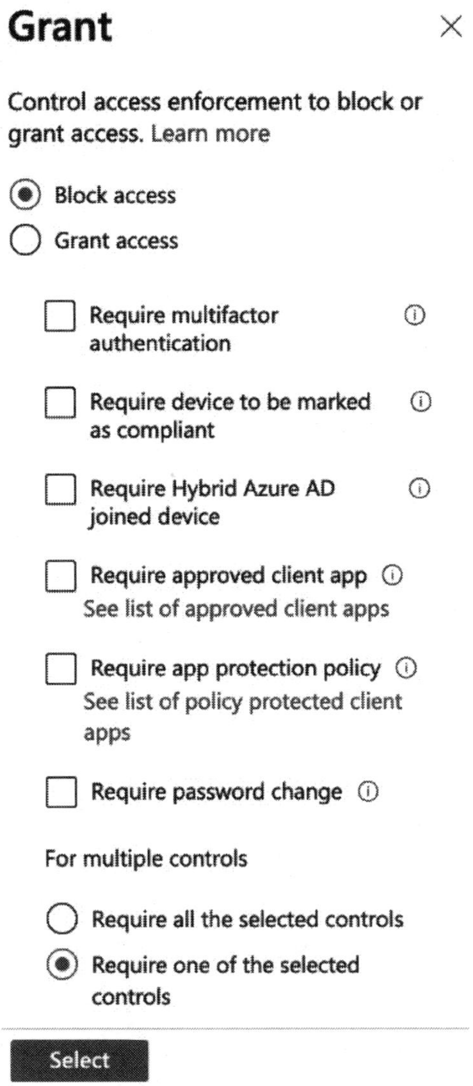

Grant   ✕

Control access enforcement to block or
grant access. Learn more

⊙ Block access

◯ Grant access

☐ Require multifactor   ⓘ
    authentication

☐ Require device to be marked   ⓘ
    as compliant

☐ Require Hybrid Azure AD   ⓘ
    joined device

☐ Require approved client app ⓘ
    See list of approved client apps

☐ Require app protection policy ⓘ
    See list of policy protected client
    apps

☐ Require password change ⓘ

For multiple controls

◯ Require all the selected controls

⊙ Require one of the selected
    controls

[Select]

Figure 3.15: Access controls

9. Click **Select**. This is the final selection for the policy, which should now look as follows:

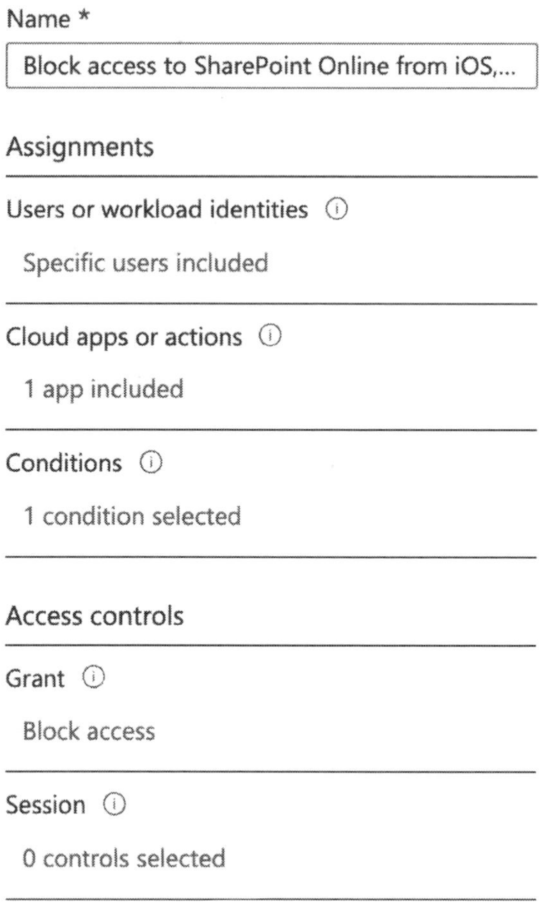

Name *

Block access to SharePoint Online from iOS,...

Assignments

Users or workload identities ⓘ

Specific users included

Cloud apps or actions ⓘ

1 app included

Conditions ⓘ

1 condition selected

Access controls

Grant ⓘ

Block access

Session ⓘ

0 controls selected

Figure 3.16: All policy controls set

10. To enable and apply this policy, select **Enable policy** and click **Create**:

Figure 3.17: Enabling the policy

11. The policy is successfully created and appears in the list of policies, as shown in the following screenshot:

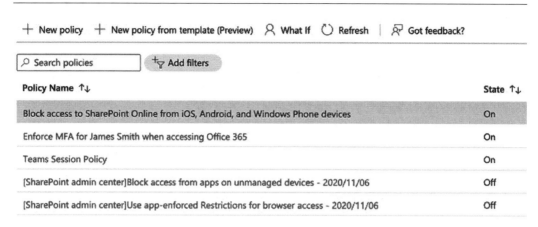

Figure 3.18: List of policies

Now, you can test whether the policy works. To do this, assume that the user Jane Bloggs is logging in with her Microsoft 365 credentials and trying to access SharePoint Online.

First, consider what would happen if this was done from an Apple macOS device via the web browser. The Conditional Access policy should not block this, which is confirmed by the following screenshot:

Figure 3.19: Access to SharePoint via the macOS web browser

However, if Jane attempts the same action from her Apple iOS device, the following is displayed:

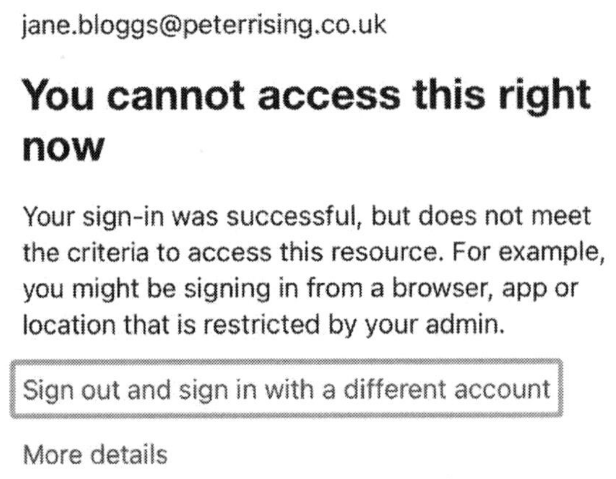

jane.bloggs@peterrising.co.uk

You cannot access this right now

Your sign-in was successful, but does not meet the criteria to access this resource. For example, you might be signing in from a browser, app or location that is restricted by your admin.

Sign out and sign in with a different account

More details

Figure 3.20: Access to SharePoint blocked on the iOS device

This indicates that the policy works exactly as expected. As you will have noticed from the earlier screenshots, there are many ways to tailor assignments and access controls in your Conditional Access policies.

The following section discusses app-based Conditional Access.

App-based Conditional Access

With Microsoft Intune, app protection policies can also be created that enforce **app-based Conditional Access**. This ensures that only apps that support these policies can access Microsoft 365 services.

This is particularly useful when dealing with BYOD devices. This is because this kind of policy further protects your Microsoft 365 environment from requests sent by apps on non-corporate-owned devices.

Creating an app-based Conditional Access policy

In order to create an app-based Conditional Access policy, you need to perform the following steps:

1. First, ensure that you have an app protection policy applied to any apps that you use. To do this, log in to the Intune admin center and select **Apps** | **App protection policies**:

Figure 3.21: App protection policies

2. Click on **Create policy**. For this example, create a policy for Microsoft Outlook on Apple devices named and described as follows:

    *   **Name**: Outlook on iOS and iPadOS

    *   **Description**: Policy for settings and access requirements when using the Outlook App on Apple iOS or iPadOS devices

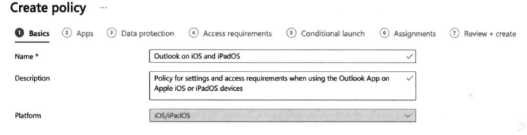

Figure 3.22: Setting up an app protection policy

3. On the **Apps** screen, ensure that **Microsoft Outlook** is selected in the **Target policy to** section as shown in the following screenshot:

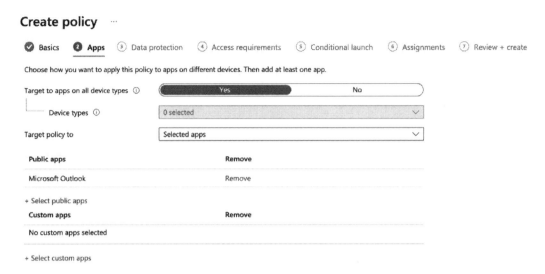

Figure 3.23: Target policy to apps

4. Next, configure the available settings for the policy. Follow the wizard through all the steps and review and complete the required options for your policy. These are **Data protection**, **Access requirements**, **Conditional launch**, and **Assignments**:

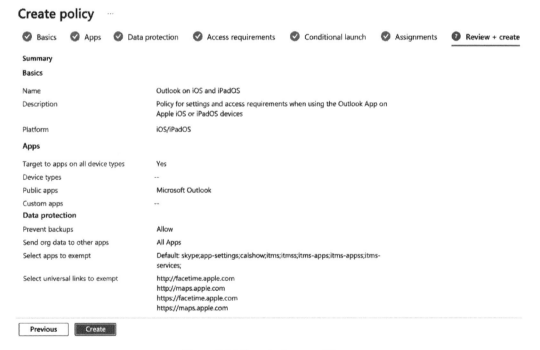

Figure 3.24: Targeted apps settings

5.   Once you are happy with your selections, click **Create**.

Now that you have your app protection policy, you can proceed to create the app-based Conditional Access policy:

1.   Navigate to **Conditional Access | Policies | New Policy**. Name this policy `Outlook App Policy`:

2.   Under **Assignments**, you can configure the desired settings and apply them to the required users and groups. Mobile Application Management can only be applied to iOS or Android devices, so you must also choose the selected device platforms from the **Conditions | Device platforms** section:

Figure 3.25: Device platform settings

3.   Next, under **Access controls | Grant**, select **Grant Access** and **Require approved client app**:

Grant   ✕

Control access enforcement to block or
grant access. Learn more

◯ Block access

◉ Grant access

⬜ Require multifactor   ⓘ
authentication

⬜ Require device to be marked   ⓘ
as compliant

⬜ Require Hybrid Azure AD   ⓘ
joined device

☑ Require approved client app ⓘ
See list of approved client apps

⬜ Require app protection policy ⓘ
See list of policy protected client
apps

⬜ Require password change ⓘ

For multiple controls

◉ Require all the selected controls

◯ Require one of the selected
controls

Select

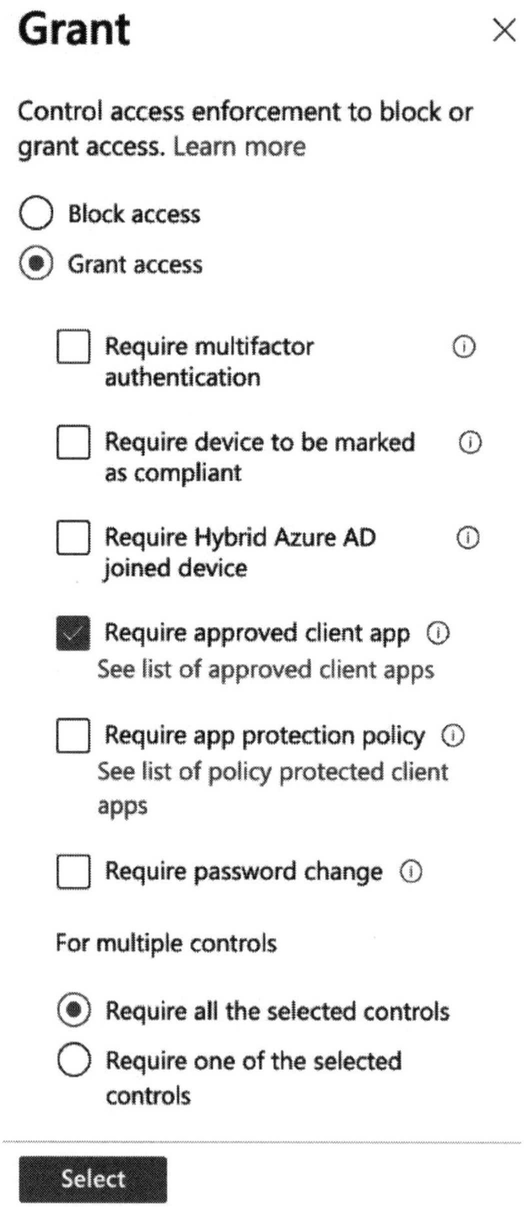

Figure 3.26: Require approved client app

4.   Click **Select**, ensure that **Enable policy** is set to **On**, and click **Create**. You will now see the new
policy added to your list of existing Conditional Access policies:

Policy Name ↑↓	State ↑↓
Teams Session Policy	On
Enforce MFA for James Smith when accessing Office 365	On
Block access to SharePoint Online from iOS, Android, and Windows Phone devices	On
Outlook App Policy	On
[SharePoint admin center]Block access from apps on unmanaged devices - 2020/11/06	Off
[SharePoint admin center]Use app-enforced Restrictions for browser access - 2020/11/06	Off

Figure 3.27: Outlook app policy enabled

> **Note**
> In order to create Conditional Access policies, an Azure AD Premium license is required.

The following sections explain how you can monitor Conditional Access events in Azure AD.

Monitoring Conditional Access events

As a security admin, an important part of your job will be to monitor and interpret any events that are recorded in relation to Conditional Access to ensure that it is doing its job correctly. In order to monitor and search for Conditional Access policy matches in Azure AD, you need to take the following steps:

1. From the Azure portal, select **Azure Active Directory** and choose **Sign-in logs** from the **Monitoring** section:

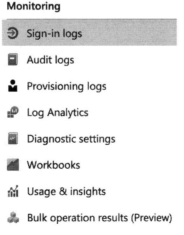

Figure 3.28: Monitoring Conditional Access

2.   From the results displayed, filter by **Conditional access**:

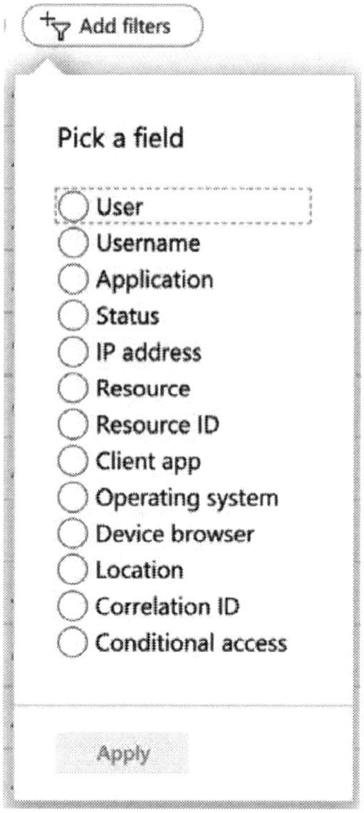

Figure 3.29: Filtering by Conditional access

3.   You can further filter the results by **Success**, **Failure**, or **Not Applied**:

Figure 3.30: Filtering results

> **Note**
>
> You can also monitor the device compliance status from the Microsoft Intune admin center by selecting **Compliance status** from the **Devices | Overview** section.

In this section, we examined how administrators can monitor Conditional Access events in the Azure AD portal. This is an extremely useful capability and a great way to ensure that your Conditional Access policies are appropriately configured and working as expected.

Summary

In this chapter, you were introduced to Conditional Access policies in Azure AD. You learned how Conditional Access helps you address traditional security requirements with a modern approach; instead of configuring a firewall (which is not possible in a Microsoft 365 environment), you can configure policies in Azure AD and Microsoft Intune to provide additional protection for users and resources. You also learned how to create a simple Conditional Access policy as well as app-based and device-based policies integrated with Microsoft Intune. In addition, you explored how to utilize the Azure AD Sign-ins page to track successful, failed, and unapplied Conditional Access policy events.

> **Note**
>
> Azure AD Conditional Access also integrates with Azure AD Identity Protection and Microsoft Defender for Cloud Apps. These topics will be covered in later chapters of this book.

The next chapter will show you how role assignment and privileged identities can be used in Azure AD to ensure that the correct access is provided to your users. You will also learn about the principles of Azure AD Entitlement Management and Azure AD Access Reviews.

Questions

1. Which of the following is not a possible response to a Conditional Access policy being triggered?

    A. Requiring Microsoft Defender for Identity

    B. Requiring MFA

    C. Requiring an approved client app

    D. Requiring a device to be marked as compliant

2. True or false? Conditional Access is included with an Azure AD Premium P1 license.

    A. True

    B. False

3. Which of the following may be used to configure Conditional Access Policies? Choose two options.

   A. Microsoft Intune Admin center

   B. Microsoft 365 Admin center

   C. The Azure Portal under **Azure Active Directory | Security**

   D. Microsoft 365 Compliance center

4. What are the two possible methods of bypassing Conditional Access?

   A. Setting named locations in Azure AD

   B. Using **Role-Based Access Control (RBAC)**

   C. Setting up MFA-trusted IPs

   D. Enabling self-service password reset

   E. Enabling pass-through authentication

5. True or false? With Microsoft Intune, you can use device-based compliance and app-based compliance in conjunction with Conditional Access.

   A. True

   B. False

6. Where would you look to monitor Conditional Access events?

   A. The Intune admin center under **Apps | App protection policies**

   B. The Intune admin center under **Devices | Compliance policies**

   C. The Azure portal under **Azure Active Directory | Security | Conditional Access | Policies**

   D. The Azure portal under **Azure Active Directory | Monitoring | Sign-in logs**

7. Which of the following licenses on its own does not provide Conditional Access?

   A. Office 365 E3

   B. Microsoft 365 Business Premium

   C. Microsoft 365 E3

   D. Microsoft 365 E5

   E. Azure AD Premium P1

8. True or false? With app-based Conditional Access, you can configure policies to require an approved client application to access a particular Microsoft 365 service.

    A. True

    B. False

9. Which of the following are available device platforms that can be targeted with Conditional Access policies (choose all that apply)?

    A. Android

    B. Windows Phone

    C. macOS

    D. Linux

    E. Windows

10. True or false? With Conditional Access conditions, you can apply encryption to sensitive documents.

    A. True

    B. False

Further reading

Please refer to the following links for more information:

- The following link is an example of a device compliance policy. Before configuring the device compliance policies, make sure that you are aware of all of the device types in your organization that you will need to protect: `https://learn.microsoft.com/en-gb/mem/intune/protect/quickstart-set-password-length-android?wt.mc_id=4039827`.

- The following link shows how to configure a device-based Conditional Access policy. When using these, always test them thoroughly with a small pilot group before targeting all users: `https://learn.microsoft.com/en-gb/mem/intune/protect/create-conditional-access-intune`.

- This policy helps you to set rules on your devices to allow access. The *Ways to deploy device compliance policies* section will give you a greater understanding of how to plan for device rules: `https://learn.microsoft.com/en-gb/mem/intune/protect/device-compliance-get-started`.

- This link will show you how to plan for app-based Conditional Access: `https://learn.microsoft.com/en-gb/mem/intune/protect/app-based-conditional-access-intune`.

- This link will show you how to set up app-based Conditional Access policies. Remember that you need an Azure AD Premium license to create Conditional Access policies from the Intune portal: `https://learn.microsoft.com/en-gb/mem/intune/protect/app-based-conditional-access-intune-create`.

- This link will show you how to create and assign app protection policies: `https://learn.microsoft.com/en-gb/mem/intune/apps/app-protection-policies`.

- This link will show you how you can monitor your device compliance policies. Remember that devices must always be enrolled in order to take advantage of these policies: `https://learn.microsoft.com/en-us/mem/intune/protect/compliance-policy-monitor`.

- This link explains the principles of authentication context within Conditional Access: `https://techcommunity.microsoft.com/t5/microsoft-entra-azure-ad-blog/conditional-access-authentication-context-now-in-public-preview/ba-p/1942484`.

- This link explains the principles of Workload Identities within Conditional Access: `https://learn.microsoft.com/en-us/azure/active-directory/conditional-access/workload-identity`.

4

Managing Roles and Identity Governance

In this chapter, you will learn about Azure AD **Privileged Identity Management** (**PIM**) and how it enables you to manage, control, and monitor access to resources within Azure AD. PIM can help you identify and minimize the number of people who have access to sensitive or secure information and resources within your organization.

You will also explore how to implement and manage Azure AD **entitlement management**, which can be used to grant users access to a set of applications and sites within Microsoft 365, and finally access reviews, which are designed to allow users and admins to regularly review standing access to resources and assess where there may be stale permissions that are no longer required.

This chapter will cover the following topics:

- Planning and configuring PIM
- Planning and configuring entitlement management
- Planning and configuring access reviews

Planning and configuring PIM

Azure AD PIM enables you to take greater control of your privileged accounts within Azure AD. So, what exactly is a **privileged account**? Essentially, this is any user account within your Microsoft 365 environment that grants elevated privileges above the scope of a standard user.

By default, Microsoft 365 standard user accounts are created without any sort of administrative privileges. However, it may be necessary to grant certain users elevated privileges as per their jobs. There are many built-in administrator roles within Microsoft 365 for this, including (but not limited to) the following:

- Billing Administrator
- Exchange Administrator

- Global Administrator
- Helpdesk Administrator
- Service Administrator
- SharePoint Administrator
- Teams Administrator
- User Administrator
- Privileged Role Administrator

If you'd like to know more, please refer to the *Further reading* section at the end of this chapter.

Now that you understand the purpose of PIM and some of the available roles, let's look at how you plan for PIM in your environment.

Planning PIM

PIM provides you with the ability to control and monitor access to your resources in Azure AD. It does so by minimizing the number of users who have permanent administrative access, with admin roles such as those described previously. Reducing the number of permanent administrative accounts has the obvious benefit of reducing your attack surface and thereby reducing the risk of a malicious actor gaining access to your resources.

However, there will undoubtedly be a business requirement for certain users to perform administrative tasks within Azure AD from time to time; this is where PIM comes into play. PIM can allow you to provide **just-in-time (JIT)** privileged access to your resources in Azure AD. This will help reduce the risk of access rights becoming compromised and misused in any way.

When thinking about your users who may require occasional admin access to Azure resources, consider the following features of PIM to configure them:

- JIT privileged access to activate roles
- Time-bound access (using start and end dates)
- An approval process for privileged role activation requests
- The requirement for MFA when activating certain roles
- A justification process where users must explain why they require a privileged role
- Notifications to alert you when privileged roles are activated
- Access reviews to assess ongoing requirements for privileged roles

To access the PIM feature, go to the Azure portal and search for **Azure AD Privileged Identity Management**, as follows:

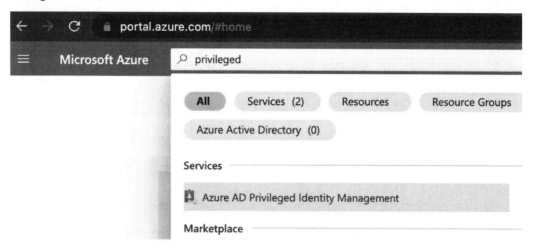

Figure 4.1: Searching for Azure AD Privileged Identity Management

Then, you will be directed to the PIM console:

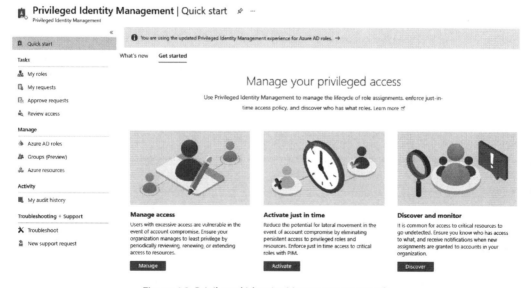

Figure 4.2: Privileged Identity Management console

In this example, you can see that the logged-in user has not only **Global Administrator** access but also two other permanently assigned admin roles. This is viewed under **Azure AD roles | Active assignments**:

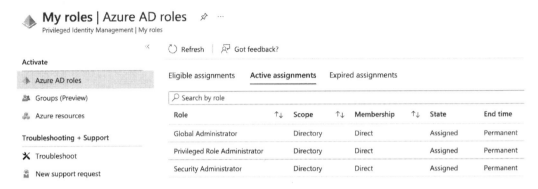

Figure 4.3: Assigned Azure AD roles

As a PIM administrator, you can grant other administrators the ability to manage **Azure AD roles**, **Privileged access groups** (which is a preview feature), and **Azure resources**, as shown in the following screenshot:

Figure 4.4: Managing roles and resources

As a PIM administrator, you can also allow other users to be approvers who can then view and approve/reject requests from users to elevate their privileges. Additionally, it is possible to make specific users eligible for privileged roles so that they can request access to them on a JIT basis.

> **Note**
> In order to use the features of Azure AD PIM in your Microsoft 365 environment, you must have an **Azure AD Premium P2**, **Enterprise Mobility + Security E5**, or **Microsoft 365 E5** license for all users who wish to leverage the feature. The Microsoft 365 E5 Security add-on may also be added to use Azure AD PIM, but this must be used in conjunction with a Microsoft 365 E3 subscription.

Now that you understand what PIM is and the considerations for planning its deployment, you can start configuring PIM.

Configuring PIM

When running PIM for the first time, open it in the Azure portal.

The actions available to you as an administrator can be viewed in the **Tasks** and **Manage** sections of the PIM portal. Let's discuss the options shown in the following screenshot in detail:

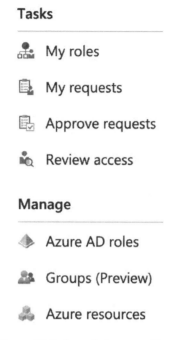

Figure 4.5: Tasks and Manage settings

The following are the options under **Tasks** within PIM:

- **My roles**: Shows the active roles assigned to you and any roles for which you are eligible. Eligible roles may be activated from here.

- **My requests**: Shows your requests to activate eligible role assignments.

- **Approve requests**: Shows a list of activation requests from other users that you will need to action, approve, or deny.

- **Review access**: Shows any access reviews assigned to you. You will see access reviews here for yourself and other users.

> **Note**
> Azure AD access reviews are covered in detail later in this chapter.

The following are the options under **Manage** within PIM:

- **Azure AD roles**: PIM administrators can use this dashboard to manage Azure AD role assignments and other Microsoft 365 online services. Only privileged role administrators can see this dashboard.

- **Groups (Preview)**: This is used to set up JIT access to members and assign owner roles to an Azure AD security group. This is an alternative way to set up PIM for both Azure AD and Azure roles but also allows the setup of PIM for services such as Intune, Azure Key Vault, and Azure Information Protection.

- **Azure resources**: PIM administrators can use this dashboard to manage Azure resource role assignments such as management groups and subscriptions. Only privileged role administrators can see this dashboard.

Now that you understand the **Tasks** and **Manage** options within PIM, you can examine PIM in action and configure some of the common settings. These include the following:

- Making a user eligible for a role

- Making the role assignment permanent

- Removing a role assignment

- Approving a role request

Making a user eligible for a role

In this example, you will assign the role of Billing Administrator to one of your users (Jane Bloggs) in Azure AD. In the first instance, you will make the user eligible for the role so that it can be activated as and when required. However, there may be occasions where the user requires the role permanently to do their job. To demonstrate this, the following steps also show how to change the role assignment so that it is permanent.

To make a user eligible for a role, do the following:

1.   Open the PIM pane in the Azure portal. Select **Manage** | **Roles**. You will be able to see a list of all the available roles that can be assigned:

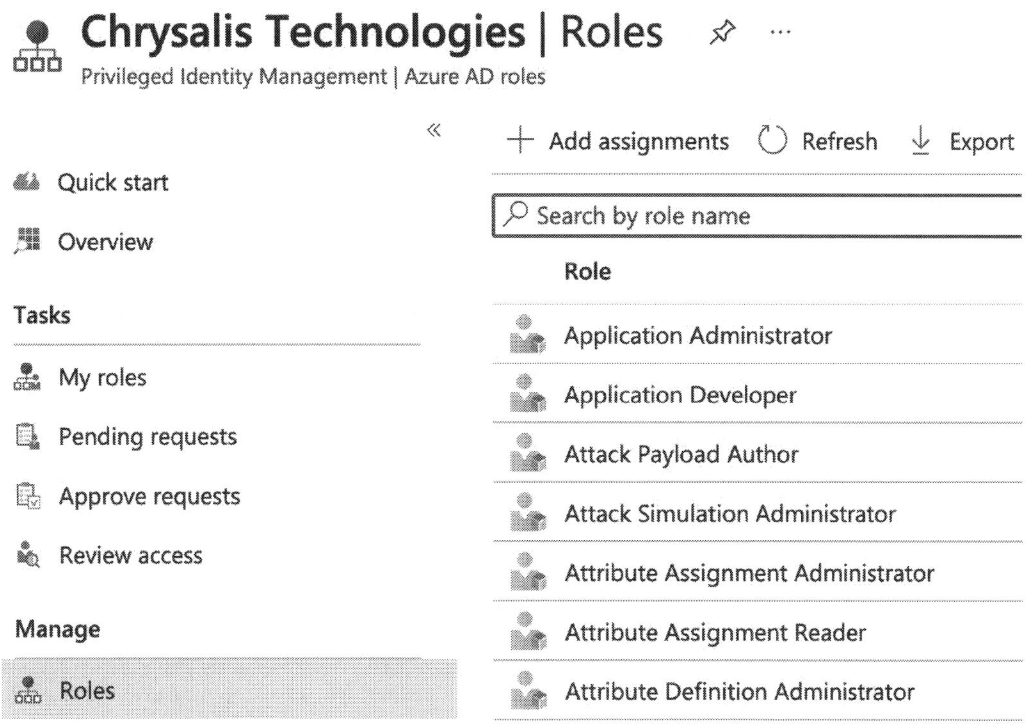

Chrysalis Technologies | Roles 📌 ⋯
Privileged Identity Management | Azure AD roles

«   + Add assignments   ◯ Refresh   ↓ Export

- 🛶 Quick start
- 🗄 Overview

Tasks

- 🔧 My roles
- 📄 Pending requests
- 📑 Approve requests
- 🔍 Review access

Manage

- 🔧 Roles

🔍 Search by role name

Role

- 👤 Application Administrator
- 👤 Application Developer
- 👤 Attack Payload Author
- 👤 Attack Simulation Administrator
- 👤 Attribute Assignment Administrator
- 👤 Attribute Assignment Reader
- 👤 Attribute Definition Administrator

Figure 4.6: Azure AD roles

> **Note**
>
> If you select **Members**, you will be able to see a list of users that are already assigned to the various roles and whether the assignments make the user eligible temporarily or permanently.

2. Now that your list of roles is available, find and select the **Billing Administrator** role from the list:

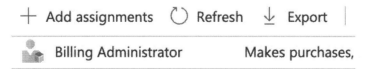

Figure 4.7: Finding a role

3. Under **Assignments**, click on **Add assignments**. This will take you to the member list for this role so that you can add the required user:

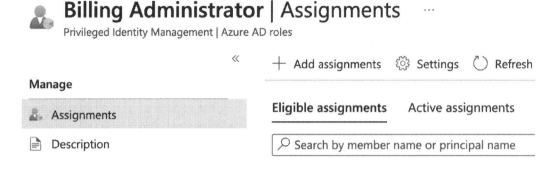

Figure 4.8: Adding the required user to the role

4.   Click on **Select members** and search for the name of the required user (in this case, **Jane Bloggs**). Click **Select**; then, click **Next**:

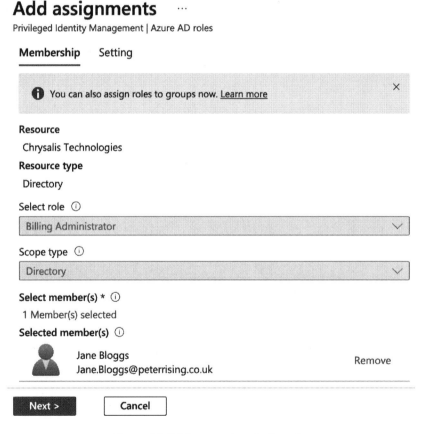

Figure 4.9: Adding members to the role

5. You can choose to make the user permanently eligible for the role here or set a duration for eligibility. For this example, make the user permanently eligible by selecting **Eligible** under **Assignment type** and choosing **Permanently eligible** under **Maximum allowed eligible duration is permanent**. Click **Assign**:

Add assignments ...

Privileged Identity Management | Azure AD roles

Membership   **Setting**

Assignment type ⓘ

⦿ Eligible

◯ Active

Maximum allowed eligible duration is permanent.

☑ Permanently eligible

Assignment starts

| 08/22/2022 | 🗓 | 1:31:01 PM |

Assignment ends

| 08/22/2023 | 🗓 | 1:31:01 PM |

| **Assign** | **< Prev** | **Cancel** |

Figure 4.10: Setting user eligibility

You will now see the user listed as eligible for this role:

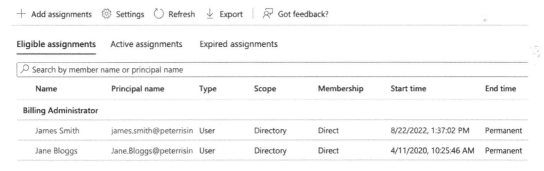

+ Add assignments   ⚙ Settings   ⟳ Refresh   ↓ Export | ⨕ Got feedback?

Eligible assignments   Active assignments   Expired assignments

🔍 Search by member name or principal name

Name	Principal name	Type	Scope	Membership	Start time	End time
Billing Administrator						
James Smith	james.smith@peterrisin	User	Directory	Direct	8/22/2022, 1:37:02 PM	Permanent
Jane Bloggs	Jane.Bloggs@peterrisin	User	Directory	Direct	4/11/2020, 10:25:46 AM	Permanent

Figure 4.11: Viewing user eligibility

Jane can now log in to the Azure portal and navigate to **Tasks | My roles**. Then, under **Azure AD roles**, she can activate her eligible role by clicking **Activate**. This is illustrated in the following screenshot:

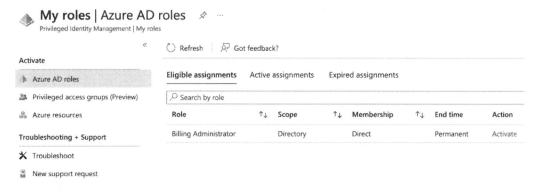

Figure 4.12: Activating a role

Next, Jane needs to choose an activation duration. The duration is set to **1 hour** initially; however, the user can set a shorter duration if less time is needed. She will also need to enter a reason for activating the role and then click on **Activate**, as shown in the following screenshot:

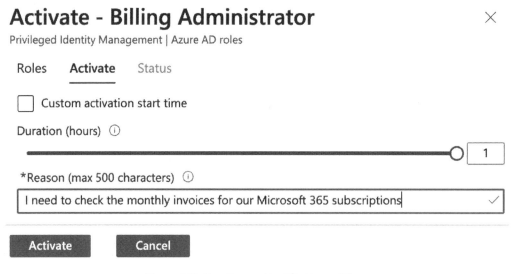

Figure 4.13: Duration and justification settings

Jane should now sign out and then log back in. By doing this, she will have access to the **Billing Administrator** role for a 1-hour duration and have permanent eligibility for the role.

> **Note**
> Eligible users will be asked to set up MFA on their Azure AD account as part of this process if they are not already registered for MFA.

If the eligibility period had not been permanent, then it would expire as per the set duration, and access to the Billing Administrator role would be removed from Jane's account.

Additionally, the administrator can track that Jane has activated the role and can check what time it is due to expire.

Removing a role assignment

Removing a role assignment is just as simple for the administrator and can be achieved as follows:

1. Open the Billing Administrator assignments page once again from Azure AD roles, as shown in *Figure 4.8*, and select the user whose role assignment you wish to remove. Click **Remove**. You will be asked to confirm the removal, as shown in the following screenshot:

Remove

Are you sure you want to remove member 'Jane Bloggs' from role 'Billing Administrator'?

Figure 4.14: Removing a role assignment

2. Click **Yes**. After this, the user will be removed as a member and will no longer have permanent access or eligibility for the selected role.

In this example, you made the user Jane Bloggs eligible for the Billing Administrator role, which was automatically activated for her when she requested it. However, this can be configured further. Let's look at this in the next section.

Approving a role request

To add another layer of protection to the role assignment process, it is possible to configure the requirement for approval for each of the role settings. The following example shows how this process works with the same user and role:

1. From PIM in the Azure portal, navigate to **Manage | Settings**, as shown in the following screenshot:

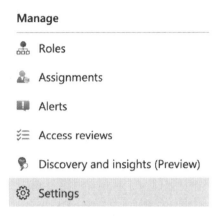

Figure 4.15: Role settings

2. Select **Billing Administrator** from the roles list, and then click **Edit**. Select the **Require approval to activate** checkbox, as shown in the following screenshot:

Figure 4.16: Approver settings

You will have the option to select a specific user to be the approver for this role. If you do not select an approver here, the PIM administrator or Global Administrators will be set as the approvers by default.

3. Click **Update** to commit the changes.

4. Next, make the user Jane Bloggs eligible for the Billing Administrator role again. Now, when she attempts to activate the role, a justification or **Reason** field will be included:

Figure 4.17: Role activation with justification and approval required

The request to activate the role can be viewed by the approver in PIM under **Tasks | Approve requests**, as shown in the following screenshot:

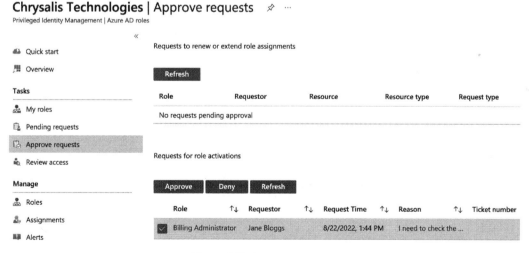

Figure 4.18: Approve requests

The approver will receive an email with a link to approve or deny the request. Alternatively, they can go to the Azure portal, access PIM, select the request, and choose **Confirm**, as shown in the following screenshot:

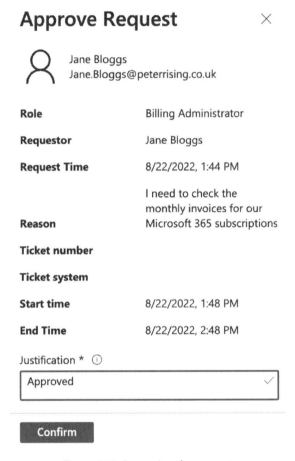

Approve Request   ✕

Jane Bloggs
Jane.Bloggs@peterrising.co.uk

Role	Billing Administrator
Requestor	Jane Bloggs
Request Time	8/22/2022, 1:44 PM
Reason	I need to check the monthly invoices for our Microsoft 365 subscriptions
Ticket number	
Ticket system	
Start time	8/22/2022, 1:48 PM
End Time	8/22/2022, 2:48 PM

Justification * ⓘ

Approved   ✓

Confirm

Figure 4.19: Approving the request

The user will receive an email confirmation and can check **Azure AD roles | Active roles** to see that the role approval and activation have been successfully completed, as shown in the following screenshot:

Eligible roles   **Active roles**   Expired roles

🔍 Search by role or resource

Role	Scope	Membership	State
Billing Administrator	Directory	Direct	Activated

Figure 20: Role approved and activated for the user

> **Note**
>
> It is also possible to use PowerShell to configure PIM. There are some references to this at the end of this chapter.

Now, you should have a good grasp of the steps required to configure PIM. You have learned about the **Task** and **Manage** features available within PIM and how to make users eligible for privileged roles, how to make the roles permanent when required, how to approve or deny user activation approval requests, and how to remove role assignments from user accounts.

Next, we will explore how to monitor PIM.

Monitoring PIM

PIM provides several ways in which you can monitor it to ensure that it is being used appropriately. Administrators can view activity, audit trails, and activation events for roles within Azure AD.

In order to view alerts within PIM, complete the following steps:

1. Open the PIM pane from the Azure portal and choose **Azure AD roles** from the **Manage** section, as shown in the following screenshot:

Figure 4.21: Managing Azure AD roles

2. Select **Alerts** from the **Manage** tab, as shown in the following screenshot:

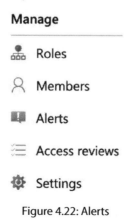

Figure 4.22: Alerts

3. Here, you can review the recorded alerts that relate to PIM. Each alert has a name and a **Risk level**, which can be **Low**, **Medium**, or **High** depending on severity, as shown in the following screenshot:

| Scan | Setting | Got feedback? |

Alert	Count	Risk level
Roles don't require multi-factor authentication for activation	1	Medium
Eligible administrators aren't activating their privileged role	1	Low
Potential stale accounts in a privileged role	3	Medium

Figure 4.23: Reviewing alerts

In this section, you learned how you can monitor PIM within your Azure AD environment. It is important to constantly monitor PIM to ensure that privileged roles are being used appropriately and that the principle of least privilege is being applied where possible.

Next, we will look at entitlement management.

Planning and configuring entitlement management

Azure AD entitlement management is Microsoft's identity governance capability through which you can automate who has access to what and for how long. In this section, we will learn how to create **access packages**, which are used to grant groups of users (both internal and external) access to a collection of roles and settings to simplify access, administration, and lifecycle management.

Entitlement management is available with an Azure AD Premium P2 license and enables organizations to do the following:

- Control access to applications, groups, teams, and SharePoint sites, using multi-stage approval, time-limited assignments, and recurring access reviews

- Automatically provide users with access to resources based on the user's properties, such as a department or location, and remove access should such properties change

- Use delegation to allow non-administrative users the ability to create access packages

- Select connected organizations whose users can request access

To start using entitlement management, perform the following steps:

1. Log on to the Azure portal as an admin and navigate to **Azure Active Directory | Identity Governance**. In the **Entitlement management** section, choose **Access packages**:

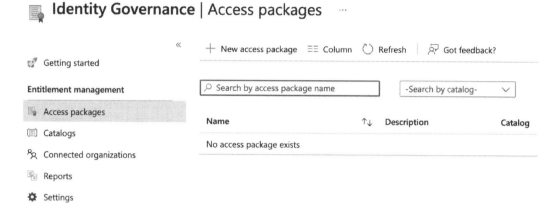

Figure 4.24: Access packages in Azure AD entitlement management

2. Click on **New access package** to start the access package creation wizard. Enter a name and description and select a catalog:

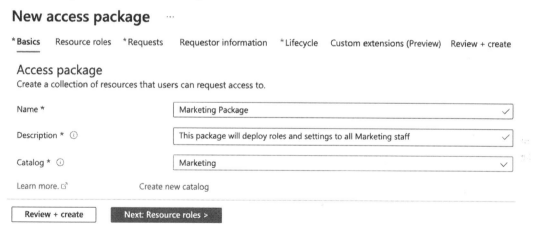

Figure 4.25: Creating an access package

3. Click **Next: Resource roles >**. Here, you can select the **Groups and Teams**, **Applications**, and **SharePoint Site** that you want to assign to users within your access package. You can also choose the role level at this stage:

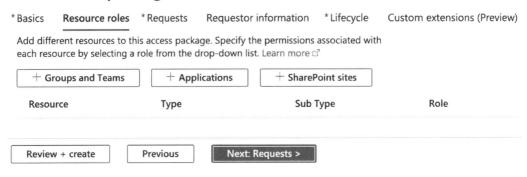

Figure 4.26: Adding resource roles to the access package

4. Click **Next: Requests >**. Here, you can choose whether the access package will be available to internal or external users to request or whether the package will be directly assigned by an admin. In this example, internal users may request access:

Figure 4.27: Specifying users who can request access

The **Requestor information** tab is optional, and is used to gather information and attributes from the requestor. For this example, skip to the **Lifecycle** tab. Here, choose **Expiration** and **Access Reviews** settings where you can set expiry assignment settings and review requirements and frequency:

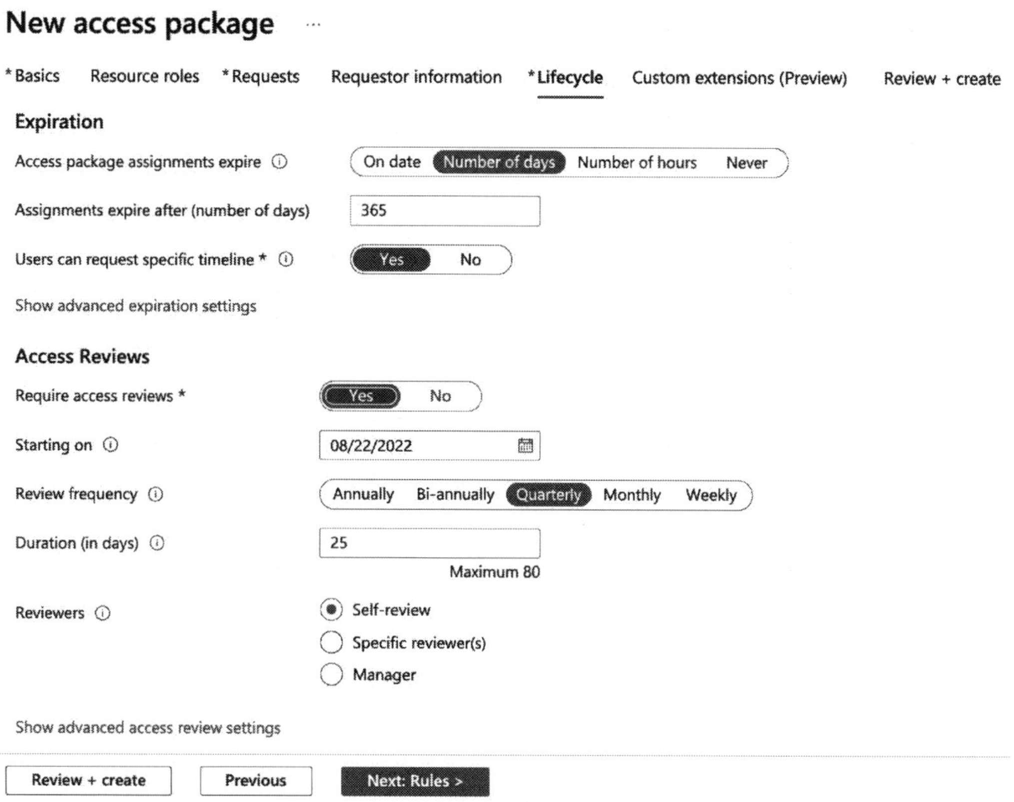

New access package ...

| * Basics | Resource roles | * Requests | Requestor information | * Lifecycle | Custom extensions (Preview) | Review + create |

Expiration

Access package assignments expire ⓘ	`On date` `Number of days` `Number of hours` `Never`
Assignments expire after (number of days)	`365`
Users can request specific timeline * ⓘ	`Yes` `No`

Show advanced expiration settings

Access Reviews

Require access reviews *	`Yes` `No`
Starting on ⓘ	`08/22/2022` 🗓
Review frequency ⓘ	`Annually` `Bi-annually` `Quarterly` `Monthly` `Weekly`
Duration (in days) ⓘ	`25`
	Maximum 80
Reviewers ⓘ	⦿ Self-review
	◯ Specific reviewer(s)
	◯ Manager

Show advanced access review settings

| Review + create | Previous | Next: Rules > |

Figure 4.28: Expiration and Access Reviews settings

5. The **Custom extensions (Preview)** tab is optional and in preview. For this example, skip to the **Review + create** tab. When you are happy with your choices, click **Create** to complete the setup of your access package:

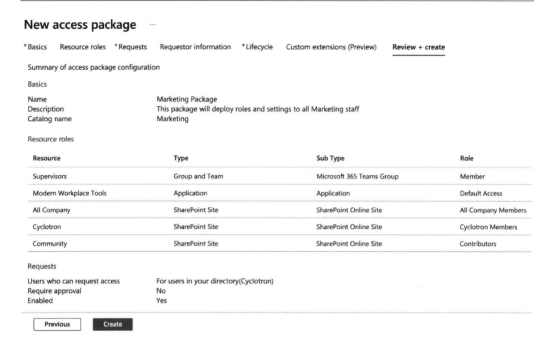

Figure 4.29: Completing the access package setup wizard

6.   Once created, the new access package shows a portal link that can be used by users to request access:

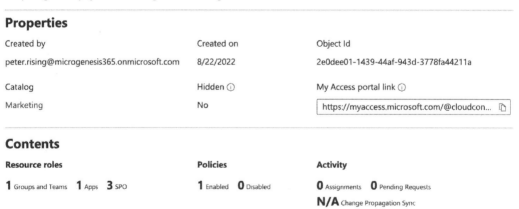

Figure 4.30: Access package portal link for users

7.   The following figure shows the dialog box in which requests for access and the required justification can be entered:

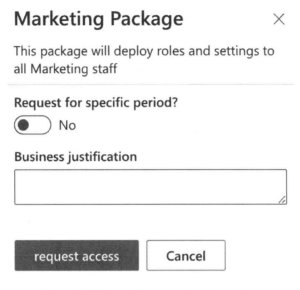

Marketing Package   ✕

This package will deploy roles and settings to all Marketing staff

Request for specific period?

(●) No

Business justification

request access   Cancel

Figure 4.31: Requesting access to the package

Access packages are the core element of Azure AD entitlement management. However, other key settings that you need to be aware of include the following:

- Catalogs
- Connected organizations
- Reports
- Settings

For more information, you can refer to the links provided in the *Further reading* section. Now that we know how to use access packages, let's look at Azure AD access reviews.

Planning and configuring access reviews

Azure AD access reviews are a feature of Azure AD Premium P2. They enable administrators to ensure that users within the tenant have the appropriate level of access. Access reviews are also useful for weeding out stale accounts or accounts that are not often used. Users can participate in this process themselves, or their supervisors can review their current level of access. Once a review is completed, changes can be made and access can be revoked from users, as deemed appropriate.

To create and execute an access review, you need to follow these steps:

1. Log in to the Azure portal as either a **Global Administrator** or a **User Administrator**. Navigate to **Azure Active Directory | Identity Governance** and select **Access reviews**.

2. Choose the **New access review** option:

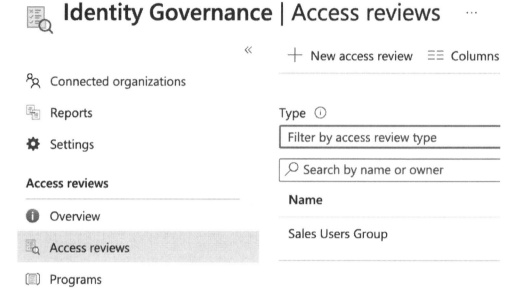

Figure 4.32: Access reviews

3. You can select either **Teams + Groups** or **Applications**. For this example, create an access review by selecting **Teams + Groups**:

New access review

*Review type   *Reviews   Settings   *Review + Create

Schedule an access review to ensure the right people have the right access to access packages, groups, apps, and privileged roles. Learn more

Select what to review *

Select Review	∨
Teams + Groups	
Applications	

Figure 4.33: Create an access review

4. This access review will be configured to run only once. It will select the members of the **Sales Users** group (alternatively, you could configure a recurring schedule for the review):

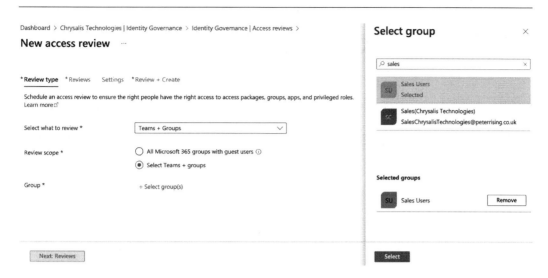

Figure 4.34: Create an access review

5. Next, specify the reviewers and the review recurrence settings (it is also possible to set a **multi-stage review** at this point – meaning that the review can go through a more stringent process with additional steps):

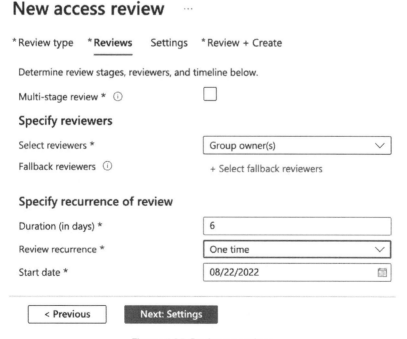

Figure 4.35: Reviewer options

6. Next, configure your preferred review settings. Here, you can select the actions that will be taken if reviewers do not respond and also configure any **Advanced settings** you may wish to apply to your review, such as requiring a justification entry, setting email notifications and reminders, and additional content for the email sent to reviewers:

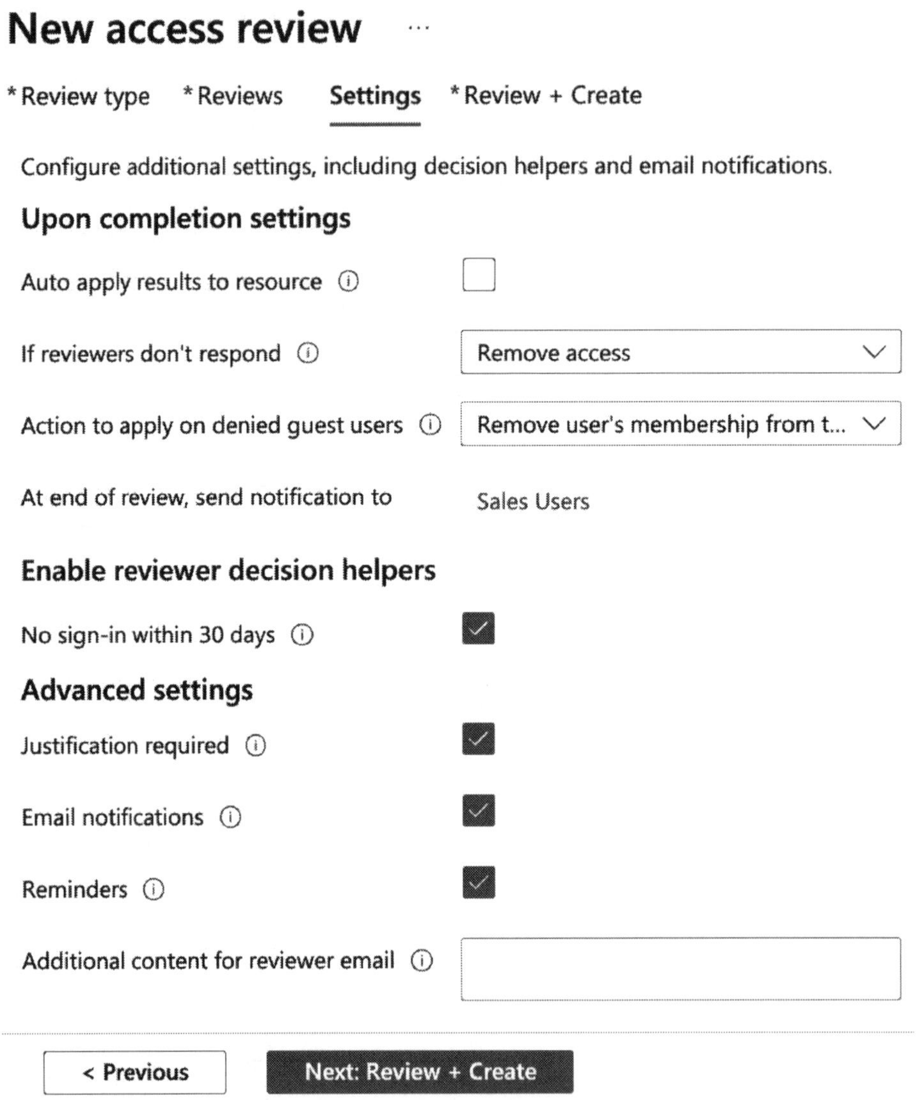

New access review   ...

* Review type   * Reviews   **Settings**   * Review + Create

Configure additional settings, including decision helpers and email notifications.

Upon completion settings

Auto apply results to resource ⓘ   ☐

If reviewers don't respond ⓘ | Remove access   ∨ |

Action to apply on denied guest users ⓘ | Remove user's membership from t... ∨ |

At end of review, send notification to   Sales Users

Enable reviewer decision helpers

No sign-in within 30 days ⓘ   ☑

Advanced settings

Justification required ⓘ   ☑

Email notifications ⓘ   ☑

Reminders ⓘ   ☑

Additional content for reviewer email ⓘ   [   ]

[< Previous]   [Next: Review + Create]

Figure 4.36: Further settings

7. Once you are happy with your access review settings, give it a **Review name** and **Description** and click **Create** to trigger it:

New access review   ...

* Review type   * Reviews   Settings   * Review + Create

Name new access review

Review name * ⓘ | Sales User Group Access Review   ✓ |

Description ⓘ | Review access to the Sales user group ✓
                                      and take appropriate action |

Confirm access review + create

Resources

Selected resource
1 group selected

Review scope
Guest users

Reviews

Reviewers
Group owner(s)

Frequency
One time

End
28/08/2022

[< Previous]   [Create]

Figure 4.37: New access review ready to be started

Once an access review is completed, the results can be viewed by Global Administrators, User Administrators, Security Administrators, or anyone who has been granted the Security Reader role. An email will be sent to all reviewers after the review is started – as long as this has option been selected under the **Advanced settings**.

> **Note**
> It is also possible to create access reviews using APIs with Microsoft Graph. Please check the *Further reading* section at the end of this chapter for further information.

Summary

This chapter introduced you to the principles of PIM, entitlement management, and access reviews. You explored the steps to diligently plan your PIM configuration and configure and assign roles to your users and resources with the principle of least privilege applied. You also learned how to make users eligible for privileged access roles to gain JIT access, how to assign permanent access to privileged roles when required, and how to remove this access when it's no longer required.

After that, you looked at the various monitoring capabilities of PIM, which enable you to be appropriately informed regarding your PIM configuration and ensure that access is granted only when it is required.

You also examined access packages to collate features and settings to be targeted to groups of users and control lifecycle and access reviews to check users' access permissions to ensure they are appropriate and remove stale access permissions.

In the next chapter, you will explore identity protection concepts in detail, along with techniques to identify and protect against risky sign-in activities, such as impossible travel and non-compliant devices.

Questions

1. Which of the following is not one of the functions of PIM?

    A. Making a user eligible for a role

    B. Making a service principal eligible for a role

    C. Removing a role assignment

    D. Approving a role request

2. True or false? You can configure Azure AD entitlement management with an Azure AD Premium P1 subscription.

    A. True

    B. False

3. In the PIM Azure AD roles page, which of the following is not one of the available options?

    A. Access

    B. Assign

    C. Approve

    D. Activate

4. Which of the following is not an available option when configuring an access package for entitlement management?

    A. For users in your directory

    B. For users not in your directory

    C. None (auto apply by policy assignment)

    D. None (administrator direct assignments only)

5. True or false? Entitlement management access packages can be targeted at users based on attributes such as their department.

    A. True

    B. False

6. When a user requires approval in order to be granted JIT access to a privileged role, which two methods can they use to see whether their request has been approved or denied?

    A. Wait for an email notification that contains the PIM approver's response to the request

    B. Wait for a text to arrive on their mobile device that contains the PIM approver's response to the request

    C. Log in to the Azure portal, navigate to **Privileged Identity Management**, and select **My requests**

    D. Log in to the Azure portal, navigate to **Privileged Identity Management**, and select **Review access**

    E. Log in to the Azure portal, navigate to **Privileged Identity Management**, and select **Approve requests**

7. Which of the following is not a reason you should use PIM?

    A. To reduce your organization's attack surface

    B. To reduce licensing costs

    C. To provide just-in-time access to privileged roles

    D. To improve your identity compliance posture

8. True or false? In Entitlement Management, it is possible to grant users access to both SharePoint sites and applications using access packages.

    A. True

    B. False

9. When configuring an access package for entitlement management, which of the following tabs in the setup wizard contain compulsory fields (choose three)?

    A. Resource roles

    B. Requestor information

    C. Requests

    D. Basics

    E. Lifecycle

10. True or false? With Entitlement Management, there is the option to add external domains in the form of Connected Organizations.

   A. True

   B. False

Further reading

Please refer to the following links for more information regarding what was covered in this chapter:

- What is Azure AD Privileged Identity Management?: `https://learn.microsoft.com/en-us/azure/active-directory/privileged-identity-management/pim-configure?wt.mc_id=4039827`

- Getting started with using Privileged Identity Management: `https://learn.microsoft.com/en-us/azure/active-directory/privileged-identity-management/pim-getting-started?wt.mc_id=4039827`

- Viewing activity and audit history for Azure resource roles in Privileged Identity Management: `https://learn.microsoft.com/en-us/azure/active-directory/privileged-identity-management/azure-pim-resource-rbac?wt.mc_id=4039827`

- What is Azure AD entitlement management? `https://learn.microsoft.com/en-us/azure/active-directory/governance/entitlement-management-overview?WT.mc_id=M365-MVP-4039827`

- Manage access to resources in Active Directory entitlement management using Microsoft Graph APIs: `https://learn.microsoft.com/en-us/graph/tutorial-access-package-api?toc=%2Fazure%2Factive-directory%2Fgovernance%2Ftoc.json&bc=%2Fazure%2Factive-directory%2Fgovernance%2Fbreadcrumb%2Ftoc.json&tabs=http`

- Manage access to resources in Azure AD entitlement management: `https://learn.microsoft.com/en-us/azure/active-directory/governance/entitlement-management-access-package-first`

- What are Azure AD access reviews? `https://learn.microsoft.com/en-us/azure/active-directory/governance/access-reviews-overview`

5

Azure AD Identity Protection

When planning an Azure AD implementation, **identity** is key. However, the importance of protecting identities should be given equal priority. **Azure AD Identity Protection** enables administrators to protect their users' identities by detecting and recording identity-based risks so that they can be analyzed and investigated, and corrective measures can be taken.

In this chapter, you will examine the principles of Azure AD Identity Protection, how it can be used to review risky events and flagged user accounts, and how to create risk-based conditional access policies to improve security. You will learn how to use this feature within the Azure portal, identify Identity Protection roles, and conduct investigations to detect risk events and vulnerabilities within your Microsoft 365 environment.

The following topics will be covered in this chapter:

- Understanding Identity Protection
- Protecting users with risk and registration policies
- Configuring alert options
- Managing and resolving risk events

Understanding Identity Protection

Azure AD Identity Protection is a feature that works on the principle of **risk detection and remediation**. It allows administrators to view risk events and detections in the Azure portal and then control what happens when risks are detected. They can also configure notifications regarding alerts about risk activities and receive a weekly report via email. Identity Protection detects and reports on risk classification events based on the following categories:

- Impossible travel
- Anonymous IP addresses
- Unfamiliar sign-in behavior

- Malware-linked IP addresses

- Leaked credentials

- Azure AD threat intelligence

- Password spray

Whenever one of these risk classifications is matched, it results in a remediation action being triggered, such as requiring the affected users to register for/respond to MFA or to perform a password reset. If a risk is deemed significant enough, the affected user can even be blocked entirely until further notice. Meanwhile, administrators can review reports in the **Azure AD Identity Protection** dashboard to respond to and resolve matches against risky users, risky sign-ins, and risk detections.

In order to view or configure Azure AD Identity Protection, you need to be a member of one of the following groups: Security Reader, Security Operator, Global Reader, or Global Administrator.

To ensure access to all the policies, reports, and notifications included with Azure AD Identity Protection, each Azure AD user who wishes to benefit from this feature must possess an Azure AD Premium P2, EM+S E5, or Microsoft 365 E5 license.

Now that we have explored the principles of Azure AD Identity Protection, let's examine the different policies that can be configured to protect users.

Protecting users with risk and registration policies

With Identity Protection, you can protect users with **risk policies**. These can be separated into the following categories:

- User risk policies

- Sign-in risk policies

It is also possible to protect your users with an MFA **registration policy**.

Let's examine each of these policies and take a look at how you can start to configure them.

Configuring user risk and sign-in risk policies

User risk policies and **sign-in risk policies** are similar in what they do. They are both capable of allowing or blocking access to Azure AD based on risk. With a user risk policy, you can block or allow access and require a password change, whereas with a sign-in risk policy, you can block or allow access and require MFA.

This difference between the two can be seen in the following screenshot in terms of the control enforcements of **Require password change** and **Block access** that can be applied:

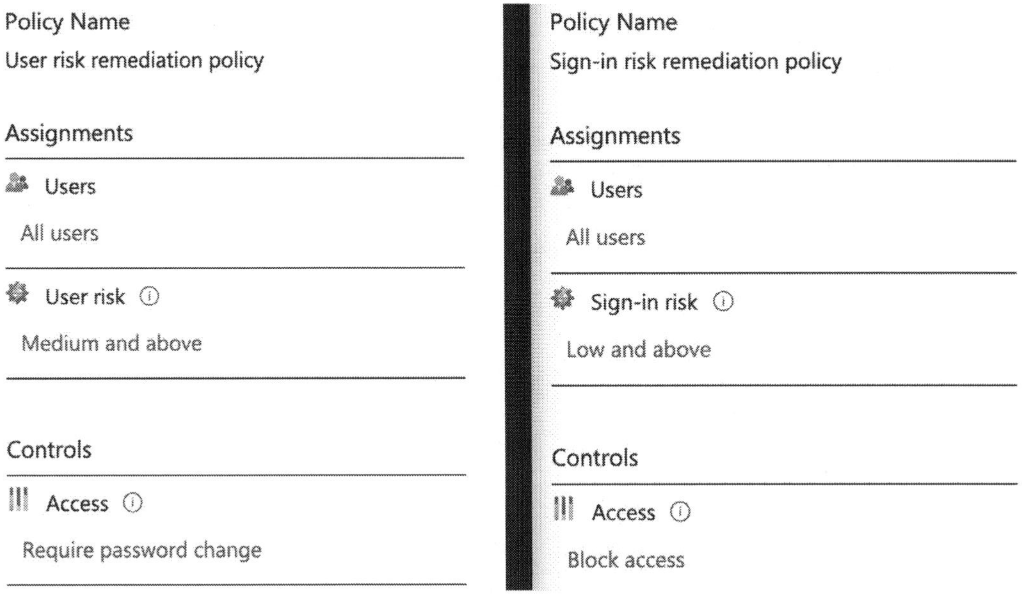

Policy Name	Policy Name
User risk remediation policy	Sign-in risk remediation policy
Assignments	**Assignments**
👥 Users	👥 Users
All users	All users
⚙ User risk ⓘ	⚙ Sign-in risk ⓘ
Medium and above	Low and above
Controls	**Controls**
⫴ Access ⓘ	⫴ Access ⓘ
Require password change	Block access

Figure 5.1: User risk policy and sign-in risk policy

The following example of a user risk policy explains how you can configure such policies. It will show you how a policy can be assigned to users, how conditions for the risk level can be applied, and whether the policy will allow the user to proceed or whether they should be blocked. Follow these steps:

1. Log in to the Azure portal (with the appropriate access, as described previously) at `https://portal.azure.com`. Search for **Azure Identity Protection** and select it. You can also access **Identity Protection** from the Microsoft Entra admin center at `https://entra.micrososoft.com` under **Azure Active Directory | Identity Protection**. All examples shown in this chapter use the Azure portal.

2. You will be taken to the **Identity Protection | Overview** screen:

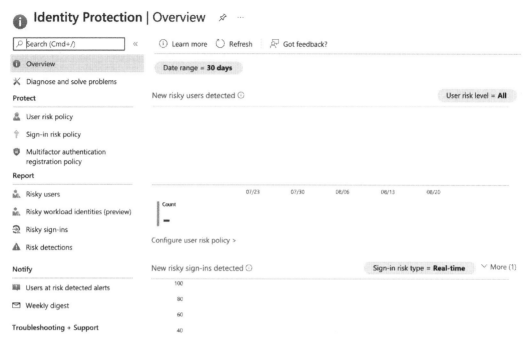

Figure 5.2: Identity Protection | Overview

3.   Under the **Protect** options, select **User risk policy**:

Figure 5.3: Protect options

4.   You will now see the following options for configuring the policy to assign to users, set the user risk, and apply the control to require a password change whenever this policy match is triggered:

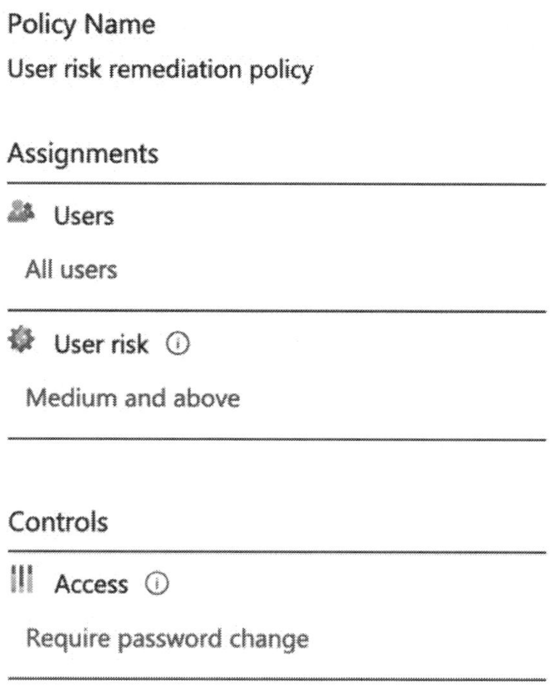

Policy Name

User risk remediation policy

Assignments

Users

All users

User risk ⓘ

Medium and above

Controls

Access ⓘ

Require password change

Figure 5.4: Policy settings

5.   Under **Users**, you can choose to include **All users** or select specific users or groups. It is also possible to exclude specific users using the **Exclude** option:

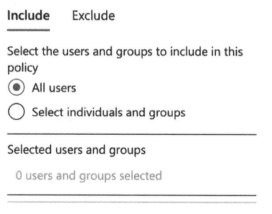

Figure 5.5: Including or excluding users

6.   Next, under **User risk**, configure the **user risk levels** needed to enforce the user risk policy. In the following screenshot, this is set to **Medium and above**:

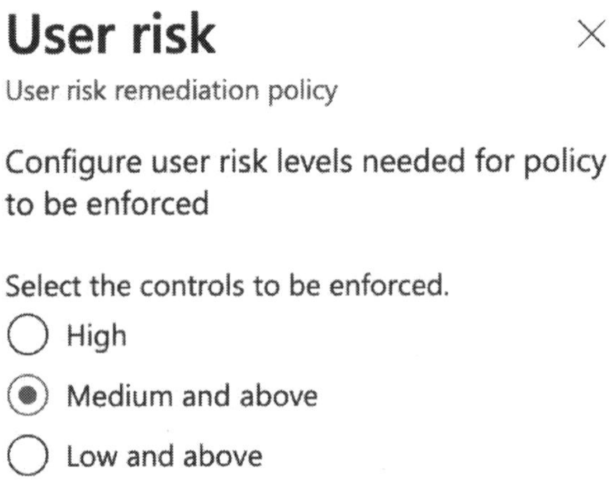

User risk   ✕

User risk remediation policy

Configure user risk levels needed for policy
to be enforced

Select the controls to be enforced.

◯ High

◉ Medium and above

◯ Low and above

Figure 5.6: User risk levels

> **Note**
>
> Make sure that you choose an acceptable risk level when making these selections. It is important
> to plan a balance between user experience and security. It is Microsoft's recommendation to
> set the user risk policy to **High** and the sign-in risk policy to **Medium and above** or higher.

7. Now, select **Access** from the **Controls** section so you can choose whether you are going to
    allow or block access when this risk policy generates a match. You can also force the user to
    complete a password reset by selecting **Require password change** here:

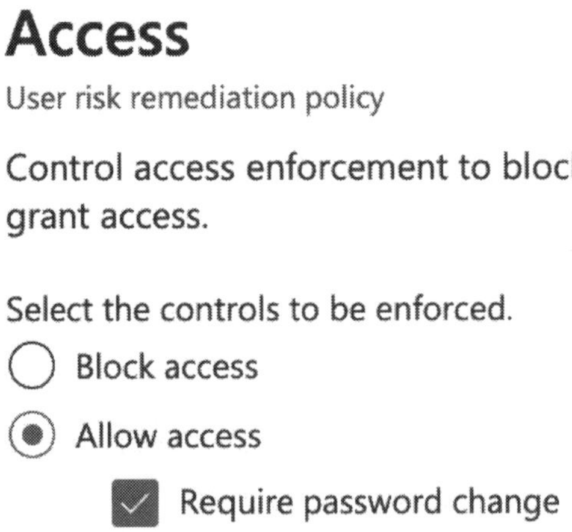

Access

User risk remediation policy

Control access enforcement to block or
grant access.

Select the controls to be enforced.

◯ Block access

◉ Allow access

        ☑ Require password change

Figure 5.7: Access enforcement options

8. With these settings and controls selected, set the **Enforce policy** option to **On** and click **Save** to
    commit your choices to the user risk policy. If the policy is set to **Off**, it will not be implemented:

Enforce policy

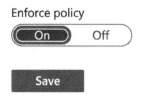

Figure 5.8: Enforce policy settings

> **Note**
>
> Only users who have registered for MFA and SSPR are ready to respond to a situation requiring remediation. Users not registered are blocked and require administrator intervention.

With that, you have configured a user risk policy. Should you wish to configure a sign-in risk policy, the process is the same, except for the sign-in risk remediation controls, wherein you can choose **Require multi-factor authentication** alongside blocking or allowing access. So, if you were configuring a sign-in risk policy, you would choose that option in *step 3* instead of **User risk policy**:

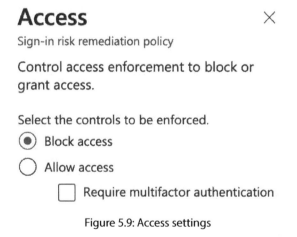

Figure 5.9: Access settings

Once you have your user and sign-in risk policies configured, they will start working to automate responses based on your risk detection settings. Some further considerations when enabling these policies are as follows:

- If you wish your users to be able to respond to Identity Protection requirements such as enforcing MFA and password changes, ensure that you enable your users for MFA and self-service password reset (as described in *Chapter 2, Authentication and Security*).

- When configuring acceptable risk levels, be aware of the possible effects on your users. For example, a high threshold will minimize the number of times a risk policy is triggered. However, this will also prevent low- and medium-risk detections, which could enable malicious actors to exploit a compromised identity within your environment.

Now you are familiar with the best practices for configuring user risk and sign-in risk policies. You learned how to create these policies, assign them to your users, and exclude certain users from them, along with how to set the required risk level for the policy and the actions to be taken if there is a policy match. Next, we will look at how to configure MFA registration policies with Azure AD Identity Protection.

Configuring MFA registration policies

MFA was already discussed in *Chapter 2, Authentication and Security*, and *Chapter 3, Implementing Conditional Access Policies*. These chapters illustrated how MFA can be enabled and enforced for your Microsoft 365 users via both the Microsoft 365 admin center and by using Conditional Access policies. It is also possible to configure an Azure MFA policy for your cloud-based users from within the **Azure AD Identity Protection** pane.

In the context of Identity Protection, it is always preferable to require Azure MFA for your user sign-ins as it does the following:

- Provides strong authentication with a choice of verification methods
- Provides your users with the option to effectively take responsibility for their own risk detections and use self-remediation

In order to configure the MFA registration policy within Azure AD Identity Protection, you need to complete the following steps:

1. From Azure AD Identity Protection, navigate to the **Protect** section and select **Multifactor authentication registration policy**:

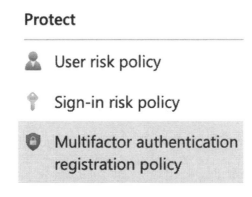

Figure 5.10: MFA registration policy

2. Next, under **Assignments**, select **Users**:

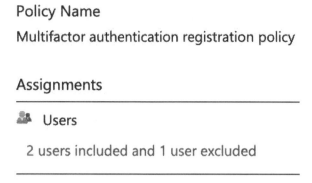

Figure 5.11: Assigning a policy to users

3. Here, you can decide whether you want to apply the requirement of MFA for all your users or whether you wish to select specific users or groups. You also have the option to explicitly exclude users from the policy:

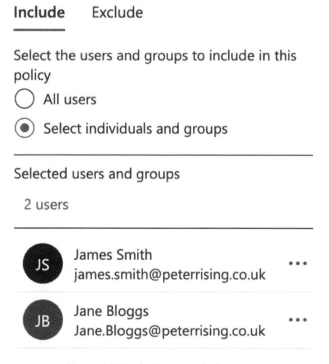

Figure 5.12: Including or excluding users

4. Next, under **Controls**, ensure that **Require Azure AD multifactor authentication registration** is selected:

Controls

 Require Azure AD multifactor
authentication registration

Figure 5.13: Access controls

5.   Next, ensure that **Enforce policy** is set to **On** and then click on **Save**:

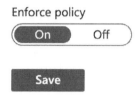

Figure 5.14: Enforcing the policy

The policy will be saved, and the affected users will be prompted to register for MFA the next time they sign in with their Microsoft 365 credentials. They will be able to bypass MFA registration and continue to log in for a period of 14 days. They will then be forced to complete the registration process or they will be unable to gain access.

With this, you examined how an MFA registration policy can be configured and deployed to your Microsoft 365 users with Azure AD Identity Protection. This will force your users to register for MFA. If you have Azure AD Premium P2 licenses available to you in your tenancy, it is highly recommended to deploy the MFA registration policy.

Next, we will examine the available alert options for Azure AD Identity Protection.

Configuring alert options

Azure AD Identity Protection is only effective if the available alert options are correctly configured, the alerts are being diligently reviewed by administrators, and the appropriate steps are being taken where needed. Identity Protection has two notification settings that can be configured to alert administrators of risk detection within Microsoft 365: **Users at risk detected alerts** and **Weekly digest**. The following sub-sections cover these in detail.

Users at risk detected alerts

This alert can be found under the **Notify** section of Azure AD Identity Protection and can be used to configure an email alert that will be sent to administrators when a user at risk is detected. The benefit of this alert is that administrators receive email notifications as soon as the risk event is detected. Follow these steps to set up these alerts:

1.   Click on **Users at risk detected alerts** to configure the relevant options:

Notify

Figure 5.15: Notification options

When you view the **Users at risk detected alerts** section, you will see that any existing Global Administrators, Security Administrators, or Security Readers are automatically included to be alerted.

2. Add any custom email addresses to be included in these alerts:

Figure 5.16: Setting the alert recipients

3. Next, choose the alert level (**Low**, **Medium**, or **High**) that you wish to configure. The choices you make here will represent the risk levels needed for policy to be enforced:

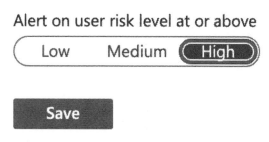

Figure 5.17: Selecting the user risk level

4. Once you have configured your preferred settings, click **Save**.

5. You can also click **Download** to generate a CSV or JSON file that contains details of the users who have been configured to receive these alerts:

IpcEmailRecipients_2022-08-22

Name	ID	Recipient	Receives digest	Receives alerts
Alert minimum risk level	Low			
Send weekly digest	Yes			
Peter Rising	f208bac9-71b2-4e69-92ab-ebbe496d8515	peter.rising@peterrising.co.uk	Yes	Yes
Admin User	176c9e8a-2245-4c56-a5b1-584ae48af068	adminuser@chrysalistech.onmicrosoft.com	Yes	Yes

Figure 5.18: Example of a CSV report

When an alert email is triggered, the included recipients will receive a notification email in the following format:

User at risk detected

We detected a new user with at least low risk in your Chrysalis Technologies directory. This might be because we noticed suspicious account activity or we found their emails and passwords posted in a public location.

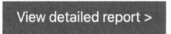

Figure 5.19: Example of an email alert

Clicking on **View detailed report** > will direct the email recipient to log in to **Azure AD Identity Protection** in the Azure portal, view the alert, and take corrective action.

Weekly digest

While the users at risk detected alerts will be generated whenever Azure AD Identity Protection detects a risk, the weekly digest works differently. It will send an email on a weekly basis to show administrators how many users have been flagged for risk and how many risk events and vulnerabilities have been detected.

The **Weekly digest** alert can also be found under the **Notify** section of Azure AD Identity Protection and can be configured as follows:

1. Click on **Weekly digest**; you will again see that any existing Global Administrators, Security Administrators, or Security Readers are automatically included to be emailed the weekly digest. Choose **Yes** or **No** to turn the weekly email digest on or off:

Figure 5.20: Weekly digest email

2. When you are happy with your selections, click **Save**. When the weekly digest email is generated, the targeted users will receive a notification email in the following format:

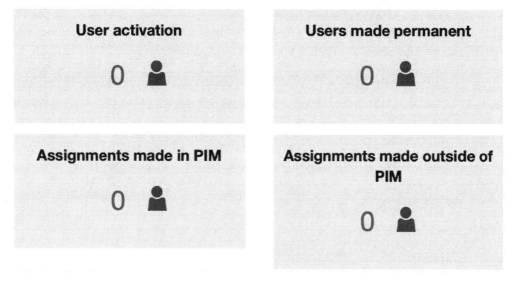

Figure 5.21: Weekly digest email format

Further options that the recipient can select from the email are as follows and show the top assigned roles and whether these roles are allocated to users on a permanent basis or whether they are simply eligible to activate the roles when needed on a just-in-time basis:

Overview of your top roles

Role	Permanent	Eligible	Action
Global Administrator	2	0	Reduce permanent >
Directory Readers	2	0	Reduce permanent >

Figure 5.22: Weekly digest email format

3. You can also choose to reduce the permanent nature of the role assignments from the email by clicking **Reduce Permanent** to make users eligible for the roles instead.

> **Note**
> Configuring the users at risk alerts and the weekly digest email will help you keep on top of your Azure AD Identity Protection. Review these emails regularly.

Next, we will learn how to manage and resolve risk events.

Managing and resolving risk events

The **Report** section of Azure AD Identity Protection provides administrators the ability to review and resolve events and detections, as shown in the following screenshot:

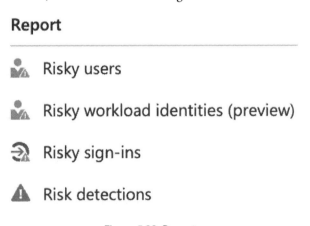

Figure 5.23: Reports

You can carry out investigations based on what is recorded through the options and take steps to resolve any risks as well as to unblock any users who may have been blocked, provided it is safe to do so.

The following covers each of the options within the **Report** section in detail.

Examining users at risk

A **risky user** is someone whose activity has matched the risk level set in Azure AD Identity Protection. When a risk is detected, alerts are sent to administrators, as discussed earlier in this chapter. However, it is important to proactively review the list of users at risk in Azure AD Identity Protection in the Azure portal and take corrective actions.

Under **Risky Users**, you will see a list of the users within your tenant (including B2B guest users) who have been determined to be at risk. You will be able to see the user's name, **Risk state**, **Risk level**, and the date that the risk was last updated. An example of this is shown in the following screenshot:

Figure 5.24: User at risk

To further examine users at risk, take the following steps:

1. Click on the three dots to the right of the status of the highlighted user to see more options. These include **User's sign-ins**, **User's risky sign-ins**, and **User's risk detections**, as shown in the following screenshot:

> User's sign-ins

> User's risky sign-ins

> User's risk detections

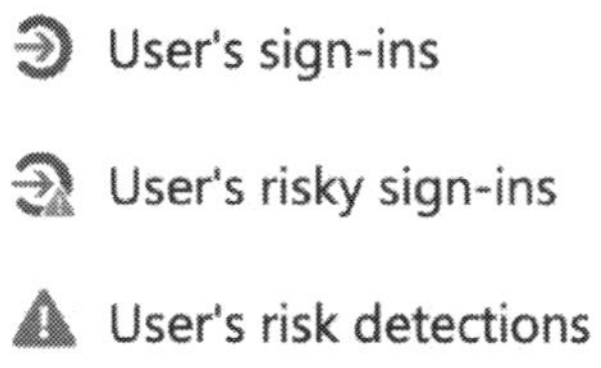

Figure 5.25: More options

2. Select an at-risk user to view the detailed summary of their sign-in activity and the actions you can take to respond and remediate.

3. Based on the information gathered from these events, you can then apply the following actions or conditions to that user:

   • Reset the user's password

   • Confirm that the user is compromised

   • Dismiss the user risk if you are confident that this is safe to do

- Block the user

- Investigate the user with Azure Defender

These options are shown in the following screenshot:

Figure 5.26: Risky user detail summary

If you select the step to confirm that a user is compromised, then that user will be moved to the **High risk** category to optimize future risk assessment, as shown in the following screenshot:

Confirm user compromised?

This confirms to Azure AD that the selected user is currently compromised. Azure AD will move the selected user to High risk and optimize future risk assessment. Note: This action cannot be reversed and may take a few minutes. Please do not resubmit this request.

Learn more

Figure 5.27: Confirming that a user is compromised

Next, we will look at risky sign-ins.

Examining risky sign-ins

A **risky sign-in** is recorded in Azure AD Identity Protection when a user signs in with their Microsoft 365 account and that activity triggers a risk event. Administrators can view and manage risky sign-in activity from the **Reports** section of Azure AD Identity Protection in the Azure portal, as follows:

1. Under **Risky sign-ins**, you can view and manage all recorded risky sign-in activity:

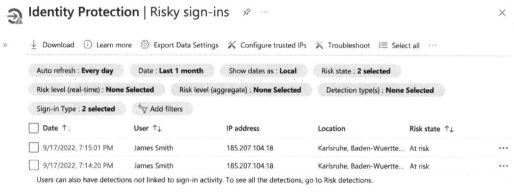

Figure 5.28: Risky sign-ins

2. Clicking an entry in this list will provide you with additional details for the sign-in event, as shown in the following screenshot:

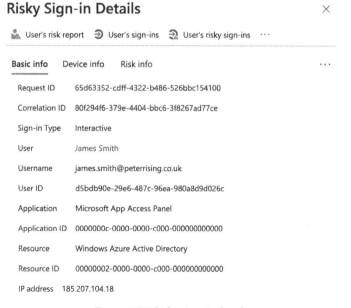

Figure 5.29: Risky sign-in details

Similar to **Risky users**, you can view risk reports, users' sign-ins, users' risky sign-ins, and sign-in risk detections from here. Upon examining the information presented here, you can confirm that the sign-in activity for the highlighted user was, in fact, compromised, as shown in the following screenshot:

Figure 5.30: Confirm sign-in compromised

3.   Additionally, by clicking the three dots, you can confirm that the sign-in was safe.

Now, let's examine how we can examine risk detections in Azure AD Identity Protection

Examining risk detections

A risk is recorded in Azure AD Identity Protection whenever any event is detected that matches a risk definition. Administrators can view and manage risk detections from the **Reports** section of Azure AD Identity Protection in the Azure portal by going to **Risk detections**. Here, you can view all recently recorded risk events:

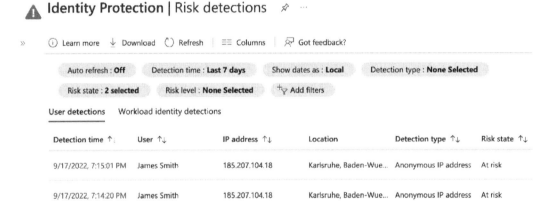

Figure 5.31: Risk detections

These events are broken down into the following sections:

- **Detection time**
- **User**

- **IP address**

- **Location**

- **Detection type**

- **Risk state**

- **Risk level**

- **Request ID**

Selecting an individual event in the list provides more details about it, as shown here:

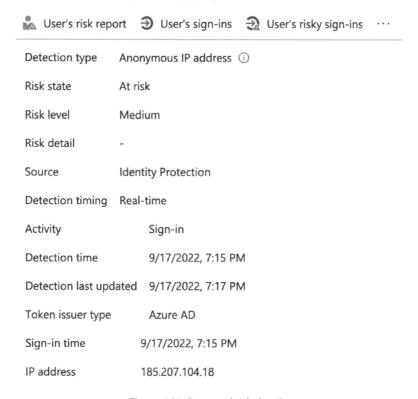

Figure 5.32: Detected risk details

Once again, from here, you can gain access to risk reports, sign-ins, and risky sign-ins, as well as risk detections.

These steps provide you with the means to effectively review and manage all risk events using Azure AD Identity Protection.

> **Note**
>
> Review, investigate, and remediate user risk events regularly to ensure you are keeping your Microsoft 365 tenant secure and protected. Resolve risk events as soon as you have reviewed them to keep the list of recorded events neat and manageable.

Risky workload identities (preview)

Azure AD Identity Protection has now been extended to support the capabilities of **workload identities**, which protect applications, service principals, and managed identities.

A workload identity is an identity that permits applications or service principals to access resources, often in the context of a user. Workload identities are different from conventional user accounts in the following ways:

- They are not MFA compatible
- They have limited or no lifecycle processes
- They need to store their credentials or secrets somewhere

Therefore, workload identities are more difficult to manage, which means they are at greater risk of compromise.

The following figure shows where you would view any **Risky workload identities**, if present:

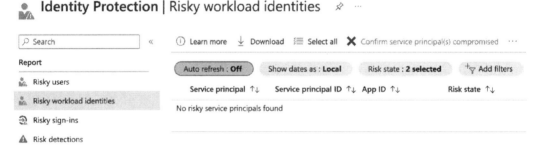

Figure 5.33: Detected risky workload identities

> **Note**
>
> Caution is urged whenever deploying preview features in Azure AD as they are subject to change or removal, often at short notice.

Risk-based Conditional Access policies

When you have Azure AD Identity Protection available in your tenant, you can configure Conditional Access policies based on risk. This is achieved when setting up a Conditional Access policy in Azure AD. To do this, follow these steps:

1. From the **Conditions** section of the policy, set the **User risk level** and **Sign-in risk level** options:

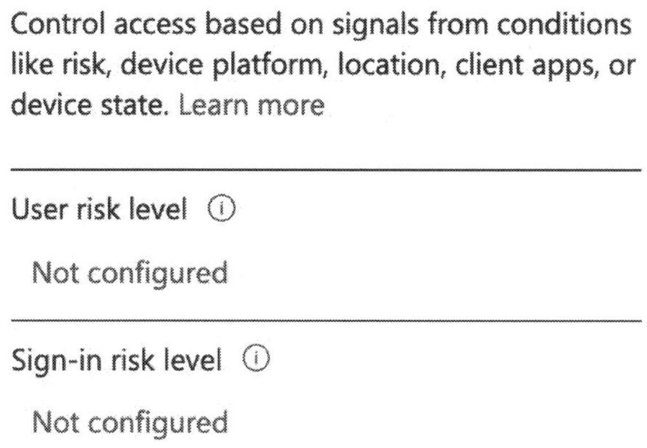

> Control access based on signals from conditions like risk, device platform, location, client apps, or device state. Learn more
>
> ---
>
> User risk level ⓘ
>
> Not configured
>
> ---
>
> Sign-in risk level ⓘ
>
> Not configured

Figure 5.34: Risk-based conditional access

2. The **User risk level** options are **High**, **Medium**, and **Low**, and can be configured depending on the risk level you wish to set. Microsoft doesn't provide specify how risk is calculated; however, each risk level brings higher confidence that the user or sign-in has been compromised:

Figure 5.35: Risk-based conditional access

3.   The **Sign-in risk level** options include **High**, **Medium**, **Low**, and **No risk**, as shown here:

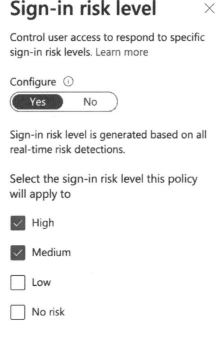

Figure 5.36: Risk-based conditional access

Note that multiple selections are permitted within risk-level setting applications.

This section explained how risk-based Conditional Access policies are supported by Azure AD Identity Protection. Now let's summarize the key lessons you've learned in this chapter.

Summary

In this chapter, we examined Azure AD Identity Protection, which can be accessed from the Azure portal. We dived into how Identity Protection detects and records risky users, risky sign-ins, and risk events, and provides us with the ability to review, investigate, and remediate these events with powerful preventative measures such as blocking user access, forcing password changes, or requiring MFA.

We also understood how reports and alerts can be generated and interpreted. Understanding these principles will enable you to effectively and diligently manage Azure AD Identity Protection in your Microsoft 365 environment and take the necessary steps to ensure that compromised users are identified and remediated in a timely fashion.

In the next chapter, we will examine the principles of **Microsoft Defender for Identity** (**MDI**), formerly known as Azure Advanced Threat Protection. The chapter will also teach you how to plan for and configure MDI, as well as how to monitor and interpret the reporting features.

Questions

1. Which of the following allows you to monitor and remediate based on service principal IDs or app IDs?

    A. Risky users

    B. Risky workload identities (preview)

    C. Risky sign-ins

    D. Risk detections

2. True or false? With Identity Protection, you can configure an MFA registration policy.

    A. True

    B. False

3. Which section of a Conditional Access policy allows you to configure user risk level or sign-in risk level?

    A. User or workload identities

    B. Cloud apps or actions

    C. Conditions

    D. Grant

    E. Session

4. Which of these licenses is required for users who need to be protected with Azure AD Identity Protection?

    A. Azure Information Protection P1

    B. Azure AD Premium P2

    C. Azure AD Premium P1

    D. Azure Information Protection P2

5. Which two formats can the users at risk detected alerts and the weekly digest emails be downloaded in?

    A. CSV

    B. TXT

    C. JSON

    D. PDF

6. Which of the following roles is not added to the users at risk detected alerts or the weekly digest emails?

    A. Global Administrator

    B. User Admin

    C. Security Reader

    D. Security Admin

7. When viewing a risky user object in Azure AD Identity Protection, which of the following is not a remediation action?

    A. Confirm user compromised

    B. Dismiss user risk

    C. Reset password

    D. Investigate with Microsoft Defender for Cloud Apps

8. True or false? With a user risk policy, it is possible to enforce MFA for a user.

    A. True

    B. False

9. Which of these is not a sign-in risk level?

    A. Low and above

    B. Medium and above

    C. Moderate

    D. High

10. True or false? When examining a risky user event, it is possible for administrators to confirm a suspected risky user as compromised, and in so doing, automatically raise the risk level of that user to High.

    A. True

    B. False

Further reading

Please refer to the following links for more information regarding what was covered in this chapter:

- Principles of Azure AD Identity Protection and understanding how to plan for its implementation: https://learn.microsoft.com/en-gb/azure/active-directory/identity-protection/overview-identity-protection

- How to configure risk policies: https://learn.microsoft.com/en-gb/azure/active-directory/identity-protection/howto-identity-protection-configure-risk-policies?wt.mc_id=4039827

- How to remediate risk events and unblock users: https://learn.microsoft.com/en-gb/azure/active-directory/identity-protection/howto-identity-protection-remediate-unblock?wt.mc_id=4039827

- How to simulate risk events: https://learn.microsoft.com/en-gb/azure/active-directory/identity-protection/howto-identity-protection-simulate-risk?wt.mc_id=4039827

- How to configure notifications for Azure AD Identity Protection: https://learn.microsoft.com/en-gb/azure/active-directory/identity-protection/howto-identity-protection-configure-notifications

- User risk-based Conditional Access policies: https://learn.microsoft.com/en-us/azure/active-directory/conditional-access/howto-conditional-access-policy-risk-user

- Conditional Access: Sign-in risk-based Conditional Access: https://learn.microsoft.com/en-us/azure/active-directory/conditional-access/howto-conditional-access-policy-risk

- Securing workload identities with Identity Protection Preview: https://learn.microsoft.com/en-us/azure/active-directory/identity-protection/concept-workload-identity-risk

- Identity Protection and B2B users: https://learn.microsoft.com/en-us/azure/active-directory/identity-protection/concept-identity-protection-b2b

- User experiences with Azure AD Identity Protection: https://learn.microsoft.com/en-us/azure/active-directory/identity-protection/concept-identity-protection-user-experience

Part 2: Implementing and Managing Threat Protection

In this part, you will learn how to configure and manage Microsoft 365 threat protection components. On completion, you will be able to describe the components of Microsoft Defender for Identity, Microsoft Defender for Endpoint, and Microsoft Defender for Office 365. You will also have learned how to monitor Microsoft 365 using Microsoft Sentinel and how to use Microsoft Defender for Cloud Apps.

This part has the following chapters:

- *Chapter 6, Configuring a Microsoft Defender for Identity Solution*
- *Chapter 7, Configuring Device Threat Protection with Microsoft Defender for Endpoint and Intune*
- *Chapter 8, Configuring Microsoft Defender for Office 365*
- *Chapter 9, Using Microsoft Sentinel to Monitor Microsoft 365 Security*
- *Chapter 10, Configuring Microsoft Defender for Cloud Apps*

6

Configuring a Microsoft Defender for Identity Solution

As you learned in *Chapter 1*, *Planning for Hybrid Identity*, the default identity method in Microsoft 365 is cloud-only. However, very few organizations are in the fortunate position to leverage cloud-only identities. Start-up businesses and organizations with minimal infrastructure find adopting this method easier than those with more complex infrastructure and a long-term reliance on on-premises Active Directory and legacy applications. The latter will likely leverage some form of hybrid identity strategy.

Organizations with this challenge need to consider how to extend the cloud-based protection features included in Microsoft 365 to their on-premises Active Directory domain controllers. This is possible with **Microsoft Defender for Identity (MDI)**, which was formerly known as **Azure Advanced Threat Protection** or **Azure ATP**. MDI is a Microsoft 365 cloud-based solution that leverages signals from your on-premises Active Directory to identify, detect, and investigate advanced threats, identity compromises, and malicious insider activities aimed at your organization.

In this chapter, you will learn how MDI works and understand the prerequisites and processes for configuring and implementing MDI. You will also review the MDI sensor settings, which are used to examine data within your MDI instance. Finally, you will examine MDI health, alerts, reports, and monitoring to interpret security alerts.

These topics will be covered in the following order:

- Identifying the organizational need for MDI
- Understanding the MDI architecture
- Setting up MDI
- Managing and monitoring MDI

Identifying the organizational need for MDI

To identify your organization's needs in relation to MDI, you first need to examine, in great detail, exactly what MDI is and what it can do. Essentially, MDI is a security solution designed for use in hybrid cloud environments that have a mixture of on-premises and cloud users, data, and resources.

MDI can monitor your on-premises domain controllers to identify and investigate advanced threats and compromised identities by using machine learning and behavioral algorithms to do the following:

- Identify suspicious activity
- Detect and identify advanced attacks and malicious activities
- Protect Azure **Active Directory** (**AD**) identities and credentials
- Provide incident reports

MDI can create behavioral profiles for your users and diligently analyze user activities and events to detect any advanced threats, compromised users, and malicious insiders that could threaten your organization. The information gathered by MDI provides recommended security best practices and helps you significantly reduce the risk in areas vulnerable to attack.

The following sections cover MDI in more detail, starting with how you can identify suspicious activity.

Understanding suspicious activity

This section will discuss what represents suspicious user activity from an MDI perspective. To further understand this concept, you must first have an awareness of the **cyber-attack kill chain**. This is a series of steps that traces the progress of a cyber-attack from the beginning (the *reconnaissance* stage) to the end (*unauthorized data exfiltration*).

MDI focuses on the phases of the kill chain to detect suspicious activities, which can include the following:

- **Reconnaissance**: The attacker gathers information about the environment by searching for usernames, group memberships, device IP addresses, and more
- **Compromised credentials**: The attacker attempts to compromise user credentials using brute force attacks, failed authentications, changes in user group membership, and other methods
- **Lateral movement**: The attacker now has access and works patiently to spread their attack and gain elevation of privileges
- **Domain dominance** (**persistence**): The attacker gains control of your environment and ensures that they have multiple points of entry to it

It is crucial to understand these phases of the kill chain to identify suspicious activities in your Microsoft 365 environment.

Exploring advanced attacks and malicious activities

By focusing on the phases of the kill chain (which is not in itself a part of MDI but rather a process within cybersecurity), MDI can protect your environment from attack vectors before they cause any damage or disruption. **Decoy accounts** can be set up to track any malicious activities within your environment and generate security alerts that can include the following:

- Suspected identity theft using pass-the-ticket

- Suspected identity theft using pass-the-hash

- Suspected brute force attacks

- Reconnaissance using the **Domain Name System** (**DNS**)

- Unusual protocols

- Suspicious service creation

The malicious activities listed here are only a few of the many that can generate security alerts within MDI.

> **Note**
>
> Please see the *Further reading* section at the end of this chapter for links to further information and greater detail on the available MDI security alerts.

Before you can start working with MDI, it is important to understand the MDI architecture. Let's delve into this in the next section.

Understanding the MDI architecture

MDI is a combination of services and components that work together to provide your Microsoft 365 **hybrid deployment** with comprehensive protection from modern threats and attacks. You can view the MDI architecture at `https://learn.microsoft.com/en-us/defender-for-identity/architecture`. Here, sensors are installed on AD FS servers and domain controllers. These sensors send signals to Microsoft 365 Defender about Active Directory entities, parsed traffic, and Windows events and traces.

MDI can function to protect your hybrid identity by leveraging the following three key components:

- The **Microsoft 365 Defender portal**, in which you create your MDI instance, as well as monitor and address any threats that have been reported.

- The **MDI sensor**, which is installed on your on-premises domain controllers and is used to monitor domain controller traffic. It can also be installed on your AD FS servers to directly monitor network traffic and authentication events.

- The **MDI cloud service**, which runs on Azure infrastructure and shares data using Microsoft's intelligent security graph.

When you create your MDI instance using the portal, it enables you to integrate with Microsoft security services. With this integration, you can configure your MDI sensor settings for your domain controllers and review the data retrieved by these sensors to interpret any suspicious activities. An MDI sensor can monitor on-premises domain controller ingress and egress traffic. It receives events from domain controllers, which can include information about on-premises users and computers. The information gathered is passed on to the MDI cloud service.

So, how does this information help you to understand and plan for your organization's need for MDI deployment? This can be broken down by answering the following questions:

- What do you need to protect?

- How can you protect it?

- How can you be certain that the protection you have applied is working?

These questions have the following simple answers:

- You need to protect your Microsoft 365 hybrid cloud users and resources by deploying an MDI instance.

- You can apply protection by installing MDI sensors on your on-premises domain controllers.

- You can verify that the protection is working by diligently monitoring MDI events and alerts to review and respond to any potentially suspicious and malicious activities.

It is Microsoft's recommended best practice to deploy MDI in three stages:

- **Stage 1**:

  - Set up MDI to protect primary environments. MDI can be deployed quickly to configure immediate protection.

  - Set sensitive accounts and honeytoken accounts, which are accounts specifically set up to trap malicious actors.

  - Review reports and potential lateral movement paths.

- **Stage 2**:

  - Protect all domain controllers and forests in your organization.

  - Monitor all alerts and investigate any lateral movement or domain dominance.

  - Use the security alert guide to understand threats.

- **Stage 3**:

  - Integrate MDI alerts into your security operation's workflows if applicable.

> **Note**
>
> For special installation scenarios, such as installing MDI for AD FS, multi-forest support, or migrating from Advanced Threat Analytics, please review the *Further reading* section at the end of this chapter. Links to configuring a standalone sensor deployment can also be found there.

The preceding steps will help you understand the principles of MDI and show you how you can prepare to configure it. Now, you are almost ready to set up your MDI instance and start taking advantage of its various features and capabilities.

Setting up MDI

Before setting up MDI, you need to be familiar with the prerequisites for using MDI in your organization. Let's take a look at these in the next section.

Prerequisites for MDI

The following prerequisites should be considered and understood prior to deploying MDI in your organization:

- **Supported Licensing:**

  - Enterprise Mobility + Security E5 (EMS E5/A5)

  - Microsoft 365 E5 (M365 E5/A5/G5) or Microsoft 365 E5/A5/G5 Security

  - Standalone Defender for Identity licenses

- **Accounts:**

  - A minimum of one Directory Service account with read access for all objects in the monitored domains

- **Permissions:**

  - Access to your Azure AD tenant with at least Global Administrator or Security Administrator access

  - Active Directory **Forest Functional Level (FFL)** of Windows 2003 and above

> **Note**
>
> Further prerequisites such as firewall and port requirements can be found in the *Further reading* section at the end of this chapter.

Once you understand the prerequisites, you can set up your MDI instance.

Installing and configuring MDI

Having ensured that you have the required licenses described in the previous section, you can now provision MDI. Your instance will be set up in Azure data centers in one of the following locations:

- Europe

- UK

- North America/Central America

- Caribbean and Asia

The data center that is geographically closest to your Azure AD tenant will be automatically selected for this.

To begin setting up MDI, log in to the Microsoft 365 Defender portal at `https://security.microsoft.com`, and complete the following steps:

1. Navigate to **Settings** from the left-hand side menu and choose **Identities**. This will start the MDI setup process:

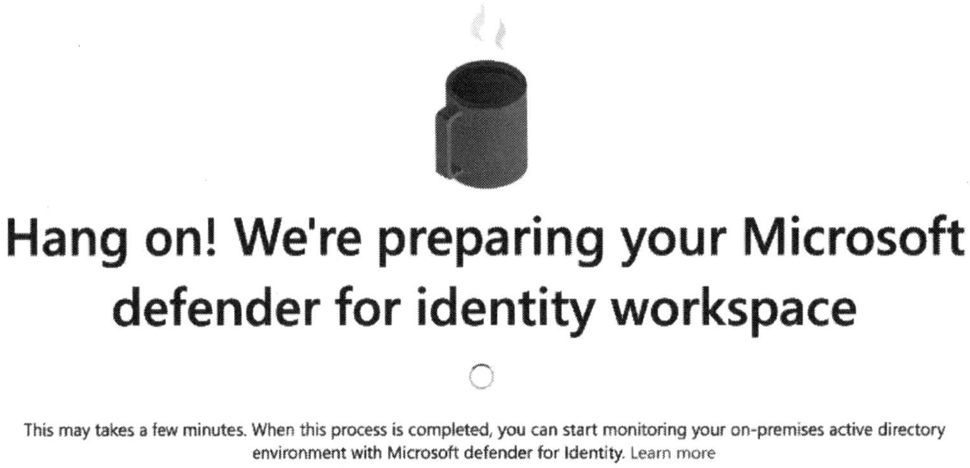

Hang on! We're preparing your Microsoft defender for identity workspace

○

This may takes a few minutes. When this process is completed, you can start monitoring your on-premises active directory environment with Microsoft defender for Identity. Learn more

Figure 6.1: Preparing the MDI workspace

2. The MDI settings page will appear as shown in the following screenshot. Your first step is to add a sensor. To do so, click on **Add sensor**:

Microsoft Defender for Identity

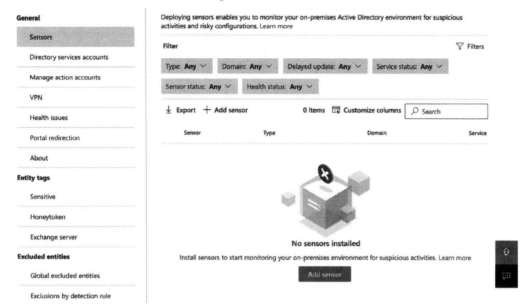

Figure 6.2: MDI settings and controls

3. Click **Download installer** and save the ZIP file to a location where you will be able to access it (like a network share) to install the sensor on your domain controller or AD FS server. You will also need to copy your **Access key** as this will also be required during setup:

Add a new sensor

Install and configure the sensor using the generated access key. Once installed, the new sensor will appear in the sensor list. Learn more

> Download installer

Access key

`xi9Wl6bCEPqRTcaVKipjlEY5zXGDke4zfOGyezHjibwB9/TKCs4cN3z383iF...`

Access key is only used during the sensor installation. Regenerating the key will invalidate the existing key and installations using the previous key will fail.

> Regenerate key

Figure 6.3: Downloading the sensor install package

> **Note**
>
> Should you ever need to regenerate your access key, you can do so without affecting the previous sensor installations.

4.   Next, from your domain controller, run MDI `Sensor Setup` (at the time of writing, the download filename still reflects MDI's previous name of `Azure ATP Sensor Setup`):

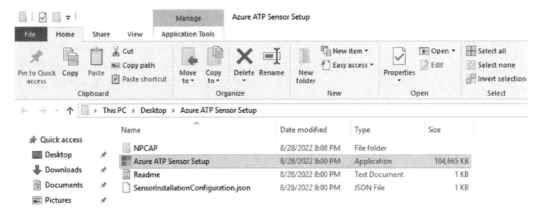

Figure 6.4: Sensor setup

5.   The installation wizard starts, and you will see the following screen. Select your chosen language and click **Next**:

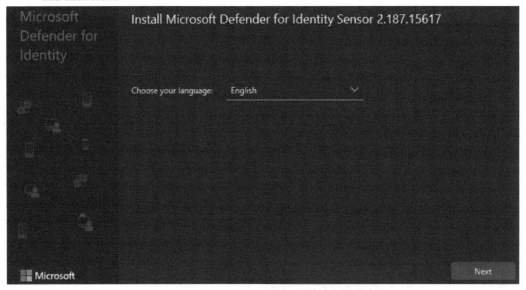

Figure 6.5: MDI sensor install wizard

6. The wizard will detect whether you are installing the sensor on a domain controller, installing a standalone sensor, or an AD FS sensor. Click **Next** again:

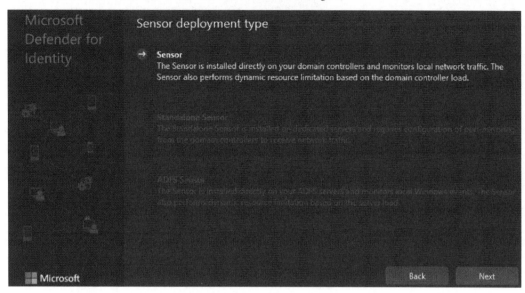

Figure 6.6: Sensor deployment type

7. Choose the installation path as shown in the following screenshot. The wizard will alert you at this point if any of the prerequisites for installing the sensor are not met, such as insufficient disk space. Click on **Install**:

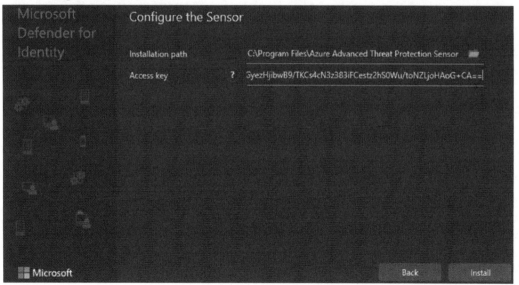

Figure 6.7: Configuring the sensor

The installation will start as follows:

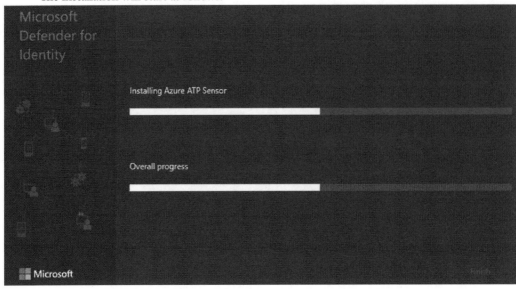

Figure 6.8: Installation progress

8. When the installation is complete, you will see the following message. Click **Finish** to exit the setup wizard:

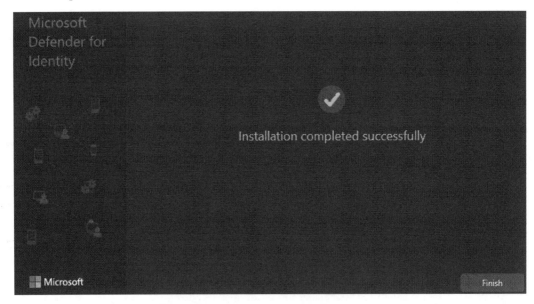

Figure 6.9: Installation is complete

9. Once the installation is complete, you can click on **Sensors** from the **General** section of the MDI portal, and you will see the first installed sensor, as shown in the following screenshot:

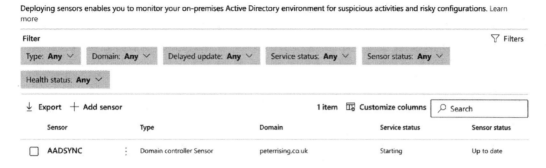

Figure 6.10: Sensors

The preceding steps complete the setup of your first MDI sensor. Should you need more sensors, you can easily add them.

Next, we will look at some of the additional configuration options available within MDI.

Additional configuration options

On the left-hand side menu of the MDI portal, you will see all the configuration options available to you within MDI. This section is divided into the following sub-sections:

*   **General**
*   **Entity Tags**
*   **Excluded entities**
*   **Notifications**

These are shown in the following screenshot:

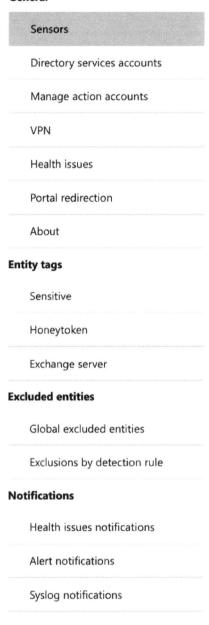

General

Sensors

Directory services accounts

Manage action accounts

VPN

Health issues

Portal redirection

About

Entity tags

Sensitive

Honeytoken

Exchange server

Excluded entities

Global excluded entities

Exclusions by detection rule

Notifications

Health issues notifications

Alert notifications

Syslog notifications

Figure 6.11: The configuration options

We will discuss these options in greater detail in the next section.

> **Note**
>
> Depending on your organizational requirements for MDI, you may not need to configure all the features within the preceding sub-sections. However, it is recommended that you familiarize yourself with all the available options.

Now that you have configured MDI, deployed the first sensor to a domain controller, and have MDI up and running, you can begin to consider how to manage your MDI instance and carry out monitoring and reporting tasks.

Managing and monitoring MDI

You can now start managing and monitoring the MDI service. From a management perspective, this means configuring settings and features such as **Entity tags** and **Excluded entities**. From a monitoring perspective, it is important to review MDI regularly by looking at **Health Issues** from the **General** section of the MDI settings page.

Some of these capabilities are presented in greater detail next

Entity tags

MDI allows you to apply **Entity tags** to sensitive accounts. The status of the tags that you define enables MDI to detect things such as sensitive group modification and lateral movement. Additionally, **honeytoken accounts** may be configured to trap malicious actors and trigger an alert.

You can configure the three following types of entity tags in MDI:

- Sensitive tags
- Honeytoken tags
- Exchange server tags

The following sections explain these tags in detail.

Sensitive tags

You can use the **Sensitive** tag to identify assets of high value. MDI considers some entities to be sensitive by default, but it is also possible to add entities manually. Default sensitive entities include AD groups such as **Domain Admins** and **Enterprise Admins** (and more).

To set up sensitive tags, go to **Entity tags** in the MDI portal and click **Sensitive**. You will see that you can define high-value assets by **Users**, **Devices**, and **Groups**, as shown in the following screenshot:

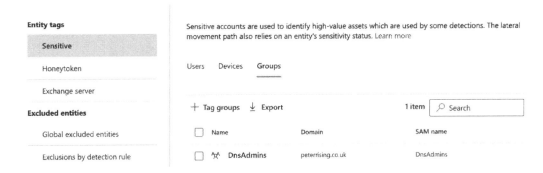

Figure 6.12: Setting up a Sensitive entity tag

With your tags defined and saved, MDI will now trigger alerts whenever there is a match.

Honeytoken tags

To set traps for malicious actors, use **Honeytoken** tags. Any authentication associated with these honeytoken entities triggers an alert in the same way as **Sensitive** tags. With **Honeytoken** tags, you can add **Users** and **Devices**:

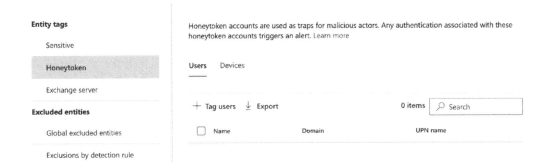

Figure 6.13: Setting up a honeytoken tag

Exchange server tags

On-premises exchange servers are considered high-value assets by MDI and are automatically tagged as **Sensitive**. It is also possible to manually tag devices as exchange servers.

To set up exchange server tags, select **Exchange server**, and you will see any devices labeled with the **Exchange server** tag:

Microsoft Defender for Identity

Entity tags	Tag devices as Exchange servers. Microsoft Defender for Identity considers Exchange servers as high-value assets and automatically tags them as Sensitive. Learn more		
Sensitive			
Honeytoken	Devices		
Exchange server			
Excluded entities	+ Tag devices ↓ Export		2 items 🔍 Search
Global excluded entities	☐ Name	Domain	SAM name
Exclusions by detection rule	☐ 🖥 CHRYSALIS04	peterrising.co.uk	CHRYSALIS04$
Notifications	☐ 🖥 CHRYSALIS03	peterrising.co.uk	CHRYSALIS03$

Figure 6.14: Setting up an exchange server tag

In the following section, you will learn about the next MDI configuration feature: excluded entities.

Excluded entities

With the excluded entities feature, it is also possible to exclude IP addresses, users, computers, or domains from the detection process in MDI if required. This feature is typically used to reduce false positives. This feature can be found in the MDI portal under **Excluded entities**. There are two types within, which are described as follows.

Global excluded entities

Global excluded entities include **Users**, **Domains**, **Devices**, and **IP addresses**, which can be added manually. In the following example, you can select the option **Exclude users**:

Microsoft Defender for Identity

Entity tags	Exclude entities from all detection rules
Sensitive	
Honeytoken	Users Domains Devices IP addresses
Exchange server	
Excluded entities	+ Exclude users ↓ Export 0 items 🔍 Search
Global excluded entities	☐ User Domain name
Exclusions by detection rule	

Figure 6.15: Global excluded entities

The other exclusion option is to use detection rules.

Exclusions by detection rule

Excluding by detection rule allows you to choose an exclusion type by entity. Depending on the rule, you will see different choices of entity types. In the following screenshot, the detection rule for **Suspected overpass-the-hash attack (Kerberos)** provides exclusion options of **devices** and **IP addresses**:

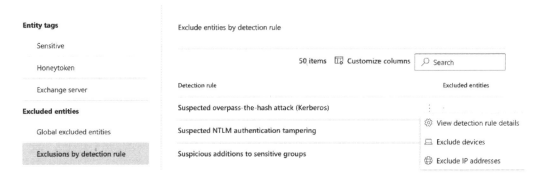

Figure 6.16: Exclusions by detection rule

The other possible options you will see in the other rules are domains and users.

Next, we will look at how you can monitor health, alerts, and notifications in MDI.

Monitoring MDI

In MDI, you should regularly check for health issues and ensure that you have alerts set up correctly so that admins are informed when incidents occur. There are several areas in the MDI portal where you can check for health issues and set up alert notifications.

Health issues

In MDI, under the **General** section, you can view **Health issues**. This lets you know when there is a problem with your identity instance by raising a health alert. Alerts are split into three categories: **Open**, **Closed**, and **Suppressed**, as shown in the following screenshot:

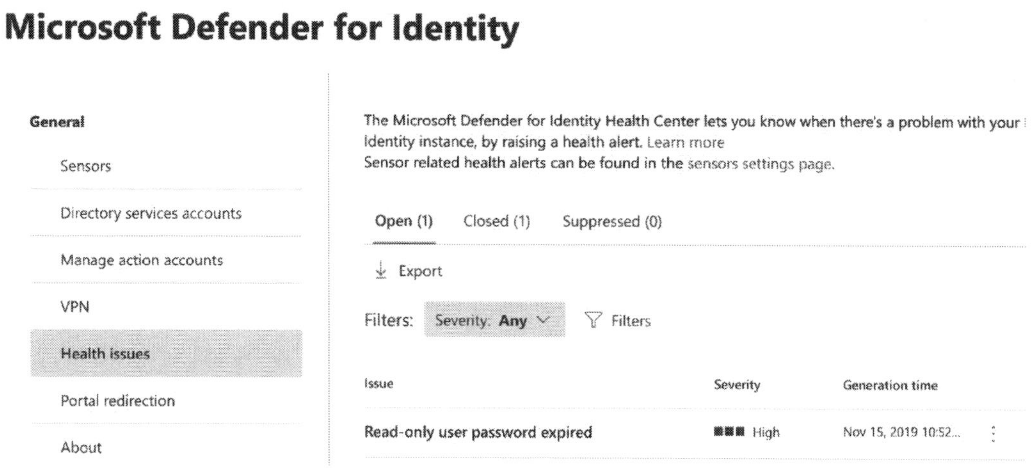

Microsoft Defender for Identity

General

Sensors

Directory services accounts

Manage action accounts

VPN

Health issues

Portal redirection

About

The Microsoft Defender for Identity Health Center lets you know when there's a problem with your Identity instance, by raising a health alert. Learn more
Sensor related health alerts can be found in the sensors settings page.

Open (1)   Closed (1)   Suppressed (0)

⬇ Export

Filters: Severity: **Any** ∨   ▽ Filters

Issue	Severity	Generation time	
Read-only user password expired	■■■ High	Nov 15, 2019 10:52...	⋮

Figure 6.17: MDI Health issues

Clicking on one of the issues will expand the details, as shown in the following screenshot. Here, you can examine the **Description** of the issue, act on the recommended steps, and then choose to close or suppress the issue as appropriate:

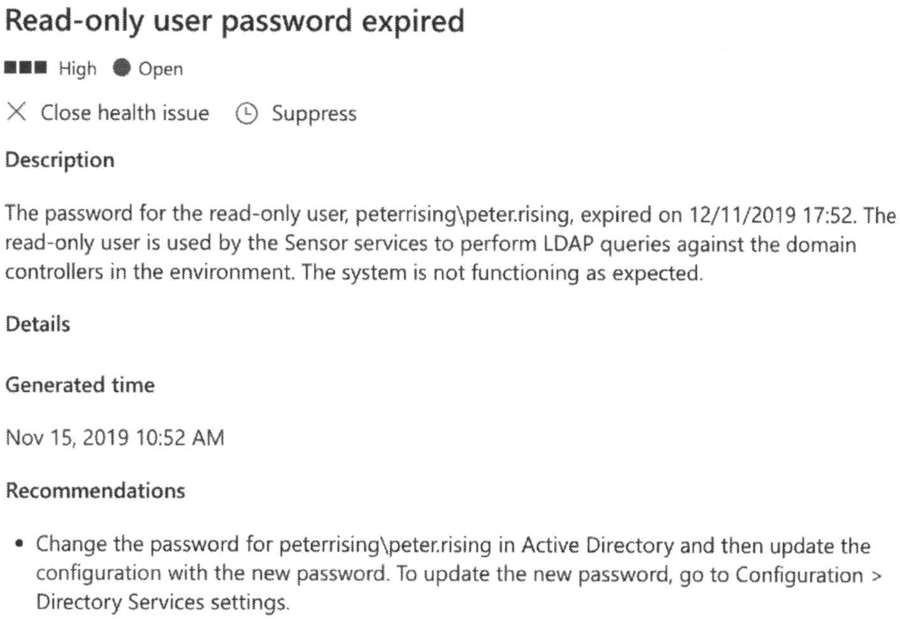

Read-only user password expired

■■■ High   ● Open

✕ Close health issue   🕐 Suppress

Description

The password for the read-only user, peterrising\peter.rising, expired on 12/11/2019 17:52. The read-only user is used by the Sensor services to perform LDAP queries against the domain controllers in the environment. The system is not functioning as expected.

Details

Generated time

Nov 15, 2019 10:52 AM

Recommendations

- Change the password for peterrising\peter.rising in Active Directory and then update the configuration with the new password. To update the new password, go to Configuration > Directory Services settings.

Figure 6.18: Health issue details

Next, we will examine the available notification options in MDI.

Notifications

Configuring notifications in MDI allows you to generate emails to chosen recipients for MDI health alerts and newly detected alerts. You can also configure syslog notifications, which can be used to generate a message in your syslog infrastructure solution.

Health issues notifications are configured by adding a recipient email address(es) as shown in the following screenshot:

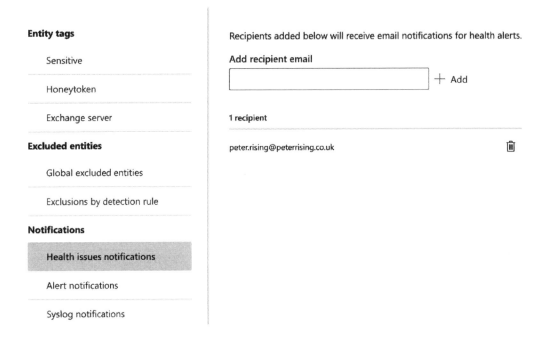

Figure 6.19: Health issues notifications

Alert notifications are configured in the same way as health issues notifications, that is, by adding a recipient email address(es) again:

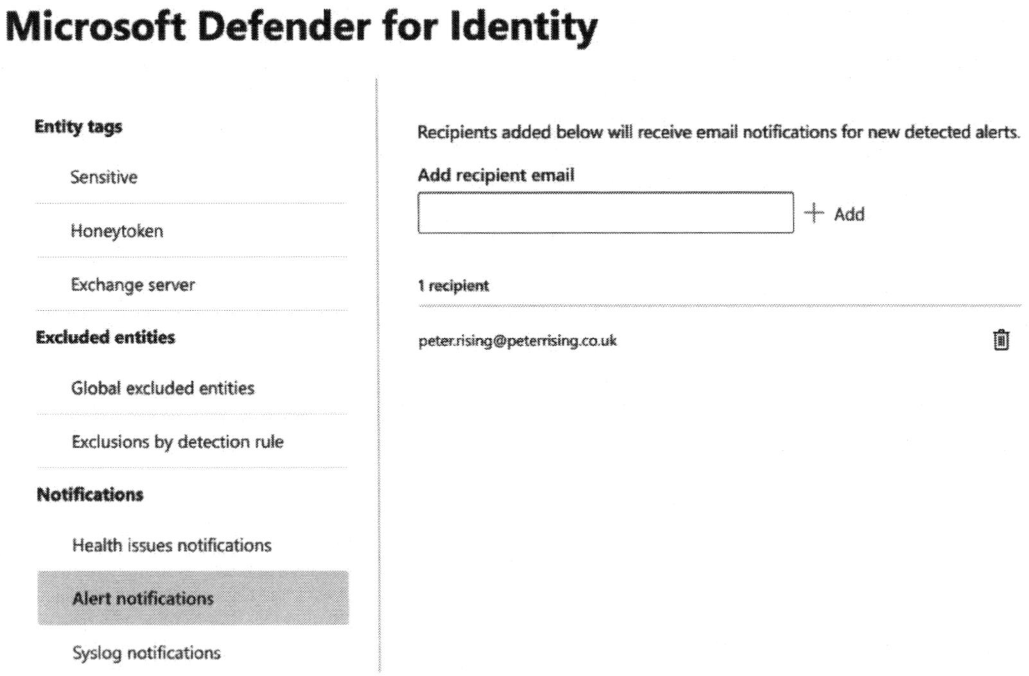

Microsoft Defender for Identity

Entity tags

Sensitive

Honeytoken

Exchange server

Excluded entities

Global excluded entities

Exclusions by detection rule

Notifications

Health issues notifications

Alert notifications

Syslog notifications

Recipients added below will receive email notifications for new detected alerts.

Add recipient email

+ Add

1 recipient

peter.rising@peterrising.co.uk

Figure 6.20: Alert notifications

Syslog notifications in MDI will notify you when suspicious activities are detected and send health and security-based alerts to your syslog server via a nominated MDI sensor.

You can view the configured settings under **Notifications | Syslog notifications**:

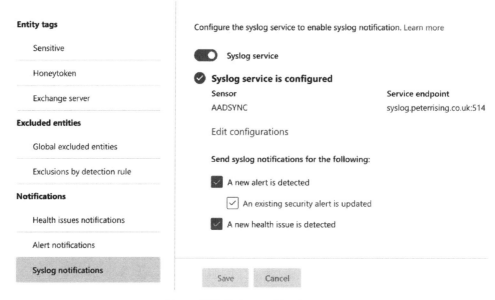

Figure 6.21: Syslog notifications

Clicking on **Edit configurations** shows you the available settings for the syslog server:

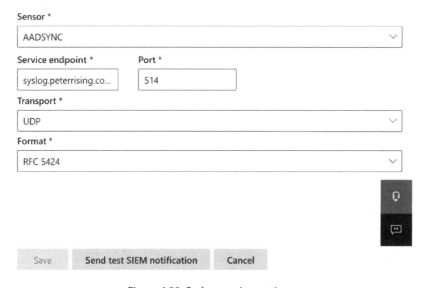

Figure 6.22: Syslog service settings

If you click on **Send test SIEM notification**, you can verify a message is generated in your syslog infrastructure solution.

In this section, we learned about the managing and monitoring capabilities in MDI, including configuring entity tags and setting up notifications.

Summary

In this chapter, we examined **Microsoft Defender for Identity** (**MDI**), which is a feature that's included with Enterprise Mobility + Security E5 and Microsoft 365 E5. It enables you to protect your Microsoft 365 hybrid cloud environment against malicious actors attempting to access vulnerable user accounts and devices and conduct reconnaissance activities to gain elevation of privilege and achieve domain dominance.

We also learned how to configure MDI in the Microsoft 365 Defender portal and install sensors on domain controllers. We looked at how entity tags can be configured to establish sensitive accounts, honeytoken accounts, and exchange servers and set to trigger alerts when matched to suspicious activity. We then considered how MDI establishes a timeline of suspicious and malicious activities, the steps that can be taken to review and resolve these within the MDI health center, and how to use notifications and alerts.

In the next chapter, we will examine the principles of Microsoft Defender for Endpoint. We will explore how to plan for and configure Microsoft Defender for Endpoint, and how it can be used to protect your organization's devices.

Questions

1. Which of the following is not a type of MDI sensor deployment type?

    A. Sensor

    B. Pass-through authentication

    C. AD FS

    D. Standalone

2. Where do you go to configure MDI?

    A. The Microsoft Purview compliance center

    B. The Microsoft 365 Defender portal

    C. The Microsoft 365 admin center

    D. The Endpoint Manager admin center

3. True or false? You can migrate an instance of **Advanced Threat Analytics (ATA)** to Microsoft Defender for Identity.

   A. True

   B. False

4. Which of the following are types of entity tags (choose three)?

   A. DNS server

   B. Exchange server

   C. Honeytoken

   D. Confidential

   E. Sensitive

5. True or false? An MDI instance is NOT automatically created in the closest geographical data center.

   A. True

   B. False

6. Which of the following are not types of alerts displayed in the MDI health center (choose two)?

   A. Open

   B. Pending

   C. Suppressed

   D. Closed

   E. Deferred

7. Which of the following are types of entity exclusion listed in the MDI portal menu (choose two)?

   A. User excluded entities

   B. Global excluded entities

   C. Device excluded entities

   D. Exceptions by detected rule

8. True or false? The syslog service CANNOT send SIEM test notifications.

   A. True

   B. False

9. Which of the following would you use to set traps for malicious actors?

    A. Sensitive entity tag

    B. Exchange server entity tag

    C. Global excluded entities

    D. Honeytoken entity tag

10. True or false? Nominated recipients will receive email alerts when there is a health alert or a new detected alert in MDI?

    A. True

    B. False

Further reading

Please refer to the following links for more information:

- MDI prerequisites: `https://learn.microsoft.com/en-us/defender-for-identity/prerequisites`

- MDI architecture: `https://learn.microsoft.com/en-us/defender-for-identity/architecture`

- MDI documentation: `https://learn.microsoft.com/en-us/defender-for-identity/what-is`

- Deploying MDI: `https://learn.microsoft.com/en-us/defender-for-identity/deploy-defender-identity`

- Download the MDI sensor: `https://learn.microsoft.com/en-us/defender-for-identity/download-sensor`

- Configure sensor settings: `https://learn.microsoft.com/en-us/defender-for-identity/configure-sensor-settings`

- Installing an MDI sensor: `https://learn.microsoft.com/en-us/defender-for-identity/install-sensor`

- Configure endpoint proxy settings for MDI: `https://learn.microsoft.com/en-us/defender-for-identity/configure-proxy`

- Manage MDI action accounts: `https://learn.microsoft.com/en-us/defender-for-identity/manage-action-accounts`

- MDI FAQs: `https://learn.microsoft.com/en-us/defender-for-identity/technical-faq`

- Sensor health alerts: `https://learn.microsoft.com/en-us/defender-for-identity/health-alerts?WT.mc_id=EM-MVP-4039827`

- MDI notifications: `https://learn.microsoft.com/en-us/defender-for-identity/notifications?WT.mc_id=EM-MVP-4039827`

- Monitored activities: `https://learn.microsoft.com/en-us/defender-for-identity/monitored-activities?WT.mc_id=EM-MVP-4039827`

- Understanding Security alerts: `https://learn.microsoft.com/en-us/defender-for-identity/understanding-security-alerts?WT.mc_id=EM-MVP-4039827`

- Detection exclusions: `https://learn.microsoft.com/en-us/defender-for-identity/exclusions`

- Entity tags: `https://learn.microsoft.com/en-us/defender-for-identity/entity-tags`

7

Configuring Device Threat Protection with Microsoft Defender for Endpoint and Intune

In the modern IT landscape, malicious actors are using more and more sophisticated methods to attack environments and devices. The average time it takes to detect a threat is believed to be approximately 250 days. Traditional anti-virus and anti-malware software are not enough to effectively defend against these attackers who are determined to cause disruption.

This is where **Microsoft Defender for Endpoint** (**MDE**) comes in. Microsoft Defender for Endpoint is a cloud-based online service that provides prevention, detection, and investigation methods that you can use to respond to advanced threats within your organization.

In this chapter, you will learn how to configure and manage MDE capabilities to provide the best protection for your organization, as well as how to enable and configure always-on protection and monitoring.

The chapter will cover these topics in the following order:

- Planning and implementing MDE
- Managing and monitoring MDE
- Implementing Microsoft Defender Application Guard, Application Control, and exploit protection
- Encrypting your Windows devices using BitLocker
- Implementing application protection policies

Planning and implementing MDE

The MDE security platform enables organizations to investigate and respond to advanced threats that target their enterprise networks. It does so by providing information about advanced attack detections based on behavioral patterns. The threats detected by MDE are interpreted in terms of a forensic timeline. This timeline is then used to build and maintain a threat intelligence knowledge base.

This is achieved by using **endpoint behavioral sensors** that collect signals from the Windows operating system and send that data to MDE. Then, **cloud security analytics** use machine learning techniques to translate the collected data into insights and provide recommendations on how to resolve advanced threats. Finally, **threat intelligence** activities are carried out by Microsoft hunters and security experts. This allows MDE to recognize the tools and methods employed by malicious actors and to alert administrators when similar behavior is detected.

MDE provides both preventative and post-breach detection and performs the following functions:

- Reduces the attack surface

- Provides next-generation protection

- Conducts **endpoint detection and response** (EDR)

- Conducts automated investigation and remediation

- Provides core Defender vulnerability management

- Carries out advanced hunting to provide custom threat intelligence

To benefit from the MDE service, users must have one of the following licenses:

- MDE Plan 1 (P1) standalone user (also included as part of Microsoft 365 E3/A3)

- MDE Plan 2 (P2) standalone user, which is also included as part of the following plans:

  - Windows 11 Enterprise E5/A5

  - Windows 10 Enterprise E5/A5

  - Microsoft 365 E5/A5/G5 (includes Windows 10 or Windows 11 Enterprise E5)

  - Microsoft 365 E5/A5/G5/F5 Security

  - Microsoft 365 F5 Security & Compliance

With the required licensing in place, MDE can now be configured via the Microsoft security center cloud portal by completing the following steps:

1. Go to `https://securitycenter.windows.com/` and log in with your Microsoft 365 Global Administrator credentials. The portal will appear as shown here:

Figure 7.1: Microsoft Defender security center

2. Scroll down the menu on the left side and choose **Settings**:

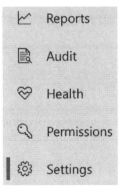

Figure 7.2: Security portal settings

3. In the settings, click on **Microsoft 365 Defender**:

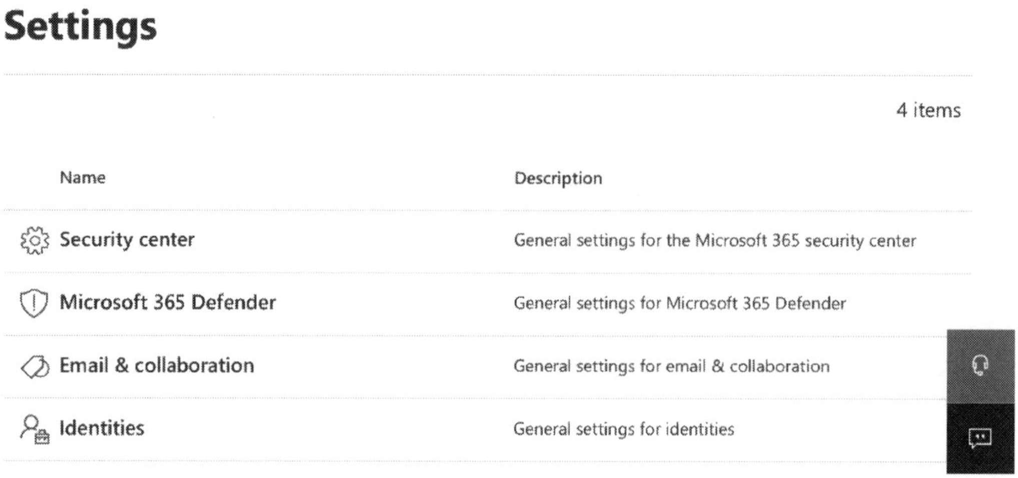

Settings

	4 items
Name	**Description**
⚙️ Security center	General settings for the Microsoft 365 security center
🛡️ Microsoft 365 Defender	General settings for Microsoft 365 Defender
🗨️ Email & collaboration	General settings for email & collaboration
👤 Identities	General settings for identities

Figure 7.3: Settings configuration

You will now see the following message that new spaces for your data are being prepared. You may need to wait for this stage to complete:

Hang on! We're preparing new spaces for your data and connecting them.

Loading...

Figure 7.4: Preparing Microsoft 365 Defender

4. When complete, the **Settings** section will have additional options. Select **Endpoints**:

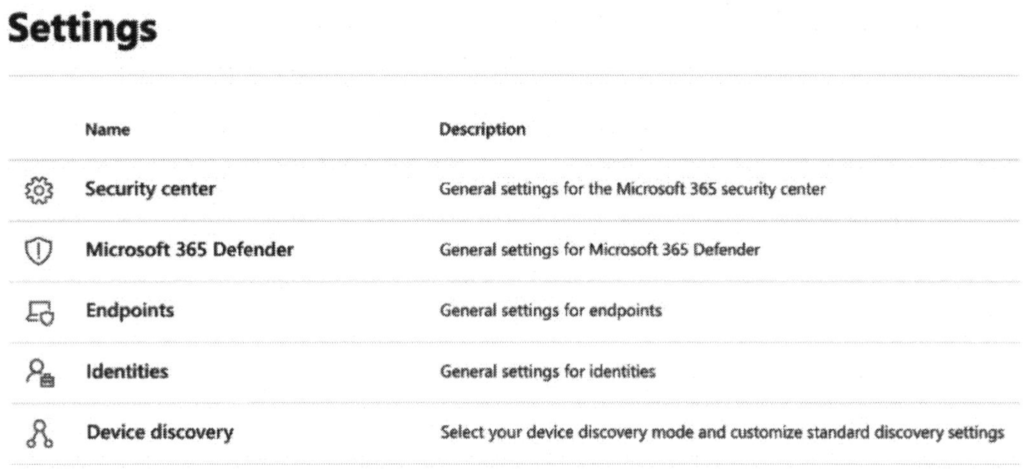

Settings

	Name	Description
⚙️	**Security center**	General settings for the Microsoft 365 security center
🛡️	**Microsoft 365 Defender**	General settings for Microsoft 365 Defender
🖥️	**Endpoints**	General settings for endpoints
👤	**Identities**	General settings for identities
⚗️	**Device discovery**	Select your device discovery mode and customize standard discovery settings

Figure 7.5: Endpoints now available in Settings

5.   Clicking on **Endpoints** shows you the available settings you can configure:

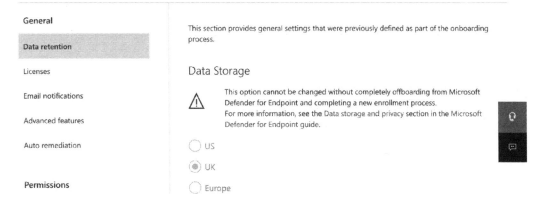

Figure 7.6: Defender for Endpoint settings options

The security portal will now show a new menu in the left pane called **Endpoints**:

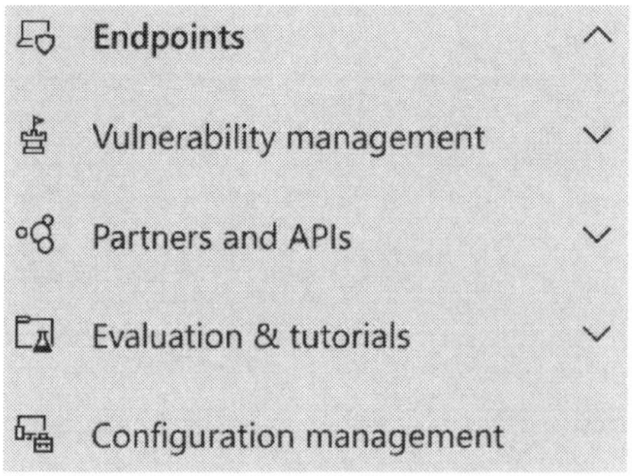

Figure 7.7: Endpoints section in the security center

With this initial setup completed, you can customize the settings for Defender for Endpoint to your organization's requirements using the **Settings | Endpoints** menu in the security portal. You can modify the available configuration options as shown in the following table:

Setting	Description
General settings	Modify general settings that were defined as part of the onboarding process
Permissions	Manage access to the portal using role-based access control device groups
APIs	Enable threat intelligence and integration with SIEM
Rules	Set rules for suppression and automation settings
Device management	Onboard and offboard devices
Network assessments	Select devices to regularly be scanned and added to the device inventory

Table 7.1: Endpoint settings and their description

> **Note**
>
> The contents of the **Endpoints** settings section are so vast that it is impractical to cover them all in detail. This chapter will instead cover the **Device Management** settings only. For more details about all other sections in the preceding table, please refer to the *Further reading* section at the end of this chapter.

When your settings are customized as required, you can plan policies for MDE security management to be targeted to the supported device platforms. These include the following:

- Windows 10 Professional/Enterprise (with KB5006738)

- Windows 11 Professional/Enterprise

- Windows Server 2012 R2 with Microsoft Defender for down-level devices
- Windows Server 2016 with Microsoft Defender for down-level devices
- Windows Server 2019 (with KB5006744)
- Windows Server 2022 (with KB5006745)

The next section covers how to onboard devices with MDE.

Onboarding devices

This section will explain the different methods for onboarding devices to MDE in your organization.

Deploying MDE is a two-step process:

- Onboard devices to the service.
- Configure the capabilities of the service.

Let's look at some of the available configuration tools for onboarding devices with MDE.

Configuration tools for onboarding

Several tools are available to onboard the supported operating systems to MDE. Some of these are shown in the following table:

Operating system	Available tools
Windows Client	**Mobile Device Management (MDM)**/Microsoft Intune Group Policy Local script (maximum of 10 devices) VDI script
Windows Server	Microsoft Intune Group Policy VDI script MDE service

Operating system	Available tools
macOS	Local script Microsoft Intune JAMF Pro MDM
Linux Server	Local script Puppet Ansible
iOS	Microsoft Intune
Android	Microsoft Intune

Table 7.2: Configuration tools for onboarding to MDE

> **Note**
>
> Devices that are not managed by Microsoft Intune or Microsoft Endpoint Configuration Manager can use Security Management for Defender for Endpoint. This will enable them to receive security configurations for Microsoft Defender directly from Intune.

Device onboarding

To onboard devices to MDE, you need to navigate to the Microsoft security center. Appropriate steps, guidance, and deployment tool options will be provided depending on the supported device type you choose to onboard.

To onboard a device to MDE, take the following steps:

1. Go to the Microsoft 365 Defender security center and log on as an administrator. Navigate to **Devices** and select **Onboard devices**. You can also reach the onboarding options by navigating to **Settings** | **Endpoints** | **Device management** | **Onboarding**:

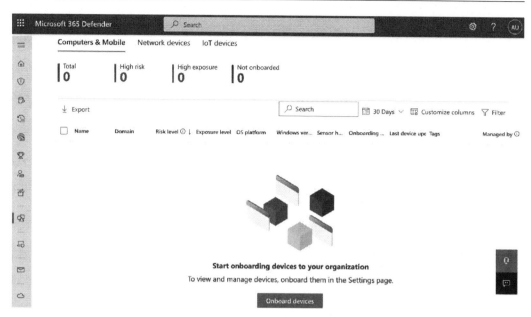

Figure 7.8: Onboarding a device in the security center

2. The first option you see is the **operating system** selection. There are several choices here. For this example, select **Windows 10 and 11**:

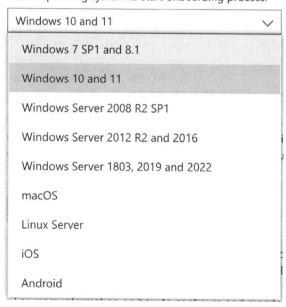

Figure 7.9: Selecting an operating system

3.   From the **Onboard a device** section, click on the **Deployment method** dropdown:

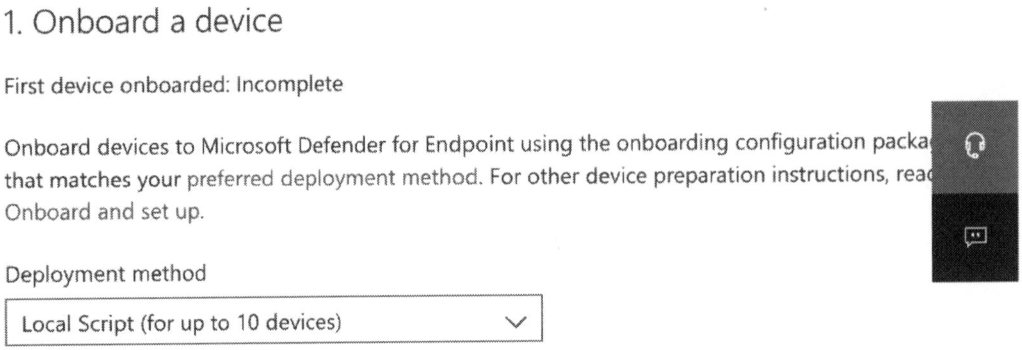

1. Onboard a device

First device onboarded: Incomplete

Onboard devices to Microsoft Defender for Endpoint using the onboarding configuration packa
that matches your preferred deployment method. For other device preparation instructions, read
Onboard and set up.

Deployment method

Local Script (for up to 10 devices)   ⌄

Figure 7.10: Choose a deployment method

4.   Choose the desired deployment method. For this example, choose **Local Script (for up to 10 devices)** – you might select this option if you only have a few devices to configure:

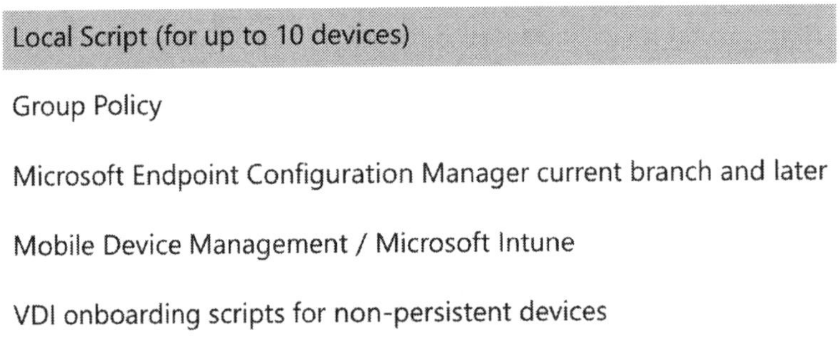

Local Script (for up to 10 devices)

Group Policy

Microsoft Endpoint Configuration Manager current branch and later

Mobile Device Management / Microsoft Intune

VDI onboarding scripts for non-persistent devices

Figure 7.11: Choosing the deployment method

For details on the other options, refer to the links provided in the *Further reading* section at the end of this chapter.

5.   Next, click **Download onboarding package**. You will use this to install Defender for Endpoint on your device:

↓ Download onboarding package

Figure 7.12: Downloading your deployment package

6.   Copy the downloaded package file to the machine (or a network location the machine can access) and double-click to run it. The installer package will run as shown here:

Figure 7.13: Running a local script file to install Defender for Endpoint

7. Next, to verify that the device is properly onboarded and reporting to the service, open Command
    Prompt on your machine and run the following command:

```
powershell.exe -NoExit -ExecutionPolicy Bypass -WindowStyle
Hidden $ErrorActionPreference= 'silentlycontinue';(New-Object
System.Net.WebClient).DownloadFile('http://127.0.0.1/1.exe',
'C:\\test-WDATP-test\\invoice.exe');Start-Process 'C:\\test-
WDATP-test\\invoice.exe'
```

8. If all steps were completed successfully, you will see the machine displayed in the **Device
    Inventory** section as shown here:

Figure 7.14: Device successfully onboarded

> **Note**
>
> For guidance on the other methods of installing Defender for Endpoint for different operating
> systems, please refer to the *Further reading* section at the end of this chapter.

Next, we will examine how to configure the capabilities of the Defender for Endpoint service.

Configuring the capabilities of MDE

Once devices are onboarded, the **endpoint detection and response (EDR)** capabilities of MDE are enabled. However, there are other settings in the service that must be configured to get maximum protection for your environment. These are listed and described in the following table:

Setting	Description
Microsoft Defender Vulnerability Management	Defender Vulnerability Management provides the following benefits to your administrators and security teams: • Real-time EDR insights correlated with endpoint vulnerabilities • Context for device vulnerability during incident investigations • Inbuilt remediation processes using Intune and Configuration Manager
Next-generation protection	Next-generation protection for desktops, laptops, and servers is provided by Microsoft Defender Antivirus. This is a built-in anti-malware solution that includes the following: • Cloud-provided protection to near-instantly detect and block both new and emerging threats. This includes machine learning and the Intelligent Security Graph. • Real-time protection with always-on scanning that leverages advanced file and process behavior monitoring, plus other heuristics. • Protection updates that leverage machine learning, manual and automated big data analysis, and comprehensive threat resistance research.
Attack surface reduction	MDE also includes attack surface reduction capabilities, which are designed to protect your organization's devices and apps from new and emerging threats.
Auto investigation and remediation	Automated investigations are used to reduce the number of alerts that need to be individually investigated manually.
Microsoft Threat Experts	Microsoft Threat Experts is a managed hunting service. It provides SOCs with expert analysis and monitoring.

Table 7.3: MDE settings and descriptions

In the next section, we will explore how you can use MDE to monitor and manage the prevention and detection of threats in your environment.

Managing and monitoring MDE

Now that you have MDE set up and deployed to one or more workstations, there are several ways in which you can fine-tune the capabilities and monitor the service.

To maximize security protection in your environment, it is vital that you regularly and diligently monitor and manage your MDE instance. The following sections demonstrate how you can make the most of some of the available options. You can access these through the Microsoft 365 Defender security center at `https://security.microsoft.com` by navigating to the **Endpoints** section:

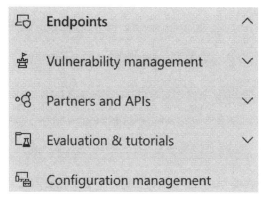

Figure 7.15: Endpoint configuration options in the security center

The following sections will discuss each of these items in detail.

Vulnerability management

The **Vulnerability management** section includes the items shown in the following screenshot:

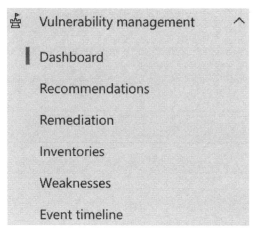

Figure 7.16: Vulnerability management

The **Dashboard** section shows you your overall exposure score, a breakdown of security recommendations, and much more. You can use the dashboard as a bird's-eye view of your vulnerability status and make the necessary plans to improve your scores. The intent should be to reduce the **Exposure score** value and increase the **Microsoft Secure Score for Devices** value:

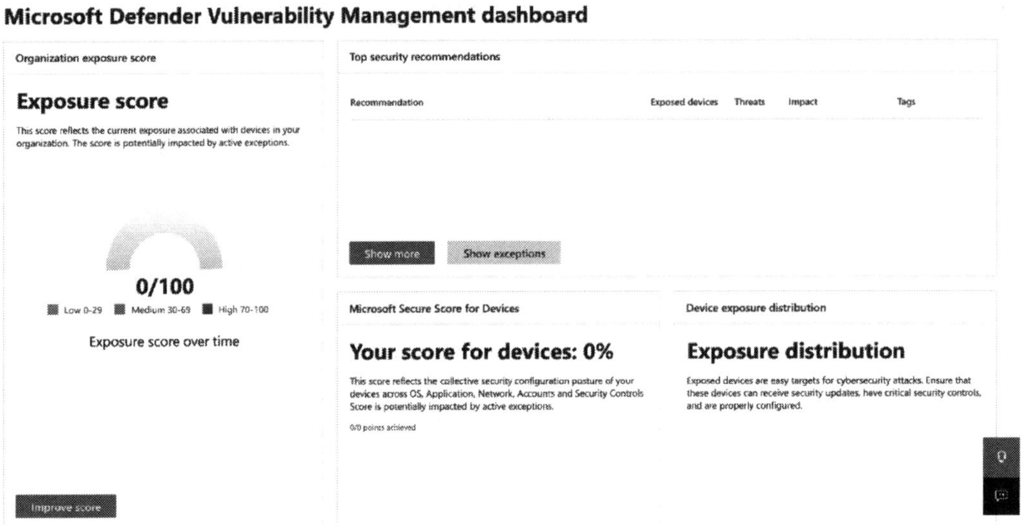

Microsoft Defender Vulnerability Management dashboard

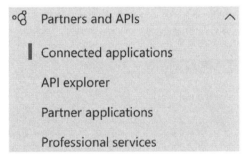

Figure 7.17: Vulnerability management dashboard

For a more detailed analysis, you can use the other sections within **Vulnerability management**; for more information, refer to the *Further reading* section.

Partners and APIs

Under **Partners and APIs**, you can see the following options:

Figure 7.18: Partners and APIs

These options serve the following purposes:

- **Connected applications** will show the applications that are connected

- You can use **API explorer** to test MDE capabilities by using sample queries to get started

- You can view the supported **Partner applications** connectors, which when added can enhance your detection, investigation, and threat intelligence capabilities

- Through **Professional services**, you can view a catalog of supported partner connections, which include things such as Microsoft Managed Desktop and Microsoft Defender Experts

Take the time to go through these sections and assess their relevance to your MDE roadmap.

Evaluation & tutorials

With **Evaluation & tutorials**, you can evaluate various labs and simulations:

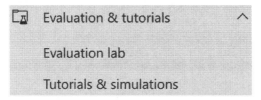

Figure 7.19: Evaluation & tutorials

This is a useful way to experience MDE in action with onboarded test devices that can detect sophisticated attacks. This allows you to experience how MDE detects and facilitates efficient investigation and response.

Configuration management

The **Configuration management** menu item (shown in *Figure 7.15*) will show you several options that you can explore in order to manage the configuration options for MDE in your organization:

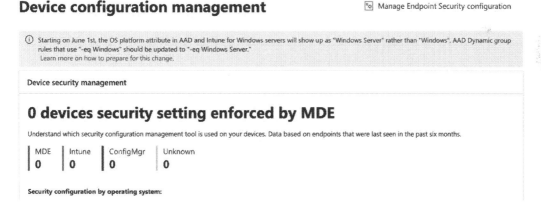

Figure 7.20: Configuration management settings

The following features are available under **Configuration management** and perform the following functions:

- **Device configuration management** enables you to understand which security configuration management tool is used on your devices. The data is based on endpoints that were seen in the past 6 months.

- **Control security setting management** lets you view the security setting management in Microsoft Intune enforced by MDE.

- **Onboarded devices** displays the onboarding of Intune-managed devices to MDE.

- **Compliance of Windows clients to the MDE baseline** in Microsoft Intune shows the configuration of Microsoft Intune 10 and 11 devices that have been assigned the MDE security baseline.

- **Device attack surface management** lets you view predictive analysis and tuning of attack surfaces on your devices.

- **Web protection coverage** helps you ensure that you have web protection and deploy network protection using the MDE security baseline.

> **Note**
>
> Further details on all the settings described in the preceding paragraphs can be found in many of the links included in the *Further reading* section at the end of this chapter.

To recap, this section showed you how to install, configure, and monitor MDE within your Microsoft 365 environment. The subsequent sections will show you how to further refine the service by implementing additional features, such as Microsoft Defender Application Guard, Application Control, and exploit protection.

Implementing Microsoft Defender Application Guard, Application Control, and exploit protection

Now that you know how to manage and monitor MDE, let's take a look at some of its associated features, starting with Microsoft Defender Application Guard.

Configuring Microsoft Defender Application Guard

Microsoft Defender Application Guard is a system designed to isolate devices so that malicious actors are unable to use their attack methodologies against them. It protects your company's users on Windows, specifically on the Microsoft Edge browser, by isolating untrusted sites when users browse the internet.

Microsoft Defender Application Guard empowers Microsoft 365 security administrators to explicitly define the following categories:

- Trusted websites
- Trusted cloud resources
- Trusted internal networks

A **zero-trust methodology** is employed to ensure that anything that is not defined in the preceding categories is considered untrusted and is blocked. So, how does this work?

Essentially, when a user protected by Microsoft Defender Application Guard attempts to access a website that is not trusted, via Microsoft Edge, the site is opened in an isolated container.

The result of this is that the user's PC remains unaffected even if the website contains malicious code or content. Subsequently, a potential attack is prevented, and malicious actors cannot carry out any reconnaissance that could lead to the elevation of privilege and domain dominance.

Microsoft Defender Application Guard can be deployed to domain-joined computers on your organization's network by using either System Center Configuration Manager or Microsoft Intune.

It is also possible to deploy Microsoft Defender Application Guard to **bring your own device (BYOD)** or personal Windows devices. While these devices are not domain-joined, it is possible to protect them with Application Guard if they are managed by Intune.

When you configure Microsoft Defender Application Guard to be deployed to your Windows devices, it enables the following features, which can be found under **Control Panel | Programs and Features | Install Windows Features**:

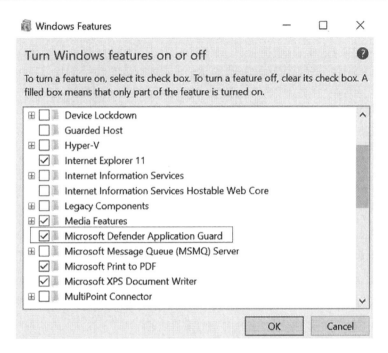

Figure 7.21: Turning Windows features on or off

Once enabled, clicking on the menu bar within Microsoft Edge will show the **New window** and **New Application Guard window** options, as shown in the following screenshot:

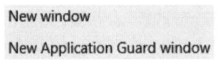

Figure 7.22: The Edge browser experience

When a user selects the **New Application Guard window** option, they can browse safely and any malicious code or content lurking on a website will not be able to harm the workstation as the browser session will be completely isolated. Simply clicking **New Window** will not add this protection.

Configuring Microsoft Defender Application Control

Microsoft Defender Application Control can restrict the applications on your network from accessing the system kernel. Microsoft Defender Application Control can also block scripts that are unsigned as well as MSIs.

You can create Application Control policies via an MDM solution, such as Microsoft Intune. It is also possible to use Group Policy to deploy Application Control policies.

To create a Microsoft Defender Application Control policy using Intune, follow these steps:

1. Open `https://endpoint.microsoft.com`, click on **Device Configuration | Profiles**, and select **Create profile**. Select **Windows 10 and later** as the **Platform**, and **Templates** as the **Profile type**. Choose **Endpoint protection** from the list of templates and click **Create**:

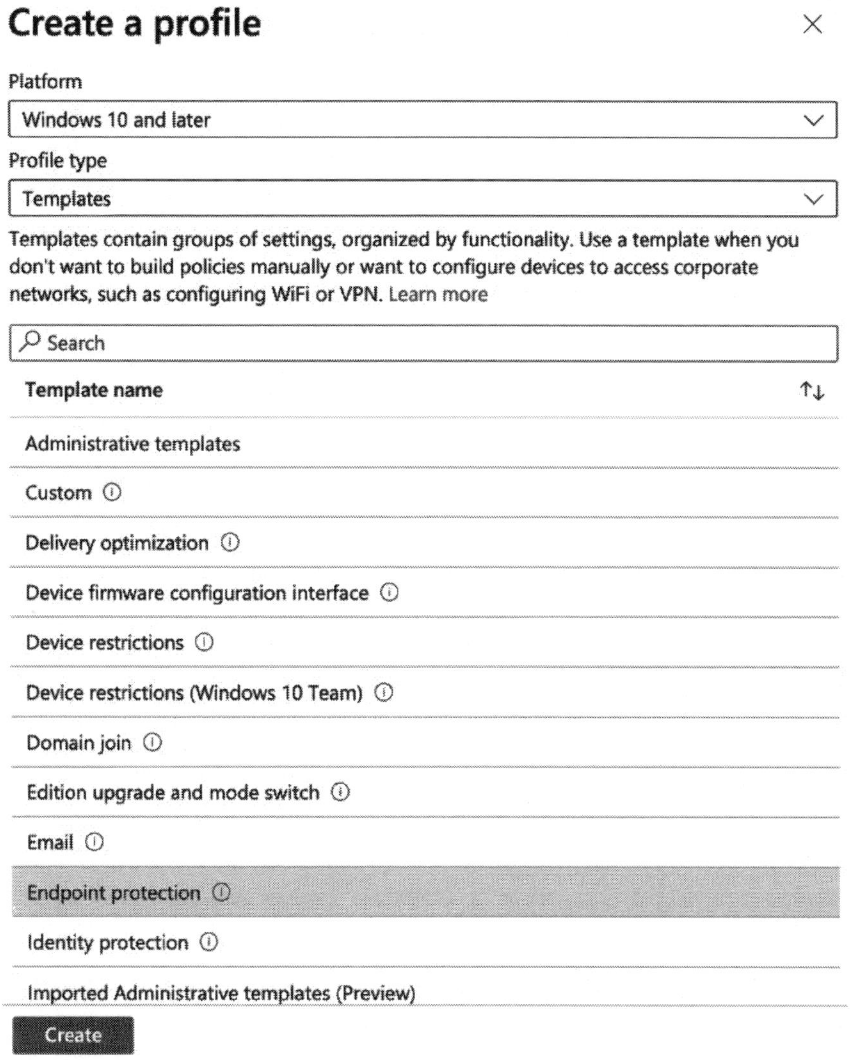

Create a profile   ✕

Platform

| Windows 10 and later | ⌄ |

Profile type

| Templates | ⌄ |

Templates contain groups of settings, organized by functionality. Use a template when you don't want to build policies manually or want to configure devices to access corporate networks, such as configuring WiFi or VPN. Learn more

🔍 Search

Template name	↑↓
Administrative templates	
Custom ⓘ	
Delivery optimization ⓘ	
Device firmware configuration interface ⓘ	
Device restrictions ⓘ	
Device restrictions (Windows 10 Team) ⓘ	
Domain join ⓘ	
Edition upgrade and mode switch ⓘ	
Email ⓘ	
Endpoint protection ⓘ	
Identity protection ⓘ	
Imported Administrative templates (Preview)	

Create

Figure 7.23: Creating a profile

2. Scroll down to **Microsoft Defender Application Guard**, choose your preferred settings for **Application Guard**, and click **Next**:

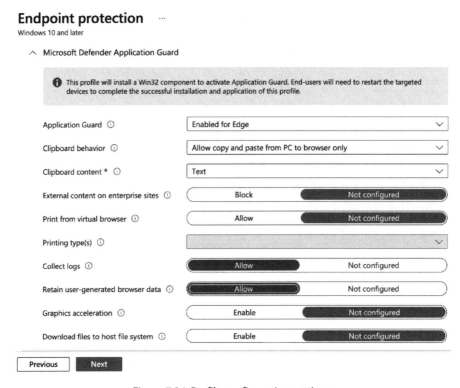

Figure 7.24: Profile configuration settings

3. Follow the wizard through; choose the edition or version of Windows that you wish to apply the profile to and click **Create**. Your new profile will appear as shown in the following screenshot:

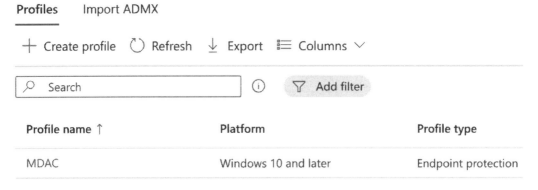

Figure 7.25: Profile overview

You can monitor your Microsoft Defender Application Control profile from the **Monitor** section on the left-hand side of the profile.

Configuring Microsoft Defender Exploit Guard

Microsoft Defender Exploit Guard provides intrusion detection capabilities in Windows. You can use Microsoft Defender Exploit Guard to protect your apps and reduce the attack surface of your apps. This can be achieved by using rules designed to prevent malware attacks.

You can also use Microsoft Defender Exploit Guard to protect your users against social engineering attacks by using Microsoft Defender SmartScreen within Microsoft Edge. Additionally, you can use **Controlled** folder access to protect files within your system folders to prevent them from being changed by malicious actors.

As with Application Control, Microsoft Defender Exploit Guard can be enabled and deployed using the same method shown for Application Control; the available configuration settings are as follows:

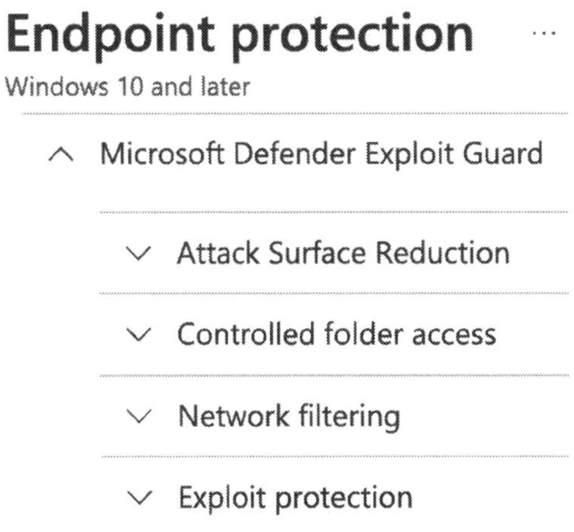

Endpoint protection   ⋯
Windows 10 and later

∧   Microsoft Defender Exploit Guard

∨   Attack Surface Reduction

∨   Controlled folder access

∨   Network filtering

∨   Exploit protection

Figure 7.26: Microsoft Defender Exploit Guard

There are several configuration settings that can be applied to your devices for Microsoft Defender Application Guard, Microsoft Defender Application Control, and Microsoft Defender Exploit Guard. You will find links to articles on how you can configure these features in the *Further reading* section at the end of this chapter.

Encrypting your Windows devices using BitLocker

In the modern IT landscape, it is more crucial than ever to protect your organization's devices against data theft in case a device is stolen or lost. **BitLocker** is a feature that can be used to address this by encrypting Windows devices.

BitLocker Drive Encryption provides integrated data protection features for your Windows devices to combat the threat of stolen, lost, or poorly decommissioned Windows devices. BitLocker is most effective when used with **Trusted Platform Module (TPM)** version 1.2 or later. However, it also works on computers that do not have TPM version 1.2 or later by using a USB startup key instead. You can also apply a form of multi-factor authentication with BitLocker with the ability to block device startup until one of the following responses has been provided:

- A user PIN

- A removable device that contains a startup key

These methods help to ensure that the device does not start until the appropriate prompt has been issued and the response to it is valid.

So, how is BitLocker configured? It can be deployed to devices using either Group Policy or Microsoft Intune. For deployment via Intune, create a profile by performing the following steps:

1. Go to https://intune.microsoft.com and navigate to **Device Configuration | Profiles | Create Profile**. Select **Windows 10 and later** as the **Platform**, and **Templates** as the **Profile type**. Choose **Endpoint protection** from the list of templates and click **Create**. Then, scroll down to **Windows Encryption**, choose your preferred settings for BitLocker, and click **Next**:

Endpoint protection ...
Windows 10 and later

| ∨ Microsoft Defender Application Guard |
| ∨ Microsoft Defender Firewall |
| ∨ Microsoft Defender SmartScreen |
| ∧ Windows Encryption |

Windows Settings ⓘ

| Encrypt devices ⓘ | Require | Not configured |
| Encrypt storage card (mobile only) ⓘ | Require | Not configured |

BitLocker base settings ⓘ

Warning for other disk encryption ⓘ	Block	Not configured
Allow standard users to enable encryption during Azure AD Join ⓘ	Allow	Not configured
Configure encryption methods ⓘ	Enable	Not configured

[Previous] [Next]

Figure 7.27: Creating a profile

2. Follow the wizard through to select OS versions and device assignments and click **Create**.

    There are many options to encrypt your Windows devices available in this section, and how you choose to configure these will depend on the security requirements of your organization.

3. Once you have configured the required settings for your BitLocker policy, click on **OK**, then **OK** again, and finally, click on **Create**.

BitLocker will now be deployed to your targeted devices. You can now monitor device and user status from within Intune to ensure that all required devices have the appropriate BitLocker data encryption settings applied.

To recap, BitLocker protects your Windows devices against loss or theft by ensuring that the devices are encrypted by settings that can be deployed by either Group Policy or Microsoft Intune.

Next, we examine application protection policies.

Implementing application protection policies

You cannot use BitLocker to configure and manage non-Windows device encryption. Instead, you need to use **application protection policies**. This approach comprises rules that ensure data safety within a managed app. This is done through the configuration of **Mobile Application Management** (**MAM**) policies in Microsoft Intune.

App protection policies may be configured for apps running on devices that are enrolled either in Microsoft Intune or in a third-party MDM solution. These devices are typically corporate-owned but personal devices can also be enrolled.

To create an app protection policy, go to the Intune admin center, browse to **Apps | App Protection policies**, and choose **Create policy**. The options available are shown in the following screenshot:

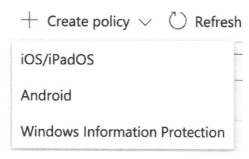

Figure 7.28: Policy creation options

As there are many different ways you can configure app protection policies, and three OS platforms you can choose from, listing instructions or examples here would be exhaustive. Therefore, please review the *Further reading* section at the end of this chapter, where you will find a link to app protection policies.

> **Note**
>
> Microsoft has announced the discontinuation of Windows Information Protection. They advise using Microsoft Purview Information Protection and Microsoft Purview Data Loss Prevention instead. These are topics that will be covered in *Chapters 11* and *12*.

In this section, you learned that application protection policies in Microsoft Intune can be used to protect non-Windows devices that cannot be encrypted with Windows encryption technology such as BitLocker.

Summary

In this chapter, we examined how MDE can be used to protect your organization's devices. You learned how to plan your MDE implementation by being aware of the licensing requirements and compatible operating systems, how to create your MDE instance, and how to manage and monitor the service. We also examined Microsoft Defender Application Guard and Microsoft Defender Exploit Guard, and learned about how these features can complement the core features and can be deployed by different methods, including System Center Configuration Manager, Group Policy, and Microsoft Intune. Finally, we explored how BitLocker can apply data protection and encryption to your Windows devices in order to safeguard them from loss, theft, or poor decommissioning practices, and how application protection policies can be used to protect non-Windows devices.

The next chapter will discuss message protection with **Microsoft Defender for Office 365**. You will learn how you can protect your emails in Exchange Online and apply anti-spoofing and anti-impersonation settings and anti-spam and anti-malware policies. You will also learn how to configure safe attachments and safe links within the Microsoft 365 security center.

Questions

1. Which of the following is not one of the features of MDE?

    A. Attack surface reduction

    B. Next-generation protection

    C. File encryption

    D. Endpoint detection and response

    E. Automated investigation and remediation

2. True or false? Microsoft Defender Application Guard can be used with the Google Chrome browser.

    A. True

    B. False

3. Which of the following URLs can be directly used to access device configuration profiles?

    A. `admin.microsoft.com`

    B. `endpoint.microsoft.com`

    C. `compliance.microsoft.com`

    D. `portal.azure.com`

4. Which template type do you need to configure to create a BitLocker deployment policy?

    A. Network boundary

    B. Endpoint protection

    C. Identity protection

    D. Trusted certificate

    E. Domain join

5. Where would you go on a Windows device to enable Microsoft Defender Application Guard?

    A. **Control Panel | Windows Features**

    B. **Access work or school**

    C. **Settings**

    D. **Control Panel | Application Guard**

6. True or false? macOS devices cannot be onboarded to MDE via the use of a local script.

    A. True

    B. False

7. Which of the following is not a feature of Microsoft Defender Vulnerability Management?

    A. Real-time EDR insights correlated with endpoint vulnerabilities

    B. Built-in remediation processes with Intune and Configuration Manager

    C. Protection updates that leverage machine learning, human and automated big data analysis, and comprehensive threat resistance research

    D. Device vulnerability context during incident investigations

8. Which of the following is not an option in Microsoft Defender Application Guard?

    A. Trusted websites

    B. Trusted WAN interfaces

    C. Trusted internal networks

    D. Trusted cloud resources

9. True or false? You can download a package to manually onboard a limited number of machines to MDE.

    A. True

    B. False

10. BitLocker supports a form of multi-factor authentication that includes which of the following methods (choose two)?

    A. Security questions

    B. A user PIN

    C. A text message

    D. A removable device that contains a startup key

Further reading

Please refer to the following links for more information:

- MDE: `https://learn.microsoft.com/en-us/microsoft-365/security/defender-endpoint/microsoft-defender-endpoint?view=o365-worldwide`

- Onboarding devices: `https://learn.microsoft.com/en-au/microsoft-365/security/defender-endpoint/onboard-configure?WT.mc_id=EM-MVP-4039827&view=o365-worldwide`:

    - Onboarding Windows clients: `https://learn.microsoft.com/en-au/microsoft-365/security/defender-endpoint/onboard-windows-client?view=o365-worldwide`

    - Onboarding Windows servers: `https://learn.microsoft.com/en-au/microsoft-365/security/defender-endpoint/onboard-windows-server?view=o365-worldwide`

    - Onboarding non-Windows devices: `https://learn.microsoft.com/en-au/microsoft-365/security/defender-endpoint/configure-endpoints-non-windows?view=o365-worldwide`

- Onboarding for Mac: `https://learn.microsoft.com/en-au/microsoft-365/security/defender-endpoint/microsoft-defender-endpoint-mac?view=o365-worldwide`

- Onboarding for Linux: `https://learn.microsoft.com/en-au/microsoft-365/security/defender-endpoint/microsoft-defender-endpoint-linux?view=o365-worldwide`

- General settings: `https://learn.microsoft.com/en-us/microsoft-365/security/defender-endpoint/preferences-setup?view=o365-worldwide`

- Configuring attack surface reduction: `https://learn.microsoft.com/en-us/microsoft-365/security/defender-endpoint/overview-attack-surface-reduction?view=o365-worldwide`

- Microsoft Defender Application Guard: `https://learn.microsoft.com/en-us/windows/security/threat-protection/microsoft-defender-application-guard/md-app-guard-overview`

- Microsoft Defender Exploit Guard: `https://www.microsoft.com/ security/blog/2017/10/23/windows-defender-exploit-guard-reduce-the-attack-surface-against-next-generation-malware/`

- BitLocker Encryption: `https://learn.microsoft.com/en-us/windows/security/information-protection/bitlocker/bitlocker-overview`

- How to create and assign app protection policies: `https://learn.microsoft.com/en-us/mem/intune/apps/app-protection-policies`

- App protection policies overview: `https://learn.microsoft.com/en-us/mem/intune/apps/app-protection-policy?WT.mc_id=EM-MVP-4039827`

8

Configuring Microsoft Defender for Office 365

Even with the ascendance of Microsoft Teams, **Exchange Online** remains one of the core features of the Microsoft 365 platform. The majority of businesses with a Microsoft 365 tenant rely heavily on email as one of their primary methods of communication, both internally and with customers, suppliers, and other external correspondents. In the ever-changing security landscape where attackers are becoming more sophisticated and more determined to cause chaos and disruption, it is crucial to provide as much protection to your users as possible when they are using Exchange Online for their emails. **Microsoft Defender for Office 365** addresses this requirement.

Microsoft Defender for Office 365 is a cloud-based email filtering service designed to safeguard your organization and protect you from threats within emails, links, and even collaboration tools such as Microsoft Teams. Microsoft Defender for Office 365 includes extensive reporting and URL trace capabilities that provide administrators insight into the types of attacks that may threaten your organization.

In this chapter, you will learn the steps required to implement and manage Microsoft Defender for Office 365 under the following topics:

- Protecting users and domains with anti-phishing protection and policies
- Configuring Safe Attachments options and policies
- Configuring Safe Links options, blocked **Uniform Resource Locators** (**URLs**), and policies
- Monitoring and remediating with Microsoft Defender for Office 365 reports
- Running simulated attacks with Microsoft Defender for Office 365
- Further attack simulation configuration policies

Protecting users and domains with anti-phishing protection and policies

Phishing is a practice utilized by malicious actors to trick email users into revealing personal or sensitive information, such as passwords or credit card numbers. Phishing is a form of what is known as **social engineering**. In this type of attack, emails are sent by what appear to be genuine and reputable email domains from well-known and trusted organizations, but in fact originate from malicious sources.

It is extremely difficult to prevent phishing attacks, as the average email user is not trained to look for clues and signs that would alert trained IT professionals that an email is not genuine. Educating your users on the principles of phishing and what they need to be aware of is certainly a good start in trying to minimize phishing attacks within your environment. However, education alone is not enough, and this is where Microsoft Defender for Office 365 comes in.

Microsoft Defender for Office 365 includes **anti-phishing protection**. Anti-phishing policies can be set up by organization management administrators or security administrators to protect your Exchange Online email domains and users from malicious, impersonation-based, phishing attacks.

Microsoft Defender for Office 365 is available in the form of the following Microsoft 365 subscriptions:

- **Microsoft Defender for Office 365 Plan 1**, included as part of Microsoft 365 Business Premium
- **Microsoft Defender for Office 365 Plan 2**, included as part of Office 365 E5, Office 365 A5, and Microsoft 365 E5

Microsoft Defender for Office 365 Plan 1 and Defender for Office 365 Plan 2 are also both available as an add-ons for certain subscriptions.

Anti-phishing protection and policies are included in all these licenses and can be configured from the Microsoft 365 Defender portal, which can be accessed at `https://security.microsoft.com`.

We will now take a look at how to set up an anti-phishing policy in the security center.

Setting up an anti-phishing policy

Configuring an anti-phishing policy is crucial for protecting your domains and users against phishing attacks. To do this, take the following steps:

1. Go to the Microsoft 365 Defender portal at `https://security.microsoft.com`, which is shown as follows:

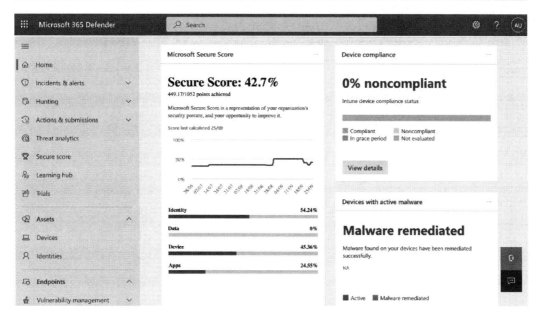

Figure 8.1: Microsoft 365 Defender portal

2. Navigate to **Policies | Email & collaboration | Policies & rules**:

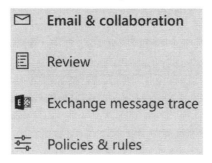

Figure 8.2: Policies & rules

3. Next, select **Threat policies | Anti-phishing**, or you can navigate straight to `https://security.microsoft.com/antiphishing`. You will now see the following page:

Anti-phishing

By default, Microsoft 365 includes built-in features that help protect your users from phishing attacks. Set up anti-phishing polices to increase this protection. For example, you can refining the settings to better detect and prevent impersonation and spoofing attacks. The default policy applies to all users within the organization. You can create custom, higher priority policies for specific users, groups or domains. Learn more about anti-phishing policies

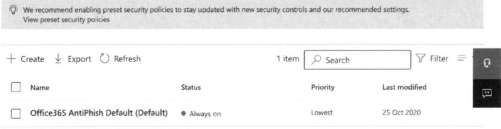

Figure 8.3: Anti-phishing policy section

4.   Click on **Create** to set up a new policy. This takes you to the policy setup wizard. Enter a **Name** and **Description** for your policy and click **Next**. In this instance, we are creating a policy to protect our email domains:

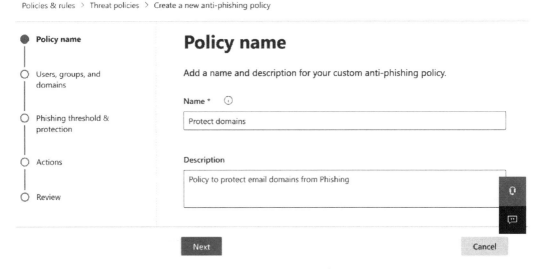

Figure 8.4: Naming your policy

5.   This takes you to the **Users, groups, and domains** screen, where you can add the ones that you wish to protect. For this example, select a domain(s) that you wish to protect. You also have the option to explicitly exclude users, groups, and domains if applicable. Once you have made your selections, click **Next**:

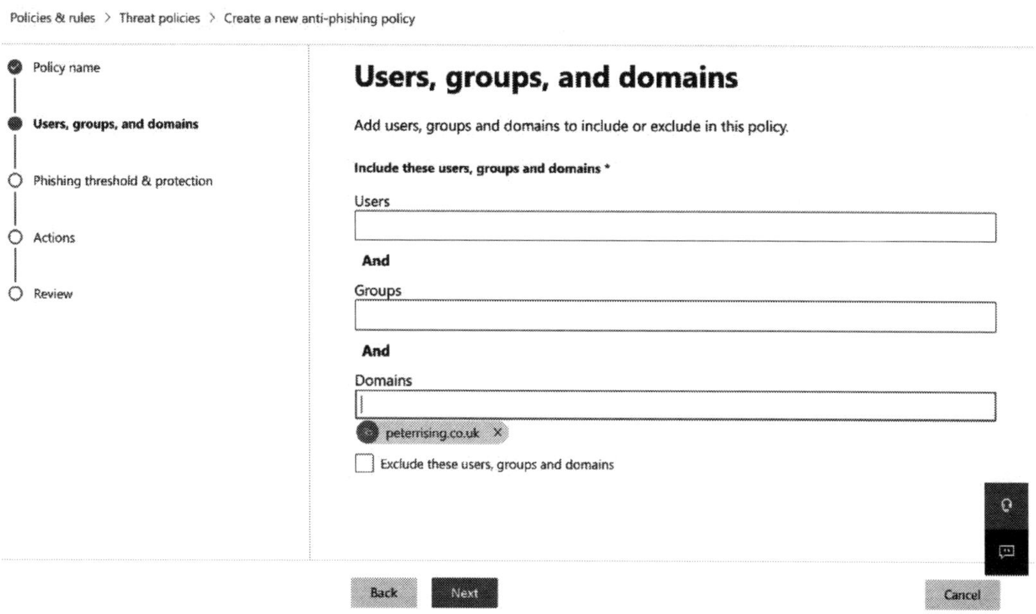

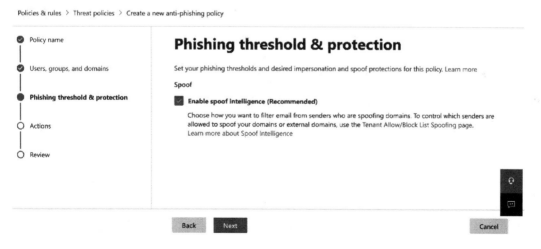

Figure 8.5: Adding a domain to protect

6. In the **Phishing threshold & protection** section, choose **Enable spoof intelligence (Recommended)**. Before you proceed further through the wizard, you may wish to fine-tune how you wish to filter email from senders who are spoofing domains. To do this, click on the link to the **Tenant Allow/Block List Spoofing** page:

Policies & rules > Threat policies > Create a new anti-phishing policy

✓ Policy name	# Phishing threshold & protection
✓ Users, groups, and domains	Set your phishing thresholds and desired impersonation and spoof protections for this policy. Learn more
● Phishing threshold & protection	Spoof
	☑ Enable spoof intelligence (Recommended)
○ Actions	Choose how you want to filter email from senders who are spoofing domains. To control which senders are allowed to spoof your domains or external domains, use the Tenant Allow/Block List Spoofing page. Learn more about Spoof Intelligence
○ Review	

Back   Next   Cancel

Figure 8.6: Enabling spoof intelligence

7. Here, you can see a list of **Spoofed senders**. Add your own domain pairs here or access the other tabs to block any domains and email addresses, URLs, and files as needed. You may also click **View spoofing activity**:

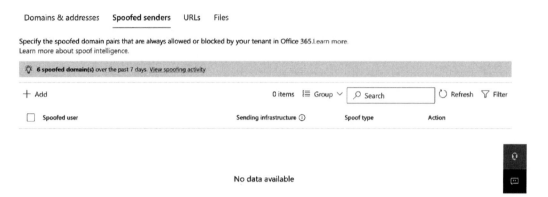

Figure 8.7: Tenant Allow/Block Lists

The **Spoof Intelligence Insight** page shows you a list of suspicious domains. Review and export this list:

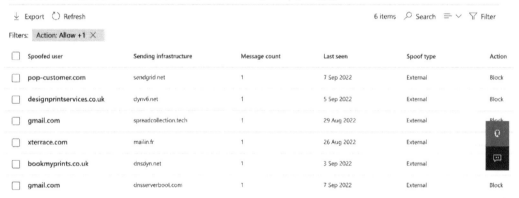

Figure 8.8: Spoof Intelligence Insight page

8. Having reviewed the spoof intelligence settings, return to the setup wizard shown in *Figure 8.6* and click **Next**. You will now see the **Actions** page, as shown in the following figure:

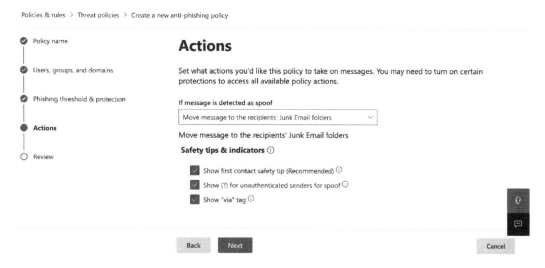

Figure 8.9: Select policy actions

9. There are two spoof detection options. For this example, choose the default option, **Move message to the recipients' Junk Email folders**, and click **Next**:

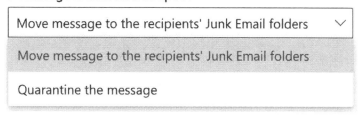

Figure 8.10: Spoof detection options

Note that if you select the **Quarantine** option, the message will be sent to a central quarantine area; for more information, refer to the *Further reading* section at the end of this chapter.

10. Review the settings you have configured for your policy and click **Submit**:

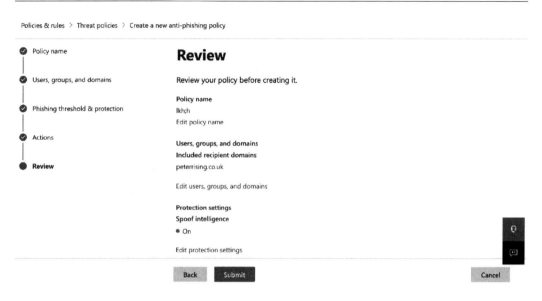

Figure 8.11 – Review policy settings

11. The policy is now created and is visible on the **Anti-phishing** policy page.

Anti-phishing

By default, Microsoft 365 includes built-in features that help protect your users from phishing attacks. Set up anti-phishing polices to increase this protection. For example, you can refining the settings to better detect and prevent impersonation and spoofing attacks. The default policy applies to all users within the organization. You can create custom, higher priority policies for specific users, groups or domains. Learn more about anti-phishing policies

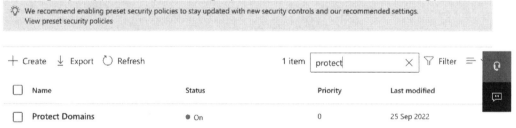

Figure 8.12: New policy created and visible on the Anti-phishing policy page

In this section, we learned how to configure an anti-phishing policy for our domains and users in Microsoft 365. Next, we will look at how to configure options for Safe Attachments policies.

Configuring Safe Attachments options and policies

Safe Attachments is a Microsoft Defender for Office 365 feature that allows you to protect your users from opening attachments that may contain malicious code. This works through the use of a virtual environment that Safe Attachments uses to check the attachments in inbound emails. This takes place after the attachment has been scanned by Exchange Online anti-malware protection. Safe Attachments policies are configured either in the Microsoft 365 Defender portal or in PowerShell.

A Safe Attachments policy comprises the following:

- **Safe Attachments policy**: Defines and sets actions for unknown malware detection and can be set to send messages with malware attachments to a specific email address. The policy will also determine whether to deliver messages if attachment scanning cannot be completed.

- **Safe Attachments rule**: Defines the priority and filters to which recipients the policy will apply.

In this section, we will learn how to manage Safe Attachments by setting up policies in the Microsoft 365 Defender portal and by using Windows PowerShell.

Creating a Safe Attachments policy

To create a Safe Attachments policy, you must be a member of one of the following role groups:

- Organization Management
- Security Administrator

Next, complete the following steps:

1. From the Microsoft 365 Defender portal at `https://security.microsoft.com`, navigate to **Policies & Rules** | **Threat policies** | **Policies** | **Safe attachments**. This will show you the following screen:

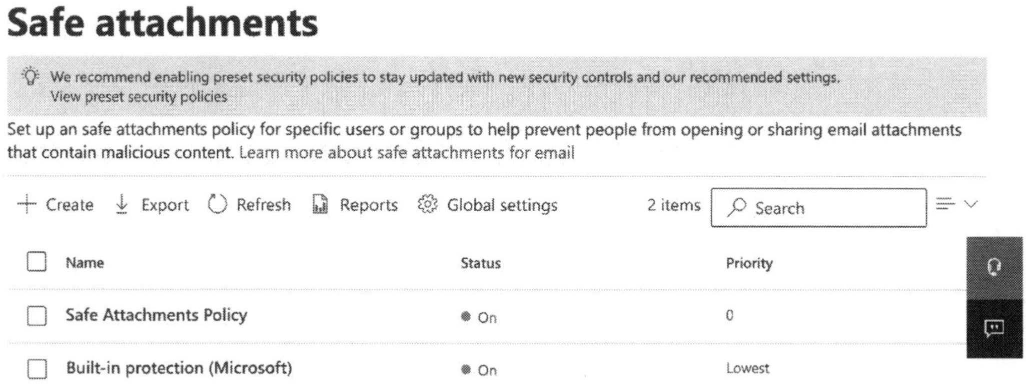

Figure 8.13: Safe attachments

2. Click on **Global settings** on the main toolbar to configure settings to protect files in SharePoint, OneDrive, and Microsoft Teams. You can also help users to stay safe when trusting a file to open outside of the protected view in Office applications:

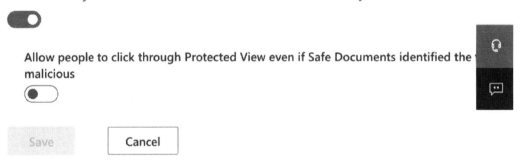

Global settings   ✕

Use this page to protect your organization from malicious content in email attachments and files in SharePoint, OneDrive, and Microsoft Teams.

Protect files in SharePoint, OneDrive, and Microsoft Teams

If a file in any SharePoint, OneDrive, or Microsoft Teams library is identified as malicious, Safe Attachments will prevent users from opening and downloading the file. Learn more

Turn on Defender for Office 365 for SharePoint, OneDrive, and Microsoft Teams

Help people stay safe when trusting a file to open outside Protected View in Office applications.

Before a user is allowed to trust a file opened in a supported version of Office, the file will be verified by Microsoft Defender for Endpoint. Learn more about Safe Documents.

Turn on Safe Documents for Office clients. Only available with *Microsoft 365 E5* **or** *Microsoft 365 E5 Security* license. Learn more about how Microsoft handles your data.

Allow people to click through Protected View even if Safe Documents identified the **malicious**

Save   Cancel

Figure 8.14: Global settings for Safe Attachments

The **Built-in protection (Microsoft)** policy contains preset security policies that are applied to all users in your organization. This policy may not be edited:

Built-in protection (Microsoft)

● Policy on | Priority Lowest

☐ View preset security policies

Description   ⌃

Built-in Microsoft Office 365 security applied to all users in your organization to protect against malicious links and attachments.

Note: Built-in protection is enabled only for paid Microsoft Defender for Office 365 tenants.

Learn more about built-in protection

Exclude from built-in protection   ⌃

Figure 8.15: Preset security policy

You can, however, choose to create your own policy for Safe Attachments or edit one that you have previously created.

3. For this instance, create a new Safe Attachments policy by clicking **Create**. Enter a **Name** and **Description** for your policy and click **Next**:

Policies & rules › Threat policies › Create Safe Attachments policy

● Name your policy

○ Users and domains

○ Settings

○ Review

Name your policy

Name *

| Org-Wide Safe Attachments policy |

Description

This is the default policy for Safe Attachments for all users, groups, and domains in the organization

[Next]   [Cancel]

Figure 8.16: Create a new Safe Attachments policy

4. Enter the names of the required **Users**, **Groups**, and **Domains** for the policy and click **Next**:

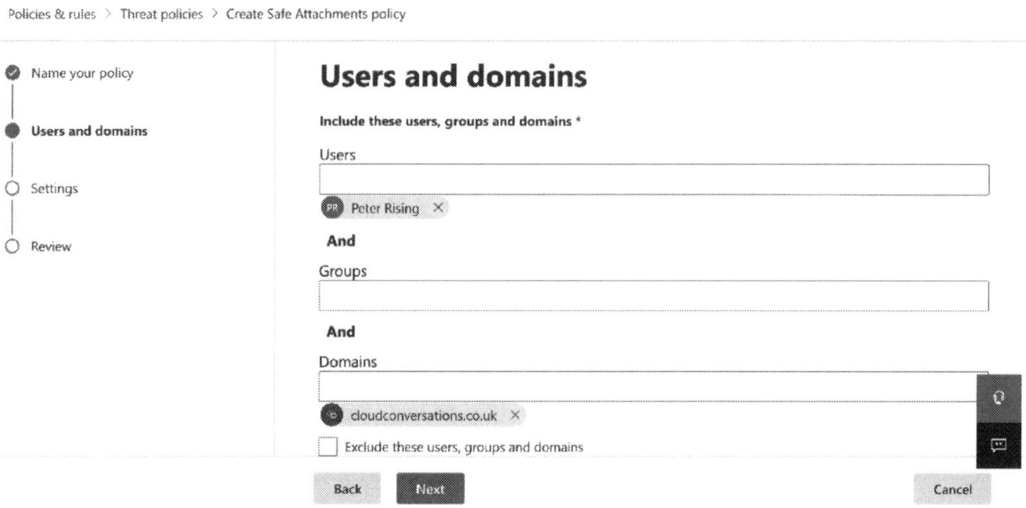

Policies & rules > Threat policies > Create Safe Attachments policy

✓ Name your policy	**Users and domains**
● **Users and domains**	Include these users, groups and domains *
○ Settings	Users
○ Review	

PR Peter Rising ✕

And

Groups

And

Domains

🌐 cloudconversations.co.uk ✕

☐ Exclude these users, groups and domains

Back   Next   Cancel

Figure 8.17: Set users, groups, and domains for the policy

5. Now you need to choose the action you wish the policy to take for unknown malware in attachments. There are five options to choose from, based on your preference. For this example, select **Dynamic Delivery (Preview messages)**:

Safe Attachments unknown malware response

Select the action for unknown malware in attachments. Learn more

Warning

- **Monitor**, **Replace** and **Block** actions might cause a significant delay in message delivery.Learn more
- **Dynamic Delivery** is only available for recipients with hosted mailboxes.Learn more
- For **Block**, **Replace**, or **Dynamic Delivery**, messages with detected attachments are quarantined and can only be released by an admin.

○ Off - Attachments will not be scanned by Safe Attachments.

○ Monitor - Deliver the message if malware is detected and track scanning results.

○ Block - Block current and future messages and attachments with detected malware.

○ Replace - Block attachments with detected malware, but deliver the message.

◉ Dynamic Delivery (Preview messages) - Immediately deliver the message without attachments. Reattach files after scanning is complete.

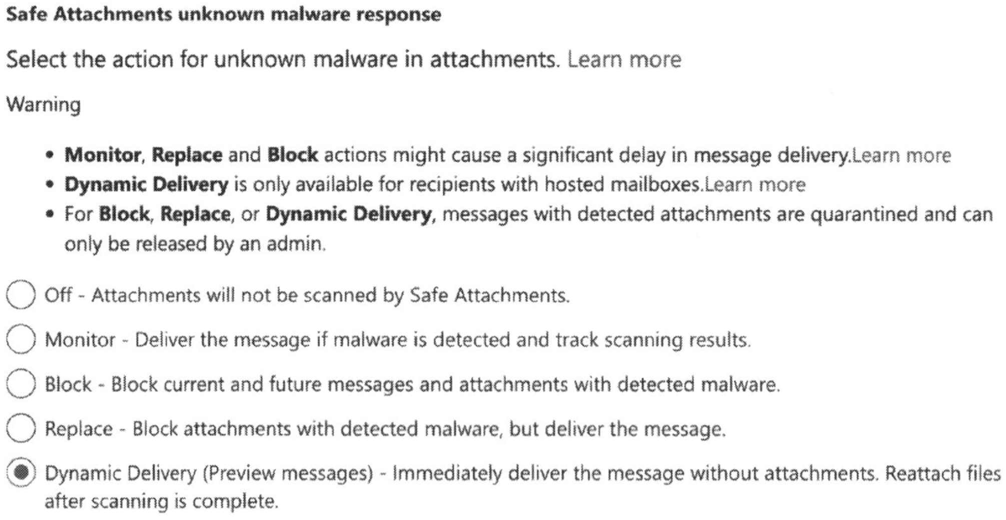

Figure 8.18: Setting the Safe Attachments delivery method

This selection will deliver the message to the recipient immediately, without the attachment. This option is designed to minimize the delivery time. When the user opens the email and clicks the attachment placeholder, the attachment will be detonated and tested in an isolated manner and delivered if safe. Other options include **Off**, **Monitor**, **Block** and **Replace**. For more details on these options, refer to the *Further reading* section at the end of this chapter.

6. Scroll down and select the **Quarantine**, **Redirect**, and **Safe Attachments detection response** to your policy, then click **Next**:

Quarantine policy

| AdminOnlyAccessPolicy   ⌄ |

Permission to release quarantined messages will be ignored for messages with malware detected and we will fall back to release request instead

Redirect messages with detected attachments

☑ Enable redirect ⓘ

Send messages that contain blocked, monitored, or replaced attachments to the specified email address.

| James.smith@peterrising.co.uk   🎧 |

☑ Apply the Safe Attachments detection response if scanning can't complete (timeout or errors).

Back   Next   Cancel

Figure 8.19: Attachment quarantine and redirection options

7. Review the settings you have selected for your policy and click **Submit**:

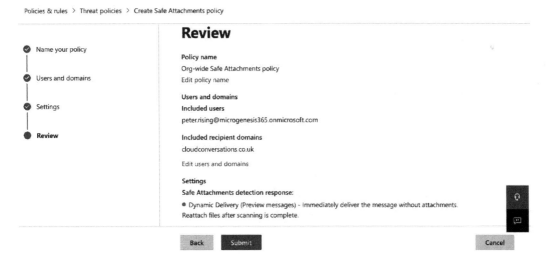

Policies & rules > Threat policies > Create Safe Attachments policy

Review

✓ Name your policy

✓ Users and domains

✓ Settings

● **Review**

Policy name
Org-wide Safe Attachments policy
Edit policy name

Users and domains
Included users
peter.rising@microgenesis365.onmicrosoft.com

Included recipient domains
cloudconversations.co.uk

Edit users and domains

Settings
Safe Attachments detection response:
● Dynamic Delivery (Preview messages) - Immediately deliver the message without attachments. Reattach files after scanning is complete.

Back   Submit   Cancel

Figure 8.20: Review policy settings and submit

The policy will now be visible in the list of Safe Attachments policies and will begin to take effect.

The following section presents some PowerShell commands that can be used to create a Safe Attachments policy.

Creating a Safe Attachments policy using Windows PowerShell

Safe Attachments policies may also be configured with the following PowerShell commands once connected to Exchange Online PowerShell:

- `Get-SafeAttachmentPolicy`: Use this command to examine the Safe Attachments policy settings
- `Set-SafeAttachmentPolicy`: Use this command to modify the existing Safe Attachments policy settings
- `New-SafeAttachmentPolicy`: Use this command to set up an entirely new and custom Safe Attachments policy
- `Remove-SafeAttachmentPolicy`: Use this command to remove any custom Safe Attachments policies you may have configured

You may also apply rules to your Safe Attachments policies using PowerShell. A rule defines the conditions, and a policy defines the actions. The following PowerShell commands are available for Safe Attachments rules:

- `Get-SafeAttachmentRule`: Use this command to examine the Safe Attachments rule settings
- `Set-SafeAttachmentRule`: Use this command to modify the current Safe Attachments rule settings
- `New-SafeAttachmentRule`: Use this command to set up an entirely new and custom Safe Attachments rule
- `Remove-SafeAttachmentRule`: Use this command to remove any custom Safe Attachments rules you may have configured

In this section, we discussed how to configure Safe Attachments using the Microsoft 365 Defender portal and Exchange Online PowerShell. We also learned that Safe Attachments policies can be created and applied for your Microsoft 365 users, groups, and domains, and that rules, conditions, and exceptions may be applied to these policies.

Next, we will see how the Safe Links feature can be used to protect your Microsoft 365 users from suspicious links within emails and within Microsoft Office applications.

Configuring Safe Links options, blocked URLs, and policies

Safe Links is a feature that allows you to protect your users from links they receive that may contain malicious code. You can manage Safe Links in Microsoft 365 by setting up a **Safe Links policy** that will be targeted to specific users, groups, or domains. Safe Links policies can be managed both in the Microsoft 365 Defender portal and by using Windows PowerShell.

Creating a new Safe Links policy

To create a new Safe Links policy, complete the following steps:

1. From the Microsoft 365 Defender portal at `https://security.microsoft.com`, navigate to **Policies & Rules | Threat policies | Policies | Safe links**. This will show you the following screen:

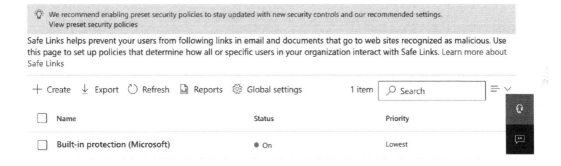

Figure 8.21: Safe links

2. You will again see that there is a built-in protection policy that applies to the entire organization, and you can also once again view **Global settings**. For this example, however, create a new policy by clicking **Create**:

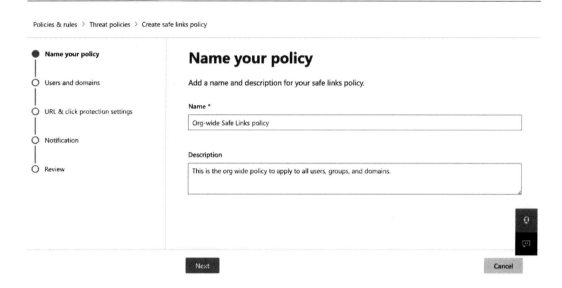

Figure 8.22: Creating a Safe Links policy

3. Next, set the **Users**, **Groups**, and **Domains** you wish to include in the Safe Links policy and click **Next**:

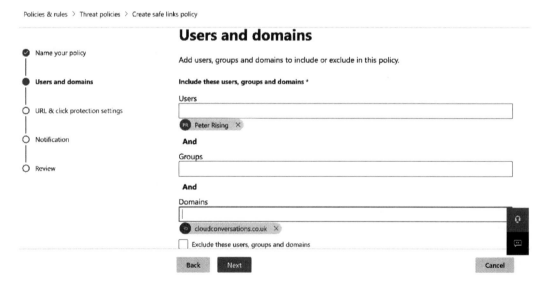

Figure 8.23: Configure Users, Groups, and Domains

4. On the **URL & click protection settings** page, set your preferred settings for **Email**, shown as follows, where settings for Safe Links are set to **On: Safe Links checks a list of known, malicious links when users click links in an email. URLs are rewritten by default** and **Apply Safe Links to email messages sent within the organization**. The other checkbox options listed can be configured as per organizational policy or preference:

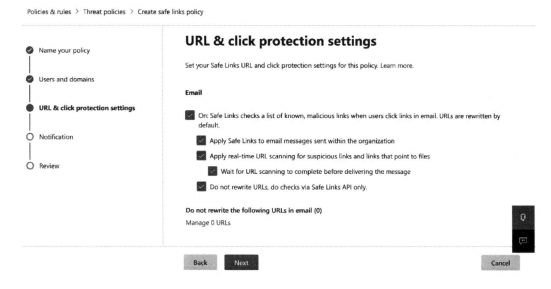

Figure 8.24: Safe Links email settings

5. Scroll down and select your required settings for **Teams**, **Office 365 Apps**, and **Click protection settings** and click **Next**:

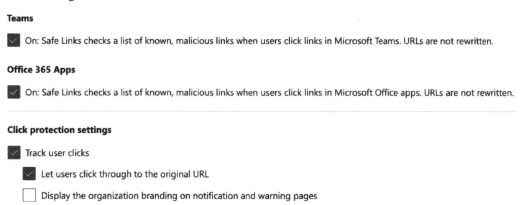

Figure 8.25: Safe Links Teams, Office 365 Apps, and Click protection settings

6. Under **Notification**, select **Use the default notification text** that will be sent to users if there is a policy match. Alternatively, you can select **Use custom notification text** and enter custom text of your own. Once you've selected your preferred setting, click **Next**:

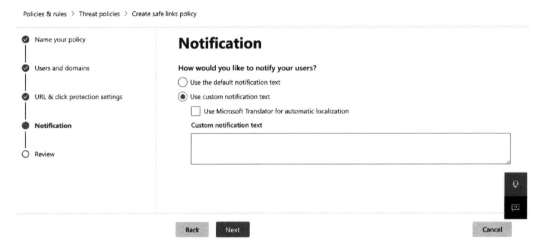

Figure 8.26: Safe Links notification settings

7. Finally, review and verify the policy settings you have chosen and, once you're satisfied, click **Submit**:

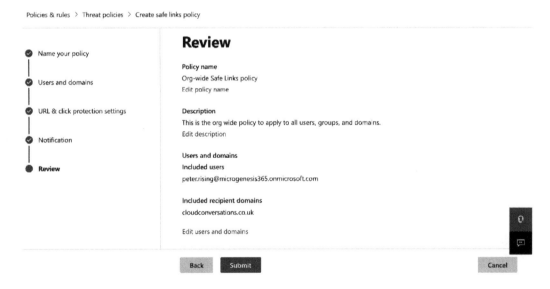

Figure 8.27: Safe Links policy settings

The Safe Links policy is now created and will start to take effect.

The following section details some of the PowerShell commands that can be used to create a Safe Links policy.

Creating a Safe Links policy using Windows PowerShell

Safe Links policies may also be configured with the following PowerShell commands, which can be executed when you are connected to Exchange Online PowerShell:

- `Get-SafeLinksPolicy`: View Safe Links policy settings
- `Set-SafeLinksPolicy`: Edit existing Safe Links policy settings
- `New-SafeLinksPolicy`: Create a custom Safe Links policy
- `Remove-SafeLinksPolicy`: Delete a custom Safe Links policy

In the same manner as Safe Attachments, you may also apply rules to your Safe Links policies using PowerShell. Once again, the rule defines the conditions, and the policy defines the actions. The following PowerShell commands are available for Safe Links rules:

- `Get-SafeLinksRule`: View Safe Links rule settings
- `Set-SafeLinksRule`: Edit existing Safe Links rule settings
- `New-SafelinksRule`: Create a custom Safe Links rule
- `Remove-SafelinksRule`: Delete a custom Safe Links rule

This section covered Safe Links in Microsoft Defender for Office 365. We learned about the built-in Safe Links policy that will apply to all users in your tenant, and that new Safe Links policies can be created with more customized settings and applied to specific users, groups, and domains. In addition, we learned that we can manage Safe Links by using the Microsoft 365 Defender portal as well as by connecting to the Exchange Online PowerShell tool.

Next, we will examine the monitoring and remediation options available with Microsoft Defender for Office 365 reports.

Monitoring and remediating with Microsoft Defender for Office 365 reports

With Microsoft Defender for Office 365, you can access a selection of security-related reports. To view and use these reports, you need to be a member of one of the following role groups:

- Organization Management
- Security Administrator

- Security Reader

- Global Reader

You can then view and download the reports from the Microsoft 365 Defender portal as follows:

1. Go to `https://security.microsoft.com` and navigate to **Reports | Email & collaboration | Email & collaboration reports** or access it directly via `https://security. microsoft.com/emailandcollabreport`:

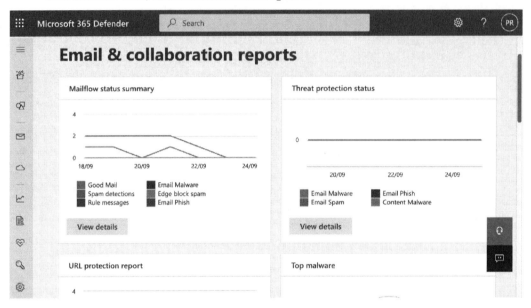

Figure 8.28: Email & collaboration reports

2. Click on **View details** to view any report, as per the example of the Mailflow status summary report that follows:

Mailflow status report

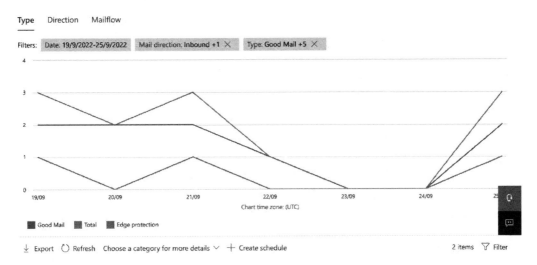

Figure 8.29: Mailflow status report

From here, you can export the details to a `.csv` file, break down the report by specific category, or even create custom schedules to run the report. Such a custom schedule will result in that report being available for download from `https://security.microsoft.com/ReportsForDownload?viewid=custom`. Some of the reports that you may find available in this location are as follows:

- Mailflow status summary

- Threat protection status

- URL protection report

- Top malware

- Spoof detections

- Compromised users

- Mail latency report

- User-reported messages

- Submissions

- Top senders and recipients

It is also possible to acquire reports using PowerShell. A sample command for running one of these reports (specifically the **Top senders and recipients** report) is as follows:

```
Get-MailTrafficSummaryReport -Category TopSpamRecipient -StartDate
06/13/2022 -EndDate 06/15/2022
```

When executed, this command will return the top spam recipient statistics between June 13, 2022 and June 15, 2022. For in-depth information on the available reports and commands, please refer to the *Further reading* section in this chapter.

In the next section of this chapter, we will examine the option to test the users in your organization with simulated attacks.

Running simulated attacks with Microsoft Defender for Office 365

One of the great features available to global and security administrators with Microsoft 365 E5 or Microsoft Defender for Office 365 Plan 2 is the ability to carry out **simulated attack training** to run realistic attack scenarios in your organization. These simulations can help you identify your most vulnerable users and educate them before a real attack could cause a serious compromise.

To use these capabilities, take the following steps:

1. From the Microsoft 365 Defender portal at `https://security.microsoft.com`, navigate to **Email & collaboration | Attack simulation training**, or you can access this directly from `https://security.microsoft.com/attacksimulator`. This takes you to the following page:

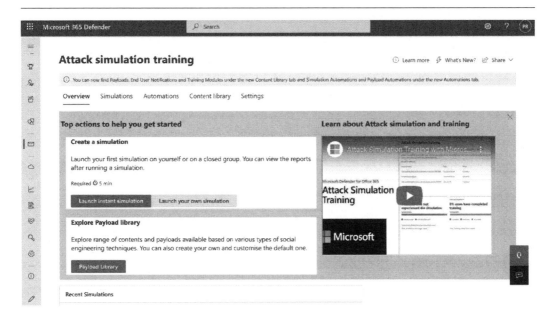

Figure 8.30: Attack simulation overview page

When using the attack simulator section for the first time, you can access helpful resources to guide you to create a simulation and learn more about attack simulation training. Scrolling further down the page will show you further information, such as **Recent Simulations**, **Recommendations**, and **Simulation coverage**:

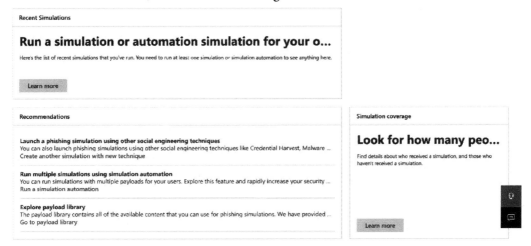

Figure 8.31: Attack simulation overview page

2. To configure and launch a simulation, go to the **Simulations** tab and select **Launch a simulation**:

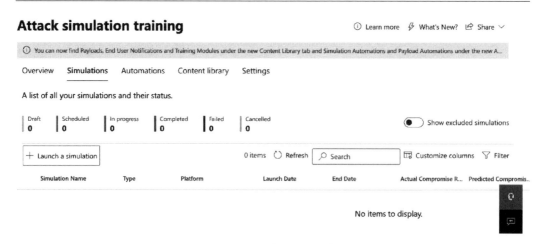

Figure 8.32: Launching a simulation

3. There are several simulation techniques you can choose from. For this example, we will be using the **Credential Harvest** technique. In a credential harvest, an attacker sends a message designed to trick the recipient into clicking on a URL:

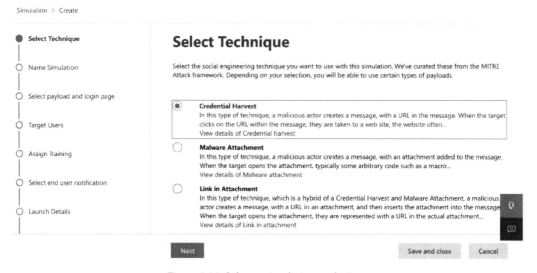

Figure 8.33: Select a simulation technique

4. Next, select a payload type for your simulation. A **payload** refers to the subject name and content of the email that users will receive. You can create your own or choose one provided by Microsoft. In this case, let's select **Account disconnection**:

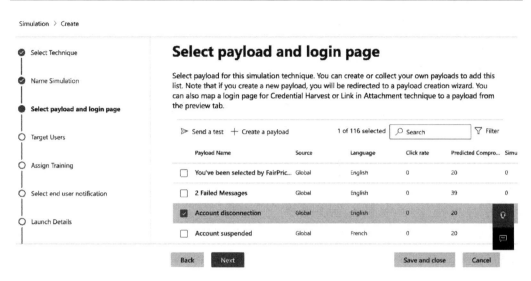

Figure 8.34: Select a payload type

5. Now, select the users or groups you wish to target in the simulated attack. In this example, a user named **Rachel Greene** is selected:

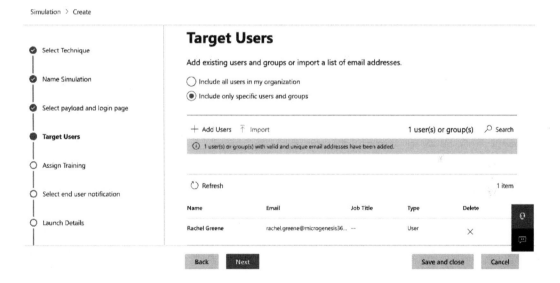

Figure 8.35: Target Users

6. Following a successful attack simulation, users can be assigned training exercises, either recommended by Microsoft or chosen by you. For this example, select the Microsoft-recommended option **Assign training for me (Recommended)** and set the due date to 30 days after the end of the simulation:

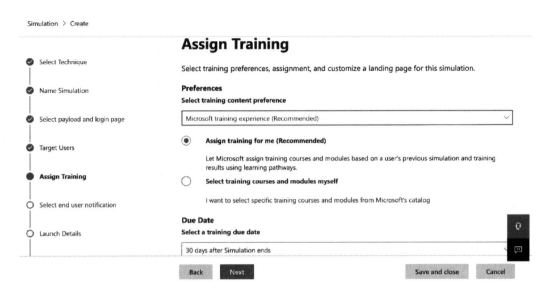

Figure 8.36: Assigning post-simulation awareness training

7.   Next, select the logos and layouts to include in your training communications:

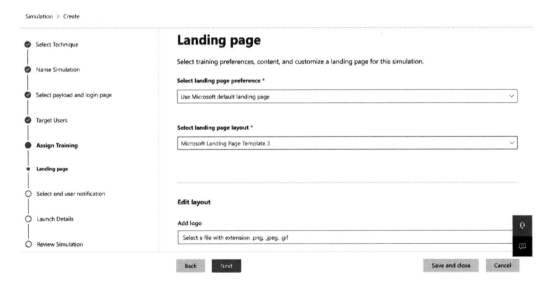

Figure 8.37: Set landing page preferences

8. Now choose the **end user notification** preferences for your simulation:

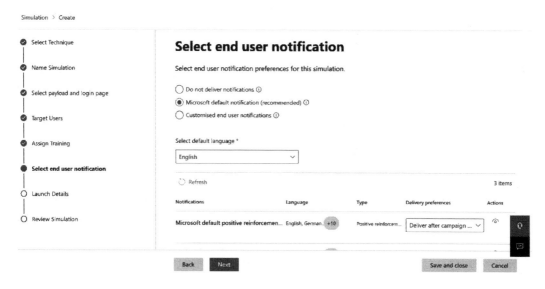

Figure 8.38: Select end user notification

9. Choose when to launch your simulation. For this example, choose **Launch this simulation as soon as I'm done**:

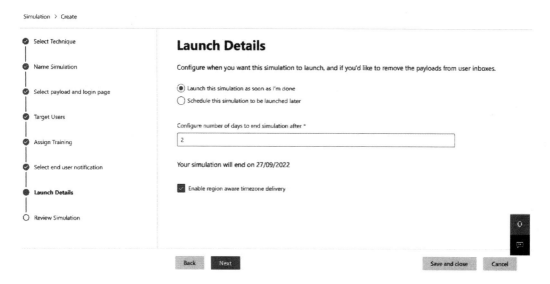

Figure 8.39: Attack simulation page

10. On the final page of the simulation wizard, review your settings and make any final changes. You can also send a test email of the simulation to yourself at this point to see what the users receiving it will experience. When you are happy with your selections, click **Submit**:

Figure 8.40: Review and submit the attack simulation

11. The simulation is now scheduled for launch:

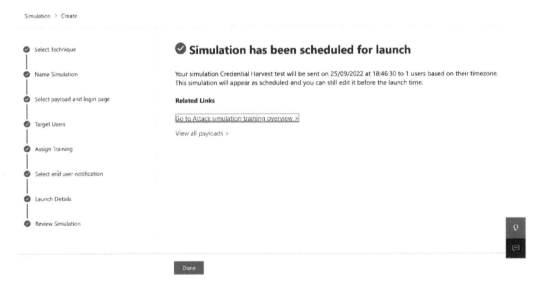

Figure 8.41: Attack simulation scheduled for launch

12. Back on the main **Simulations** tab, you will now see the simulation you created is in progress:

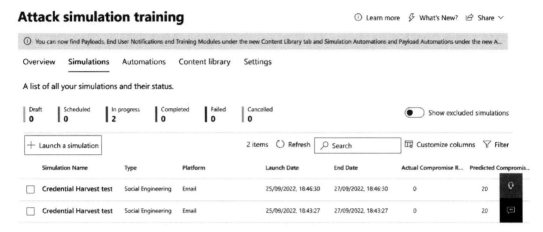

Figure 8.42: Simulation shown in progress

13. Now, the targeted user (Rachel, in this example) will receive an email in her inbox, as shown in the following screenshot:

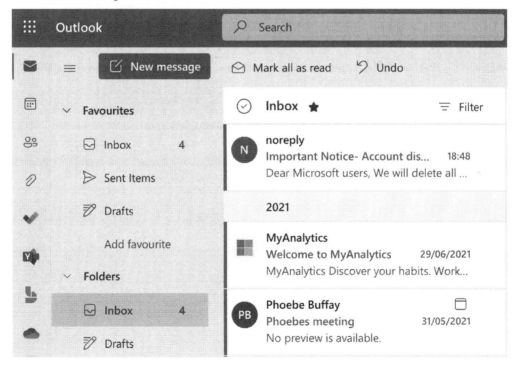

Figure 8.43: Simulation email arrives in the user's mailbox

14. The user opens the message. The content is shown in the following screenshot, with a message designed to scare the user into taking immediate action:

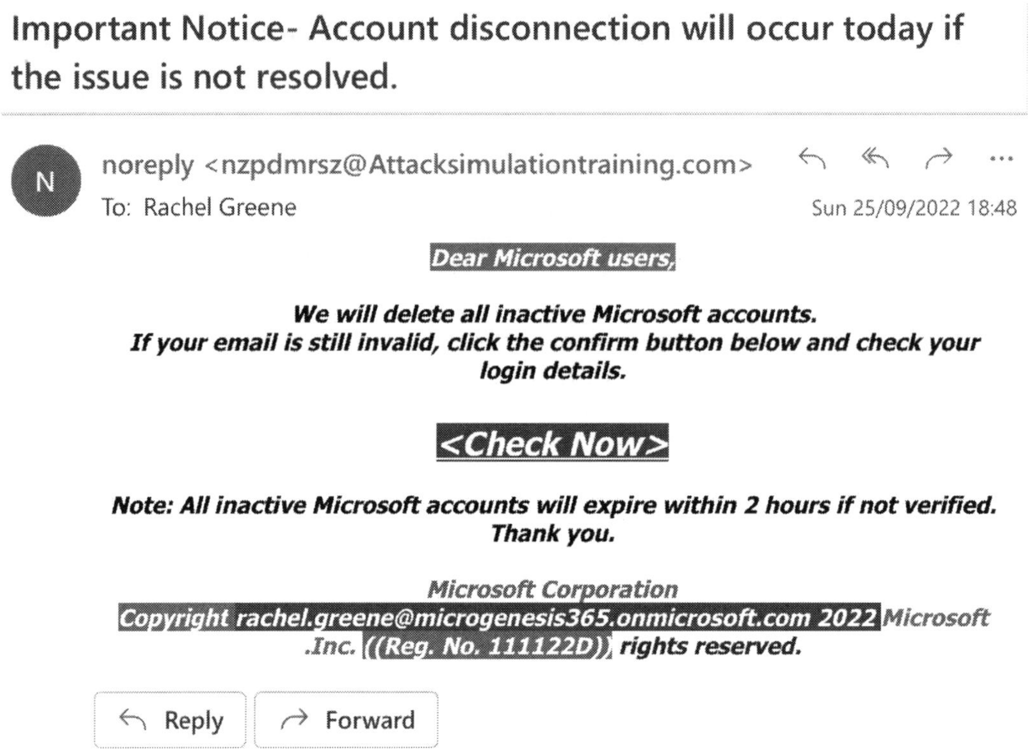

Important Notice- Account disconnection will occur today if the issue is not resolved.

noreply <nzpdmrsz@Attacksimulationtraining.com>   ↩ ↩ ↪ ⋯

To: Rachel Greene   Sun 25/09/2022 18:48

Dear Microsoft users,

We will delete all inactive Microsoft accounts.
If your email is still invalid, click the confirm button below and check your
login details.

<Check Now>

Note: All inactive Microsoft accounts will expire within 2 hours if not verified.
Thank you.

Microsoft Corporation
Copyright rachel.greene@microgenesis365.onmicrosoft.com 2022 Microsoft
.Inc. ((Reg. No. 111122D)) rights reserved.

↩ Reply   ↪ Forward

Figure 8.44: Attack simulation message content

15. The user clicks on the link in the message and is prompted to enter her Microsoft 365 credentials on what looks like a genuine Microsoft login page. However, note the URL!

Figure 8.45: Simulated Microsoft login page

16. The user enters their username and password and logs in. They immediately see that this is a simulation:

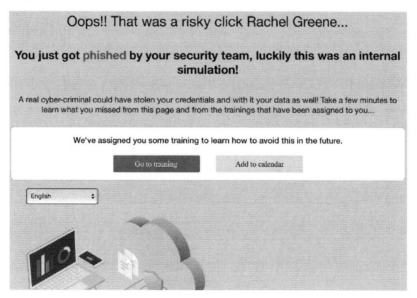

Figure 8.46: User fails simulation training

17. Back in the Microsoft 365 Defender portal, the administrator opens the simulation and sees that one user has been compromised by entering credentials:

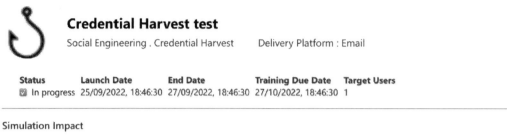

Credential Harvest test

Social Engineering . Credential Harvest   Delivery Platform : Email

Status	Launch Date	End Date	Training Due Date	Target Users
☑ In progress	25/09/2022, 18:46:30	27/09/2022, 18:46:30	27/10/2022, 18:46:30	1

Simulation Impact

1 of 1 users compromised by entering credentials

Compromised

■ Entered credentials   ■ Did not enter credentials

View users

Figure 8.47: User compromised by entering credentials

18. Scrolling down further, the administrator can see all the matching user activity for the attack simulation:

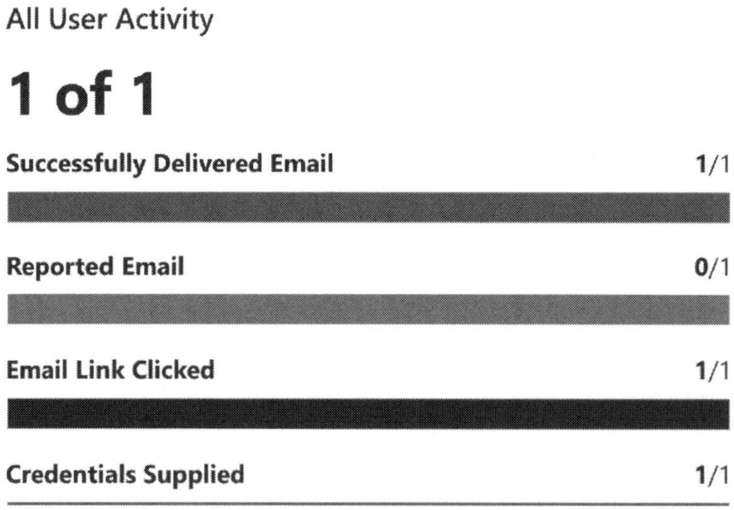

All User Activity

1 of 1

Successfully Delivered Email   1/1

Reported Email   0/1

Email Link Clicked   1/1

Credentials Supplied   1/1

Figure 8.48: Attack simulation user activity

19. Finally, by clicking on **View users**, the administrator can see that the user has been reported as compromised and has been assigned awareness training that they have not yet started:

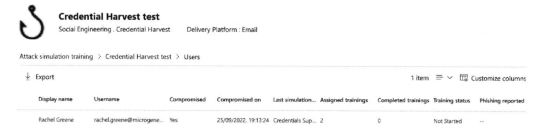

Credential Harvest test
Social Engineering . Credential Harvest   Delivery Platform : Email

Attack simulation training > Credential Harvest test > Users

↓ Export   1 item ≡ ∨ ▦ Customize columns

Display name	Username	Compromised	Compromised on	Last simulation...	Assigned trainings	Completed trainings	Training status	Phishing reported
Rachel Greene	rachel.greene@microgene...	Yes	25/09/2022, 19:13:24	Credentials Sup...	2	0	Not Started	--

Figure 8.49: Compromised user details

So, this concludes the attack simulation process. In the final section of this chapter, we will briefly examine some other options available on the **Attack simulation training** page.

Further attack simulation configuration options

There are three other tabs on the attack simulation page that have not been discussed yet. These are listed and described as follows:

- **Automations**: There are two types of automation available:

  - **Simulation automations** are flows that are automated and use specific techniques and payloads that run when the specified conditions are met and launch simulations

  - **Payload automations** are automated flows that can be used to collect payloads to launch simulations

- **Content library**: The **Content library** section contains **Payloads**, which are phishing emails and web pages available for you to use when launching simulations. Payloads can be manually created or automatically collected with automation. Also within **Content library** are login pages, which are the entities used in the credential harvesting and link in attachment techniques to create a phishing login page. Finally, **End user notifications** are messages delivered to users during simulated attacks, such as appreciating users for reporting phishing.

- **Settings**: The settings page has two areas. The first is **Repeat offender threshold**, which is the number of simulations in a row where a user is compromised that it takes to flag them as a repeat offender. The **Simulations excluded from reporting** option allows admins to view any such simulations that are not included in reporting for any reason. The **Settings** tab is shown in the following screenshot:

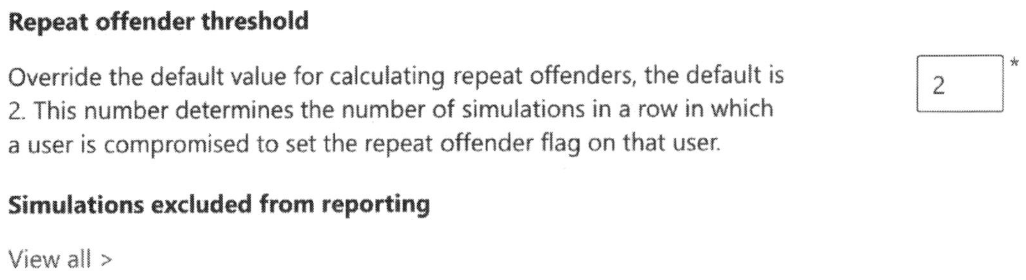

Repeat offender threshold

Override the default value for calculating repeat offenders, the default is
2. This number determines the number of simulations in a row in which
a user is compromised to set the repeat offender flag on that user.

2 *

Simulations excluded from reporting

View all >

Figure 8.50: The Settings tab on the attack simulation page

> **Note**
>
> The **Automations** and **Content library** tabs contain many settings and options that you will
> need to be familiar with. Please consult the *Further reading* section at the end of this chapter
> for more details on these features.

This section demonstrated the methods and results of launching a simulated attack against a user in
your Microsoft 365 organization with Microsoft Defender for Office 365.

Summary

In this chapter, we examined how Microsoft Defender for Office 365 can be used to protect your
organization's users, groups, and domains from malicious content. We then learned how anti-phishing
policies can be created to protect your users from spoofing. We also created Safe Attachments and
Safe Links policies to protect users, groups, and domains by using the Microsoft 365 Defender portal
and also by using Exchange Online PowerShell. Additionally, we learned about the reporting options
within Microsoft Defender for Office 365 and how to configure and execute attack simulation training
for users to improve their awareness of threats and vulnerabilities within emails and attachments.

In the next chapter, we will examine the principles of **Microsoft Sentinel** and learn how to plan and
implement Microsoft Sentinel in your organization to monitor Microsoft 365 security. We will also
learn how to configure playbooks and manage and monitor them using Microsoft Sentinel and how to
respond to threats.

Questions

1. Which of the following is not a feature of Microsoft Defender for Office 365?

    A.   Safe Attachments

    B.   Safe Emails

C. Safe Links

D. Simulated Attacks

2. True or false? One of the delivery methods for Safe Attachments is called **Static Delivery**.

A. True

B. False

3. Which of the following is a valid PowerShell command for creating a Safe Links rule?

A. `Set-SafeLinksRule`

B. `New-SafeLinksRule`

C. `Get-SafeLinksRule`

D. `Start-SafeLinksRule`

4. Which of the following are technique options within an attack simulation (choose three)?

A. Link in attachment

B. Dynamic delivery

C. Link to malware

D. Credential harvest

E. Monitor

5. True or false? Safe Links can be enabled for Microsoft Teams.

A. True

B. False

6. Which section of the Microsoft 365 Defender portal would you access to manage anti-phishing policies?

A. **Threat management | Activity alerts**

B. **Threat management | Alert policy**

C. **Policies & rules | Threat policies**

D. **Threat management | Manage advanced alerts**

7. Where in the Microsoft 365 Defender portal would you go to configure/examine reports for Microsoft Defender for Office 365?

A. **Reports | Messaging**

B. **Reports | Email & collaboration**

    C. **Reports | General**

    D. **Reports | Communication**

8. True or false? Spoofed senders can be configured via the Tenant Allow/Block lists?

    A. True

    B. False

9. Which of the following are valid actions that can be applied to the Safe Attachments unknown malware response (choose three)?

    A. Block

    B. Dynamic delivery

    C. Edit

    D. Monitor

    E. Scan

10. True or false? **Drive-by URL** is a technique that can be used within a Microsoft Defender for Office 365 attack simulation.

    A. True

    B. False

Further reading

Please refer to the following links for more information:

- Microsoft Defender for Office 365: `https://learn.microsoft.com/en-us/microsoft-365/security/office-365-security/defender-for-office-365?view=o365-worldwide#microsoft-defender-for-office-365-plan-1-and-plan-2`

- Introduction to Microsoft Defender for Office 365: `https://learn.microsoft.com/en-us/training/modules/m365-threat-remediate/introduction`

- Microsoft Defender for Office 365 Security Operations Guide: `https://learn.microsoft.com/en-us/microsoft-365/security/office-365-security/mdo-sec-ops-guide?view=o365-worldwide`

- Configure anti-phishing policies in Microsoft Defender for Office 365: `https://learn.microsoft.com/en-us/microsoft-365/security/office-365-security/configure-mdo-anti-phishing-policies?view=o365-worldwide`

- Anti-spoofing protection: https://learn.microsoft.com/en-us/microsoft-365/ security/office-365-security/anti-spoofing-protection?view=o365-worldwide

- Manage the tenant allow/block list: https://learn.microsoft.com/en-us/ microsoft-365/security/office-365-security/manage-tenant-allow-block-list?view=o365-worldwide

- Set up Safe Attachments policies: https://learn.microsoft.com/en-us/ microsoft-365/security/office-365-security/set-up-safe-attachments-policies?WT.mc_id=M365-MVP-4039827&view=o365-worldwide

- Set up Safe Links policies: https://learn.microsoft.com/en-us/microsoft-365/ security/office-365-security/set-up-safe-links-policies?WT.mc_id=M365-MVP-4039827&view=o365-worldwide

- View Defender for Office 365 reports in the Microsoft 365 Defender portal: https://learn.microsoft.com/en-us/microsoft-365/security/office-365-security/ view-reports-for-mdo?WT.mc_id=M365-MVP-4039827&view=o365-worldwide

- Get started with attack simulation training in Defender for Office 365: https://learn.microsoft.com/en-us/microsoft-365/security/office-365-security/ attack-simulation-training-get-started?WT.mc_id=M365-MVP-4039827&view=o365-worldwide

- Assign quarantine policies in supported policies in the Microsoft 365 Defender portal: https://learn.microsoft.com/en-us/microsoft-365/security/office-365-security/quarantine-policies?view=o365-worldwide#assign-quarantine-policies-in-supported-policies-in-the-microsoft-365-defender-portal

- Reports via PowerShell: https://learn.microsoft.com/en-us/microsoft-365/ security/office-365-security/reports-defender-for-office-365?WT.mc_id=M365-MVP-4039827&view=o365-worldwide#additional-reports-to-view

9

Using Microsoft Sentinel to Monitor Microsoft 365 Security

Microsoft Sentinel is a cloud-based **security information and event management** (**SIEM**) tool that enables the analysis of vast quantities of data both within Microsoft 365 and from external sources using **artificial intelligence**. Microsoft Sentinel allows you to gather data and detect potential threats, and then investigate and respond to those threats.

In this chapter, you will learn how to plan and implement Microsoft Sentinel in your organization, understand and configure playbooks, manage and monitor signals across Microsoft 365 and other sources using Microsoft Sentinel, and respond to threats. You will also be able to access and enable Microsoft Sentinel in the Azure portal, set up a Log Analytics workspace, and connect to Microsoft and third-party data sources.

This chapter will cover the following topics:

- Planning and configuring Microsoft Sentinel
- Configuring playbooks in Microsoft Sentinel
- Managing and monitoring your Microsoft Sentinel instance

Planning and configuring Microsoft Sentinel

The first steps you need to take when planning to use Microsoft Sentinel for your organization are to open Microsoft Sentinel and then connect it to a workspace and thereby to your organization's data sources. Microsoft Sentinel has several native Microsoft connectors that enable integration with other Microsoft services, such as Azure Active Directory, Office 365, Microsoft Defender for Identity, and **Microsoft Defender for Cloud Apps** (**MDA**). Ingestion from Microsoft connectors is free of charge.

It is also possible to configure Microsoft Sentinel to connect to non-Microsoft services, and use connection methods such as Syslog, REST API, or the **Common Event Format** (**CEF**). It is important to note that using non-Microsoft connections will incur ingestion charges. For more information on how to plan for and track your usage costs, use the Sentinel pricing calculator at `https://learn.microsoft.com/en-us/azure/sentinel/billing?tabs=commitment-tier`.

Knowing what objectives you are looking to achieve by deploying Microsoft Sentinel within your Microsoft 365 environment will help you to plan which connectors you need to accomplish them. Once you know which data sources you need, you can connect to them and use several available workbooks that provide insights into your data.

So, how do we get started with Microsoft Sentinel? Let's find out in the next section.

Connecting Microsoft Sentinel to a workspace

The first step we need to take with Microsoft Sentinel is to connect to an existing workspace or create a new workspace in the Azure portal. In this instance, we will create a new workspace as part of the starting process of Microsoft Sentinel.

> **Note**
>
> You must have contributor permissions for the Azure subscription where you plan to deploy your Microsoft Sentinel workspace.

To enable Microsoft Sentinel, you need to complete the following steps:

1. Go to the Azure portal at `https://portal.azure.com` and search for and select **Microsoft Sentinel**:

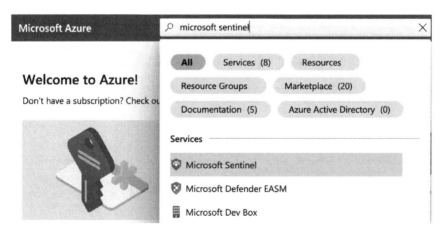

Figure 9.1: Searching for Microsoft Sentinel in the Azure portal

2. You will now see the **Microsoft Sentinel** screen, as shown in the following screenshot. Click on **Create Microsoft Sentinel**:

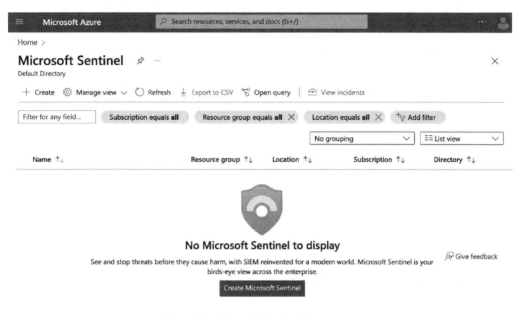

Figure 9.2: Microsoft Sentinel home page

3. If any suitable workspaces were available, they would be visible here. In this example, there are no available workspaces, so you need to click on + **Create a new workspace**:

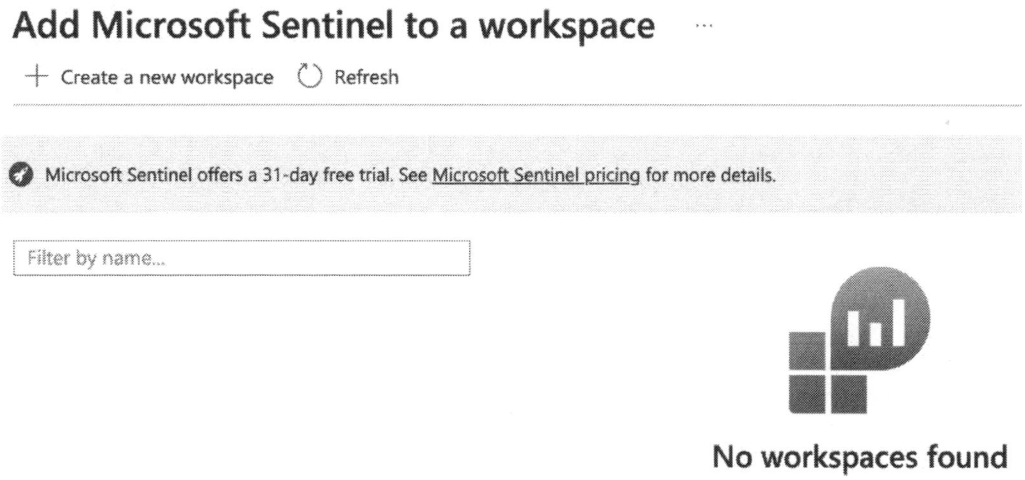

Add Microsoft Sentinel to a workspace ⋯

  + Create a new workspace   ○ Refresh

ⓘ Microsoft Sentinel offers a 31-day free trial. See Microsoft Sentinel pricing for more details.

Filter by name...

No workspaces found

Figure 9.3: Choosing your workspace for Microsoft Sentinel

4. Complete the fields to choose your **Subscription** and **Resource group**, give your instance a **Name** (in this example, we are naming it MyOrgWorkspace), select a **Region**, and then click **Next: Tags >**:

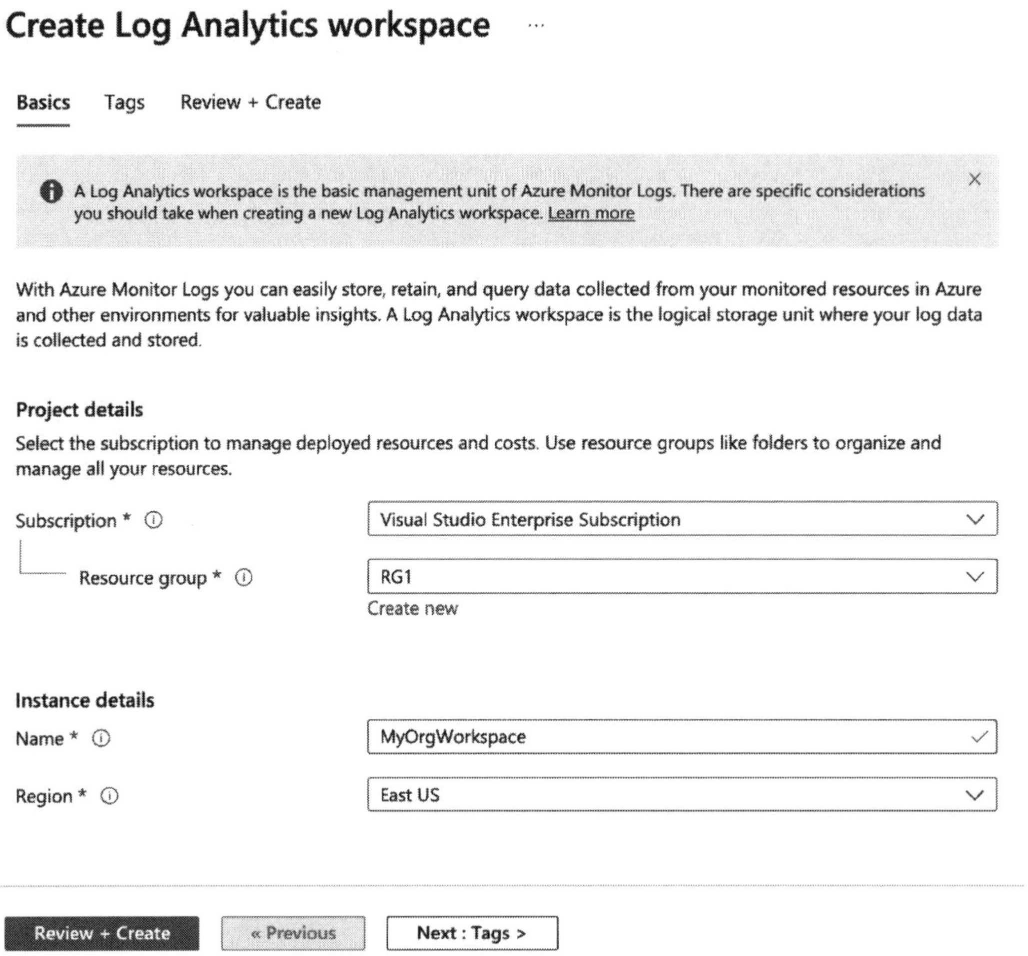

Create Log Analytics workspace   ...

Basics   Tags   Review + Create

> ⓘ A Log Analytics workspace is the basic management unit of Azure Monitor Logs. There are specific considerations   ✕
> you should take when creating a new Log Analytics workspace. Learn more

With Azure Monitor Logs you can easily store, retain, and query data collected from your monitored resources in Azure and other environments for valuable insights. A Log Analytics workspace is the logical storage unit where your log data is collected and stored.

Project details

Select the subscription to manage deployed resources and costs. Use resource groups like folders to organize and manage all your resources.

Subscription * ⓘ	Visual Studio Enterprise Subscription ∨
Resource group * ⓘ	RG1 ∨
	Create new

Instance details

Name * ⓘ	MyOrgWorkspace ✓
Region * ⓘ	East US ∨

Review + Create	« Previous	Next : Tags >

Figure 9.4: Creating a Log Analytics workspace

5. In the next part of the wizard, you may optionally add tags to help you categorize resources. Add tags if required, then click **Next: Review + Create**:

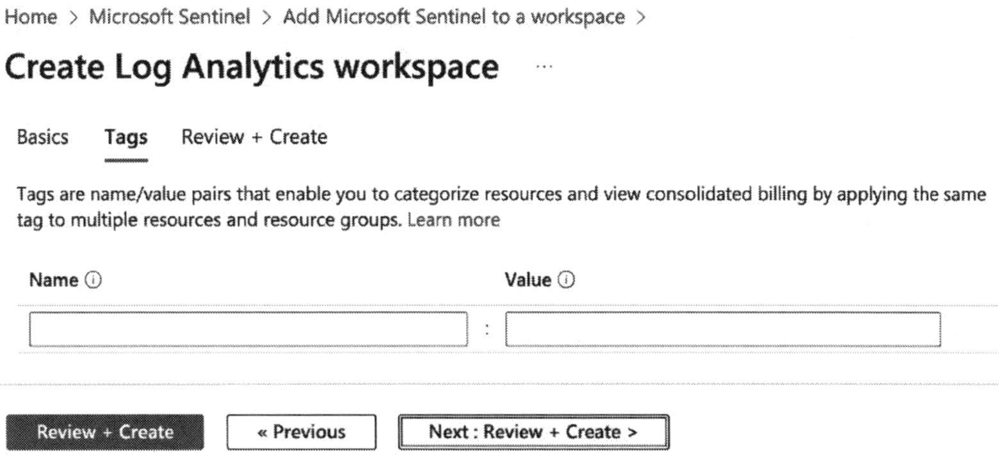

Home > Microsoft Sentinel > Add Microsoft Sentinel to a workspace >

Create Log Analytics workspace   ...

Basics   **Tags**   **Review + Create**

Tags are name/value pairs that enable you to categorize resources and view consolidated billing by applying the same tag to multiple resources and resource groups. Learn more

Name ⓘ   **Value** ⓘ

┌──────────────────────────────┐ : ┌──────────────────────────────┐
└──────────────────────────────┘   └──────────────────────────────┘

┌─────────────────────┐ ┌─────────────────┐ ┌──────────────────────────┐
│ Review + Create   │ │ « Previous   │ │ Next : Review + Create >│
└─────────────────────┘ └─────────────────┘ └──────────────────────────┘

Figure 9.5: Optionally adding tags to your workspace

6.   Next, review your selections and then click on **Create**, as shown in the following screenshot:

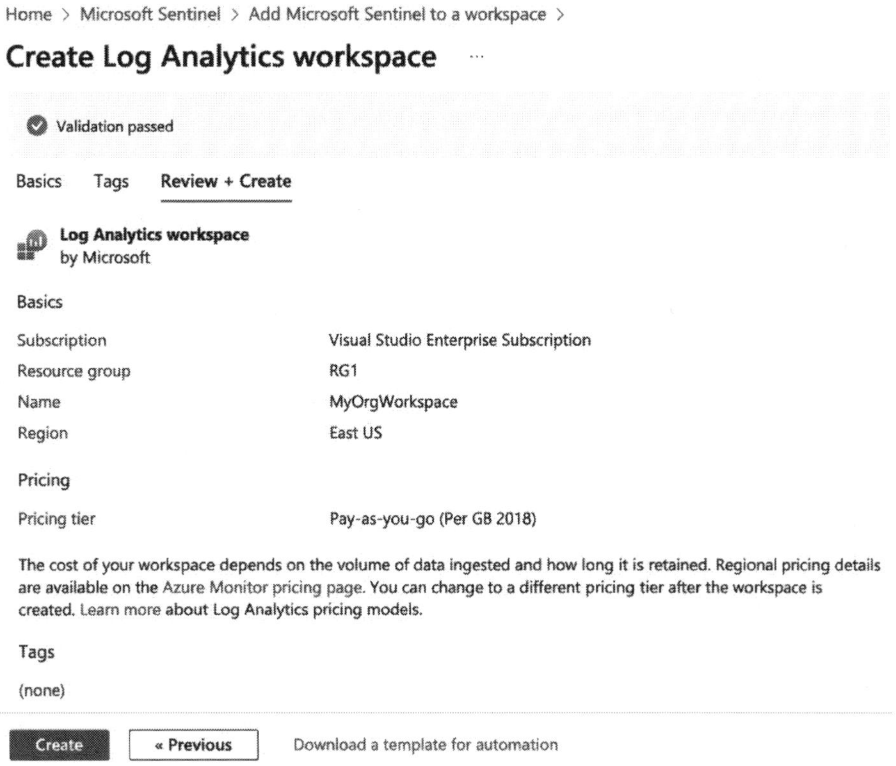

Home > Microsoft Sentinel > Add Microsoft Sentinel to a workspace >

Create Log Analytics workspace   ...

✓ Validation passed

Basics   Tags   **Review + Create**

Log Analytics workspace
by Microsoft

Basics

Subscription	Visual Studio Enterprise Subscription
Resource group	RG1
Name	MyOrgWorkspace
Region	East US

Pricing

Pricing tier	Pay-as-you-go (Per GB 2018)

The cost of your workspace depends on the volume of data ingested and how long it is retained. Regional pricing details are available on the Azure Monitor pricing page. You can change to a different pricing tier after the workspace is created. Learn more about Log Analytics pricing models.

Tags

(none)

┌─────────────┐ ┌─────────────┐
│ Create   │ │ « Previous │   Download a template for automation
└─────────────┘ └─────────────┘

Figure 9.6: Reviewing settings and creating your workspace

The new workspace deployment proceeds and a **Deployment succeeded** message is displayed, as shown in the following screenshot:

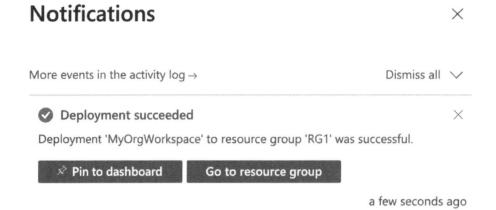

Figure 9.7: The created Microsoft Sentinel workspace

7.   You may need to refresh the page at this point. Once you have done so, you will see your new workspace available for selection. Highlight the workspace, then click **Add**:

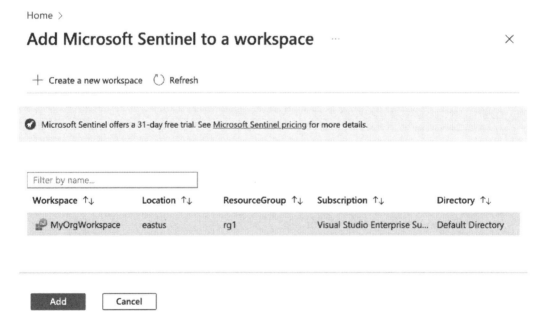

Figure 9.8: Adding Sentinel to the new workspace

Microsoft Sentinel is now enabled and connected to your chosen workspace, and you will be taken to the **News & guides** section, as shown in the following screenshot:

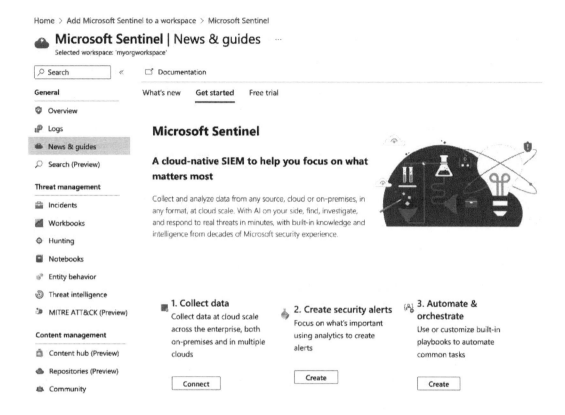

Figure 9.9: Azure Sentinel is enabled and connected to the workspace

Now that you have enabled Microsoft Sentinel within the Azure portal and connected it to your chosen workspace, the next step is to connect Sentinel to some data sources.

Connecting Microsoft Sentinel to data sources

Now that Microsoft Sentinel is enabled, it is time to go through the process of collecting data by connecting it to data sources. This is achieved by completing the following steps:

1. Go to Microsoft Sentinel in the Azure portal and select **Configuration | Data connectors**. The following screenshot shows an extensive list of data source connectors that you can configure with Microsoft Sentinel, with connectors for both Microsoft and third-party data sources:

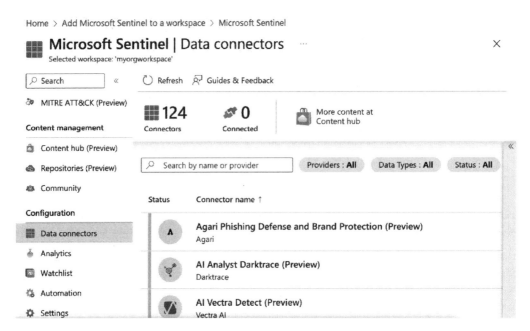

Figure 9.10: Using data connectors

2. You may filter data connectors by **Providers**, **Data Types**, and **Status**. For this example, filter and select the **Microsoft** data source. Then, click **Apply**:

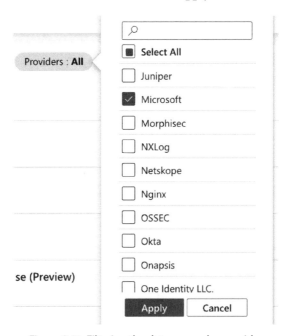

Figure 9.11: Filtering the data source by provider

3. You will now see the list of Microsoft data connectors. Scroll down to select the **Office 365** connector. Doing so will open the connector description on the right side of the screen, and you will see that this connector provides you with insights into ongoing user activities. Click on **Open connector page**:

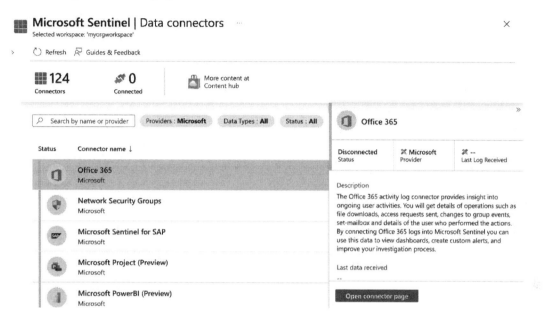

Figure 9.12: Choosing the Office 365 connector

4. Under **Instructions**, you will see some prerequisites listed for using the connector:

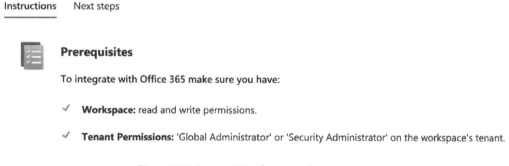

Figure 9.13: Prerequisites for using the connector

5. Scrolling down, you will next see the **Configuration** options for the connector. For this example, select all three options, which are **Exchange**, **SharePoint**, and **Teams**. Then, click **Apply Changes**:

Configuration

Connect Office 365 activity logs to your Microsoft Sentinel.

Select the record types you want to collect from your tenant and click **Apply Changes**.

☑ Exchange

☑ SharePoint

☑ Teams

Apply Changes

Figure 9.14: Connector configuration options

6. Scroll down further. You will see that the final option allows you to search for any **Previously connected tenants**. This feature provides the ability to search for and view any Office 365 tenants that you may have previously had connected to Microsoft Sentinel, and you can view and modify which logs you collect from each tenant:

2. Previously connected tenants

Microsoft Sentinel now enables Office 365 single-tenant connection. You can modify your previously connected tenants and click **Save**.

✎ Save   ⟳ Refresh

🔍 Search

Tenant

No results

Figure 9.15: Previously connected tenants option

7. Go to the **Next steps** tab; you will see **Recommended workbooks**, which you can use to view logs relating to your data connector. Workbooks provide you with a way to monitor your data in Office 365. There are several built-in workbook templates that you can choose from, or you can create your own custom workbooks:

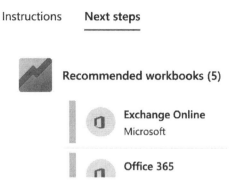

Figure 9.16: Viewing recommended workbooks

8. Scroll down to see some useful **Query samples**, which can be used to investigate data gathered by your connector. These can include things like gathering log files from services in Microsoft 365 such as Teams, Exchange, SharePoint, and OneDrive:

Figure 9.17: Viewing recommended query samples

9. Finally, scroll down further to see some relevant **analytics templates** from which you can create rules based on the various relevant data sources you may have. These rules will have tactics to respond to or combat specific vulnerabilities:

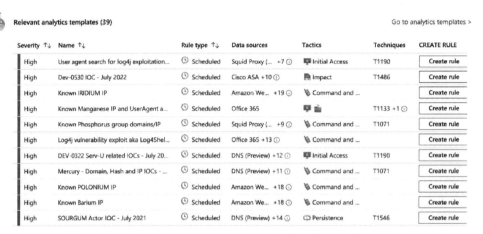

Figure 9.18: Viewing recommended analytics rule templates

10. Select one of the available workbooks to see what the workbook is designed to do. If you want to add it to Microsoft Sentinel, just click **Save**. The following screenshot shows the **Exchange Online** workbook selected:

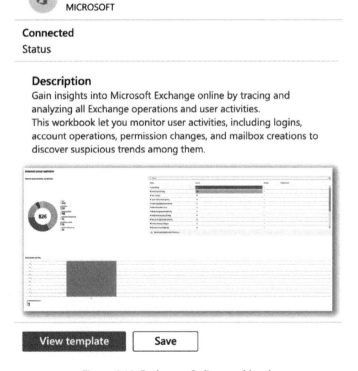

Figure 9.19: Exchange Online workbook

11. Next, choose the location where you wish to save the workbook and click **OK**:

Figure 9.20: Choosing your workbook location

12. Now, click on **View saved workbook** (you may also view any workbooks that you save via the Microsoft Sentinel portal under **Workbooks | My workbooks**):

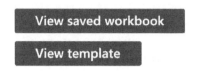

Figure 9.21: Click to view your saved workbook

The workbook is opened and looks as shown in the following screenshot. You will not see any matched activities immediately:

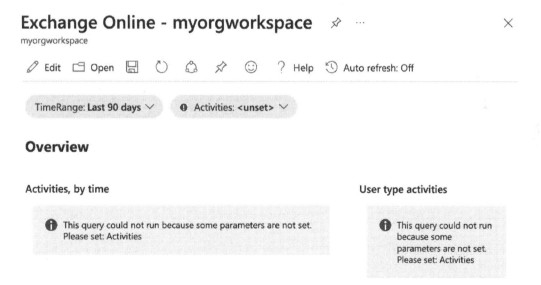

Figure 9.22: A new Azure Sentinel workbook

13. Click the **Activities** drop-down menu to check the **All** option. Then click the **Save** icon:

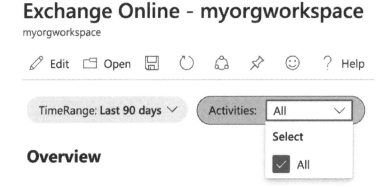

Figure 9.23: Selecting all activities

The workbook will now appear as shown in the following screenshot. There may not be any query results at this stage:

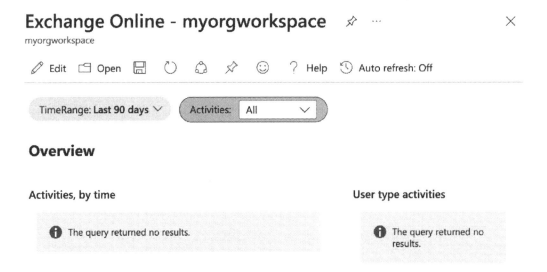

Figure 9.24: Workbook saved with all activities targeted for analysis by the data connector

This is how you enable Microsoft Sentinel in the Azure portal and connect it to a workspace and data connectors.

> **Note**
>
> Microsoft Sentinel is an extremely complex service within the Microsoft Azure portal and this chapter will only cover its basic principles. Should you wish to gain a more advanced understanding, you may consult the references included in the *Further reading* section at the end of this chapter.

Next, we will learn about Microsoft Sentinel playbooks.

Configuring playbooks in Microsoft Sentinel

In Microsoft Sentinel, **playbooks** are collections of responses and actions that can be run like a routine. Playbooks automate and orchestrate threat responses and can be integrated with other systems, both internal and external. They can be configured to run manually or automatically in response to specific alerts or incidents. An example of an automated trigger for a playbook is an **automation rule**.

Automation rules enable users to centrally manage incident automation. This includes the ability to assign playbooks to incidents and automate responses for multiple analytics rules at once. Additionally, you can automatically tag, assign, or close incidents without requiring a playbook. You can also control the order of the actions executed.

Playbooks are based on **Azure Logic Apps**. Microsoft Sentinel can leverage the following logic app types:

- **Consumption**: This is the more classic Azure Logic Apps experience
- **Standard**: This is the new type that runs in the redesigned Azure Logic Apps engine

The newer Standard logic app type provides benefits including the following:

- Enhanced performance
- A fixed pricing structure
- Multiple workflow capabilities
- An improved API connections management experience
- Native network capabilities (including support for virtual networks and private endpoints)
- Improved Visual Studio Code integration
- An updated workflow designer

Standard playbooks may be used in the same ways that you use Consumption playbooks: by attaching them to automation rules and/or analytics rules. They can be run on demand from incidents and alerts, and they can be managed in the **Active Playbooks** tab within Microsoft Sentinel.

> **Note**
>
> Standard workflows are *not* supported by playbook templates. This means that a Standard workflow-based playbook cannot be directly created in Microsoft Sentinel. The workflow must be created directly within Azure Logic Apps, after which it will appear as a playbook in Microsoft Sentinel.

As Standard workflows are the newer experience, we will use this workflow experience and learn how to do the following:

- Create an automation rule
- Create a playbook
- Add actions to a playbook
- Attach a playbook to an automation rule or an analytics rule to automate threat response

> **Note**
>
> Only playbooks based on the **incident trigger** can be called by automation rules. Playbooks based on the **alert trigger** must be defined to run directly in analytics rules. Both types can also be run manually.

Creating a simple playbook

To create a simple playbook, complete the following steps:

1. From the Microsoft Sentinel portal, select **Configuration | Automation**:

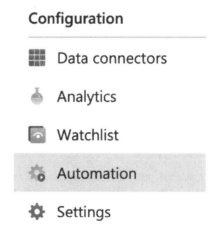

Figure 9.25: Opening the Automation section to configure a playbook

The **Automation** page opens as shown here:

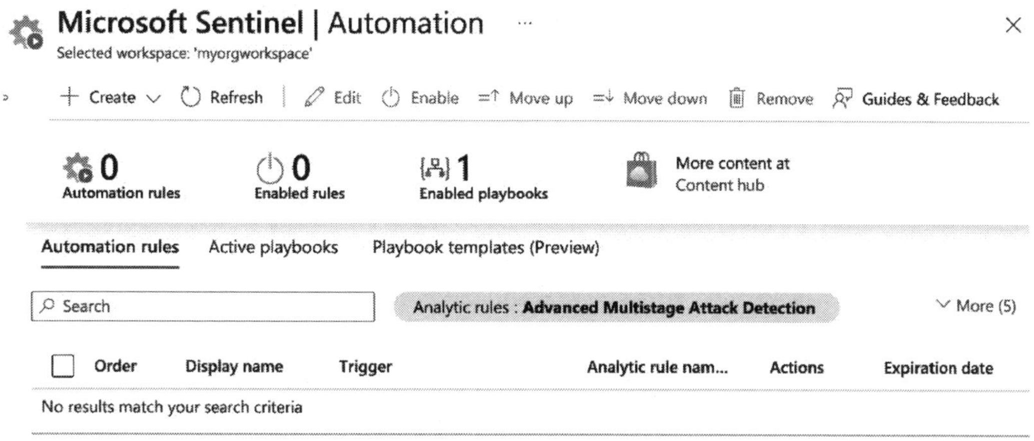

Microsoft Sentinel | Automation ...   ✕
Selected workspace: 'myorgworkspace'

＋ Create ⌄   ↻ Refresh | ✎ Edit ⏻ Enable =↑ Move up =↓ Move down 🗑 Remove ⤳ Guides & Feedback

⚙ **0**   ⏻ **0**   {⌗} **1**   More content at
Automation rules   **Enabled rules**   **Enabled playbooks**   Content hub

Automation rules   Active playbooks   Playbook templates (Preview)

🔍 Search   Analytic rules : **Advanced Multistage Attack Detection**   ⌄ More (5)

☐   Order   Display name   Trigger   Analytic rule nam...   Actions   Expiration date

No results match your search criteria

Figure 9.26: The Microsoft Sentinel Automation page

2.   Click on **Create**. You will see the following options:

＋ Create ⌄   ↻ Refresh

Automation rule

Playbook with incident trigger

Playbook with alert trigger

Blank playbook

Figure 9.27: Options to create automation rules and playbooks

Select the **Blank playbook** option, which is the option for the newer Standard Logic Apps experience. Then, the **Create Logic App** experience launches. Complete the fields shown in the following screenshot; choose an Azure **Subscription**, choose a **Resource group**, and enter a **Logic App name**. Choose a **Publish** method – either **Workflow** or **Docker Container**. **Workflow** will offer one of the custom app service plans, but does not allow the selection of an existing app service. Docker containers are supported with custom locations. For this example, we are using **Workflow**. Finally, choose a **Region** (**Central US** for this example):

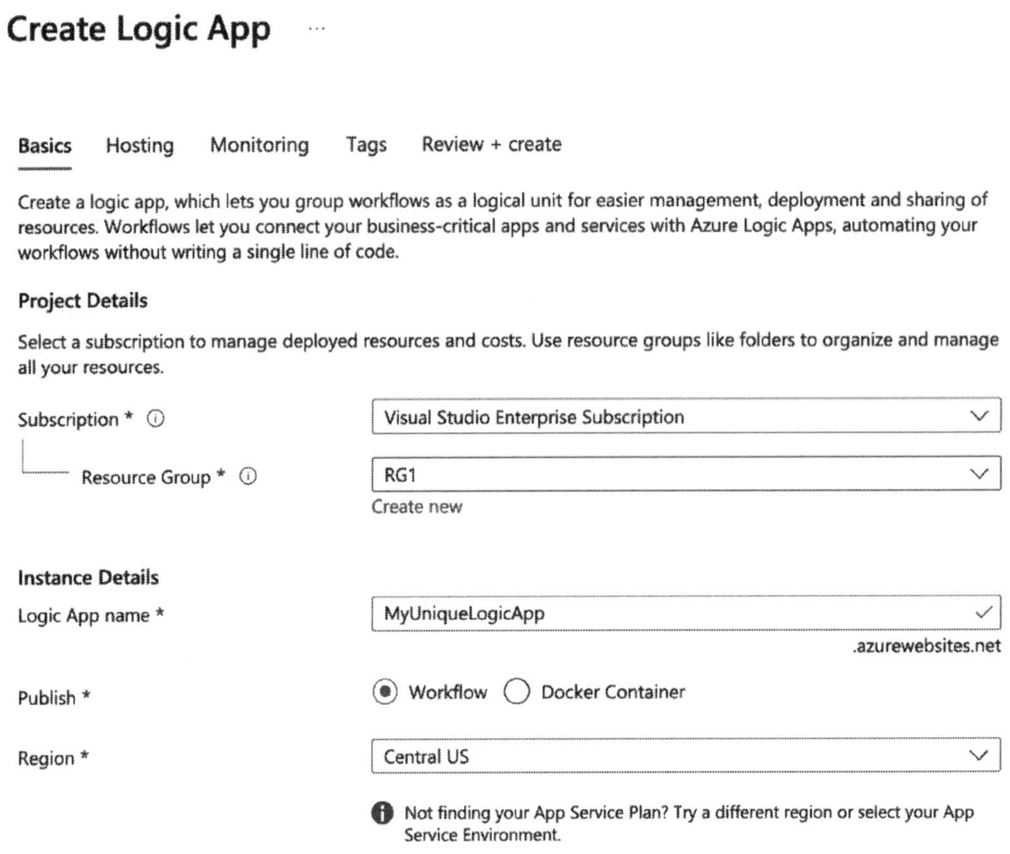

Create Logic App   ...

Basics Hosting Monitoring Tags Review + create

Create a logic app, which lets you group workflows as a logical unit for easier management, deployment and sharing of resources. Workflows let you connect your business-critical apps and services with Azure Logic Apps, automating your workflows without writing a single line of code.

Project Details

Select a subscription to manage deployed resources and costs. Use resource groups like folders to organize and manage all your resources.

Subscription * ⓘ	Visual Studio Enterprise Subscription ⌄
└─ Resource Group * ⓘ	RG1 ⌄
	Create new

Instance Details

Logic App name *	MyUniqueLogicApp ✓
	.azurewebsites.net
Publish *	◉ Workflow ◯ Docker Container
Region *	Central US ⌄

ⓘ Not finding your App Service Plan? Try a different region or select your App Service Environment.

Figure 9.28: Create Logic App

3. Scroll down and select the options as shown. You can choose between the **Standard** option, which is appropriate for enterprise-level, serverless applications, where event-based scaling and network location are relevant, or **Consumption**, which is appropriate for situations where you need to pay for only what you want to use in your workflow. Once done, click **Next: Hosting**:

Plan

The plan type you choose dictates how your app scales, what features are enabled, and how it is priced. Learn more

Plan type *

    ◉ **Standard:** Best for enterprise-level, serverless applications, with
       event-based scaling and networking isolation.

    ◯ **Consumption:** Best for entry-level. Pay only as much as your
       workflow runs.

Windows Plan (Central US) * ⓘ

| ASP-RG1-a295 (WS1) | ⌄ |

Create new

Sku and size *

Workflow Standard WS1
210 total ACU, 3.5 GB memory

Zone redundancy

An App Service plan can be deployed as a zone redundant service in the regions that support it. This is a deployment time only decision. You can't make an App Service plan zone redundant after it has been deployed Learn more

Zone redundancy

    ◯ **Enabled:** Your App Service plan and the apps in it will be zone
       redundant. The minimum App Service plan instance count will be three.

    ◉ **Disabled:** Your App Service Plan and the apps in it will not be zone
       redundant. The minimum App Service plan instance count will be one.

| Review + create | | < Previous | | Next : Hosting > |

Figure 9.29: Select plan and redundancy options

4.   On the **Hosting** page, select your **Storage type** and **Storage account**. Then click **Next: Monitoring**:

Create Logic App ···

Basics   **Hosting**   Monitoring   Tags   Review + create

Storage

When creating a logic app, you must create or link to an external storage, which is used to store workflow state, run history, and artifacts.

Storage type *

| Azure Storage | ⌄ |

Storage account * ⓘ

| rg19881 (v1) | ⌄ |

Create new

| Review + create | | < Previous | | Next : Monitoring > |

Figure 9.30: Select Azure storage type and storage account

5.   Now select the **Yes** radio button to **Enable Application Insights** and choose an option from the **Application Insights** drop-down menu. Click **Next: Tags >**:

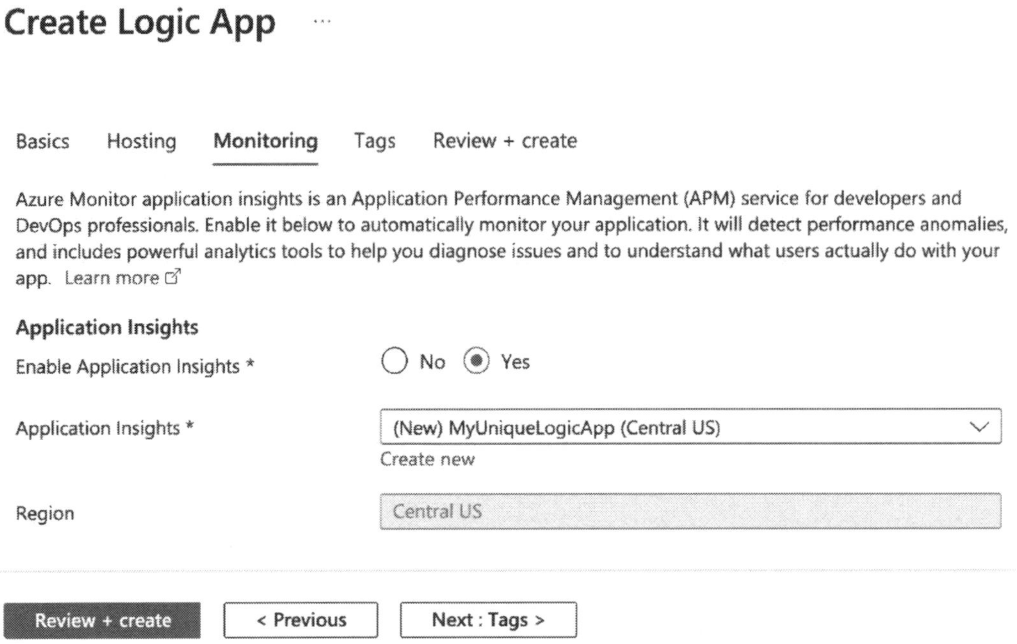

Create Logic App   ⋯

Basics   Hosting   **Monitoring**   Tags   Review + create

Azure Monitor application insights is an Application Performance Management (APM) service for developers and DevOps professionals. Enable it below to automatically monitor your application. It will detect performance anomalies, and includes powerful analytics tools to help you diagnose issues and to understand what users actually do with your app. Learn more ⌕

Application Insights

Enable Application Insights *   ◯ No ⦿ Yes

Application Insights *   (New) MyUniqueLogicApp (Central US)   ⌄
                               Create new

Region   Central US

[Review + create]   [< Previous]   [Next : Tags >]

Figure 9.31: Configure monitoring settings

6.   You may optionally create tags. If you need tags, create them and move to the **Review + Create** page. Once you have reviewed your configuration and made any final adjustments, click on **Create**:

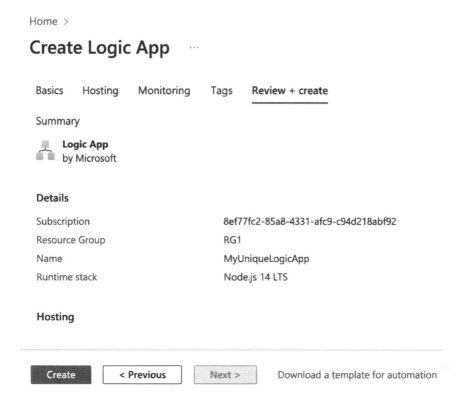

Home >

Create Logic App   ···

Basics   Hosting   Monitoring   Tags   **Review + create**

Summary

Logic App
by Microsoft

Details

Subscription	8ef77fc2-85a8-4331-afc9-c94d218abf92
Resource Group	RG1
Name	MyUniqueLogicApp
Runtime stack	Node.js 14 LTS

Hosting

Create   < Previous   Next >   Download a template for automation

Figure 9.32: Review and create the logic app

7. Deployment of the logic app will now commence. Once successfully completed, click on **Go to resource**, as shown in the following window:

✓ Your deployment is complete

Deployment name: Microsoft.Web-LogicAp...   Start time: 10/1/2022, 6:55:57 PM
Subscription: Visual Studio Enterprise Subsc...   Correlation ID: a52362e0-e649-4c77-89ca-
Resource group: RG1

∨ **Deployment details**

∧ **Next steps**

Go to resource

Figure 9.33: Logic app deployment completed

8.   Within your new **Logic App**, select **Workflows** from the left menu, then click +**Add**:

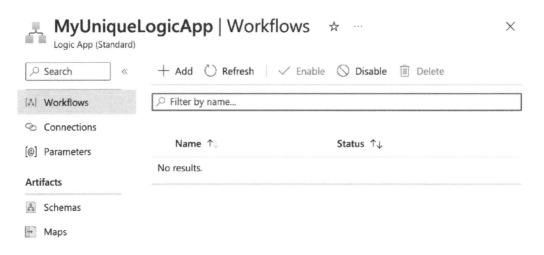

Figure 9.34: Adding a workflow to the logic app

9.   Name your workflow, choose a **State type** (in this case **Stateful**), and click **Create**:

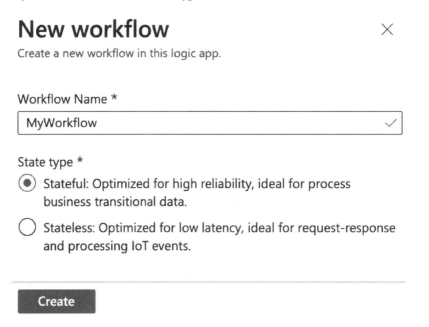

Figure 9.35: Configuring the workflow

Now that your workflow has been created, select it from the list to enter it.

10. Click on the **Designer** option in the left pane, and you will see the workflow designer trigger options as shown here:

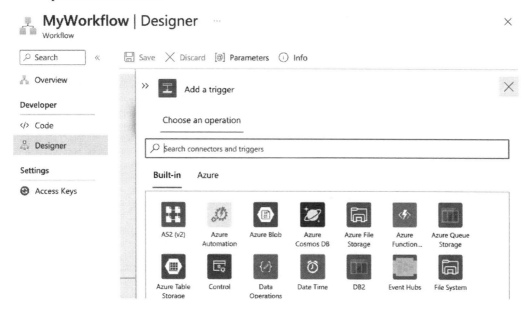

Figure 9.36: Workflow designer trigger options

11. Now, you can start to configure the trigger actions for your workflow. Select the **Azure** tab and search for `sentinel` as shown. Click on **Microsoft Sentinel** in the results:

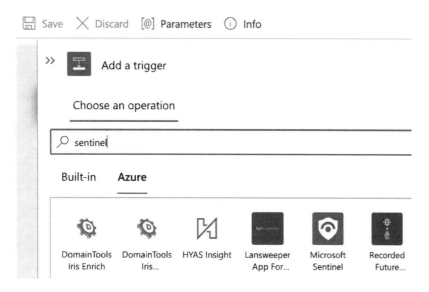

Figure 9.37: Searching for the Microsoft Sentinel trigger

12. Select the **Microsoft Sentinel incident (preview)** option, which will be used in this example. Click on the **Save** button:

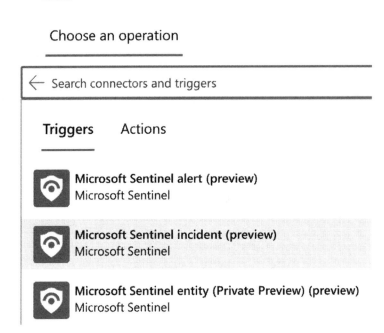

Figure 9.38: Selecting the Microsoft Sentinel incident trigger

Now you can start to build your incident triggers:

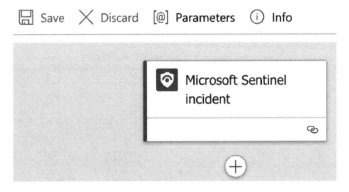

Figure 9.39: Build out the workflow

13. For this example, add a simple workflow to send an email when a new member is added to a team in Microsoft Teams:

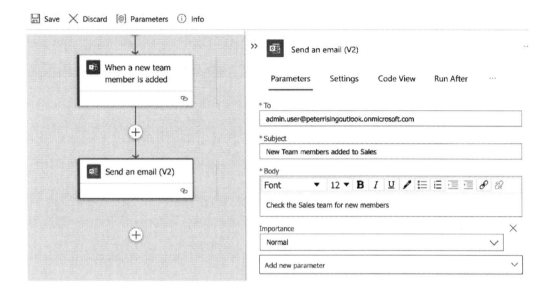

Figure 9.40: Build out the workflow

14. When you have completed your workflow setup, the playbook will show in the **Active playbooks** section:

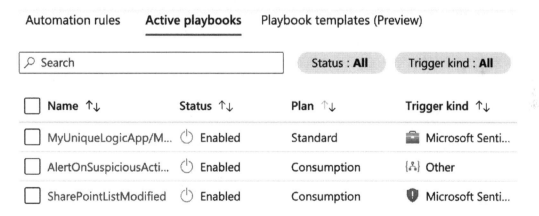

Figure 9.41: Standard logic app-based playbook created successfully

15. If you open the playbook, you can trigger the workflow by clicking **Run Trigger | Run**:

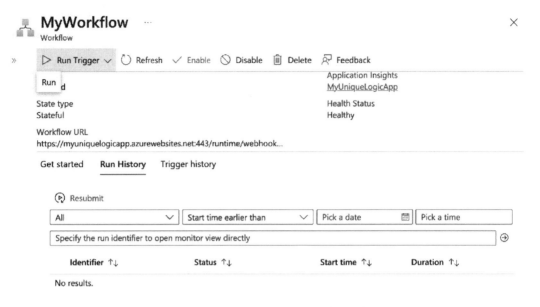

Figure 9.42: Manually trigger the playbook

When completed, the **Run History** tab will show a **Succeeded** status:

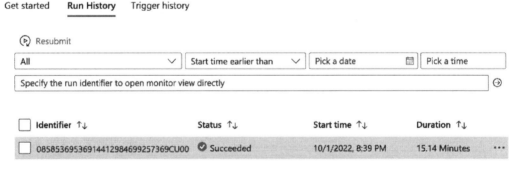

Figure 9.43: Playbook run successfully

With the playbook successfully executed, the required email alert is sent to the intended recipient:

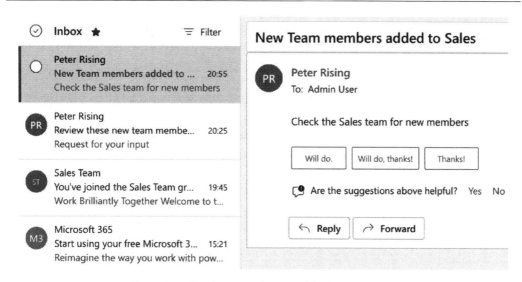

Figure 9.44: Email triggered successfully from playbook

The playbook you just created is a very simple example just to demonstrate the principle. It is useful to familiarize yourself with all types of playbooks and triggers. Use a trial Azure subscription to try these for yourself.

Creating a playbook using templates

Also available from within the **Automation** section of Microsoft Sentinel is the option to create playbooks using templates. You can access this option by going to the **Playbook templates (Preview)** tab:

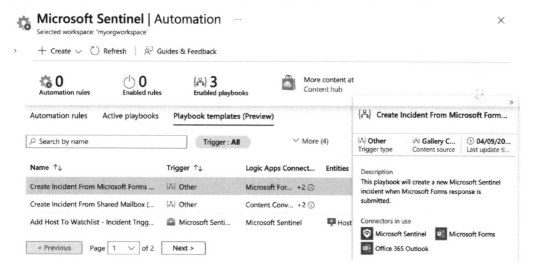

Figure 9.45: Using a playbook template

The example playbook template selected is **Create Incident from Microsoft Forms Response**. Using the **Create playbook** option shown in the following screenshot, you can create a new Microsoft Sentinel incident by submitting the Microsoft Forms response:

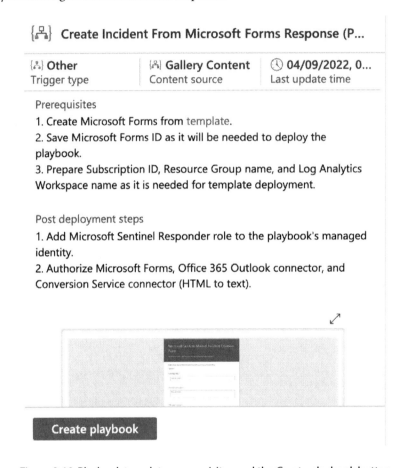

Figure 9.46: Playbook template prerequisites and the Create playbook button

Playbook templates are a very useful way to get started with some simple but effective playbooks, and they can be customized to your needs.

In the next section, we will cover automation rules in Microsoft Sentinel.

Creating and using automation rules to manage responses

Automation rules in Microsoft Sentinel are used to manage and orchestrate responses to threats. They can be set using **triggers** and **actions**, such as when an incident is created. In this case, this would be the trigger, and running a playbook in response would be the action. To create an automation rule, complete the following steps:

1. In Microsoft Sentinel, navigate to **Automation** | **Create** | **Automation rule**. The **Create new automation rule** panel will open as shown here:

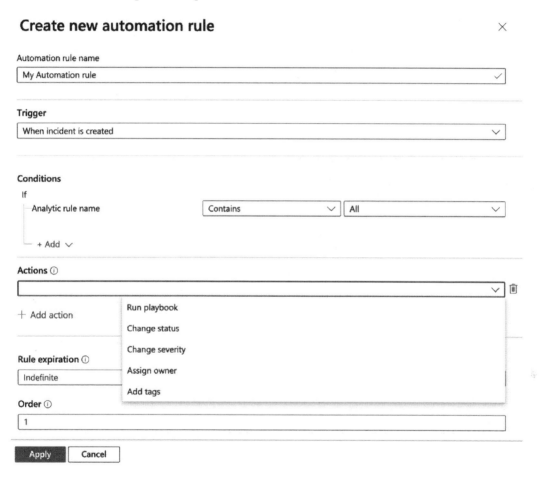

Figure 9.47: Configuring an automation rule

2. Set a name for your rule and select a trigger action based on incident creation, incident update, or alert creation. Add any required conditions (for more information on this, refer to the *Further reading* section at the end of this chapter), and then select the action you wish to perform when there is a match. The available actions are as follows:

    - Run playbook

    - Change status level

    - Change severity level

    - Assign owner

    - Add tags

Automation rules are extremely useful when you want to automatically run a playbook that would otherwise need to be triggered manually.

Now that you have configured your Microsoft Sentinel instance and set up some workbooks and playbooks, it is important to know how to manage and monitor Microsoft Sentinel.

Managing and monitoring your Microsoft Sentinel instance

Managing and monitoring our Microsoft Sentinel instance ensures that we are regularly reviewing and responding to any threats and taking any corrective action that may be required. Some of the methods available to manage and monitor Microsoft Sentinel are as follows:

- **Microsoft Sentinel Overview screen**: From the **Microsoft Sentinel | Overview** section, you can review a selection of alerts and metrics, such as recent incidents, events, and alerts over time, as shown in the following screenshot:

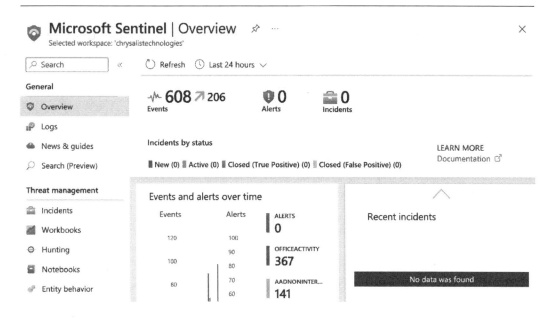

Figure 9.48: Microsoft Sentinel Overview screen

Here you can review events, alerts, usage, and metrics.

- **Microsoft Sentinel logs**: From the **Microsoft Sentinel | Logs** section, you can choose from a large number of built-in queries under **Log Analytics** workspaces and see information on things such as **Applications** and **Azure Monitor**, as shown in the following screenshot:

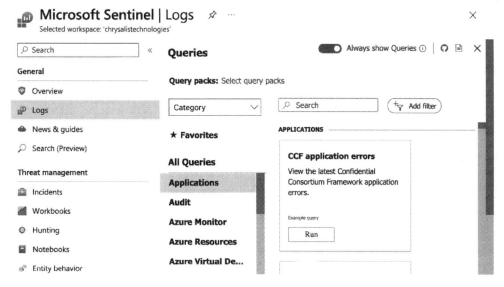

Figure 9.49: Microsoft Sentinel Logs

From the **Logs** page, you can access tables, queries, and filters. You can also choose from a list of Log Analytics workspaces to run any queries you may require.

- **Threat management tools**: When you navigate to **Microsoft Sentinel | Threat management**, you will see options to help you to manage and monitor activities within Microsoft Sentinel. From the **Microsoft Sentinel** page, you may leverage a number of threat management tools, as shown in the following screenshot:

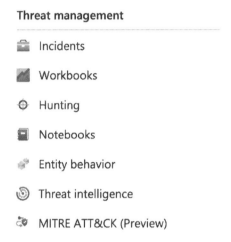

Figure 9.50: Azure Sentinel Threat management options

It is highly recommended that Microsoft Sentinel administrators regularly review the events and alerts that are reported in the **Overview** section, along with the Microsoft Sentinel logs and the tools that are included in the **Threat management** section of Microsoft Sentinel.

Summary

This chapter introduced Microsoft Sentinel, which is a cloud-based SIEM tool that allows you to analyze large amounts of data from both Microsoft and third-party sources. We discussed how to enable Microsoft Sentinel and connect it to a new or existing Log Analytics workspace. We also learned how to set up and configure Microsoft Sentinel playbooks, which use triggers and actions to send alerts on a multitude of events.

In the next chapter, we will discuss the principles of MDA. We will learn how to configure MDA, create snapshot Cloud Discovery reports, discover custom cloud apps, and add them to Cloud App Discovery. In addition, we will learn how to use App Connectors to enable visibility and control over the apps we connect to and apply policies to them, and how to interpret and analyze alerts, reports, and dashboards.

Questions

1. True or false? Automation rules can be used in Microsoft Sentinel to trigger a playbook.

   A. True

   B. False

2. Where in the Microsoft Sentinel portal would you configure a log connector?

   A. **Configuration | Data Connectors**

   B. **Configuration | Automation**

   C. **Configuration | Settings**

   D. **Threat management | Workbooks**

3. What is the first step after enabling Microsoft Sentinel?

   A. Create a playbook

   B. Set up a data connector

   C. Connect to a playbook

   D. Connect to a workspace

4. Which of the following is not a type of playbook that you can use with Microsoft Sentinel?

   A. Playbook with incident trigger

   B. Playbook with PowerShell trigger

   C. Blank playbook

   D. Playbook with alert trigger

5. True or false? Playbook templates are available with Microsoft Sentinel.

   A. True

   B. False

6. Which Microsoft portal must you access to configure Azure Sentinel?

   A. `https://portal.office.com`

   B. `https://portal.azure.com`

   C. `https://security.microsoft.com`

   D. `https://compliance.microsoft.com`

7.   True or false? Microsoft Sentinel does not require a Log Analytics workspace.

   A.   True

   B.   False

8.   Which of the following would you find in the Threat management section of Microsoft Sentinel (choose three)?

   A.   **Workbooks**

   B.   **Logs**

   C.   **Hunting**

   D.   **Entity behavior**

   E.   **Automation**

9.   From which section of Microsoft Sentinel can you run queries?

   A.   **Threat management | Workbooks**

   B.   **Configuration | Settings**

   C.   **Threat management | Notebooks**

   D.   **General | Logs**

10.   True or false? With Microsoft Sentinel workbooks, you can view more options via Content Hub.

   A.   True

   B.   False

Further reading

Please refer to the following links for more information regarding what was covered in this chapter:

- Overview of Microsoft Sentinel: `https://learn.microsoft.com/en-us/azure/sentinel/overview`

- Pre-deployment activities: `https://learn.microsoft.com/en-us/azure/sentinel/prerequisites`

- Plan costs and billing: `https://learn.microsoft.com/en-us/azure/sentinel/billing?tabs=commitment-tier`

- Onboarding Microsoft Sentinel: `https://learn.microsoft.com/en-us/azure/sentinel/quickstart-onboard`

- Best practices for Microsoft Sentinel: `https://learn.microsoft.com/en-us/azure/sentinel/best-practices`

- Microsoft Sentinel data connectors: `https://learn.microsoft.com/en-us/azure/sentinel/connect-data-sources`

- Creating a Log Analytics workspace: `https://learn.microsoft.com/en-us/azure/azure-monitor/logs/quick-create-workspace?tabs=azure-portal`

- Investigating incidents with Microsoft Sentinel: `https://learn.microsoft.com/en-us/azure/sentinel/investigate-cases`

- Using playbooks with automation rules in Microsoft Sentinel: `https://learn.microsoft.com/en-us/azure/sentinel/tutorial-respond-threats-playbook?tabs=LAC`

- Using triggers and actions in playbooks: `https://learn.microsoft.com/en-us/azure/sentinel/playbook-triggers-actions`

- Workspace architecture: `https://learn.microsoft.com/en-us/azure/sentinel/best-practices-workspace-architecture`

- Logic app types: `https://learn.microsoft.com/en-us/azure/sentinel/automate-responses-with-playbooks#logic-app-types`

- Create automation rules to manage responses: `https://learn.microsoft.com/en-us/azure/sentinel/create-manage-use-automation-rules`

10

Configuring Microsoft Defender for Cloud Apps

When you move your organization's apps and services to the cloud, you gain greater flexibility for your users and administrators. However, this is a double-edged sword as a traditional firewall cannot be wrapped around the Microsoft 365 platform. The need to protect your Microsoft 365 apps and services remains absolutely crucial though, and this is where **Microsoft Defender for Cloud Apps (MDA)** comes in.

MDA is a **Cloud Access Security Broker (CASB)**. CASBs provide you with the visibility and control to protect your organization's cloud and third-party apps from cyber threats and shadow IT (which is where users feel they do not have the tools to do their jobs, so they look for other, unapproved applications). MDA supports functionalities such as log collection, API connectors, and reverse proxy.

This chapter will cover the following topics:

- Planning your MDA implementation
- Configuring MDA
- Managing Cloud App Discovery
- Managing the MDA catalog
- Managing apps and app connectors in MDA
- Configuring policies and templates
- Using Conditional Access App Control with MDA
- Reviewing and interpreting alerts, reports, and dashboards

Planning your MDA implementation

In this section, you will learn how to plan for and configure MDA. It is a CASB solution designed to provide Microsoft 365 administrators with visibility of all **Software-as-a-Service (SaaS)** applications within their organization and alert them to risky cloud app usage.

The framework of MDA enables you to discover shadow IT activities (for further information, please refer to the *Further reading* section at the end of this chapter), as well as identify, classify, and protect sensitive information stored in the cloud. It also detects anomalous behavior within cloud apps to protect you from cyber threats. This in turn helps you ensure that industry standards for security and compliance are applied to your cloud apps to protect them against data leakage.

> **Note**
>
> MDA was previously known as **Microsoft Cloud App Security**. It is not to be confused with **Office 365 Cloud App Security**, which is a subset of the features of MDA. Office 365 Cloud App Security and MDA are two distinct products and while the former is available with Office 365 Enterprise E5, MDA is available with EM+S E5 and Microsoft 365 E5.
>
> Office 365 Cloud App Security provides visibility into and control over native Office 365 cloud apps only, whereas MDA contains features that provide enhanced visibility and control across a wider range of third-party SaaS solutions.

With MDA, administrators can complete the following tasks:

- **Using Cloud Discovery**: Cloud Discovery allows you to discover the cloud apps used in your organization by uploading logs from your firewall or proxies; these logs are analyzed by MDA to detect cloud app usage. This can be achieved by manually uploading the logs from firewalls or proxies or by configuring log collectors to automate regular log reports.

- **Sanctioning or unsanctioning cloud apps**: The MDA app catalog consists of over 25,000 cloud apps, which are available for use within your Microsoft 365 environment. Microsoft ranks these apps based on industry standards and applies a risk score to each app. This helps you assess how risky an app may be for your organization, thereby allowing you to make informed decisions as to whether you should sanction these apps on your tenant.

- **Using app connectors to gain visibility and control of third-party apps**: If you wish to approve and use non-Microsoft cloud apps in your organization, app connectors allow you to do this. They integrate third-party cloud apps with MDA and extend Microsoft 365 security and protection to these additional apps. This is achieved using APIs issued from the cloud app provider, which allows the app to be accessed and controlled by MDA.

- **Using Azure AD Conditional Access App Control in conjunction with MDA**: MDA can also leverage the powerful capabilities of Azure AD Conditional Access to control cloud apps by using reverse-proxy architecture. Conditional Access App Control allows you to avoid data leakage, enforce encryption, monitor activities on unmanaged devices, and control any access from external networks or IP ranges that may constitute a risk.

- **Using built-in policies or creating custom policies to control SaaS app usage**: MDA comes with a selection of pre-configured policy templates that can be applied to users in your organization when risky activity or behavior is detected within the SaaS apps allowed by your Microsoft 365 tenant.

One example of this kind of policy is detecting multiple failed user login attempts to a cloud app. You can set these templates or create your own custom policies to detect single-instance or repeated behavior, select filters and alerts, and apply governance actions when cloud app activity matches a policy.

Now that you understand what MDA is and the steps you need to consider when planning for it, the next sections will show you how to configure MDA.

Configuring MDA

Now that you understand the principles of MDA, take a look at how you can configure it to gain visibility of your SaaS applications. First, you need to be aware of the following prerequisites for using MDA:

- A valid license to use the MDA service. MDA is available with a variety of Microsoft 365 subscriptions. For more information, please refer to the *Further reading* section at the end of this chapter.

- A **Global Administrator** or **Security Administrator** role.

> **Note**
>
> Once access has been assigned with the required licenses and roles, you may need to wait approximately 15 minutes before you can log in to the MDA portal.

Once you have fulfilled these prerequisites, you can proceed to configure your Cloud Discovery settings. To configure MDA, complete the following steps:

1. Log in to the Microsoft 365 Defender portal at `https://security.microsoft.com` and, from the left menu navigation, choose **Settings**:

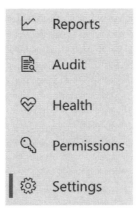

Figure 10.1: The Settings menu in Microsoft 365 Defender

2.   Next, select **Cloud Apps**:

Settings

	Name	Description
	Security center	General settings for the Microsoft 365 security center
	Microsoft 365 Defender	General settings for Microsoft 365 Defender
	Endpoints	General settings for endpoints
	Identities	General settings for identities
	Device discovery	Select your device discovery mode and customize standard discovery settings
	Cloud Apps	General settings for Cloud apps

6 items

Figure 10.2: Cloud Apps settings

This takes you to the full list of Cloud Apps settings – you need to check or configure these before you can begin using MDA. These include the following:

- System
- Cloud Discovery
- Connected Apps
- Information Protection
- Conditional Access App Control

The following screenshot shows some of these settings (you'll have to scroll down to see the others):

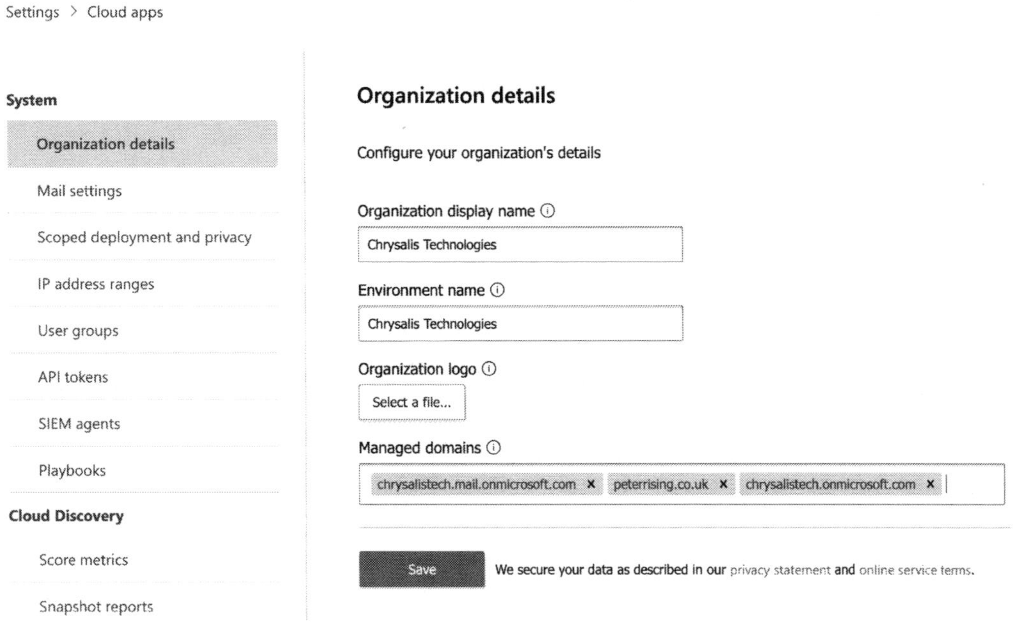

Settings > Cloud apps

System

Organization details

Mail settings

Scoped deployment and privacy

IP address ranges

User groups

API tokens

SIEM agents

Playbooks

Cloud Discovery

Score metrics

Snapshot reports

Organization details

Configure your organization's details

Organization display name ⓘ

Chrysalis Technologies

Environment name ⓘ

Chrysalis Technologies

Organization logo ⓘ

Select a file...

Managed domains ⓘ

chrysalistech.mail.onmicrosoft.com ✕   peterrising.co.uk ✕   chrysalistech.onmicrosoft.com ✕

Save   We secure your data as described in our privacy statement and online service terms.

Figure 10.3: Cloud Apps settings

To progress through a basic setup before using MDA, you should at least configure the settings in the **Organization details** area of the **System** settings, as discussed in the next steps.

3.   Fill in an **Organization display name** for your organization. This will be displayed on emails and web pages sent from the system.

4.   Fill in an **Environment name** (tenant). This information is important when managing more than one tenant.

5.   Upload an image under **Organization logo**, which will be displayed in email notifications and web pages sent from the system.

6.   Add a list of all your **Managed domains** to identify internal users. This is a critical configuration step as MDA uses these to determine which users are internal, which are external, and where files can and cannot be shared. This information is also used for reporting and alerting.

7.   When you have configured the required settings for your organizational needs, click on **Save** to complete the configuration.

Note

There are many more sections and settings within the **Cloud Apps** settings in the Microsoft Defender 365 portal. You can familiarize yourself with all of these using the resources linked in the *Further reading* section at the end of this chapter.

Now that you have completed your basic MDA configuration, you can proceed to the next stage, which is managing Cloud App Discovery.

Managing Cloud App Discovery

With Cloud App Discovery, you can manually upload traffic logs from your firewall and proxies and analyze for cloud app activity. Additionally, you can automate regular log collection. This is done by completing the following steps:

1. Log in to the MDA portal at `https://security.microsoft.com` as a Global Administrator or a Security Administrator and navigate to **Cloud apps | Cloud Discovery**:

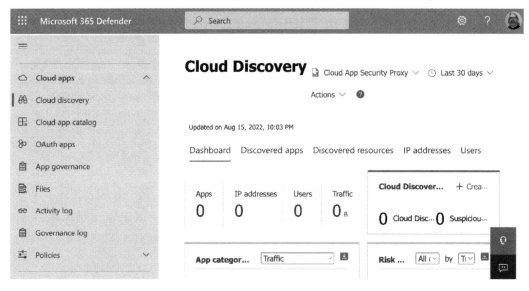

Figure 10.4: Cloud Discovery

2. The first thing to do is to create a **snapshot report** to provide ad hoc visibility into a set of traffic logs you manually upload from your firewalls and proxies. To do this, click on **Cloud App Security Proxy** and choose **Create snapshot report**:

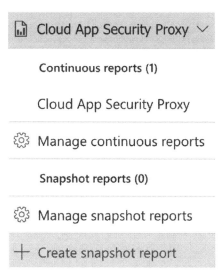

Figure 10.5: Creating a snapshot report

3. Enter a report name and description for your report. You also have the **Anonymize private information** option, as shown in the following screenshot. This should be selected if you need to hide the names of your users:

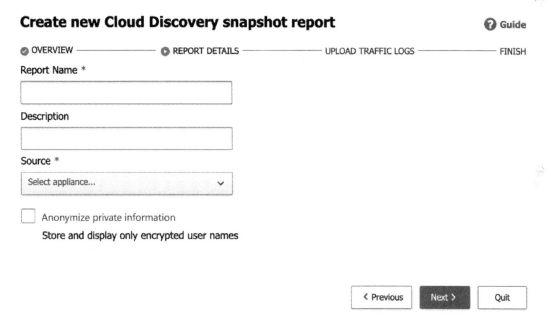

Figure 10.6: The details for creating a snapshot report

4. Click **Select appliance…** under **Source**. You will be able to select your appliance from the list of default values, as shown here:

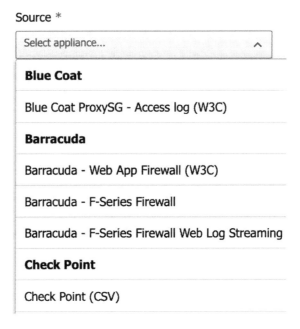

Figure 10.7: Choosing your appliance

5. Browse to your log file and then click **Upload logs >**:

Figure 10.8: Uploading traffic logs

No appliance is available for the purpose of this example; therefore, this process cannot be fully demonstrated. For details on how this can be done, refer to the *Further reading* section.

In addition to snapshot reports, you can also create a **continuous report** to analyze all logs that are forwarded from your network using MDA.

6. Go to **Cloud App Security Proxy | Manage Continuous reports | Create continuous report**:

Create continuous report

Create a customized continuous report for your Cloud Discovery data

Report name *

[   ]

Comments

[   ]

Data sources

◉ All data sources

◯ Specific data sources

Filters

☐ User group ⓘ

☐ IP address tags

☐ IP address ranges ⓘ

ⓘ The custom report can be viewed in the report selector only after the new data is processed.
This may take a while.

[Create]   [Cancel]

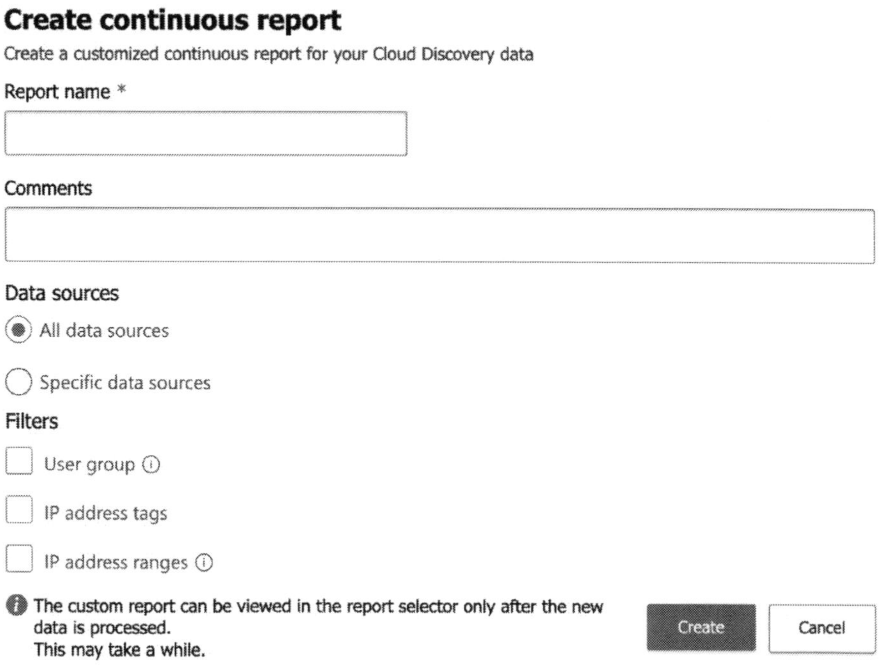

Figure 10.9: Creating a continuous report

You can also automatically collect and upload traffic logs at regular intervals. This is done from the MDA settings (shown earlier in this chapter in *Figure 10.2*).

7. Choose **Automatic log upload** from the **Cloud Discovery** section. Click on the **Add data source…** button from the **Data Sources** tab to add your data source:

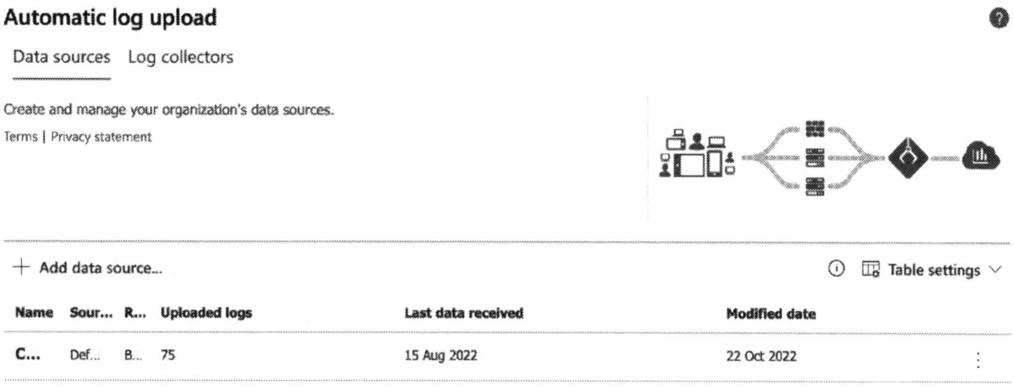

Automatic log upload   ❓

Data sources   Log collectors

Create and manage your organization's data sources.
Terms | Privacy statement

+ Add data source...   ⓘ 🗔 Table settings ∨

Name	Sour...	R...	Uploaded logs	Last data received	Modified date	
C...	Def...	B...	75	15 Aug 2022	22 Oct 2022	⋮

Figure 10.10: Automatic log upload

8. Enter the name for your data source and choose your source and receiver settings in the **Add data source** section, shown here:

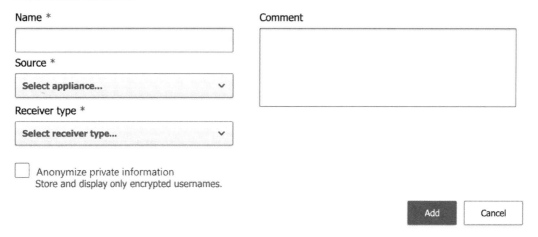

Figure 10.11: Adding a data source

9. Repeat *steps 7* and *8* but this time choose the **Log Collectors** tab and complete the details in the **Create log collector** fields:

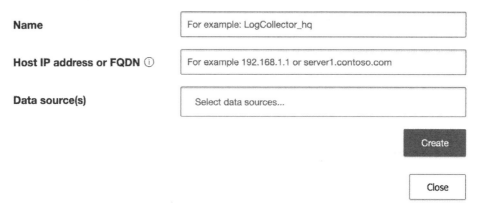

Figure 10.12: Adding the log collector settings

Uploading your traffic logs will provide you with valuable intelligence on your cloud app usage. Next, you will learn how to manage the Cloud Apps catalog in MDA.

Managing the MDA catalog

MDA includes a vast **app catalog** consisting of both native Microsoft 365 and third-party cloud applications. Microsoft assigns a risk score to each of these cloud apps, which you can assess to decide whether to sanction an app for use within your Microsoft 365 environment.

To access the app catalog, carry out the following steps in the MDA portal at `https://security.microsoft.com`:

1. Navigate to **Cloud Apps | Cloud app catalog**. Each app has a risk score, and you can mark an app as sanctioned or unsanctioned using the two icons to the right of each app listing, under **Actions**:

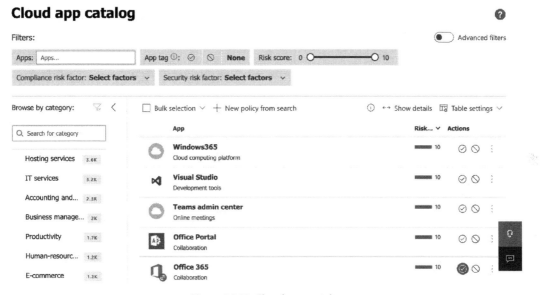

Figure 10.13: Cloud app catalog

2. Clicking on the three dots to the right will also provide you with further actions you can take for the apps in the app catalog, such as tagging apps, app deployment options, and viewing the app score and app details. This is shown in the following screenshot; for more details, please refer to the *Further reading* section at the end of the chapter:

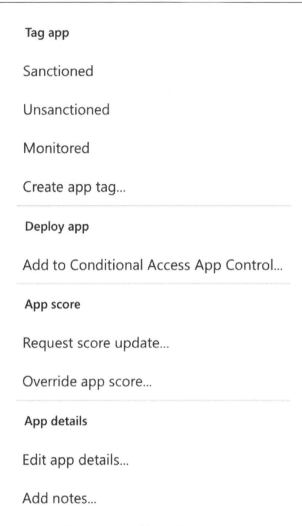

Tag app

Sanctioned

Unsanctioned

Monitored

Create app tag...

Deploy app

Add to Conditional Access App Control...

App score

Request score update...

Override app score...

App details

Edit app details...

Add notes...

Figure 10.14: Additional app options

The next section will examine how to connect an app using MDA.

Managing apps and app connectors in MDA

You can connect apps in MDA to provide greater visibility by taking the following steps:

1. From the Microsoft 365 Defender portal at `https://security.microsoft.com`, navigate to **Settings** | **Cloud Apps** | **Connected Apps** | **App Connectors**. This will take you to the connected apps section, as shown in the following screenshot:

App Connectors

App connectors provide you with greater visibility and control over your cloud apps.   ❓

Filters: 🔘 Advanced filters

App: **Select apps** ⌄	App category: **Select category** ⌄	Connected by: **Select users** ⌄

➕ Connect an app ⌄   ⓘ   ↔ Show details   ▽ Hide filters   ▦ Table settings ⌄

	App	Status	Was connect...	Last activity	Accounts ⌄	
▣	**Office 365** Collaboration	✅ Connected	17 Mar 2019 0...	22 Oct 2022 1...	596	⋮
✖	**Dropbox -Sales** Cloud storage	⚠ ...	10 Feb 2020 1...	—	0	⋮

Figure 10.15: Connected apps

2. Click on the **Connect an app** option. You will be given the option to add connected apps, as shown here:

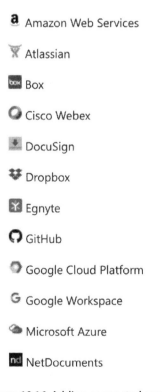

ⓐ Amazon Web Services

▽ Atlassian

▨ Box

◯ Cisco Webex

⬇ DocuSign

✖ Dropbox

☒ Egnyte

◉ GitHub

⬡ Google Cloud Platform

G Google Workspace

☁ Microsoft Azure

▪ NetDocuments

Figure 10.16: Adding connected apps

3.   Select **Microsoft Azure** to connect to MDA for this example:

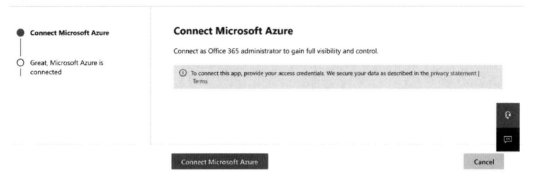

Figure 10.17: Connecting an app

4.   Click on **Connect Microsoft Azure**. You will see the following:

Figure 10.18: Connecting an app

5.   Click on **Done**. You will see your connected app in the list of connected apps, as in the following screenshot:

App	Status	Was conn...	Last activ...	Accou... ∨	
Office 365 Collaboration	✓ ...	17 Mar 2...	22 Oct 20...	596	⋮
Microsoft Azure Cloud computing platform	✓ ...	22 Oct 20...	19 Oct 20...	3	⋮

Figure 10.19: The list of connected apps

The next section will explain how MDA allows you to control your cloud apps by applying built-in or custom policies.

Configuring policies and templates

With MDA policies, you can control your cloud apps with governance and compliance actions. This can be achieved by completing the following steps:

1. From the Microsoft 365 Defender portal, select **Cloud apps | Policies**, as in the following screenshot:

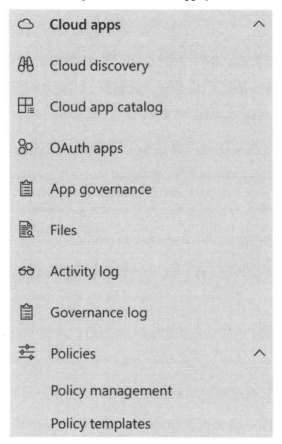

Figure 10.20: MDA policies

2. Choose **Policy management**. You will see a list of active MDA policies. These can be filtered by risk category for ease of use, as shown in the following screenshot. From this view, you can choose to view or edit the policy settings by double-clicking on the policy or choosing the cog wheel to the right of the policy. You can also choose to view all matches or alerts for the policy:

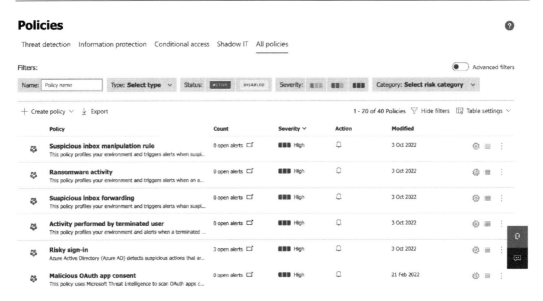

Figure 10.21: MDA policy management

3. Viewing all matches for the risky sign-in policy returned the results shown in the following screenshot. From the action menu (the three dots to the right), you can then make decisions relating to the match:

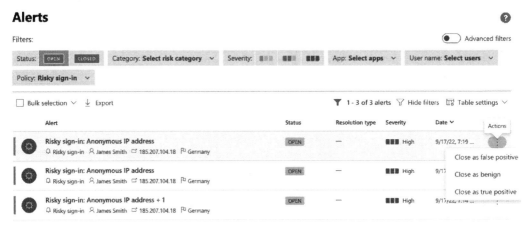

Figure 10.22: Policy match alerts

4. You can create new policies from the policy management section by clicking **Create policy**:

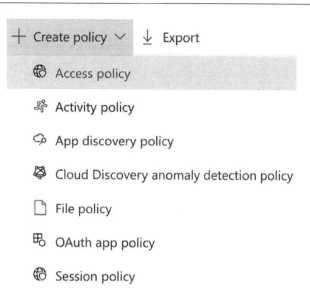

Figure 10.23: Policy creation

MDA also includes several built-in policy templates from which you can create policies. In the steps that follow, you will create a policy based on one of these available templates:

5. Select **Policy templates** from the **Policies** section of MDA. You will see the policy templates displayed as shown:

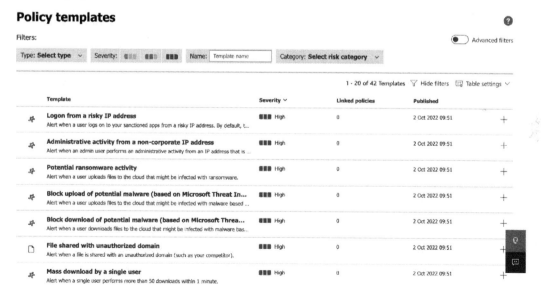

Figure 10.24: Policy templates

6. Use the example of **Mass download by a single user** to create a policy from this template by clicking the + symbol to the right of the policy. You will see that the type of policy created with this template is an activity policy. You can optionally change the policy template, alter the policy name and description, and choose the category and policy severity from here if desired:

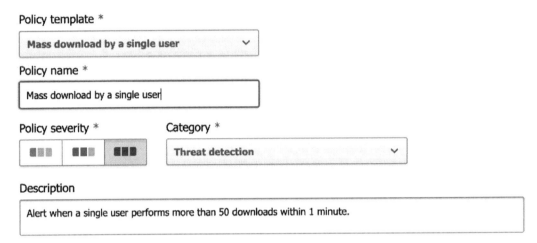

Figure 10.25: Creating an activity policy

The next few options all appear on the same screen but have been separated into different images as there are many to choose from. You will need to scroll through the policy settings options one by one.

7. Configure the filtering settings for your policy, as in the following screenshot:

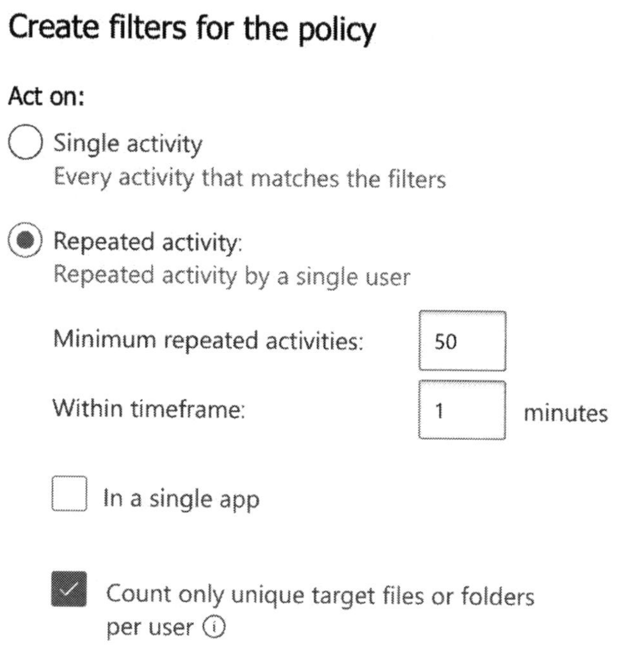

Create filters for the policy

Act on:

○ Single activity
Every activity that matches the filters

● Repeated activity:
Repeated activity by a single user

Minimum repeated activities: `50`

Within timeframe: `1`   minutes

☐ In a single app

☑ Count only unique target files or folders per user ⓘ

Figure 10.26: Creating policy filters

8. Next, scroll down to view and modify the activity-matching settings for your policy. This can be used to include any and all detail you want to include, such as users, groups, activity types, and more, as shown in the following screenshot:

Figure 10.27: Modifying the activity-matching settings

Scroll further, and you can also configure alerts to notify users or administrators when there is a policy match, as shown:

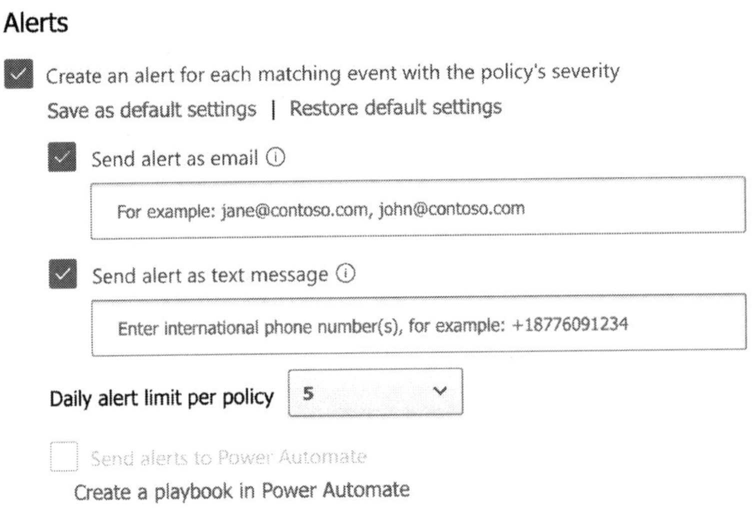

Alerts
Create an alert for each matching event with the policy's severity
Save as default settings | Restore default settings
Send alert as email
For example: jane@contoso.com, john@contoso.com
Send alert as text message
Enter international phone number(s), for example: +18776091234
Daily alert limit per policy
5
Send alerts to Power Automate
Create a playbook in Power Automate

Figure 10.28: Configuring alerts

9. Finally, scroll down further and choose which governance actions are applied when a policy match occurs. These can be set for either all apps or just Office 365 apps. The **Governance actions** options are shown in the following screenshot:

Governance actions
All apps
Notify user
Notify additional users
Suspend user
For Azure Active Directory users
Require user to sign in again
For Azure Active Directory users
Confirm user compromised
For Azure Active Directory users
Office 365
Suspend user
Require user to sign in again
Confirm user compromised

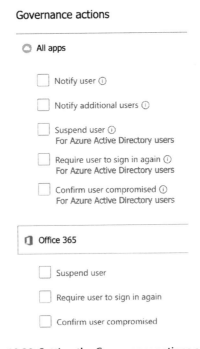

Figure 10.29: Setting the Governance actions options

10. When you are happy with your policy settings, click on **Create** to complete the setup of your policy. Your policy is created, and you can search for it in **MDA** under **Policy Management** by clicking on the three dots. You can then modify the policy if required, as well as clicking on **View all matches** to see any instances where your policy has been triggered:

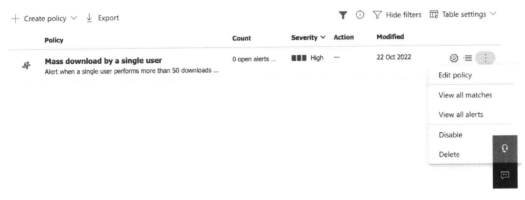

Figure 10.30: Viewing all matches

The policy templates available to you in MDA provide many useful options to alert you to cloud app activity and respond by applying governance actions.

Next, we will examine how Conditional Access App Control can be used with MDA to prevent data leakage, enforce encryption, and control access to your cloud applications in Microsoft 365.

Using Conditional Access App Control with MDA

MDA can integrate with Azure AD Conditional Access to control access to your Microsoft 365 cloud apps. Conditional Access App Control allows you to specify conditions where users can be informed that their access is being monitored, blocked from downloading content, or forced to use only online web apps.

To view Conditional Access App Control apps, complete the following steps:

1. From the Microsoft 365 Defender portal, go to **Settings | Connected Apps** and select **Conditional Access App Control apps**. This takes you to the page shown in the following screenshot, where you can see native Microsoft 365 apps included. It is also possible to add a SAML application from your identity provider:

Conditional Access App Control apps

The Conditional Access App Control adds real-time monitoring and control capabilities for your apps.
To enable Conditional Access App Control capabilities on your apps, follow the deployment instructions.

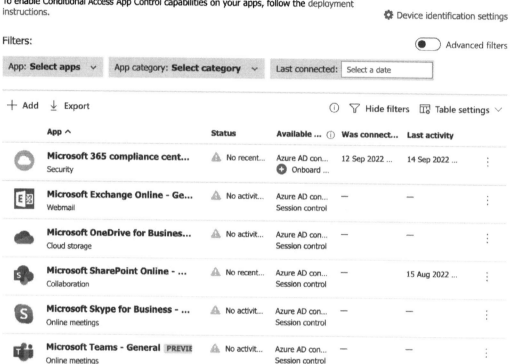

Figure 10.31: Conditional Access App Control

2. Using the Exchange Online app as an example, create a Conditional Access policy to use session controls. To do this, go to https://portal.azure.com and navigate to **Azure Active Directory | Security | Conditional Access**. Set up a new policy or edit an existing policy.

3. Click on **Access Controls | Session** within the policy settings to choose your session controls. Under the **Use Conditional Access App Control** option, there are three available settings. For this example, set it to **Monitor only (Preview)**. The session control settings are shown in the following screenshot:

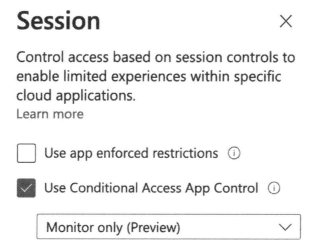

Session   ✕

Control access based on session controls to enable limited experiences within specific cloud applications.
Learn more

☐ Use app enforced restrictions ⓘ

☑ Use Conditional Access App Control ⓘ

┌─────────────────────────────────┐
│ Monitor only (Preview)   ⌄ │
└─────────────────────────────────┘

Figure 10.32: Session controls

4. After saving your Conditional Access policy, sign in to Exchange Online as a user targeted by the policy. Log in via `https://outlook.office.com` and enter your credentials. Now that you have enabled session controls on the Conditional Access policy, you will be warned that access to Exchange Online is monitored:

Access to Microsoft Exchange Online is monitored

For improved security, your organization allows access to **Microsoft Exchange Online** in monitor mode.

Access is only available from a web browser.

 Getting ready...

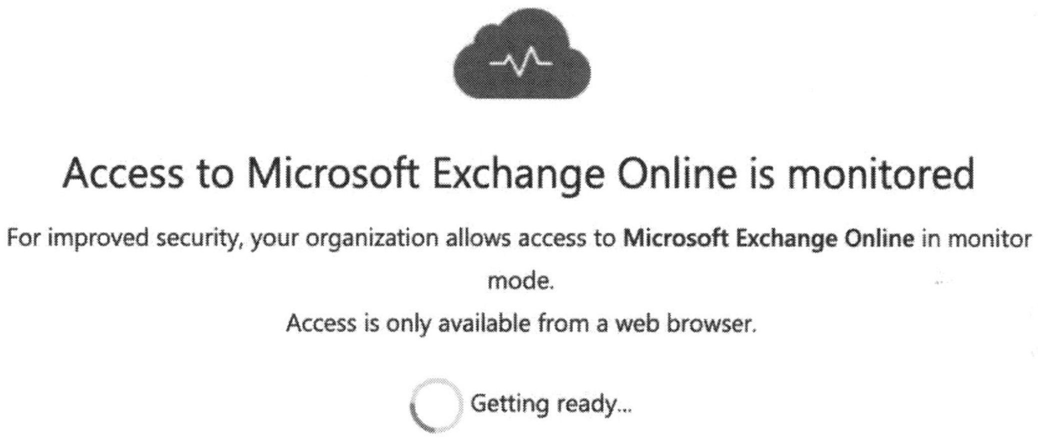

Figure 10.33: User warning of monitoring activity

5. Now that you have logged in and completed the Conditional Access requirements, return to the **Conditional Access App Control apps** setting within MDA. You will see that **Microsoft Exchange Online - General** is showing as **Connected** and also has some recent activity:

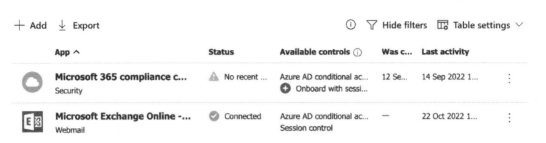

Figure 10.34: Exchange Online app connected

6.   Click on the app to inspect the available tabs, which contain information related to this cloud
     app. Click on **Activity log** to see the corresponding user activity:

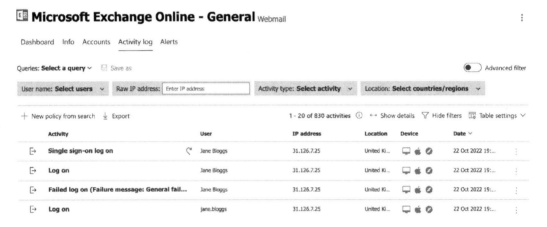

Figure 10.35: Exchange Online user activity in Conditional Access App Control

Conditional Access App Control extends MDA with controls to help you monitor and protect your
Microsoft 365 cloud apps. In the preceding example, we used Exchange Online in a Conditional Access
policy and enforced session controls to make the activities visible in the MDA portal. There are many
other apps to which Conditional Access App Control can be applied, and you can take more aggressive
actions than simply monitoring user activity, such as blocking downloads.

In the final section of this chapter, we will review the MDA dashboard and learn how reports and logs
can be used to gather vital intelligence on cloud app activity within the Microsoft 365 environment.

Reviewing and interpreting alerts, reports, and dashboards

With MDA, you can review information on file activity within your cloud applications by completing the following steps:

1. From the Microsoft 365 Defender portal, go to **Cloud Apps | Files**, as shown in the following screenshot:

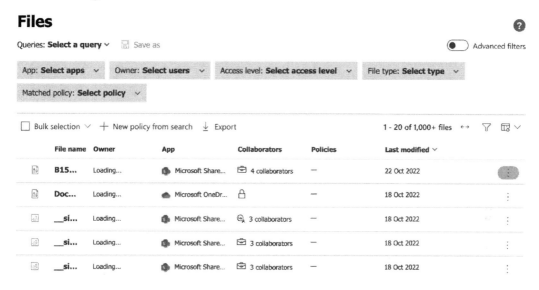

Figure 10.36: Investigating files

2. Click on an individual file to see information related to it. Additionally, selecting the three dots next to an individual file item will show you the recent file activity in this area for your cloud apps, such as related alerts and governance, and allow you to apply the required response actions:

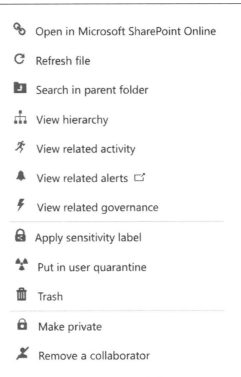

Figure 10.37: The available file actions

3.   From the same section of the Microsoft 365 Defender portal, you can also access the **Activity log**:

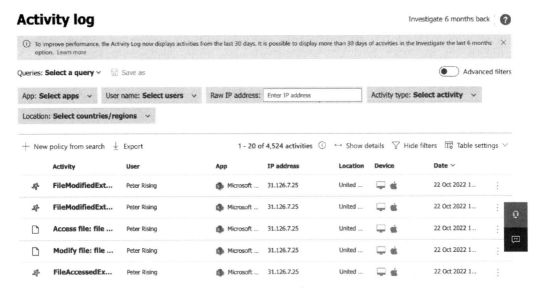

Figure 10.38: Activity log

4. Use the queries and filters at the top of the activity log to view specific log activity. Expanding each log entry displays additional details related to the recorded activity. Clicking the three dots to the right of each log entry shows you the following options: **View activity of the same type**, **View all user activity**, **View activity from the same IP address**, and **View activity from the same country/region**:

Figure 10.39: Activity log line options

In this section, we examined the available options in MDA to view file activities, alerts, and activity logs, and the associated actions on offer.

Summary

This chapter provided an introduction to MDA. We learned about the two variations of MDA and how Office 365 Cloud App Security is a subset of the broad array of features available in MDA. We learned how MDA can provide visibility of your cloud app usage within your Microsoft 365 environment, both with native Microsoft 365 apps and third-party cloud apps. We also examined how to discover cloud activity by uploading traffic logs from your firewalls and proxies, along with how to sanction and unsanction cloud apps and connect third-party cloud apps using the app connector. The chapter also demonstrated how policies can be applied from built-in templates and policy management creation to control cloud app usage. Finally, we learned how Azure AD Conditional Access can be integrated with MDA using session controls and how to view alerts, file activity, and activity logs.

The next chapter will introduce the features of sensitivity labels in **Microsoft Purview**. We will learn how to plan your organization's deployment of sensitivity labels. In addition, we will learn how to create labels and label policies, how to configure and use Activity Explorer, and how to use sensitivity labels with Teams, SharePoint, OneDrive, and Office apps.

Questions

1. Which of the following is not a possible application of Conditional Access App Control?

    A. Monitoring access

    B. Blocking uploads

    C. Blocking downloads

2. True or false: Defender for Cloud Apps policies can be used to apply sensitivity labels to content.

    A. True

    B. False

3. Which of the following are names of Defender for Cloud Apps policies? (Choose three)

    A. Access policy

    B. Device compliance policy

    C. File policy

    D. App Protection policy

    E. Activity policy

4. True or false: Office 365 Cloud App Security contains all the features of Microsoft Defender for Cloud Apps.

    A. True

    B. False

5. Where in the MDA portal would you go to sanction or unsanction an app?

    A. **Cloud App Control | Policies**

    B. **Cloud app catalog | Cloud Apps**

    C. **Cloud Apps | Cloud app catalog**

    D. **Cloud Discovery | Cloud app catalog**

6. When configuring a policy template, which of the following alerts can be configured? (Choose three)

    A. Send alert as email

    B. Send alert via Microsoft Teams

    C. Send alert as text message

    D. Send alert via RSS feed

    E. Send alert to Power Automate

7. Which of the following Microsoft 365 admin roles can be used to configure Cloud App Security? (Choose two)

   A. Security Administrator

   B. Global Reader

   C. Global Administrator

   D. User Administrator

   E. Service Administrator

8. True or false? When you create a Cloud Discovery snapshot report, you have the option to anonymize private information.

   A. True

   B. False

9. Which of the following URLs could you use to access Microsoft Defender for Cloud Apps? (Choose two)

   A. `https://security.microsoft.com`

   B. `https://admin.cloudappsecurity.com`

   C. `https://microsoft.cloudappsecurity.com`

   D. `https://portal.cloudappsecurity.com`

10. What does CASB stand for?

    A. Cloud Access Security Broker

    B. Cloud Activity Security Broker

    C. Cloud Active Sensitivity Broker

    D. Cloud Access Security Bridge

Further reading

Please refer to the following links for more information:

- Top 20 CASB use cases: `https://query.prod.cms.rt.microsoft.com/cms/api/am/binary/RE3nibJ`

- Defender for Cloud Apps overview: `https://learn.microsoft.com/en-us/defender-cloud-apps/what-is-defender-for-cloud-apps`

- Comparing Office 365 Cloud App Security and Microsoft Defender for Cloud Apps: `https://learn.microsoft.com/en-us/defender-cloud-apps/editions-cloud-app-security-o365?WT.mc_id=EM-MVP-4039827`

- *Set up Cloud Discovery*: `https://learn.microsoft.com/en-us/defender-cloud-apps/set-up-cloud-discovery`

- *Add custom apps to Cloud Discovery*: `https://learn.microsoft.com/en-us/defender-cloud-apps/cloud-discovery-custom-apps?WT.mc_id=EM-MVP-4039827`

- Setting up Microsoft Defender for Cloud Apps: `https://learn.microsoft.com/en-us/defender-cloud-apps/general-setup?wt.mc_id=4039827`

- Cloud App Discovery: `https://learn.microsoft.com/en-us/defender-cloud-apps/create-snapshot-cloud-discovery-reports?wt.mc_id=4039827`

- Connecting apps: `https://learn.microsoft.com/en-us/defender-cloud-apps/enable-instant-visibility-protection-and-governance-actions-for-your-apps?wt.mc_id=4039827`

- *Activity filters and queries*: `https://learn.microsoft.com/en-us/defender-cloud-apps/activity-filters-queries?WT.mc_id=EM-MVP-4039827`

- Microsoft Defender for Cloud Apps policies: `https://learn.microsoft.com/en-us/defender-cloud-apps/control-cloud-apps-with-policies?wt.mc_id=4039827`

- Conditional Access App Control: `https://learn.microsoft.com/en-gb/defender-cloud-apps/proxy-intro-aad`

- Reports: `https://learn.microsoft.com/en-us/defender-cloud-apps/built-in-reports?wt.mc_id=4039827`

- Investigating alerts: `https://learn.microsoft.com/en-us/defender-cloud-apps/managing-alerts?wt.mc_id=4039827`

- What is SaaS: `https://azure.microsoft.com/en-gb/resources/cloud-computing-dictionary/what-is-saas`

- Tagging apps: `https://learn.microsoft.com/en-us/defender-cloud-apps/discovered-app-queries`

- Working with risk score: `https://learn.microsoft.com/en-us/defender-cloud-apps/risk-score`

Part 3: Implementing and Managing Information Protection

In this part, you will learn how to configure and manage Microsoft 365 Information Protection. On completion, you will be able to describe and implement secure data access within Microsoft 365 and manage sensitivity labels and policies, **Data Loss Prevention** (**DLP**), and features for data life cycle management, such as retention labels and policies and record management.

This part has the following chapters:

- *Chapter 11, Managing Sensitive Information*
- *Chapter 12, Managing Microsoft Purview Data Loss Prevention*
- *Chapter 13, Managing Microsoft Purview Data Lifecycle Management*

11

Managing Sensitive Information

With data protection being more critical than it has ever been before, Microsoft 365 administrators need to consider how to protect their organization's data and ensure that only those that are authorized can consume it. **Microsoft Purview** (which is the umbrella term for compliance in Microsoft 365) provides **Information Protection** features to respond to these requirements. Information Protection enables the use of sensitivity labels and policies to allow users to apply permissions and content marking to the data with which they are working. This includes documents and emails, teams, groups and sites, and much more. When you protect content with a sensitivity label, encryption is applied, ensuring that the content may only be accessed by those who have permission.

This chapter will introduce the features and capabilities of sensitivity labels in Microsoft Purview. You will learn how to plan your organization's sensitivity label solution, understand **sensitive information types (SITs)**, and create labels and label policies. Additionally, you will learn how to configure and use **Activity explorer**, and how to use sensitivity labels with Teams, SharePoint, OneDrive, and Office apps.

We will cover the following main topics:

- Planning a sensitivity label solution for your organization
- Creating and managing SITs
- Setting up sensitive labels and policies
- Configuring and using **Activity explorer**
- Using sensitivity labels with Teams, SharePoint, OneDrive, and Office apps

> **Note**
> In the Microsoft documentation, you will often find the terms *Azure Information Protection* and *Microsoft Information Protection* used to describe the same technology. For the purposes of this book, I will use the newer term, *Microsoft Purview Information Protection*.

Planning a sensitivity label solution for your organization

To effectively plan for the deployment of sensitivity labels in your organization and decide which Microsoft 365 subscriptions you are going to require for your users, you first need to understand how Microsoft Purview Information Protection is licensed. The following list identifies the relevant subscription options for performing specific tasks in Microsoft Purview Information Protection:

- **Manual sensitivity labeling**: The following licenses will provide the required user rights:

  - Microsoft 365 E5/A5/G5

  - Microsoft 365 E3/A3/G3

  - Microsoft 365 F1/F3

  - Microsoft Business Premium (Information Protection for Office 365 – Standard should be enabled if only an E5 license has been assigned)

  - Enterprise Mobility + Security E3/E5

  - Office 365 E5/A5/E3/A3

  - Azure Information Protection Plan 1

  - Azure Information Protection Plan 2

- **Automatic sensitivity labeling (client and service side)**: The following licenses will provide the required user rights:

  - Microsoft 365 E5/A5/G5

  - Microsoft 365 E5 Compliance

  - Microsoft 365 E5/A5/G5 Information Protection and Governance

  - Office 365 E5/A5/G5

- **Automatic sensitivity labeling (client side only)**: The following licenses will provide the required user rights:

  - Enterprise Mobility + Security E5/A5/G5

  - Azure Information Protection Plan 2

- **Power BI and export from Power BI to Excel, PowerPoint, or PDF**: The following licenses will provide the required user rights:

  - Microsoft 365 E5/A5/G5

  - Microsoft 365 E3/A3/G3

  - Microsoft 365 F1/F3

- Microsoft Business Premium

- Enterprise Mobility + Security E3/E5

- Azure Information Protection Plan 1

- Azure Information Protection Plan 2

Once you have determined your licensing requirements and acquired the necessary licenses for your users, you may proceed to create your sensitivity labels and policies and apply them as required.

However, before creating your labels and policies, it is important to understand SITs, which are relevant not only to auto-labeling with Microsoft Purview Information Protection but also to **data loss prevention** (**DLP**) (which will be covered in the next chapter – *Chapter 12, Managing Microsoft Purview Data Loss Prevention*). Let's explore SITs in the following section.

Creating and managing SITs

SITs are pattern-based classifiers that can detect information such as credit card numbers to identify sensitive items under your organization's control. Microsoft Purview provides you with the following methods to identify these items so that they can be classified manually by users, or by using automated pattern recognition and machine learning processes.

An SIT is defined by a pattern that can be identified by the following characteristics:

- Regular expressions or functions

- Dictionary keyword

- Checksums

- Confidence levels

- Proximity

There are many built-in SITs available as part of Microsoft Purview. These can be viewed in the Microsoft Purview compliance portal at `https://compliance.microsoft.com` under the **Data classification** section, as shown in the following screenshot:

Data classification

Overview   Trainable classifiers   **Sensitive info types**   EDM classifiers   Content explorer   Activity explorer

The sensitive info types here are available to use in your security and compliance policies. These include a large collection of types we provide, spanning regions around the globe, as well as any custom types you have created.

+ Create sensitive info type   ○ Refresh   307 items   🔎 Search

Name ↑	Type	Publisher
☐ ABA Routing Number	Entity	Microsoft Corporation
☐ ASP.NET Machine Key	Credential	Microsoft Corporation
☐ All Credential Types	BundledCredential	Microsoft Corporation
☐ All Full Names	BundledEntity	Microsoft Corporation
☐ All Medical Terms And Conditions	BundledEntity	Microsoft Corporation
☐ All Physical Addresses	BundledEntity	Microsoft Corporation

Figure 11.1: Built-in SITs

However, there may also be occasions wherein organizations need to add one or more custom SITs to allow the identification and protection of information, which is not covered by the built-in options.

To create a custom SIT in the Microsoft Purview compliance portal, you will need to have either Global Administrator or Compliance Administrator permissions. Then, complete the following steps:

1. Go to the **Sensitive info types** tab and click **Create sensitive info type**, as shown in the following screenshot:

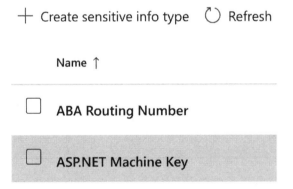

Figure 11.2: Creating an SIT

2. Enter a name and description for your new SIT and then click on **Next**, as shown in the following screenshot. Here, let's create an entry for Bank Account Number:

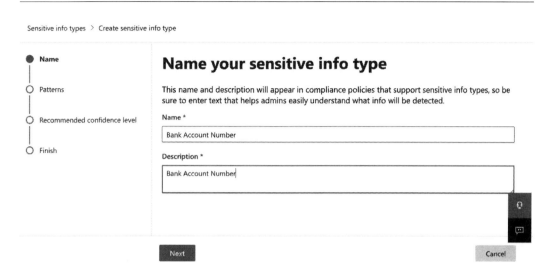

Figure 11.3: Choosing a name and description

3. Go to the **Patterns** section. Here you need to define the patterns that will be used for this SIT. Click on **Create pattern**:

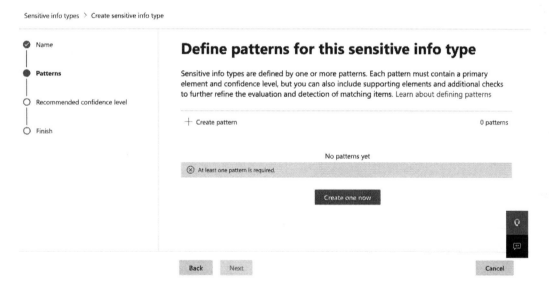

Figure 11.4: Defining patterns for the sensitive info type

4. The **New pattern** dialog box appears. Choose your settings for mandatory fields, including **Confidence level** and **Primary element**. You can optionally complete fields for **Character proximity**, **Supporting elements**, and **Additional checks**:

New pattern

At minimum, a pattern should have a confidence level and primary element to detect. Adding supporting elements, character proximity, and additional checks will help increase accuracy.

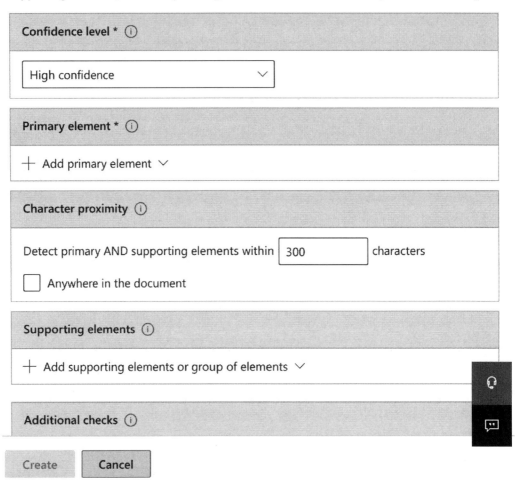

Figure 11.5: Defining patterns for the sensitive info type

5. First, choose the **Confidence level** setting. This setting will be used to reflect the confidence of the match. Typically, the confidence level will increase when you add supporting elements to your SIT. The more supporting elements are specified, the higher the confidence level you should select. For this example, set a **High confidence** level, and then in the steps that follow, define the supporting elements:

Figure 11.6: Setting the confidence level

6. Next, click on **Add primary element**, and you will see the element types you can choose from. **Keyword lists** and **keyword dictionaries** are the simplest to set up, but **regular expressions** are usually the most efficient. For this example, choose **Regular expression**:

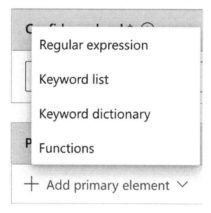

Figure 11.7: Add a regular expression as a primary element

> **Note**
>
> Understanding and creating regular expressions is a complex subject and beyond the scope of this book. To learn more about how regular expressions work and how to create them, there are many online sources you can consult, such as https://regex101.com/.

7. Give your regular expression an ID; for this example, we've used Bank Account Number. For the **Regular expression** field, enter the value of \d(8). Complete this section with weight values of 2,4,6,1,3,5,7,0 and values of 8 for **Position of the checksum digit** and 9 for **Mod**. To better understand why we are choosing these values, refer to the *Further reading* section at the end of this chapter. Click **Done**:

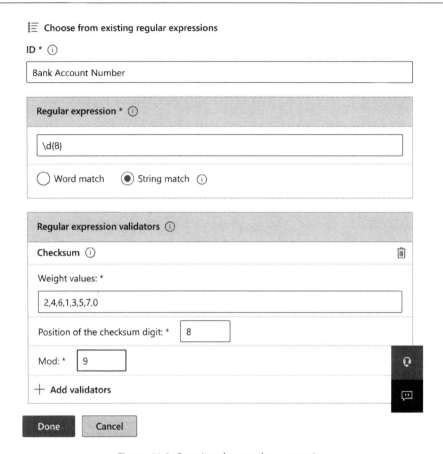

Figure 11.8: Creating the regular expression

8. Next, set **Character proximity**. When the primary element (defined in *Figure 11.8*) is matched, any supporting elements will match only when found within this proximity to the primary element. The closer the primary and supporting elements are to each other, the more likely the detected content will be what you are looking for. For this example, leave the value as 300, which is the default value in this case:

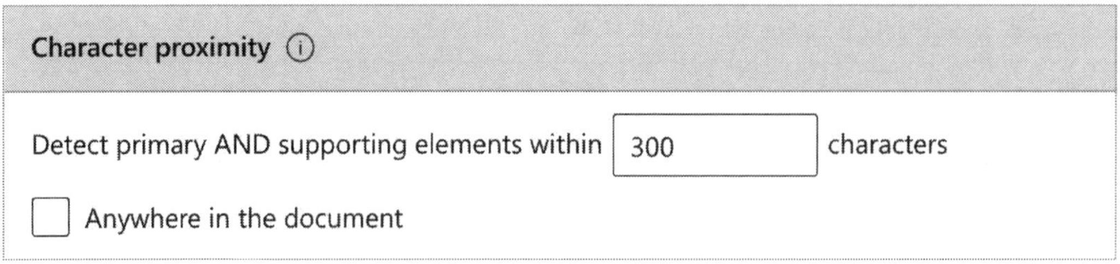

Character proximity ⓘ

Detect primary AND supporting elements within [300]   characters

☐ Anywhere in the document

Figure 11.9: Setting the character proximity

9. Next, move to **Supporting elements** and click **Add supporting elements or group of elements**:

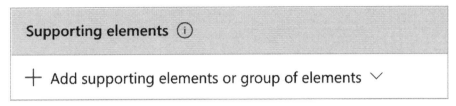

Figure 11.10: Setting the supporting elements

10. The following options appear where you can choose **Elements** or **Groups**. For this example, select **Keyword list**:

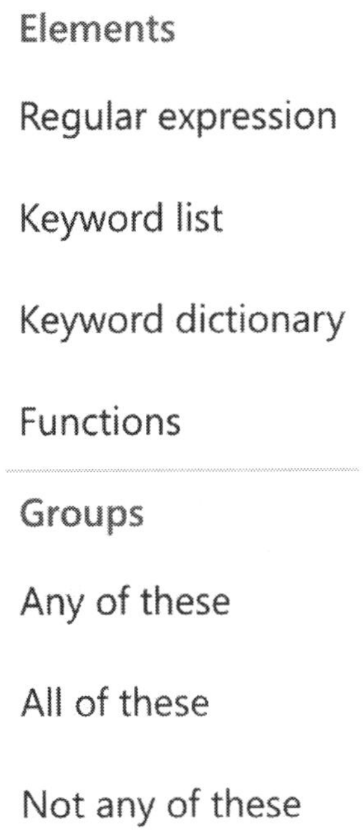

Elements

Regular expression

Keyword list

Keyword dictionary

Functions

Groups

Any of these

All of these

Not any of these

Figure 11.11: Available supporting element types

11. Enter an ID and, for this example, choose from a list of **Case sensitive** and/or **Case insensitive** keyword groups, as shown. Then, click **Done**:

Add a keyword list

Keyword lists identify the words and phrases you want this info type to detect. For example, the keyword list to identify Netherlands VAT numbers is 'VAT number, vat no, vat number, VAT#'. Learn how to create keyword lists

:≡ Choose from existing keyword lists

ID * ⓘ

Bank Account Number

Keyword group #1 * ⓘ   🗑

Case insensitive

Bank Account Number

Case sensitive

Bank account number

◉ Word match   ◯ String match

+ **Add another keyword group**
+ Add proximity for this element

[Done] [Cancel]

Figure 11.12: Adding a keyword list

12. Finally, if required, you may use the **Additional checks** options to exclude or include certain values. To do this, click on **Add additional checks**:

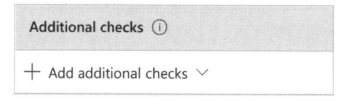

Figure 11.13: Adding additional checks

13. You will see the list shown in the following screenshot. For this example, select **Include or exclude prefixes**:

Exclude specific values

Starts or doesn't start with characters

Ends or doesn't end with characters

Exclude duplicate characters

Include or exclude prefixes

Include or exclude suffixes

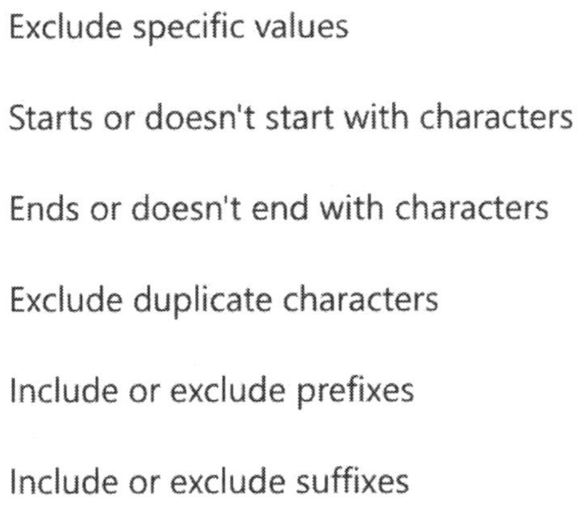

Figure 11.14: Specifying an additional value

14. For this example, include the Acc no prefix as an additional value. Click **Done**:

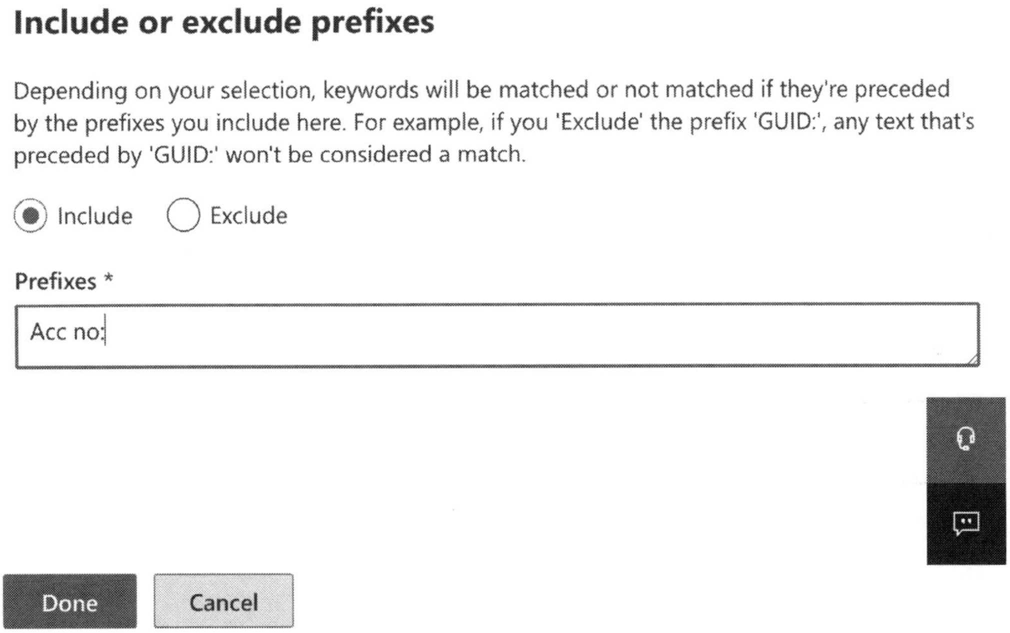

Include or exclude prefixes

Depending on your selection, keywords will be matched or not matched if they're preceded by the prefixes you include here. For example, if you 'Exclude' the prefix 'GUID:', any text that's preceded by 'GUID:' won't be considered a match.

◉ Include   ○ Exclude

Prefixes *

Acc no:

Done   Cancel

Figure 11.15: Include or exclude prefixes

15. All the required pattern options have now been set. Click **Create**:

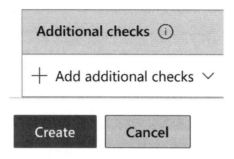

Figure 11.16: Create the pattern

16. You will see the pattern created. Click **Next**:

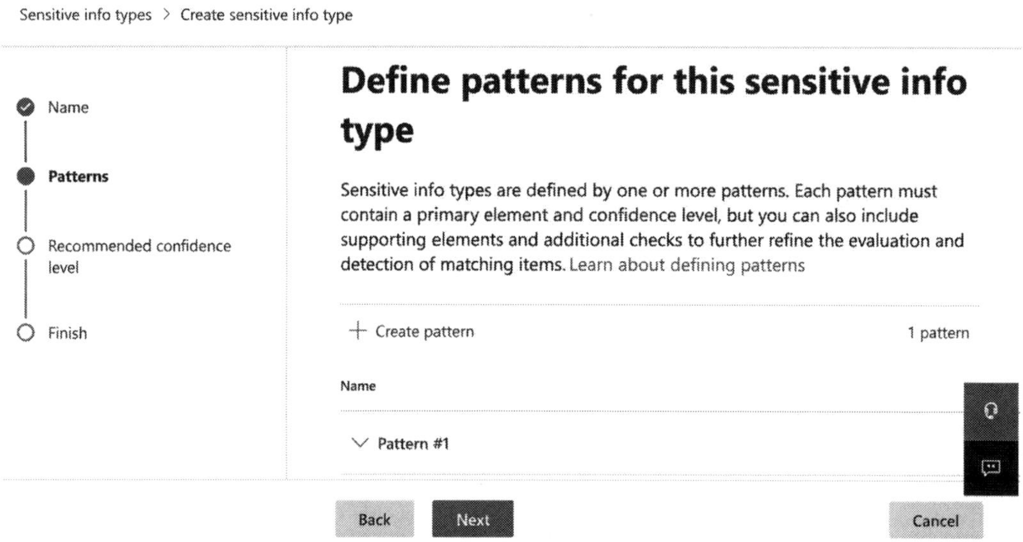

Sensitive info types > Create sensitive info type

✅ Name

● **Patterns**

○ Recommended confidence level

○ Finish

Define patterns for this sensitive info type

Sensitive info types are defined by one or more patterns. Each pattern must contain a primary element and confidence level, but you can also include supporting elements and additional checks to further refine the evaluation and detection of matching items. Learn about defining patterns

+ Create pattern   1 pattern

Name

⌄ Pattern #1

Back   Next   Cancel

Figure 11.17: Created pattern

17. Choose the recommended confidence level and click **Next**:

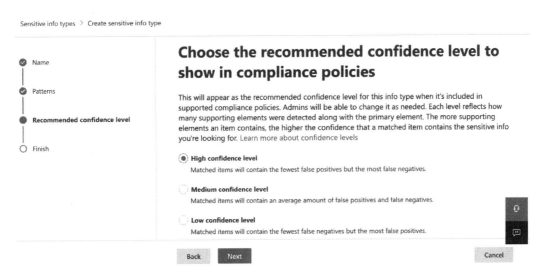

Figure 11.18: Choose the recommended confidence level

18. Review your settings and click **Create**:

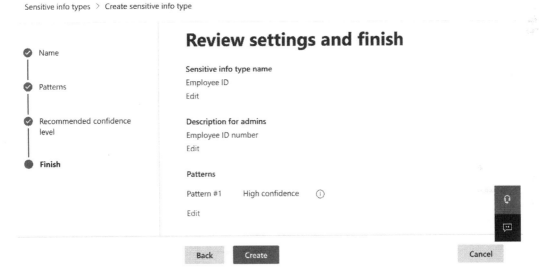

Figure 11.19: Review settings and finish

19. When the wizard finishes, click **Done**:

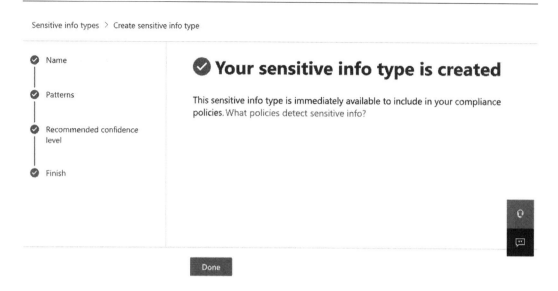

Figure 11.20: SIT successfully created

20. Your custom SIT is now set up and available. It is recommended that you test this before informing your Microsoft 365 users that it is available to them. A custom SIT can be added to a new auto-labeling policy:

Data classification

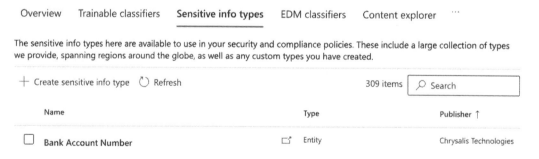

Figure 11.21: SIT shown in Data classification

In this section, we learned that while the built-in SITs included in the Microsoft Purview compliance portal will usually fulfill most requirements, it may also be necessary on some occasions to create one or more custom SITs. We learned how to create a custom SIT by using a regular expression.

Next, we will learn how to set up sensitivity labels and policies.

Setting up sensitivity labels and policies

The core functionality of Microsoft Information Protection is based on sensitivity labels and policies. Microsoft 365 administrators can define **sensitivity labels** in the Microsoft Purview compliance portal. These labels can be configured with protection settings and visual markings (such as watermarks). Furthermore, depending on your subscriptions, they may also include conditions (using the SITs described in the previous section) so that a label can be automatically applied.

Once labels have been created, policies may then be defined in order to determine which users will be able to see and use the labels within their Microsoft Office applications.

Now, let's take a look at how sensitivity labeling works, starting with setting up labels from the Microsoft Purview Compliance portal.

Setting up labels

To create a label in Microsoft Purview, complete the following steps:

1. Navigate to **Information protection**, as shown in the following screenshot:

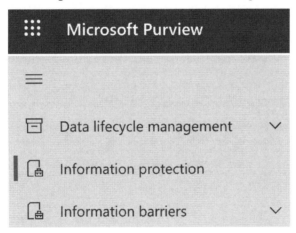

Figure 11.22: Information protection in Microsoft Purview

2. Click on the **Labels** tab. If there are any labels already created in your tenant, they will appear as shown in the following screenshot, which are sample Microsoft labels. Labels are processed in order from 0 upward; therefore, label order is important. Label 0 should be your least restrictive label, and the highest number should be the most restrictive. To create a new label, click **Create a label**:

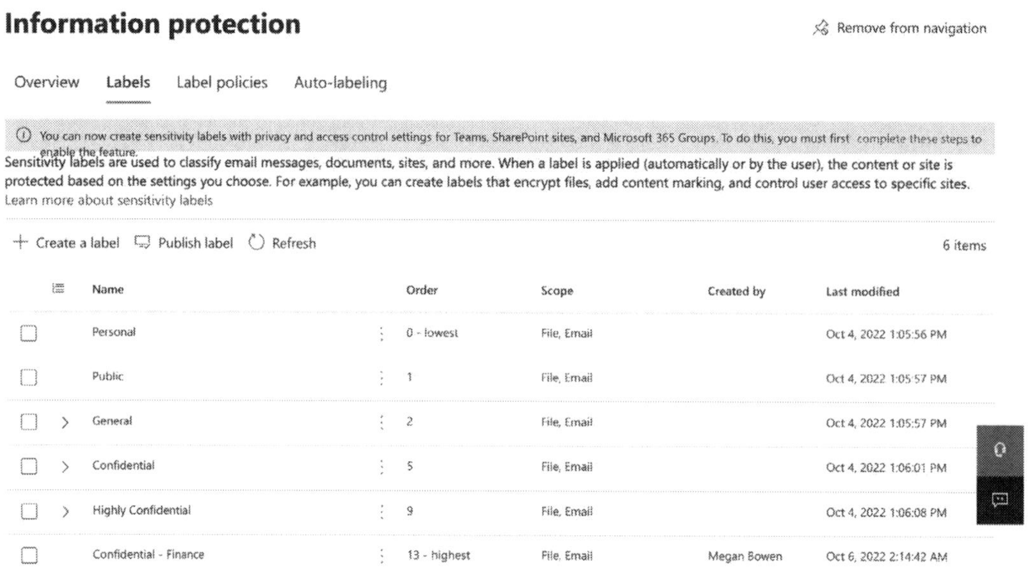

Information protection

🖋 Remove from navigation

Overview   **Labels**   Label policies   Auto-labeling

ⓘ You can now create sensitivity labels with privacy and access control settings for Teams, SharePoint sites, and Microsoft 365 Groups. To do this, you must first complete these steps to enable the feature.

Sensitivity labels are used to classify email messages, documents, sites, and more. When a label is applied (automatically or by the user), the content or site is protected based on the settings you choose. For example, you can create labels that encrypt files, add content marking, and control user access to specific sites. Learn more about sensitivity labels

\+ Create a label   ⬓ Publish label   ⟳ Refresh   6 items

	Name	Order	Scope	Created by	Last modified
☐	Personal	⋮ 0 - lowest	File, Email		Oct 4, 2022 1:05:56 PM
☐	Public	⋮ 1	File, Email		Oct 4, 2022 1:05:57 PM
☐ ﹥	General	⋮ 2	File, Email		Oct 4, 2022 1:05:57 PM
☐ ﹥	Confidential	⋮ 5	File, Email		Oct 4, 2022 1:06:01 PM
☐ ﹥	Highly Confidential	⋮ 9	File, Email		Oct 4, 2022 1:06:08 PM
☐	Confidential - Finance	⋮ 13 - highest	File, Email	Megan Bowen	Oct 6, 2022 2:14:42 AM

Figure 11.23: Creating a label

3. For this example, create a label called `Leadership team only`. Complete all the mandatory fields, which are **Name**, **Display name**, and **Description for users**, and enter thorough descriptions, then click **Next**:

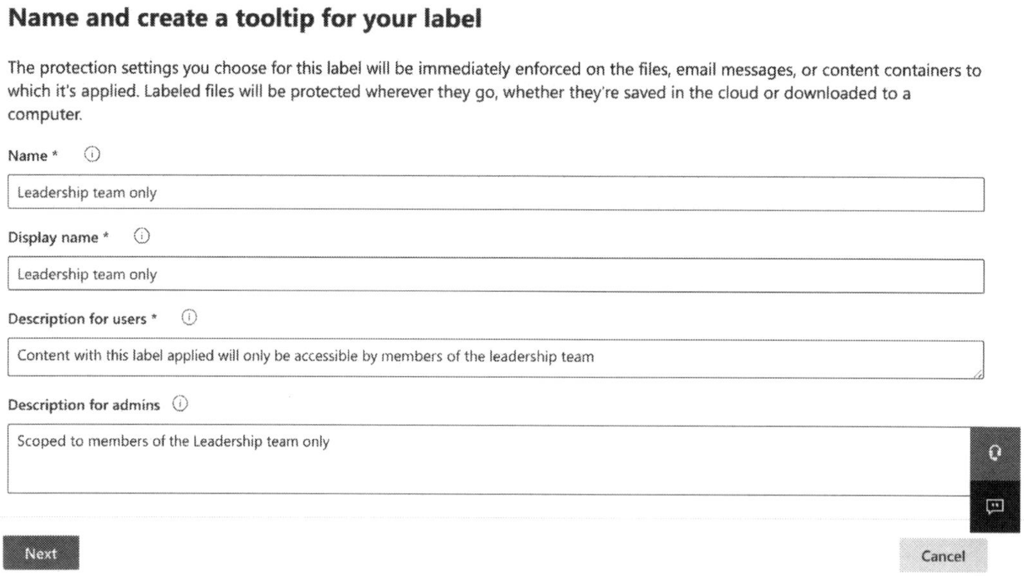

Name and create a tooltip for your label

The protection settings you choose for this label will be immediately enforced on the files, email messages, or content containers to which it's applied. Labeled files will be protected wherever they go, whether they're saved in the cloud or downloaded to a computer.

Name *   ⓘ

Leadership team only

Display name *   ⓘ

Leadership team only

Description for users *   ⓘ

Content with this label applied will only be accessible by members of the leadership team

Description for admins   ⓘ

Scoped to members of the Leadership team only

Next   Cancel

Figure 11.24: Entering label details

4. Next, define the scope for your label. There are three options available here. Select **Items** and **Groups & sites**. These options will allow you to configure your label for use with the most common use cases, such as emails, documents, teams, groups, and sites. **Schematized data assets (preview)** will apply (if selected) to more niche targets, such as SQL, Azure SQL, and AWS. Therefore, for this example, exclude this option. Click **Next**:

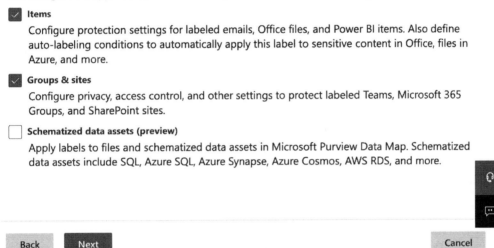

Define the scope for this label

Labels can be applied directly to files, emails, containers like SharePoint sites and Teams, Power BI items, schematized data assets, and more. Let us know where you want this label to be used so you can configure the applicable protection settings. Learn more about label scopes

✓ **Items**
Configure protection settings for labeled emails, Office files, and Power BI items. Also define auto-labeling conditions to automatically apply this label to sensitive content in Office, files in Azure, and more.

✓ **Groups & sites**
Configure privacy, access control, and other settings to protect labeled Teams, Microsoft 365 Groups, and SharePoint sites.

☐ **Schematized data assets (preview)**
Apply labels to files and schematized data assets in Microsoft Purview Data Map. Schematized data assets include SQL, Azure SQL, Azure Synapse, Azure Cosmos, AWS RDS, and more.

Back   Next   Cancel

Figure 11.25: Defining the label scope

> **Note**
>
> To use **Groups & sites** with your sensitivity labels, you first need to enable the feature in the Security & Compliance PowerShell by running the `Execute-AzureAdLabelSync` command.

5. Now choose what you want this label to do when it is applied to content. The options available to you are **Encrypt items** and **Mark items**. These are not mandatory selections, and sometimes a label can be just a label. However, most labels will be created to apply encryption at the very least. For this example, check the box to select both options and click **Next**:

Choose protection settings for labeled items

Configure encryption and content marking settings to protect labeled items.

☑ **Encrypt items**
Control who can access emails (and meeting invites if enabled), Office files, and Power BI files that have this label applied.

☑ **Mark items**
Add custom headers, footers, and watermarks to emails and Office files that have this label applied.

Back   Next   Cancel

Figure 11.26: Defining the label protection settings

6. Next, you will see the available encryption settings. You can set a label to remove encryption from protected files and emails if required. However, for this instance, select the default option of **Configure encryption settings**:

Encryption

Control who can access files and email messages that have this label applied. Learn more about encryption settings

◯ Remove encryption if the file or email is encrypted

◉ Configure encryption settings

ⓘ Turning on encryption impacts Office files (Word, PowerPoint, Excel) that have this label applied. Because the files will be encrypted for security reasons, performance will be slow when the files are opened or saved, and some SharePoint and OneDrive features will be limited or unavailable. Learn more

Assign permissions now or let users decide?

| Assign permissions now | ⌄ |

The encryption settings you choose will be automatically enforced when the label is applied to email and Office files.

User access to content expires ⓘ

| Never | ⌄ |

Allow offline access ⓘ

| Always | ⌄ |

Assign permissions to specific users and groups * ⓘ

Back   Next   Cancel

Figure 11.27: Configuring encryption settings

7. The default selection under **Assign permissions now or let users decide?** is **Assign permissions now**. Click the dropdown and set this to **Let users assign permissions when they apply the label**. In most scenarios, this setting will be left as the default option:

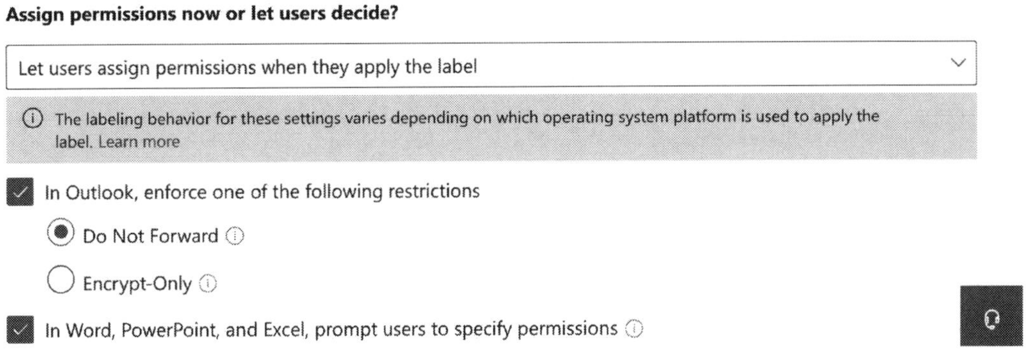

Assign permissions now or let users decide?

Let users assign permissions when they apply the label	∨

ⓘ The labeling behavior for these settings varies depending on which operating system platform is used to apply the label. Learn more

☑ In Outlook, enforce one of the following restrictions

    ◉ Do Not Forward ⓘ

    ◯ Encrypt-Only ⓘ

☑ In Word, PowerPoint, and Excel, prompt users to specify permissions ⓘ

Figure 11.28: Permission assignment options

8. Scroll down the label setup wizard further and choose a setting for **User access to content expires**:

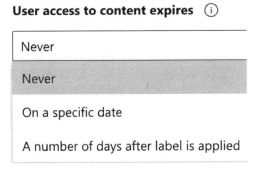

User access to content expires ⓘ

Never
Never
On a specific date
A number of days after label is applied

Figure 11.29: Label content expiration settings

9. Now you need to assign permissions to your label. Click on **Assign permissions**:

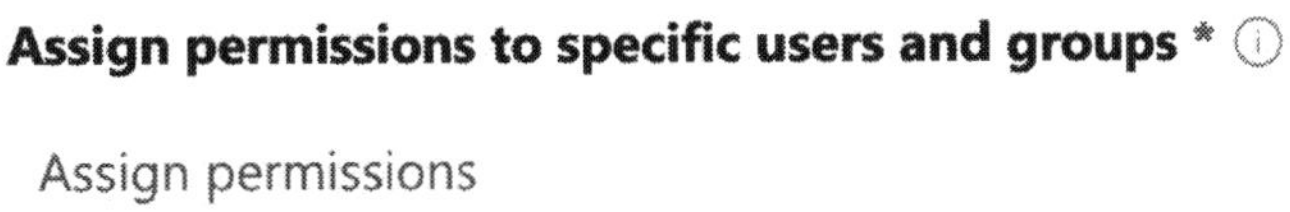

Assign permissions to specific users and groups * ⓘ

Assign permissions

Figure 11.30: Assign label permissions

10. There are four options you can choose from here. For this example, select the **Add users or groups** option to choose specific users in your organization:

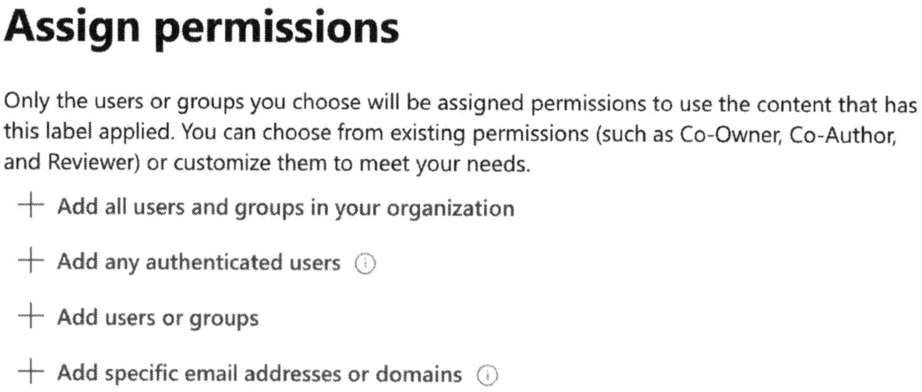

Assign permissions

Only the users or groups you choose will be assigned permissions to use the content that has this label applied. You can choose from existing permissions (such as Co-Owner, Co-Author, and Reviewer) or customize them to meet your needs.

$+$ Add all users and groups in your organization

$+$ Add any authenticated users ⓘ

$+$ Add users or groups

$+$ Add specific email addresses or domains ⓘ

Figure 11.31: Assigning label permissions

11. Next, choose which level of permissions you want to assign to the users or groups who will have permissions to use content assigned this label. You can choose from **Co-Author**, **Co-Owner**, **Reviewer**, **Viewer**, and **Custom**. For this example, let's choose **Co-Author**:

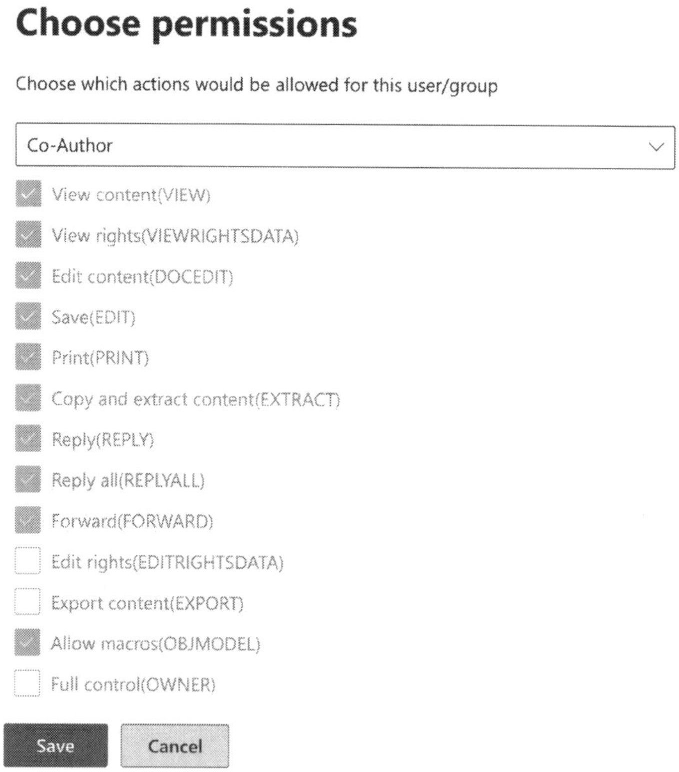

Choose permissions

Choose which actions would be allowed for this user/group

Co-Author	∨

☑ View content(VIEW)

☑ View rights(VIEWRIGHTSDATA)

☑ Edit content(DOCEDIT)

☑ Save(EDIT)

☑ Print(PRINT)

☑ Copy and extract content(EXTRACT)

☑ Reply(REPLY)

☑ Reply all(REPLYALL)

☑ Forward(FORWARD)

☐ Edit rights(EDITRIGHTSDATA)

☐ Export content(EXPORT)

☑ Allow macros(OBJMODEL)

☐ Full control(OWNER)

[Save] [Cancel]

Figure 11.32: Defining the label permissions

12. The users and permissions you select will be shown. Click **Save**:

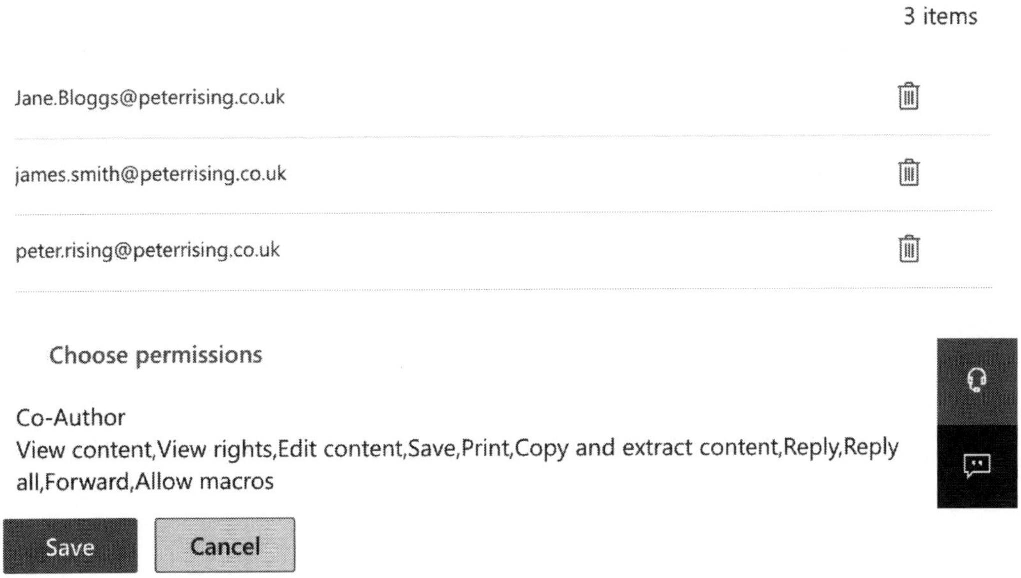

3 items

Jane.Bloggs@peterrising.co.uk   🗑

james.smith@peterrising.co.uk   🗑

peter.rising@peterrising.co.uk   🗑

Choose permissions

Co-Author
View content,View rights,Edit content,Save,Print,Copy and extract content,Reply,Reply all,Forward,Allow macros

Save   Cancel

Figure 11.33: Saving the label permission settings

13. The final setting on this section of the label wizard allows you to optionally choose **Use Double Key Encryption**. This will only be required if your organization has a regulatory requirement to do so. Click **Next**:

Users and groups

Jane.Bloggs@peterrising.co.uk

jame   For regulatory reasons, you can use two additional keys to secure
        your most sensitive documents. You manage one key in Azure
        RMS and the other key in the double key encryption (DKE)
pete   service. The key you manage in the DKE service is inaccessible to
        Microsoft. Learn more

✓ Use Double Key Encryption ⓘ

Back   Next

Figure 11.34: Double key encryption option

14. Now that you have completed the encryption settings, you can optionally configure any of the settings under **Content marking** that you want your label to apply:

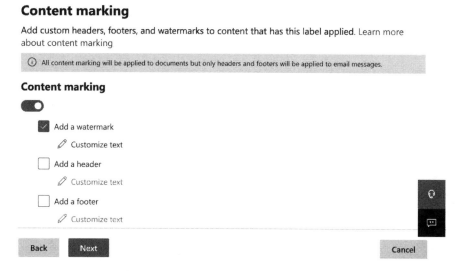

Figure 11.35: Label content marking settings

As an example, you can see how you could configure the watermark settings by entering watermark text, font size, font color, and text layout, as shown in the following screenshot:

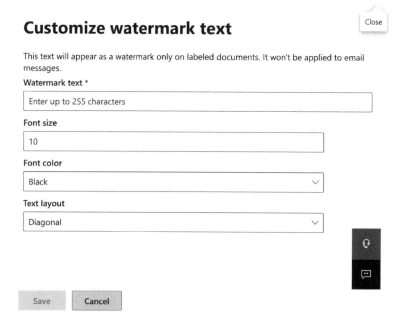

Figure 11.36: Customize watermark settings

15. Next, you have the option to configure auto-labeling to apply to your files and emails. Move the slider to the **On** position to configure these settings:

Auto-labeling for files and emails

When users edit Office files or compose, reply to, or forward emails from Outlook that contain content matching the conditions you choose here, we'll automatically apply this label or recommend that they apply it themselves. Learn more about auto-labeling for Microsoft Purview

> ⓘ To automatically apply this label to files that are already saved (in SharePoint and OneDrive) or emails that are already processed by Exchange, you must create an auto-labeling policy. Learn more about auto-labeling policies

Auto-labeling for files and emails

Figure 11.37: Auto-labeling options

16. For auto-labeling, select an SIT to match against. For this example, select the custom **Bank Account Number** SIT you created earlier in this chapter:

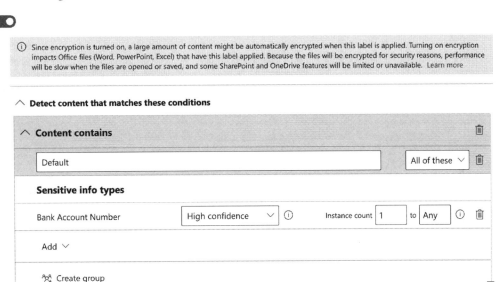

Figure 11.38: Selecting an SIT for auto-labeling

17. Scroll down and choose the action you want to perform when the content matches the conditions. You have the **Automatically apply the label** or **Recommend that users apply the label** option. Choose **Automatically apply the label** in this instance:

When content matches these conditions

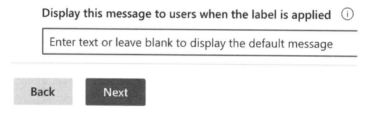

Figure 11.39: Selecting label actions for content match

18. The final option in the auto-labeling section is to enter text to display a user message when the label is applied:

Display this message to users when the label is applied ⓘ

Enter text or leave blank to display the default message

[Back]   [Next]

Figure 11.40: Displaying a user message

19. Next, you need to configure protection settings for groups and sites. There are two available options here, as shown in the following screenshot. Select both options and click **Next**:

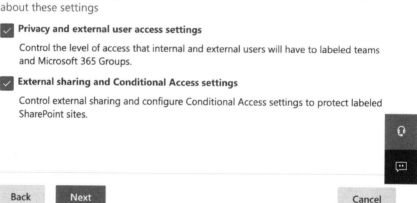

Define protection settings for groups and sites

These settings apply to teams, groups, and sites that have this label applied. They don't apply directly to the files stored in those containers. Learn more about these settings

☑ **Privacy and external user access settings**

Control the level of access that internal and external users will have to labeled teams and Microsoft 365 Groups.

☑ **External sharing and Conditional Access settings**

Control external sharing and configure Conditional Access settings to protect labeled SharePoint sites.

[Back]   [Next]   [Cancel]

Figure 11.41: Define protection settings for groups and sites

20. The first option you selected in the previous screen is **Privacy and external user access settings**. Once you are directing to this page, you select options to apply to all Microsoft groups and teams that have the label applied. The options are **Public**, **Private**, and **None**. For this example, select **Private**. You can also choose whether you wish to allow external user access. Then, click **Next**:

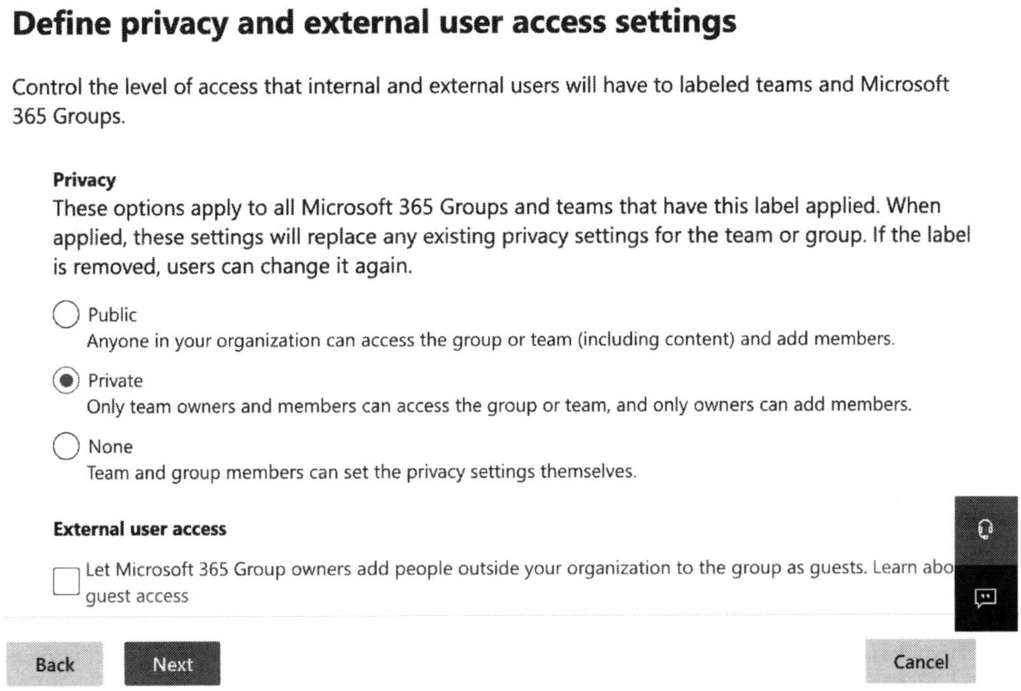

Define privacy and external user access settings

Control the level of access that internal and external users will have to labeled teams and Microsoft 365 Groups.

Privacy
These options apply to all Microsoft 365 Groups and teams that have this label applied. When applied, these settings will replace any existing privacy settings for the team or group. If the label is removed, users can change it again.

◯ Public
   Anyone in your organization can access the group or team (including content) and add members.

◉ Private
   Only team owners and members can access the group or team, and only owners can add members.

◯ None
   Team and group members can set the privacy settings themselves.

External user access

☐ Let Microsoft 365 Group owners add people outside your organization to the group as guests. Learn abo
   guest access

Back   Next   Cancel

Figure 11.42: Define privacy and external user access settings

21. For the next selection, you can choose the **Define external sharing and conditional access settings** option, as shown. Take great care when configuring these settings as they will replace any existing external sharing settings on SharePoint sites:

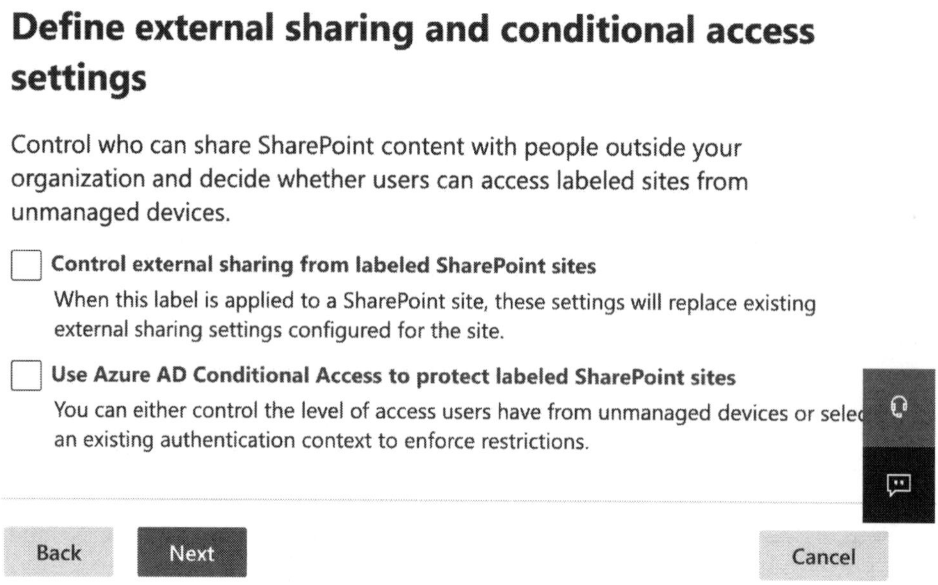

Define external sharing and conditional access settings

Control who can share SharePoint content with people outside your organization and decide whether users can access labeled sites from unmanaged devices.

☐ **Control external sharing from labeled SharePoint sites**
When this label is applied to a SharePoint site, these settings will replace existing external sharing settings configured for the site.

☐ **Use Azure AD Conditional Access to protect labeled SharePoint sites**
You can either control the level of access users have from unmanaged devices or selec
an existing authentication context to enforce restrictions.

Back   Next   Cancel

Figure 11.43: Defining external sharing and Conditional Access settings

22. The next page shows options for **Auto-labeling for schematized data assets (preview)**. Due to the focus of this book being on Microsoft 365 as opposed to Azure, this option was not chosen in the label configuration, so just click **Next**:

Auto-labeling for schematized data assets (preview)

Automatically apply this label to schematized data assets in Microsoft Purview Data Map that contain the sensitive info types you choose here. You can automatically label database columns in SQL, Azure SQL, Azure Synapse, Azure Cosmos, AWS RDS, and various other data sources governed by Microsoft Purview Data Map. Learn more about auto-labeling for schematized data assets

Auto-labeling for schematized data assets (preview)

Back   Next   Cancel

Figure 11.44: Skip through the auto-labeling for schematized data assets

23. You will now see a summary of the label settings you have chosen. When you are happy with these selections, click on **Create label**:

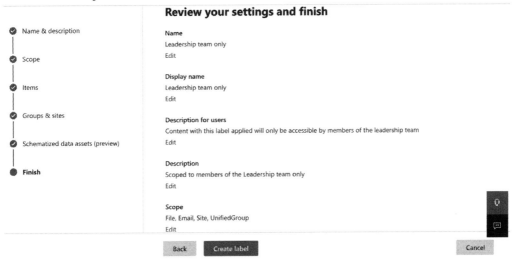

Figure 11.45: Creating the label

You will now see your new label displayed in the list of labels. If you click to select your label, you can either move it up or down the list of labels to alter its priority number or create sub-labels on your label:

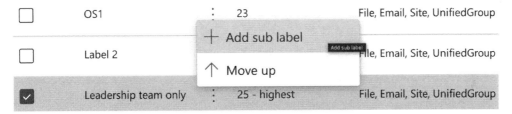

Figure 11.46: New label successfully created

Now that we have created a label, let's take a look at setting up a label policy.

Setting up label policies

Once you have one or more labels defined, the next step is to set up or apply an existing label policy to your users and groups in Azure AD. Label policies can be found in the same location as labels in the Microsoft Purview compliance portal at `https://compliance.microsoft.com` in the **Information protection** section.

To set up a label policy, complete the following steps:

1. In the **Label policies** tab, you will see any existing policies that have been created. Edit them as required and add/remove labels from them. For this example, create a new policy by selecting **Publish label**:

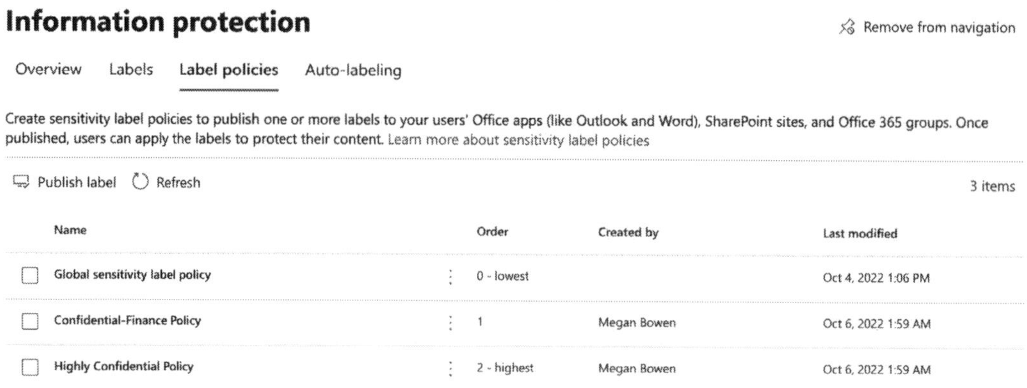

Information protection
Remove from navigation
Overview
Labels
Label policies
Auto-labeling
Create sensitivity label policies to publish one or more labels to your users' Office apps (like Outlook and Word), SharePoint sites, and Office 365 groups. Once published, users can apply the labels to protect their content. Learn more about sensitivity label policies
Publish label
Refresh
3 items
Name
Order
Created by
Last modified
Global sensitivity label policy
0 - lowest
Oct 4, 2022 1:06 PM
Confidential-Finance Policy
1
Megan Bowen
Oct 6, 2022 1:59 AM
Highly Confidential Policy
2 - highest
Megan Bowen
Oct 6, 2022 1:59 AM

Figure 11.47: Creating a label policy

2. Click on **Choose sensitivity labels to publish**:

Sensitivity label policy > Create policy
Labels to publish
Users and groups
Settings
Name
Finish
Choose sensitivity labels to publish
When published, the labels you choose here will be available in specified users' Office apps (Word, Excel, PowerPoint, and Outlook), SharePoint and Teams sites, and Microsoft 365 Groups.
Sensitivity labels to publish
Choose sensitivity labels to publish
Next
Cancel

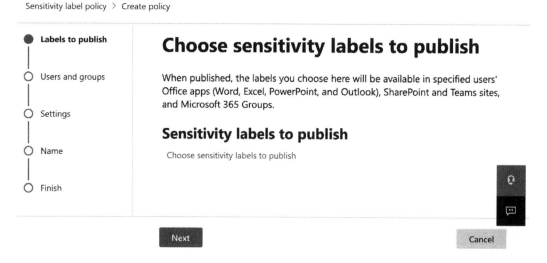

Figure 11.48: Choosing labels for the policy

3. Select your required labels for your policy and click **Add**:

Sensitivity labels to publish

🔍 Search for specific labels

5 selected

Label

☑ Personal

☑ Public

☑ General

General/Anyone (unrestricted)

General/All Employees (unrestricted)

☑ Confidential

Add   Cancel

Figure 11.49: Choosing labels for the policy

4. Next, choose the users and groups to which you wish to publish the policy by clicking **Choose user or group**. Once chosen, click **Next**:

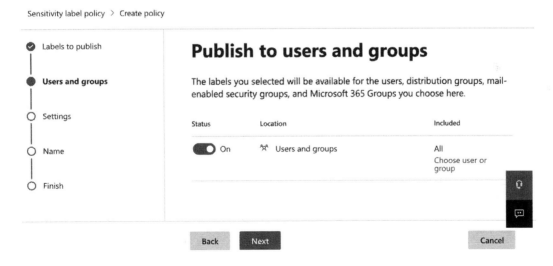

Sensitivity label policy > Create policy

✓ Labels to publish	# **Publish to users and groups**
● **Users and groups**	The labels you selected will be available for the users, distribution groups, mail-enabled security groups, and Microsoft 365 Groups you choose here.
○ Settings	
○ Name	
○ Finish	

Status	Location	Included
🔘 On	🖈 Users and groups	All Choose user or group

Back   Next   Cancel

Figure 11.50: Choosing users for the policy

5. Now choose the policy settings you wish to apply. Review these carefully and familiarize yourself with what they do. For this example, select **Users must provide a justification to remove a label or lower its classification**. Then, click **Next**:

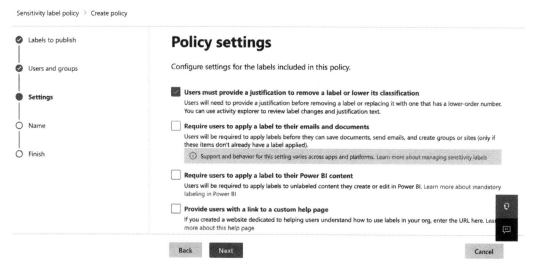

Figure 11.51: Choosing the policy settings

6. You can optionally choose to apply a default label to all documents. This can be a good practice if you do not have auto-labeling capabilities and you do not trust your users to apply a label to all content. This way, at least all content will be labeled. Click **Next**:

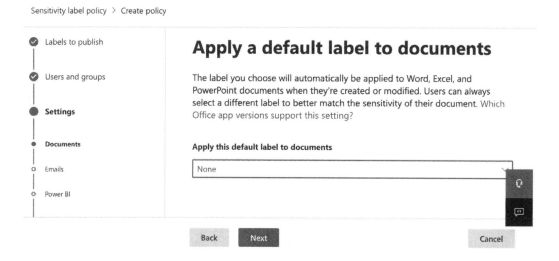

Figure 11.52: Applying a default label

7. Now set a name and description for your policy and click **Next**:

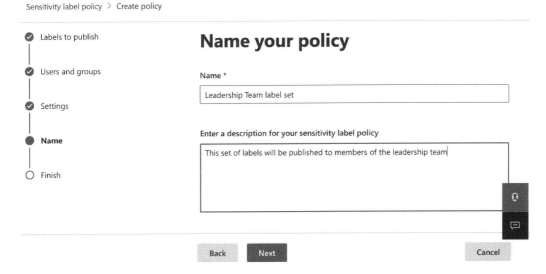

Figure 11.53: Naming the policy

8. Finally, review your settings and click **Submit**:

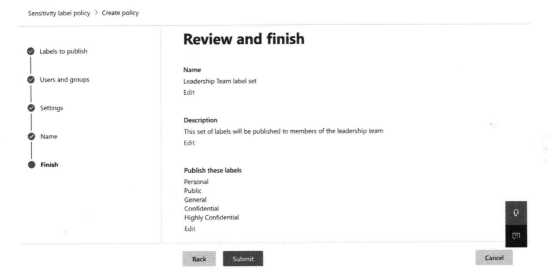

Figure 11.54: Submit the policy

9. The policy is created. You may expect to wait up to 24 hours for the labels to be visible in the users' applications. Click **Done**:

Sensitivity label policy > Create policy
Labels to publish
Users and groups
Settings
Name
Finish
New policy created
It can take up to 24 hours to publish the labels to the selected users' apps.
Next steps
Review data classification reports to see how labels are being used
Read guidance on how to educate users about sensitivity labels
Done

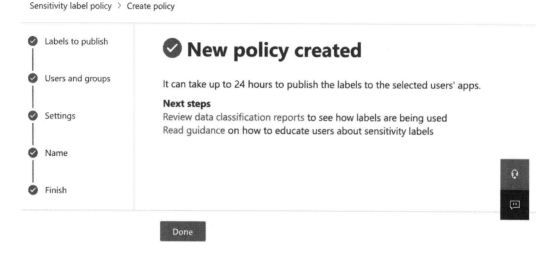

Figure 11.55: Policy successfully created

The policy is now visible in your policy list:

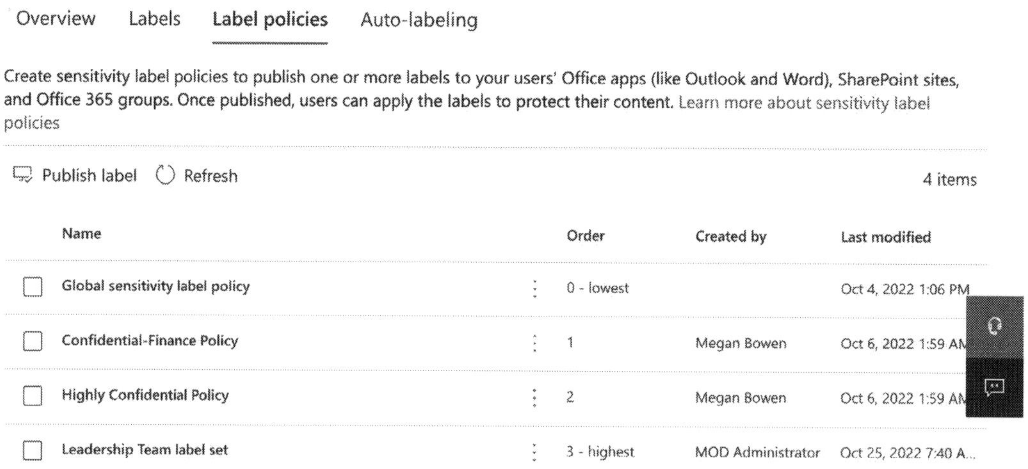

Overview
Labels
Label policies
Auto-labeling
Create sensitivity label policies to publish one or more labels to your users' Office apps (like Outlook and Word), SharePoint sites, and Office 365 groups. Once published, users can apply the labels to protect their content. Learn more about sensitivity label policies
Publish label
Refresh
4 items
Name
Order
Created by
Last modified
Global sensitivity label policy
0 - lowest
Oct 4, 2022 1:06 PM
Confidential-Finance Policy
1
Megan Bowen
Oct 6, 2022 1:59 AM
Highly Confidential Policy
2
Megan Bowen
Oct 6, 2022 1:59 AM
Leadership Team label set
3 - highest
MOD Administrator
Oct 25, 2022 7:40 A...

Figure 11.56: Full list of existing label policies

You also have the **Auto-labeling** option where you can run through settings similar to that shown earlier in *Figure 11.38*. In this case, you have the option to first run your auto-labeling choices in simulation mode so you can review the items that will be auto-labeled when the policy is fully activated.

10. Click on **Create auto-labeling policy** to begin this process:

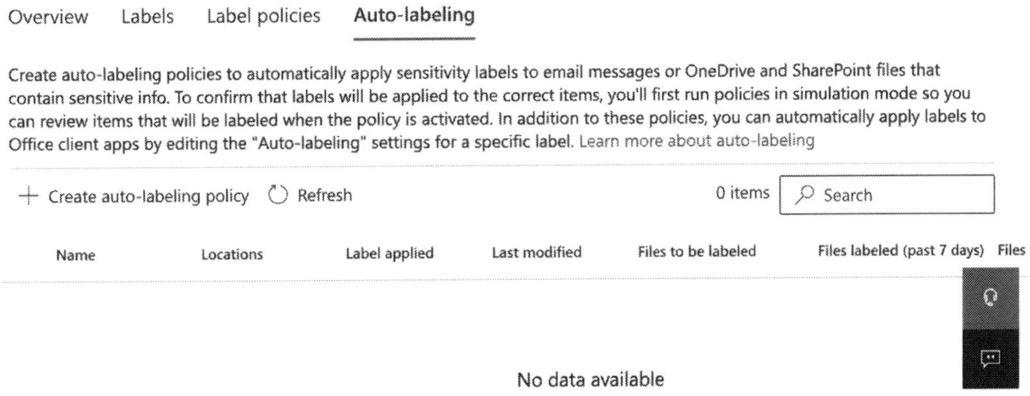

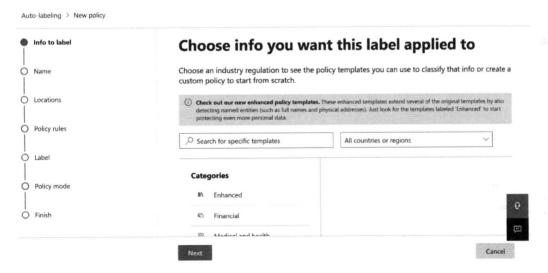

Figure 11.57: Auto-labeling options

11. Work through the wizard to choose from SITs and apply your auto-labeling policy to the required locations with the desired rules:

Figure 11.58: The auto-labeling policy wizard

These steps showed you how to create a new label policy and set up an auto-labeling policy. The next section will cover user experience.

Using sensitivity labels

When users are targeted by label policies, they will see the sensitivity button available within their Microsoft Office applications. This button, when expanded, will show the users the **Sensitivity** labels available to them. This is shown in the following screenshot:

Figure 11.59: Sensitivity labels in Microsoft Word

The experience will differ slightly depending on the platform or operating system. Next, take a look at how you can use **Activity explorer** to view label activity in your Microsoft 365 tenant.

Configuring and using Activity explorer

Activity explorer is a feature available in the **Data classification** section of the Microsoft Purview compliance portal that allows administrators to monitor what is being done with their labeled content. Thirty days' worth of content is stored in **Activity explorer**:

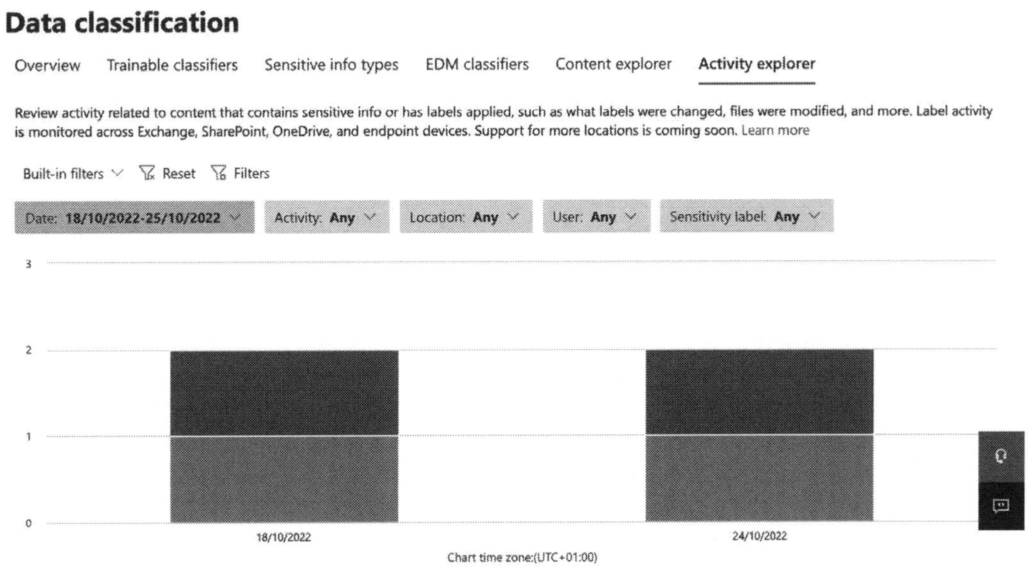

Data classification

Overview   Trainable classifiers   Sensitive info types   EDM classifiers   Content explorer   **Activity explorer**

Review activity related to content that contains sensitive info or has labels applied, such as what labels were changed, files were modified, and more. Label activity is monitored across Exchange, SharePoint, OneDrive, and endpoint devices. Support for more locations is coming soon. Learn more

Built-in filters ∨   ⧨ Reset   ⧨ Filters

Date: **18/10/2022-25/10/2022** ∨ | Activity: **Any** ∨ | Location: **Any** ∨ | User: **Any** ∨ | Sensitivity label: **Any** ∨

Chart time zone:(UTC+01:00)

Figure 11.60: Activity explorer

Activity explorer is part of the premium features of Microsoft Purview. The configuration steps are minimal and only relate to the available licensing you have in your tenant. Each Microsoft 365 account that accesses and uses data classification features such as **Activity explorer** needs to have one of the following licenses assigned:

- Microsoft 365 (E5)

- Office 365 (E5)

- Advanced Compliance (E5) add-on

- Advanced Threat Intelligence (E5) add-on

- Microsoft 365 E5/A5 Info Protection & Governance

- Microsoft 365 E5/A5 Compliance

Further, to use **Activity explorer**, you must be assigned one of the following roles:

- Information Protection Admin

- Information Protection Analyst

- Information Protection Investigator

- Information Protection Reader

- Global Administrator

- Compliance Administrator

- Security Administrator

- Compliance Data Administrator

Activity explorer will gather information from the audit logs for labeling activity, including **Label applied**, **Label changed**, **Auto-labeling simulation**, and **File read**:

	Activity	File	Location	User	Happened	Policy
☐	**Label changed**	https://chrysalistech-my.sharepoint.com/person...	OneDrive	peter.rising@peterrising.co.uk	24 Oct 2022 16:08	
☐	**Label applied**	https://chrysalistech-my.sharepoint.com/person...	OneDrive	peter.rising@peterrising.co.uk	24 Oct 2022 16:06	
☐	**Label changed**	https://chrysalistech-my.sharepoint.com/person...	OneDrive	peter.rising@peterrising.co.uk	18 Oct 2022 11:24	
☐	**Label applied**	https://chrysalistech-my.sharepoint.com/person...	OneDrive	peter.rising@peterrising.co.uk	18 Oct 2022 11:24	

Figure 11.61: Activity explorer label events

Monitoring **Activity explorer** will help you to monitor the effectiveness of your labeling strategy and make fine-tuned adjustments to the process where required. For example, a user may have changed a label to a lower priority, and you may not have chosen the requirement to provide a justification when they do so. **Activity explorer** would only show the label had been changed by the user in this instance. It would not show an audited explanation.

In the final section of this chapter, you will learn about using sensitivity labels with Teams, SharePoint, OneDrive, and Office apps.

Using sensitivity labels with Teams, SharePoint, OneDrive, and Office apps

In *Figure 11.25* of this chapter, we configured a sensitivity label to be applied to **Groups & sites**. This means that when published, you can apply sensitivity labels to a team in Microsoft Teams, a SharePoint Online site or OneDrive, or a Microsoft 365 group in Outlook on the web.

The experience will show available sensitivity labels in each of these services. In Microsoft Teams, when a new team is created, users with labels applied in this way can choose the sensitivity setting of the team. When doing so, the available privacy options for creating the team will be displayed as shown in the following screenshot:

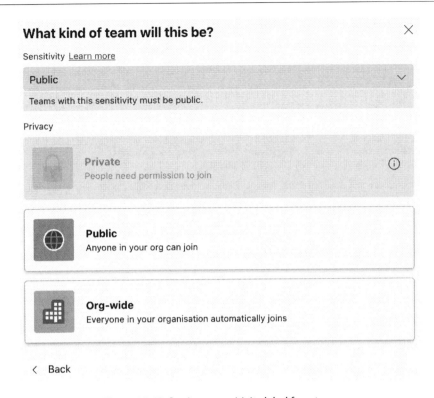

Figure 11.62: Setting a sensitivity label for a team

When the team is created, the sensitivity label appears in the top-right corner:

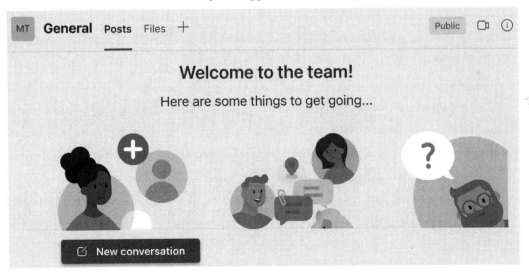

Figure 11.63: Team with sensitivity label applied

The same sensitivity label will automatically be set for the Microsoft 365 group and the connected SharePoint team site. The same principles shown for teams also apply to setting labels at the SharePoint site, OneDrive, and Microsoft 365 group level.

Summary

This chapter introduced you to the principles of managing sensitive information in Microsoft 365. We learned how to understand built-in SITs and create custom ones as well. We then created a sensitivity label with settings to apply to items, groups, and sites, and assigned it to users with a label policy. We also saw how to create an auto-labeling policy. Next, we learned how to use **Activity explorer** to track the labeling activity within your organization. Finally, you learned how you can apply sensitivity labels to Teams, SharePoint sites, OneDrive, and Microsoft 365 groups.

In the next chapter, you will explore DLP and how it can be used to safeguard your users from accidentally sharing sensitive content. This is done using rules and conditions that help users make the correct decisions when working with sensitive information.

Questions

1. Which of the following is not a method of creating a custom sensitive information type?

    A. Regular expression

    B. Keyword list

    C. Keyword group

    D. Keyword dictionary

2. True or false? You can apply a sensitivity label to a team within Microsoft Teams.

    A. True

    B. False

3. Which section in the Microsoft Purview compliance portal would you go to to configure sensitivity labels and policies?

    A. **Insider risk management**

    B. **Information protection**

    C. **Data lifecycle management**

    D. **Data classification**

4. Which of the following is not a visual marking setting available for a sensitivity label?

   A. Watermark

   B. Highlight

   C. Header

   D. Footer

5. True or false? Labels are processed in order of highest value to lowest.

   A. True

   B. False

6. What would you configure if you wanted to record in **Activity explorer** the reason why a label was changed to a lower level?

   A. **Configure a custom help link**

   B. **Configure a sensitive information type**

   C. **Require a justification**

   D. **Require a label**

7. Which of the following actions can a label perform (choose two)?

   A. Delete content

   B. Rename content

   C. Apply content marking

   D. Encrypt content

8. True or false? When applied, sensitivity labels can be set to allow or prevent offline access to content.

   A. True

   B. False

9. Which of the following PowerShell commands would you run to activate labeling for groups and sites in your tenant?

   A. `Execute-AzureAdLabelPolicySync`

   B. `Enable-AzureAdLabelPolicySync`

   C. `Execute-AzureAdLabelSync`

   D. `Enable-AzureAdLabelSync`

10. Which of the following roles will not give access to use **Activity explorer**?

    A.   Information Protection Administrator

    B.   Global Administrator

    C.   SharePoint Administrator

    D.   Compliance Administrator

Further reading

Please refer to the following links for more information:

- *Learn about sensitive information types*: `https://learn.microsoft.com/en-us/microsoft-365/compliance/sensitive-information-type-learn-about?view=o365-worldwide`

- *Create custom sensitive information types in the compliance portal*: `https://learn.microsoft.com/en-us/microsoft-365/compliance/create-a-custom-sensitive-information-type?view=o365-worldwide`

- *Sensitive information type REGEX validators and additional check*: `https://learn.microsoft.com/en-us/microsoft-365/compliance/sit-regex-validators-additional-checks?view=o365-worldwide`

- *Create and configure sensitivity labels and their policies*: `https://learn.microsoft.com/en-us/microsoft-365/compliance/create-sensitivity-labels?WT.mc_id=EM-MVP-4039827&view=o365-worldwide`

- *Get started with sensitivity labels*: `https://learn.microsoft.com/en-us/microsoft-365/compliance/get-started-with-sensitivity-labels?WT.mc_id=M365-MVP-4039827&view=o365-worldwide`

- *Get started with activity explorer*: `https://learn.microsoft.com/en-us/microsoft-365/compliance/data-classification-activity-explorer?WT.mc_id=M365-MVP-4039827&view=o365-worldwide`

- *Use sensitivity labels to protect content in Microsoft Teams, Microsoft 365 groups, and SharePoint sites*: `https://learn.microsoft.com/en-us/microsoft-365/compliance/sensitivity-labels-teams-groups-sites?WT.mc_id=M365-MVP-4039827&view=o365-worldwide`

- *Manage sensitivity labels in Office apps*: `https://learn.microsoft.com/en-us/microsoft-365/compliance/sensitivity-labels-office-apps?WT.mc_id=M365-MVP-4039827&view=o365-worldwide`

- *Analytics and reporting for Azure Information Protection*: https://learn.microsoft.com/en-us/azure/information-protection/reports-aip?WT.mc_id=M365-MVP-4039827

- Licensing guidance for sensitivity labels: https://learn.microsoft.com/en-us/office365/servicedescriptions/microsoft-365-service-descriptions/microsoft-365-tenantlevel-services-licensing-guidance/microsoft-365-security-compliance-licensing-guidance#microsoft-purview-information-protection-sensitivity-labeling

- *Conditional access policy for SharePoint sites and OneDrive*: https://learn.microsoft.com/en-us/sharepoint/authentication-context-example

- Label order: https://learn.microsoft.com/en-us/microsoft-365/compliance/sensitivity-labels?view=o365-worldwide#label-priority-order-matters

12
Managing Microsoft Purview Data Loss Prevention

Data loss prevention (**DLP**) in Microsoft 365 is designed to allow administrators to protect users from accidentally sharing sensitive information from your organization. This is achieved by creating policies that can be applied to your users and groups across multiple Microsoft 365 services. These policies use built-in or custom **sensitive information types** (**SITs**) that can then be detected within the content that your users are working on. They can also be used to trigger user policy tips to provide guidance on sharing information. These policies can also block content more aggressively when a policy match is detected and alert and report on such instances. This chapter will show you how to effectively plan and implement your DLP policies. It will also demonstrate how you can manage the reporting features and alert settings available and create policies from built-in templates, or create custom policies to meet your requirements using simple or advanced settings. Finally, you will examine how to apply the principles of DLP at a device level by implementing **Endpoint DLP**.

In this chapter, we will cover the following main topics:

- Planning and implementing DLP
- Creating DLP policies for Microsoft 365 workloads
- DLP reporting and alerting capabilities
- Implementing Endpoint DLP

Planning and implementing DLP

In order to effectively plan for your Microsoft 365 DLP deployment, you need to understand any existing or potential data leakage within your organization. DLP can initially be configured with policies that run in test mode only. This is a good starting point for acquiring the information you need to determine your DLP strategy. But before you can create your test policies, it is important that you understand how DLP works, what sort of information can be detected, and which Microsoft 365 services can be protected.

A good starting point is to examine the SITs used by DLP policies. There are several built-in SITs available in Microsoft 365. You explored sensitive info types in more detail in *Chapter 11, Managing Sensitive Information*, but as a quick reminder, you can find these in the Microsoft Purview compliance center at `https://compliance.microsoft.com` under **Data classification | Sensitive info types**:

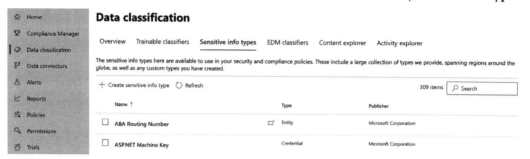

Figure 12.1: Sensitive info types

The DLP policies that you create in the Microsoft Purview compliance center can be applied to the following Microsoft 365 locations:

- **Exchange email**

- **SharePoint sites**

- **OneDrive accounts**

- **Teams chat and channel messages**

- **Devices**

- **Microsoft Defender for Cloud Apps**

- **On-premises repositories**

- **Power BI (preview)**

In the following example, you can see that you have the option to protect all available locations or only those you wish to select:

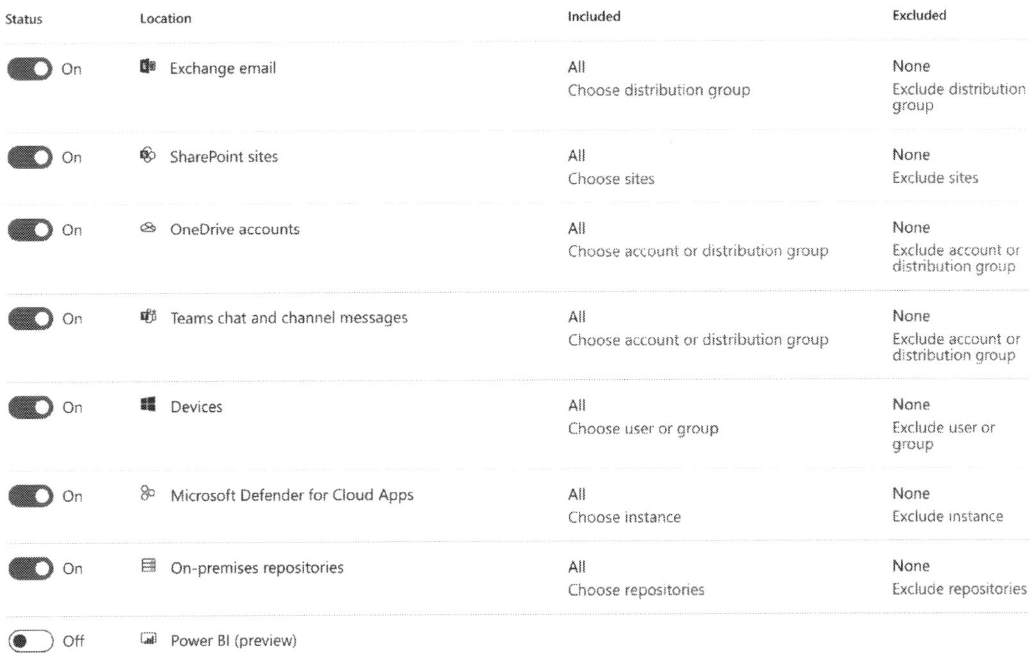

Status	Location	Included	Excluded
On	Exchange email	All Choose distribution group	None Exclude distribution group
On	SharePoint sites	All Choose sites	None Exclude sites
On	OneDrive accounts	All Choose account or distribution group	None Exclude account or distribution group
On	Teams chat and channel messages	All Choose account or distribution group	None Exclude account or distribution group
On	Devices	All Choose user or group	None Exclude user or group
On	Microsoft Defender for Cloud Apps	All Choose instance	None Exclude instance
On	On-premises repositories	All Choose repositories	None Exclude repositories
Off	Power BI (preview)		

Figure 12.2: Protecting Office 365 locations

DLP policies can be configured with conditions and actions, including the following:

- **Notify users when content matches the policy settings**
- **Detect when a specific amount of information is being shared at one time**
- **Send incident reports to Global Admins**
- **Restrict access or encrypt the content**

Choosing only the **Notify users when content matches the policy settings** option is a good way of testing your DLP policies. Users will receive policy tips in their Microsoft Office applications, and a corresponding alert will be generated in the Microsoft Purview compliance center. However, no further action will be taken, and no encryption or access restrictions will be applied.

When you have finished setting up your DLP policy, you have the option to place the policy in test mode, and users will see policy tips when there is a match:

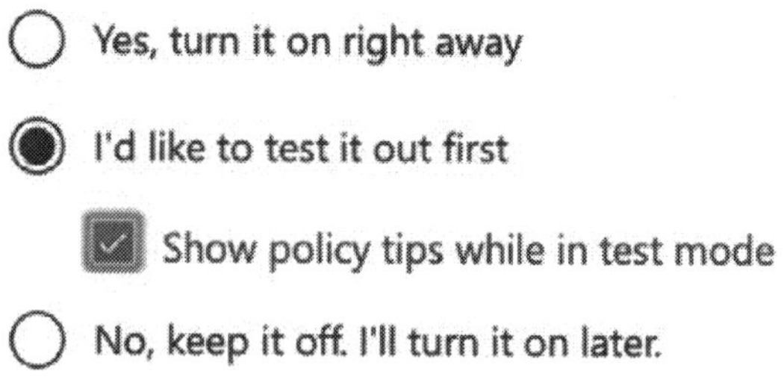

○ Yes, turn it on right away

◉ I'd like to test it out first

☑ Show policy tips while in test mode

○ No, keep it off. I'll turn it on later.

Figure 12.3: Setting the policy in test mode

This is good practice as it will help your users become familiar with the principles of DLP before you fully enable it and will also help administrators experience typical alerts and matches and understand how to take corrective measures.

> **Note**
>
> Policy tips are currently only available for users with Microsoft Office applications running on Windows computers, Outlook on the web, documents in SharePoint Online or OneDrive for Business, and Excel, PowerPoint, and Word (when the document is stored on a site targeted by a DLP policy).

In this section, we learned the basic principles of planning and implementing your DLP policies in Microsoft 365 to protect your Microsoft 365 locations. Next, we will explore how to create DLP policies and assign them to users and groups in Microsoft 365.

Managing DLP policies for Microsoft 365 workloads

Now that you understand the core components that make up a DLP policy, you can go ahead and work with an actual DLP policy.

Creating a DLP policy

To create a DLP policy, you can use a template and assign it to the chosen Microsoft 365 locations. To do this, complete the following steps:

1. Log in to the Microsoft Purview compliance center, which can be accessed by administrators at `https://compliance.microsoft.com`, and navigate to **Data loss prevention |** **Policies**, shown in the following screenshot. You will see a list of any existing DLP policies described by name, order of priority, last modified date, and the status of the policy. To create your new DLP policy, click on **Create policy**:

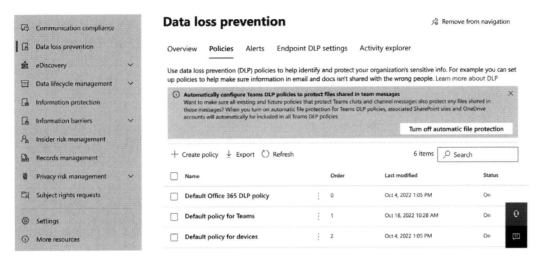

Figure 12.4: Policy

2. You have several options to create your policy. You can use a template or create your own custom policy. Templates are broken down into categories such as **Enhanced**, **Financial**, **Medical and health**, **Privacy**, and **Custom**. A template consists of one or more SITs.

3. For this example, configure a **Financial** policy from a template for an organization in the United Kingdom. Select **United Kingdom** from the drop-down pane on the right. Then, under **Categories**, choose **Financial**, and under **Templates**, choose **U.K. Financial Data**. You will see a description of the template and the SITs included in the template. Then, click **Next**:

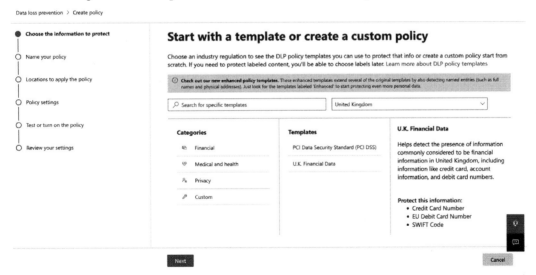

Figure 12.5: Creating a policy from a template

4.   Next, enter a name and description for your policy. You can either use the recommended name and description or enter your own. When complete, click **Next**:

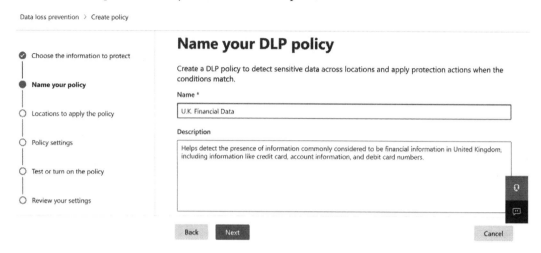

Figure 12.6: Setting a name and description for the policy

5.   Next, choose the locations you wish to protect. For this example, include **Exchange email**, **SharePoint sites**, **OneDrive accounts**, and **Teams chat and channel messages**. Exclude all other locations. Optionally, you can filter each location by what you wish to include or exclude. For this example, choose a specific Exchange distribution group and exclude a specific OneDrive account. Once your options are selected, click **Next**:

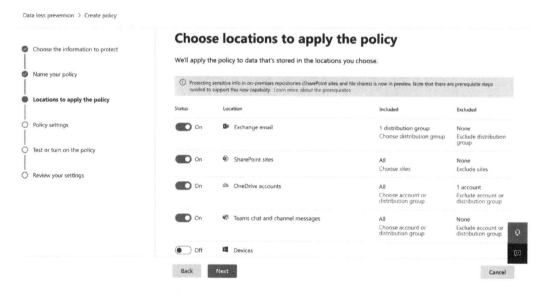

Figure 12.7: Choosing which locations to apply the policy to

6. Now, define your policy settings. You have the option here to choose **Review and customize default settings from the template** or **Create or customize advanced DLP rules**. For this example, select the default option. Then, click **Next**:

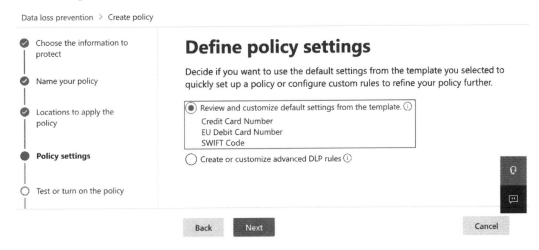

Figure 12.8: Defining the policy settings

To learn how to use advanced DLP rules, please check the *Further reading* section at the end of this chapter.

7. Now, you choose how you want your DLP policy to detect content shared from Microsoft 365. In this example, select **With people outside my organization**, and click **Next**:

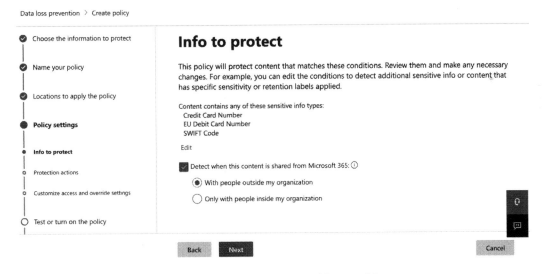

Figure 12.9: Protect content matching conditions

8. Now you will see the protection actions available to you. These include the option to show policy tips to users when content matches the policy, detecting when a specific amount of sensitive information is being shared at one time, whether to send incident reports in an email to the policy creator and Global Administrators, sending alerts if there is a policy match, and choosing to restrict access or encrypt content. When you are happy with your selections, click **Next**:

Protection actions

We'll automatically create detailed activity reports so you can review the content that matches this policy. What else do you want to do?

☑ **When content matches the policy conditions, show policy tips to users and send them an email notification**

Tips appear to users in their apps (like Outlook, OneDrive, and SharePoint) and help them learn how to use sensitive info responsibly. You can use the default tip or customize it to your liking. Learn more about notifications and tips

Customize the tip and email

☑ **Detect when a specific amount of sensitive info is being shared at one time**

At least [10] or more instances of the same sensitive info type

☑ **Send incident reports in email**

By default, you and your global admin will automatically receive the email. Incident reports are supported only for activity in Exchange, SharePoint, OneDrive, and Teams.

Choose what to include in the report and who receives it

☑ **Send alerts if any of the DLP rules match**

By default, you and any global admins will automatically be alerted if a DLP rule is matched.

Customize alert configuration

☐ **Restrict access or encrypt the content in Microsoft 365 locations**

Back   Next   Cancel

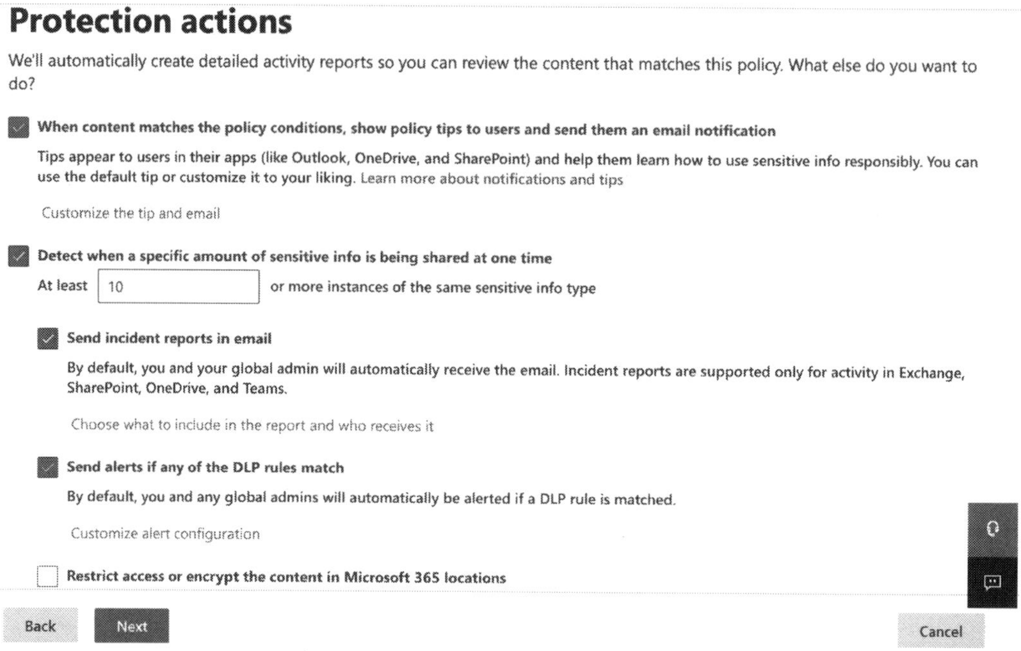

Figure 12.10: Choosing protection actions

9. Next, you will see the **Restrict access or encrypt the content in Microsoft 365 locations** option. Here, choose whether you want to restrict users receiving the content being shared if there is a policy match. This can be set to **Block everyone** or **Block only people outside your organization**. For this example, select **Block only people outside your organization**.

You can also choose whether you wish people to see a policy tip, whether they can override the policy, and whether they are required to enter a justification for overriding the policy. Finally, set to automatically override the DLP rule if the user reports it as a false positive. Once you are happy with your selections, click **Next**:

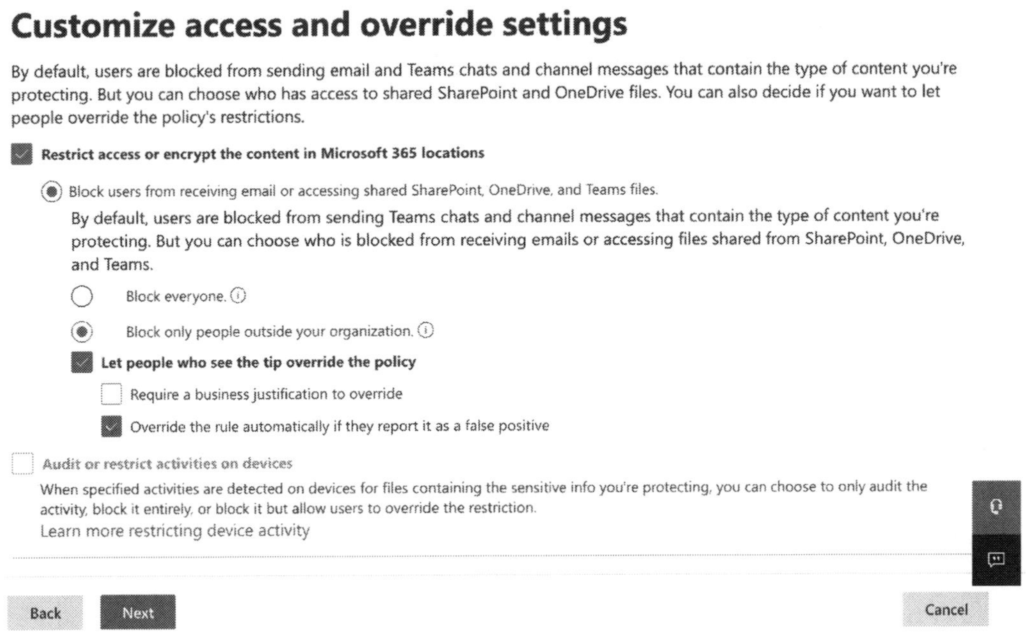

Customize access and override settings

By default, users are blocked from sending email and Teams chats and channel messages that contain the type of content you're protecting. But you can choose who has access to shared SharePoint and OneDrive files. You can also decide if you want to let people override the policy's restrictions.

☑ **Restrict access or encrypt the content in Microsoft 365 locations**

   ◉ Block users from receiving email or accessing shared SharePoint, OneDrive, and Teams files.

     By default, users are blocked from sending Teams chats and channel messages that contain the type of content you're protecting. But you can choose who is blocked from receiving emails or accessing files shared from SharePoint, OneDrive, and Teams.

     ◯   Block everyone. ⓘ

     ◉   Block only people outside your organization. ⓘ

     ☑ **Let people who see the tip override the policy**

       ☐ Require a business justification to override

       ☑ Override the rule automatically if they report it as a false positive

☐ Audit or restrict activities on devices

   When specified activities are detected on devices for files containing the sensitive info you're protecting, you can choose to only audit the activity, block it entirely, or block it but allow users to override the restriction.
   Learn more restricting device activity

[Back] [Next]   [Cancel]

Figure 12.11: Customize access and override settings

> **Note**
>
> In this section, you will see some grayed-out options relating to auditing and restricting activities on devices. These settings relate to Endpoint DLP, which will be covered later in this chapter.

10. Next, choose how you wish the policy to be applied. It can be enabled immediately, placed in test mode, or turned off for later use. For this example, select the **Test it out first** option, and also choose **Show policy tips while in test mode**, as shown in the following screenshot. Click **Next**:

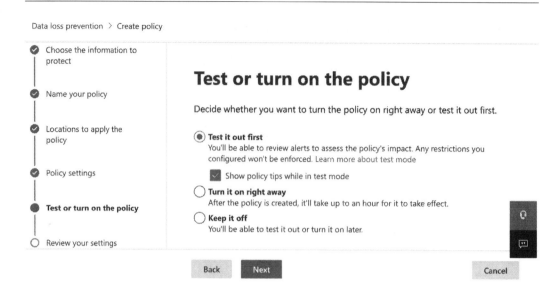

Figure 12.12: Test or turn on the policy

11. The final step when creating your policy is reviewing your policy to ensure you are happy with the settings you have chosen. Make any last-minute changes from here. When you are satisfied that the policy is configured as required, click **Submit**:

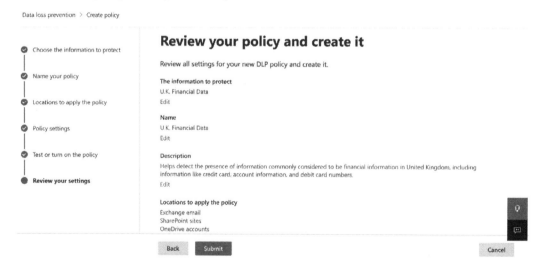

Figure 12.13: Submitting the policy for creation

In this list of DLP policies, you can now view or search for your new policy. You will see it has a status of **Test with notifications**:

Data loss prevention

        ✂ Remove from navigation

Overview   **Policies**   Alerts   Endpoint DLP settings   Activity explorer

Use data loss prevention (DLP) policies to help identify and protect your organization's sensitive info. For example you can set up policies to help make sure information in email and docs isn't shared with the wrong people. Learn more about DLP

+ Create policy   ↓ Export   ◌ Refresh   1 item   🔍 u.k. fin   ✕

	Name	Order	Last modified	Status
☐	U.K. Financial Data	⋮ 6	Nov 5, 2022 10:52 AM	Test with notifications

Figure 12.14: New DLP policy successfully created

This policy is set to detect content in specific Microsoft 365 locations matching a DLP template containing SITs relating to financial data for the UK. When there is a match, alerts will be sent to administrators, and the users who are attempting to share the content will see a policy tip to guide them on why this has been flagged, and what (if any) actions they can take. As the policy is only in test mode at this time, the restrictions in the policy will not actually be applied. This will occur only when the policy is fully turned on.

How do you know whether this is all working correctly, though? You need to test the user experience.

Testing your DLP policy

Now that your DLP policy has been created, it should take effect after approximately one hour and start detecting genuine policy matches. You can manually trigger the policy by sending an email with matching content from an email account that is bound by the policy or adding matching content to a OneDrive document, a document in a SharePoint site, or a Teams chat or channel message.

In our example, we created conditions to apply the policy when UK financial data was detected. It is important to note that DLP is intelligent enough to know when a random set of numbers is entered to represent a debit or credit card number. However, there are some websites that provide genuine test card numbers to conduct successful testing.

An example of this can be seen in the following screenshot, in which a policy tip appears when a user tries to send an email that contains a credit card number to an external recipient:

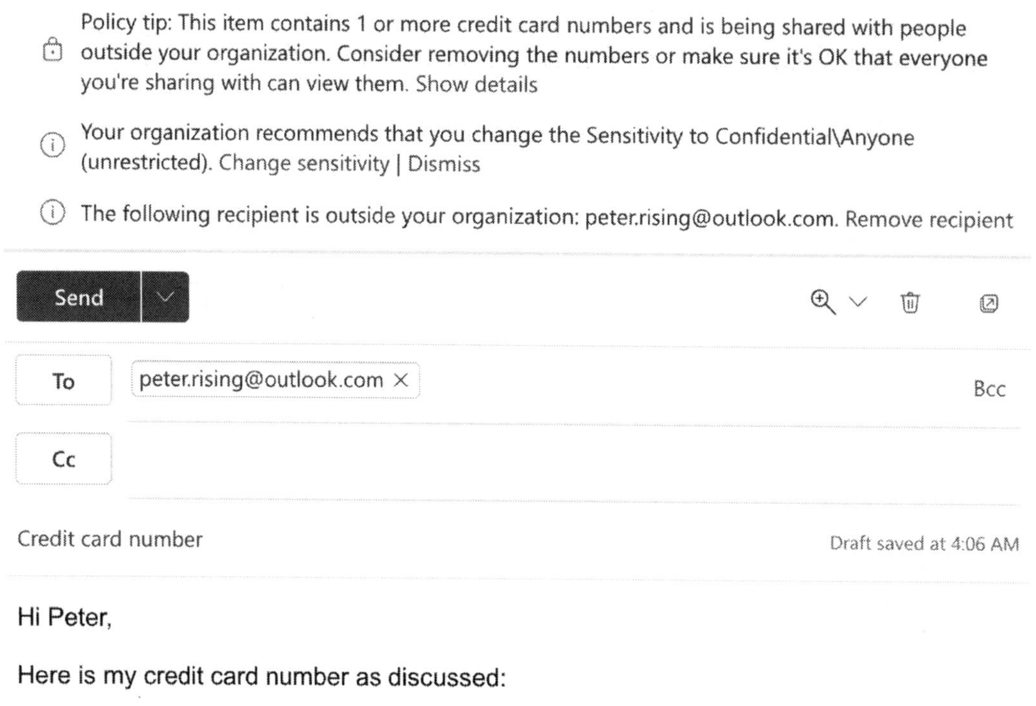

Policy tip: This item contains 1 or more credit card numbers and is being shared with people outside your organization. Consider removing the numbers or make sure it's OK that everyone you're sharing with can view them. Show details

Your organization recommends that you change the Sensitivity to Confidential\Anyone (unrestricted). Change sensitivity | Dismiss

The following recipient is outside your organization: peter.rising@outlook.com. Remove recipient

| Send | ∨ | | | ⊕ ∨ | 🗑 | 🗗 |

| To | peter.rising@outlook.com ✕ | | Bcc |

| Cc | | |

Credit card number   Draft saved at 4:06 AM

Hi Peter,

Here is my credit card number as discussed:

Figure 12.15: Policy tip in Outlook

Once the credit card number is entered, the policy tip appears (even before the email is sent). The policy tip reads: **This item contains 1 or more credit card numbers and is being shared with people outside your organization. Consider removing the numbers or make sure it's OK that everyone you're sharing with can view them.**.

Since you set up the policy so that it only runs in test mode at this time, the user will still be able to successfully send the email regardless of any restrictions set in the policy.

> **Note**
>
> **Microsoft Purview** and **Microsoft Defender for Cloud Apps** (**MDA**) both provide DLP capabilities. MDA allows organizations to implement DLP policies for data in motion through session policies on web applications, and file policies for data at rest. MDA also protects data in third-party apps as well as Microsoft apps. Microsoft Purview DLP (which is what we are covering in this chapter) is primarily used to enforce DLP controls on Microsoft apps, which include native apps and web applications.

Once the user has sent the email, an email alert will be sent to them:

Figure 12.16: Email notification of policy match

A copy of the original email is also attached to the alert.

So, if you initially configure your DLP policies in test mode with policy tips in this way, it will give you a good opportunity to assess the accuracy and effectiveness of your policies when you decide to fully activate and enforce them.

Editing your DLP policy

When testing your DLP policy, you may find that you need to go back and make some changes if the results are not as expected. You can change the conditions, actions, user notifications, user overrides, and incident report settings within your policy while editing.

To edit the policy, complete the following steps:

1. Select the policy and select **Edit policy**:

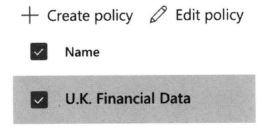

Figure 12.17: Editing a DLP policy

2. The policy wizard opens and provides the same options you saw when creating the policy. Click **Next** through each stage and make changes to the description of your policy and the locations targeted. When you come to the **Advanced DLP rules** section of the policy editing wizard, you will see that you have options to edit low- and high-volume detected content rule settings:

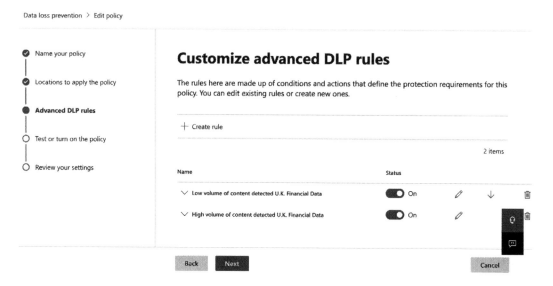

Figure 12.18: Low- and high-volume content options

> **Note**
> These rules were automatically created when you selected the default option to create your DLP policy earlier in *Figure 12.8*. If you had chosen the **Create or customize advanced DLP rules** option when setting up your policy earlier, you would have seen these same options at that point.

3. Clicking the down arrow next to each role expands them, and you will see what conditions and actions apply to each role. The following screenshot shows that when a lower volume of content is detected, less aggressive actions are taken. When a higher volume is detected by the policy, more restrictions will apply:

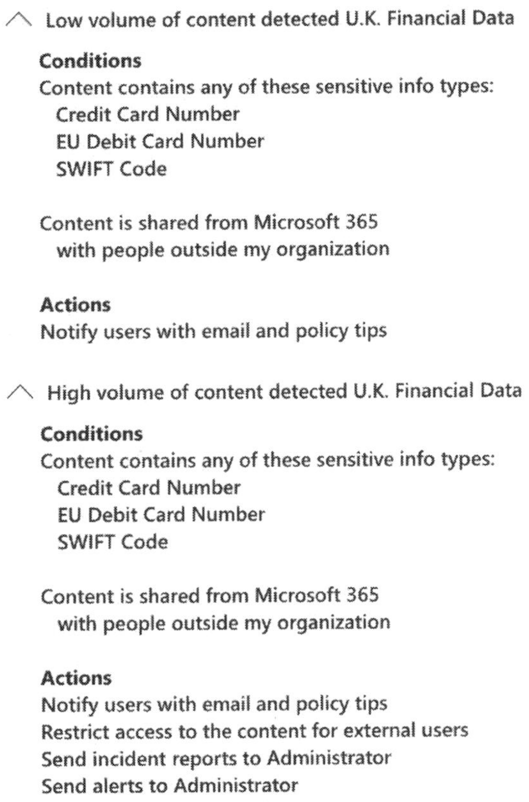

⌃ Low volume of content detected U.K. Financial Data

Conditions
Content contains any of these sensitive info types:
   Credit Card Number
   EU Debit Card Number
   SWIFT Code

Content is shared from Microsoft 365
   with people outside my organization

Actions
Notify users with email and policy tips

⌃ High volume of content detected U.K. Financial Data

Conditions
Content contains any of these sensitive info types:
   Credit Card Number
   EU Debit Card Number
   SWIFT Code

Content is shared from Microsoft 365
   with people outside my organization

Actions
Notify users with email and policy tips
Restrict access to the content for external users
Send incident reports to Administrator
Send alerts to Administrator

Figure 12.19: Low- and high-volume content options

4. For this example, modify the high-volume content rule by clicking the edit button (a pen symbol) to the right of the rule. There is a lot of content that can be edited within rules, so you will have to scroll through each section. The first section you can modify is the description. The name cannot be changed:

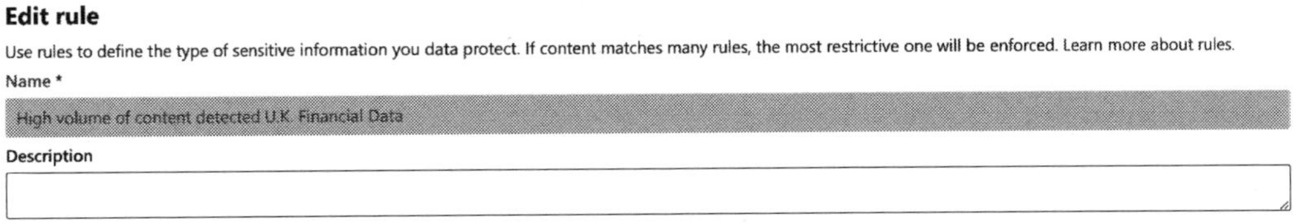

Edit rule

Use rules to define the type of sensitive information you data protect. If content matches many rules, the most restrictive one will be enforced. Learn more about rules.

Name *

High volume of content detected U.K. Financial Data

Description

Figure 12.20: Editing the rule description

5. Next, edit the conditions of the rule. Here, you will see **Sensitive info types** specified for the rule. You can add, edit, or remove these as required and modify their confidence level and **Instance count** values:

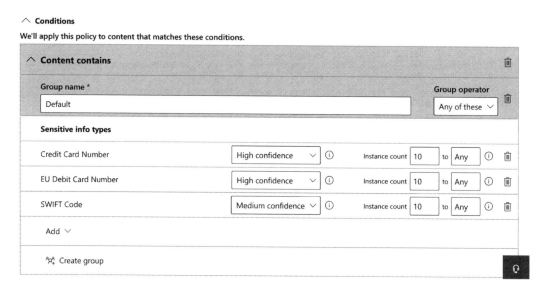

Figure 12.21: Editing the rule conditions

6. Scrolling down further, edit the setting you chose to detect content that matches the policy that is shared either within or outside the organization:

Figure 12.22: Editing the rule trigger

7. Add any exceptions you would like to make to the policy rule:

Figure 12.23: Setting exceptions for the policy rule

8. Scrolling further down the rule, choose whether access will be restricted or encrypted and users will be blocked from receiving content that is a match for this policy rule:

Figure 12.24: Editing the rule description

9. Next, choose how or whether you want your users to be notified with policy tips if there is a policy rule match:

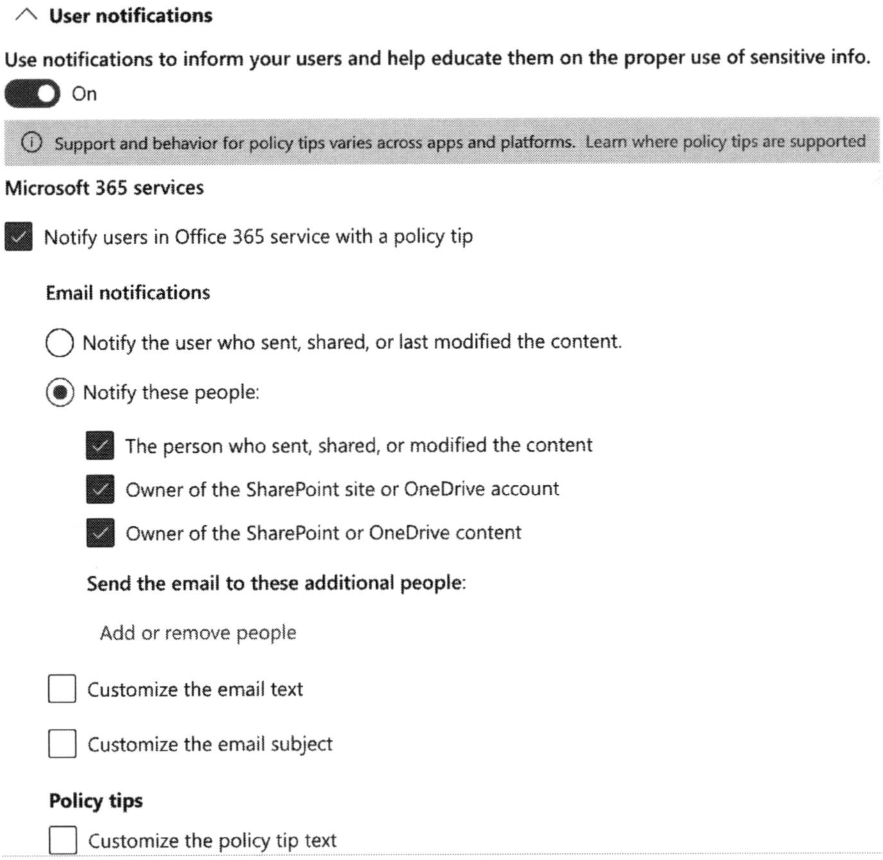

∧ **User notifications**

Use notifications to inform your users and help educate them on the proper use of sensitive info.

⬤ On

ⓘ Support and behavior for policy tips varies across apps and platforms. Learn where policy tips are supported

Microsoft 365 services

☑ Notify users in Office 365 service with a policy tip

Email notifications

◯ Notify the user who sent, shared, or last modified the content.

⦿ Notify these people:

☑ The person who sent, shared, or modified the content

☑ Owner of the SharePoint site or OneDrive account

☑ Owner of the SharePoint or OneDrive content

Send the email to these additional people:

Add or remove people

☐ Customize the email text

☐ Customize the email subject

Policy tips

☐ Customize the policy tip text

Figure 12.25: Setting user notification options

10. For this example, allow user overrides, and optionally require the user to enter a business justification if they override a policy tip. Also, there is the **Override the rule automatically if the user reports it as a false positive** option:

Figure 12.26: Setting user override options

11. Next, choose your settings for **Incident reports**. Here, you can choose the severity level of admin alerts and reports, set the alert frequency based on the volume of matched activity, and use email incident reports to receive a notification when a policy match occurs:

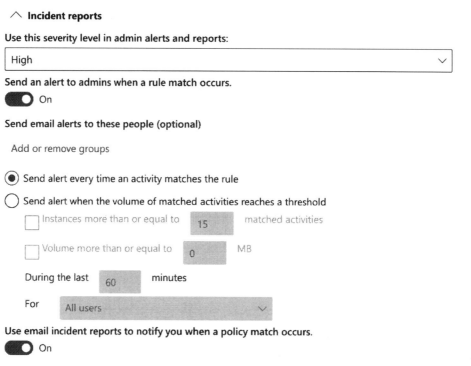

Figure 12.27: Configuring incident reports

Further incident report settings options include the ability to include specific information in the report, such as the name of the person who was the last to modify the content, the SITs that matched the rule, and the rule's severity level.

12. When you have configured these settings, you will have reached the end of the editing capabilities for the rule. Click **Save**:

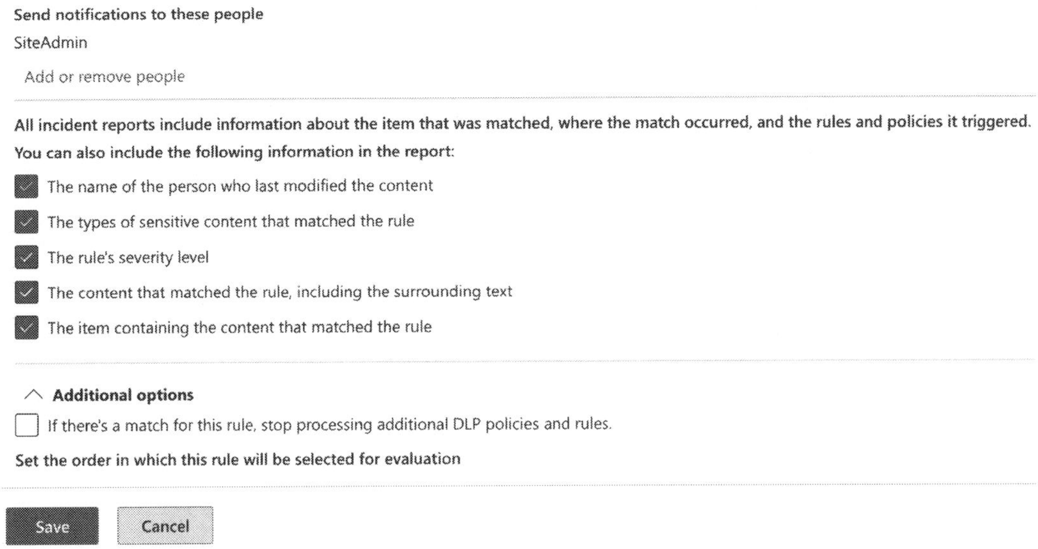

Send notifications to these people

SiteAdmin

Add or remove people

All incident reports include information about the item that was matched, where the match occurred, and the rules and policies it triggered. You can also include the following information in the report:

☑ The name of the person who last modified the content

☑ The types of sensitive content that matched the rule

☑ The rule's severity level

☑ The content that matched the rule, including the surrounding text

☑ The item containing the content that matched the rule

∧ **Additional options**

☐ If there's a match for this rule, stop processing additional DLP policies and rules.

Set the order in which this rule will be selected for evaluation

Save   Cancel

Figure 12.28: Setting notifications

The changes to the policy will now be saved and should take effect in a short period of time.

In this section, we learned how to create a DLP policy and assign it to a selection of Microsoft 365 locations. We observed that we can keep our new policy turned off until we are ready to test or activate it, as well as how to enable it in test mode with user notifications and policy tips. We also learned how to edit our DLP policies after creating them and modify them with the advanced policy settings.

Next, we will explore the reporting and alerting capabilities of DLP.

DLP reporting and alerting capabilities

There are several reporting and alerting capabilities for DLP available within the Microsoft Purview compliance center. Regularly reviewing these will give Microsoft 365 administrators valuable insights into how effectively DLP is configured and working. The reports that are available are as follows:

- **DLP Policy Matches**: This section shows a count of recent policy matches, all of which you can filter by date, location, policy, or action. Policy matches are shown in this report at a rule level, meaning that the report is better for identifying matches with specific rules and fine-tuning your DLP policies. Clicking into the tile will give you a broader view of the DLP policy match activity, along with related reports on **DLP Incidents** and **DLP false positives and overrides**.

- **DLP Incidents**: This report shows you policy matches over time at an item level. An example of this would be where an email matches different rules but the report shows only one item for that content. This report improves the detection of specific content causing issues for DLP policies.

- **DLP false positives and overrides**: This will show you a count of any detected false positives and overrides (if allowed). This report can be filtered and examined to analyze this activity and apply any required corrective measures. For example, if DLP policy overrides are allowed in your organization and you are seeing a high volume of overrides and user justifications, this may need to be addressed.

- **Third-party DLP policy matches**: This will redirect you to the MDA portal where you can see any third-party DLP activity if relevant.

You can view the available DLP reports from the compliance center by navigating to **Reports** and scrolling down to the **Organizational data** section:

Figure 12.29: DLP policy reports

All the DLP reports available in the compliance center can store information for up to four months prior to the current date. However, the most recent DLP activity may take up to 24 hours to be included in these reports.

In addition to the Microsoft Purview dashboard, you can use Windows PowerShell to get information relating to DLP. Let's look at this in the next section.

Using PowerShell with DLP reporting

To use the DLP PowerShell reporting cmdlets, you need to complete the following steps:

1. Connect to **Security & Compliance PowerShell** at https://learn.microsoft.com/ en-us/powershell/exchange/connect-to-scc-powershell. This is achieved by running the following command:

    ```
    Connect-IPPSSession -UserPrincipalName username@tenantname.
    onmicrosoft.com
    ```

2. Once connected, use the following cmdlets:

    *   Get-DlpDetailReport

    *   Get-DlpDetectionsReport

    *   Get-DlpSiDetectionsReport

For more details on using PowerShell for DLP reporting, please refer to the *Further reading* section at the end of this chapter.

Now, let's review the permissions required to view DLP reports.

Required permissions for DLP reports

You must be assigned the following permissions to view the DLP reports in the Microsoft Purview compliance portal or via Windows PowerShell:

*   The **Security Reader** role in the Exchange admin center

*   The **View-Only DLP Compliance Management** role in the Microsoft Purview compliance portal

*   The **View-Only Recipients** role in the Exchange admin center

Now let's look at some additional ways in which we can view DLP activity.

Further alerting capabilities

In addition to the options already described, you can also view DLP alerts and activity right from within the DLP section of the Microsoft Purview compliance center. To do this, navigate to the **Data Loss Prevention | Alerts** section, as shown in the following screenshot. Here, you will see any relevant alerts relating to DLP. Click on **View details**:

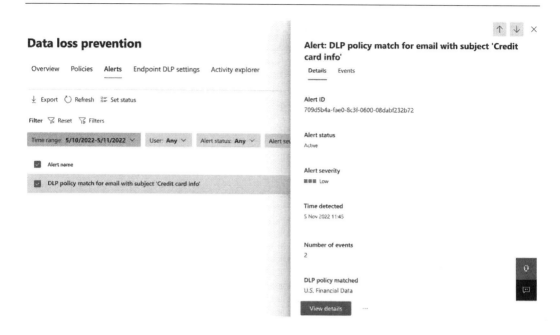

Figure 12.30: DLP alerts

You will now see more detailed information on the alert, including the user who performed the actions that led to the alert. You can take actions to alter the status of the alert, add comments, and assign it to another admin user to remediate the alert:

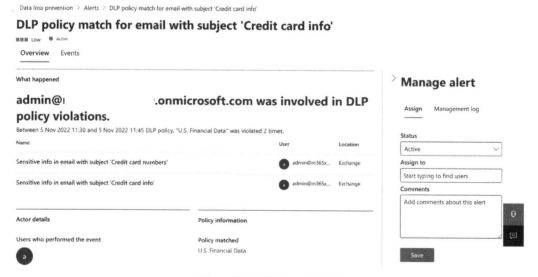

Figure 12.31: DLP alert detail

Similarly, if you click on the **Activity Explorer** section of DLP, you can view and filter statistics on DLP rule match activity:

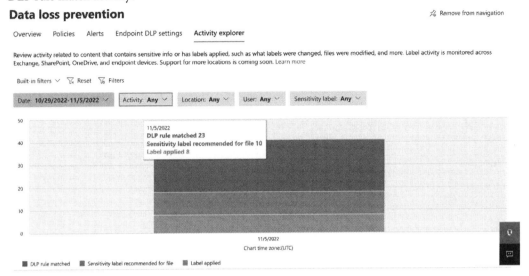

Figure 12.32: DLP Activity explorer

Scroll down to view individual line items and select each one to view more details about the activity:

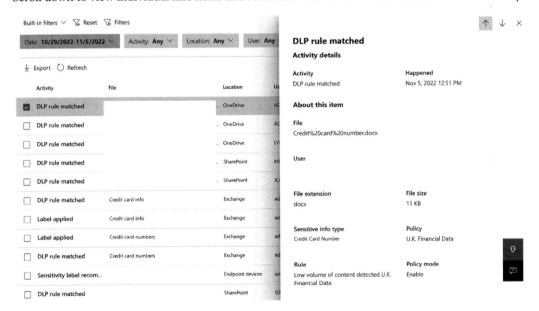

Figure 12.33: DLP Activity explorer detail

In this section, we learned how to view and interpret alerts and reports relating to Microsoft Purview DLP using the Purview compliance center and Windows PowerShell.

In the final section of this chapter, you will be introduced to Endpoint DLP.

Implementing Endpoint DLP

Endpoint DLP enables you to protect sensitive content stored on your Windows 10, Windows 11, and macOS devices using DLP policies. In order to use DLP policies with devices, you must have those devices onboarded that you want your policies to target. To do this, complete the following steps:

1. From the Microsoft Purview compliance center, go to **Settings | Device onboarding** and click on **Turn on device onboarding**:

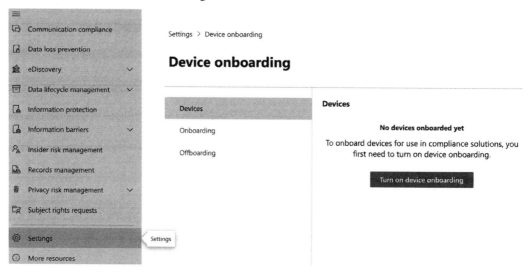

Figure 12.34: Turning on device onboarding in the Purview compliance center

2. You will be informed that when turning this feature on, any devices already onboarded to Microsoft Defender for Endpoint will appear in the list of devices. Click **OK**:

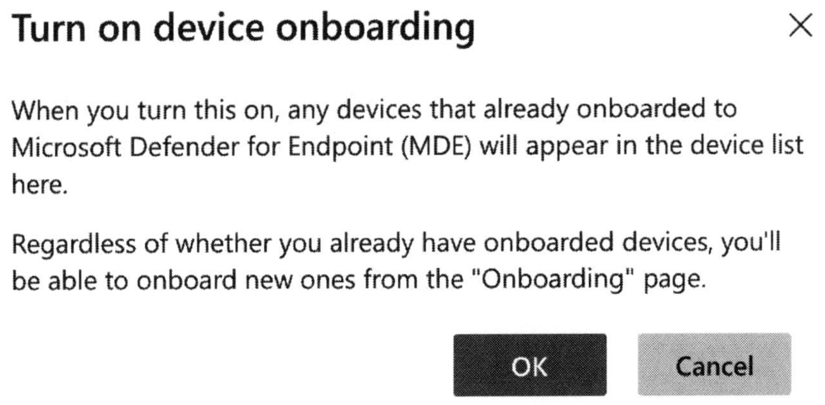

Turn on device onboarding

When you turn this on, any devices that already onboarded to Microsoft Defender for Endpoint (MDE) will appear in the device list here.

Regardless of whether you already have onboarded devices, you'll be able to onboard new ones from the "Onboarding" page.

Figure 12.35: Turning on device onboarding

3. Be aware that it could take some time for device onboarding to be fully enabled. You will be warned of this, as shown in the following screenshot. Acknowledge the warning by clicking **OK**:

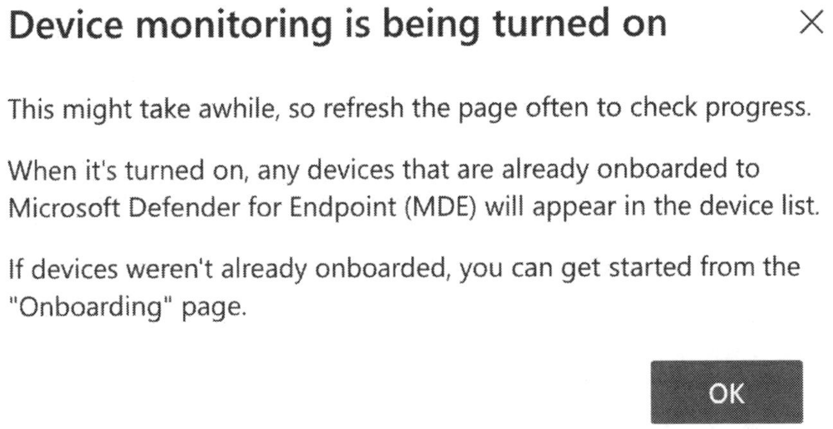

Device monitoring is being turned on

This might take awhile, so refresh the page often to check progress.

When it's turned on, any devices that are already onboarded to Microsoft Defender for Endpoint (MDE) will appear in the device list.

If devices weren't already onboarded, you can get started from the "Onboarding" page.

Figure 12.36: Turning on device onboarding

Once device onboarding is enabled, you may create a DLP policy targeted to devices. This is done in exactly the same way as described earlier in the chapter in the *Creating a DLP policy* section.

4. When you get to the section of the policy creation wizard where you must choose the locations to which you want to apply your policy, select **Devices**, then filter by the users or groups that you wish to either explicitly include or exclude from the policy. Then, click **Next**:

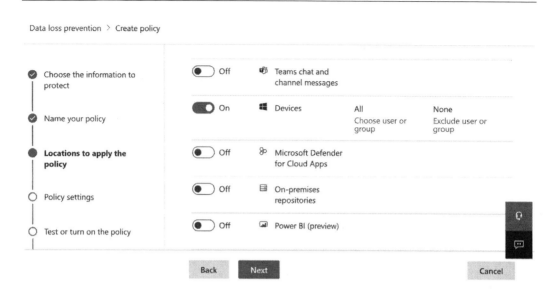

Figure 12.37: Choosing devices as the target for applying a DLP policy

5. Now that you have device onboarding enabled, the options that were previously grayed out, as shown in *Figure 12.11*, will be available to you. Select **Audit or restrict activities on devices**:

☑ **Audit or restrict activities on devices**

When specified activities are detected on devices for files containing the sensitive info you're protecting, you can choose to only audit the activity, block it entirely, or block it but allow users to override the restriction.
Learn more restricting device activity

Service domain and browser activities

Detects when protected files are blocked or allowed to be uploaded to cloud service domains based on the 'Allow/Block cloud service domains' list in endpoint DLP settings.

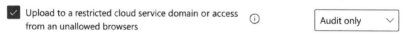

Figure 12.38: Audit or restrict activities on devices

6. Scroll down to see all the available actions you can apply with an endpoint DLP policy. Each option available for selection has three possible settings: **Audit only**, **Block with override**, and **Block**. You can select the option you need for your policy:

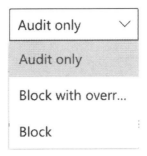

Figure 12.39: Available settings within an Endpoint DLP policy

7.   Scroll down to the **File activities for all apps** section. Here, you can control the behavior on your onboarded devices and restrict activities, including **Copy to clipboard**, **Copy to a USB removable media**, **Copy to a network share**, **Print**, **Copy or move using unallowed Bluetooth app**, and **Copy or move using RDP**:

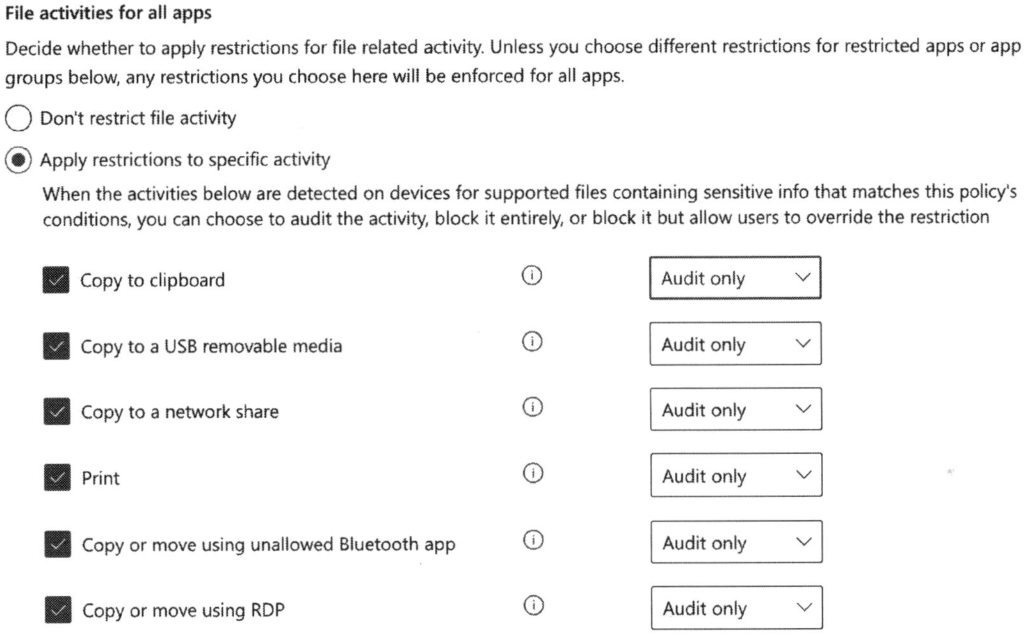

File activities for all apps

Decide whether to apply restrictions for file related activity. Unless you choose different restrictions for restricted apps or app groups below, any restrictions you choose here will be enforced for all apps.

◯ Don't restrict file activity

⦿ Apply restrictions to specific activity

When the activities below are detected on devices for supported files containing sensitive info that matches this policy's conditions, you can choose to audit the activity, block it entirely, or block it but allow users to override the restriction

☑ Copy to clipboard	ⓘ	Audit only ⌄
☑ Copy to a USB removable media	ⓘ	Audit only ⌄
☑ Copy to a network share	ⓘ	Audit only ⌄
☑ Print	ⓘ	Audit only ⌄
☑ Copy or move using unallowed Bluetooth app	ⓘ	Audit only ⌄
☑ Copy or move using RDP	ⓘ	Audit only ⌄

Figure 12.40: Apply restrictions to specific activity

8.   Scroll down, and you will find the option to add a restricted app group. Define a group for this purpose and then select it. Then, select **Copy to clipboard**, **Copy to a USB removable media**, **Copy to a network share**, or **Print** to restrict file activity for group members:

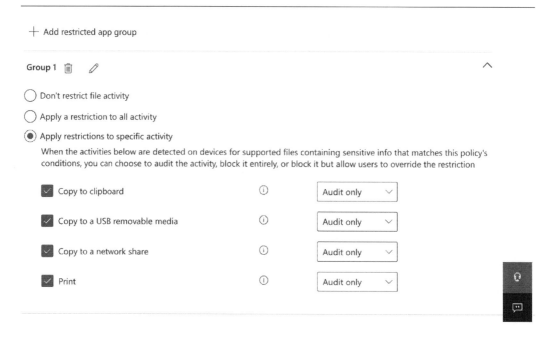

Figure 12.41: Apply restrictions to specific activity using an app group

9. Scroll down to the **Restrict app activities** section. Here, choose how you want the tenant-wide Endpoint DLP policy to act when apps that are on the restricted apps list attempt to access protected files on a device:

Restricted app activities

Detects when apps that are on the restricted apps list (as defined in Endpoint DLP settings) attempt to access protected files on a device.

Figure 12.42: Restricting app activities

If you scroll down further, you will also see options for restricting third-party apps. This would need to be configured in conjunction with MDA. For the purposes of this example, we will skip this section. More information can be found in the *Further reading* section at the end of the chapter.

10. Click on **Next** and proceed through the wizard to complete setting up your Endpoint DLP policy (in test mode of course):

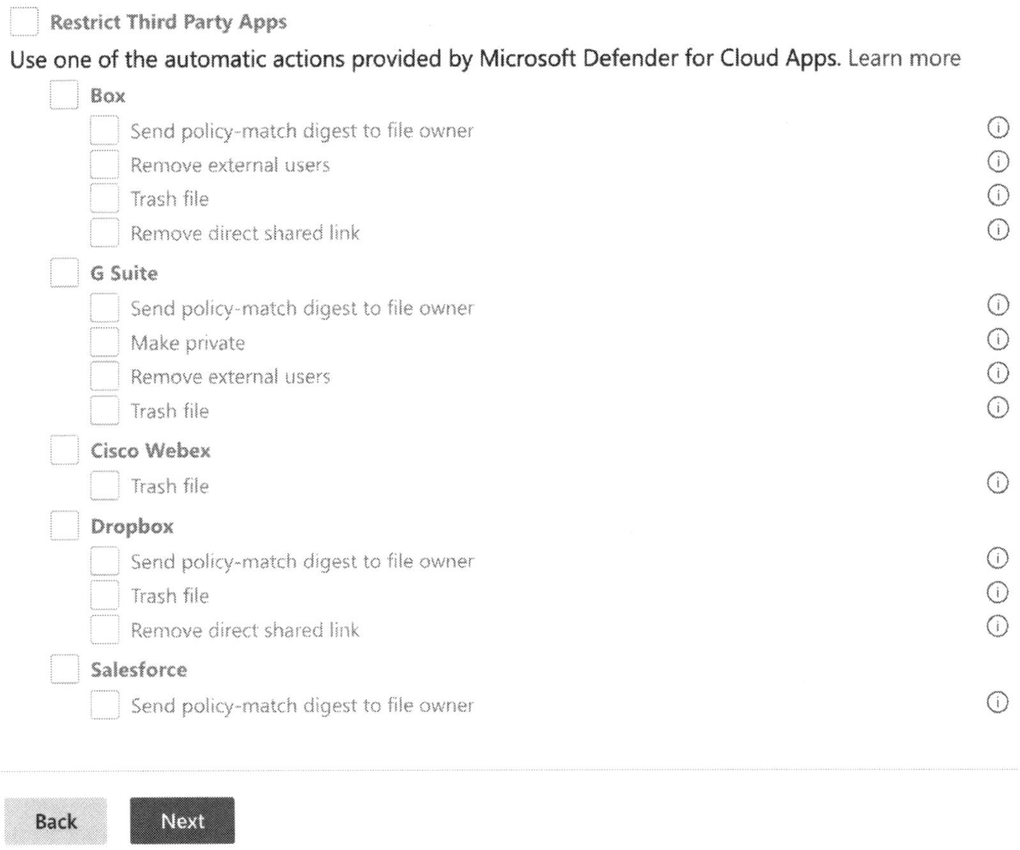

Figure 12.43: Restricting third-party apps

11. With your Endpoint DLP policy created, you also need to be sure that your tenant-wide endpoint DLP settings (referenced in *Figure 12.42*) are configured as required. To do this, click on **Endpoint DLP settings**:

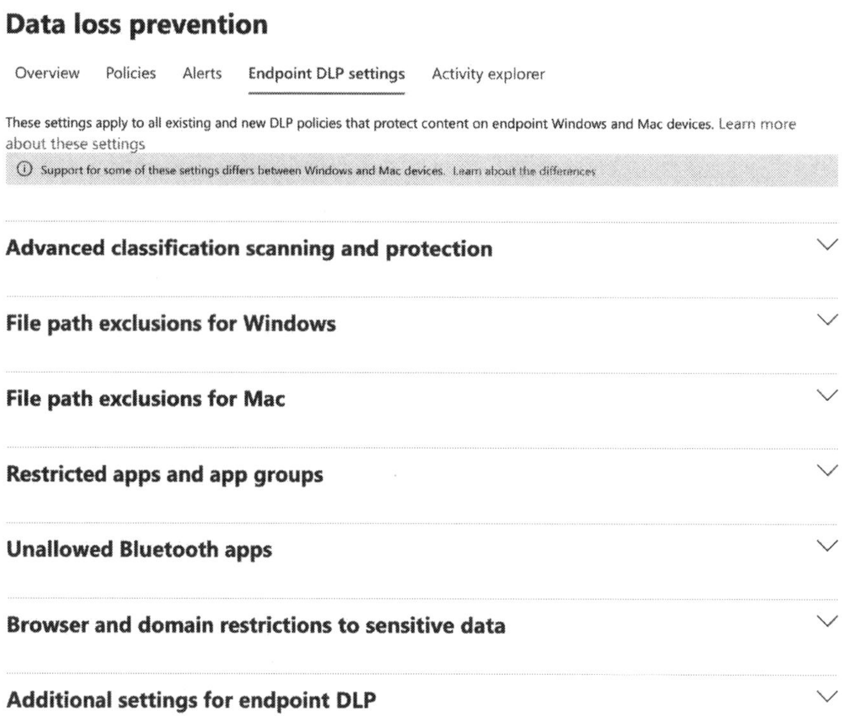

Data loss prevention

Overview   Policies   Alerts   **Endpoint DLP settings**   Activity explorer

These settings apply to all existing and new DLP policies that protect content on endpoint Windows and Mac devices. Learn more about these settings

ⓘ Support for some of these settings differs between Windows and Mac devices. Learn about the differences

Advanced classification scanning and protection   ⌄

File path exclusions for Windows   ⌄

File path exclusions for Mac   ⌄

Restricted apps and app groups   ⌄

Unallowed Bluetooth apps   ⌄

Browser and domain restrictions to sensitive data   ⌄

Additional settings for endpoint DLP   ⌄

Figure 12.44: Tenant-wide Endpoint DLP settings

Let's discuss each of these settings in detail:

- The **Advanced classification scanning and protection** option allows Microsoft 365 to scan and classify items, and return the results to the local device. Classification features such as exact data match and named entities can be used in your DLP policies with this feature:

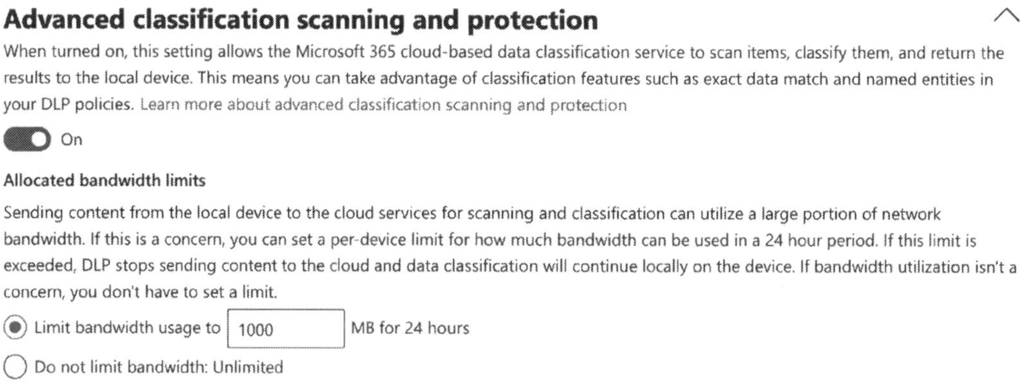

Advanced classification scanning and protection   ⌃

When turned on, this setting allows the Microsoft 365 cloud-based data classification service to scan items, classify them, and return the results to the local device. This means you can take advantage of classification features such as exact data match and named entities in your DLP policies. Learn more about advanced classification scanning and protection

🔘 On

Allocated bandwidth limits

Sending content from the local device to the cloud services for scanning and classification can utilize a large portion of network bandwidth. If this is a concern, you can set a per-device limit for how much bandwidth can be used in a 24 hour period. If this limit is exceeded, DLP stops sending content to the cloud and data classification will continue locally on the device. If bandwidth utilization isn't a concern, you don't have to set a limit.

◉ Limit bandwidth usage to [1000] MB for 24 hours

◯ Do not limit bandwidth: Unlimited

Figure 12.45: Advanced classification scanning and protection

- The **File path exclusions for Windows** section allows you to add file paths on Windows devices that will be excluded from the policy. The same option is available for macOS devices:

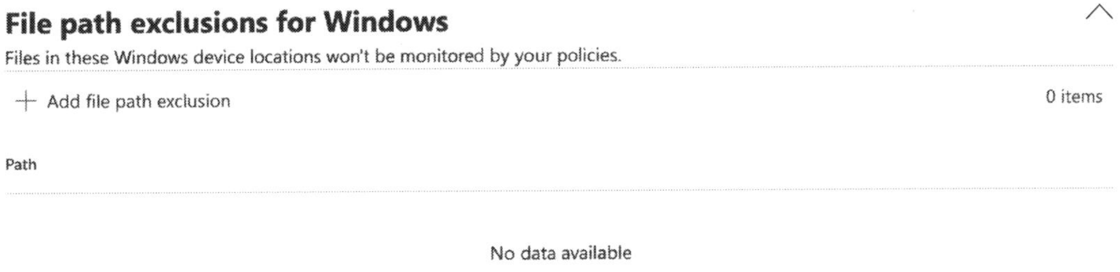

File path exclusions for Windows

Files in these Windows device locations won't be monitored by your policies.

+ Add file path exclusion   0 items

Path

No data available

Figure 12.46: File path exclusion options

- The **Restricted apps and app groups** section allows you to control the level of access of specific apps to the sensitive content detected in your DLP policies. Create groups of apps to enforce different access restrictions for each group or add apps individually to one list to apply the same restrictions to them all:

Restricted apps and app groups

Control the level of access that specific apps have to the sensitive content detected in your DLP policies. Create groups of apps to enforce different access restrictions for each group or add apps individually to one list to apply the same restrictions to them all. Learn more about restricted apps

> ⓘ If a policy blocks restricted apps from accessing files, cloud apps like OneDrive might show repeated notifications to users as the app continuously attempts to access the files. To prevent this, specify a location on user's devices to quarantine files, then select the 'Autoquarantine' option when adding apps. Learn more about auto-quarantine ✕

Restricted app groups

You can use app groups in your DLP policies to enforce different access restrictions on Windows devices.

+ Add app group   1 group

App group name	Included apps	Number of apps	Auto-quarantine ⓘ		
Group 1	Notepad++.exe	1	☐	✏	🗑

Restricted apps

The restriction enforced by the 'Access by restricted apps' setting in DLP policies will apply to all apps in this list.

+ Add or edit restricted apps   2 apps

App name	Executable name	Auto-quarantine ⓘ	
Notepad++	notepad++.exe	☐	🗑
Atom	atom.bat	☐	🗑

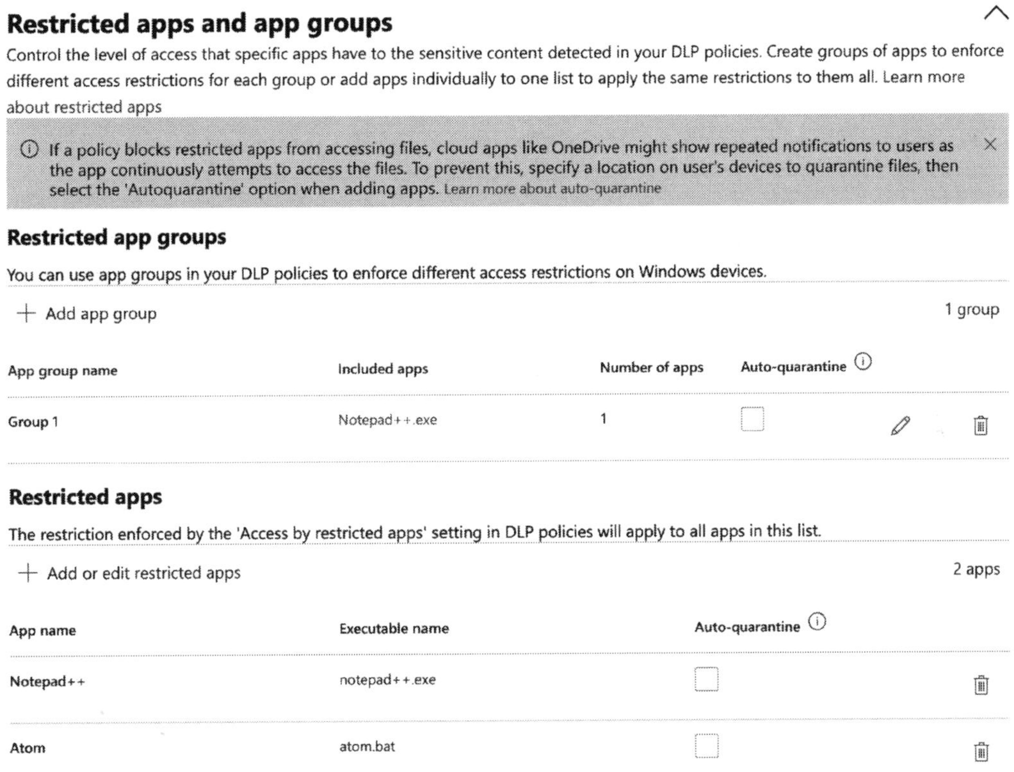

Figure 12.47: Restricted apps and app groups options

- **Auto-quarantine settings** allows you to specify a location on users' devices where files should be quarantined if they are blocked from accessing an unallowed app that has the **Auto-quarantine** option selected. You can also replace the blocked file with a custom text file to let users know why the file was blocked and where it was moved:

Auto-quarantine settings

Edit these settings to specify a location on user's devices where files should be quarantined if they're blocked from accessing an unallowed app that has the 'Auto-quarantine' option selected. You can also replace the blocked file with a custom text file to let users know why the file was blocked and where it was moved to.

Auto-quarantine status: **On**

🖉 Edit auto-quarantine settings

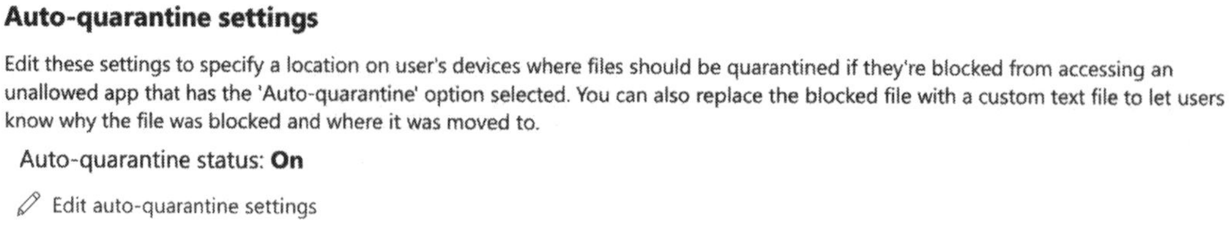

Figure 12.48: Auto-quarantine settings

- The **Unallowed Bluetooth apps** section enables you to prevent people from using specified Bluetooth apps to copy or move protected files to another location:

Unallowed Bluetooth apps   ⌃

Prevent people from using specified Bluetooth apps to copy or move protected files to another location.

+ Add or edit unallowed Bluetooth apps   0 items

Include Bluetooth apps recommended by Microsoft: **On** Edit ⓘ

App	Executable name

No data available

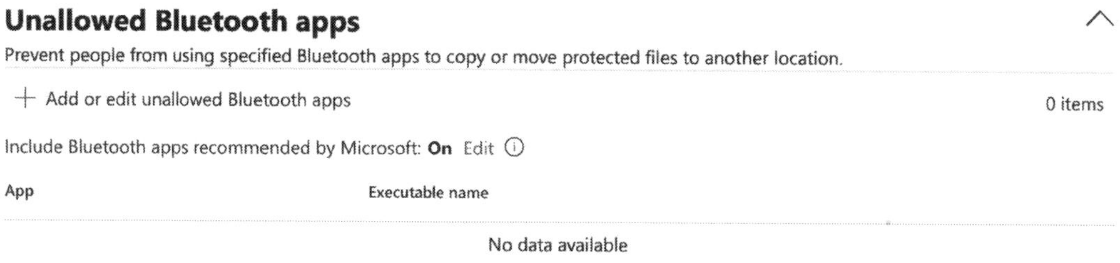

Figure 12.49: Unallowed Bluetooth apps settings

- The **Browser and domain restrictions to sensitive data** section allows you to restrict sensitive files that match your policies from being shared with unallowed browsers and service domains:

Browser and domain restrictions to sensitive data   ⌃

Restrict sensitive files that match your policies from being shared with unallowed browsers and service domains.

Unallowed browsers

Unallowed browsers will be blocked from accessing files protected by your policies. When blocked, users will be prompted to access the files using Microsoft Edge, where they'll be able to interact with the content but be prevented from uploading to unallowed service domains.

ⓘ Users who have the Microsoft Purview extension installed on their devices won't be blocked when using Chrome, even if Chrome is listed as an unallowed browser.

+ Add or edit unallowed browsers   0 items

Browser	Executable name

No data available

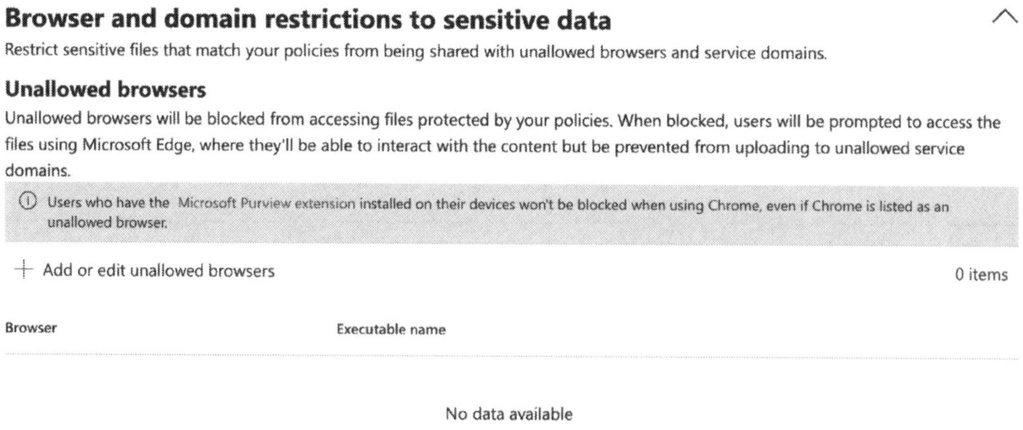

Figure 12.50: Browser and domain restrictions to sensitive data options

- Under **Additional settings for endpoint DLP**, you can configure **Business justification in policy tips** to control how users can proceed when a policy setting is set to **Block with override**:

Additional settings for endpoint DLP

Business justification in policy tips

Control how users interact with the business justification option in policy tip notifications that appear on devices. This option appears when users perform an activity that's protected by the "Block with override" setting in a DLP policy. Learn more

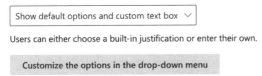

Users can either choose a built-in justification or enter their own.

Figure 12.51: Business justification in policy tips settings

- Finally, the setting for **Always audit file activity for devices** controls whether device activity is to be audited only when onboarded devices are included in an active policy. Note that file activity will always be audited for onboarded devices regardless of whether they are included in an active policy or not:

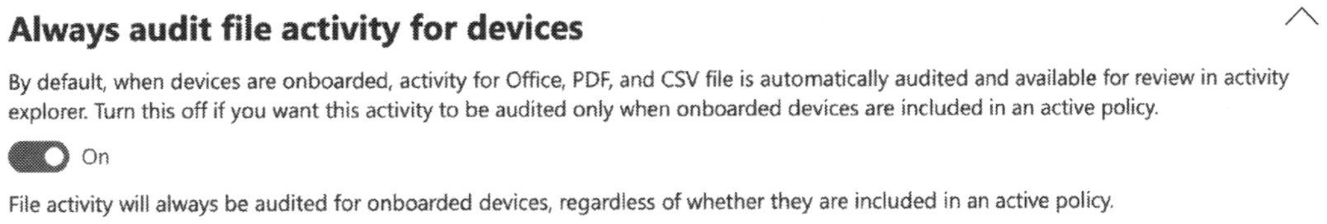

Always audit file activity for devices   ⌃

By default, when devices are onboarded, activity for Office, PDF, and CSV file is automatically audited and available for review in activity explorer. Turn this off if you want this activity to be audited only when onboarded devices are included in an active policy.

🔘 On

File activity will always be audited for onboarded devices, regardless of whether they are included in an active policy.

Figure 12.52: Always audit file activity for devices control

This section introduced the principles of Endpoint DLP. We learned that to use Endpoint DLP, you need to have device onboarding settings enabled in Microsoft Purview. Thereafter, we can configure DLP policies targeted to those devices. We also learned how to set tenant-wide Endpoint DLP settings. Now let's wrap up this chapter with a brief recap.

Summary

This chapter explained how DLP in Microsoft 365 can help create policies based on built-in and custom SITs. This prevents users in an organization from accidentally sharing sensitive information. We learned how to set up and modify a DLP policy and apply it to all or selected Microsoft 365 locations. We also learned how to effectively plan a DLP rollout by creating policies in test mode only, as well as how to view and interpret the reports that are available in the Microsoft Purview compliance center and also Windows PowerShell. Finally, we learned how Endpoint DLP is used to protect Windows 10 and 11 devices as well as macOS devices with device onboarding settings and DLP policies.

The next chapter will introduce the principles of data governance and retention. We will learn how to view and interpret data life cycle management reports and dashboards, configure retention labels and policies, configure retention within Microsoft 365 workloads, find and recover deleted Office 365 data, and configure and use Microsoft Purview Records Management.

Questions

1. What do you need to do before you can use Endpoint DLP in Microsoft Purview?

   A. Enable device synchronization

   B. Enable device onboarding

   C. Enable device scanning

   D. Enable Microsoft Defender for Cloud Apps

2. Which of the following device types can be protected using Endpoint DLP (select three)?

   A. Windows 11

   B. Linux

   C. Windows 10

   D. macOS

   E. iOS

   F. Android

3. Which of the following is not one of the possible settings for a DLP policy in Microsoft Purview?

   A. Test (with notifications)

   B. On

   C. Test (without notifications)

   D. Test in simulation mode

   E. Off

4. Which of the following are categories of templates that can be selected when setting up a DLP policy (choose two)?

   A. Legal

   B. Financial

   C. Government

   D. Medical and health

5. True or False? DLP policies can be applied to Teams chat and channel messages.

    A. True

    B. False

6. Where do you configure DLP policies?

    A. The Azure portal

    B. The Microsoft 365 Defender portal

    C. The Microsoft Purview compliance portal

    D. The Microsoft 365 admin center

7. True or False? When a DLP policy is set to test with policy tips, the policy and its rule will be enforced.

    A. True

    B. False

8. What can DLP protect within Microsoft Teams (select two)?

    A. Calendar

    B. Teams chat

    C. Channel messages

    D. Apps

9. Which of the following is not one of the configuration sections of DLP?

    A. **Content Explorer**

    B. **Activity Explorer**

    C. **Endpoint DLP**

    D. **Policies**

10. True or False? Apps and app groups can be used to control user actions on devices with Endpoint DLP.

    A. True

    B. False

Further reading

Please refer to the following links for more information regarding what was covered in this chapter:

- *Learn about data loss prevention*: `https://learn.microsoft.com/en-gb/microsoft-365/compliance/dlp-learn-about-dlp?view=o365-worldwide`

- Viewing reports for DLP: `https://learn.microsoft.com/en-gb/microsoft-365/compliance/view-the-dlp-reports?view=o365-worldwide`

- *Connecting to Security & Compliance PowerShell*: `https://learn.microsoft.com/en-us/powershell/exchange/connect-to-scc-powershell?view=exchange-ps`

- DLP PowerShell commands: `https://learn.microsoft.com/en-us/powershell/module/exchange/get-dlpcompliancepolicy?view=exchange-ps`

- *Get started with Endpoint data loss prevention*: `https://learn.microsoft.com/en-us/microsoft-365/compliance/endpoint-dlp-getting-started?view=o365-worldwide`

- *Learn about Endpoint data loss prevention*: `https://learn.microsoft.com/en-us/microsoft-365/compliance/endpoint-dlp-learn-about?WT.mc_id=M365-MVP-4039827&view=o365-worldwide`

- *Create a DLP policy scoped to a non-Microsoft cloud app*: `https://learn.microsoft.com/en-us/microsoft-365/compliance/dlp-use-policies-non-microsoft-cloud-apps?view=o365-worldwide#create-a-dlp-policy-scoped-to-a-non-microsoft-cloud-app`

13

Managing Microsoft Purview Data Lifecycle Management

Planning the **lifecycle** of your organization's data is a crucial task for Microsoft 365 compliance administrators, and it is vital to have the correct strategy in place to ensure that your organization is protected and compliant. There are several ways to manage the lifecycle of the data hosted in your Microsoft 365 environment, the principles of which will be introduced in this chapter. You will learn how to view and interpret Data Lifecycle Management reports and dashboards, configure retention labels and policies, configure retention within Microsoft 365 workloads, find and recover deleted Office 365 data, and configure and use adaptive scopes.

These topics will be covered in the following order:

- Planning for data lifecycle management

- Analyzing reports and dashboards

- Configuring retention labels and policies

- Planning and implementing adaptive scopes

- Finding and recovering deleted Microsoft 365 data

Planning for data lifecycle management

The complexity and volume of data that is stored and processed by organizations is ever increasing. Data can be stored within email messages, documents, Teams chat and channel messages, and more. It has never been more crucial to effectively manage and govern the data that you store in order to do the following:

- Comply with internal policies or industry regulations and retain content for only as long as it is needed

- Permanently delete old and unnecessary content to reduce risk in the event of a security breach or litigation

- Ensure that your organization's employees work only with content that is current and relevant

The starting point for compliance administrators when planning for data lifecycle management is retention. With retention labels and policies in Microsoft 365, you can take actions that will either retain or delete content in line with the set retention periods. This will result in the following outcomes:

- **Retain-only**: Retain content forever or for a specified time period

- **Delete-only**: Permanently delete content after a specified time period

- **Retain and then delete**: Retain content for a specified time period and then delete it permanently

When content is targeted by a retention label or policy, the user who is working on that content can make any necessary changes unimpeded. However, the retention actions will make a copy of the original content, which will be retained for the duration of that retention schedule. This works across the various Microsoft 365 services as follows:

- **SharePoint Online and OneDrive**: A copy of the original content is retained in the `Preservation Hold` library

- **Email and public folders**: A copy of the original content is retained in the `Recoverable Items` folder

- **Teams**: A copy of chat content is stored in Exchange Online

> **Note**
>
> If your organization is bound by more restrictive regulations, then you may be required to configure retention policies using the **Preservation Lock** feature. When Preservation Lock is applied to a retention policy, the policy cannot be turned off or set to lesser restriction settings by anyone (including Microsoft 365 administrators).

When thinking about data lifecycle management, it is also important to be aware of your organization's records management requirements. Let's explore these in the next section.

Records management

Microsoft Purview includes capabilities for records management in the form of **file plan retention labels**. File plan retention labels are more appropriately used when your organization is obliged to mark items as a record or regulatory record. Declaring records in this way allows you to implement a single and consistent strategy for managing records across your Microsoft 365 environment. When disposing of content at the end of a retention period, it may be necessary to perform what is known as a **disposition review**. In this type of review, reviewers in your organization are tasked with reviewing content at the end of its retention period and deciding whether it can be deleted or whether it needs to be reprocessed.

The following statements apply when an item is declared a record:

- Restrictions are applied to the item in terms of what actions are allowed or blocked

- Further activities about the item are logged

- Your organization will have proof of disposition when the item is deleted at the end of the designated retention period

In this section, you learned that retention is a core principle when it comes to data lifecycle management in Microsoft 365. Once you have your retention schedule defined and approved, you can start to plan and roll out retention labels and policies. This will be covered later in the chapter in the *Configuring retention labels and policies* section. Next, we will learn how to analyze reports and dashboards in relation to data lifecycle management.

Analyzing reports and dashboards

Microsoft provides administrators with a great deal of information relating to data lifecycle management, which can be accessed from the Microsoft Purview compliance portal. Regularly reviewing this information enables you to stay one step ahead in ensuring that your organization meets its compliance and regulatory obligations. It also allows you to make logical adjustments to the existing compliance settings that you have already configured. The Microsoft Purview **Data classification** page provides you with visibility on the following details:

- Items classified as a **sensitive information type** (**SIT**) and what those classifications are

- The most frequently applied sensitivity labels

- The most frequently applied retention labels

- A summary of activities that users are carrying out on your sensitive content

- The locations of your sensitive and retained data

In order to view this information in the Microsoft Purview compliance portal, complete the following steps:

1. Navigate to `https://compliance.microsoft.com` and log in as a Global Administrator, Compliance Administrator, Compliance Data Administrator, or Security Administrator. Navigate to **Data classification** from the left-hand side menu bar. You will see the **Overview** tab:

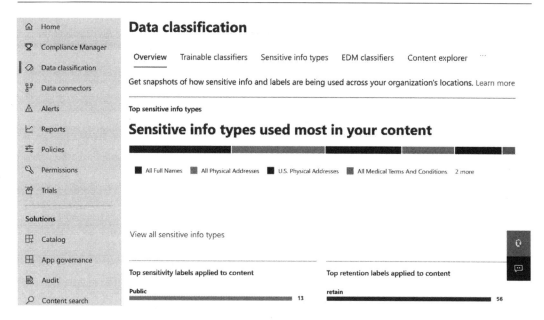

Figure 13.1: The Data classification dashboard

The **Overview** page contains cards showing statistics on data classification. The **Sensitive info types used** card shows the top SITs identified and labeled across your organization. Sensitive info types can be used with auto-labeling policies in retention.

2. Hover over one of the SITs on the graph to view the number of matched items:

Figure 13.2: Sensitive info types used in your organization

3. Another card relating to data lifecycle management is **Top retention labels applied to content**:

Top retention labels applied to content

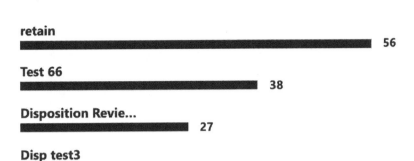

retain
56

Test 66
38

Disposition Revie...
27

Disp test3
2

RCN
1

Figure 13.3: The top retention labels applied to content

4. View the **Locations where retention labels are applied** card and hover over the pie chart to see the number of matches per location:

Locations where retention labels are applied

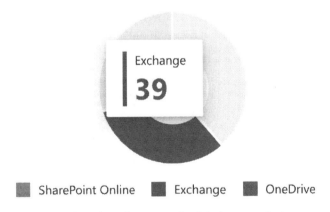

Exchange
39

■ SharePoint Online   ■ Exchange   ■ OneDrive

Figure 13.4: Location where retention labels are applied

Expanding these cards to see more details takes you to **Content explorer**, where you can view what has been discovered and labeled and where that content is stored. Let's explore this in the next section.

Content explorer

Content explorer enables you to view any items summarized in the cards on the **Overview** page. When you select the **Content explorer** tab, you will see categories on the left side and location types on the right:

Data classification

Overview   Trainable classifiers   Sensitive info types   EDM classifiers   **Content explorer**   Activity explorer

Explore the email and docs in your organization that contain sensitive info or have labels applied. You drill down further by reviewing the source content that's currently stored in Exchange, SharePoint, and OneDrive. Support for more locations is coming soon. Learn more

	Sensitive info types			All locations		
		⌄		↓ Export		4 items
	All Full Names	2685			Name	Files
	All Physical Addresses	2429		Exchange		2354 ›
	U.S. Physical Addresses	1990		OneDrive		75 ›
	All Medical Terms And Conditions	1347		SharePoint		186 ›
	Diseases	1230		Teams		70 ›
	U.K. Physical Addresses	355				

🔍 Filter on labels, info types, or categories

Figure 13.5: Content explorer

You can filter by (or scroll down to) **Retention labels**, select a specific label, and navigate to the locations and items where the label has been applied. This is shown in the following screenshot, where the **retain** label has been selected and the **OneDrive** location has been chosen. Expanding the folder would take the administrator to a list of files with this label applied:

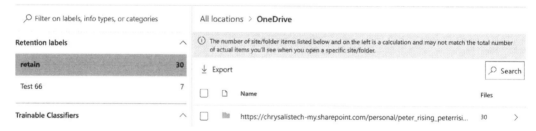

Figure 13.6: Location where retention labels are applied

Another way to monitor labeled content is through **Activity explorer**.

Activity explorer

While the **Overview** and **Content explorer** tabs allow you to see content (and the location of that content) that has been discovered and labeled, **Activity explorer** enables you to see what actions are being taken by users in your organization with labeled content on up to 30 days' worth of data.

When you select the **Activity explorer** tab, you will see a chart showing matches to metrics such as DLP rules, sensitivity labels, and, in relation to data lifecycle management, label activity:

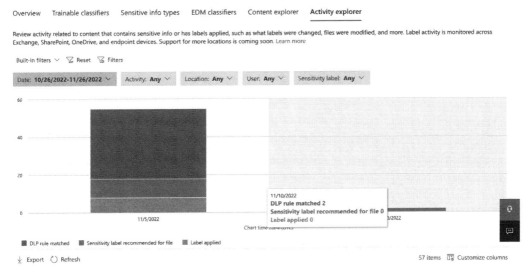

Figure 13.7: Activity explorer

Scroll down, and you will see line items for activities—for example, when a retention label was applied. Clicking to expand the detail shows who applied the label and which label was applied:

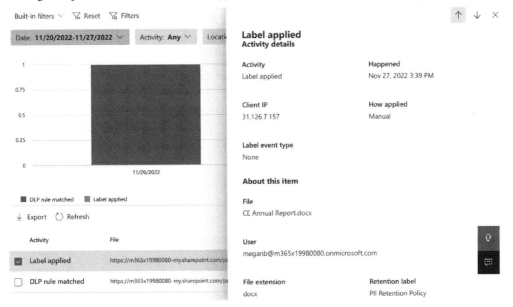

Figure 13.8: Retention label applied and shown in Activity explorer

Retention labels may be applied either manually by users or automatically by a retention label policy. The following screenshot shows the user experience of selecting a retention label manually:

Figure 13.9: User experience applying a retention label manually

Users can view the retention labels available to them from within a SharePoint document library or OneDrive folder by selecting the file and viewing its details. The **Properties** bar is then displayed showing the labels.

> **Note**
> **Activity explorer** does not monitor retention activity for Exchange Online.

So, as you can see, there are many ways you can track your organization's data lifecycle actions and activities by accessing the areas and dashboards described. In this section, we learned about the available methods to view information and dashboards relating to data lifecycle management. Next, we will explore the steps to configure retention labels and policies.

Configuring retention labels and policies

In this section, we will learn how to create **retention labels**, **retention label policies**, and **retention policies** and apply them to Microsoft 365 workloads, including Exchange Online, SharePoint Online, OneDrive, and Teams, from the Microsoft Purview compliance portal.

Retention labels are generally intended for when you need exceptions to your retention policies. Typically, you would use retention labels to retain specific items for longer periods than an applied retention policy. For example, you may set retention policies on SharePoint sites to retain content for five years. However, you may also have some documents within the SharePoint site that need to be retained for a longer period—say seven years—for regulatory compliance reasons. Retention labels could be applied to that content. First, we will see how retention labels are used at the item level and applied to content with retention label policies, and then how retention policies apply at the service level and apply to sites and mailboxes.

The next sections will take a look at retention labels and policies in more detail.

Creating a retention label

To create **retention labels**, use the Microsoft Purview compliance portal at `https://compliance.microsoft.com`. While the Global Admininstrator role has full permissions to create retention labels, it is recommended to assign the Compliance Administrator role to those within your organization who need to create and manage retention labels and their policies.

> **Note**
>
> If you need to use retention labels to manage records or regulatory records, you will need to create your retention labels using a file plan from the **Records management** section of the Microsoft Purview compliance portal.

In this example, you will create a retention label using **Data lifecycle management** by completing the following steps:

1. From the Microsoft Purview compliance portal, navigate to **Data lifecycle management |
    Microsoft 365**:

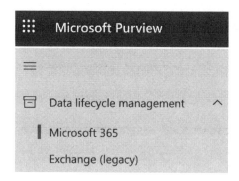

Figure 13.10: Data lifecycle management in the Microsoft Purview compliance portal

2.   Select **Labels | Create a label**:

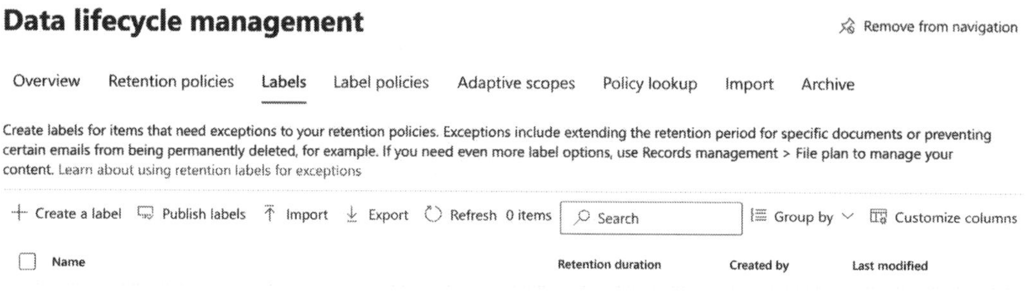

Data lifecycle management

✂ Remove from navigation

Overview   Retention policies   **Labels**   Label policies   Adaptive scopes   Policy lookup   Import   Archive

Create labels for items that need exceptions to your retention policies. Exceptions include extending the retention period for specific documents or preventing certain emails from being permanently deleted, for example. If you need even more label options, use Records management > File plan to manage your content. Learn about using retention labels for exceptions

+ Create a label   ▭ Publish labels   ⤒ Import   ⤓ Export   ◯ Refresh 0 items | 🔍 Search | ≡ Group by ∨   🖽 Customize columns

☐   Name   Retention duration   Created by   Last modified

Figure 13.11: Creating a retention label

3.   When the label creation wizard starts, add the name `Personal Financial PII` for your
     label. Then, enter the description `Personally identifiable information (PII)`
     `that, when used alone or with other relevant data, can identify an`
     `individual.` for both users and admins. This is shown in the following screenshot. Click **Next**:

Create retention label

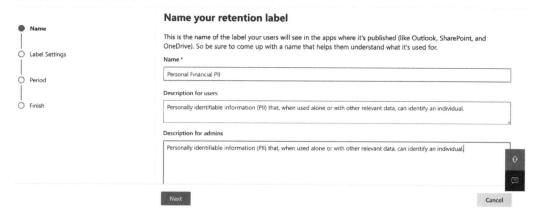

Figure 13.12: Set the name and descriptions for your retention label

4. Define the settings for your label. You have the following three options here:

   - **Retain items forever or for a specific period**

   - **Enforce actions after a specific period**

   - **Just label items**

   These options are shown in the following screenshot. For this example, choose **Retain items forever or for a specific period** and click **Next**:

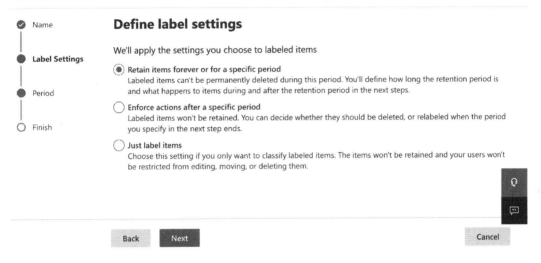

Figure 13.13: Defining your retention label settings

5. Now define the retention period. You can choose to retain items for 5, 7, or 10 years, or forever. Alternatively, you may choose to enter a custom value. Here, you also need to choose whether to start the retention period based on the following parameters:

   - **When items were created**

   - **When items were last modified**

   - **When items were labeled**

   - An event type (created by you), such as an employee leaving the organization

   For this example, select a custom value of three years and choose to start retention based on **When items were created**:

Create retention label

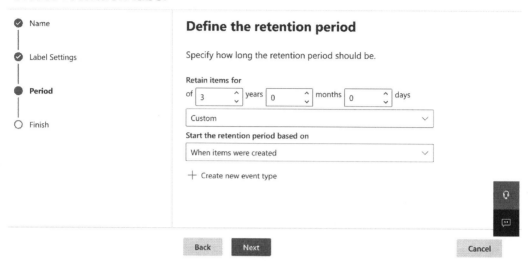

Figure 13.14: Defining the retention period

6.   Next, decide what happens after the retention period. The available options are as follows:

- **Delete items automatically**

- **Upgrade to trigger a disposition review** (if you have Microsoft 365 E5 this will simply read **Trigger a disposition review**)

- **Change the label**

- **Run a Power Automate flow**

- **Deactivate retention settings**

For this example, select **Delete items automatically** and click **Next**:

These settings determine what happens to items when the retention period ends.

Choose what happens after the retention period

◉ **Delete items automatically**
   We'll permanently remove labeled items from wherever they're stored.

○ **Upgrade to trigger a disposition review**
Assign disposition reviewers to check whether items can be safely deleted. Learn more about disposition reviews or try Microsoft 365 E5 for free to activate the feature.
 Learn more about disposition reviews
 and
upgrading to E5

○ **Change the label**
   You can extend the period by choosing an existing label to replace this one with. Learn more about relabeling items

○ **Run a Power Automate flow**
   Customize what happens to labeled items with a Power Automate flow. You can run a flow to meet a specific business need, such as moving labeled items to a certain location or sending email notifications. Learn more about running a Power Automate flow

○ **Deactivate retention settings**
   Labeled items won't be retained or deleted when their retention settings are deactivated. You'll have to manually remove any items that you want deleted.

[Back] [Next]   [Cancel]

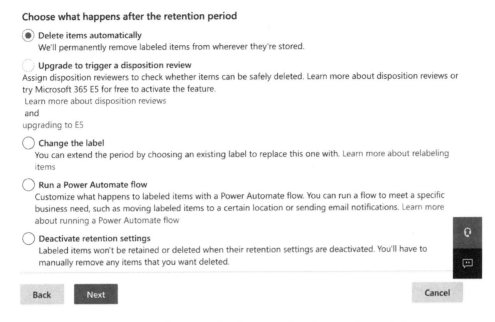

Figure 13.15: Choosing what happens after the retention period

7. Review the selections you have made and make any final changes. When you are ready, click **Create label**:

Create retention label

Review and finish

✓ Name

✓ Label Settings

✓ Period

● **Finish**

Name

Name
Name
Personal Financial PII
Edit

Description for users
Personally identifiable information (PII) that, when used alone or with other relevant data, can identify an individual
Edit

Description for admins
Personally identifiable information (PII) that, when used alone or with other relevant data, can identify an individual
Edit

Retention settings

[Back] [Create label]   [Cancel]

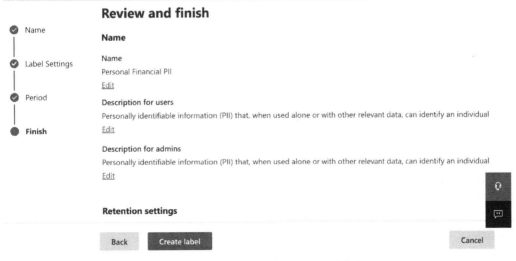

Figure 13.16: Creating the retention label

Your retention label will now be created, and you will have the following three options:

- **Publish this label to Microsoft 365 locations**: This option will take you into the label policy wizard to make the label available for users to manually apply it to content or set it as a default label for SharePoint document libraries or email folders.

- **Upgrade to automatically apply labels to specific content** (If you have Microsoft 365 E5, this option will read **Auto-apply this label to a specific type of content**): This option allows you to create a policy that will label content matching certain conditions, such as content containing an SIT.

- **Do Nothing**.

For this example, select **Do Nothing** and then click **Done**:

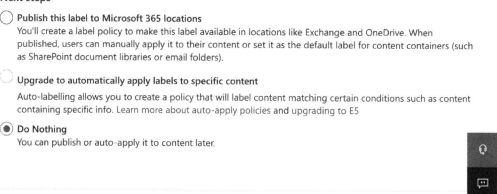

Figure 13.17: Completing the creation of the retention label

Your retention label is now created. In order for the label to be made available to users, you must create a retention label policy. This process is covered in the next section.

Creating a retention label policy

A **retention label policy** is created to assign retention labels to Microsoft 365 locations so your users can manually apply them to content. Complete the following steps to create a retention label policy using the retention label created in the previous section:

1. From **Data lifecycle management** within **Microsoft Purview**, choose the **Label policies** tab. You will see the following two options:

    - **Publish labels**: This option allows you to create a policy to publish selected retention labels to users and groups, allowing them to manually apply the labels.

    - **Auto-apply a label**: This option allows you to create a policy in which content is automatically labeled based on matching conditions, such as an SIT, a word or phrase, a trainable classifier, or cloud attachments shared in Exchange or Teams.

    For this example, choose the first option, **Publish labels**:

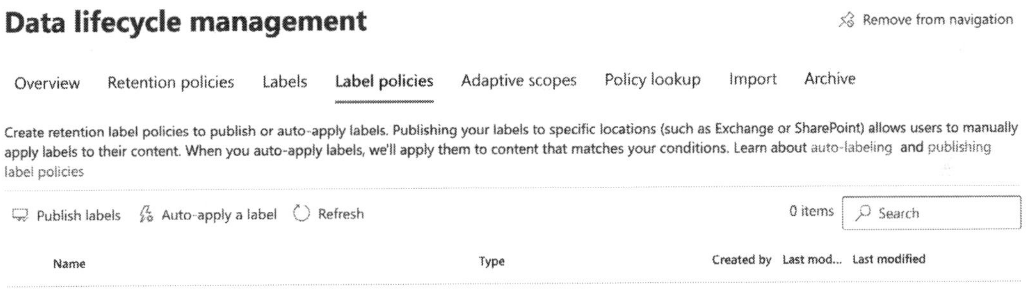

Data lifecycle management

⤬ Remove from navigation

| Overview | Retention policies | Labels | **Label policies** | Adaptive scopes | Policy lookup | Import | Archive |

Create retention label policies to publish or auto-apply labels. Publishing your labels to specific locations (such as Exchange or SharePoint) allows users to manually apply labels to their content. When you auto-apply labels, we'll apply them to content that matches your conditions. Learn about auto-labeling and publishing label policies

🖵 Publish labels   ⅍ Auto-apply a label   ◯ Refresh   0 items   🔍 Search

| Name | | Type | | Created by | Last mod... | Last modified |

Figure 13.18: Creating a retention label policy

2. The **Publish labels** wizard starts. Click on **Choose labels to publish** and select the label(s) you wish to include in your policy:

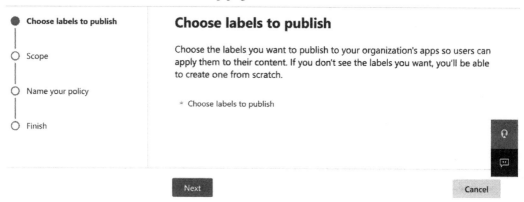

Figure 13.19: Choosing labels to publish

In this example, the `Retain for 7 years` and `Personal Financial PII` labels were already chosen for the policy.

3. Once you have chosen your labels, they will be shown as per the following screenshot. Click **Next**:

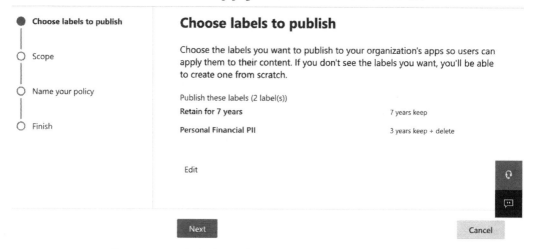

Figure 13.20: Labels chosen for inclusion in retention label policy

4. Now, choose the scope type for your policy. The choices are **Adaptive** or **Static**. Choose **Static** and click **Next**:

Publish labels so users can apply them to their content.

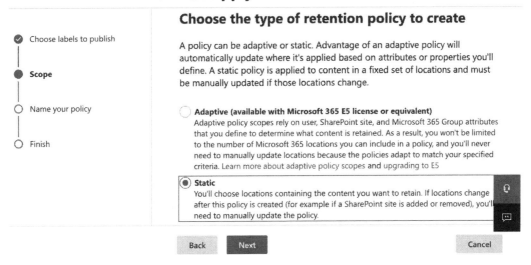

Figure 13.21: Setting the scope for your retention label policy

Adaptive scopes are covered later in this chapter in the *Planning and implementing adaptive scopes* section.

5. Next, you must choose the locations to publish your policy. The **Let me choose specific locations** option allows you to filter your choices. For this example, choose **All locations. Includes content in Exchange email, Office 365 groups, OneDrive and SharePoint documents**. Click **Next**:

Publish labels so users can apply them to their content.

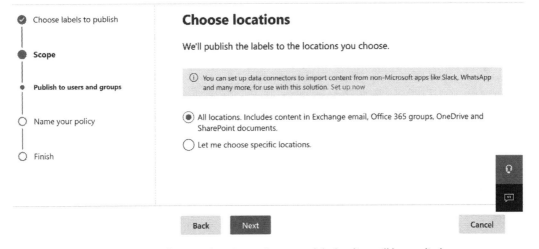

Figure 13.22: Choosing locations where your label policy will be applied

6.   Enter a name and description for your policy. Click **Next**:

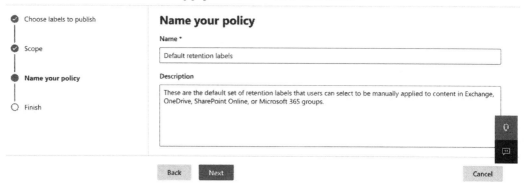

Figure 13.23: Setting a name and description for your retention label policy

7.   Review your choices and, when you're satisfied, click **Submit**:

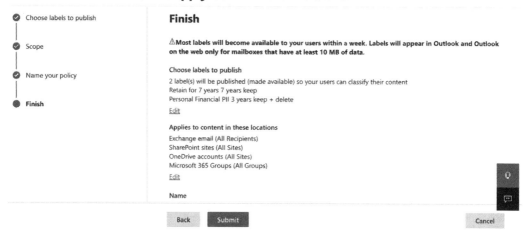

Figure 13.24: Submitting the retention label policy

8.   Finally, you are shown some related tasks you can perform, such as **Publish another retention label**, **Upgrade to automatically apply labels to specific content**, and **Create a retention label**. It is not mandatory to select these options, so for this example, click **Done** to complete the publish labels wizard:

Publish labels so users can apply them to their content.

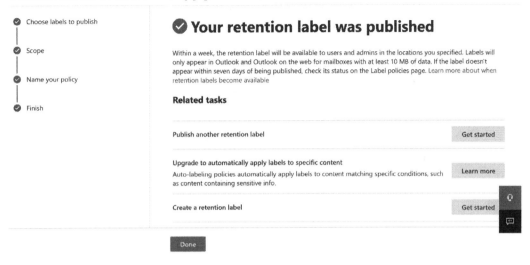

Figure 13.25: Viewing related tasks

9.   Your label policy is now created and can be found in the **Label policies** tab within **Data lifecycle management** in Microsoft Purview:

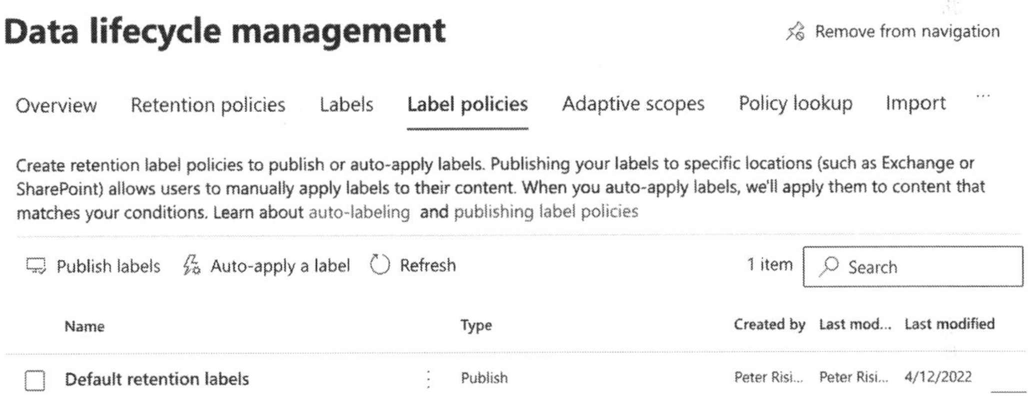

Data lifecycle management

✄ Remove from navigation

Overview   Retention policies   Labels   **Label policies**   Adaptive scopes   Policy lookup   Import   ...

Create retention label policies to publish or auto-apply labels. Publishing your labels to specific locations (such as Exchange or SharePoint) allows users to manually apply labels to their content. When you auto-apply labels, we'll apply them to content that matches your conditions. Learn about auto-labeling and publishing label policies

🖵 Publish labels   ⚡ Auto-apply a label   ◯ Refresh   1 item   🔍 Search

Name	Type	Created by	Last mod...	Last modified
☐ Default retention labels	⋮ Publish	Peter Risi...	Peter Risi...	4/12/2022

Figure 13.26: Retention label policy shown in Microsoft Purview

---

Note

When retention labels are published to SharePoint Online or OneDrive, they usually appear for users within one day. However, you should allow up to seven days, especially when publishing retention labels to Exchange Online, which can take longer.

Now let's look at how users can apply the retention labels you have made available to content in Microsoft 365.

Applying retention labels

Within SharePoint or OneDrive libraries, users can manually choose and apply retention labels by highlighting a document, clicking the three dots, and choosing the **Details** option from the menu:

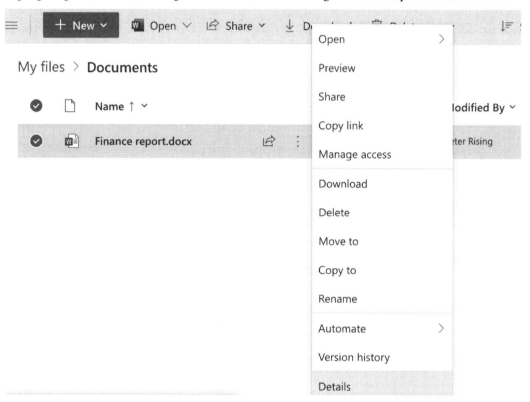

Figure 13.27: User experience choosing a retention label in SharePoint or OneDrive

On the right side of the screen, a side menu appears from which the user can choose the **Apply label** option:

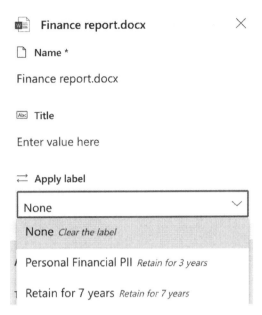

Figure 13.28: Retention labels available to users

Hovering over the label will show the user the description that you entered when you created the label:

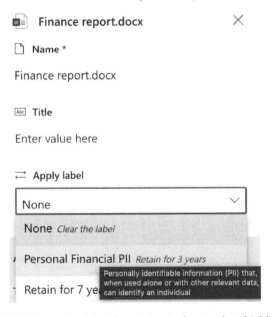

Figure 13.29: Retention label description is shown when highlighted

Next, we will look at retention policies and how to apply them.

Creating a retention policy

As stated earlier in the chapter, **retention policies** are used to retain content at the service or container level. This means that retention is applied broadly and, as already demonstrated, you can make any exceptions using retention labels. Also note that users never have the option to apply retention policies themselves. It is something that happens automatically without any user involvement. Administrators must create retention policies based on organizational policies or regulatory obligations.

To create retention policies within Microsoft Purview, complete the following steps:

1. Log in to the Microsoft Purview compliance portal at `https://compliance.microsoft.com`, then navigate to **Data lifecycle management** | **Microsoft 365** and click on the **Retention policies** tab. You will then see the list of policies, as shown in the following screenshot:

Data lifecycle management

⚴ Remove from navigation

Overview   **Retention policies**   Labels   Label policies   Adaptive scopes   Policy lookup   Import   Archive

Your users create a lot of content every day, from emails to Teams and Yammer conversations. Use retention policies to keep the content you want and get rid of what you don't need. Learn about creating retention policies

＋ New retention policy   ↓ Export   ✉ Inactive mailbox   ⟳ Refresh   2 items   🔍 Search

Name		Created by	Last modified
☐ **Teams Retention Policy**	⋮	Peter Rising	7 Apr 2020 18:19
☐ **Test Policy**	⋮	Peter Rising	3 Aug 2017 10:01

Figure 13.30: Retention policies tab in the Microsoft Purview Data lifecycle management section

2. Click on **New retention policy**. Give your policy a descriptive name and description. Click **Next**:

Figure 13.31: Creating a new retention policy

3. Similar to the retention label options, you can choose between an **Adaptive** or **Static** scope type. Select **Static** and click **Next**:

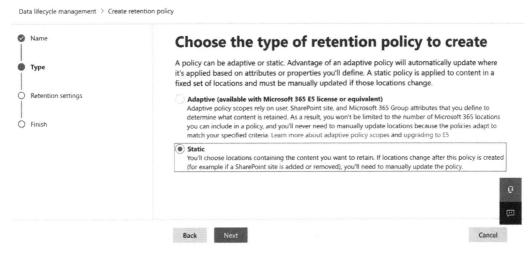

Figure 13.32: Choosing the retention policy type

4. Choose which Microsoft 365 locations you can apply the policy to. These include **Exchange email**, **SharePoint sites**, **OneDrive accounts**, and **Microsoft 365 Groups**. Slide the locations on or off and filter the location selections to include or exclude recipients, accounts, or sites as required:

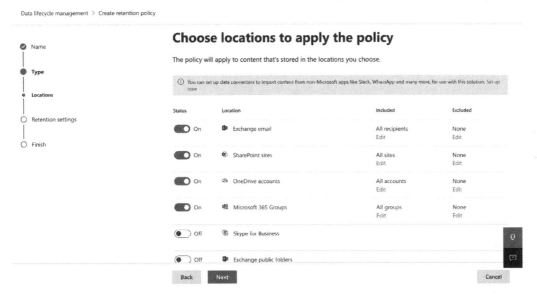

Figure 13.33: Choose the location to apply the policy to

5. Scroll down the list to see the complete set of locations you can choose from. They include **Skype for Business, Exchange public folders, Teams channel messages, Teams chats, Teams private channel messages, Yammer community messages,** and **Yammer user messages.** Choose your location selections and click **Next**:

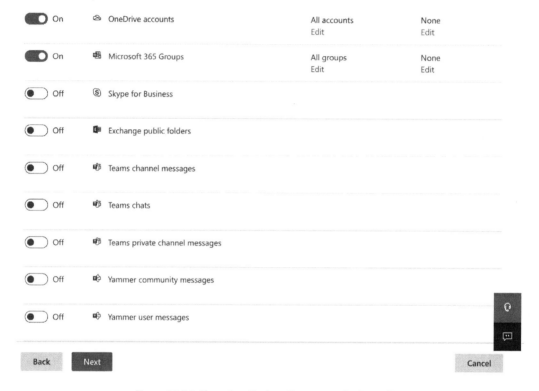

Figure 13.34: Choosing the locations to apply the policy

> **Note**
> A separate retention policy must be created for Teams channel messages and Teams chats. If you select either or both of these, all the sliders for the other locations will automatically move to **Off**. Similarly, Teams private channel messages can only be included in a policy that has no other locations selected.

6. Choose the retention settings you wish to apply. These are similar to the settings when creating a retention label. For this example, select the following options:

    - **Retain items for a specific period | 7 years**

    - **Start the retention period based on | When items were created**

    - **Delete items automatically**

When you have configured these settings, click **Next**:

Data lifecycle management > Create retention policy
Name
Type
Retention settings
Finish
Decide if you want to retain content, delete it, or both
Retain items for a specific period
Items will be retained for the period you choose.
Retain items for a specific period
7 years
Start the retention period based on
When items were created
At the end of the retention period
Delete items automatically
Do nothing
Retain items forever
Items will be retained forever, even if users delete them.
Only delete items when they reach a certain age
Items won't be retained, but when they reach the age you choose, we'll delete them from where they're stored.
Back
Next
Cancel

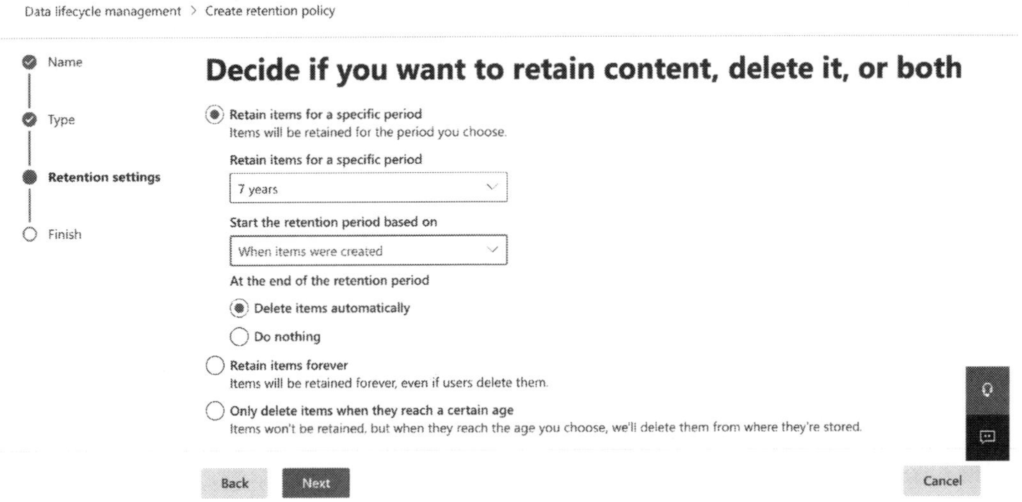

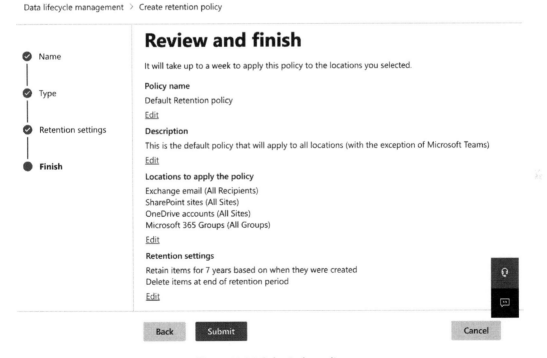

Figure 13.35: Choosing the retention settings

7. Review the choices you have made for your retention policy and click **Submit**:

Data lifecycle management > Create retention policy
Name
Type
Retention settings
Finish
Review and finish
It will take up to a week to apply this policy to the locations you selected.
Policy name
Default Retention policy
Edit
Description
This is the default policy that will apply to all locations (with the exception of Microsoft Teams)
Edit
Locations to apply the policy
Exchange email (All Recipients)
SharePoint sites (All Sites)
OneDrive accounts (All Sites)
Microsoft 365 Groups (All Groups)
Edit
Retention settings
Retain items for 7 years based on when they were created
Delete items at end of retention period
Edit
Back
Submit
Cancel

Figure 13.36: Submit the policy

8.   The retention policy is successfully created. Click **Done**:

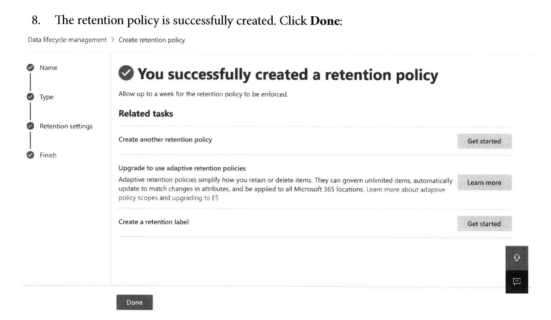

Figure 13.37: The retention policy successfully created

9.   You will see your new retention policy in the list of policies within **Data lifecycle management**:

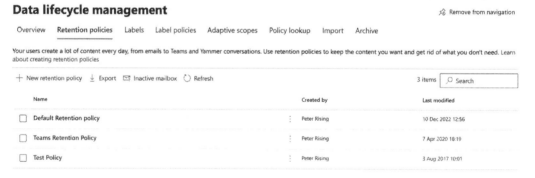

Figure 13.38: New retention policy shown in Microsoft Purview Data lifecycle management

In this section, we learned how retention policies can be used to retain (or retain then delete) content across our Microsoft 365 locations based on the criteria set in our policies. Next, we will explore the planning and implementation of adaptive scopes.

Planning and implementing adaptive scopes

As you have already seen in this chapter, when you create a retention policy or retention label policy, you are required to choose between adaptive and static scope types to define the scope of the policy. In previous examples, you have used **static scopes** wherein the administrator chooses the locations and the criteria for retention. Static scopes have more limited configuration options, such as including or excluding locations and instances within those locations.

With **adaptive scopes**, you can specify queries that enable the dynamic inclusion of users who should be targeted by the scope. Adaptive scopes run daily to pick up any changes that may apply, such as a new user account being added to Microsoft 365 that has a department field selection or a job title selection that matches an adaptive scope query. It is possible to use multiple adaptive scopes within a single policy.

Some advantages of using adaptive scopes include the following:

- There are no limitations on the number of items per policy. This increases flexibility and means you can potentially configure fewer policies.

- You can assign different retention settings to users based on their geographical location. This is facilitated by Azure **Active Directory** (**AD**) attributes.

- You can use query-based membership to provide resilience against organizational changes that might not be accurately reflected in static group memberships.

- A single retention policy can include locations for both Microsoft Teams and Yammer. Static scopes do not support this.

- Specific retention settings can be applied to only inactive mailboxes. This is not possible with static scopes that do not support the specific inclusion of recipients with inactive mailboxes.

To configure an adaptive scope, first plan the type of scope you need to create and the attributes and values you will need to use. For example, it may be necessary for you to work collaboratively with a SharePoint Administrator if you need to reference custom site properties within your scope.

Adaptive scopes may be created in the Microsoft Purview compliance portal at `https://compliance.microsoft.com`, either from the **Records management** or **Data lifecycle management** sections. In this example, you will use the **Data lifecycle management** section by completing the following steps:

1. From **Data lifecycle management | Microsoft 365**, navigate to **Adaptive scopes** and select **Create scope**:

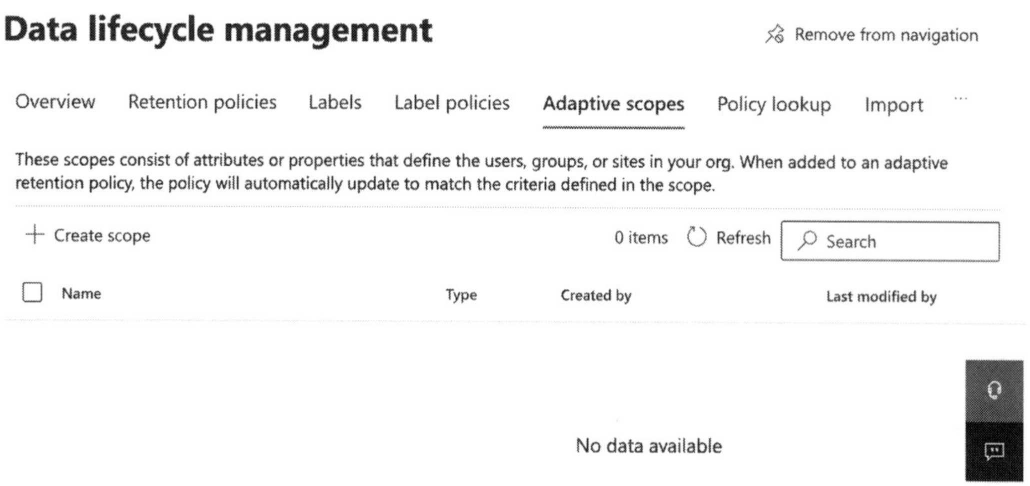

Data lifecycle management
Remove from navigation
Overview
Retention policies
Labels
Label policies
Adaptive scopes
Policy lookup
Import
These scopes consist of attributes or properties that define the users, groups, or sites in your org. When added to an adaptive retention policy, the policy will automatically update to match the criteria defined in the scope.
Create scope
0 items
Refresh
Search
Name
Type
Created by
Last modified by
No data available

Figure 13.39: Adaptive scopes in Microsoft Purview Data lifecycle management

> **Note**
>
> You will only see the **Create scope** option here if you have the appropriate licensing to support adaptive scopes. This is a Microsoft 365 E5 requirement.

2. For this example, create a simple adaptive policy scope targeted to an organization's Marketing department. Enter a name and description that reflect your policy scope and click **Next**:

Data lifecycle management > Create adaptive scope
Name
Scope type
Finish
Name your adaptive policy scope
Name *
Marketing department
Description
This scope will be used in retention label policies and retention policies targeted to the marketing department
Next
Cancel

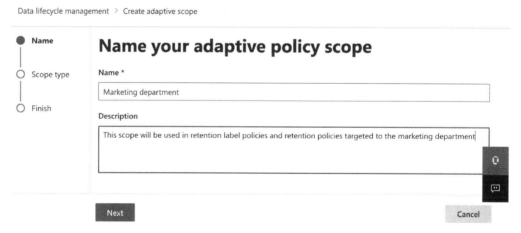

Figure 13.40: Naming your adaptive scope

3. Now choose the type of scope you want to create. The choices are **Users**, **SharePoint sites**, and **Microsoft 365 Groups**. Users and groups use Azure AD attributes, while SharePoint sites use SharePoint properties. For this example, select **Users**. Click **Next**:

Data lifecycle management > Create adaptive scope

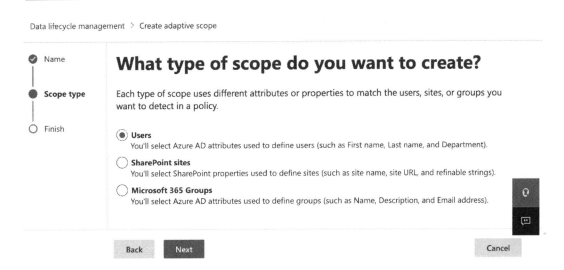

Figure 13.41: Selecting the scope type

4. Enter the user attributes you wish to use. For this example, add **Department is equal to Marketing**. You can add further and/or attributes if required, but this example has been kept simple. Click **Next**:

Data lifecycle management > Create adaptive scope

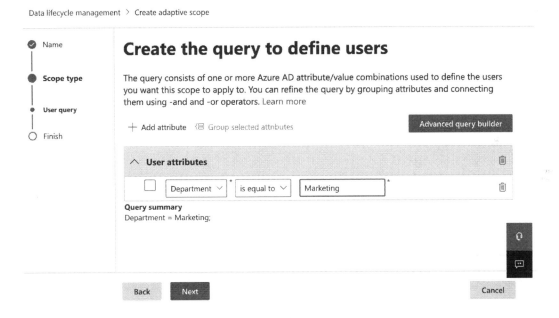

Figure 13.42: Defining the scope query attributes

5.   Review your settings and, when satisfied, click **Submit**:

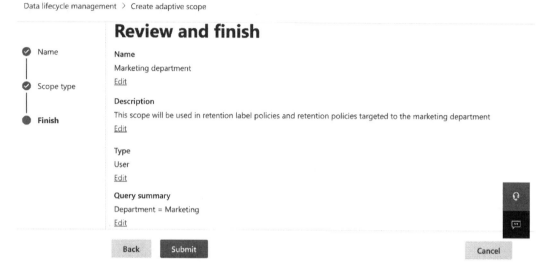

Figure 13.43: Submitting the adaptive scope

6.   Your scope is now created. Click **Finish**:

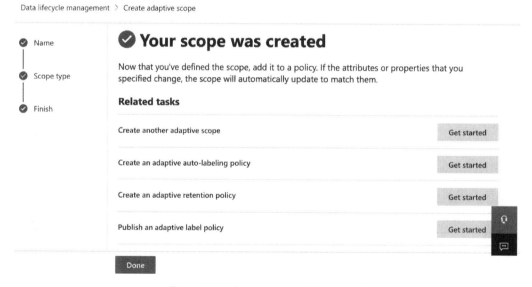

Figure 13.44: Scope successfully created

7. You will now see your new adaptive scope within **Data lifecycle management**:

Data lifecycle management

⤨ Remove from navigation

Overview   Retention policies   Labels   Label policies   **Adaptive scopes**   Policy lookup   Import   Archive

These scopes consist of attributes or properties that define the users, groups, or sites in your org. When added to an adaptive retention policy, the policy will automatically update to match the criteria defined in the scope.

+ Create scope   1 item ○ Refresh   🔎 Search

Name	Type	Created by	Last modified by	Last modified
☐ Marketing department	User	Peter Rising	Peter Rising	10 Dec 2022 14:25

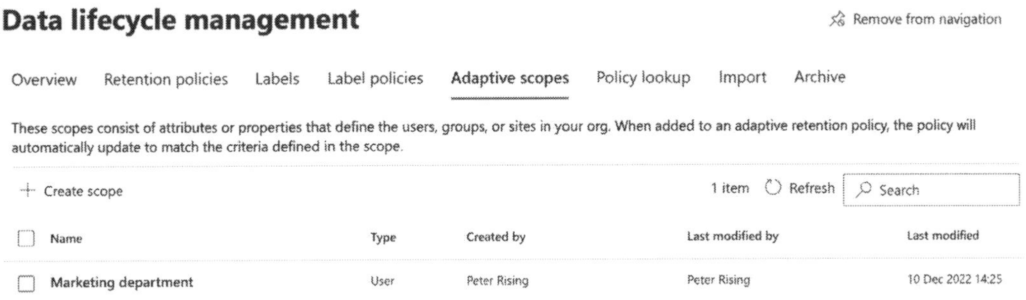

Figure 13.45: New adaptive scope shown in Microsoft Purview Data lifecycle management

8. *Figure 13.42* also shows the option to choose **Advanced query builder**. Selecting this option allows you to specify your own queries. For **User** and **Microsoft 365 Group** scopes, use the **OPATH filtering syntax**. For **SharePoint sites** scopes, use **Keyword Query Language** (**KQL**).

   For example, to create a user scope that defines its membership by department and country, you would enter a value such as (Department -eq "Marketing") -and (CountryOrRegion -eq "United Kingdom"):

Create the query to define users

The query consists of one or more Azure AD attribute/value combinations used to define the users you want this scope to apply to. You can refine the query by grouping attributes and connecting them using -and and -or operators. Learn more

Simple query builder

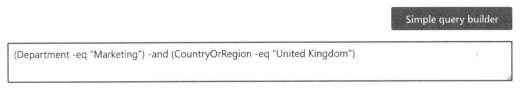

(Department -eq "Marketing") -and (CountryOrRegion -eq "United Kingdom")

Figure 13.46: Using advanced query builder

9. Once your adaptive scopes are created and available, you can set up retention policies and retention label policies using the **Choose adaptive policy scopes and locations** option. Click on **Add scopes**:

Publish labels so users can apply them to their content.

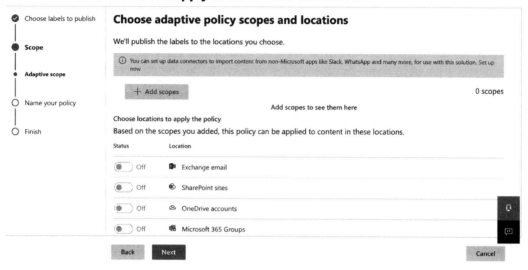

Figure 13.47: Choosing adaptive policy scopes and locations

10. Select the scope you created earlier—as per this example, **Marketing department**. Click **Add**:

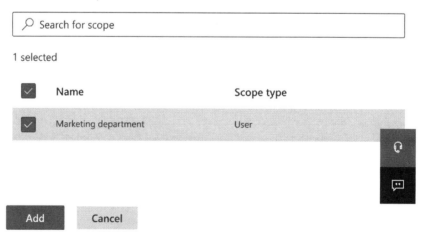

Figure 13.48: Choosing the adaptive scope

You will see that the locations that will apply to the policy will be automatically set based on the selection you made in your adaptive scope:

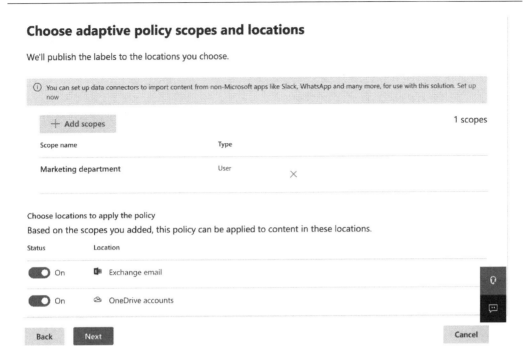

Figure 13.49: Adaptive scope applied to policy

11. You can then follow the policy wizard through to the end in the same way as previously demonstrated for static scopes.

In the final section of this chapter, we will look at finding and recovering deleted Microsoft 365 data.

Finding and recovering deleted Microsoft 365 data

In addition to retention, it is important to have an understanding of what happens when content is deleted from locations in Microsoft 365 and what steps you can take to recover that content. First, let's take a look at how this applies to user mailboxes.

User mailboxes

There are two types of deleted Exchange Online user mailboxes. These are **hard-deleted mailboxes** and **soft-deleted mailboxes**:

- A hard-deleted mailbox is a mailbox that has been soft-deleted for more than 30 days, and the associated Azure AD user has been hard-deleted. There are various scenarios that can apply to hard-deleted mailboxes. Refer to the *Further reading* section for links to more information about this. Hard-deleted mailboxes cannot be recovered.

- A soft-deleted mailbox is one that has been deleted either via the Microsoft 365 admin center or using the `Remove-Mailbox` PowerShell cmdlet, after which it has remained in the Azure AD recycle bin for a period shorter than 30 days. Soft-deleted user mailboxes can be defined as mailboxes that have been deleted under the following circumstances:

  - The Azure AD user account associated with the user mailbox is soft-deleted.

  - The Azure AD user account associated with the user mailbox is hard-deleted. However, a Litigation Hold or an eDiscovery-based hold was applied to the Exchange Online mailbox prior to deletion.

  - The Azure AD user account associated with the user mailbox has been completely purged during the last 30 days. Exchange Online preserves the mailbox as soft-deleted prior to it being permanently purged. The mailbox cannot be recovered at this point.

As specified earlier in this section, soft-deleted mailboxes can be recovered. To recover a soft-deleted mailbox, complete the following steps:

1. Log on to the Microsoft 365 admin center at `https://admin.microsoft.com` and navigate to **Users** | **Deleted users**. You will see any users who have been deleted within the last 30 days:

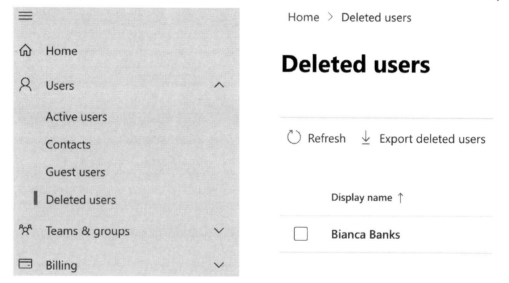

Figure 13.50: Viewing deleted users in Microsoft 365 admin center

2. To restore the user, select their name and click **Restore user**, then click **Restore**:

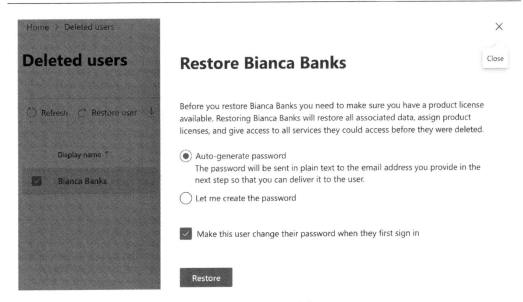

Figure 13.51: Restoring a deleted user

3.   Alternatively, use Exchange Online PowerShell to restore the user by running the following cmdlet:

```
Undo-SoftDeletedMailbox username@domain.com -WindowsLiveID
username@domain.com -Password (ConvertTo-SecureString -String
'Pa$$word1' -AsPlainText -Force)
```

Now that you understand the principles of deleting and recovering mailboxes, we will learn about the same principles as they relate to OneDrive.

OneDrive

Similar to mailboxes, when you delete a user in the Microsoft 365 admin center, the user's OneDrive will be retained for the default setting of 30 days unless you have specifically changed this. Within the 30-day period, the content within OneDrive remains accessible to users who are granted access at the point of deletion. Once that 30-day period has passed, the OneDrive content will be in a deleted state for 93 days and can only be restored by a Global Administrator or a SharePoint Administrator. If any of the deleted content was subject to retention label policies or retention policies, however, the content is preserved and can be searched for with tools such as eDiscovery (which will be covered in *Chapter 15, Planning For, Conducting, and Managing eDiscovery Cases*).

If the user was deleted within a period of 30 days, the account can be restored along with all their data from the Microsoft 365 admin center in the same way as shown earlier for user mailboxes.

If the 30-day period has elapsed, PowerShell must be used to recover the content within the stated 93-day period. Detailed information can be found on this within the *Further reading* section at the end of this chapter.

Summary

In this chapter, we were introduced to the principles of data lifecycle management and retention within Microsoft 365. We learned how to use Microsoft Purview dashboards for data classification, view **Content explorer** to see where sensitive info is detected in Microsoft 365 locations, and utilize **Activity explorer** to view user activity such as applying a label. We also learned how retention policies in Microsoft Purview are used to retain content at the container level to comply with organizational policies and regulatory requirements, and how retention labels can be used as exceptions to those policies when item-level content such as individual documents need different retention settings from those more broadly applied by retention policies. Finally, we learned how content can be recovered if deleted from Microsoft 365, such as mailboxes and OneDrive.

In the next chapter, we will learn about managing and analyzing audit logs in Microsoft Purview. We will examine the concepts of reporting and how to plan our auditing and reporting strategy, as well as using audit logs to investigate compliance activities, creating and using alert policies to trigger alerts against specific activities, and configuring auditing retention policies.

Questions

1. When a user object is soft-deleted from Microsoft 365, how many days do you have to recover the user mailbox before it is permanently deleted?

    A. 60 days

    B. 30 days

    C. 120 days

    D. 90 days

2. True or false? Retention labels can be used as exceptions to your retention policies.

    A. True

    B. False

3. Which of the following locations cannot be present in a retention policy designed to cover all Microsoft 365 locations? (Choose all that apply)

    A. Exchange email

    B. Teams chat

    C. SharePoint sites

    D. Teams channel messages

    E. OneDrive

    F. Teams private channel messages

4. Which feature in Microsoft Purview would you use to identify Microsoft 365 data containing sensitive info?

    A. Activity explorer

    B. Content explorer

    C. Alert policies

    D. Assessments

5. True or false? Adaptive scopes require an M365 E5 license.

    A. True

    B. False

6. Which two sections in Microsoft Purview can be used to configure retention labels?

    A. **Data classification**

    B. **Data lifecycle management**

    C. **Records management**

    D. **Compliance manager**

7. What will happen if you try to include Teams channel messages and Teams chats in the same retention policy as other services, such as Exchange Online, SharePoint Online, and OneDrive?

    A. You will receive a warning that you should create separate retention policies but you will be allowed to proceed

    B. The retention policy will successfully be applied to all selected services

    C. The other services will be automatically de-selected from the policy

    D. The Teams selections will automatically be de-selected from the policy

8. True or false? When creating a retention policy, you can both delete and retain content based on the settings you configure.

    A. True

    B. False

9. Which of the following is not one of the available options for defining retention label settings?

    A. Enforce actions after a specific period

    B. Retain items forever or for a specific period

    C. Just label items

    D. Do nothing

10. True or false? You can use data lifecycle management retention labels to mark items as regulatory records.

    A. True

    B. False

Further reading

Please refer to the following links for more information:

- *How to use the Microsoft data classification dashboard*: https://learn.microsoft.com/en-us/microsoft-365/compliance/data-classification-overview?WT.mc_id=M365-MVP-4039827&view=o365-worldwide

- *Get started with activity explorer*: https://learn.microsoft.com/en-us/microsoft-365/compliance/data-classification-activity-explorer?view=o365-worldwide

- *Learn about retention policies and retention labels*: https://learn.microsoft.com/en-us/microsoft-365/compliance/retention?WT.mc_id=M365-MVP-4039827&view=o365-worldwide

- *Common settings for retention policies and retention label policies*: https://learn.microsoft.com/en-us/microsoft-365/compliance/retention-settings?WT.mc_id=M365-MVP-4039827&view=o365-worldwide

- *Create and configure retention policies*: https://learn.microsoft.com/en-us/microsoft-365/compliance/create-retention-policies?WT.mc_id=M365-MVP-4039827&view=o365-worldwide

- *Create retention labels for exceptions to your retention policies*: https://learn.microsoft.com/en-us/microsoft-365/compliance/create-retention-labels-data-lifecycle-management?view=o365-worldwide

- *Publish retention labels and apply them in apps*: https://learn.microsoft.com/en-us/microsoft-365/compliance/create-apply-retention-labels?view=o365-worldwide#manually-apply-retention-labels

- *Get started with data lifecycle management*: https://learn.microsoft.com/en-us/microsoft-365/compliance/get-started-with-data-lifecycle-management?view=o365-worldwide

- *Use file plan to create and manage retention labels*: https://learn.microsoft.com/en-us/microsoft-365/compliance/file-plan-manager?view=o365-worldwide

- *Learn about records management*: https://learn.microsoft.com/en-us/microsoft-365/compliance/records-management?WT.mc_id=M365-MVP-4039827&view=o365-worldwide

- *Learn about auto-expanding archiving*: https://learn.microsoft.com/en-us/microsoft-365/compliance/autoexpanding-archiving?WT.mc_id=M365-MVP-4039827&view=o365-worldwide

- *Learn about connectors for third-party data*: https://learn.microsoft.com/en-us/microsoft-365/compliance/archiving-third-party-data?WT.mc_id=M365-MVP-4039827&view=o365-worldwide

- *Restore a deleted OneDrive*: https://learn.microsoft.com/en-us/sharepoint/restore-deleted-onedrive?WT.mc_id=M365-MVP-4039827

- *Restore a deleted Microsoft 365 group*: https://learn.microsoft.com/en-us/microsoft-365/admin/create-groups/restore-deleted-group?WT.mc_id=M365-MVP-4039827&view=o365-worldwide&tabs=outlook

- *Delete or restore user mailboxes in Exchange Online*: https://learn.microsoft.com/en-us/exchange/recipients-in-exchange-online/delete-or-restore-mailboxes?WT.mc_id=M365-MVP-4039827

Part 4:
Managing Compliance Features in Microsoft 365

In this part, you will learn how to configure and manage Microsoft 365 governance and compliance features. On completion, you will be able to configure and analyze security reporting, respond to compliance queries, and manage regulatory compliance and insider risk solutions.

This part has the following chapters:

- *Chapter 14, Managing and Analyzing Audit Logs and Reports in Microsoft Purview*
- *Chapter 15, Planning For, Conducting, and Managing eDiscovery Cases*
- *Chapter 16, Managing Regulatory and Privacy Requirements*
- *Chapter 17, Managing Insider Risk Solutions in Microsoft 365*

14

Monitoring and Analyzing Audit Logs and Reports in Microsoft Purview

When you consider the importance of security, compliance, and best practice configuration in your Microsoft 365 environment, the configuration of your Microsoft 365 services is only as effective as the analytical, auditing, and reporting capabilities that are available to (and diligently used by) Microsoft 365 administrators. When you configure, review, and take any required actions by using these capabilities, you can gain vital intelligence on the activities within your environment.

In this chapter, we will be introduced to the principles and capabilities of **analysis and reporting** within Microsoft Purview. We will learn how to plan our auditing and reporting strategy as well as how to use **audit logs** to carry out investigations into compliance-related activities. We will also review the available **compliance reports** and **dashboards** and consider how we might configure **alert policies** and **auditing retention policies**. This chapter will provide you with the information you need to effectively monitor and analyze audit logs and reports in Microsoft Purview.

These topics will be covered in the following order:

- Planning for auditing and reporting
- Investigating compliance activities by using audit logs
- Reviewing and interpreting compliance reports and dashboards
- Configuring alert policies
- Configuring audit retention policies

Planning for auditing and reporting

Tracking user and administrator activities is a crucial capability for any organization using Microsoft 365, and there are several auditing and reporting capabilities available that you will need to be aware of. But what sort of things do you need to consider? What activities should you be tracking and have visibility of? Examples may include the following:

- Documents changed by users
- Tenant configuration altered by admins

You can monitor such activities from the various Microsoft 365 admin portals to ensure that you have a robust strategy in place to mitigate any risks and ensure that your organization is fulfilling any regulatory compliance obligations.

Using tools such as the Microsoft Purview compliance portal and the Microsoft 365 Defender portal, you can access the appropriate navigation panes for features, which include the following:

- Alerts
- Permissions
- Data Lifecycle Management
- Threat management
- Mail flow
- Data privacy
- Search and investigation
- Reports
- Service assurance

It is important to understand these features and how they can affect your compliance posture. In the following sections of this chapter, we will learn how to leverage and respond to the information available to us through these features.

First, we will take a look at using audit logs to investigate compliance activities.

Investigating compliance activities by using audit logs

The Microsoft Purview compliance portal grants administrators the ability to search the **unified audit log** to view user and administrator activity in your organization. This is a Purview feature that provides further and deeper insight into Microsoft 365 activities. So, as an example, if you need to find out whether a user deleted an email or accessed a specific document, the unified audit log should be your first port of call.

It is often asked why this is known as the unified audit log. This is simply due to the fact that you can use it to search for activities across different Microsoft 365 services and features. A few examples of these features include the following:

- Azure Active Directory
- **Data Loss Prevention (DLP)**
- eDiscovery
- Exchange Online
- Microsoft 365 Defender
- Microsoft Teams
- Sensitivity labels
- Threat Intelligence
- Yammer

> **Note**
>
> These are only a few of the locations available to the unified audit log. Links to the full list can be found in the *Further reading* section at the end of this chapter.

Before you search the audit log, you should be aware that the audit log is turned on by default for all Microsoft 365 tenants. There was a time when this was not the case, and therefore, if your tenant has been in use for several years, you may need to explicitly enable the audit log. To check whether the audit log search capability is turned on, run the following command in Exchange Online PowerShell:

```
Get-AdminAuditLogConfig | FL UnifiedAuditLogIngestionEnabled
```

A value of `True` indicates that auditing is enabled, while `False` indicates it is not enabled. To enable auditing, enter the following cmdlet:

```
Set-AdminAuditLogConfig -UnifiedAuditLogIngestionEnabled $true
```

With auditing enabled, you will be able to search for user and administrator activities within your tenant for a period of up to 90 days.

To do so, you must be a member of the **Compliance Management** or **Organization Management** role groups within Microsoft 365. **Global Administrators** are automatically added as members of the **Organization Management** role group.

Now that you have checked that auditing is enabled, you have access to perform an audit log search.

Performing an audit log search

To run an **audit log search**, complete the following steps:

1. Log in to the Microsoft Purview compliance portal at `https://compliance.microsoft.com` and navigate to **Solutions | Audit**:

Figure 14.1: Audit within Microsoft Purview

2. The **Audit** page is now displayed. The page has three tabs. These are **New Search**, **Classic Search**, and **Audit retention policies**:

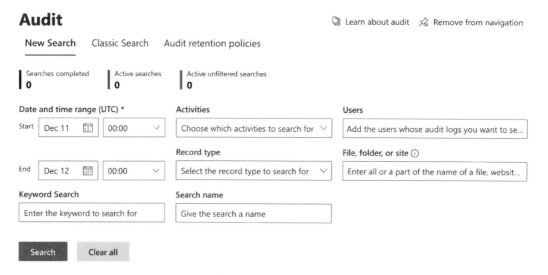

Figure 14.2: The Audit page in Microsoft Purview

3. In this example, you will configure a search from the **New Search** tab. The **Classic Search** experience remains available for now but has less functionality. We will look at **Audit retention policies** later in the chapter in the *Configuring audit log retention policies* section. For reference, the **Classic Search** experience is shown in the following screenshot, and includes the ability to search **Date and time range**, **Activities**, **Users**, and **File, folder, or site**:

New Search   **Classic Search**   Audit retention policies

Date and time range (UTC) *   **Activities**   **File, folder, or site** ⓘ

Start | Sat Dec 10 📅 | 00:00 ∨ | | Choose which activities to search for ∨ | | Enter all or a part of the name of a file, we... |

Users

End | Sat Dec 17 📅 | 00:00 ∨ | | Add the users whose audit logs you want t... |

| Search | | Clear all |

Figure 14.3: The Classic audit search experience

4. The **New Search** experience, as used in this example, provides all the same search capabilities as the Classic experience, but additionally includes **Keyword Search**, **Record type**, and **Search name**.

5. Complete a simple audit search by setting a date and time range and choosing some activities relating to retention labels and policies. Set **Date and time range** to between November 1st and December 17th.

6. Under **Activities**, enter the search keyword retention and select **Changed retention label for a file**, **Created retention label**, **Created retention policy**, and **Configured settings for a retention policy**:

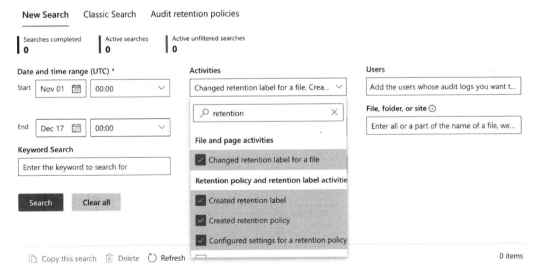

Figure 14.4: Configuring settings for a new search

7. With your selections completed, the **New Search** pane appears, as shown in the following screenshot. You can optionally add a keyword search, record type, user(s), file, folder, or site to filter your results. You may also add a search name. For this example, however, keep this search simple and click **Search**:

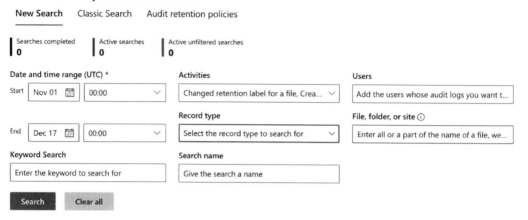

Figure 14.5: Search selections ready to be submitted

8. At the bottom of the **Audit search** page, you will see a list of any current or previous search jobs and their status and progress. Initially, **Job status** will show as **Queued**:

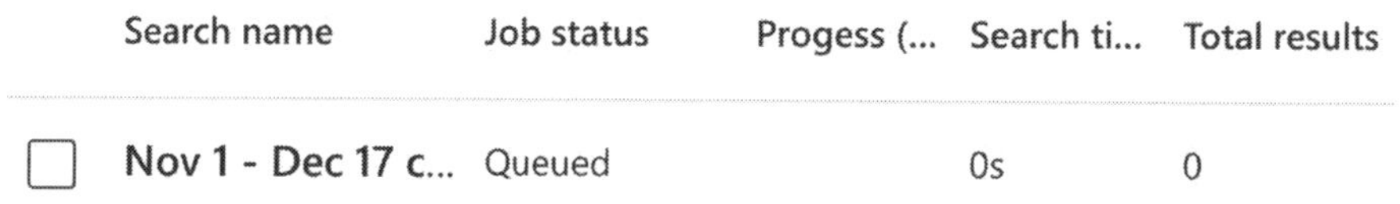

Search name	Job status	Progess (...	Search ti...	Total results
Nov 1 - Dec 17 c...	Queued		0s	0

Figure 14.6: The audit search queued

Depending on the complexity of your search and the number of matching results, the search times will vary, but when completed, **Job status** will show as **Completed**.

9. Click on the search to see the results:

Search name	Job status	Progess (...	Search ti...	Total results
Nov 1 - Dec 12 ...	Completed	100%	7m, 47s	0
Oct 12 - Dec 12 ...	Completed	100%	10m, 2s	1

Figure 14.7: The audit search completed

10. The details of the search query are shown at the top of the results. Scroll down and click **Export**. Once complete, you will get a message that your search results are ready to download, as shown in the following screenshot. You can download them as a .csv file. In this example, you can see there is one match referring to the creation of a retention label:

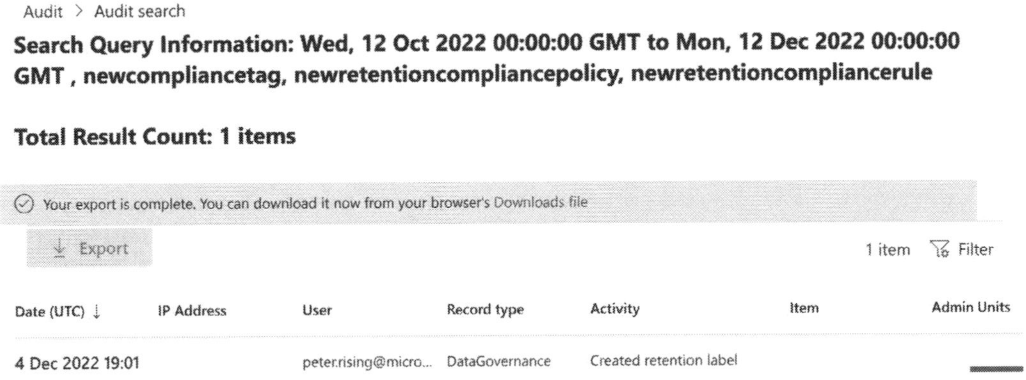

Audit > Audit search

Search Query Information: Wed, 12 Oct 2022 00:00:00 GMT to Mon, 12 Dec 2022 00:00:00 GMT , newcompliancetag, newretentioncompliancepolicy, newretentioncompliancerule

Total Result Count: 1 items

⊘ Your export is complete. You can download it now from your browser's Downloads file

⬇ Export   1 item   ⅛ Filter

Date (UTC) ↓	IP Address	User	Record type	Activity	Item	Admin Units
4 Dec 2022 19:01		peter.rising@micro...	DataGovernance	Created retention label		▬

Figure 14.8: The completed audit search results

11. Click on each search item result to see more details in a flyout panel. You can scroll through to get further information on the search match item, such as **Date**, **IP Address**, **Users**, **Activity**, **Item**, **Detail**, **CreationTime**, and **Id**:

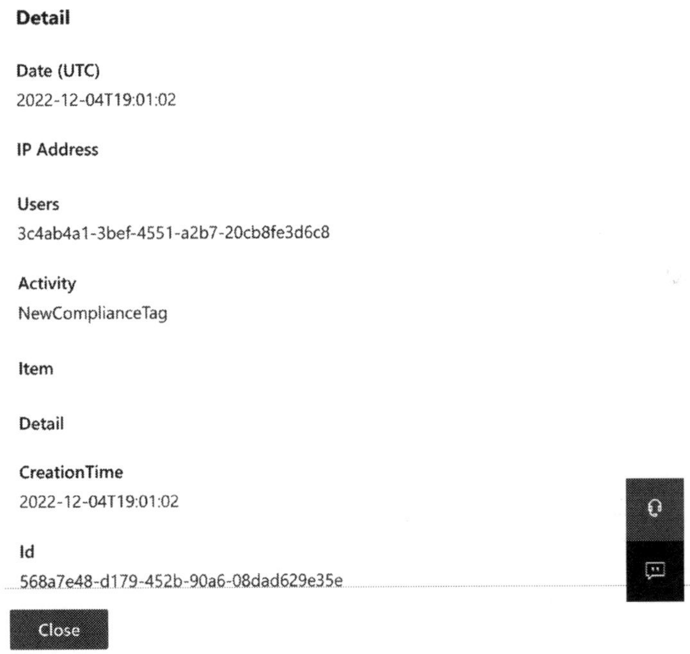

Detail

Date (UTC)
2022-12-04T19:01:02

IP Address

Users
3c4ab4a1-3bef-4551-a2b7-20cb8fe3d6c8

Activity
NewComplianceTag

Item

Detail

CreationTime
2022-12-04T19:01:02

Id
568a7e48-d179-452b-90a6-08dad629e35e

Close

Figure 14.9: Search item detail

12. Scroll down further to see more details, such as **Operation**, **OrganizationID**, **RecordType**, **UserKey**, **UserType**, **Version**, **Workload**, **UserID**, **ExtendedProperties**, **ObjectType**, and **Parameters**.

> **Note**
>
> You can download a maximum of 50,000 entries from a single audit log search to a `.csv` file. Should your export have 50,000 entries, you can presume that your search results are, in fact, in excess of 50,000. Use filtering options within your search to reduce the number of search results.

In this section, we examined only a basic example from a comprehensive list of possible activities that can be inspected using the audit log. Next, we will look at how to review and understand compliance reports and dashboards.

Reviewing and interpreting compliance reports and dashboards

As an administrator with responsibility for Microsoft Purview settings, policies, and activities, it is important for you to be aware of the **compliance reports** that are available. Reports can be accessed from within the Microsoft Purview compliance portal by navigating to **Reports**:

Figure 14.10: Reports section within Microsoft Purview

The **Reports** section is shown in the following screenshot:

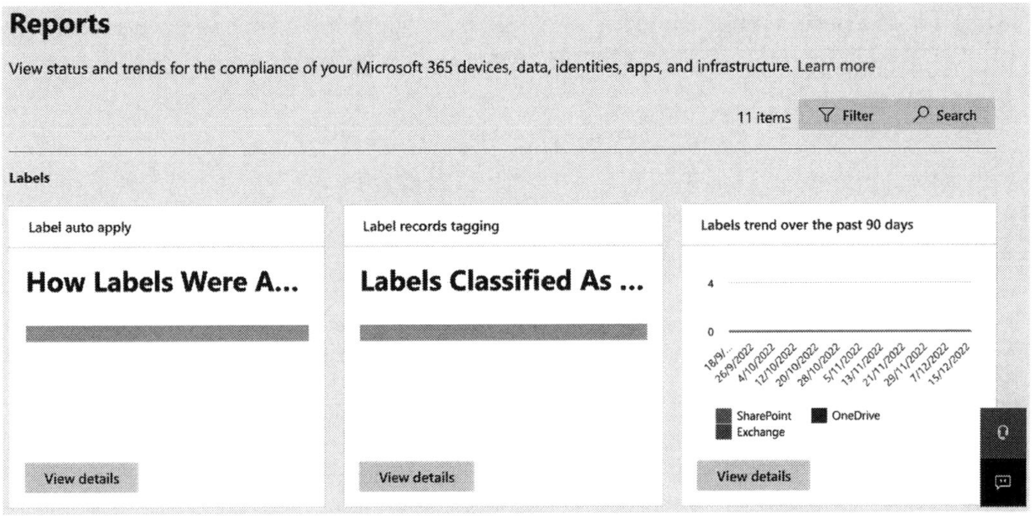

Figure 14.11: Microsoft Purview Reports

The reports are divided into two distinct categories: **Labels** and **Organizational Data**.

> **Note**
> The options that you see in the **Reports** section will depend on the level of licensing within your Microsoft 365 tenant. In this example, the tenant used has Microsoft 365 E5 licensing.

With Microsoft 365 E5, under the **Labels** section, you can see the following report tiles:

- **Label auto apply**
- **Label records tagging**
- **Labels trend over the past 90 days**
- **Label usage over the past 90 days**
- **Retention label usage**
- **Sensitivity label usage**
- **Retention label changes**

Again, with Microsoft 365 E5, under the **Organizational Data** section, the following report tiles are accessible:

- **DLP policy matches**
- **DLP incidents**

- **DLP false positives and overrides**

- **Encryption report**

Click on **View details** on any of the tiles to expand the report details.

In the following example, you can see the **DLP Policy Matches** tile opened and any matching entries for when a DLP policy has been triggered. Here, you can see that a user attempted to send credit card details via Exchange email:

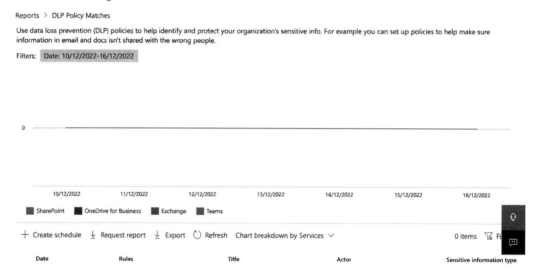

Figure 14.12: DLP Policy Matches

You can also request or download a report from here.

So, now you understand how you can view the available reports, we can look toward the configuration of policies to alert us when certain incidents or activities take place. This is covered in the following section.

Configuring alert policies

Microsoft Purview **alert policies** are used to generate and categorize alerts when users perform activities matching the alert policies you configure. Alert policies can be created by users with the **Manage Alerts** role or the **Organization Configuration** role. It can take up to 24 hours after you create an alert policy for alerts to start triggering from the policy.

Note

The more advanced features available with alert policies will require an E5 subscription, an E1 / E3 subscription with E5 compliance, or the E5 eDiscovery add-on. More information can be found in the links included at the end of the chapter.

Alert policies are made up of rules and conditions comprising the activity that will generate the alert.

To create an alert policy, complete the following steps:

1. Log in to the Microsoft Purview compliance portal at `https://compliance.microsoft.com` and navigate to **Policies** | **Alert policies**:

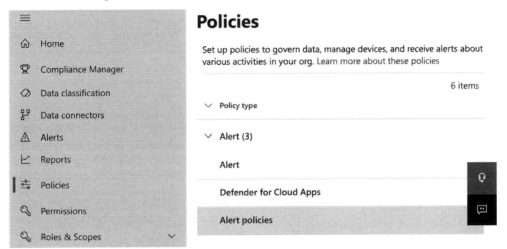

Figure 14.13: Alert policies in Microsoft Purview

You will see a list of existing and/or default policies. Default policies will have some editing restrictions:

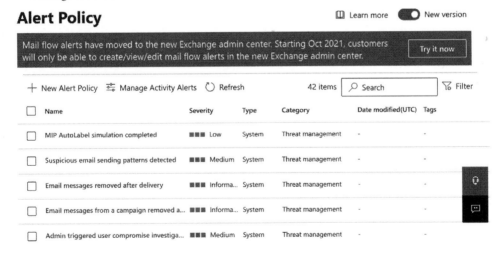

Figure 14.14: List of alert policies in Microsoft Purview

To understand alert policies most effectively, you will need to create a new one.

2. Click **New Alert Policy**. For this example, you will set up a policy to trigger an alert when a user shares a file from SharePoint.

3. In the **Name** field, enter User shares a file. Under **Description**, enter User shares a file from SharePoint. Choose the **Severity** level for this alert. The options are **Low**, **Medium**, and **High**. Choose **Medium**. For **Category**, choose **Information governance**. Click **Next**:

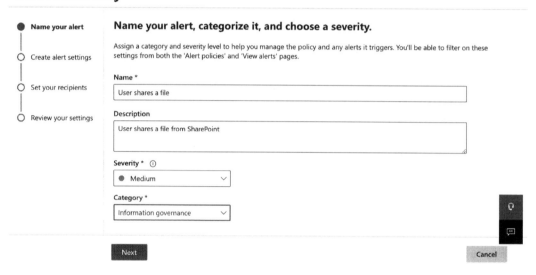

Figure 14.15: Setting up a new alert policy

4. Now, you need to choose the activity to match with the alert policy. In the **Activity is** search, enter the word share. You will see relevant options that you can add related to sharing file or folder content:

New Alert Policy

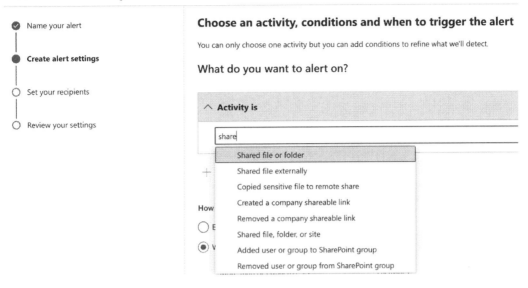

Figure 14.16: Setting an activity to trigger the alert policy

5. Next, you can optionally add further conditions to tailor the trigger conditions for the alert policy. These include **General: IP address is**, **User: User is**, **User: User tags are**, **File: File name is**, **File: Site collection URL is**, and **File: File extension is** (for details about these conditions, refer to the *Further reading* section):

$+$ Add condition $\vee$

General: IP address is

User: User is

User: User tags are

File: File name is

File: Site collection URL is

File: File extension is

Figure 14.17: Adding conditions to the activity set in the policy

6. Choose how you want the alert to be triggered. You can choose from the following options: **Every time an activity matches the rule**, **When the volume of matched activities reaches a threshold**, or **When the volume of matched activities becomes unusual**. For this example, select the option to trigger when activities reach a threshold based on **More than or equal to 15 activities**, **During the last 60 minutes**, and set it to **On** for **All users**. Click **Next**:

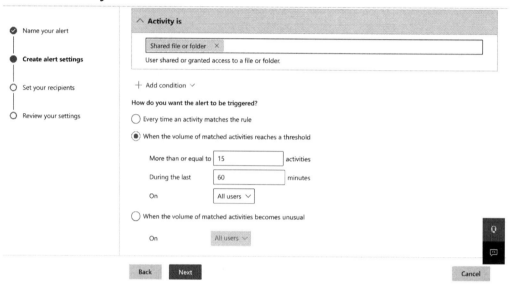

Figure 14.18: Choosing how the alert policy is triggered

7. Choose whether you want to allow others to be able to opt-in for email notifications. Set the email recipients who will receive the alerts and the daily notification limit. Click **Next**:

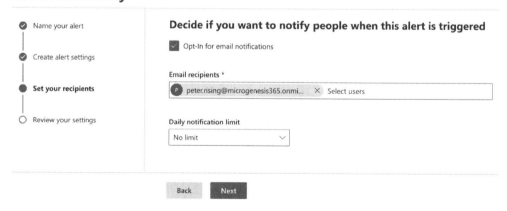

Figure 14.19: Adding recipient options for the policy

8. Finally, review the settings you have chosen for your alert policy, and click **Submit** to create the policy:

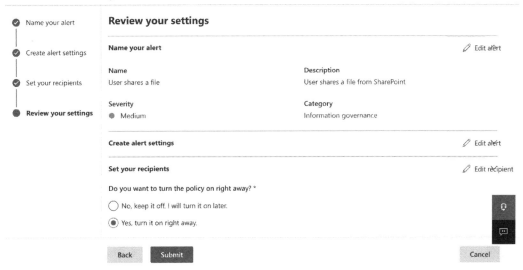

Figure 14.20: Submitting the alert policy for creation

The new policy is now shown in the list of alert policies. You will see the policy name, the severity level, the policy type, the policy category, the date modified, tags, status, and the actions (three vertical dots, which, when selected, allow you to edit or delete the policy):

Figure 14.21: New alert policy shown in Microsoft Purview

Any alerts generated by the alert policy will appear in the **Alerts** section of the Microsoft Purview compliance portal. They will also be emailed to the recipients you selected when configuring your alert policy:

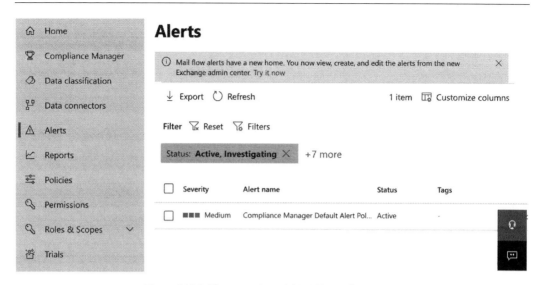

Figure 14.22: Alerts section within Microsoft Purview

Alert policies are an effective way to generate specific alerts that you are interested in and ensure that the correct individuals in your organization are notified if there is a policy match.

> **Note**
>
> Consider your policy severity levels when setting up alert policies. Set a higher severity for activities that could result in data loss such as the viewing of sensitive or classified data.

In this section, we learned about Microsoft Purview alert policies and how to create them. The final section of this chapter will focus on the configuration of audit log retention policies.

Configuring audit log retention policies

With audit retention policies in Microsoft Purview, you can specify how long to retain your audit logs within your organization. This is a Premium feature and requires the E5 license. If your organization does not have access to a Premium subscription, then audit logs will be retained for 90 days. With the advanced features of audit log retention policies, however, you can retain your audit logs for a period of up to 10 years. You can audit log policies based on the following:

- All activities within Microsoft 365 services

- Specified activities within Microsoft 365 services

- A priority level that specifies the policy that takes precedence; this is applicable only if you have multiple policies in your organization

To create an audit log retention policy, you need the **Organization Configuration** role in the Microsoft Purview compliance portal. You can create up to 50 such policies in your organization.

To create an audit log retention policy, complete the following steps:

1. Log in to the Microsoft Purview compliance portal at `https://compliance.microsoft.com`. From the left pane, select **Audit** and click on the **Audit retention policies** tab. Now, click on **Create audit retention policy**:

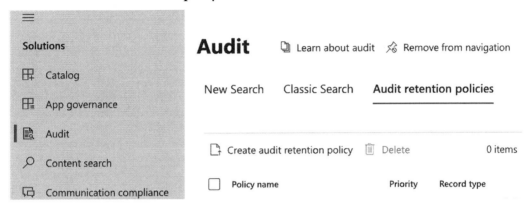

Figure 14.23: Audit retention policies in Microsoft Purview

2. Complete the fields on the flyout page, which include the following:

   - **Policy name**
   - **Description**
   - **Users** (must be selected if **Record type** is not selected)
   - **Record type** (must be selected if **Users** is not selected)
   - **Duration**
   - **Priority**

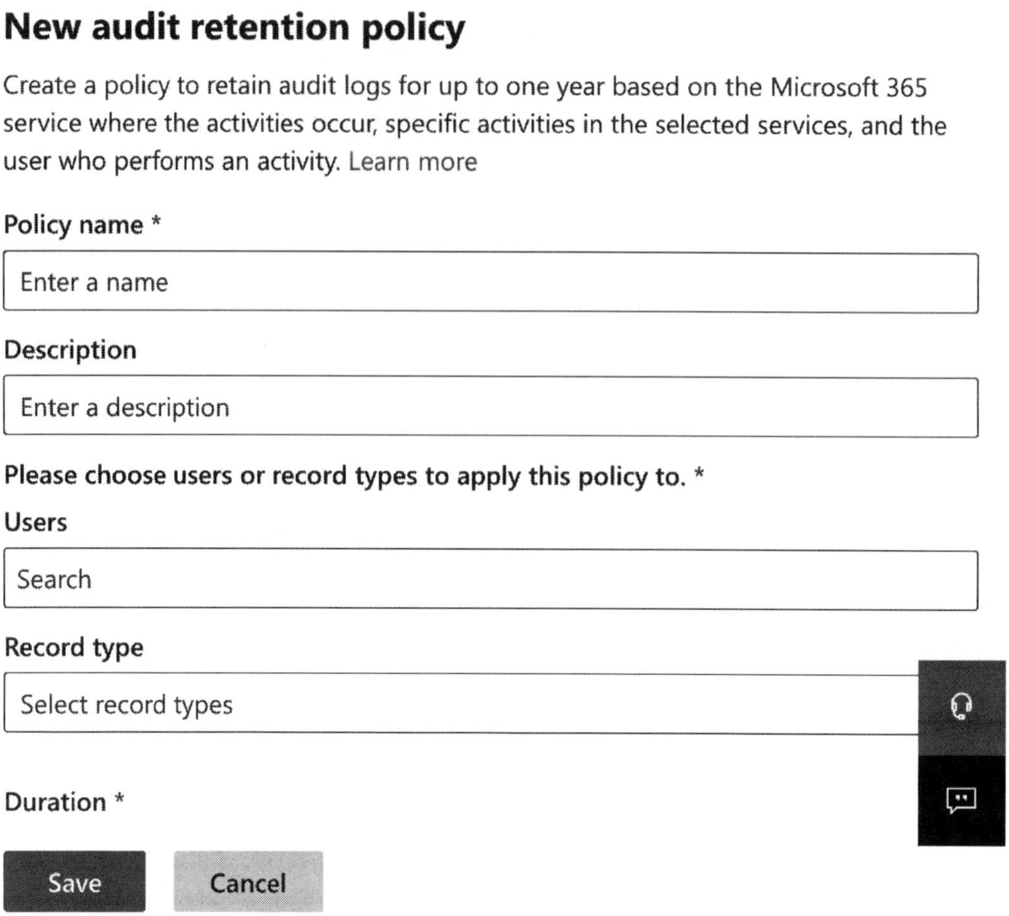

New audit retention policy

Create a policy to retain audit logs for up to one year based on the Microsoft 365 service where the activities occur, specific activities in the selected services, and the user who performs an activity. Learn more

Policy name *

> Enter a name

Description

> Enter a description

Please choose users or record types to apply this policy to. *

Users

> Search

Record type

> Select record types

Duration *

[Save]   [Cancel]

Figure 14.24: Fields within the new audit log retention policy

3. Enter a policy name and a description. You must also select values for either **Users** or **Record type** or a combination of both. For this example, set the policy to retain audit entries related to sensitivity labeling. The duration is set to **10 Years**, and the priority is set to 1. This means that audit log entries relating to sensitivity label activities for Peter Rising will be retained for a duration of 10 years. The priority of this policy means it will be processed before any other audit log retention policies. Click **Save** to create the policy:

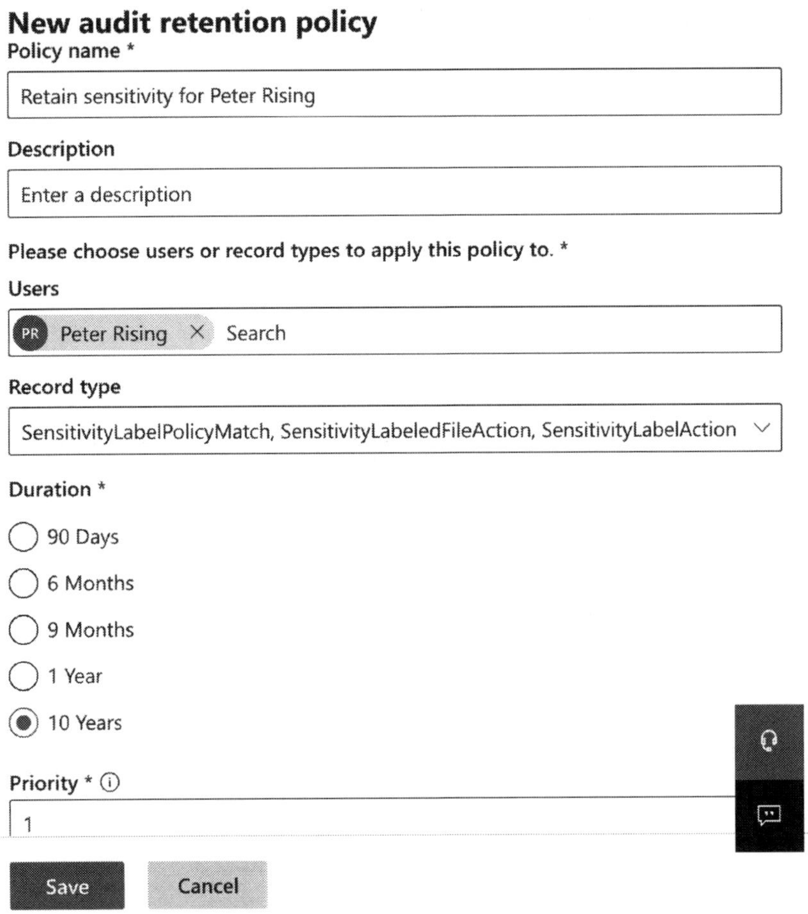

New audit retention policy
Policy name *

> Retain sensitivity for Peter Rising

Description

> Enter a description

Please choose users or record types to apply this policy to. *

Users

> PR Peter Rising ✕ Search

Record type

> SensitivityLabelPolicyMatch, SensitivityLabeledFileAction, SensitivityLabelAction ⌄

Duration *

○ 90 Days

○ 6 Months

○ 9 Months

○ 1 Year

◉ 10 Years

Priority * ⓘ

> 1

[Save] [Cancel]

Figure 14.25: Completed fields within the new audit log retention policy

The policy is now visible in the list of audit log retention policies:

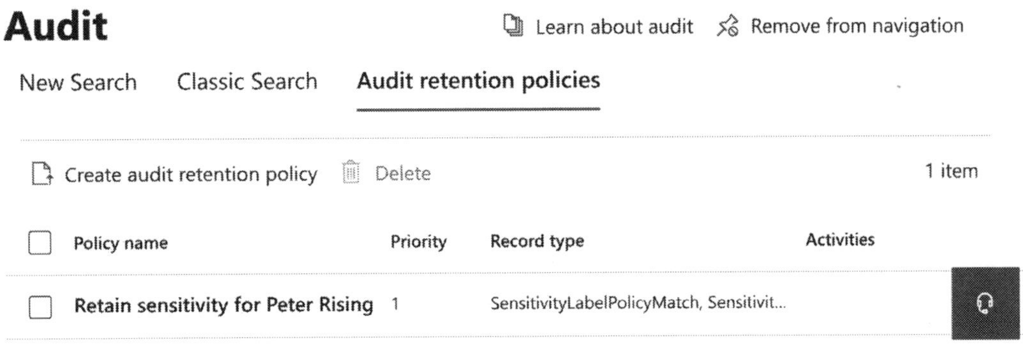

Audit
📋 Learn about audit   ⚂ Remove from navigation

New Search   Classic Search   **Audit retention policies**

🗋 Create audit retention policy   🗑 Delete   1 item

	Policy name	Priority	Record type	Activities
☐	**Retain sensitivity for Peter Rising**	1	SensitivityLabelPolicyMatch, Sensitivit...	

Figure 14.26: New audit log retention policy successfully created

Thus, audit log retention policies can be extremely useful for applying different retention periods against users and/or record types in Microsoft 365. This more granular approach is far more flexible than the standard 90-day retention for all audit log activity.

Summary

This chapter covered the principles of planning for auditing and reporting in Microsoft 365 using the Microsoft Purview compliance portal. We learned about the available reports, tools, and dashboards, as well as how to investigate compliance activities by running audit log searches. We also learned how to configure alert policies that can be set up to email chosen users when an activity matching the policy is triggered, and how audit retention policies enable you to retain audit log activity based on users and/or specified record types within Microsoft Purview.

The next chapter will introduce content search and eDiscovery in Microsoft Purview.

Questions

1. Which of the following is NOT one of the available reports in Microsoft Purview?

    A. Label auto apply

    B. Retention label changes

    C. SharePoint files

    D. DLP policy matches

2. True or false? In an audit log search, the keyword search field is mandatory:

    A. True

    B. False

3. Which of the following URLs grants you access to the audit log?

    A. `https://admin.microsoft.com`

    B. `https://compliance.microsoft.com`

    C. `https://portal.office365.com`

    D. `https://portal.azure.com`

4. Which of the following PowerShell commands is used to enable audit logging in your tenant?

    A. `Set-AdminAuditLogConfig -UnifiedAuditLogIngestionEnabled $yes`

B. `Set-AdminAuditLogConfig -UnifiedAuditLogIngestion`

   `$enabled`

C. `Set-AdminAuditLog -UnifiedAuditLogIngestionEnabled`

   `$true`

D. `Set-AdminAuditLogConfig -UnifiedAuditLogIngestionEnabled`

   `$true`

5. True or false? It can take up to 24 hours after you create an alert policy for alerts to start triggering from the policy:

   A. True

   B. False

6. Where in the Microsoft Purview compliance portal would you set up an alert policy?

   A. **Policies | Alert Policies**

   B. **Policies | Alert**

   C. **Policies | Defender for Cloud Apps**

7. Which of the following is not one of the available category types when creating a new alert policy?

   A. Threat Management

   B. Permissions

   C. Information Protection

   D. Information Governance

8. True or false? You can configure an alert policy based on when the volume of matched activities meets a particular threshold:

   A. True

   B. False

9. What is the maximum amount of entries from an audit log search that you can download from a `.csv` file?

   A. 20,000

   B. 70,000

   C. 30,000

   D. 50,000

10. True or false? Advanced audit log capabilities allow organizations to retain audit logs for up to 10 years:

A. True

B. False

Further reading

Please refer to the following links for more information:

- Auditing and reporting in Microsoft cloud services: `https://learn.microsoft.com/en-us/compliance/assurance/assurance-auditing-and-reporting-overview?WT.mc_id=M365-MVP-4039827&view=o365-worldwide`

- Search the audit log in the compliance portal: `https://learn.microsoft.com/en-us/microsoft-365/compliance/audit-log-search?WT.mc_id=M365-MVP-4039827&view=o365-worldwide`

- Microsoft 365 reports in the admin center: `https://learn.microsoft.com/en-us/microsoft-365/admin/activity-reports/activity-reports?WT.mc_id=M365-MVP-4039827&view=o365-worldwide`

- Alert policies in Microsoft 365: `https://learn.microsoft.com/en-us/microsoft-365/compliance/alert-policies?WT.mc_id=EM-MVP-4039827&view=o365-worldwide`

- Manage audit log retention policies: `https://learn.microsoft.com/en-us/microsoft-365/compliance/audit-log-retention-policies?WT.mc_id=ES-MVP-4039827&view=o365-worldwide`

- Turn auditing on or off: `https://learn.microsoft.com/en-us/microsoft-365/compliance/audit-log-enable-disable?view=o365-worldwide`

15

Planning For, Conducting, and Managing eDiscovery Cases

Organizations may often be required to respond to legal investigations to locate and export data contained in their Microsoft 365 environment. The **eDiscovery** and **Content search** tools provide you with these capabilities. This chapter will explain the principles of Content search and eDiscovery in Microsoft Purview. We will learn the differences between **eDiscovery (Standard)** and **eDiscovery (Premium)** and when to use them. We will also examine how to plan for content searches and eDiscovery cases and how to delegate permissions to use search and discovery tools. Additionally, we will learn how to use these tools to discover data and respond to investigations and how to manage your eDiscovery cases.

After reading this chapter, you will know about the tools available to you in Microsoft 365 for search and discovery and the scenarios in which you need to use them.

These topics will be covered in the following order:

- Recommending eDiscovery (Standard) or eDiscovery (Premium)
- Planning for content searches and eDiscovery
- Delegating the required permissions to use search and discovery tools
- Creating eDiscovery cases
- Managing eDiscovery cases

Recommending eDiscovery (Standard) or eDiscovery (Premium)

eDiscovery is a feature within Microsoft Purview that allows you to identify and provide information pertaining to any legal cases or internal investigations that may be in progress within your organization. Compliance administrators can set controls for who can create and manage eDiscovery cases in your environment to search for content within the following Microsoft 365 locations:

- Exchange Online

- OneDrive for Business

- SharePoint Online

- Microsoft Teams

- Microsoft 365 Groups

- Yammer

If your organization is just beginning its journey into using search and discovery tools, it is important to know about the ones that are available and which of those are suitable for your needs.

Within Microsoft Purview, the following three solutions fall under the category of eDiscovery: **Content search**, **eDiscovery (Standard)**, and **eDiscovery (Premium)**. Which of these solutions you will use will be based on your organization's requirements and obligations. If your organization is heavily regulated and/or is likely to be required to respond to regular and potentially complex internal or legal investigations, then at the very least, you will likely need to implement eDiscovery (Standard). However, an increasing number of organizations are finding that eDiscovery (Premium) provides the level of functionality required to respond to such investigations in a timely, detailed, and accurate manner.

There is no correct or incorrect solution, but each organization will need to understand its requirements and obligations and then leverage the eDiscovery solution that best suits its needs. Content search and eDiscovery (Standard) will fulfill some requirements, whereas eDiscovery (Premium) will fulfill most, if not all, of them.

Now that you know the available eDiscovery solutions and how they are licensed, we will examine how to plan for our content searches and eDiscovery cases.

Planning for content searches and eDiscovery

The first step is to consider the reasons that your organization needs to respond to a legal case and who is involved. Examples of those who may need to be involved in a case include (but are not limited to) the following:

- Executives
- Employees
- Legal teams
- Compliance managers
- Data protection officers
- IT teams

Note that the preceding examples would by no means have the same roles within the case. Executives and employees, for instance, will more likely be the subject of the case, while the other examples may be part of the teams responsible for conducting the investigation. This does *not* mean that this is a clandestine process. In most cases, the subjects of investigations will be notified that their email, documents, and collaboration activity are subject to being placed on hold, meaning that their content must be retained for the duration of the investigation. An example of such a notification is the communication process that is included within eDiscovery (Premium).

The most important consideration, however, is to establish *who* in your organization will be charged with carrying out these investigations. Large and heavily regulated organizations will inevitably have more structure relating to legal and compliance matters and will likely have dedicated departments responsible for these functions.

In smaller organizations, the IT teams will often be charged with this responsibility. IT teams invariably will not have the appetite or the understanding of this process beyond assigning the appropriate role group access to enable the searches to be completed. However, they may reluctantly find themselves running the cases from start to conclusion simply because there is no other function to do so.

Regardless of any of the aforementioned scenarios, the key to successfully planning for and executing an end-to-end investigation—using tools such as Content search and eDiscovery—will rely on the following:

- Setting roles and responsibilities
- Working as a team
- Knowing your organization's data
- Protecting and governing your organization's data

The governance of organizational data is key to this process. In *Chapter 13, Managing Microsoft Purview Data Lifecycle Management*, you learned about the importance of retaining data for only as long as you are obligated to do so. The requirement to conduct content searches and eDiscovery cases is only as effective as your organization's defined retention schedule.

Once you have diligently considered your organizational roles and obligations, you will be better placed to run legal investigations whenever they occur. For example, you will be able to manage legal investigations by performing the following tasks:

- Creating and using eDiscovery cases for all legal investigations submitted to your organization
- Assigning the required eDiscovery roles and permissions to control who can create and manage eDiscovery cases in your organization
- Controlling content locations that eDiscovery managers can search with compliance boundaries
- Searching for and exporting any relevant content in your organization

Carefully considering the steps and principles outlined in this section will increase your organization's chances of planning for and executing effective content searches and eDiscovery cases.

Next, we will see how to assign the appropriate permissions in the Microsoft Purview compliance portal to control who has access to the powerful search and discovery features within our Microsoft 365 environment.

Delegating the required permissions to use search and discovery tools

Before you start using the eDiscovery cases and content hold features, it is important to assign the appropriate permissions to the users who need access to these tools. This section will demonstrate how to do this from the Microsoft Purview compliance portal by adding users to the correct role group. The role used to control access is called **eDiscovery Manager**. This role also contains the following two subgroups:

- **eDiscovery Manager**: Can only view and edit cases that the user has access to
- **eDiscovery Administrator**: Can view and edit all cases regardless of permissions

To assign these roles to users in your organization, you will need to be a member of the **Organization Management** role group. When you have the correct access, complete the following steps to assign eDiscovery permissions to the required users:

1. Log in to the Microsoft Purview compliance portal at `https://compliance.microsoft.com` and, in the left pane, select **Permissions**:

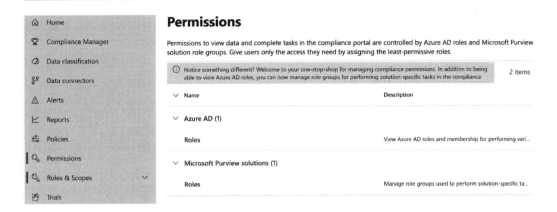

Figure 15.1: Permissions in the Microsoft Purview compliance portal

2. Under **Microsoft Purview solutions**, select **Roles**. You will now see **Role groups for Microsoft Purview solutions**, as shown in the following screenshot:

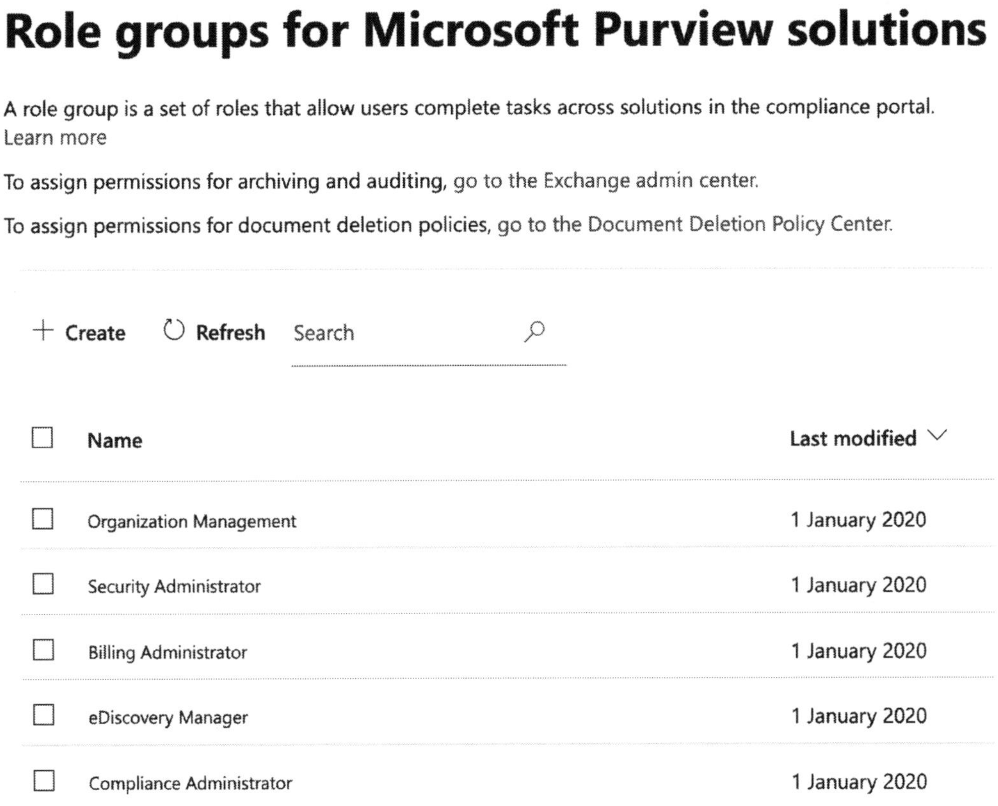

Role groups for Microsoft Purview solutions

A role group is a set of roles that allow users complete tasks across solutions in the compliance portal. Learn more

To assign permissions for archiving and auditing, go to the Exchange admin center.

To assign permissions for document deletion policies, go to the Document Deletion Policy Center.

	Name	Last modified ∨
☐	Organization Management	1 January 2020
☐	Security Administrator	1 January 2020
☐	Billing Administrator	1 January 2020
☐	eDiscovery Manager	1 January 2020
☐	Compliance Administrator	1 January 2020

Figure 15.2: Role groups for Microsoft Purview solutions

3. Scroll down the page and select **eDiscovery Manager**. The following screenshot shows the flyout menu that appears, which contains **Description** and **Assigned roles**:

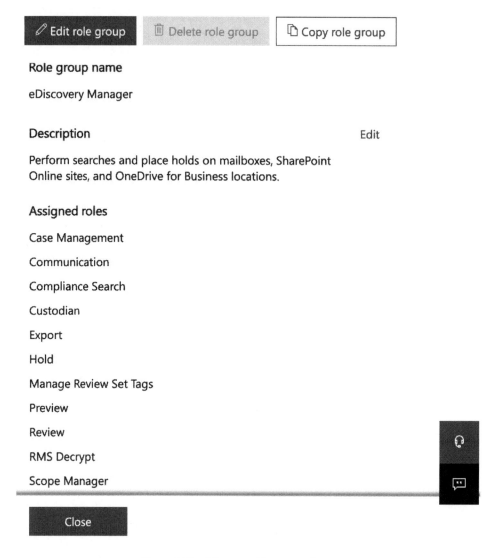

Figure 15.3: eDiscovery Manager role group

4. Scroll down the flyout to see the **eDiscovery Manager** and **eDiscovery Administrator** sub-role groups:

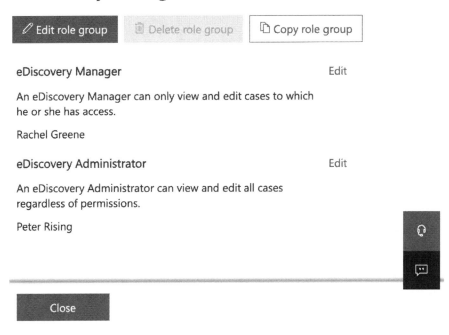

Figure 15.4: eDiscovery Manager role group

5.   Click **Edit** on either the **eDiscovery Manager** or **eDiscovery Administrator** group. Select **Edit** again, add the required user accounts to the chosen role, and then click **Save**:

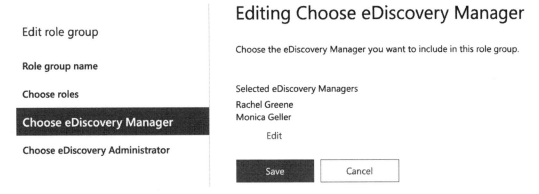

Figure 15.5: Adding members to eDiscovery role sub-groups

You can also use the Add-eDiscoveryCaseAdmin PowerShell cmdlet to assign a user as an eDiscovery Administrator. An example of the command to do this is Add-eDiscoveryCaseAdmin -User username@domainname.com.

> **Note**
>
> The **Compliance Administrator**, **Organization Management**, and **Reviewer** role groups also have permission to carry out activities relating to Microsoft Purview eDiscovery.

Now that you are familiar with the roles and permissions required for eDiscovery, the next step is to examine how to use eDiscovery (Premium) cases to create a case that will be used to search and investigate content within Microsoft 365.

Creating eDiscovery cases

In this section, you will learn how to use eDiscovery (Premium) to set up a case that will allow you to perform search and investigation tasks to discover and respond to internal investigations and legal cases.

To configure an eDiscovery (Premium) case in Microsoft Purview, you must complete the following steps:

1. Log in to the Microsoft Purview compliance portal at `https://compliance.microsoft.com` and navigate to **eDiscovery | Premium** from the left menu pane:

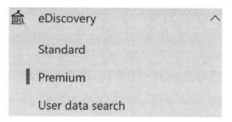

Figure 15.6: eDiscovery menu pane in Microsoft Purview

You will see any existing eDiscovery (Premium) cases listed here (based on your role group access):

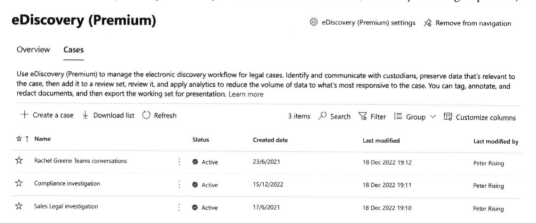

Figure 15.7: eDiscovery (Premium) case list in Microsoft Purview

2. Select **Create a case**, and the case creation wizard will open. You must enter a name for your case at this stage. Make sure that you give the case a descriptive name that is relevant to your investigation. You may change the case name later if you wish. The two optional fields here are **Description** and **Number**. Enter a detailed description relevant to the case. If you define a case numbering system, you may enter it here if required.

You will notice that, under **Case format**, the **New (recommended)** option is automatically selected. Below that, the option of **Classic (this format will be deprecated soon)** is shown. Any cases previously created under the older Classic case format will still be accessible, but you can now only create any new cases using the new format.

For this example, set **Name** as Marketing legal investigation and the optional **Description** as Investigation against activity from the Marketing department after claims of plagiarism from one of our competitors. Do not enter a case number in this example. Most organizations will have a numbering system, however. Once done, click **Next**:

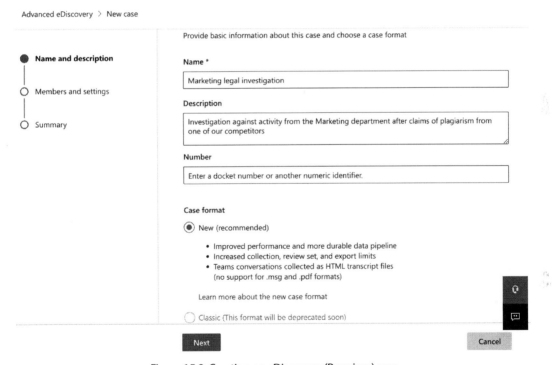

Figure 15.8: Creating an eDiscovery (Premium) case

3.   Next, you will see the **Members and settings** page. Complete the following fields if required:

- **Team members**: Choose any users and groups that you need to be assigned to the case

- **Search and analytics**: Select the options to reduce duplicates, group items by theme, or create a saved query whenever analytics is performed

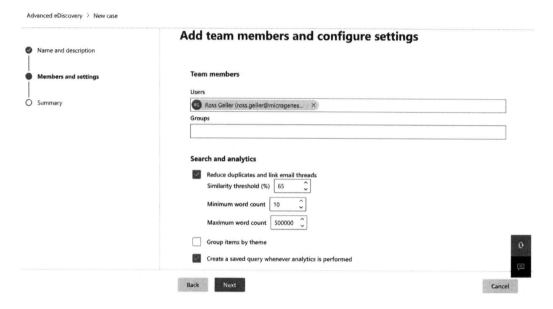

Figure 15.9: Members and settings case options

4.   Scroll down to select more options in the **Members and settings** section:

- **Text to ignore**: Add actual text or a regular expression to explicitly ignore in the case. This can be applied to **Near-duplicates**, **Email threads**, or **Themes**.

- **Optical character recognition (OCR)**: Choose whether you want to detect text within images during advanced indexing.

Click **Next**:

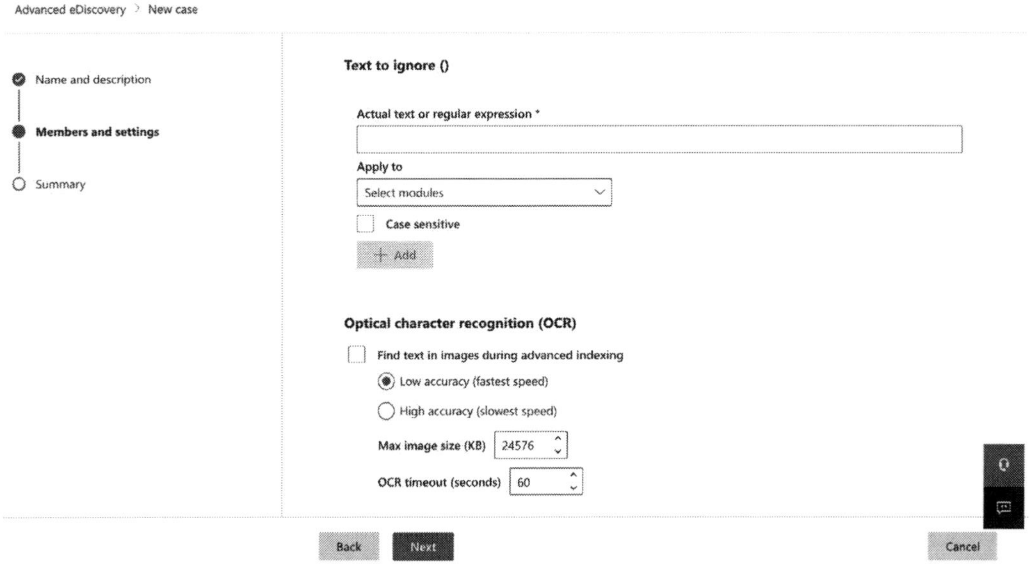

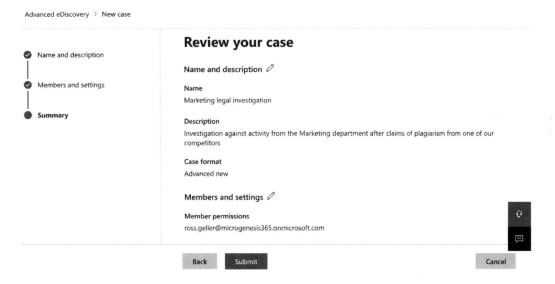

Figure 15.10: Members and settings case options

5. Now you will see the **Summary** page. Here, you can review the settings you entered for the case and make any changes if required. Click **Submit** to create your new case:

Advanced eDiscovery > New case

Name and description ✔

Members and settings ✔

Summary ●

Review your case

Name and description ✎

Name
Marketing legal investigation

Description
Investigation against activity from the Marketing department after claims of plagiarism from one of our competitors

Case format
Advanced new

Members and settings ✎

Member permissions
ross.geller@microgenesis365.onmicrosoft.com

Back   Submit   Cancel

Figure 15.11: Reviewing case settings and submitting the case for investigation

You have now completed the required steps to create an eDiscovery (Premium) case. You set up the case with a name, description, case members, search and analytics settings, text to ignore, and OCR settings.

With your case now ready for use, the next step is to manage its workflow. Let's take a look at this process in the next section.

Managing eDiscovery cases

Now that you have created your eDiscovery (Premium) case with its base settings, you need to create the workflow for your case so it can search for content and return results for you to analyze, filter, and export. The process to follow as part of your eDiscovery (Premium) case workflow will consist of some or all of the following steps:

- Add custodians to your case

- Collect content from data sources

- Create a collection and commit the content to a review set

- Access, analyze, and filter data within your review set

- Export and download your case data

We will now go through this process step by step by opening the case we created in the previous section and setting the required features.

Adding custodians

To add custodians to your case, complete the following tasks:

1. From the Microsoft Purview compliance portal, open **eDiscovery (Premium)**, as shown in the previous section, navigate to **Cases**, and click to open the case that you created. In this example, the case name is `Marketing legal investigation`. The case opens in the **Overview** tab:

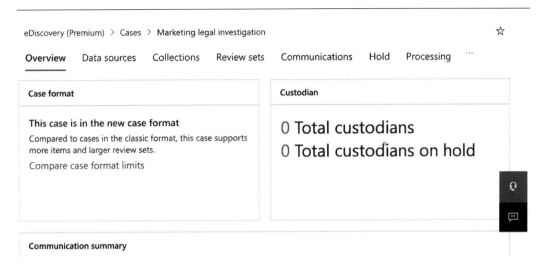

eDiscovery (Premium) > Cases > Marketing legal investigation ☆

Overview   Data sources   Collections   Review sets   Communications   Hold   Processing   ···

Case format

This case is in the new case format

Compared to cases in the classic format, this case supports more items and larger review sets.

Compare case format limits

Custodian

0 Total custodians
0 Total custodians on hold

Communication summary

Figure 15.12: eDiscovery case overview screen

2. Click on the **Data sources** tab to complete your first step in the workflow, which is to add a custodian(s) to your eDiscovery case. A **custodian** is a user in your organization who has control of content that may be relevant to your case. Additionally, you can add data sources that are not associated with a specific user but that may be relevant to the case. These are both *optional* steps, but it is common to have custodians set in eDiscovery cases.

    To add custodians, click on **Add data source**:

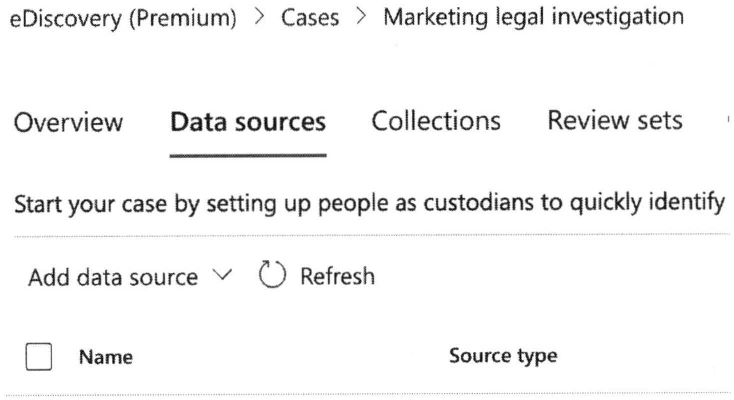

    eDiscovery (Premium) > Cases > Marketing legal investigation

    Overview   **Data sources**   Collections   Review sets   ¹

    Start your case by setting up people as custodians to quickly identify

    Add data source ∨   ⟳ Refresh

    ☐   Name   Source type

    Figure 15.13: eDiscovery case Data sources tab

3. You will see the options shown in the following screenshot. These are **Add new custodians**, **Import custodians**, and **Add data locations**. If you need to add a large number of custodians to your case, you could add them to a `.csv` file and use the **Import custodians** option. However, for this example, choose **Add new custodians**:

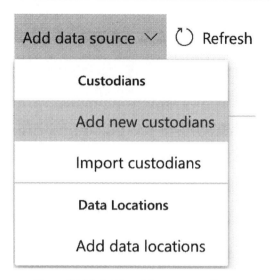

Figure 15.14: Adding data source options

4.   The **New custodian** wizard opens. Under **Select custodian**, type in the names of the custodians you wish to add and then click **Next**:

New custodian

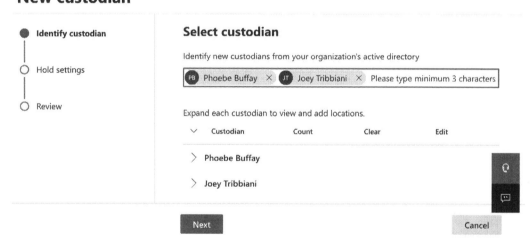

Figure 15.15: Adding custodians to an eDiscovery case

5.   On the **Hold settings** page, choose which of your custodians you want to place on hold. During an investigation, it is common for users to be placed on hold to prevent any of their data from being deleted while the investigation is in progress. Make your selections, then click **Next**:

New custodian

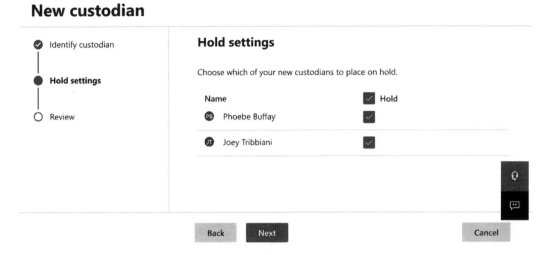

Figure 15.16: Configuring custodian hold settings

6.   Review your custodian settings and click **Submit**:

New custodian

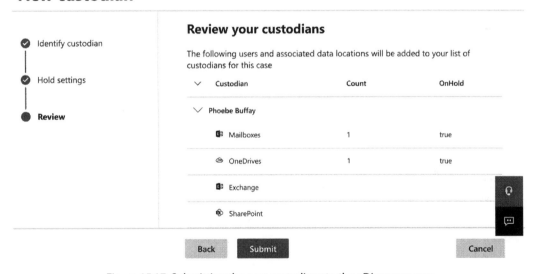

Figure 15.17: Submitting the new custodians to the eDiscovery case

7.   Click **Done** to complete the process of creating your custodians:

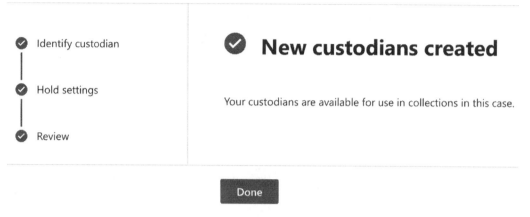

New custodian

Figure 15.18: New custodians successfully created

Your new custodians will now be shown within the **Data sources** section of the eDiscovery (Premium) case:

Name	Source type	Status
⊘ Joey Tribbiani	Custodian	✓ Active
⊘ Phoebe Buffay	Custodian	✓ Active

Add data source ⌄   ↻ Refresh   2 items   🔍

Figure 15.19: New custodians shown in the eDiscovery case Data sources section

8.   Next (again, optionally), click on **Add data source | Add data locations** to add new non-custodial data locations to your case. You may choose from **SharePoint**, **Exchange**, and **M365 connected apps**. For this example, select **SharePoint | Edit SharePoint sites**:

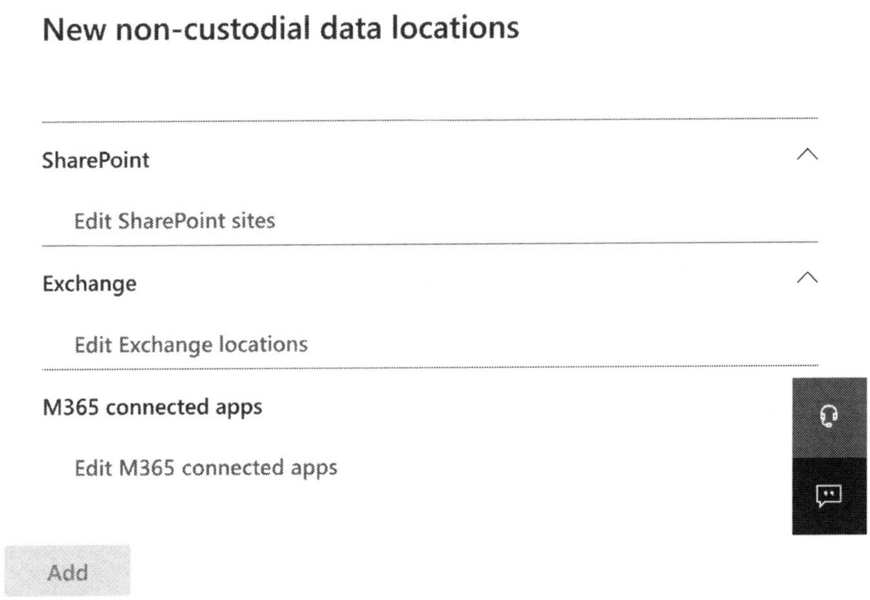

New non-custodial data locations

SharePoint   ∧

   Edit SharePoint sites

Exchange   ∧

   Edit Exchange locations

M365 connected apps

   Edit M365 connected apps

Add

Figure 15.20: Adding non-custodial data locations

9. Choose the sites you want to include and click **Add**:

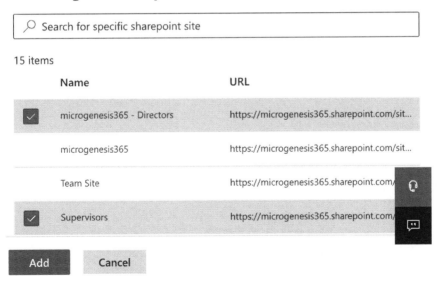

Figure 15.21: Adding non-custodial data sources

10. The sites you selected are shown. Click **Add** again:

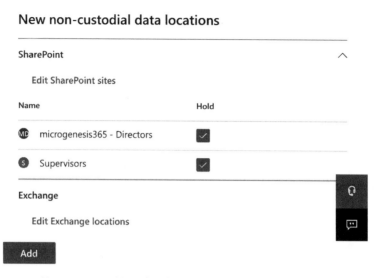

Figure 15.22: Adding the chosen non-custodial data sources

11. Finally, click **OK** to finish the process of adding the non-custodial data sources:

Figure 15.23: Completing adding non-custodial data sources

You will see a list of all the data sources you have added:

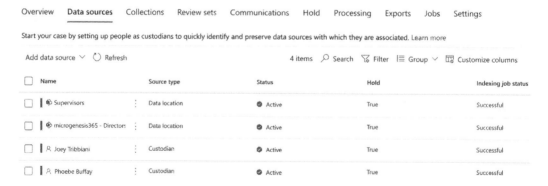

Figure 15.24: All added data sources

So, now you have added some data sources to your eDiscovery (Premium) case. The next step in the process is to collect data.

Collecting data

To do this from the data sources you've added, create a collection by completing the following steps:

1. In your eDiscovery case, go to the **Collections** tab and choose **New collection**:

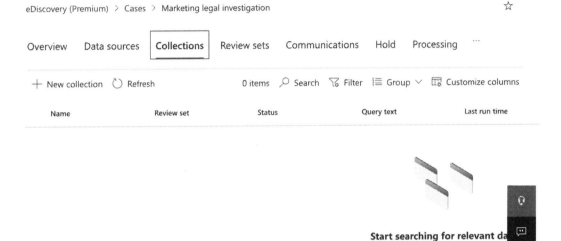

Figure 15.25: Creating a collection

2. Enter a name and description for your new collection. Click **Next**:

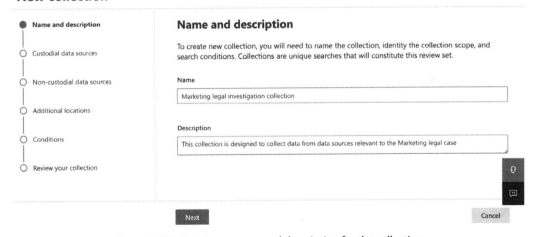

Figure 15.26: Entering a name and description for the collection

3. Choose the custodial data sources that you wish to add to the collection. You can choose either **Select custodians** to select specific custodians or, as in this example, move the slider to **Select all**. Click **Next**:

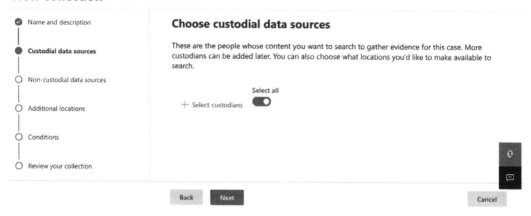

Figure 15.27: Adding custodial data sources to the collection

4. Choose the non-custodial data sources that you wish to add to the collection. You can choose either **Select non-custodial sources** to select specific non-custodial sources or, as in this example, move the slider to **Select all**. Click **Next**:

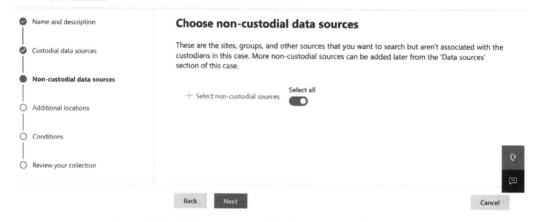

Figure 15.28: Adding non-custodial data sources to the collection

5. Next, if required, add additional locations to your collection.

An **additional location** is a data source that is not associated with the custodians that you previously selected for the collection. **Additional locations** can include **Exchange mailboxes** (including **Microsoft 365 Groups**, **Teams**, and **Yammer user messages**), **SharePoint sites** (including **OneDrive sites**, **Microsoft 365 Group sites**, **Team Sites**, and **Yammer Networks**), and **Exchange public folders**. For this example, no additional locations have been selected. Click **Next**:

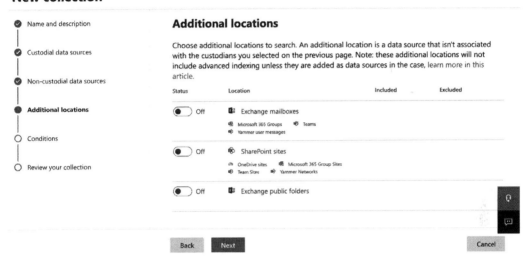

Figure 15.29: Adding additional locations to the collection

6. Next, define the conditions for your collection. These are the search conditions that apply to the data sources you have defined and will be used to populate your collection. You can add conditions either by keyword search or by using a **Keyword Query Language** (**KQL**) editor to enter KQL queries. For this example, use a simple **Condition card builder** keyword search and search with the four keywords `Marketing`, `Report`, `Data`, and `Statistics`. Click **Next**:

New collection

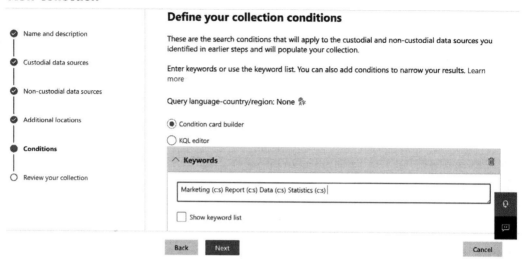

Figure 15.30: Defining search conditions for the collection

7.   Finally, review your collection settings and click **Submit**:

New collection

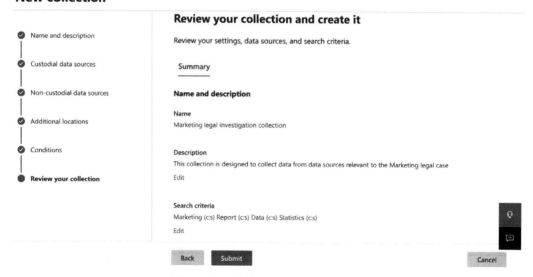

Figure 15.31: Submitting the collection

8. The collection is successfully created. Click **Done**:

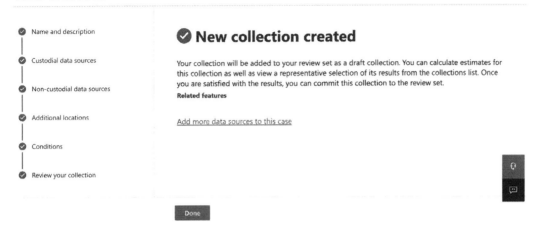

Figure 15.32: New collection successfully created

The collection is shown in the following screenshot:

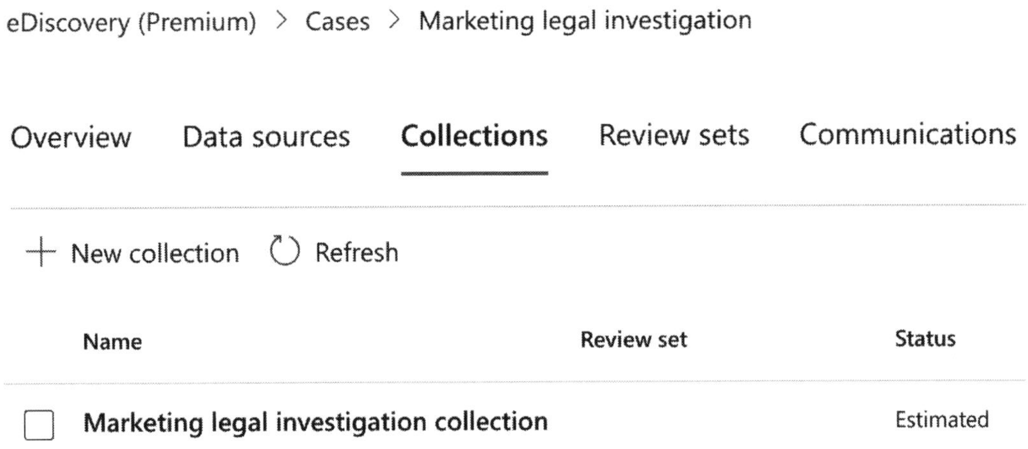

eDiscovery (Premium) > Cases > Marketing legal investigation

Overview   Data sources   **Collections**   Review sets   Communications

+ New collection   ⟳ Refresh

Name	Review set	Status
☐ **Marketing legal investigation collection**		Estimated

Figure 15.33: New collection shown under the Collections tab

9. Select the collection to see a summary of it. You now need to submit the collection to run. Click on **Actions**:

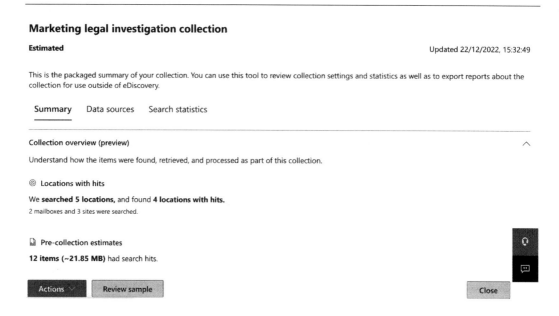

Figure 15.34: Committing the collection to run

10. You will see the options available to you for this collection. You can edit, commit, or delete the collection, as well as refresh the estimates, export a report, and make a copy of this collection as a new collection.

    For this case, select **Commit collection**:

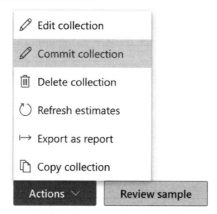

Figure 15.35: Committing the collection to run

11. When a collection searches for data, it presents that data to a review set. You can create a new review set or choose **Add to an existing review set**. For this example, choose **Add to a new review set** and enter the name Review set 1.0.

12. Some additional **Collections** settings are available that allow you to collect Teams and Yammer messages in a contextual manner. This means that conversations can be viewed in the results. You can also collect any cloud attachments in the results and can choose to collect all versions of SharePoint items (which can significantly increase the volume of items added to your review set).

13. Finally, you have the choice to add the entire collection to the review set or choose **Add only collection sample to review set**. For this example, choose **Add all of collection to review set**.

14. Click **Commit** to start the addition of collection sources to your review set:

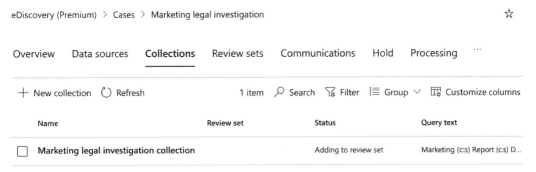

Figure 15.36: Committing the collection to run

15. Now that the collection is committed, you can track its progress by monitoring the **Status** column of the set, which initially will show as **Adding to review set**. Click the **Refresh** button to update the status. Depending on the number of data sources and search criteria you entered, the search process can take quite some time:

eDiscovery (Premium) > Cases > Marketing legal investigation   ☆

| Overview | Data sources | **Collections** | Review sets | Communications | Hold | Processing | ··· |

+ New collection   ○ Refresh   1 item   ⌕ Search   ⊽ Filter   ☰ Group ∨   ▦ Customize columns

Name	Review set	Status	Query text
☐ **Marketing legal investigation collection**		Adding to review set	Marketing (c:s) Report (c:s) D...

Figure 15.37: Collection adding to a review set

16. Use the **Jobs** tab within your eDiscovery case to see the status of the review set data population. In this example, with a minimal amount of data added, the process is completed in under 10 minutes.

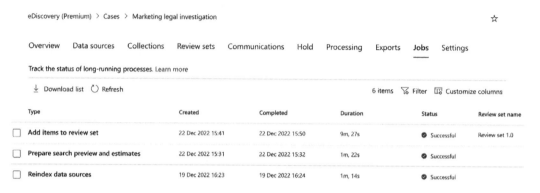

Figure 15.38: Monitoring committed collections in the Jobs tab

When completed, the collection job shows the name of the review set in the **Review set** column:

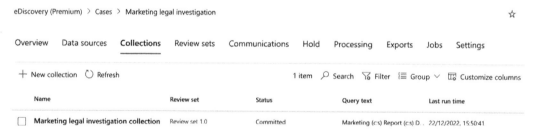

Figure 15.39: Collection mapped to review set

So, to recap the steps you have just taken, you created a collection, selected the data sources to include, and committed the collection to a newly created review set. With this process now completed, the next step is to open the review set and inspect the results.

Analyzing the review set results

To examine the review set results, complete the following steps:

1. From your eDiscovery case, go to the **Review sets** tab and click to select the review set that has been created:

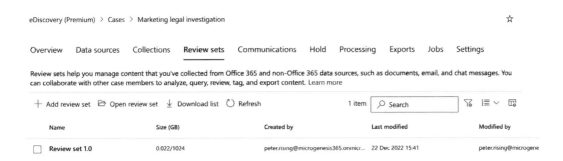

Figure 15.40: Selecting the new review set

2. You will now see any matching search results that your collection gathered from the data sources and presented to the review set. The following screenshot shows results including Teams chat messages, documents, and Word documents. Items with an arrow next to them can be expanded to show the context of a conversation:

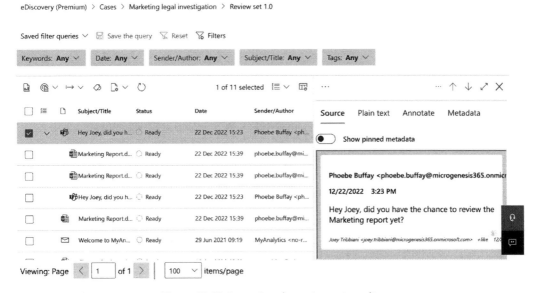

Figure 15.41: Accessing the review set results

3. Highlight a line item to see the content of that item in the right-hand side pane. There are four tabs in this pane, as shown in the preceding screenshot. **Source** shows you the default search content view. You can also view the content in **Plain text**, you can choose to annotate the content by highlighting or redacting text (in the **Annotate** tab), and you can view any metadata associated with the content in **Metadata**. Use the filtering options to filter large quantities of search results by **Keywords**, **Date**, **Sender/Author**, **Subject/Title**, or **Tags**.

Next, let's look at how to export and download data from the case.

Exporting and downloading case data

The toolbar buttons shown in the following screenshot allow you to perform certain tasks on the data presented in the review set:

Figure 15.42: Review set tools

These options on the toolbar include the following:

- Running document and email analytics
- Showing reports
- Exporting and downloading review set content
- Committing any redactions to a PDF file
- Adding content to another review set
- Tagging files
- Managing the upload of non-Office 365 data

Next, let's examine some further tasks you can complete within your eDiscovery case.

Additional tasks

Note that within an eDiscovery case, there are some other tabs available. These are described as follows:

Tab Name	Description
Communications	The **Communications** tab allows the distribution and tracking of legal hold notifications. Case admins can manage and automate initial notifications, reminders, and escalations to custodians when they are the subject of a case, and their content is placed on hold.
Hold	The **Hold** tab allows the creation of holds to preserve content. Hold policies can be linked with custodians and additional locations.
Processing	The **Processing** tab shows advanced custodian indexing information. From here, you can examine processing errors with file identification, expansion of embedded documents and attachments, and text extraction.
Exports	The **Exports** tab is where any exports you create from your review sets can be accessed.

Tab Name	Description
Jobs	It is through the **Jobs** tab that you track the status of running processes such as adding data to a review set, applying holds, and preparing search previews and estimates.
Settings	In the **Settings** tab, you can configure case information, access and permissions settings, and search and analytics settings for the case. This includes things such as duplication and identification grouping, OCR settings, and text to ignore within a case.

Table 15.1: eDiscovery (Premium) additional case tabs

Managing eDiscovery cases using eDiscovery (Premium) in Microsoft Purview is a powerful way of complying with investigations of all types. With the ability to create cases with the settings and permissions that you need and features such as custodian management, review sets, and more, your organization will be able to plan an effective strategy for managing the workflow of cases from end to end.

Summary

This chapter introduced the principles of eDiscovery in Microsoft Purview. We learned that we need to assign the eDiscovery Manager role to any users that we want to manage eDiscovery cases and that we can then create eDiscovery cases from the Microsoft Purview compliance portal. After creating an eDiscovery case, we learned how to associate custodians (users) and other data locations with our eDiscovery case and apply holds to content in these locations. Then, we examined how to create a collection, which is a search for content against the data sources we define, and commit those search results to a review set. Finally, the chapter demonstrated that once a review set is completed and available, we can preview the results and tag, annotate, filter, and export the results so they can be presented as part of regulatory processes or legal investigations.

In the next chapter, we will explore how to plan for regulatory compliance and privacy obligations within Microsoft Purview. We will study the principles of Microsoft Priva, which is Microsoft's privacy tool and includes capabilities for risk management and responding to subject rights requests.

Questions

1. Which of the following are *not* the names of eDiscovery tools in Microsoft Purview? Choose two:

    A. eDiscovery (Business)

    B. eDiscovery (Premium)

    C. eDiscovery (Basic)

    D. eDiscovery (Standard)

2. Which feature of an eDiscovery (Premium) case allows you to review, tag, annotate, and export content?

    A. Collections

    B. Holds

    C. Data sources

    D. Review sets

3. True or false? The eDiscovery Manager role group includes two subgroups called eDiscovery Managers and eDiscovery Administrators:

    A. True

    B. False

4. Which of the following roles or role groups should be used to review an eDiscovery case, using the principle of least privilege?

    A. Compliance Administrator

    B. Reviewer

    C. Organization Management

    D. Global Administrator

5. True or false? In eDiscovery (Premium) cases, it is possible to view search results in review sets in a conversational context view:

    A. True

    B. False

6. In which tab in an eDiscovery (Premium) case would you configure case information?

    A. **Settings**

    B. **Overview**

    C. **Data sources**

    D. **Communications**

7. True or false? When adding custodians to an eDiscovery case, you must place the custodians' content on hold:

    A. True

    B. False

8. Which of the following are examples of non-custodial data sources? Choose three:

   A. M365 connected apps

   B. Exchange locations

   C. Power BI

   D. SharePoint sites

9. True or false? With the **Communications** option in an eDiscovery case, it is possible to configure escalation notification messages?

   A. True

   B. False

10. Which of the following is *not* one of the available options from the **Data sources** tab in an eDiscovery (Premium) case?

    A. **Add data locations**

    B. **Import data sources**

    C. **Import custodians**

    D. **Add new custodians**

Further reading

Please refer to the following links for more information:

- *Microsoft Purview eDiscovery solutions*: https://learn.microsoft.com/en-us/microsoft-365/compliance/ediscovery?WT.mc_id=M365-MVP-4039827&view=o365-worldwide

- *Manage legal investigations in Microsoft 365*: https://learn.microsoft.com/en-us/microsoft-365/compliance/manage-legal-investigations?WT.mc_id=M365-MVP-4039827&view=o365-worldwide

- *Assign eDiscovery permissions in the compliance portal*: https://learn.microsoft.com/en-us/microsoft-365/compliance/assign-ediscovery-permissions?WT.mc_id=M365-MVP-4039827&view=o365-worldwide

- *Get started with eDiscovery (Standard)*: https://learn.microsoft.com/en-us/microsoft-365/compliance/get-started-core-ediscovery?WT.mc_id=M365-MVP-4039827&view=o365-worldwide

- *Search for content in a eDiscovery (Standard) case*: https://learn.microsoft.com/en-us/microsoft-365/compliance/search-for-content-in-core-ediscovery?WT.mc_id=M365-MVP-4039827&view=o365-worldwide

- *Get started with eDiscovery (Premium)*: `https://learn.microsoft.com/en-us/microsoft-365/compliance/get-started-with-advanced-ediscovery?view=o365-worldwide`

- *Set up attorney-client privilege detection in eDiscovery (Premium)*: `https://learn.microsoft.com/en-us/microsoft-365/compliance/attorney-privilege-detection?view=o365-worldwide`

- *Create and manage an eDiscovery (Premium) case*: `https://learn.microsoft.com/en-us/microsoft-365/compliance/create-and-manage-advanced-ediscoveryv2-case?view=o365-worldwide`

- *Use the new case format in eDiscovery (Premium)*: `https://learn.microsoft.com/en-us/microsoft-365/compliance/advanced-ediscovery-new-case-format?view=o365-worldwide`

- *Export Content search results*: `https://learn.microsoft.com/en-us/microsoft-365/compliance/export-search-results?WT.mc_id=M365-MVP-4039827&view=o365-worldwide`

- *Add-eDiscoveryCaseAdmin*: `https://learn.microsoft.com/en-us/powershell/module/exchange/add-ediscoverycaseadmin?view=exchange-ps`

- *Work with communications in eDiscovery (Premium)*: `https://learn.microsoft.com/en-us/microsoft-365/compliance/ediscovery-managing-custodian-communications?view=o365-worldwide`

16
Managing Regulatory and Privacy Requirements

Organizations need to be keenly aware of their obligations in relation to **regulatory compliance**. This can be challenging, especially for smaller businesses that may not have a dedicated compliance or data protection officer. It is important to recognize and implement the correct settings and controls in Microsoft Purview to ensure that you are observing the appropriate standards and regulations.

Equally (and increasingly) important is the awareness and implementation of **privacy settings** and **controls**. Data subjects have the right to privacy and are entitled to the expectation that data relating to them is appropriately protected, not overexposed, and only retained for as long as it is needed.

In this chapter, we will explore the available technologies in Microsoft Purview that allow you to plan for regulatory compliance and privacy within Microsoft 365. We will learn how to use the rich features of **Compliance Manager** within Microsoft Purview, including improvement actions, assessments, and assessment templates. We will also study the principles of **Microsoft Priva**, which includes policies and settings for risk management and responding to subject rights requests. After reading this chapter, you will have a better understanding of the compliance and privacy requirements that organizations need to be aware of.

These topics will be covered in the following order:

- Planning your regulatory compliance journey in Microsoft 365
- Managing regulatory compliance in Microsoft Purview Compliance Manager
- Implementing privacy risk management with Microsoft Priva
- Implementing and managing subject rights requests with Microsoft Priva

Planning your regulatory compliance journey in Microsoft 365

To start planning for regulatory compliance using Microsoft 365, organizations should be aware of the rules and regulations to which they need to adhere to be considered compliant by regulatory bodies and standards. These include the **General Data Protection Regulation (GDPR)**, which comprises rules for organizations that offer goods and services to people in the **European Union (EU)** or ones that collect and analyze data for EU residents regardless of where they or their organization may be located. The GDPR provides individuals with the right to manage any personal data that relates to them that has been collected by an organization. The individual can exercise these rights by lodging a **Data Subject Request (DSR)**. The organization must respond in a timely fashion to DSRs and also perform **Data Protection Impact Assessments (DPIAs)**.

Some of the terms and references you may encounter in relation to GDPR include the following:

- **Data Controller**: A data controller can be a legal professional or a public/other body that determines the reason and methodology of processing personal data.

- **Personal Data and Data Subject**: This is defined as any information that relates to an identified or identifiable natural person (data subject).

- **Processor**: A processor is defined as a natural or legal person or a public authority that processes personal data.

- **Customer Data**: This is data that is created and retained in relation to the needs of running your business.

- **Data Subject Request (DSR)**: This is a formal request by a data subject to an organization in relation to their personal data. The request can include an action that must be performed by the organization such as a change or a restriction.

- **Data Protection Impact Assessment (DPIA)**: DPIAs comprise an assessment of any operational data that, as stated in Article 35(1) of the GDPR, is "likely to result in a high risk to the rights and freedoms of natural persons."

GDPR is one of the more prominent examples of many regulatory standards that exist to protect data and individuals around the world. Such standards can be based on global, government, industry, or regional regulations. Links to further examples recommended by Microsoft are included in the *Further reading* section at the end of this chapter.

To better understand and implement these standards in your organization, you can use Microsoft Purview Compliance Manager. Compliance Manager has many pre-built assessments for various regulations that can be leveraged by organizations with Microsoft 365 E5 subscriptions. In the next section, we will examine how to access the Compliance Manager feature in Microsoft Purview and how to implement improvement actions and use the available assessments and assessment templates.

Managing regulatory compliance in Microsoft Purview Compliance Manager

In this section, we will learn about Microsoft Purview Compliance Manager – first by accessing this feature and the required roles and permissions, then by viewing and implementing improvement actions, as well as the available assessments and assessment templates.

Access to Compliance Manager

Compliance Manager is accessed via the **role-based access control** (**RBAC**) model. When using Compliance Manager for the first time, it is recommended to log in as a global admin and then set the required access permissions to other users. To set the required access for Compliance Manager, complete the following steps:

1. Log in to the Microsoft Purview compliance portal at `https://compliance.microsoft.com` and navigate to **Permissions** from the menu pane on the left:

Figure 16.1: Permissions within Microsoft Purview Compliance Manager

2.   Under **Microsoft Purview solutions**, select **Roles**:

Permissions

Permissions to view data and complete tasks in the compliance portal are controlled by Azure AD roles and Microsoft Purview solution role groups. Give users only the access they need by assigning the least-permissive roles.

		2 items
ⓘ Notice something different? Welcome to your one-stop-shop for managing compliance permissions. In addition to being able to view Azure AD roles, you can now manage role groups for performing solution-specific tasks in the compliance portal.		

∨ Name	Description
∨ **Azure AD (1)**	
Roles	View Azure AD roles and membership for performing various tas…
∨ **Microsoft Purview solutions (1)**	
Roles	Manage role groups used to perform solution-specific tasks in th

Figure 16.2: Selecting roles in Microsoft Purview solutions

The available role groups for Microsoft Purview solutions will be shown, as follows:

Role groups for Microsoft Purview solutions

A role group is a set of roles that allow users complete tasks across solutions in the compliance portal. Learn more

To assign permissions for archiving and auditing, go to the Exchange admin center.

To assign permissions for document deletion policies, go to the Document Deletion Policy Center.

+ Create ↻ Refresh Search 🔎	
☐ Name ∧	Last modified
☐ Billing Administrator	1 January 2020
☐ Communication Compliance	1 January 2020
☐ Communication Compliance Administrators	1 January 2020
☐ Communication Compliance Analysts	1 January 2020
☐ Communication Compliance Investigators	1 January 2020
☐ Communication Compliance Viewers	1 January 2020

Figure 16.3: Microsoft Purview solutions role groups

3. Scroll down, or search for `Compliance Manager`. The following are the four Compliance Manager-related role groups:

   - **Compliance Manager Administrators**: Manage template creation and modification

   - **Compliance Manager Assessors**: Create assessments, implement improvement actions, and update test status for improvement actions

   - **Compliance Manager Contributors**: Create assessments and perform work to implement improvement actions

   - **Compliance Manager Readers**: View all Compliance Manager content except for administrator functions

   These role groups are shown in the following figure:

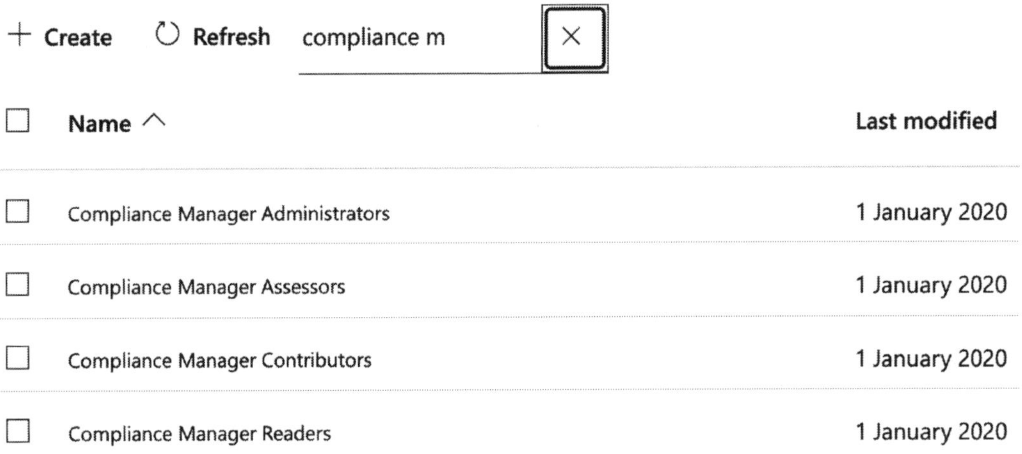

$+$ Create $\circlearrowright$ Refresh compliance m $\boxed{\times}$	
☐ **Name** $\wedge$	**Last modified**
☐ Compliance Manager Administrators	1 January 2020
☐ Compliance Manager Assessors	1 January 2020
☐ Compliance Manager Contributors	1 January 2020
☐ Compliance Manager Readers	1 January 2020

   Figure 16.4: Compliance Manager role groups

4. Select each role group to open a flyout pane that shows you more details about what the role group is for and any sub-roles contained within the group. For example, if you select the **Compliance Manager Administrators** role group, you can see the following details:

   - **Role group name**: The name of the role group

   - **Description**: The description of the role group

   - **Assigned roles**: Which roles are included within the role group

   - **Members**: Who has access to the role group

To add someone to the role group, select **Edit** under **Members**:

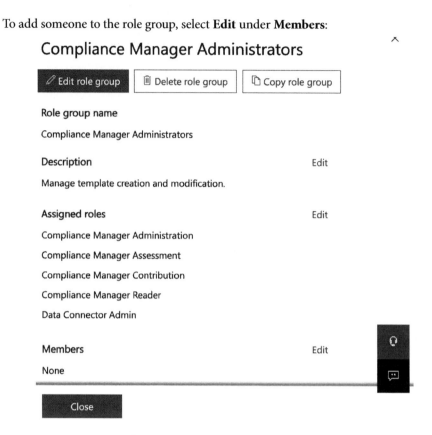

Figure 16.5: Viewing role group details

5. Under the **Choose members** option in the pane on the left, select **Choose members**:

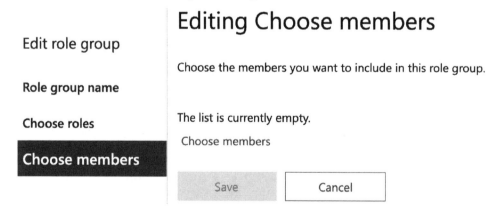

Figure 16.6: Choosing members for the role group

6. Click **Add**, then click **Add** again. Select the users you want as role group members, click **Add** for a third time, then click **Done**. The newly added members will be shown, as you can see in the following screenshot. Click **Save**:

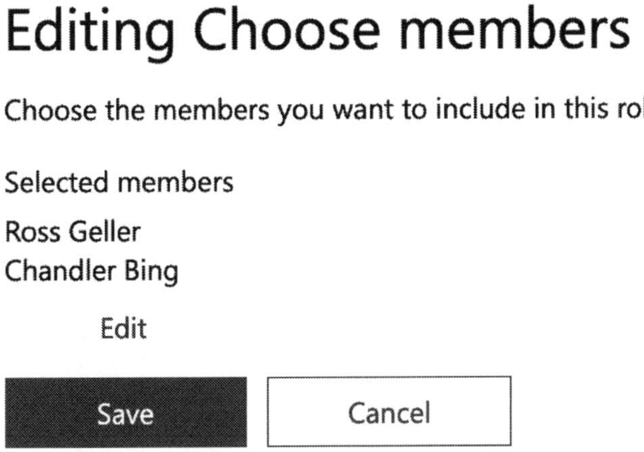

Editing Choose members

Choose the members you want to include in this role group.

Selected members

Ross Geller

Chandler Bing

Edit

Save   Cancel

Figure 16.7: New members added to the role group

Users will now have access to Compliance Manager with the level of permission according to the role group to which you assigned them.

Next, we will take a look at the **Improvement actions** page within Microsoft Purview.

Improvement actions

The **Improvement actions** tab within Microsoft Purview compliance portal provides a central point for you to manage your compliance activities. Each listed improvement action provides you with the details and guidance on how to implement the required standards and thereby conform with data protection standards and regulations.

You may assign actions to users to test and then implement. Additionally, you may add notes and documents to record the activities that have been completed in relation to improvement score items. These notes and documents can act as evidence or an audit trail that your organization can use to prove the status of your compliance. All improvement actions are listed on the **Improvement actions** page, which you can access by completing the following steps:

1. Log in to the Microsoft Purview compliance portal at https://compliance.microsoft.com and navigate to **Compliance Manager** from the menu pane on the left:

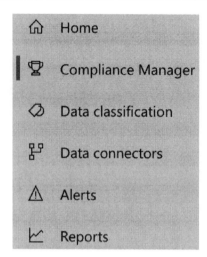

Figure 16.8: Accessing Microsoft Purview Compliance Manager

Compliance Manager will open and you will be taken to an overview screen where you can see a high-level view of your compliance posture and the option to start a trial for some premium assessment templates that are available. There are seven tabs at the top of the page, which are as follows:

- **Overview**: Gives a high-level view of your compliance posture

- **Improvement actions**: Shows the available actions you can take to improve your posture

- **Solutions**: Shows a line-by-line breakdown of all the solutions within Microsoft Purview and how they make up your compliance posture score

- **Assessments**: The purpose of this tab is to assist you with the implementation of controls relating to data protection. **Assessments** comprises actions derived from **Assessment templates**.

- **Assessment templates**: Compliance Manager's assessment templates help to track compliance with over 300 industry and government regulations around the world.

- **Alerts**: View and manage alerts for events that can affect your organization's compliance score. You can update the conditions for generating alerts on the **Alert policies** page.

- **Alert policies**: Alert policies help you monitor and receive notifications about events in Compliance Manager that are of importance to you. You can create or modify policies, change their activation status, and control alert frequency and severity.

The area you want to begin with is **Improvement actions**:

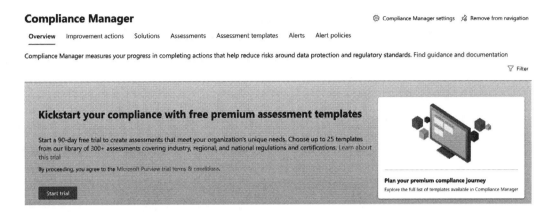

Figure 16.9: Compliance Manager Overview screen

2. Select **Improvement actions**, and you will see the options shown in the following screenshot:

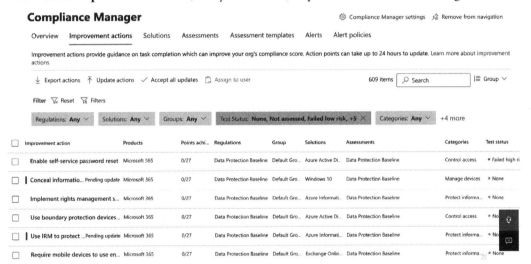

Figure 16.10: Compliance Manager Improvement actions page

Each improvement action is broken down into columns including the following:

- **Improvement action**: The description of the improvement action.

- **Products:** The products to which the improvement action will apply – for example, Microsoft 365.

- **Points achieved**: The number of points that will be achieved for your compliance score by implementing the improvement action.

- **Regulations**: The industry regulation that the improvement action is tied to – for instance, **Data Protection Baseline Assessment**.

- **Group**: The group name to which the improvement action is tied. There is one group already created called **Default Group**. You can create and use your own groups to organize your improvement actions.

- **Solutions**: The solutions that the improvement action will apply to – for instance, Windows 10, Exchange Online, and Azure Active Directory.

- **Assessments**: The assessments to which the improvement actions relate.

- **Categories**: The categories to which the improvement actions relate – for instance, **Manage devices** and **Control access**.

- **Test status**: Shows the current testing process stage.

- **Action type**: The type of action that is required – for instance, **Technical**, **Documentation**, and **Operational**.

- **Assigned to**: Shows who the improvement action has been assigned to for testing and implementation.

- **Testing source**: Indicates how the action is tested and implemented – that is, **Automatic** or **Manual**.

- **Role type**: The role type usually shows as **Admin**.

To view an improvement action, click to open it. This takes you to the details page for that improvement action:

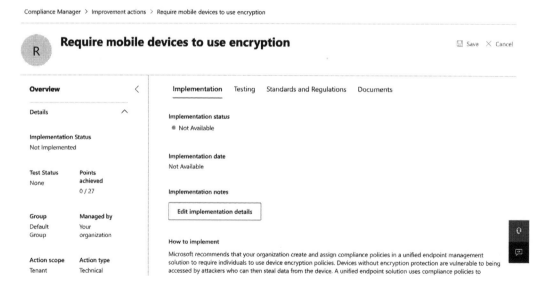

Figure 16.11: Opening an improvement action

3. Scroll through the **Overview** section of the improvement action to see more details and actions you can take. These include **Assign action**, which allocates this task to another user, and **Testing Source**, which, in this case, is set to **Manual**. The other option you can select for testing source is **Parent**, which, when selected, allows you to tie this improvement action to another improvement action so they will be implemented together:

Overview
Products
Microsoft 365
Documents
0
Assigned to
None
Assign action
Testing Source
Manual

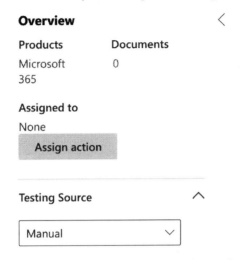

Figure 16.12: Improvement action Overview options

4. In the pane on the right, you will see the **Implementation** tab highlighted. Here, you will see information related to how you implement the improvement action. Click on **Edit implementation details** if you want to edit it:

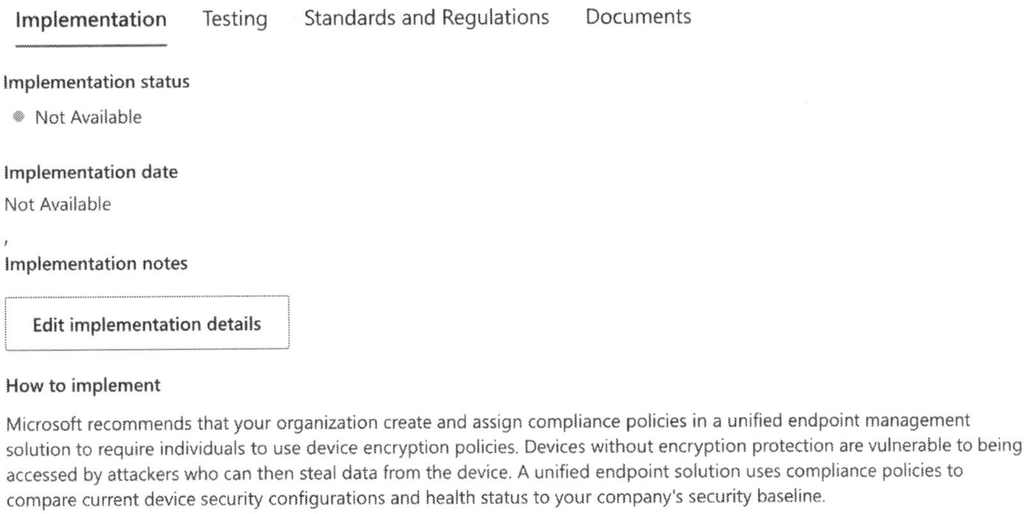

Implementation
Testing
Standards and Regulations
Documents
Implementation status
Not Available
Implementation date
Not Available
Implementation notes
Edit implementation details
How to implement
Microsoft recommends that your organization create and assign compliance policies in a unified endpoint management solution to require individuals to use device encryption policies. Devices without encryption protection are vulnerable to being accessed by attackers who can then steal data from the device. A unified endpoint solution uses compliance policies to compare current device security configurations and health status to your company's security baseline.

Figure 16.13: Improvement action implementation options

5. Scroll down further to see more implementation instruction details. Additionally, depending on the type of implementation (with some you can go straight to the portal to configure, and some will contain a list of implementation instructions), you will see a **Launch Now** button. If present, this will take you to the Microsoft 365 service where you can configure the settings appropriate to the improvement action. In this example, it takes you to the Exchange Online admin center to implement the action:

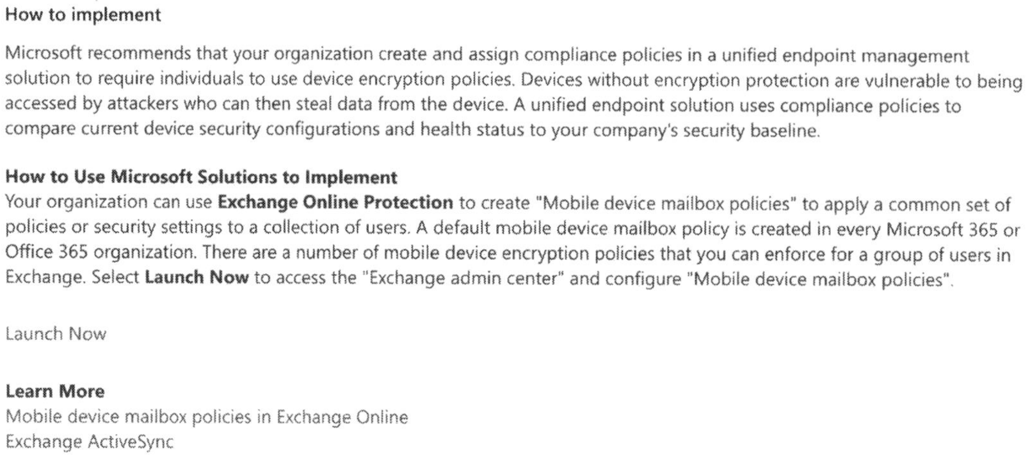

How to implement
Microsoft recommends that your organization create and assign compliance policies in a unified endpoint management solution to require individuals to use device encryption policies. Devices without encryption protection are vulnerable to being accessed by attackers who can then steal data from the device. A unified endpoint solution uses compliance policies to compare current device security configurations and health status to your company's security baseline.
How to Use Microsoft Solutions to Implement
Your organization can use Exchange Online Protection to create "Mobile device mailbox policies" to apply a common set of policies or security settings to a collection of users. A default mobile device mailbox policy is created in every Microsoft 365 or Office 365 organization. There are a number of mobile device encryption policies that you can enforce for a group of users in Exchange. Select Launch Now to access the "Exchange admin center" and configure "Mobile device mailbox policies".
Launch Now
Learn More
Mobile device mailbox policies in Exchange Online
Exchange ActiveSync

Figure 16.14: Improvement action implementation options

6. Under **Testing**, you will see the stage of the testing and you can export the testing history. Under **Standards and Regulations**, you can see which regulatory standards apply to the improvement action. Finally, under **Documents**, click **Add evidence** to add a document or a link to support the fact that you have implemented the improvement action in your organization:

Compliance Manager > Improvement actions > Require mobile devices to use encryption
R
Require mobile devices to use encryptio
Implementation
Testing
Standards and Regulations
Documents
+ Add evidence
Download all
Evidence name
Type
Add evidence
Add evidence to the improvement action
Evidence type
Document
Link
Upload file
Select a file
Browse

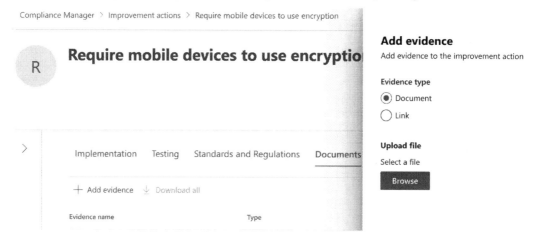

Figure 16.15: Improvement action Documents options

Improvement actions are a quick and simple way to manage the updates and settings you need to apply to be compliant and maintain a high compliance score in Microsoft Purview.

You can also easily manage and customize your experience within **Improvement actions** by filtering the items presented. Additionally, you can use **Export actions** to export the list of actions to a `.csv` file and look at any additional steps you may need to take by clicking on the **Update actions** button. By doing so, you will see any additional guidance on that particular improvement action that you may need to consider. Choose **Accept all updates**, which means any improvement action with **Pending update** as part of its description will be updated to the latest definition from Microsoft:

Improvement actions provide guidance on task completion which can improve your org's compliance score. Action points can take up to 24 hours to update. Learn more about improvement actions

↓ Export actions ⤒ Update actions ✓ Accept all updates 📋 Assign to user   1 of 609 selected | 🔍 Search | ≔ Group ⌄

Filter ⛛ Reset ⛛ Filters

| Regulations: **Any** ⌄ | Solutions: **Any** ⌄ | Groups: **Any** ⌄ | Test Status: **None, Not assessed, Failed low risk, +5** ✕ | Categories: **Any** ⌄ |

| Testing Source: **Any** ⌄ | Products: **Any** ⌄ | Assigned To: **Any** ⌄ | Role type: **Any** ⌄ | Show less |

Figure 16.16: Improvement actions additional options

The next section will demonstrate how to use assessments and assessment templates to add other data protection standards and regulations to Microsoft Purview Compliance Manager. We will also examine how this will add further improvement actions related to those standards.

Assessments and assessment templates

With Microsoft Purview Compliance Manager, you can create assessments to assess your compliance posture against industry regulations relevant to your organization. Assessments are underpinned by assessment templates. These templates comprise controls, improvement actions, and Microsoft actions that will be used to complete an assessment. To start using assessments and assessment templates, take the following steps:

1. From the Microsoft Purview compliance portal, select **Compliance Manager** and then choose **Assessments**. The following screenshot shows a default assessment provided by Microsoft called **Data Protection Baseline**:

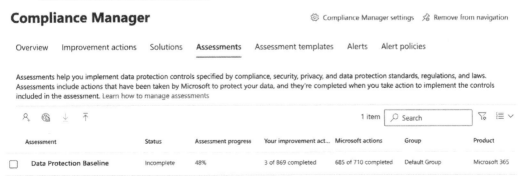

Compliance Manager

⚙ Compliance Manager settings   ⚄ Remove from navigation

Overview   Improvement actions   Solutions   **Assessments**   Assessment templates   Alerts   Alert policies

Assessments help you implement data protection controls specified by compliance, security, privacy, and data protection standards, regulations, and laws. Assessments include actions that have been taken by Microsoft to protect your data, and they're completed when you take action to implement the controls included in the assessment. Learn how to manage assessments

🧍 🗐 ↓ ⤒   1 item | 🔍 Search   ⛛ ≔ ⌄

Assessment	Status	Assessment progress	Your improvement act...	Microsoft actions	Group	Product
☐ Data Protection Baseline	Incomplete	48%	3 of 869 completed	685 of 710 completed	Default Group	Microsoft 365

Figure 16.17: Assessments in the Microsoft Purview compliance portal

2. Click to view this assessment, and you will see the **Progress** tab showing the progress of the assessment and the key improvement actions:

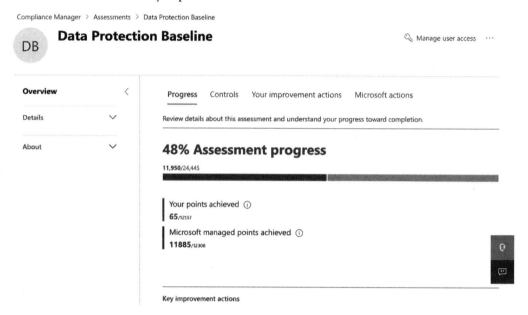

Figure 16.18: Data Protection Baseline Assessment progress status

3. Select the **Controls** tab to see the standards that are included in the assessment and their implementation progress:

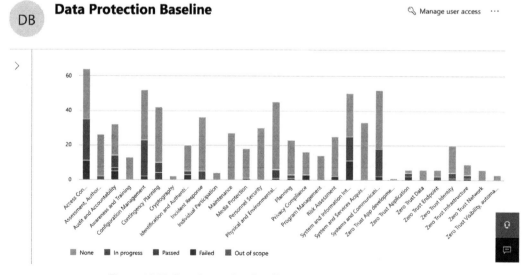

Figure 16.19: Data Protection Baseline Assessment control status

4. Go to the **Your improvement actions** tab to view and implement the actions. You can assign improvement actions to others as well:

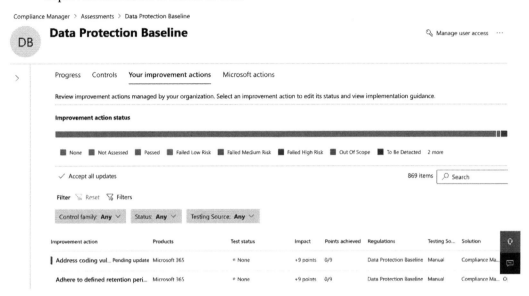

Figure 16.20: Data Protection Baseline Assessment improvement actions

5. Finally, go to the **Microsoft actions** tab to review the progress of the improvement actions managed by Microsoft:

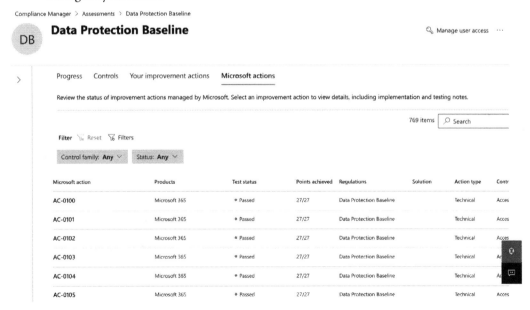

Figure 16.21: Data Protection Baseline Assessment Microsoft actions

Now let's look at how we can create assessments and groups.

Creating an assessment

When creating an assessment yourself, you will assign it to a **group**. Groups are a means of organizing assessments. To create a group, you must first create an assessment, as follows:

1.   From **Compliance Manager**, choose the **Assessments** tab, then click on **Add assessment**:

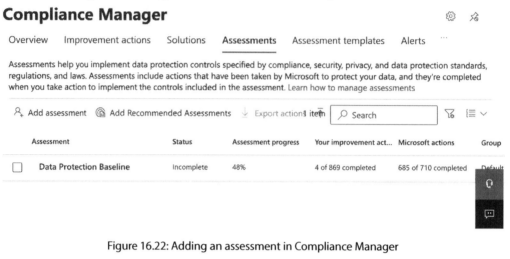

Figure 16.22: Adding an assessment in Compliance Manager

2.   The assessment creation wizard starts. Now click on **Select template**:

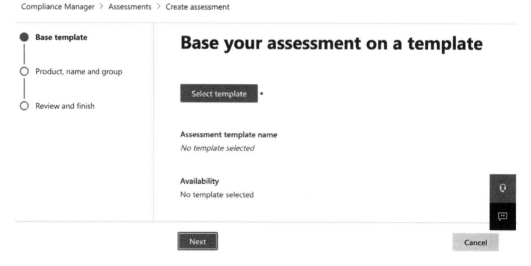

Figure 16.23: Selecting an assessment template

3. Scroll through the available templates. You will see that some are included with your current subscription and others are **Premium**, which you have to purchase. However, you can get a free trial of the **Premium** templates:

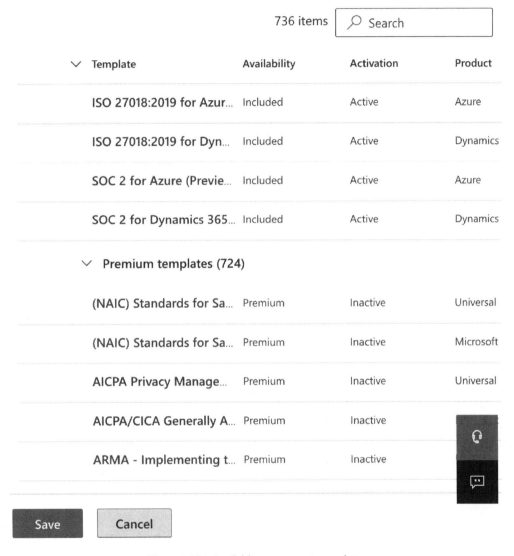

	736 items	Search		
∨ Template	Availability		Activation	Product
ISO 27018:2019 for Azur...	Included		Active	Azure
ISO 27018:2019 for Dyn...	Included		Active	Dynamics
SOC 2 for Azure (Previe...	Included		Active	Azure
SOC 2 for Dynamics 365...	Included		Active	Dynamics
∨ Premium templates (724)				
(NAIC) Standards for Sa...	Premium		Inactive	Universal
(NAIC) Standards for Sa...	Premium		Inactive	Microsoft
AICPA Privacy Manage...	Premium		Inactive	Universal
AICPA/CICA Generally A...	Premium		Inactive	
ARMA - Implementing t...	Premium		Inactive	

Save   Cancel

Figure 16.24: Available assessment templates

For this example, select the **ISO 27018:2019 for Azure** template and then add it by clicking **Save**:

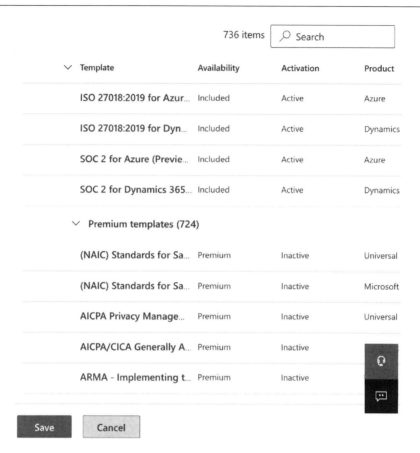

Figure 16.25: Saving an assessment template for an assessment

4. Under **Product, name and group**, select either **Choose existing product** or **Create new product**. In some cases, depending on the template you select, these choices will be grayed out, like in this example, as there are no choices to be made:

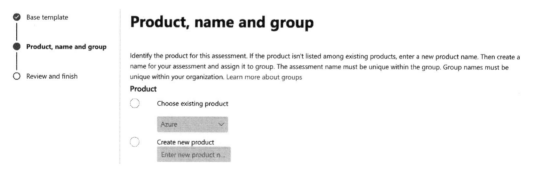

Figure 16.26: Entering the product, name ,and group details

5. Scroll down and enter **Assessment name** as ISO Assessments. Next, select either **Use existing group** or **Create new group**. For this example, choose **Create new group** and enter the group name ISO Assessments. Optionally, you can choose **Copy data from an existing group**. For this example, skip that option and click **Next**:

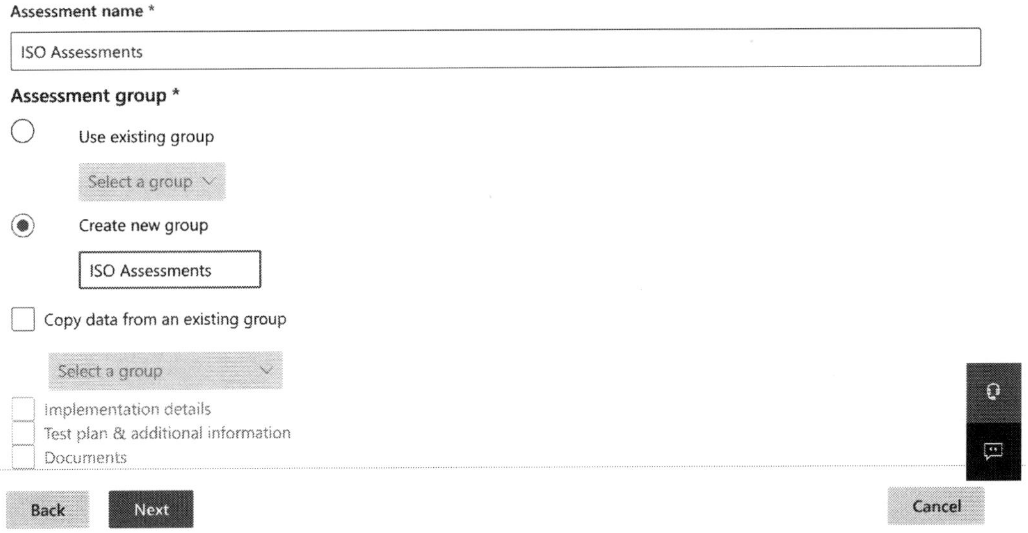

Assessment name *

ISO Assessments

Assessment group *

○   Use existing group

     Select a group ∨

◉   Create new group

     ISO Assessments

☐ Copy data from an existing group

     Select a group ∨

☐ Implementation details
☐ Test plan & additional information
☐ Documents

Back   Next   Cancel

Figure 16.27: Entering the assessment name and group details

6. Check your details on the **Review and finish** page, then click **Create assessment**:

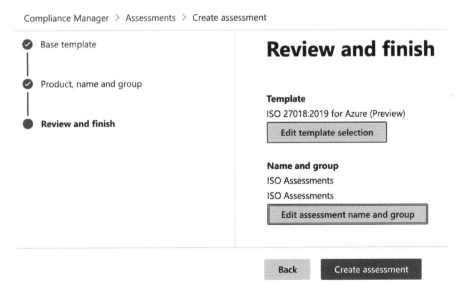

Figure 16.28: Creating the new assessment

7.   The assessment is now created. Click **Done**:

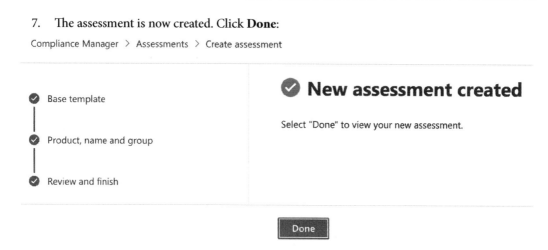

Figure 16.29: New assessment successfully created

You will be taken straight into your new assessment where you can immediately get to work by viewing progress, assessing the relevant controls, viewing and assigning improvement actions, and viewing Microsoft actions:

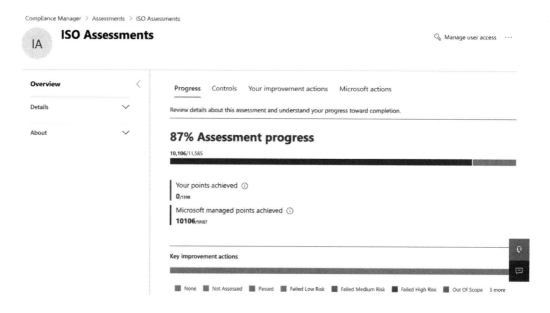

Figure 16.30: The Progress tab of the new assessment

Return to the list of assessments and you will now see the new one you just created. Note in the following screenshot that the **Group** column shows as **ISO Assessments** for the new assessments. Any new assessments that you create of a similar nature can be added to this group for ease of organization:

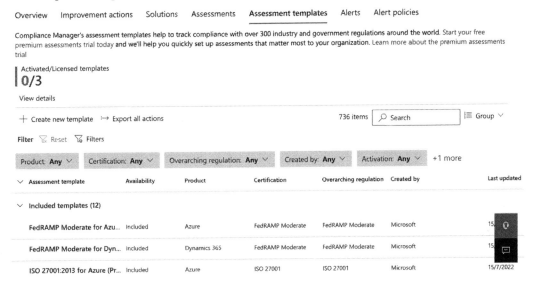

	Assessment	Status	Assessment progress	Your improvement act...	Microsoft actions	Group	Product
☐	ISO Assessments	Incomplete	87%	0 of 466 completed	564 of 567 completed	ISO Assessments	Azure
☐	Data Protection Baseline	Incomplete	48%	4 of 869 completed	685 of 710 completed	Default Group	Microsoft 365

Figure 16.31: New assessment shown with newly created group assignment

Creating assessments is a straightforward process and is a powerful way to start making an impact on your organization's compliance posture. You can also view the available templates for assessments from the **Assessment templates** tab. It will show you which templates in the list are licensed and activated, and you can quickly filter the views to find the templates that you need. You can also create new templates if required:

Overview   Improvement actions   Solutions   Assessments   **Assessment templates**   Alerts   Alert policies

Compliance Manager's assessment templates help to track compliance with over 300 industry and government regulations around the world. Start your free premium assessments trial today and we'll help you quickly set up assessments that matter most to your organization. Learn more about the premium assessments trial

Activated/Licensed templates
0/3

View details

+ Create new template   ⇥ Export all actions   736 items   🔍 Search   ≡ Group ∨

Filter   🏷 Reset   🏷 Filters

Product: **Any** ∨   Certification: **Any** ∨   Overarching regulation: **Any** ∨   Created by: **Any** ∨   Activation: **Any** ∨   +1 more

∨ Assessment template	Availability	Product	Certification	Overarching regulation	Created by	Last updated
∨ Included templates (12)						
FedRAMP Moderate for Azu...	Included	Azure	FedRAMP Moderate	FedRAMP Moderate	Microsoft	15,...
FedRAMP Moderate for Dyn...	Included	Dynamics 365	FedRAMP Moderate	FedRAMP Moderate	Microsoft	15,...
ISO 27001:2013 for Azure (Pr...	Included	Azure	ISO 27001	ISO 27001	Microsoft	15/7/2022

Figure 16.32: The Assessment templates tab

When creating your own new template, you can base it on a sample that you may download to create your own custom template. Alternatively, you can choose to extend one of the Microsoft templates to customize it for your needs:

Choose template type

Choose one of the options below to start creating your template. Create a custom template with your own contols and actions for building a custom assessment. Or, extend an existing Microsoft template with modifications to suit your needs. Learn more about custom templates

◯ **Create a custom template**

Download the sample file to see a formatted example. Fill out your template data using these instructions. You'll upload your file on the next screen.

◯ **Extend a Microsoft template**

Add controls, improvement actions, or dimensions to an existing Microsoft template. Extending a template ensures you'll receive updated guidance by Microsoft as regulations change. View the existing Microsoft templates

Figure 16.33: Creating an assessment template

In this section, we learned how to use Microsoft Purview Compliance Manager to manage regulatory compliance using improvement actions, assessments, and assessment templates. Next, we will examine how to use Microsoft Priva to implement privacy risk management policies.

Exploring Microsoft Priva

Microsoft Priva is one of the newer additions to the Microsoft Purview suite of products. Although privacy is a category of its own, strictly speaking, and not really under the banner of compliance as such, the Priva solutions are included within the Microsoft Purview compliance portal. This is an understandable decision from Microsoft considering that there is no dedicated privacy admin portal at this point in time. In the absence of a privacy admin center, Purview is the logical location for these solutions.

There are currently two Priva solutions: **Privacy Risk Management** and **Subject Rights Requests**. These solutions are not part of any existing subscription such as Microsoft 365 E5 and must be enabled as add-on licenses. First, let's take a look at Privacy Risk Management.

Implementing privacy risk management

Microsoft Priva **Privacy Risk Management** allows organizations to set up policies to identify any privacy risks in their Microsoft 365 environment and apply the required remediation. Risk Management policies provide the ability to do the following:

- Detect overexposed personal data
- Detect and limit the transfer of personal data across departments or regions
- Identify data minimization to reduce any unused personal data that your organization may be storing

To access and use Privacy Risk Management, complete the following steps:

1. Log in to the Microsoft Purview compliance portal at `https://compliance.microsoft.com` as a global admin or a member of the **Privacy Management** role group (which has access to all the features of Priva). Navigate to **Privacy risk management | Overview**:

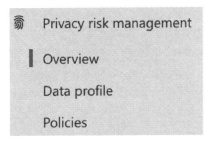

Figure 16.34: Accessing Privacy risk management from Microsoft Purview

If you are not licensed for Microsoft Priva, you will see the following message:

Figure 16.35: Message seen if not licensed for Microsoft Priva

However, once licensed, and with some policies set up, the **Privacy risk management overview** page will appear:

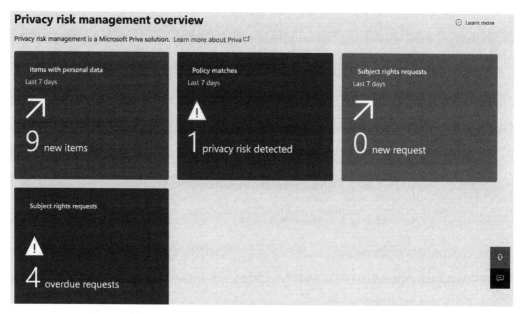

Figure 16.36: Privacy risk management overview screen

This page has tiles to show a high-level view of **Items with personal data**, and **Policy matches** over the past 7 days. There are also tiles relating to **Subject rights requests**, which we will examine in the next section.

2.   From the **Data profile** page, view the summary of the personal data type instances that are detected in your Microsoft 365 locations, such as **Teams**, **OneDrive**, **Exchange**, and **SharePoint**:

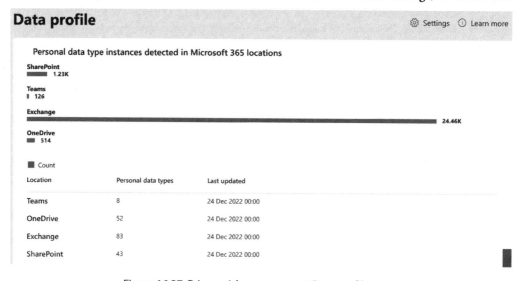

Figure 16.37: Privacy risk management Data profile page

3. Scroll down further to see a high-level view of the top personal data types across your organization and personal data type instances by region. Click on **Explore** beneath any of these views to examine more details within the content explorer:

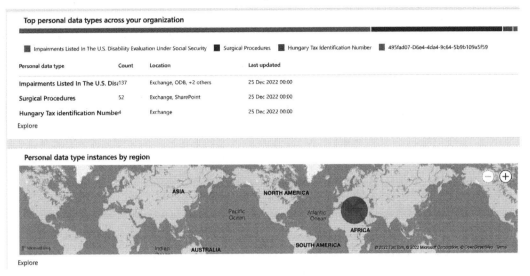

Figure 16.38: Privacy risk management Data profile page

4. Go to the **Policies** tab to view most of the detailed information and configuration for **Privacy risk management**. Here, you have tiles at the top of the page for **Policy status**, **Alerts**, and **Issues**. Scroll down to see the three default policies included in this solution. These policies are as follows:

- **Default data minimization**: This policy looks for data that has not been modified within a defined timeframe. When a match is detected, users can be notified by email with remediation instructions such as marking items for deletion, notifying the owners of the content, or tagging items to be further reviewed.

- **Default data transfers**: This policy detects personal data transfers outside of your organization or internal transfers between departments or geographic locations. If there is a policy match, you can configure user email notifications and they can remediate from within the email by making the content private or tagging items to be reviewed.

- **Default data overexposure**: This policy allows you to detect and manage organizational data stored in Microsoft 365 locations that are insufficiently secure, such as an internal SharePoint site being open to too many people, which could lead to a breach.

Select any of these three default policies to go to their settings:

Figure 16.39: Privacy risk management Policies page

5. Examine the **Overview** page for high-level policy status information. Go to the **Matched items** page to examine, filter, and export any matched items in an experience similar to that of eDiscovery Premium:

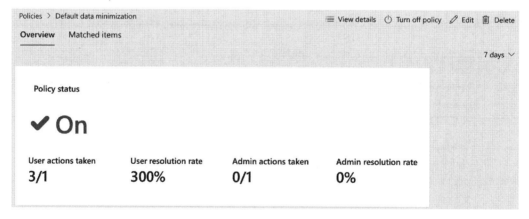

Figure 16.40: Default data minimization policy Overview page

6. Select the options at the top right of the page to view details of the policy, turn off the policy to deactivate it, edit the policy to make changes to the settings, or delete the policy completely.

When editing the policy, you can change things such as the description, the sensitive info types and classification groups that you want to monitor, the users and groups the policy will apply to, and much more by navigating through the options on the left of the screen:

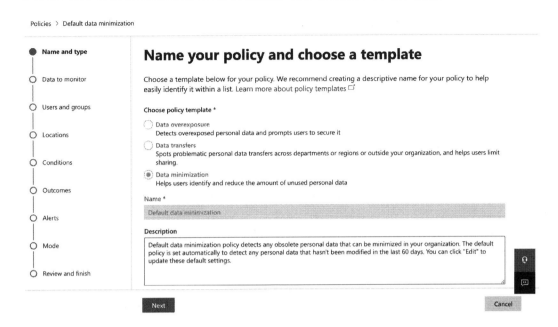

Figure 16.41: Editing a policy

An example of the type of notification email a user may receive in relation to privacy risk management is shown in the following screenshot:

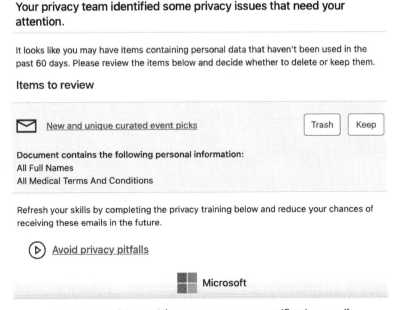

Figure 16.42: Privacy risk management user notification email

It is also possible to create your own policies, although the three default policies do contain most of the configuration settings you will need. Let's take a look at how this can be done.

Creating a custom policy

To create your own policy from the **Privacy risk management policies** page, follow these steps:

1. Click on the **Create a policy** button at the top right of the page:

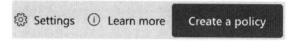

Figure 16.43: Creating a new Privacy risk management policy

2. You will be given the option to create your new policy from four templates. The first three are based on the three default policies that already exist. The fourth option is to create a **Custom** policy, which you will choose for this example:

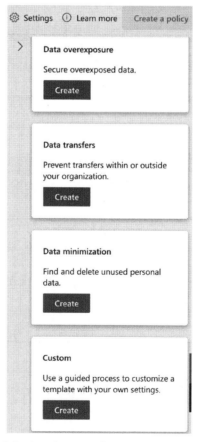

Figure 16.44: Selecting the type of Privacy risk management policy

3. When creating a custom policy, you will see the same options as you would when editing one of the existing policies. Choose between the three same templates of **Data overexposure**, **Data transfers**, and **Data minimization**:

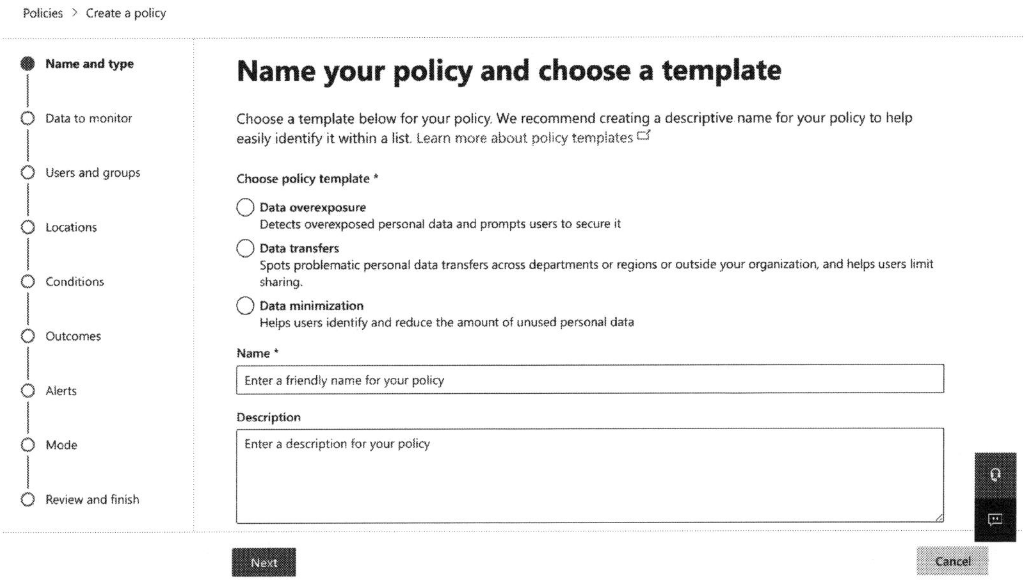
Policies > Create a policy
Name and type
Data to monitor
Users and groups
Locations
Conditions
Outcomes
Alerts
Mode
Review and finish
Name your policy and choose a template
Choose a template below for your policy. We recommend creating a descriptive name for your policy to help easily identify it within a list. Learn more about policy templates
Choose policy template *
Data overexposure
Detects overexposed personal data and prompts users to secure it
Data transfers
Spots problematic personal data transfers across departments or regions or outside your organization, and helps users limit sharing.
Data minimization
Helps users identify and reduce the amount of unused personal data
Name *
Enter a friendly name for your policy
Description
Enter a description for your policy
Next
Cancel

Figure 16.45: Creating a new custom Privacy risk management policy

From this, you have now seen that there are limited combinations for the types of policies you can create apart from the three standard templates. The value in creating your own custom policies is tied to whether you need to specify combinations of sensitive info types with certain users or groups or with certain Microsoft 365 locations such as Exchange mailboxes, Teams, SharePoint sites, or OneDrive folders.

Privacy Risk Management is a powerful feature, however, and is one that will undoubtedly continue to develop and receive further functionality and investment from Microsoft.

In the following section, we will take a look at Microsoft Priva Subject Rights Requests.

Implementing and managing Subject Rights Requests with Microsoft Priva

The other component of Microsoft Priva is **Subject Rights Requests**, which is a solution designed to reduce the effort and complexity required from organizations to respond to data subject inquiries.

You can manage your subject rights requests in Microsoft Purview by completing the following steps:

1. Log in to the Microsoft Purview compliance portal at `https://compliance.microsoft.com` as a global admin or a member of the **Privacy Management** role group (which has access to all the features of Priva). Navigate to **Subject rights requests** from the menu pane on the left:

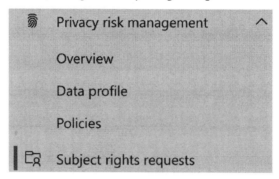

Figure 16.46: Accessing Microsoft Priva Subject rights requests in Microsoft Purview

2. If you are not licensed for **Subject rights requests**, you will see the options shown in the following screenshot, where you can buy the licensing required:

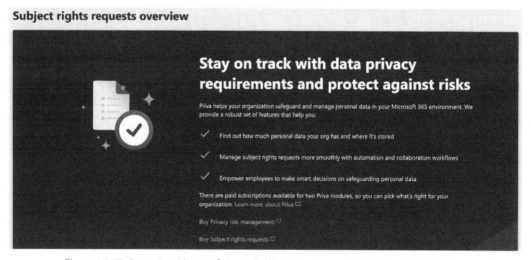

Figure 16.47: Accessing Microsoft Priva Subject rights requests in Microsoft Purview

3. Click on **Buy Subject rights requests** to go straight to the **Purchase services** section of the Microsoft 365 admin center. You can also access this by navigating to `https://admin.microsoft.com`.

    As shown in the following figure, the purchase of 1 Priva Subject Rights Requests SKU provides you with the ability to create 10 requests:

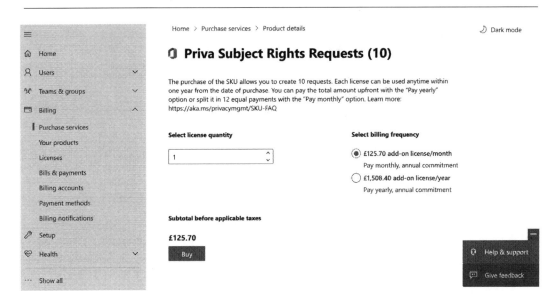

Figure 16.48: Options to purchase Priva Subject Rights Requests

4. In some instances, it is possible to acquire a trial of Subject Rights Requests. There is also the option to provision a demo tenant—which you can do if you have a Microsoft 365 account with a Microsoft Partner or if you are a Microsoft MVP—to enable the provisioning of the trial options shown in the following screenshot. Demo tenants can be created if you have access to demos.microsoft.com, as shown in the following screenshot:

Add-ons

Get even more value from the subscriptions you already have.

Privacy Management - subject rights request (50) Trial

Helps automate and manage subject rights requests at scale. This trial license allows you to create subject rights requests for free. You can create upto 50 subje...

Trial

Details   ☐ Compare

Priva Subject Rights Requests (10)

The purchase of the SKU allows you to create 10 requests. Each license can be used anytime within one year from the date of purchase. You can pay the total...

From $166.65 add-on licenses/month

Details   ☐ Compare

Privacy Management - subject rights request (50) Trial

Helps automate and manage subject rights requests at scale. This trial license allows you to create subject rights requests for free. You can create upto 50 subje...

Trial

Details   ☐ Compare

Priva Subject Rights Requests (100)

The purchase of the SKU allows you to create 100 requests. Each license can be used anytime within one year from the date of purchase. You can pay the total...

From $1,666.65 add-on licenses/month

Details   ☐ Compare

Priva Subject Rights Requests (1)

The purchase of the SKU allows you to create 1 request. Each license can be used anytime within one year from the date of purchase. You can pay the total...

From $16.65 add-on licenses/month

Details   ☐ Compare

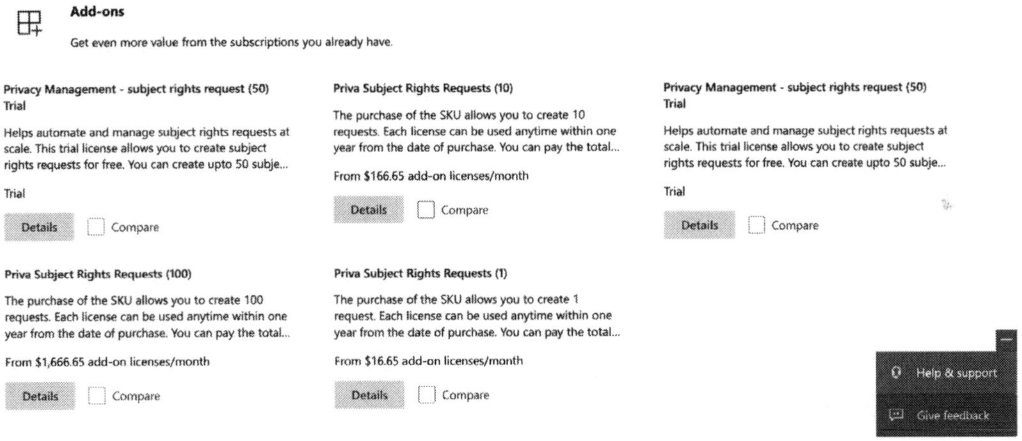

Figure 16.49: Trial options for Microsoft Priva Subject Rights Requests

5.   When you enable a trial for Priva Subject Rights Requests, you do not assign any licenses for users. The service is enabled tenant-wide, and when you return to the Microsoft Purview compliance portal, you will have Subject Rights Requests available:

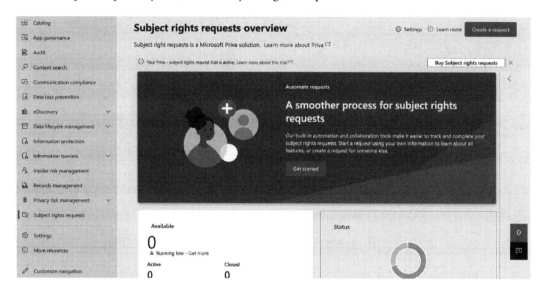

Figure 16.50: Subject rights requests overview page in Microsoft Purview

6.   Choose **Create a request** to start your first Subject rights request. The **Data request templates** flyout page will appear. You can choose to base your request on one of the following templates:

- **Data access**: To provide a summary of content containing personal data related to the data subject

- **Data export**: To provide a summary and exported list of content containing personal data related to the data subject

- **Data deletion (Preview)**: To facilitate the deletion of content related to the data subject

- **Data tagged for further action**: To tag files for follow-up actions, such as data updates, on identified items

- **Custom**: Use a guided process to complete the full request creation experience

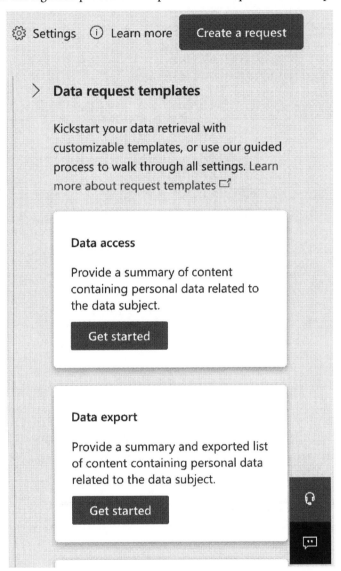

Figure 16.51: Data request templates

For this example, select **Data access**. A flyout page will appear:

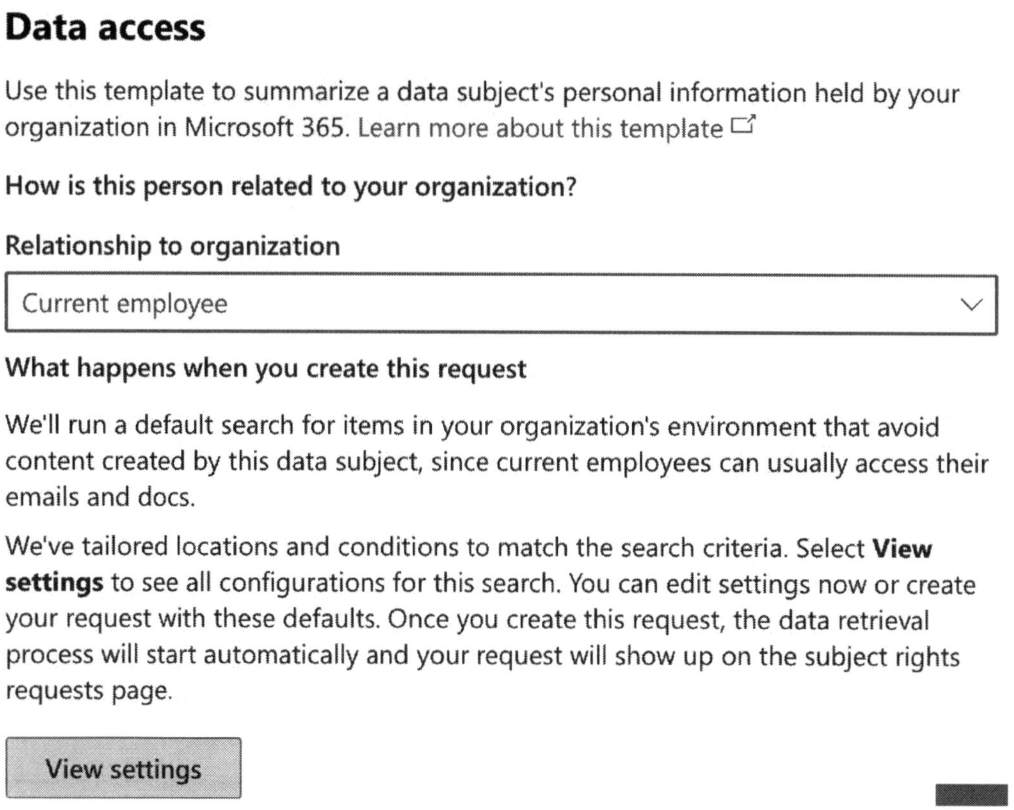

Data access

Use this template to summarize a data subject's personal information held by your organization in Microsoft 365. Learn more about this template ⬀

How is this person related to your organization?

Relationship to organization

Current employee	⌄

What happens when you create this request

We'll run a default search for items in your organization's environment that avoid content created by this data subject, since current employees can usually access their emails and docs.

We've tailored locations and conditions to match the search criteria. Select **View settings** to see all configurations for this search. You can edit settings now or create your request with these defaults. Once you create this request, the data retrieval process will start automatically and your request will show up on the subject rights requests page.

View settings

Figure 16.52: Data access template wizard

7. First, choose what type of data subject you need to add. This will depend on the nature of the request of course. Click the dropdown for **Relationship to organization** to see the options. The choices are as follows:

    - **Customer**
    - **Current employee**
    - **Former employee**
    - **Prospective employee**
    - **Other**

    For details on these options, you can refer to the *Further reading* section. For this example, choose **Current employee**:

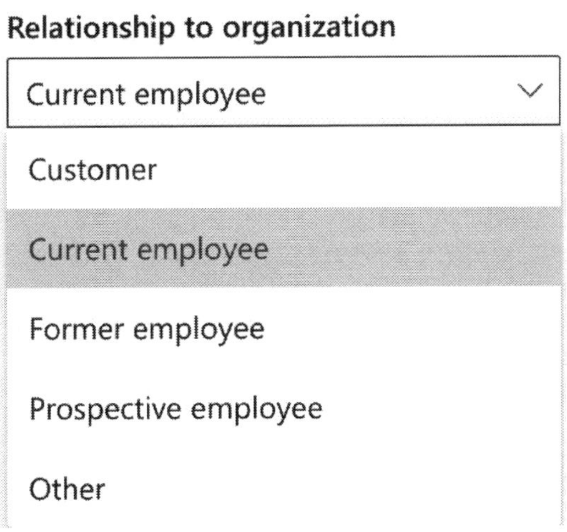

Relationship to organization

| Current employee ⌄ |

Customer

Current employee

Former employee

Prospective employee

Other

Figure 16.53: Organization relationship options

8.   Scroll down and click **View settings**:

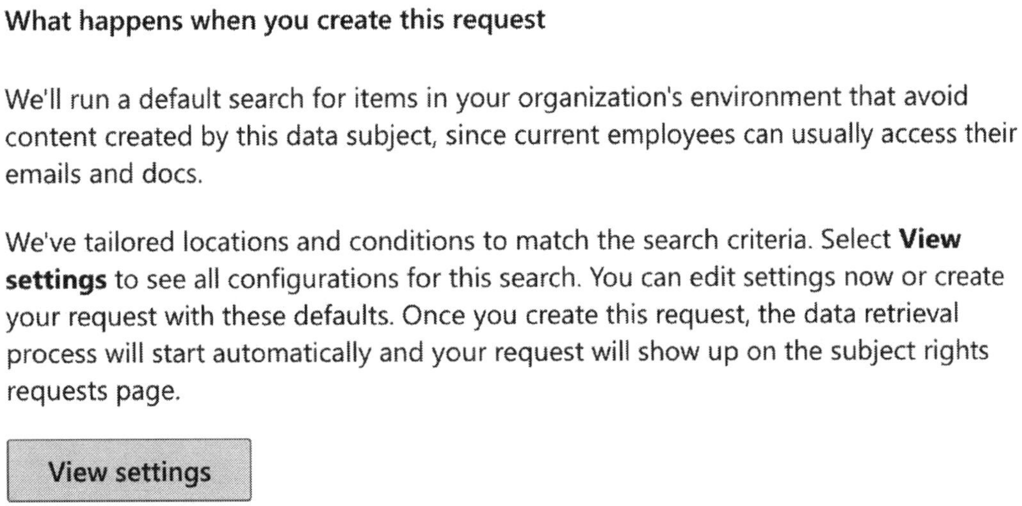

What happens when you create this request

We'll run a default search for items in your organization's environment that avoid content created by this data subject, since current employees can usually access their emails and docs.

We've tailored locations and conditions to match the search criteria. Select **View settings** to see all configurations for this search. You can edit settings now or create your request with these defaults. Once you create this request, the data retrieval process will start automatically and your request will show up on the subject rights requests page.

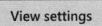

Figure 16.54: View settings for the request

9.   Now click on **Edit settings**:

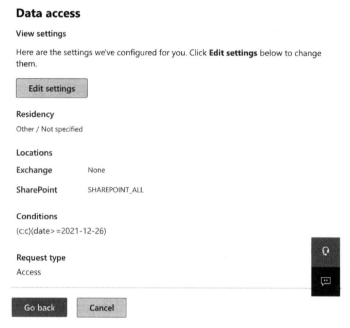

Figure 16.55: Edit settings for the request

10. This launches the full request wizard. Here, confirm the **First name**, **Last name**, and **Email address** details for the data subject, along with how the subject is connected to the organization. For this example, a user within the organization as a current employee, named `Adele Vance`, is set as the subject. Click **Next**:

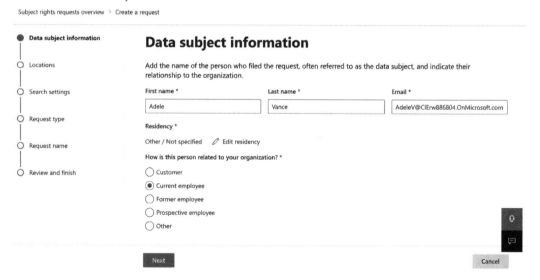

Figure 16.56: Entering Data subject information

11. On the **Locations** page, choose the **Exchange** and **SharePoint** locations you want to include. Exchange includes Exchange mailboxes and individual or group Teams chats, while SharePoint includes SharePoint sites, OneDrive for Business sites, and Teams channels. Click **Next**:

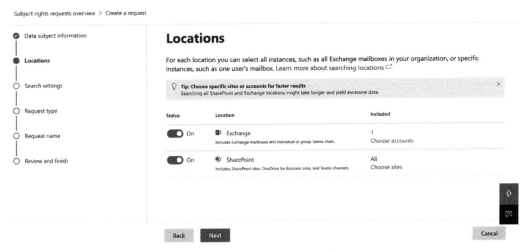

Figure 16.57: Choosing locations for the request

12. Click on **Define search settings for this request**. The options you select here will determine additional responses you need to enter as you continue through this wizard. Select **Refine your search** to provide additional search conditions to refine your results. Select **Include content authored by the data subject** to include files created by or uploaded to SharePoint by the data subject. However, this option may result in the return of significantly more data.

For this example, the remaining options are not selected. These are **Include all versions of items**, which would add all versions of SharePoint items instead of just current items, and **Get an estimate first**, which you would select to see how much data is expected to be found before committing to the full process. Click **Next**:

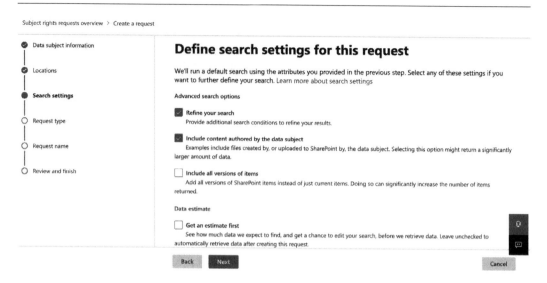

Figure 16.58: Defining search settings for the request

13. Now, add personal attributes such as names, nicknames, and email addresses:

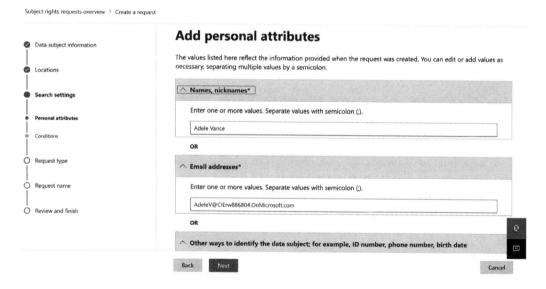

Figure 16.59: Adding personal attributes

14. Scroll down and optionally select other ways to identify the data subject, such as ID or phone numbers. You can also add an **Address** value. Once you have completed the required fields, click **Next**:

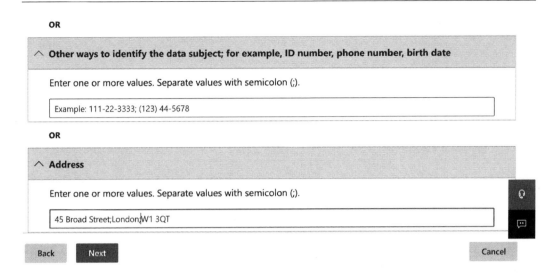

Figure 16.60: Adding more personal attributes

15. On the **Set conditions for the search** page, choose the timeframe you wish to work with. Click on **Add condition** to further tailor the conditions:

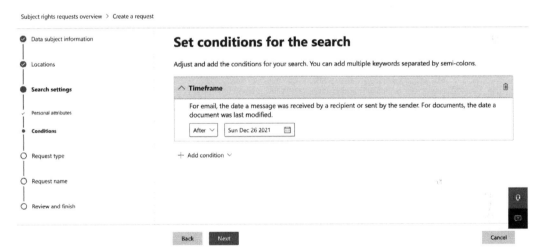

Figure 16.61: Setting conditions for the search

16. In the **Add conditions** flyout pane, choose from the following conditions:

- **Item name**
- **Retention labels**
- **Participants**

- **Recipients**
- **Sender**
- **Subject**
- **Title**
- **Shared externally**
- **Personal data type**
- **Created**

In this example, no extra conditions are selected. Click **Next**:

Item name

Retention labels

Participants

Recipients

Sender

Subject

Title

Shared externally

Personal data type

Created

$+$ Add condition $\vee$

Figure 16.62: Setting conditions for the search

17. Next, the **Select the type of request** section appears. This was already selected earlier in the process in *step 6*, but you can change your selections here if needed. For this example, leave the settings the same as earlier, with **Access** selected as the type of request. Under **Does this request relate to a specific data privacy regulation?**, click **No/not specified**. Finally, choose a date deadline till which the request will run. Click **Next**:

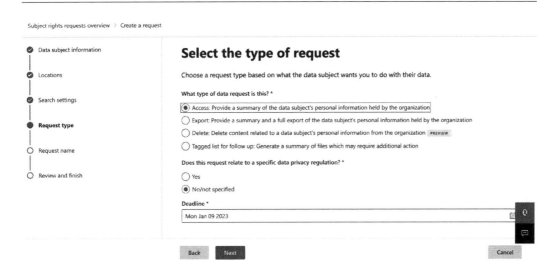

Figure 16.63: Setting the request type

18. Next, enter a name and description for the request. Click **Next**:

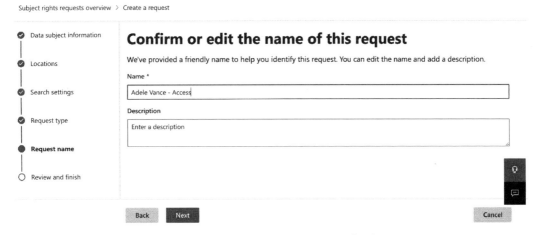

Figure 16.64: Setting the name and description for the request

19. Review the choices you have made and click **Create request**:

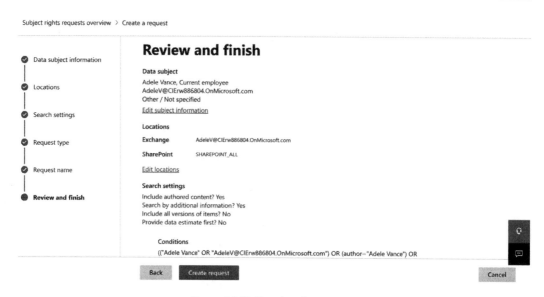

Figure 16.65: Creating the request

20. The request is submitted. Click **Done** to complete the wizard:

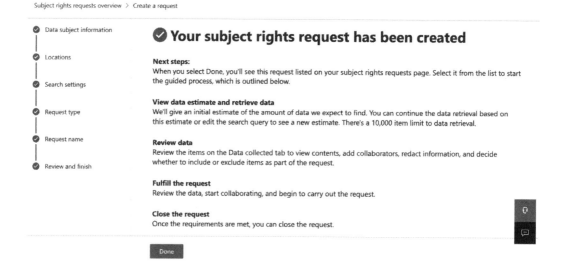

Figure 16.66: Subject rights request successfully created

The request will be shown at the bottom of the **Subject rights requests overview** page. Initially, its **Stage** value will appear as **Data estimate**:

Request name	Status	Stage	Origin	Deadline	Days remaining
☐ Adele Vance - Ac... ⋮	● Active	Data estimate	Microsoft 365	Jan 9, 2023 5:57 PM	14

Figure 16.67: Subject rights request shown on the overview page

The request will progress through the various stages, as illustrated in *Figure 16.68*.

21. Click to open your Subject Rights Request, and it will be displayed as shown in the following screenshot. Here, you can track the progress of the request. Refresh the page or keep checking back to see the progress of the request:

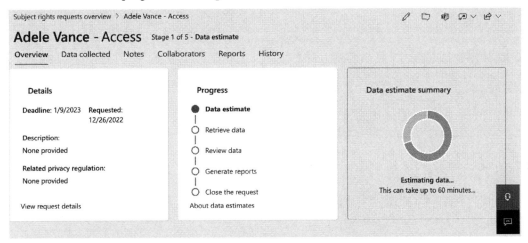

Figure 16.68: Tracking the progress of the Subject rights request

22. When the **Retrieve data** stage has completed, the progress will move to **Review data**. At this stage, start examining the results by clicking on the **Data collected** tab:

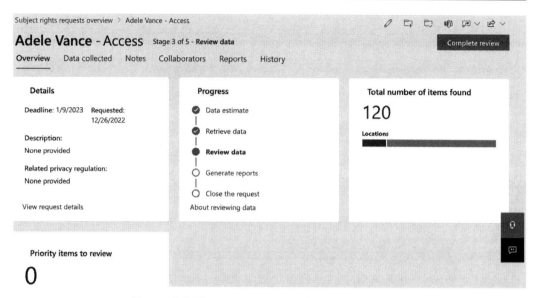

Figure 16.69: The request is now at the review data stage

23. In the **Data collected** tab, highlight each item to see details. Note that the Word document highlighted contains an address that matches the criteria entered earlier in the process:

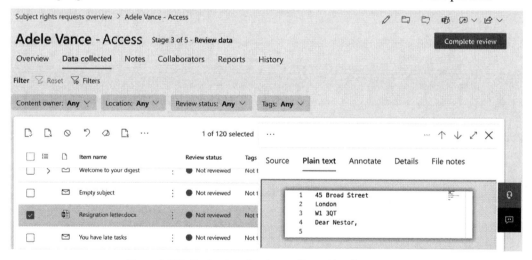

Figure 16.70: Reviewing the data collected by the request

24. Click the ellipsis next to an item to see the options you can apply to it. These are **Include**, **Exclude**, **Not a match**, **Reset status**, **Apply tags**, and **Download**. For the item with the matching address, choose **Include**:

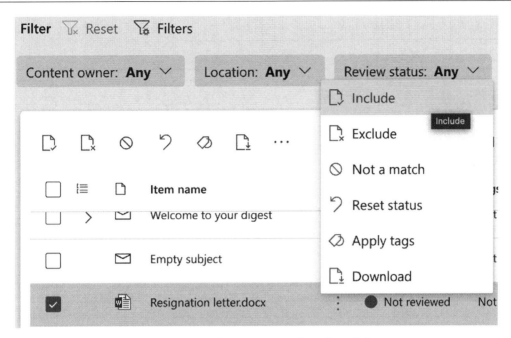

Figure 16.71: Applying actions to the collected data

25. After selecting the **Include** option, enter notes as shown in the following figure. Click **Submit**:

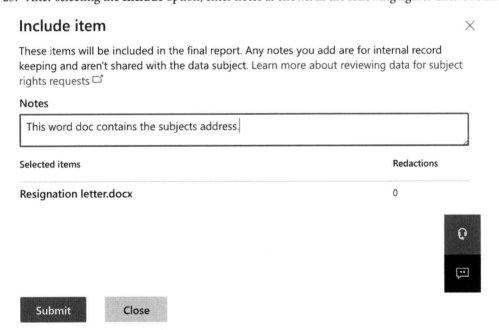

Figure 16.72: Entering notes and submitting the item for inclusion

26. In the **Review status** column of the data collected, the item will now be marked as **Included**:

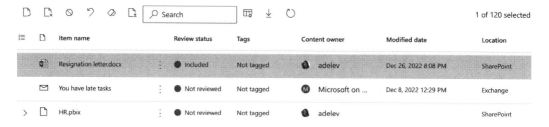

Figure 16.73: Item shown as Included in the Review status column

27. Click the **Notes** tab to add or view any case notes connected with the request:

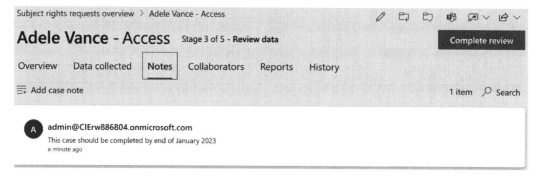

Figure 16.74: Adding or viewing case notes for the request

28. Navigate to the **Collaborators** tab to add individuals with whom you need to collaborate as part of the case. Click **Add collaborator** to include those you require:

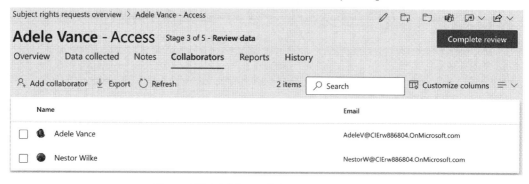

Figure 16.75: Adding collaborators to the case

When you add collaborators, a team is created in Microsoft Teams with the collaborators as members of that team:

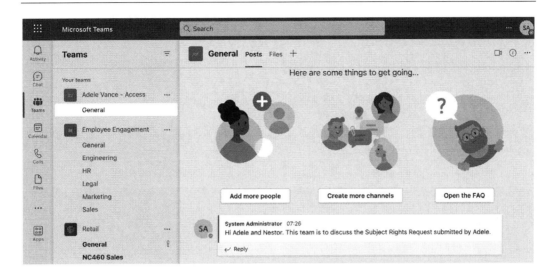

Figure 16.76: Team created for collaborators

29. Go to the **Reports** tab to see all the actions you have taken with the data collected, such as files tagged for follow-up, included, excluded, or tagged as a false positive:

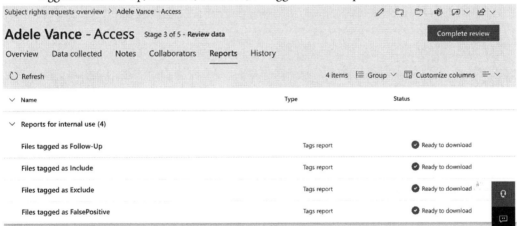

Figure 16.77: Viewing items in the Reports tab

30. Click on an item in the **Reports** tab to see more details and download information about the content:

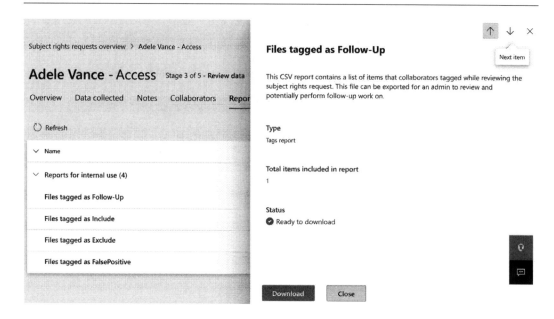

Figure 16.78: Reports tab item detail

31. Go to the **History** tab to see the complete history of actions taken during the case, such as adding team members and notes:

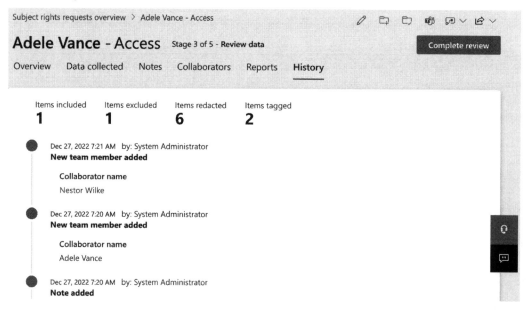

Figure 16.79: Viewing the History tab

32. The toolbar shown at the top right of the Subject Rights Request provides you with additional options you have in relation to the case. Here, you can edit the case, import files, close the request, collaborate in Teams, manage Power Automate flows, share the content in an email, or copy a link to the content as needed:

Figure 16.80: Toolbar options for the case

33. Beneath the toolbar is the **Complete review** button. Click this when you are ready to complete the case:

Figure 16.81: Completing the review

34. Enter notes to provide details on the case and click **Complete review**:

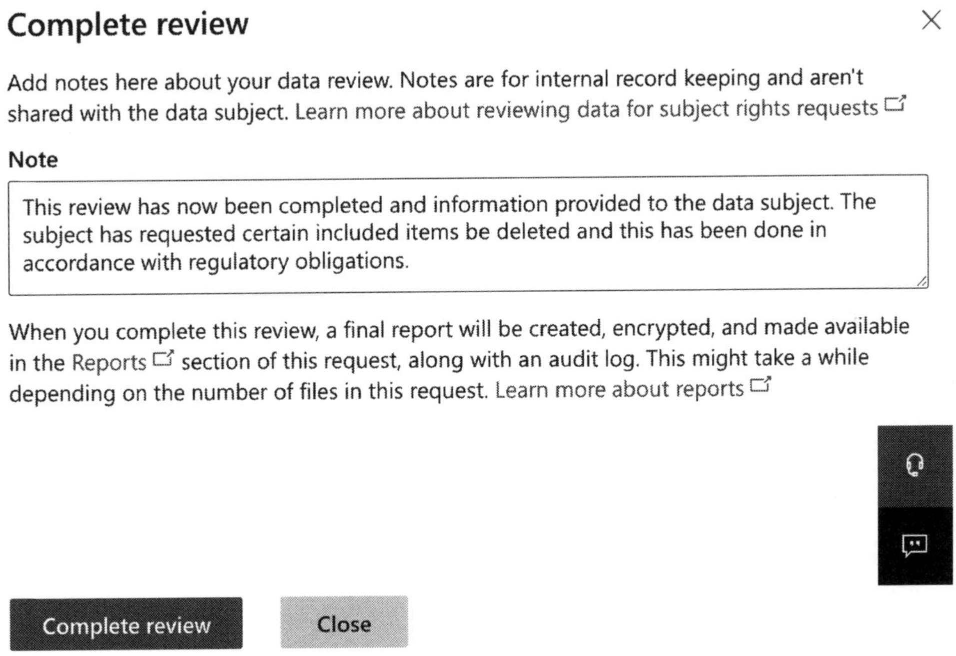

Complete review   ✕

Add notes here about your data review. Notes are for internal record keeping and aren't shared with the data subject. Learn more about reviewing data for subject rights requests ⤢

Note

> This review has now been completed and information provided to the data subject. The subject has requested certain included items be deleted and this has been done in accordance with regulatory obligations.

When you complete this review, a final report will be created, encrypted, and made available in the Reports ⤢ section of this request, along with an audit log. This might take a while depending on the number of files in this request. Learn more about reports ⤢

Complete review   Close

Figure 16.82: Completing the review

35. Go back to the **Overview** screen. The progress of the subject rights request will now appear at the **Generate reports** stage:

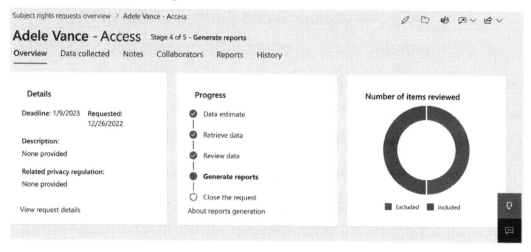

Figure 16.83: Subject rights request progress shown at the Generate reports stage

36. Close the request from the toolbar by clicking the **Close the request** button:

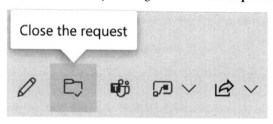

Figure 16.84: Closing the request

37. Enter any notes you wish to add and click **Close the request**:

Close the request   ✕

When you close this subject rights request, a final report will be created, encrypted, and made available in the Reports ⊏ section of this request. This might take a while depending on the number of files in this request. An audit log will also be available in the Reports ⊏ section. Learn more ⊏

Add notes here about closing this request. Notes are for internal record keeping and aren't shared with the data subject.

Note

> This request is now complete.

[Close the request]   [Cancel]

Figure 16.85: Closing the request

38. The **Overview** screen will now show the case at the **Close the request** stage:

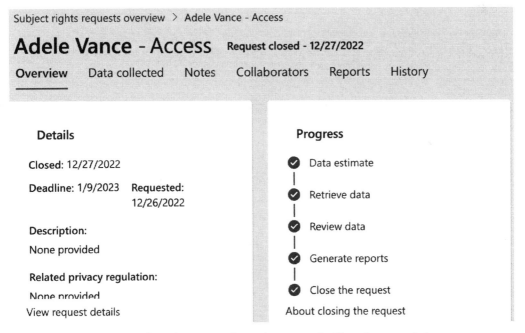

Figure 16.86: Overview screen shows the case at the Close the request stage

This concludes the process of creating, managing, processing, and closing a Subject Rights Request within Microsoft Priva in the Microsoft Purview compliance portal. This is a powerful tool for any organization that needs to respond to such requests from data subjects and is very simple and intuitive to use.

In this section, we were introduced to Microsoft Priva Subject Rights Requests. We learned how to license Subject Rights Requests, and how to create a case, analyze and process data, and collaborate with relevant participants while managing the case to conclusion.

Summary

This chapter introduced the principles of managing regulatory and privacy requirements using the features and solutions available in Microsoft Purview. We learned how to plan an organizational compliance journey in adherence to regulatory standards such as GDPR. We also learned about the capabilities of the Microsoft Purview Compliance Manager and how it can be used to work with improvement actions, assessments, and assessment templates to improve your compliance posture and score. Finally, we learned how to use Microsoft Priva to manage our privacy requirements in Microsoft 365 and how to create, manage, and edit policies to minimize and manage risks such as data exposure. We also examined how, with Subject Rights Requests, we can respond to requests from data subjects regarding any personal data that our organization may be storing about them.

The next chapter will cover the principles of managing the **Insider Risk Management** controls and policies in Microsoft Purview and how to implement features including Customer Lockbox, Communication Compliance policies, Insider Risk policies, Information Barrier policies, and Privileged Access Management.

Questions

1. Which of the following is not one of the options within an assessment in Compliance Manager?

    A. Microsoft actions

    B. Controls

    C. Custom actions

    D. Your improvement actions

2. Which of the following are available policy templates in Microsoft Priva Privacy Risk Management (choose two)?

    A. Data compliance

    B. Data management

    C. Data overexposure

    D. Data minimization

3. True or false? Microsoft Priva Subject Rights Requests licensing must be allocated on a per-user basis:

    A. True

    B. False

4. What should you create to batch assessments together?

    A. An improvement action

    B. A group

    C. A product

    D. A template

5. True or false? Users with the Privacy Management role group can access all the features of Microsoft Priva:

    A. True

    B. False

6. Which of the following are types of assessment templates (choose two)?

    A. Premium templates

    B. Included templates

    C. Standard templates

    D. Advanced templates

7. True or false? Improvement actions can be assigned to other users to test and implement:

    A. True

    B. False

8. How many hours can action points in an improvement action take?

    A. Up to 48 hours

    B. Up to 12 hours

    C. Up to 24 hours

    D. Up to 96 hours

9. True or false? When running a Subject Rights Request, it is possible to run a custom request:

    A. True

    B. False

10. When working with a Subject Rights Request, which of the following is *not* one of the main toolbar options?

    A. Edit the case

    B. Forward the case

    C. Close the request

    D. Collaborate in teams

Further reading

Please refer to the following links for more information:

- *Microsoft compliance offerings*: https://learn.microsoft.com/en-us/compliance/regulatory/offering-home?view=o365-worldwide

- *Microsoft 365 GDPR action plan – Top priorities for your first 30 days, 90 days, and beyond*: https://learn.microsoft.com/en-us/compliance/regulatory/gdpr-action-plan?WT.mc_id=M365-MVP-4039827&view=o365-worldwide

- *General Data Protection Regulation Summary*: https://learn.microsoft.com/en-us/compliance/regulatory/gdpr?WT.mc_id=M365-MVP-4039827&view=o365-worldwide

- *Office 365 Data Subject Requests for the GDPR and CCPA*: https://learn.microsoft.com/en-us/compliance/regulatory/gdpr-dsr-Office365?WT.mc_id=M365-MVP-4039827&view=o365-worldwide

- *Get started with Compliance Manager*: https://learn.microsoft.com/en-us/microsoft-365/compliance/compliance-manager-setup?WT.mc_id=M365-MVP-4039827&view=o365-worldwide

- *Build and manage assessments in Compliance Manager*: https://learn.microsoft.com/en-us/microsoft-365/compliance/compliance-manager-assessments?WT.mc_id=M365-MVP-4039827&view=o365-worldwide

- *Working with improvement actions in Compliance Manager*: https://learn.microsoft.com/en-us/microsoft-365/compliance/compliance-manager-improvement-actions?WT.mc_id=M365-MVP-4039827&view=o365-worldwide

- *Learn about Priva Privacy Risk Management*: https://learn.microsoft.com/en-us/privacy/priva/risk-management?WT.mc_id=ES-MVP-4039827

- *Learn about Priva Subject Rights Requests*: https://learn.microsoft.com/en-us/privacy/priva/subject-rights-requests?WT.mc_id=ES-MVP-40398

17

Managing Insider Risk Solutions in Microsoft 365

All too often, security and compliance administrators focus their attention on threats from outside their organization. Oftentimes, however, threats can emanate from within, from either malicious or unwitting insiders who have access to the data that you store within Microsoft 365 locations and services. It is equally important to protect your data against such **insider threats**.

In this chapter, we will explain the principles of managing the **Insider Risk Management** solutions included with Microsoft Purview. You will learn how to implement features including **Customer Lockbox**, which is a solution that ensures that Microsoft cannot access your content without your explicit approval. You will also learn how **communication compliance policies** can be used to protect employees from harassment and threatening behavior and how **Insider Risk Management policies** can be deployed to prevent data from being put at risk by malicious insiders, such as departing employees looking to gain a competitive advantage in their next role. Additionally, we will show you how **information barrier policies** can be used to segment information between geographical and organizational boundaries and how Privileged Access Management is used to allow granular access control over privileged admin tasks within Microsoft 365 and protect against breaches that use existing privileged admin access to sensitive data or critical configuration settings.

After reading this chapter, you will understand how to protect your Microsoft 365 environment from a range of insider threats.

We will cover these topics in the following order:

- Implementing Customer Lockbox
- Implementing and managing communication compliance policies
- Implementing and managing Insider Risk Management policies
- Implementing and managing information barrier policies
- Implementing and managing Privileged Access Management

Implementing Customer Lockbox

Customer Lockbox is a feature that provides an extra layer of control to organizations when they need to contact Microsoft for support and Microsoft needs to access the Microsoft 365 tenant to perform troubleshooting. It works by giving the organization the ability to provide explicit access authorization to Microsoft. Implementing Customer Lockbox ensures that the organization has full control and can be an indicator that they follow compliance regulations such as FedRAMP or HIPAA.

To benefit from and use Customer Lockbox, an organization must have some flavor of E5 licensing in place. The license options that provide the rights for a user to benefit from Customer Lockbox are the following:

- Office 365 E5

- Microsoft 365 E5

- Microsoft 365 E5 Compliance

- Microsoft 365 F5 Security & Compliance

- Microsoft 365 E5 Insider Risk Management

With Customer Lockbox, Microsoft support can request access to data in Exchange Online, SharePoint Online, OneDrive for Business, and Microsoft Teams, but they will need an organization's explicit approval to do so, and the activity can be recorded and audited. To implement Customer Lockbox, you must complete the following steps:

1. Log in to the Microsoft 365 admin center at `https://admin.microsoft.com` as either a global administrator or a user who has the Customer Lockbox access approver role assigned and navigate to **Settings | Org settings | Security & privacy**. Click **Customer lockbox**:

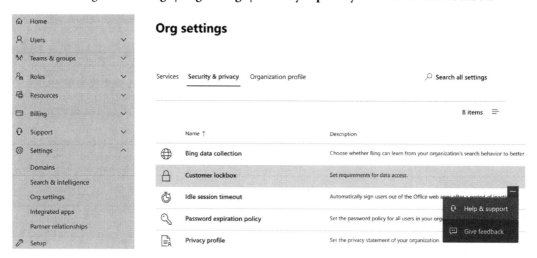

Figure 17.1: Customer lockbox in the Microsoft 365 admin center

2. Check the box next to **Require approval for all data access requests** and click **Save**:

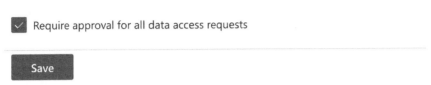

Figure 17.2: Requiring approval for all data access requests

3. Once activated, anyone who has the Customer Lockbox access approver role can respond to Customer Lockbox requests from Microsoft by navigating to **Support | Customer Lockbox Requests** in the Microsoft 365 admin center:

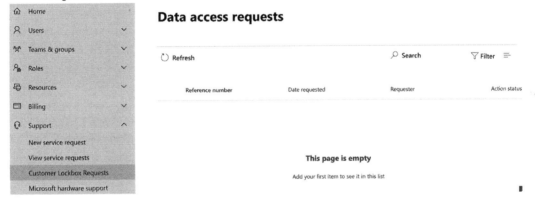

Figure 17.3: Customer Lockbox Requests

Any requests from Microsoft will show on the **Data access requests** page shown in the preceding screenshot, and Customer Lockbox access approvers can open the requests and either approve or deny them as appropriate. If the request is denied or no response from the organization is received within 12 hours, the request will expire.

4. Once approved, a Microsoft engineer has a four-hour window with access to the content to troubleshoot the issue. When the four hours are up, the access is revoked. Any activities carried out by the Microsoft engineer will be logged in the audit log, and you can search for and review these audit records. Any such results in the audit log will be visible in the **User** column of the search results as **Microsoft Operator**.

Customer Lockbox is simple to implement and use and gives you an extra layer of compliance in situations where you need support from Microsoft. Next, we will look at Communication Compliance policies.

Implementing and managing Communication Compliance policies

Communication Compliance is a Microsoft Purview feature that is part of the insider risk solution. It is designed to minimize communication risks in your organization and helps you to detect and manage inappropriate messages in your organization. Communication Compliance is straightforward to implement thanks to a set of pre-defined policies provided by Microsoft that enable you to check for internal and external communications and investigate policy matches against Exchange email, Microsoft Teams, Yammer, or third-party communications.

To manage Communication Compliance and configure initial permissions, you need to be either a **Global Administrator**, **Compliance Administrator**, or part of the **Organization Management**, **Communication Compliance**, or **Communication Compliance Admins** role group.

To use Communication Compliance in your Microsoft 365 tenant, you can use the following subscriptions:

- Microsoft 365 E5

- Microsoft 365 E3 and the Microsoft 365 E5 Compliance add-on

- Microsoft 365 E3 and the Microsoft 365 E5 Insider Risk Management add-on

- Office 365 Enterprise E5

- Office 365 Enterprise E3 subscription and the Office 365 Advanced Compliance add-on (no longer available for new subscriptions)

Communication compliance settings and policies for Microsoft 365 organizations can be created in the Microsoft Purview compliance portal at `https://compliance.microsoft.com` by completing the following steps:

1. From the **Solutions** section of the left menu pane, choose **Communication compliance**. The first thing you see is a helpful checklist of items to get you started. You can work through these and mark them as complete when done:

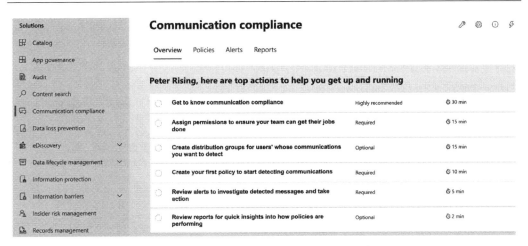

Figure 17.4: Communication compliance in Microsoft Purview

2. The first required step is **Assign permissions to ensure your team can get their jobs done**. When you select this item, you will see the flyout panel illustrated in the following screenshot. It advises that anyone in your organization who needs to be responsible for managing communication compliance features must be assigned the relevant permissions. Click **Go to Permissions** and add the relevant users to the required role groups:

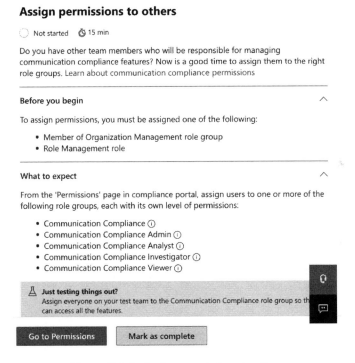

Figure 17.5: Assigning permissions to others

3. An optional but recommended step is to create distribution groups to which communication compliance policies will apply. These groups will contain the users whose communications need to be monitored. Click **Create distribution groups**:

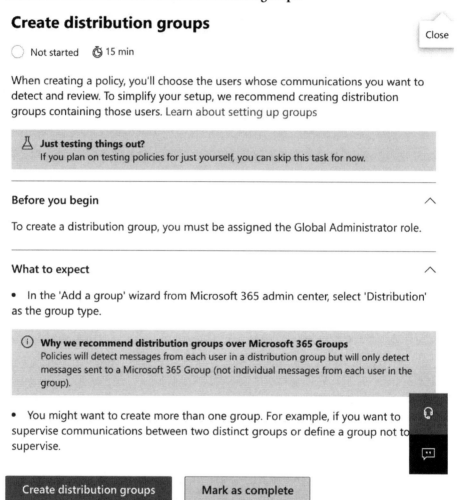

Create distribution groups

○ Not started   ⏱ 15 min

When creating a policy, you'll choose the users whose communications you want to detect and review. To simplify your setup, we recommend creating distribution groups containing those users. Learn about setting up groups

🧪 **Just testing things out?**
If you plan on testing policies for just yourself, you can skip this task for now.

Before you begin   ︿

To create a distribution group, you must be assigned the Global Administrator role.

What to expect   ︿

• In the 'Add a group' wizard from Microsoft 365 admin center, select 'Distribution' as the group type.

ⓘ **Why we recommend distribution groups over Microsoft 365 Groups**
Policies will detect messages from each user in a distribution group but will only detect messages sent to a Microsoft 365 Group (not individual messages from each user in the group).

• You might want to create more than one group. For example, if you want to supervise communications between two distinct groups or define a group not to supervise.

[Create distribution groups]   [Mark as complete]

Figure 17.6: Create distribution groups

4. You will be taken to a wizard to create a distribution group. For this example, a group was created called `Communication Compliance Marketing team`:

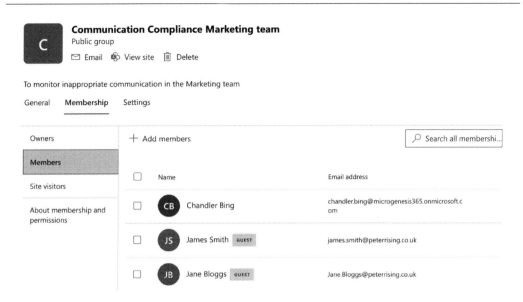

Figure 17.7: Creating a group

5.   The next required step is **Create your first policy**. At this stage of the example, let's switch away from the initial wizard and navigate to the **Policies** tab:

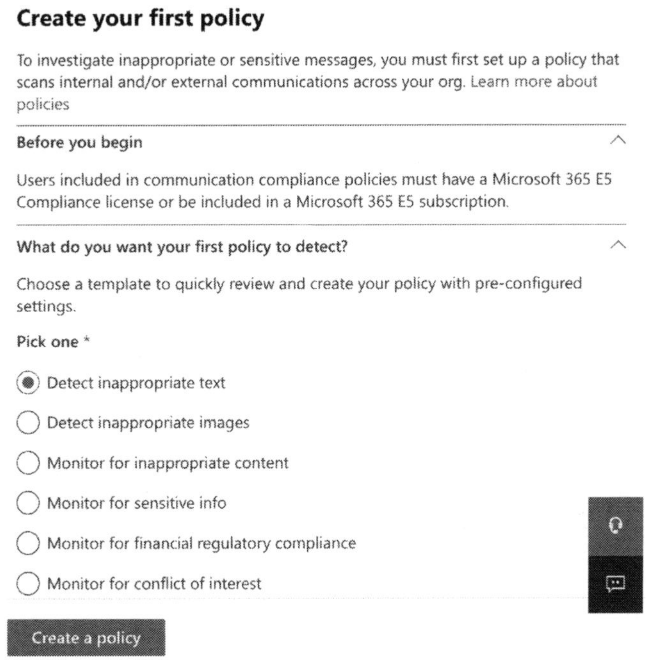

Figure 17.8: Creating your first policy

6. From the **Policies** tab, click on **Create policy** to create your first communication compliance policy. There are six choices:

-   **Detect inappropriate text**: Creates a policy that uses built-in trainable classifiers to detect inappropriate text, such as messages containing offensive or threatening language.

-   **Detect inappropriate images**: Creates a policy that uses built-in trainable classifiers to detect inappropriate images, such as messages containing adult content.

-   **Monitor for sensitive info**: Creates a policy to monitor communications containing sensitive info so you can help ensure important data isn't shared with the wrong people. To detect this info, you can choose from built-in or custom sensitive info types or upload a new keyword dictionary.

-   **Monitor for regulatory compliance**: Sets up a policy to monitor communications that might contain info that might be related to insider trading, such as messages containing credit card numbers. To detect this info, you can choose from built-in or custom sensitive info types or upload a new keyword dictionary.

-   **Monitor for conflict of interest**: Sets up a policy to monitor communications between two groups of users across locations such as Exchange, Teams, and more. Just choose the two groups whose communications you want to supervise, specify reviewers, and we'll set up the rest.

-   **Custom**: Allows you to configure a policy completely from scratch and tailored to your specific requirements.

    For this example, choose **Monitor for sensitive info**:

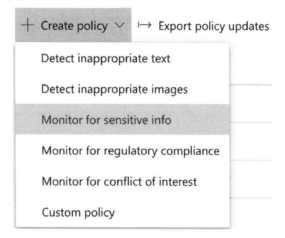

Figure 17.9: Creating a policy to detect inappropriate text

7. First, choose the **Select users** option. Here, the group created in the previous step is entered to include members of the marketing team. You must also choose any policy reviewers. Click **Create policy**:

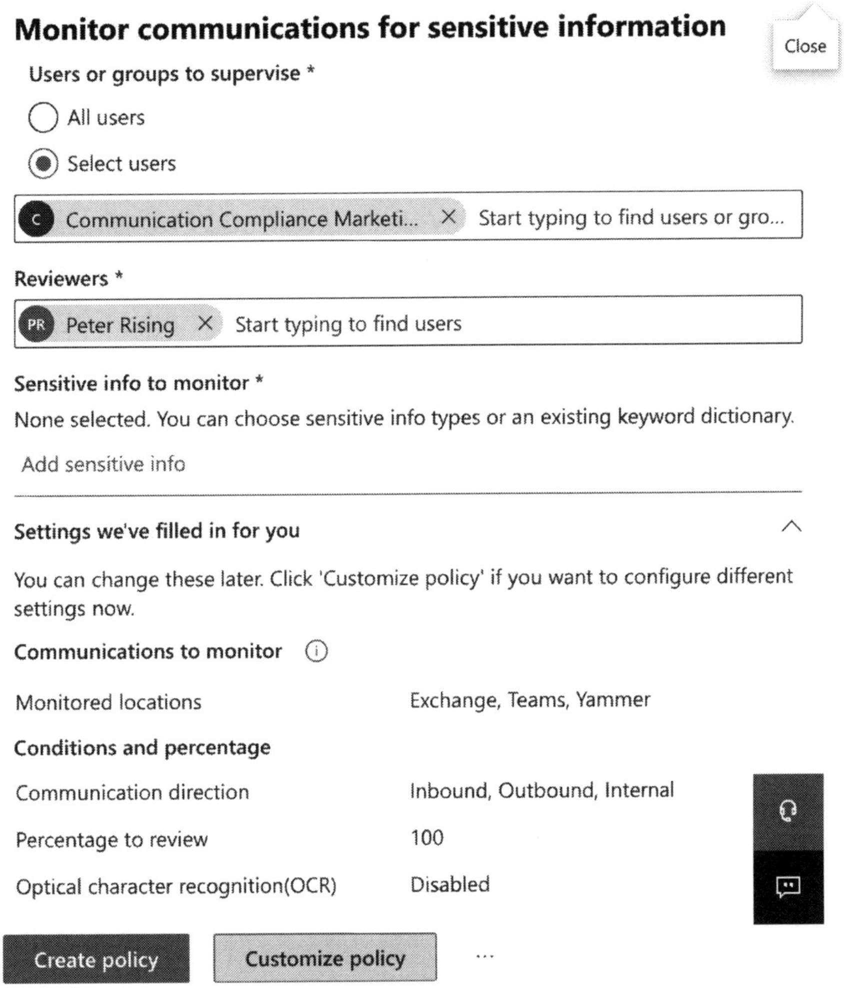

Monitor communications for sensitive information

Close

Users or groups to supervise *

◯ All users

⦿ Select users

> **C** Communication Compliance Marketi... ✕   Start typing to find users or gro...

Reviewers *

> **PR** Peter Rising ✕   Start typing to find users

Sensitive info to monitor *

None selected. You can choose sensitive info types or an existing keyword dictionary.

Add sensitive info

Settings we've filled in for you   ⌃

You can change these later. Click 'Customize policy' if you want to configure different settings now.

Communications to monitor   ⓘ

Monitored locations	Exchange, Teams, Yammer

Conditions and percentage

Communication direction	Inbound, Outbound, Internal
Percentage to review	100
Optical character recognition(OCR)	Disabled

[Create policy]   [Customize policy]   ···

Figure 17.10: Selecting users and reviewers

> **Note**
>
> If you choose **Customize policy**, you will have the option to exclude users and groups from the policy, change **Monitored locations**, and if you want to reduce the amount of content to review, you can specify a percentage, which will randomly select the amount of content from the total that matched any conditions you chose.

8. The policy is created, and you should note that it may take up to 1 hour to activate the policy. It is also important to be aware that it may take up to 24 hours for the policy to start capturing communications:

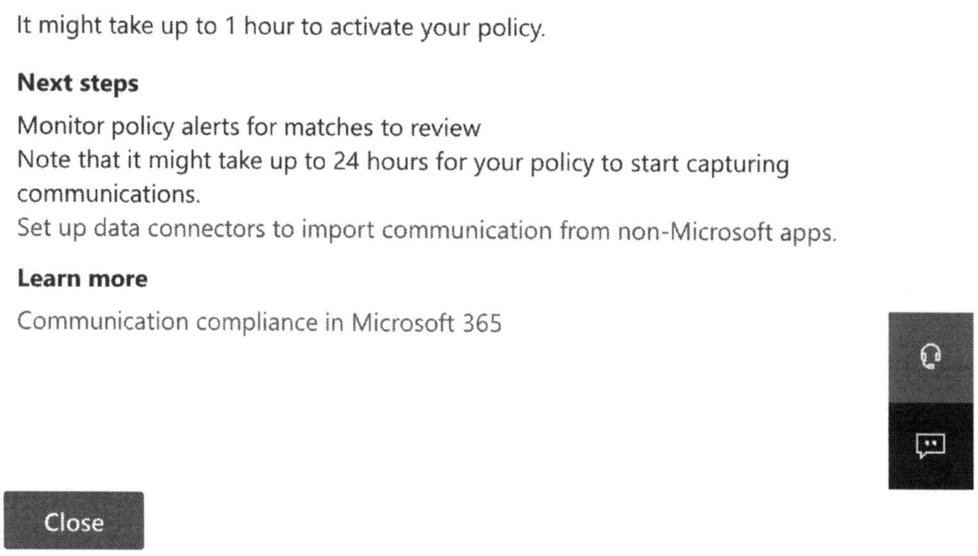

It might take up to 1 hour to activate your policy.

Next steps

Monitor policy alerts for matches to review
Note that it might take up to 24 hours for your policy to start capturing communications.
Set up data connectors to import communication from non-Microsoft apps.

Learn more

Communication compliance in Microsoft 365

Close

Figure 17.11: Policy successfully created

9. The new policy will show **Active** when the activation has been completed. The following screenshot shows three newly created policies, and 24 hours later, there is a match for the **Sensitive information** policy in the **Items pending** column:

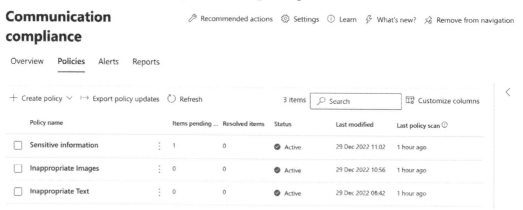

Figure 17.12: New policies created and shown as active

10. Click to open the **Sensitive information** policy. The policy opens on the **Overview** tab, while the **Pending** tab shows two detections, so keep in mind that the number of detections can change quickly:

Figure 17.13: Pending matches shown in the policy

11. Click on the **Pending** tab and you'll see the matching items in the left column. Click on one of the line items to see the details in the right pane. You can see **Source** details, **Plain Text**, and **User history**. On Teams message results, you can also view the conversation history in the full original context:

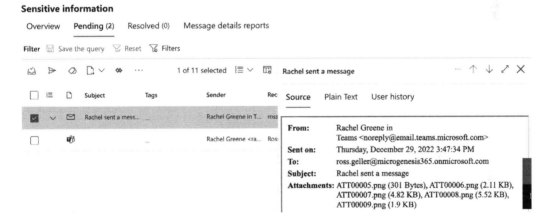

Figure 17.14: Pending matches details and options

12. To process the pending matches, you can highlight them and choose from the toolbar icons shown in the following screenshot:

- Resolve messages and remove from the Pending tab

- Use a notice template to send an email to the sender of the specified messages

- Tag messages as Compliant, Non-compliant, or Questionable

- Escalate/Escalate for investigation

- Remove messages in Teams

- Automate

- View message details

- View item history

- Download

- Refresh

Figure 17.15: Toolbar processing options

For this example, choose **Use a notice template to send an email to the sender of the specified messages**. There are no notice templates available, so you will need to create one. Under **Choose a notice template**, select **Create a new notification**:

Send a notice

Use a notice template to send an email to the sender of the specified messages.

ⓘ Don't see the notice template you are looking for? Create a new one.

Send notice to:

RG   Rachel Greene

Choose a notice template

| Create a new notification   ⌄ |

+ Create a new notification

Save   Cancel

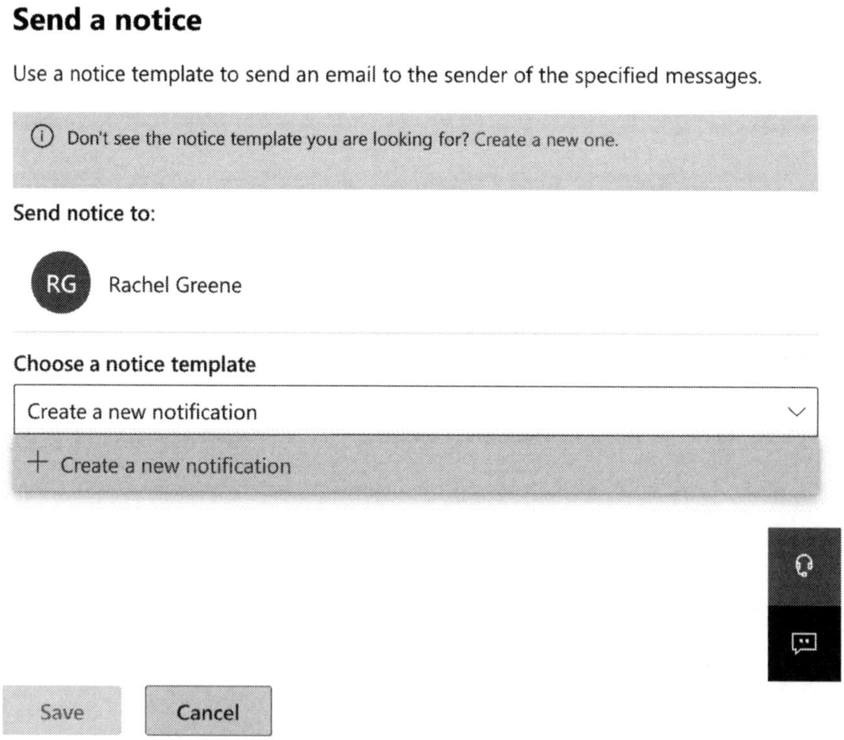

Figure 17.16: Sending a notice template email message

13. You must fill in **Template name**, the **Send from** email address, **Subject**, and **Message body**. Optionally, you can include **Cc** and **Bcc** message options. Click **Create**:

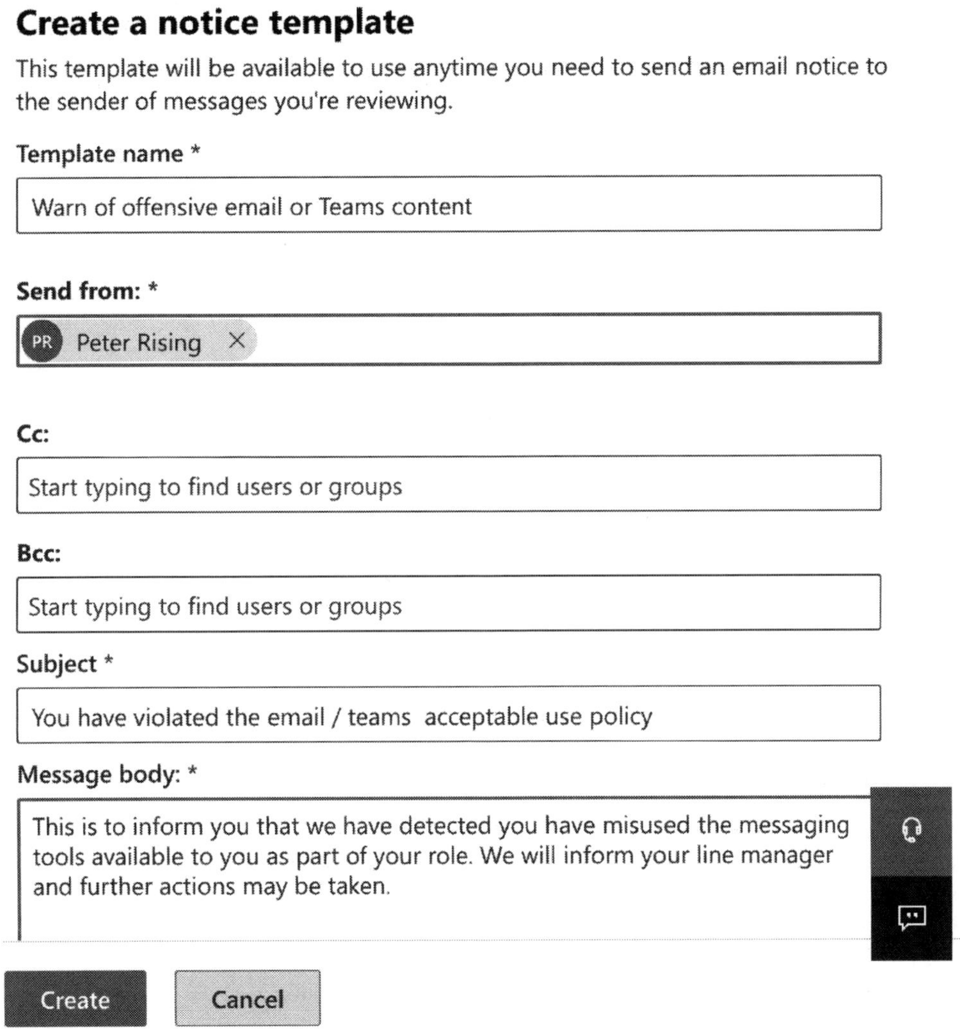

Create a notice template

This template will be available to use anytime you need to send an email notice to the sender of messages you're reviewing.

Template name *

> Warn of offensive email or Teams content

Send from: *

> PR Peter Rising   ✕

Cc:

> Start typing to find users or groups

Bcc:

> Start typing to find users or groups

Subject *

> You have violated the email / teams acceptable use policy

Message body: *

> This is to inform you that we have detected you have misused the messaging tools available to you as part of your role. We will inform your line manager and further actions may be taken.

[Create]   [Cancel]

Figure 17.17: Creating a notice template

14. After creating the template, click **Save** to send the message:

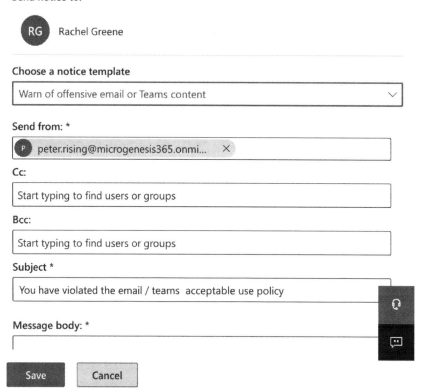

Figure 17.18: Sending the notice template message

15. The recipient receives the warning email shown in the following screenshot:

Figure 17.19: Notice template message received in the user's inbox

16. If you choose the escalate options, you can first escalate the issue via email to another party, such as the line manager of the employee who has triggered the policy. Choosing **Escalate for investigation** will take things further and allow you to create an eDiscovery Premium case right from within Communication Compliance:

Escalate for investigation

Create an eDiscovery (Premium) case for this item and notify any admins who have the eDiscovery Manager and eDiscovery Administrators roles assigned. Learn more

Name *

Investigate misconduct against employee Rachel Greene

Custodian ⓘ

Rachel Greene in Teams <noreply@email.teams.microsoft.com>

Source

Communication compliance

Selected items

1

Note *

eDiscovery investigation required.

Create case   Cancel

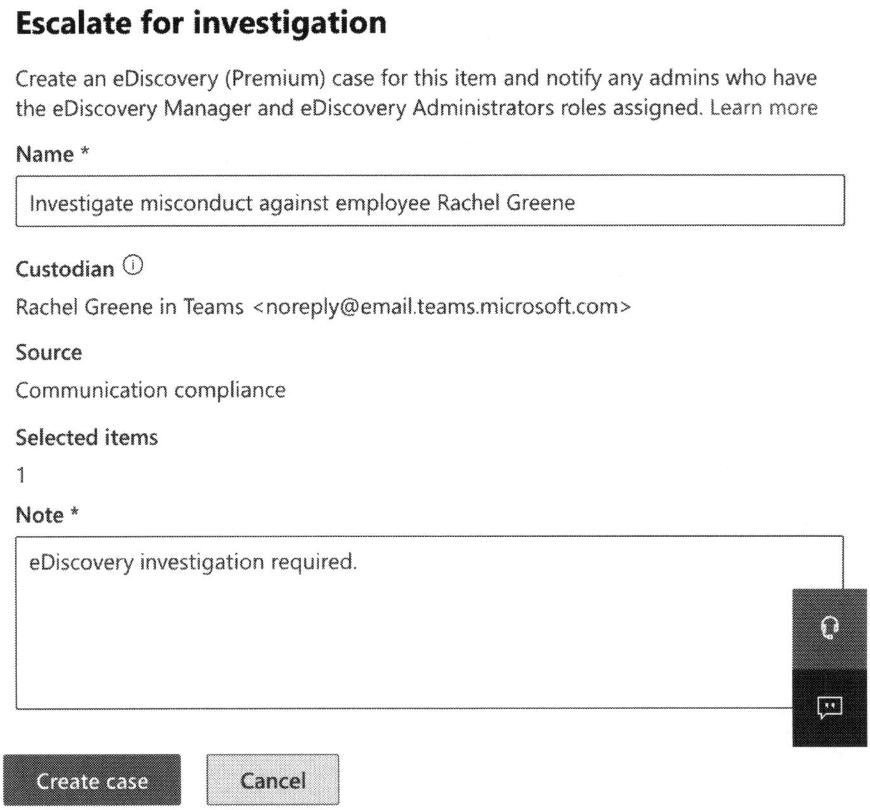

Figure 17.20: Escalating the policy match to an eDiscovery Premium case

17. The remaining tabs on the policy page are **Resolved** and **Message details reports**. When actioning items in the **Pending** tab and marking them as resolved, they are moved to the **Resolved** tab:

Sensitive information

Overview   Pending (3)   Resolved (1)   Message details reports

Figure 17.21: Sensitive information policy tabs

18. Under the **Message details reports** tab, you can create a report by selecting a report name and a date range and clicking **Create**:

Create message details report

Create a downloadable report containing details about the items matching this policy, including metadata, review status, remediation actions, and more. Creating the report can take up to few hours. When it's ready, you'll be able to download it from the 'Message details reports' tab.

Report name *

Message details reports_29-12-2022

Choose a date range

Start date

22 Dec 2022

End date

29 Dec 2022

Create   Cancel

Figure 17.22: Creating a message details report

19. When ready, you can click **Download report(s)** to download the report as a `.csv` file:

Sensitive information

Overview   Pending (3)   Resolved (1)   **Message details reports**

↓ Download report(s) ↻ Refresh   1 of 1 selected

☑	Name	Exported by	Status	Exported on
☑	Message details reports_29-12-...	peter.rising@microgenesis365.onmicrosoft.com	Ready to download	29 Dec 2022 17:04

Figure 17.23: Creating a message details report

Communication Compliance in Microsoft Purview is an extremely powerful tool that will help protect your organization and employees. Next, we will show you how you can implement insider risk management policies to minimize the threat posed by either malicious or unwitting insiders within your organization.

Implementing and managing insider risk management policies

Insider Risk Management is a Microsoft Purview feature that enables administrators to create policies that detect and identify risky activities in your organization. To manage Insider Risk Management and configure the features, you need to be either a **Global Administrator**, **Compliance Administrator**, or part of the **Organization Management, Insider Risk Management**, or **Insider Risk Management Admins** role groups.

To use Insider Risk Management in your Microsoft 365 tenant, you can use the following subscriptions:

- Microsoft 365 E5

- Microsoft 365 E3 and the Microsoft 365 E5 Compliance add-on

- Microsoft 365 E3 and the Microsoft 365 E5 Insider Risk Management add-on

- Office 365 E3, Enterprise Mobility and Security E3, and the Microsoft 365 E5 Compliance add-on

First, we will look at how we can get started with Insider Risk Management.

Getting started with Insider Risk Management policies

Insider Risk Management settings and policies for Microsoft 365 organizations can be created in the Microsoft Purview compliance portal at `https://compliance.microsoft.com`. For details on how you can plan for insider risk management, please refer to the *Further reading* section.

To get started, complete the following steps:

1. From the **Solutions** section of the left menu pane, choose **Insider risk management**. The first thing you see is the **Overview** tab, where a helpful checklist of actions is presented to get you started. You can work through these and mark them as complete when done:

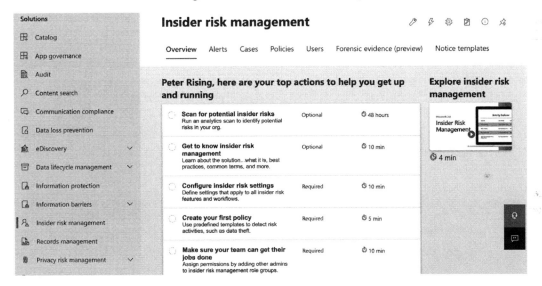

Figure 17.24: Insider risk management Overview page

2. The first step is optional but is recommended. Select the **Scan for potential insider risks** option. This will run the analytics scan to discover potential insider risks in your organization. The initial scan can take up to 48 hours to complete, and you can check the **Send an email when an analytics scan detects an insight for the first time** box. Click **Run scan**:

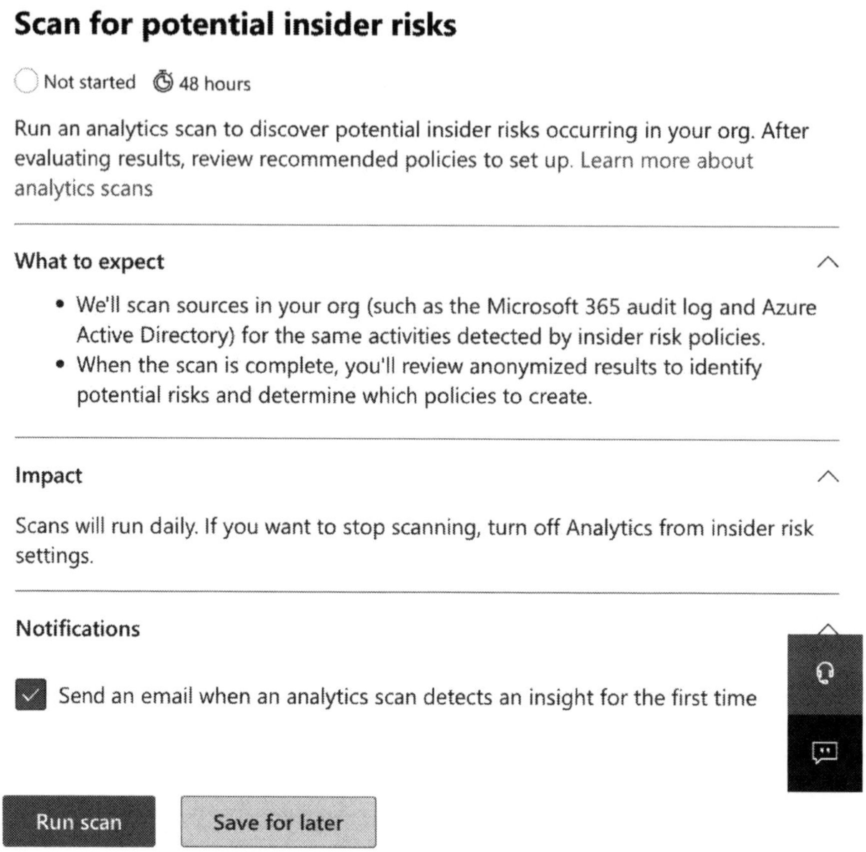

Scan for potential insider risks

◯ Not started   ⏱ 48 hours

Run an analytics scan to discover potential insider risks occurring in your org. After evaluating results, review recommended policies to set up. Learn more about analytics scans

---

What to expect   ︿

- We'll scan sources in your org (such as the Microsoft 365 audit log and Azure Active Directory) for the same activities detected by insider risk policies.
- When the scan is complete, you'll review anonymized results to identify potential risks and determine which policies to create.

Impact   ︿

Scans will run daily. If you want to stop scanning, turn off Analytics from insider risk settings.

Notifications

☑ Send an email when an analytics scan detects an insight for the first time

[Run scan]   [Save for later]

Figure 17.25: Scanning for potential insider risks

3. The first required step is to configure insider risk settings. At this point, it is suggested to leave the recommended actions list and instead navigate to the **Insider risk settings** cog wheel icon at the top right of the page:

Figure 17.26: Insider risk settings

4. The **Settings** page opens. Here you can configure the **Privacy** settings to show either real usernames or anonymized versions of usernames in policy matches to mask the identities of users from administrators investigating policy matches.

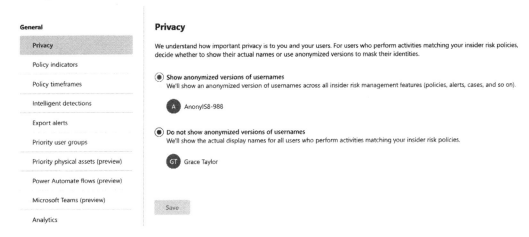

Figure 17.27: Privacy settings for Insider Risk Management

5. The most important area in the **Settings** page to configure is the **Policy indicators** page. This is where you select the types of risk activities you want to detect. These activities are divided by category and include options such as **Sharing SharePoint files with people outside the organization**:

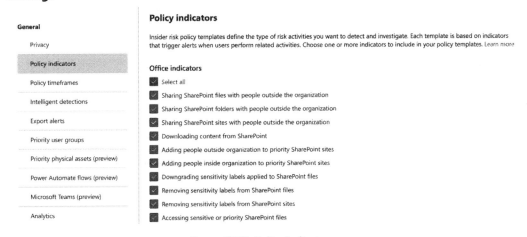

Figure 17.28: Policy indicators

The remaining settings options, as described by Microsoft in their documentation, are as follows:

- **Policy timeframes**: The timeframes you choose here go into effect for a user when they trigger a match for an insider risk policy. For example, if you set the activation window to 15 days and past activity detection to 30 days, and then a user triggers a policy match on July 1, that policy will retrieve user activity from 30 days ago (June 1) and will continue to record new activity for 15 more days (July 16).

- **Intelligent detections**: Define how the detection of risk activities is processed for insider risk alerts.

- **Export alerts**: Insider Risk Management alert information is exportable to **security information and event management (SIEM)** services by using the Office 365 Management Activity API. Turn this on to use these APIs to export insider risk alert details to other applications your organization might use to manage or aggregate insider risk data.

- **Priority user groups**: Set up priority user groups to define users in your organization whose activity requires closer inspection based on factors such as their position, level of access to sensitive information, or risk history. Once created, these groups can be included in certain policy templates that are more likely to generate high-severity alerts.

- **Priority physical assets (preview)**: These assets represent priority locations in your organization, such as company buildings or server rooms. To detect activity for these assets, related policy templates require that a physical badging connector is set up to import access events for those assets. To successfully detect this activity, the asset IDs you enter here must match the IDs specified in the connector.

- **Power Automate flows (preview)**: Use Power Automate flows to automatically manage Insider Risk Management processes and tasks. You can create flows here using built-in Insider Risk Management templates or use the Power Automate console to create custom flows.

- **Microsoft Teams (preview)**: Integrate Microsoft Teams capabilities with insider risk case management to enhance collaboration with stakeholders. Every time a case is created, an associated team will be created. Admins will also have the option to create a team for any existing cases. By default, teams will automatically include members who are assigned the **Insider Risk Management**, **Insider Risk Management Analysts**, and **Insider Risk Management Investigators** role groups. Additional contributors can be added to the team after it's created as needed.

- **Analytics**: When turned on, Microsoft will scan sources in your organization (such as the Microsoft 365 audit log) to detect the same activities used by insider risk policies. Scans will run daily, and you will be able to review anonymized results to identify potential risks and determine which policies to set up.

- **Admin notifications**: Decide whether to send email notifications and which admins will receive them.

- **Inline alert customization**: Allow the **Insider Risk Management Analyst** and **Insider Risk Management Investigator** roles to make policy edits using inline alert customization.

Once you have completed the recommended steps, including assigning any required users to appropriate role groups, then you are ready to start creating Insider Risk Management policies.

Creating Insider Risk Management policies

You can create an Insider Risk Management policy by completing the following steps:

1. Within **Insider risk management** in Microsoft Purview, navigate to the **Policies** tab and click **Create policy**:

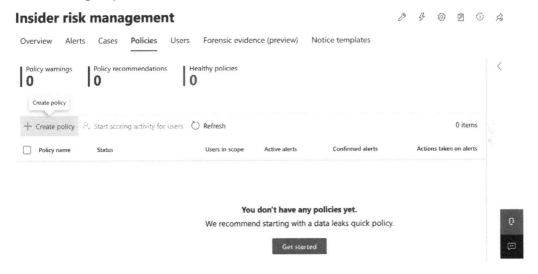

Figure 17.29: Insider risk management Policies tab

2. For this example, the **Data theft by departing users** policy is chosen. You will note that the policy templates in this area have some prerequisites. Some are recommended, others are mandatory. The selected policy in this example can also be linked to a third-party HR system if applicable. Here it is set only to trigger when a user account is deleted from Azure AD. Click **Next**:

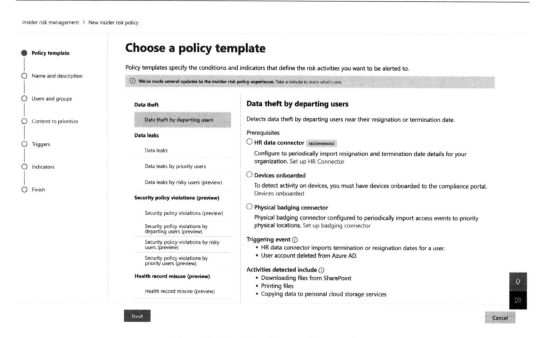

Figure 17.30: Choosing a policy template

3. Enter a name and description for your policy and click **Next**:

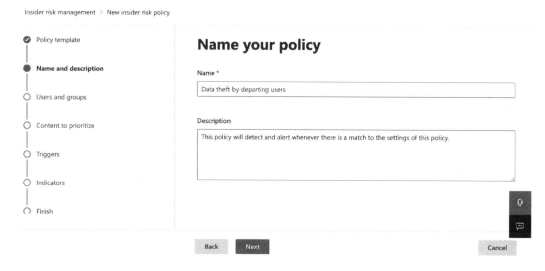

Figure 17.31: Naming your policy

4. Choose the users and groups to whom the policy will apply. In this instance, **Include all users and groups** is selected. Click **Next**:

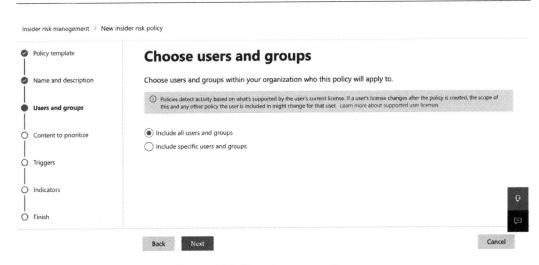

Figure 17.32: Choosing users and groups

5. Next, you can decide whether you wish to prioritize particular content. If you choose to do so, you can select from **Sharepoint sites**, **Sensitivity labels**, **Sensitive info types**, **File extensions**, or **Trainable classifiers**. For this example, only **Sharepoint sites** is selected. Click **Next**:

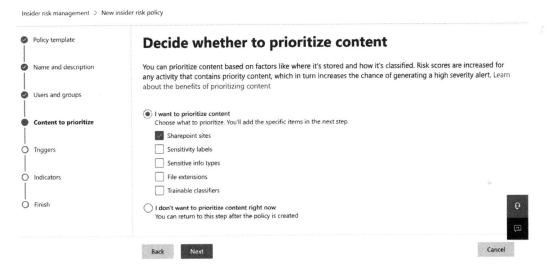

Figure 17.33: Prioritizing content

6. Next, choose the SharePoint sites you wish to prioritize. Click **Add**:

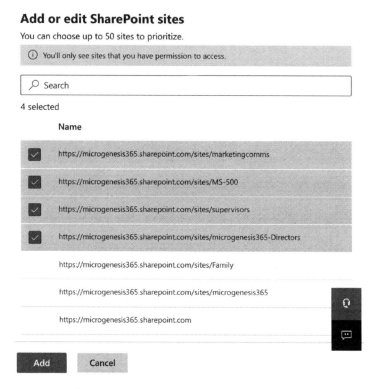

Figure 17.34: Adding or editing SharePoint sites

7.   The site selections are added. Click **Next**:

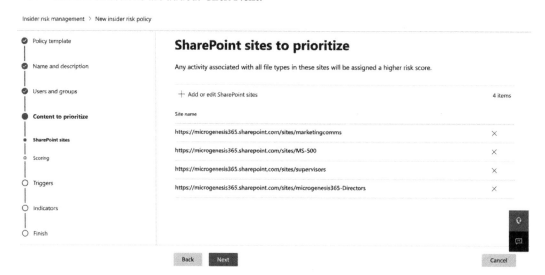

Figure 17.35: SharePoint sites selected

8. Now, you will choose to score only activity with priority content or all activity. Choose **Get alerts for all activity** and click **Next**:

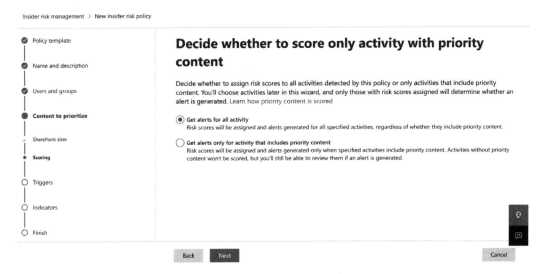

Figure 17.36: Scoring activity alerts

9. On **Triggers for this policy**, the **HR data connector events** option is grayed out as you did not select this option earlier, in *step 2*. So, the only selection you can check is **User account deleted from Azure AD**. Click **Next**:

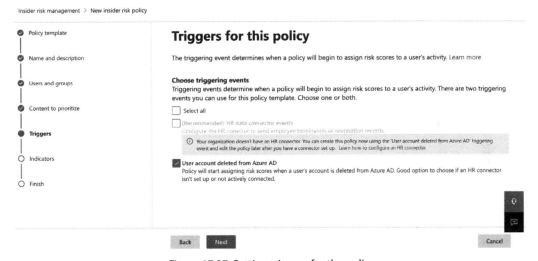

Figure 17.37: Setting triggers for the policy

10. Next, you can view the indicators that will be used to generate alerts for activity detected by the policy template you selected:

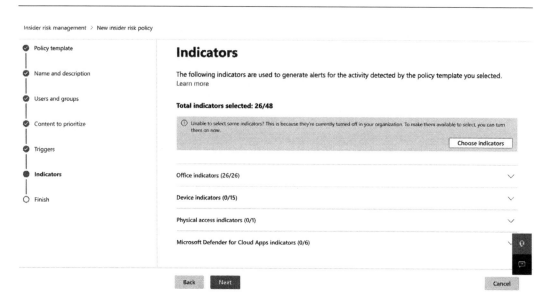

Figure 17.38: Setting policy indicators

11. If you expand **Office indicators**, you can select or deselect the ones you require or otherwise. Click **Next**:

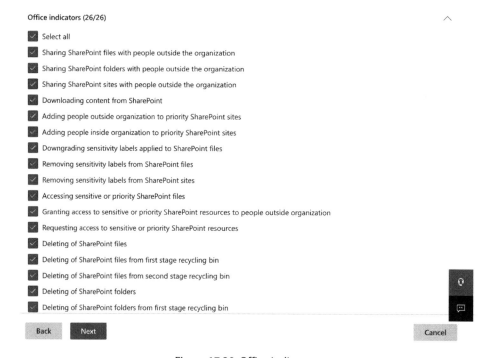

Figure 17.39: Office indicators

12. On the **Detection options** page, you can choose the advanced detection options that will be used to generate alerts for the activity detected. Some items here are grayed and cannot be selected – this is dependent on criteria such as whether you have onboarded devices into Microsoft Purview. Select the options you need, then click **Next**:

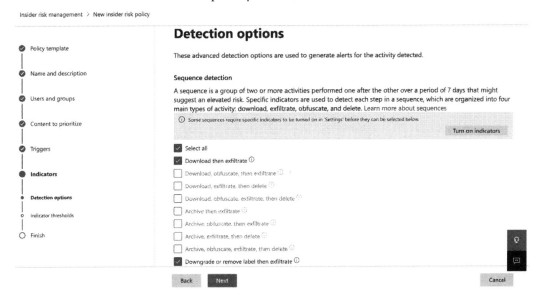

Figure 17.40: Setting detection options

13. Now, choose whether you want to use Microsoft default thresholds or select custom thresholds for the indicators. For this example, choose **Default thresholds**. Click **Next**:

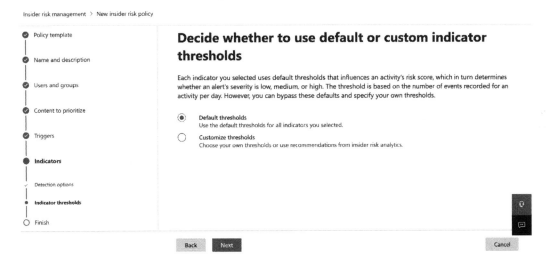

Figure 17.41: Setting thresholds

14. Finally, review your settings and click to submit the policy template:

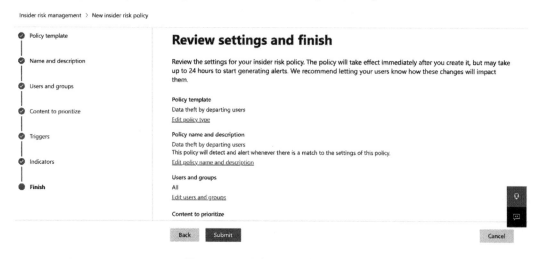

Figure 17.42: Submitting the policy

15. The policy is successfully created and can be viewed in the **Policies** tab of **Insider risk management**:

Figure 17.43: New policy successfully created

16. When your policy hits one of the thresholds to generate a match, an alert will be created in the **Alerts** tab, and you can see these in the following screenshot under the **Alerts summary** section of the **Alerts** tab:

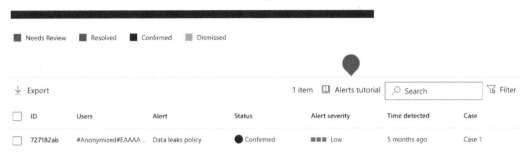

Figure 17.44: Alerts in Insider Risk Management

17. From the alerts generated, you can create cases. You can generate a new case from an alert or add an alert to an existing case:

Figure 17.45: Cases in Insider Risk Management

18. Sometimes there will be no alerts generated, but you will still see incidents related to users in the **Users** tab. The following screenshot shows an example where account deletion and data exfiltration were detected by a policy and these activities have been assigned risk scores, but none have reached the policy threshold to generate an alert:

Figure 17.46: User activity detected

19. The **User activity** tab shows the details of the captured risks. Note the anonymized data, as configured earlier in the privacy settings in *step 4*:

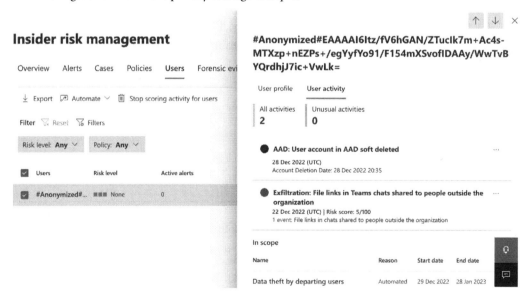

Figure 17.47: User activity details

20. There are two remaining tabs in **Insider risk management**. The first is a preview feature called **Forensic evidence (preview)**. This is an investigative tool for viewing captured user activity to help determine whether the user's actions pose a risk. When turned on, you can configure settings that apply to all users whose forensic evidence requests have been approved:

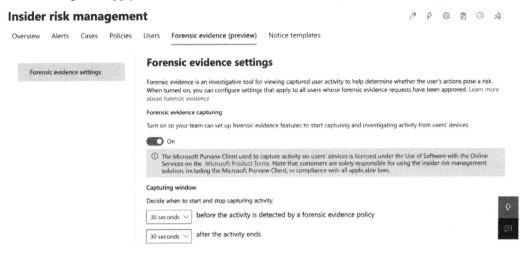

Figure 17.48: Forensic evidence settings

21. Finally, there is the **Notice templates** tab. Note the existing notice template that was created earlier when configuring Communication Compliance. Insider Risk Management uses the same process to notify users of policy matches, and you can create new notice templates to use from here:

Figure 17.49: Notice templates

Insider risk policies are a powerful means for your organization to receive alerts when risky activity by users is detected. If malicious insiders are trying to steal your data in a covert way, then you need to know. Insider Risk Management will help you to stay one step ahead of such threats.

Next, we will look at how to block communication between groups of users for compliance reasons by using information barrier policies.

Implementing and managing Information Barriers policies

With Microsoft Purview **Information Barriers**, organizations can restrict two-way communication between users and groups. This can be applied to Microsoft Teams, OneDrive, and SharePoint. Implementing Information Barriers is a process usually utilized in organizations that are strictly regulated. The aim is to avoid the possibility of a conflict of interest occurring.

Information Barriers is implemented in the form of segments and policies, which, when in place, will have the effect that one set of specified users, who should not be allowed to communicate with another set of specified users, will not be able to find, chat with, or call those users. Essentially, Information Barriers is there to prevent unauthorized communication. To use Information Barriers in your Microsoft 365 tenant, you can use the following subscriptions:

- Microsoft 365 E5

- Office 365 E5

- Office 365 Advanced Compliance add-on (no longer available for new subscriptions)

- Microsoft 365 E3 and the Microsoft 365 E5 Compliance add-on

- Microsoft 365 E3 and the Microsoft 365 E5 Insider Risk Management add-on

To manage Information Barriers, you need to be either a **Global Administrator**, **Compliance Administrator**, or part of the **IB Compliance Management** role group.

Next, we will look at creating segments and policies for Information Barriers.

Segments and policies for Information Barriers

The first step to implementing Information Barriers is understanding the **segments** and **policies** you are going to need. Any users who are to be included in your Information Barriers policies will need to belong to a segment. A user may only be in one segment, and each segment can only have one Information Barriers policy applied.

> **Note**
>
> You need to make sure that your Azure Active Directory users have populated attributes that you plan to use to define segments. You can use attributes such as **Department** or **MemberOf**. A link to the full list of supported attributes can be found in the *Further reading* section at the end of this chapter.

In the example that follows, we will configure two groups of users who should be prevented from communicating with each other. We will use the **Department** attribute to create segments for `Retail` and `Marketing`. To define segments, you need to complete the following steps:

1. Log in to the Microsoft Purview compliance portal at `https://compliance.microsoft.com` and navigate to **Information barriers | Segments**. Click on **New segment**:

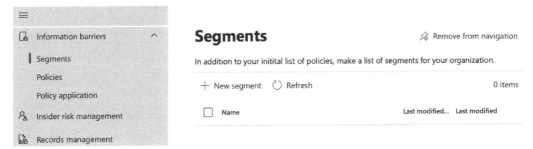

Figure 17.50: Information barriers | Segments

2. Enter the name for the segment as `Marketing`. Note that you cannot rename a segment once it is created. Click **Next**:

Figure 17.51: Naming the segment

3. On the **User group filter** page, select **Add** and choose the **Department** attribute for the segment from the list of available attributes:

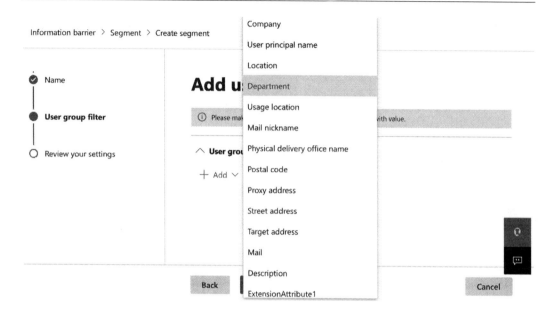

Figure 17.52: Choosing an attribute

4. Select **Equal**, then enter the value for the attribute as `Marketing`. If you want to define additional attributes for the segment, click **Add condition**. In this example, there will be no additional attributes. Click **Next**:

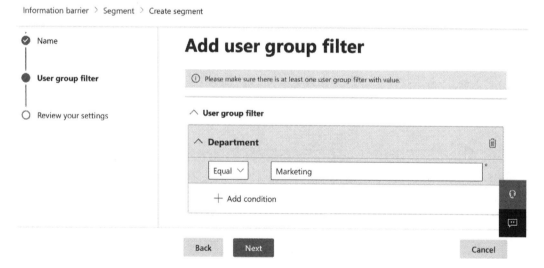

Figure 17.53: Adding a user group filter

5. On the **Review your settings** page, ensure you are happy with your selections and click **Submit** to create the segment:

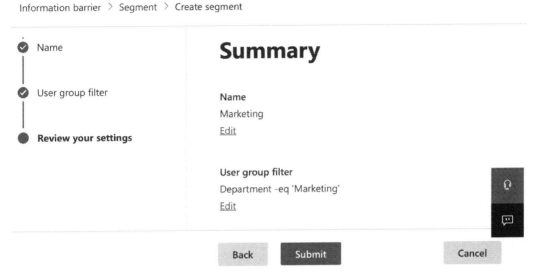

Figure 17.54: Submitting the segment

6. Repeat *steps 1-5* and create a segment with the department equal to Retail. Once complete, you will have two new segments:

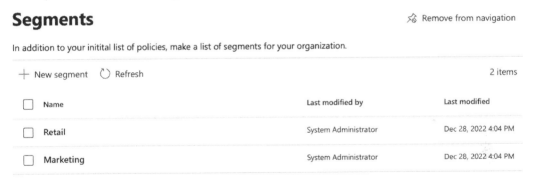

Figure 17.55: New segments created

You may also create segments using PowerShell. For example, to create the retail segment, you would enter the following cmdlet:

```
New-OrganizationSegment -Name "Retail" -UserGroupFilter "Department
-eq 'Retail'"
```

With your segments created, you may now proceed to create your Information Barriers policies. When creating policies that use segments, there are two typical methods that are used:

- Block communications between segments

- Allow a segment to communicate with only one other segment

For this example, you will create a policy in which communications are blocked between the two segments that you have created. To do this, you need to complete the following steps:

1. From the Microsoft Purview compliance portal, select **Information barriers | Policies**. Click on **Create policy**:

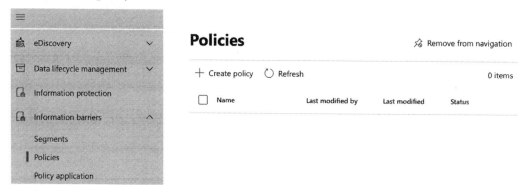

Figure 17.56: Creating an Information barrier policy

2. Provide a policy name. This example is named Block Marketing > Retail. Click **Next**:

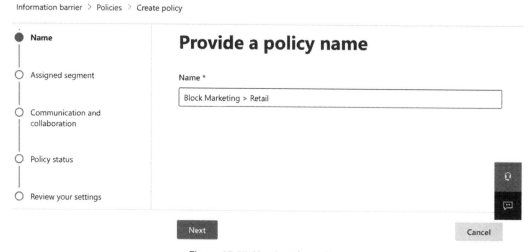

Figure 17.57: Naming the policy

3. Next, on the **Add assigned segment details** page, click **Choose segment** and select the **Marketing** segment. Click **Next**:

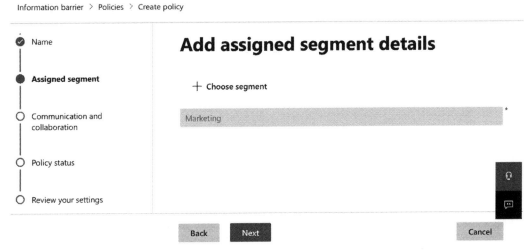

Figure 17.58: Adding assigned segment details

4. On the **Configure communication and collaboration details** page, click the **Communication and collaboration** dropdown and select **Blocked**. Then, click on **Choose segment** to select the segment you want to block. Select the **Retail** segment. Click **Next**:

Figure 17.59: Configure communication and collaboration details

5. On the **Configure policy status** page, move the slider to the **On** position when you are ready to activate your policy, and click **Next**:

Figure 17.60: Configure policy status

6. On the **Summary** page, review your settings and click **Submit**:

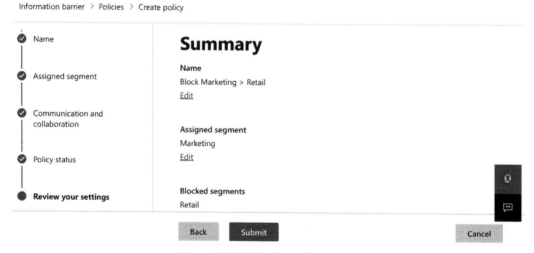

Figure 17.61: Submitting the policy

The policy is now created:

Information barrier > Policies > Create policy

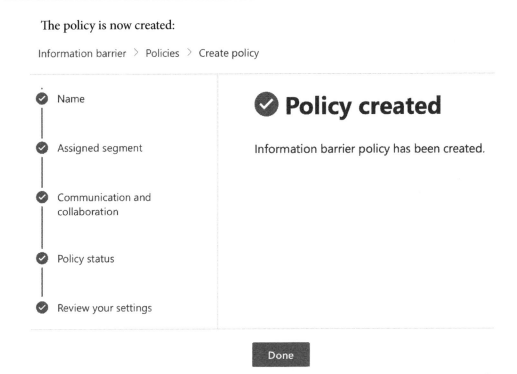

Figure 17.62: Policy created successfully

7. Repeat *steps 1-6* to create the reverse policy of Block Retail > Marketing. Once done, you will have two new Information Barriers policies, as shown in the following screenshot:

Policies

✄ Remove from navigation

+ Create policy   ○ Refresh   2 items

Name	Last modified by	Last modified	Status
☐ **Block Retail > Marketing**	System Administrator	Dec 28, 2022 4:32 PM	Active
☐ **Block Marketing > Retail**	System Administrator	Dec 28, 2022 4:30 PM	Active

Figure 17.63: New policies shown successfully created

You may also create Information Barriers policies using PowerShell. For example, to create the Block Retail > Marketing policy, you would enter the following cmdlet:

```
New-InformationBarrierPolicy -Name "Block Retail > Marketing"
-AssignedSegment "Retail" -SegmentsBlocked "Marketing" -State Active
```

With Information Barriers segments and policies logically defined and created in Microsoft Purview, you can be assured that groups of users who should not be able to communicate will not be able to find each other within Microsoft 365 services such as Microsoft Teams.

Next, we will show you how to provide users with just enough access to elevated tasks, roles, and role groups using **Privileged Access Management (PAM)**.

Implementing and managing Privileged Access Management

With Microsoft Purview PAM, it is possible to configure access control to privileged Microsoft 365 admin tasks in a granular fashion. The purpose of this is to protect your organization from any possible breaches that use existing privileged admin accounts that have existing access to settings or data.

By implementing PAM, your organization can require that your users must explicitly request just-in-time access to complete any privileged or elevated tasks. This enforces the principle of providing users with *just enough access* to complete their tasks. Doing so significantly reduces the risk of data exposure.

To use PAM in your organization, one of the following subscriptions is required:

- Microsoft 365 E5

- Microsoft 365 E3 and the Microsoft 365 E5 Compliance add-on

- Office 365 E3, Enterprise Mobility and Security E3, and the Microsoft 365 E5 Compliance add-on

- Any Microsoft 365, Office 365, Exchange, SharePoint, or OneDrive for Business subscription and the Microsoft 365 E5 Insider Risk Management add-on

- Office 365 Enterprise E5

- Office 365 Enterprise E3 and the Office 365 Advanced Compliance add-on (no longer available for new subscriptions)

You will need the **Exchange Role Management** role assigned in order to manage privileged access in Microsoft 365.

To configure PAM, you must complete the following steps:

1. Log in to the Microsoft 365 admin center at `https://admin.microsoft.com`, navigate to **Settings** | **Org settings** | **Security & privacy**, and click on **Privileged access**:

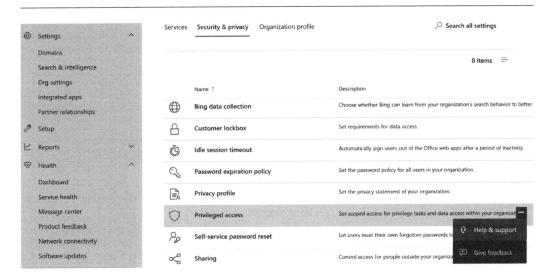

Figure 17.64: Privileged access settings in the Microsoft 365 admin center

2. Check the box that says **Allow privileged access requests and choose a default approval group**. The group you choose must be a mail-enabled security group. For this example, a group named **PAM approvals** is chosen. Click **Save**, then click the link that reads **Create policies and manage requests**:

Privileged Access

Privileged access provides a way for people in your organization to perform tasks that would otherwise require a higher level of permission or an admin role. When someone submits a request to access a privileged task, the default approval group you choose can approve or deny it.

After you choose the approval group, create policies to define the types of privileged tasks people can request access to.

Create policies and manage requests

Learn more about privileged access

Figure 17.65: Allowing privileged access requests

3. You are now taken to the **Privileged access requests** page. Before any users can request access to a privileged task, role, or role group, you must first create a policy. To do this, click on **Manage policies**:

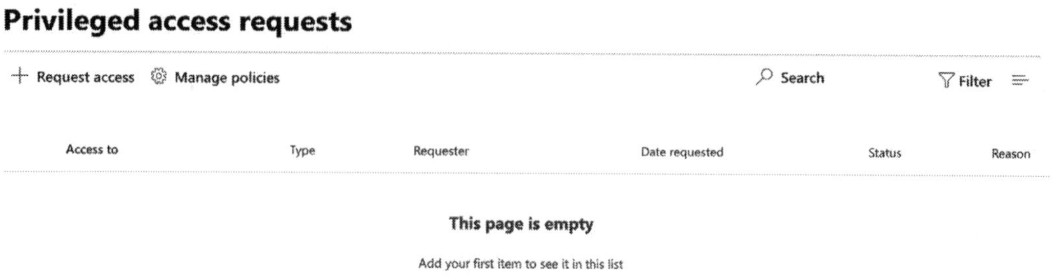

Privileged access requests

Figure 17.66: Managing policies

4. From the **Privileged access policies** page, choose **Add policy**:

Privileged access policies

Figure 17.67: Adding a policy

5. On the **Add policy** page, complete the fields to create the policy:

    *   **Policy type**: Select from **Task**, **Role**, or **Role group**.

    *   **Scope**: The scope can only be **Exchange**. No other services work with PAM yet, although Microsoft is planning to add more.

    *   **Policy name**: Select a policy name. The choices available to you here will depend upon the policy type you chose.

    *   **Approval type**: Choose between **Manual** or **Auto**. If **Auto** is selected, requestors will be automatically approved. If **Manual** is selected, you must define an approvers group. You should choose the group you created earlier for this, in *step 2*:

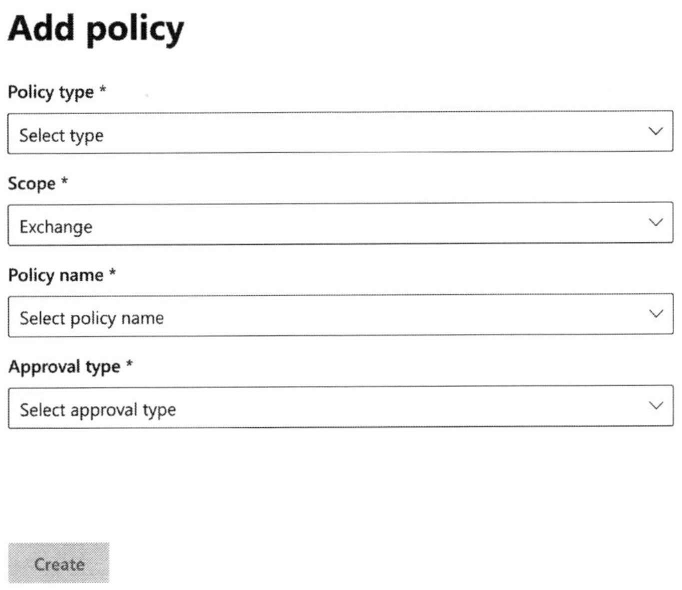

Add policy

Policy type *

Select type ⌄

Scope *

Exchange ⌄

Policy name *

Select policy name ⌄

Approval type *

Select approval type ⌄

Create

Figure 17.68: Adding a policy

6. For this example, a policy is created with a policy type of **Task**. The policy name is selected as **New Transport Rule** and the approval type is set to **Manual** with the approvers group set as **PAM approvals**. Click **Create**:

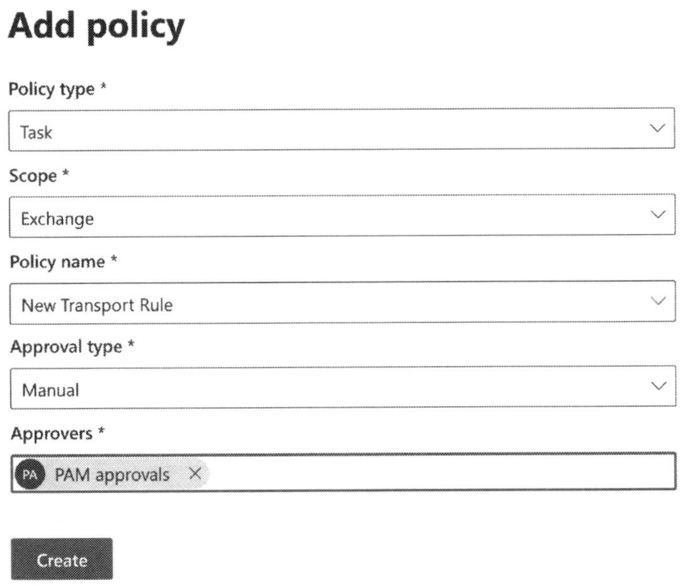

Add policy

Policy type *

Task ⌄

Scope *

Exchange ⌄

Policy name *

New Transport Rule ⌄

Approval type *

Manual ⌄

Approvers *

PA PAM approvals ✕

Create

Figure 17.69: Adding a policy

7. The policy is created and can be seen in the list of policies:

Privileged access policies

Figure 17.70: New policy created

8. Users can request access from the **Request access** page, as shown in the following screenshot:

Request access

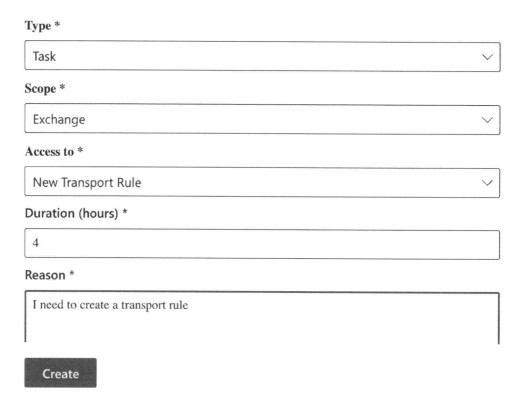

Figure 17.71: Requesting access

9. When the user access request is created, the approver group will be notified via email:

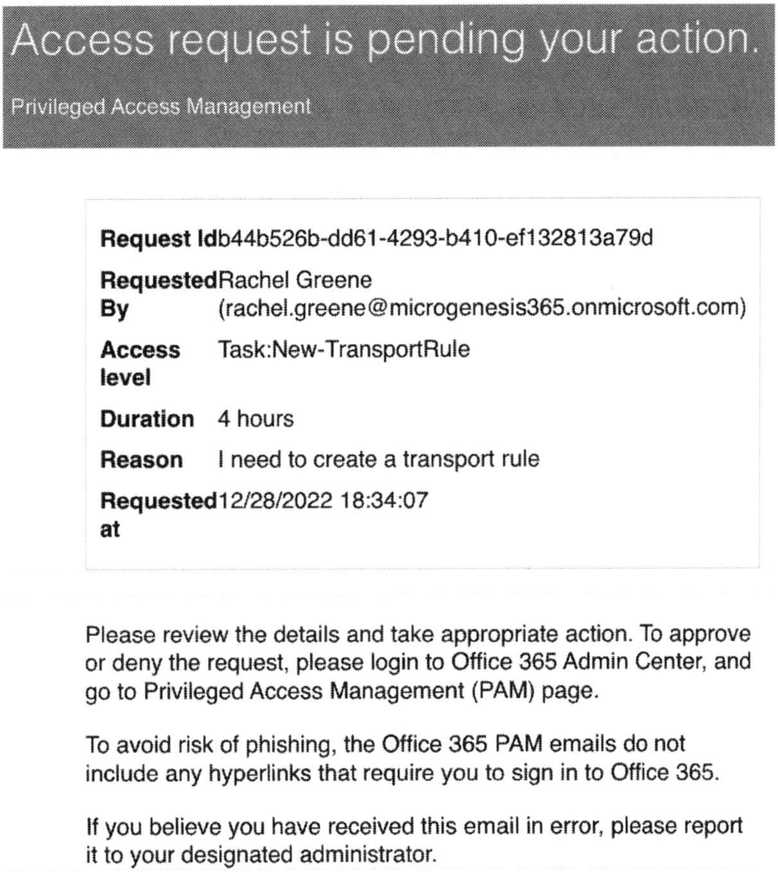

Access request is pending your action.

Privileged Access Management

Request Id	b44b526b-dd61-4293-b410-ef132813a79d
Requested By	Rachel Greene (rachel.greene@microgenesis365.onmicrosoft.com)
Access level	Task:New-TransportRule
Duration	4 hours
Reason	I need to create a transport rule
Requested at	12/28/2022 18:34:07

Please review the details and take appropriate action. To approve or deny the request, please login to Office 365 Admin Center, and go to Privileged Access Management (PAM) page.

To avoid risk of phishing, the Office 365 PAM emails do not include any hyperlinks that require you to sign in to Office 365.

If you believe you have received this email in error, please report it to your designated administrator.

Figure 17.72: Email requesting access notification to approver

10. No hyperlinks are included in the notification emails, therefore the approver must return to the **Request access** page and select the request:

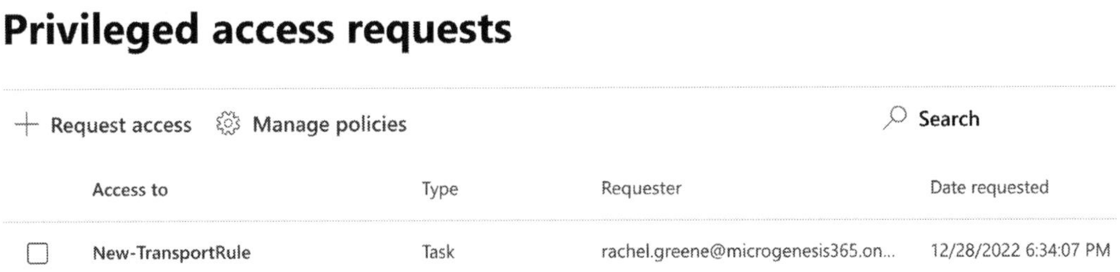

Privileged access requests

+ Request access ⚙ Manage policies			🔍 Search
Access to	**Type**	**Requester**	**Date requested**
☐ New-TransportRule	Task	rachel.greene@microgenesis365.on...	12/28/2022 6:34:07 PM

Figure 17.73: New task in Privileged access requests

11. Once the request is open, the approver can then either approve or deny the request:

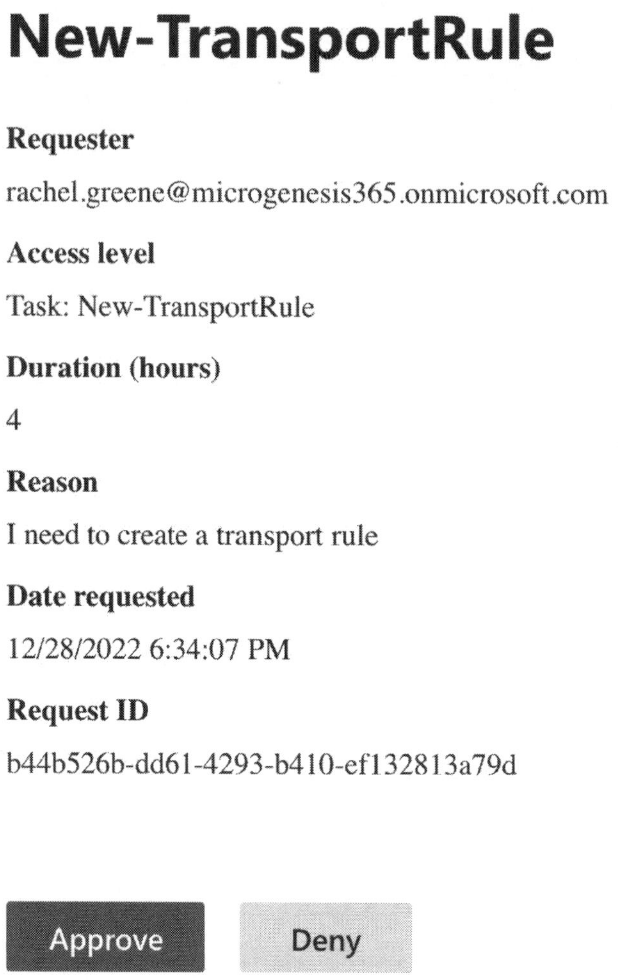

New-TransportRule

Requester

rachel.greene@microgenesis365.onmicrosoft.com

Access level

Task: New-TransportRule

Duration (hours)

4

Reason

I need to create a transport rule

Date requested

12/28/2022 6:34:07 PM

Request ID

b44b526b-dd61-4293-b410-ef132813a79d

Figure 17.74: Approving or denying the request

12. The requestor is then notified by email that their request has been approved:

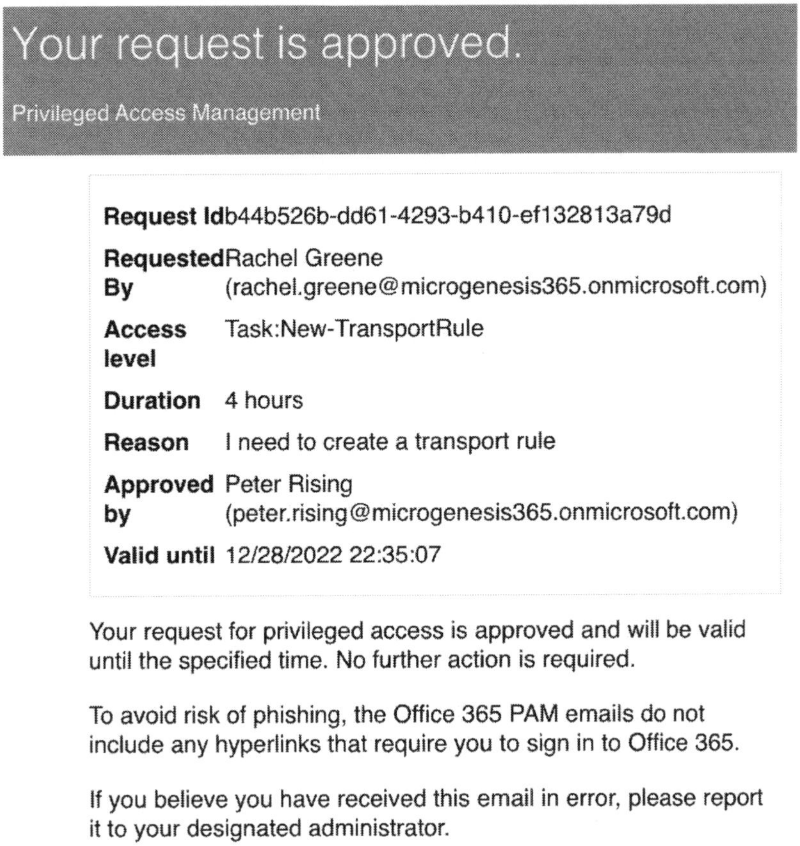

Your request is approved.

Privileged Access Management

Request Id	b44b526b-dd61-4293-b410-ef132813a79d
Requested By	Rachel Greene (rachel.greene@microgenesis365.onmicrosoft.com)
Access level	Task:New-TransportRule
Duration	4 hours
Reason	I need to create a transport rule
Approved by	Peter Rising (peter.rising@microgenesis365.onmicrosoft.com)
Valid until	12/28/2022 22:35:07

Your request for privileged access is approved and will be valid until the specified time. No further action is required.

To avoid risk of phishing, the Office 365 PAM emails do not include any hyperlinks that require you to sign in to Office 365.

If you believe you have received this email in error, please report it to your designated administrator.

Figure 17.75: Requestor notified of approval

It is also possible to manage policies and requests for PAM using Exchange Online PowerShell. Some examples include the following:

- Creating and defining an approval policy:

```
New-ElevatedAccessApprovalPolicy -Task 'Exchange\
New-TransportRule' -ApprovalType Manual -ApproverGroup
'pamapprovers@microgenesis365.onmicrosoft.com'
```

- Creating an elevation request:

```
New-ElevatedAccessRequest -Task 'Exchange\New-TransportRule'
-Reason 'Needed to route outbound mail via a third party
connector' -DurationHours 4
```

PAM is an excellent way to reduce risk and provide your users with only the access they need on demand, rather than permanently granting access to powerful privileged roles.

Summary

In this chapter, we introduced you to the principles of managing insider risk in your Microsoft 365 environment. We learned that by implementing Customer Lockbox, we can control and monitor the access that Microsoft has to our data during a support request. We also learned that with Communication Compliance policies, we can be alerted when inappropriate or abusive communications take place between users in our organizations. Additionally, we showed you how implementing and managing Insider Risk Management policies can help prevent data from being leaked outside our organization by unwitting or malicious insiders and how with Information Barriers policies, we can create segments of users who are blocked from communicating with each other for regulatory reasons. Finally, we saw that implementing and managing PAM provides granular levels of control to Exchange Online tasks, roles, and role groups and provides just enough access instead of vulnerable standing permissions.

We are now at the end of this book. We've learned about the various identity methods for Microsoft 365, how to choose them, and how to manage identity controls using Microsoft Entra. We've also learned about protecting our Microsoft 365 users, identities, and devices with the powerful suite of Microsoft Defender products, as well as how to use Microsoft Sentinel to view insights into threats and other activities and respond with playbooks and automation. Finally, we learned about the compliance features of Microsoft 365 with Microsoft Purview. You should now be able to apply what you have learned in real-world scenarios, and you can refer to this guide for support whenever you need it.

Questions

1. Which of the following are available policies in Microsoft Purview Communication Compliance? (Choose three)

    A. Detect inappropriate images

    B. Detect inappropriate video

    C. Detect inappropriate text

    D. Monitor for sensitive info

2. True or false: Using Information Barriers, you can create segments and policies to block communication and collaboration between groups of users?

    A. True

    B. False

3. In the Insider Risk Management built-in policy named **Data theft by departing users**, which of the following is not one of the available activities detected?

    A. Downloading files from SharePoint

    B. Copying data to a USB drive

    C.   Printing files

    D.   Copying data to personal cloud storage services

4.   Which of the following PowerShell commands would you use to create a PAM policy based on the task of creating a new Exchange mail flow rule where the approval process must be granted by an approver group?

    A.   `New-ElevatedAccessRequest -Task 'Exchange\New-TransportRule' -Reason 'Needed to route outbound mail via a third party connector' -DurationHours 4`

    B.   `New-ElevatedAccessApprovalPolicy -Task 'Exchange\ New-TransportRule' -ApprovalType Auto`

    C.   `New-ElevatedAccessApprovalPolicy -Task 'Exchange\ New-TransportRule' -ApprovalType Automatic -ApproverGroup 'pamapprovers@microgenesis365.onmicrosoft.com'`

    D.   `New-ElevatedAccessApprovalPolicy -Task 'Exchange\ New-TransportRule' -ApprovalType Manual -ApproverGroup 'pamapprovers@microgenesis365.onmicrosoft.com'`

5.   True or false: It can take up to 24 hours after you create a Communication Compliance policy for the policy to start capturing communications?

    A.   True

    B.   False

6.   Where do you configure Privileged Access Management?

    A.   The Microsoft 365 admin center under **Settings | Org settings**

    B.   The Microsoft Purview compliance portal under **Information Barriers | Segments**

    C.   The Microsoft 365 admin center under **Setup**

    D.   The Microsoft 365 admin center under **Settings | Integrated apps**

7.   What is the purpose of Customer Lockbox?

    A.   To ensure that any support from Microsoft is carried out in a sandboxed environment

    B.   To apply encryption to any content that is being accessed by customers

    C.   To apply controls and auditing capability to requests from Microsoft to access your tenant as part of a support request

    D.   To allow customers to share data with you in a secure manner

8. True or false: With Information Barriers policies, you can choose more than one assigned segment?

    A. True

    B. False

9. With Privileged Access Management, what type of group must be set up to process manual approvals of requests?

    A. Security group

    B. Microsoft 365 group

    C. Mail-enabled security group

10. True or false: In Insider Risk Management, it is possible to create privacy settings to anonymize user information?

    A. True

    B. False

Further reading

Please refer to the following links for more information:

- Microsoft Purview Customer Lockbox: `https://learn.microsoft.com/en-au/microsoft-365/compliance/customer-lockbox-requests?WT.mc_id=M365-MVP-4039827&view=o365-worldwide`

- Learn about communication compliance: `https://learn.microsoft.com/en-us/microsoft-365/compliance/communication-compliance?WT.mc_id=EM-MVP-4039827&view=o365-worldwide`

- Get started with communication compliance: `https://learn.microsoft.com/en-us/microsoft-365/compliance/communication-compliance-configure?WT.mc_id=EM-MVP-4039827&view=o365-worldwide`

- Create and manage communication compliance policies: `https://learn.microsoft.com/en-us/microsoft-365/compliance/communication-compliance-policies?view=o365-worldwide`

- Plan for Insider Risk Management: `https://learn.microsoft.com/en-us/microsoft-365/compliance/insider-risk-management-plan?view=o365-worldwide`

- Get started with Insider Risk Management: `https://learn.microsoft.com/en-us/microsoft-365/compliance/insider-risk-management-configure?WT.mc_id=M365-MVP-4039827&view=o365-worldwide`

- Get started with Insider Risk Management settings: `https://learn.microsoft.com/en-gb/microsoft-365/compliance/insider-risk-management-settings?view=o365-worldwide#analytics-preview`

- Create and manage insider risk policies: `https://learn.microsoft.com/en-us/microsoft-365/compliance/insider-risk-management-policies?view=o365-worldwide`

- Investigate Insider Risk Management activities: `https://learn.microsoft.com/en-gb/microsoft-365/compliance/insider-risk-management-activities?view=o365-worldwide#alert-dashboard`

- Insider Risk Management cases: `https://learn.microsoft.com/en-us/microsoft-365/compliance/insider-risk-management-cases?view=o365-worldwide`

- Get started with Information Barriers: `https://learn.microsoft.com/en-us/microsoft-365/compliance/information-barriers-policies?WT.mc_id=M365-MVP-4039827&view=o365-worldwide`

- Learn about Information Barriers: `https://learn.microsoft.com/en-us/microsoft-365/compliance/information-barriers?WT.mc_id=EM-MVP-4039827&view=o365-worldwide`

- Supported attributes for Information Barriers: `https://learn.microsoft.com/en-us/microsoft-365/compliance/information-barriers-attributes?view=o365-worldwide`

- Get started with PAM: `https://learn.microsoft.com/en-us/microsoft-365/compliance/privileged-access-management-configuration?WT.mc_id=M365-MVP-4039827&view=o365-worldwide`

Answers

Chapter 1

1 – C	6 – A
2 – B	7 – D
3 – B	8 – C
4 – A	9 – A
5 – A	10 – B

Chapter 2

1 – B	6 – A
2 – C	7 – A
3 – D	8 – C
4 – C	9 – B
5 – A	10 – A

Chapter 3

1 – A	6 – D
2 – A	7 – A
3 – A, C	8 – A
4 – A, C	9 – A, B, C, D, E
5 – A	10 – B

Chapter 4

1 – B	6 – A, C
2 – B	7 – B
3 – A	8 – A
4 – C	9 – C, D, E
5 – A	10 – A

Chapter 5

1 – B		6 – B	
2 – A		7 – D	
3 – C		8 – A	
4 – B		9 – C	
5 – A, C		10 – A	

Chapter 6

1 – B		6 – B, D	
2 – B		7 – B, D	
3 – A		8 – B	
4 – B, C, E		9 – D	
5 – B		10 – A	

Chapter 7

1 – C		6 – B	
2 – B		7 – C	
3 – B		8 – B	
4 – B		9 – A	
5 – A		10 – B	

Chapter 8

1 – B		6 – C	
2 – B		7 – B	
3 – B		8 – A	
4 – A, C, D		9 – A, B, D	
5 – A		10 – A	

Chapter 9

1 – A		6 – B	
2 – A		7 – B	
3 – D		8 – A, C, D	
4 – B		9 – D	
5 – A		10 – A	

Chapter 10

1 – B	6 – A, C, E
2 – A	7 – A, C
3 – A, C, E	8 – A
4 – B	9 – A, D
5 – C	10 – A

Chapter 11

1 – C	6 – C
2 – A	7 – C, D
3 – B	8 – A
4 – B	9 – C
5 – B	10 – C

Chapter 12

1 – B	6 – C
2 – A, C, D	7 – B
3 – D	8 – B, C
4 – B, D	9 – A
5 – A	10 – A

Chapter 13

1 – B	6 – B, C
2 – A	7 – C
3 – B, D, F	8 – A
4 – B	9 – D
5 – A	10 – B

Chapter 14

1 – C	6 – A
2 – B	7 – C
3 – B	8 – A
4 – D	9 – D
5 – A	10 – A

Chapter 15

1 – A	6 – A
2 – D	7 – B
3 – A	8 – A, B, D
4 – B	9 – A
5 – A	10 – B

Chapter 16

1 – C	6 – A, B
2 – C, D	7 – A
3 – B	8 – C
4 – B	9 – A
5 – A	10 – B

Chapter 17

1 – A, C, D	6 – A
2 – A	7 – C
3 – B	8 – B
4 – D	9 – C
5 – A	10 – A

Index

Packtpub.com

Subscribe to our online digital library for full access to over 7,000 books and videos, as well as industry leading tools to help you plan your personal development and advance your career. For more information, please visit our website.

Why subscribe?

- Spend less time learning and more time coding with practical eBooks and Videos from over 4,000 industry professionals

- Improve your learning with Skill Plans built especially for you

- Get a free eBook or video every month

- Fully searchable for easy access to vital information

- Copy and paste, print, and bookmark content

Did you know that Packt offers eBook versions of every book published, with PDF and ePub files available? You can upgrade to the eBook version at packtpub.com and as a print book customer, you are entitled to a discount on the eBook copy. Get in touch with us at customercare@packtpub.com for more details.

At www.packtpub.com, you can also read a collection of free technical articles, sign up for a range of free newsletters, and receive exclusive discounts and offers on Packt books and eBooks.

Other Books You May Enjoy

If you enjoyed this book, you may be interested in these other books by Packt:

Practical Threat Detection Engineering

Megan Roddie, Jason Deyalsingh, Gary J. Katz

ISBN: 9781801076715

- Become well versed in the detection engineering process
- Build a detection engineering test lab
- Discover how to maintain detections as code
- Find out how threat intelligence can be used to drive detection development
- Demonstrate the effectiveness of detection capabilities to business leadership
- Limit the attackers' ability to inflict damage by detecting malicious activity early

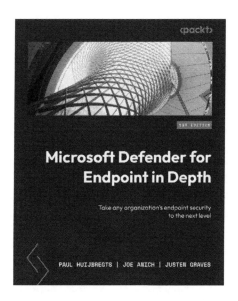

Microsoft Defender for Endpoint in Depth

Paul Huijbregts, Joe Anich, Justen Graves

ISBN: 9781804615461

- Understand the backstory of Microsoft Defender for Endpoint
- Discover different features, their applicability, and caveats
- Prepare and plan a rollout within an organization
- Explore tools and methods to successfully operationalize the product
- Implement continuous operations and improvement to your security posture
- Get to grips with the day-to-day of SecOps teams operating the product
- Deal with common issues using various techniques and tools
- Uncover commonly used commands, tips, and tricks

Packt is searching for authors like you

If you're interested in becoming an author for Packt, please visit `authors.packtpub.com` and apply today. We have worked with thousands of developers and tech professionals, just like you, to help them share their insight with the global tech community. You can make a general application, apply for a specific hot topic that we are recruiting an author for, or submit your own idea.

Share Your Thoughts

Now you've finished *Microsoft 365 Security, Compliance, and Identity Administration*, we'd love to hear your thoughts! Scan the QR code below to go straight to the Amazon review page for this book and share your feedback or leave a review on the site that you purchased it from.

`https://packt.link/r/1804611921`

Your review is important to us and the tech community and will help us make sure we're delivering excellent quality content.

Download a free PDF copy of this book

Thanks for purchasing this book!

Do you like to read on the go but are unable to carry your print books everywhere?

Is your eBook purchase not compatible with the device of your choice?

Don't worry, now with every Packt book you get a DRM-free PDF version of that book at no cost.

Read anywhere, any place, on any device. Search, copy, and paste code from your favorite technical books directly into your application.

The perks don't stop there, you can get exclusive access to discounts, newsletters, and great free content in your inbox daily

Follow these simple steps to get the benefits:

1. Scan the QR code or visit the link below

https://packt.link/free-ebook/978-1-80461-192-0

2. Submit your proof of purchase

3. That's it! We'll send your free PDF and other benefits to your email directly

Printed in Poland
by Amazon Fulfillment
Poland Sp. z o.o., Wrocław